CONTENTS

CW01507218

ILLUSTRATIONS

ABBREVIATIONS

PREFACE

INTRODUCTION

RENAISSANCE NAPLES

A Documentary History

1400–1600

RENAISSANCE NAPLES
A Documentary History
1400–1600

★

Edited by
Charlotte Nichols &
James H. McGregor

ITALICA PRESS
NEW YORK & BRISTOL
2019

ITALICA PRESS, INC.
99 Wall Street, Suite 650
New York, New York 10005
inquiries@italicapress.com

Library of Congress Cataloging-in-Publication Data
Names: Nichols, Charlotte, 1954- editor. | Mc Gregor, James H. (James
Harvey),
  1946- editor.
Title: Renaissance Naples : a documentary history, 1400/1600 / edited by
  Charlotte Nichols and James H. Mc Gregor.
Description: New York : Italica Press, [2018] | Series: A documentary history
  of Naples series | Includes bibliographical references and index.
Identifiers: LCCN 2017060514 (print) | LCCN 2017043224 (ebook) | ISBN
  9781599102573 (ebook) | ISBN 9781599102559 (hardcover : alk. paper) |
  ISBN 9781599102566 (pbk. : alk. paper)
Subjects: LCSH: Naples (Kingdom)--History--Spanish rule, 1442-1707. |
Naples
  (Italy)--History--To 1503. | Renaissance--Italy--Naples (Kingdom) |
Naples
  (Kingdom)--Civilization.
Classification: LCC DG848.1 (print) | LCC DG848.1 .R38 2018 (ebook)
| DDC
  945/.73106--dc23
LC record available at https://lccn.loc.gov/2017060514

Cover Illustration: King Alfonso's Triumphal Arch, Castel Nuovo, c.1452–
1471. Detail. Photo: Italica Press.

For a Complete List of Titles in *A Documentary History of Naples* Series
Visit our Website at: http://www.italicapress.com/index128.html.

CHAPTER 3: LITERATURE

★

ILLUSTRATIONS

★

ABBREVIATIONS

Astartita (2013)	Astarita, Tommaso, ed., *A Companion to Early Modern Naples*. Leiden: Brill, 2013.
Calabria (2002)	Calabria, Antonio. *The Cost of Empire: The Finances of the Kingdom of Naples in the Time of Spanish Rule*. Cambridge: Cambridge University Press, 2002.
CFN	Charlotte Nichols
DBI	*Dizionario Biografico degli Italiani*.
DM	Derek A.R. Moore
Hall–Willette	Hall, Marcia B., and Thomas Willette, ed. *Artistic Centers of the Italian Renaissance: Naples*. New York: Cambridge University Press, 2017.
Hughes-Buongiovanni	Hughes, Jessica, and Claudio Buongiovanni, ed. *Remembering Parthenope: The Reception of Classical Naples from Antiquity to the Present*. Oxford: Oxford University Press, 2015.
ISIME	Istituto Italiano per il Medio Evo
JHM	James H. Mc Gregor
Musto (2013)	Musto, Ronald G. *Medieval Naples: A Documentary History, 400–1400*. New York: Italica Press, 2013.
NACS	Ferraro, Italo, ed. *Napoli: Atlante della Città Storica*. 1. *Centro Storico*. Naples: CLEAN, 2002.
NN	*Napoli Nobilissima*
RGM	Ronald G. Musto
SN	*Storia di Napoli*. Ernesto Pontieri, ed. 11 vols. Naps: Società Editrice Storia di Napoli, 1967–78.
Tateo	Pontano, Giovanni. *I Trattati delle virtù sociali*. Francesco Tateo, ed. 2nd ed. Rome: Bulzoni, 1999.
TZ	Tania Zampini
Vasari, *Lives*	Vasari, Giorgio. *Lives of the Painters, Sculptors and Architects* (1568), Gaston du C. de Vere, trans. New York: Knopf, 1912, 2nd ed., repr. 1996.

PREFACE

We are pleased to present *Renaissance Naples: A Documentary History, 1400–1600* as the third part of Italica Press's five-volume Documentary History of Naples series. The publication process of this volume has been highly collaborative. Two volume editors and several other authors have been involved in its planning, discussion and implementation since its conception nearly two decades ago. This combination of disciplinary approaches and perspectives on the same historical data is especially important for the history of Renaissance Naples, an area of great richness and complexity and yet one little known outside of Italy and among European specialists. In North America, after nearly three decades of study, "Renaissance Naples" remains an emerging field and one requiring an ever-expanding circle of studies and forms of publication, from the most specialized to more general approaches. In its later phases, under Spanish domination, it has become part of the intensely studied and analyzed history of early modern Italy and Europe. Its structures and forms of thinking, expression, and reception — including its historical record — are more familiar to researchers and readers.

In that spirit the following book is intended as a general, though rigorous, introduction to the broad sweep of Naples' development during these two centuries of broad and rapid change. This is the first comprehensive English-language collection of sources to treat the history of the city from the late Angevin period through the end of the sixteenth century. It is intended for general readers, students or scholars unfamiliar with the history of the city and the types of sources available for further research. Readings cover the city's historical, economic, literary, artistic, religious and cultural life. Narrative sources predominate both to provide a historical framework and to convey the flavor of a range of both humanist and vernacular writing and of the various perspectives on the city from its rulers and administrators, through its historians, artists, and literary figures, its citizens, visitors and their guides, its boosters and its critics. We have attempted to represent the voices that came from both the palace and the street, from both the highly learned and the practically literate.

Among the 169 primary source readings presented here in English translation — many for the first time — are chronicles and histories; archival materials including financial, legal and commercial records; poetry, novelle, drama, biography, letters, travelers' accounts; treatises on government, ethics and rulership, aesthetics, patronage and artistic production; urban and topographical descriptions, chorography, the archaeological record, and displays of power, authority and culture. A final section provides a visual essay on textual cultures: manuscript production and printing in the city. An appendix reproduces the famed *Tavola Strozzi* with a key to the monuments represented in the painting and discussed in the pages below.

The introduction offers a new, comprehensive survey of historical events with a discussion of past historiography and of important current research and interpretive issues. These range from a discussions of primary sources to those of the city's changing population and the enduring question of Naples' importance as a commercial and political capital and artistic center, its developing economic and material base and the issue of its relationship to the Regno (as the kingdom of Naples continued to be called) on the one hand and to broader Mediterranean and pan-European contexts on the other. The introduction also surveys the changes in Naples' urban plan, its walls and fortifications, its port and its commercial and residential development.

This book returns again and again to two basic frames of interpretation of Naples during this period: the diachronic, or the impact of sudden changes of dynasty, of developing artistic, literary and material trends from the late fourteenth to the late sixteenth century; and the synchronic: or Naples' position vis à vis other contemporary capitals and regions both of Italy and of Europe. These frames affected both the reality and representation of all Neapolitan modes of life and culture: from its politics to its artistic styles and tastes, to its economic development. Such diachronic and synchronic frames both influenced contemporary Europeans' views of Naples and its kingdom and continue to impact our own attitudes toward the contributions and value of Naples structures of everyday life and its cultural achievements.

★

This is the series' third volume in chronological order, and the fourth to be completed. Where appropriate, we have made reference to other volumes in the series or to specific readings. We have also been fortunate to publish this volume in the wake of the groundbreaking final volume of Cambridge University Press' *Artistic Centers of the Italian Renaissance: Naples*, edited by Marcia B. Hall and Thomas Willette, for which two of the contributors to the present volume — Charlotte Nichols and Ronald G. Musto — were also authors. Through the present Documentary History their and the contributions of other experts on Renaissance Naples have provided key findings and interpretations for the present book. Throughout these pages James H. Mc Gregor brings to bear his deep knowledge of the period and its literatures to great advantage. This volume also takes advantage of the remarkable publishing achievement of the I Tatti Renaissance Library (ITRL), published by Harvard University Press beginning in 2001, under the general editorship of James Hankins. The eighty-eight volumes published to date focus on the neo-Latin literature of the period and are edited and translated by leading Renaissance scholars. As this volume goes to press, a new partnership has been created between the O'Donnell Institute of Art History (University of Texas at Dallas) and the Museo e Real Bosco di Capodimonte to facilitate the study of Naples as a globally inter-connected port city. See https://www.utdallas.edu/arthistory/port-cities.

In addition to the original translations of the volume's editors — Charlotte Nichols and James H. Mc Gregor — the readings in this volume draw from a wide range of sources, translations, methodologies and disciplines. Several of the authors translated in the following pages — including Antonio Beccadelli (Panormita), Giovanni Pontano, Jacopo Sannazaro, Pietro Summonte and Giorgio Vasari — appear in several chapters either in selections or in full texts, and various parts of the same works appear under different chapters. Others, such as Bartolomeo Facio and Notar Giacomo, appear in chapters on art. Ronald G. Musto (RGM) has provided introductory sections on historical background, forms of communication and humanist thought, along with additional readings in these areas. Sections of chapters on ecclesiastical architecture have built upon work published by Charlotte Nichols in *Artistic Centers of the Italian Renaissance: Naples* and have been duly annotated.

Each text is numbered consecutively and is preceded by an introduction contextualizing the reading and providing source bibliography. A full bibliography of primary sources and secondary works and a comprehensive index complete the volume. For consistency's sake and ease of citation, we have normalized the spellings and capitalization in many of these selections to US English usage. For the same reasons, we have also normalized the spellings of many proper and place names with the anticipation that most readers will be unfamiliar with both. To aid reading, we have also occasionally divided longer reading sections into more manageable paragraphs.

★

We would like to thank the many scholars whose translations we have excerpted and especially those who have had a hand in translating selections in this volume, including the two main editors, Charlotte Nichols and

James H. Mc Gregor. We also extend our thanks and appreciation to David Beneteau, Frederick J. Booth, Julia H. Gaiser, Anne Laidlaw, Derek Moore, Ronald G. Musto, Lilian Randall, and Tania Zampini. Unless otherwise indicated, all translations of, and references to, Vasari are from the *Lives of the Painters, Sculptors and Architects* (1568). 2 vols. Gaston Du C. de Vere, ed. and trans. (New York: Knopf, 1912, repr. 1996).

In addition to these authors and translators, we would also like to thank many scholars and institutions that have provided advice and encouragement. These include Jerry H. Bentley, Chiara De Caprio, Roger Friedman, John Marino, John Monfasani, Francesco Montuori and Francesco Senatore. Charlotte Nichols would like in particular to thank Derek Moore for his invaluable insights over many decades, Olivia Moore for cheerful patience, Kathleen Weil-Garris Brandt for setting her on the road to Naples with Claudia Pierpont, and Frederick Booth.

It is to the great loss of Neapolitan and historical studies in general that both Professors Bentley and Marino are no longer with us to see their fundamentally important researches incorporated into what we hope will be a survey of broad appeal and utility.

Ronald G. Musto
Series Editor, A Documentary History of Naples
Bristol, UK, February 2019

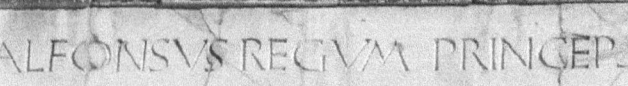

INTRODUCTION

Naples in the Renaissance has garnered relatively greater attention among scholars and readers than its medieval centuries. This is due to many causes, including the comparatively larger number of available primary sources,[1] especially as we move toward the early modern; the survival of far more of its artistic legacy in urban planning, architecture, painting, sculpture and other arts; and the broader appeal of its literature, philosophical and political thinking as Naples and the Regno (as the kingdom of Naples was called) took their place amid both the Italian balance of power and the broader structures of early modern Europe.

While both recent scholarly consensus and the chronological limits of this volume (1400–1600) might better argue to use the title, "Early Modern Naples," we have retained the term "Renaissance" both for the shorthand connotations that it summons up among scholarly and more broad readerships and because much of the political and moral philosophy, literature and arts of the period consciously based itself on ancient models and was informed by a sense of the rebirth of antiquity. While many of the material and political conditions of the city and the Regno shared the experience of early modern Europe, much of its self-consciousness remained wedded to antiquity, both in more popular forms of the legends around Virgil's presence and magical legacy in the city and its environs, and in the early modern revival of classical literatures, thought and arts.[2] Such tensions were not new: Chris Wickham explains the cognitive dissonance inherent in late antiquity's continued adherence to classical modes of thought and identity just as the means of supporting such cultural habits and ways of life were rapidly disappearing, leading to the many contradictions and apparently awkward solutions in the material culture and visual arts characteristic of the early Middle Ages.[3] So too in early modern Naples, the contradictions between its classical aspirations and the

1. See below, pp. 16–24, 30–33.

2. See Hughes–Buongiovanni.

3. See Chris Wickham, *The Inheritance of Rome: A History of Europe from 400 to 1000* (London: Penguin, 2010), 9; idem; *Early Medieval Italy: Central Power and Local Society 400–1000* (Ann Arbor: University of Michigan Press, 1989), 78, 147–52.

tensions of emerging modernity — political upheaval, population growth and urban congestion, rapid accumulation and depletion of resources and wealth — underlay and sometimes contradicted many of the artistic and cultural forms analyzed and sampled in this volume.

In the following pages Charlotte Nichols and James H. Mc Gregor provide introductions to the literature and art of Renaissance Naples and address the thorny issues of historiography and reception that continue to complicate an appreciation of Neapolitan visual culture and letters.[4] Here we will provide a basic historical introduction from the arrival of the Aragonese through the end of the sixteenth century[5] and then review the historiographical and other scholarly discussions to provide the necessary background to the chapters that follow.

HISTORICAL BACKGROUND
by Ronald G. Musto

The Aragonese, 1442–1504

During the Great Schism between the rival Roman and Avignon lines of popes (1378–1417), Queen Giovanna I, the granddaughter

4.   See John Marino, "Constructing the Past of Early Modern Naples: Sources and Historiography," in Tommaso Astarita, ed., *A Companion to Early Modern Naples* (Leiden: Brill, 2013), 11–34; idem; "Myths of Modernity and the Myth of the City: When the Historiography of Pre-modern Italy Goes South," in *New Approaches to Naples c. 1500–1800: The Power of Place*, Melissa Calaresu and Helen Hills, ed. (Farnham: Ashgate, 2013), 11–30; Ronald G. Musto, "Introduction: Naples in Myth and History," in Marcia Hall and Thomas Willette, ed., *Artistic Centers of the Italian Renaissance: Naples* (New York: Cambridge University Press, 2017), 1–33.

5.   Tommaso Astarita (2005) *and Holy Water: A History of Southern Italy* (New York and London: Norton, 2005), 69–107; Aurelio Musi, "Political History: The 'Neapolitan Nation'," in Astarita (2013), 131–51; Jeanne Chenault Porter, *Baroque Naples: A Documentary History, 1600–1800* (New York: Italica Press, 2000); Francesco Senatore, "The Kingdom of Naples." In *The Italian Renaissance State*, Andrea Gamberoni and Isabella Lazzarini, ed. (New York: Cambridge University Press, 2012), 30–49; Salvatore Tramontana, *Il Mezzogiorno medievale: Normanni, svevi, angioini, aragonesi nei secoli XI–XV* (Rome: Carocci, 2018), 163–235.

of King Robert the Wise (1307–43),[6] took the side of Clement VII of the Avignon line of popes against Urban VI, former archbishop of Bari and the Roman pope. Urban retaliated by excommunicating the queen and crowning her rival and second cousin Charles of Durazzo (Charles III). Charles conquered Naples in 1381 and had Giovanna murdered in 1382. Yet, by that time, Giovanna had adopted Duke Louis I of Anjou as her heir. He, however, died in 1384. Charles III then went off to assert the Angevin claim to the crown of Hungary and was assassinated there in 1386. Louis II of Anjou then invaded the Regno. But with the forceful help of his mother Margaret of Durazzo (queen regent 1386–93) Charles's young son, Ladislaus of Durazzo, displayed extraordinary energy and skill by fending off rebellion, invasion and rival claims, finally allying with the Roman papacy in 1399.

During this "Durazzan" period, the noble families of Naples exploited royal weaknesses by seizing the government of the city and reviving its five noble district councils or *seggi* (*sedile*) — Nido, Capuana, Montagna, Porta and Portanova — and one *seggio* of the Popolo, as the non-noble merchant class was called, as a city government and forcing concessions from King Ladislaus.[7]

With Ladislaus's death in 1414, his younger sister, Giovanna II (r. 1414–35), ascended the throne. She attempted to stave off the growing power of the Neapolitan barons and to protect the Regno from foreign threats through her alliances with a series of husbands and lovers. Heirless, in 1421 she adopted Alfonso V, king of Aragon and Sicily since 1416, but she disowned him and drove him out in 1423, naming as her heirs her cousin, Louis III of Anjou (d. 1434), and then his brother, René of Anjou.

On Giovanna II's death in 1435, claims to the Regno were contested between King René of Anjou and Alfonso of Aragon. Aragon had long been a major Mediterranean power since it had

6.   For the following narrative, see Musto (2013), 256–302.

7.   On the Durazzan period up to the year 1442, see Georges Peyronnet, "I Durazzo e Renato d'Angiò, 1281–1442," SN 3:335–436; Musi (2013), 131–51.

consolidated its own kingdom in the eleventh century and then conquered Catalonia with Barcelona, the Balearics, Sardinia, Sicily, and portions of Greece. Though the Angevins had some military and diplomatic success, René, held prisoner until 1438 by Philip the Good, duke of Burgundy, could not match Alfonso's initiative or resources.

In 1442, after Alfonso had been laying siege to Naples for weeks, a Neapolitan showed him the very same aqueduct used by Belisarius to enter Naples 900 years before.[8] On June 6, Alfonso took the city and René soon abandoned the kingdom.[9] Despite the Neapolitans' loyalty to the Angevins and their hostility to the Catalans, Alfonso the Magnanimous[10] followed up his conquest by showering mercy and favors on the city, making Naples his new capital[11] and a major center of the new visual culture of the quattrocento. As Alfonso I of Naples (r. 1442–58),[12] he built new piazzas, water systems, and fountains, and he repaired walls and streets, palaces, and religious institutions.

Alfonso established Naples as a humanist center,[13] focused on the razed and rebuilt Castel Nuovo and at the revived *Studium*,

8. See Musto (2013), xxiv–xxvii, 13–28.

9. For these events see chapter 1, reading 2, pp. 59–61.

10. For Alfonso's reign and the Aragonese, see G. D'Agostino, "Il mezzogiorno aragonese (Napoli dal 1458 al 1503)," SN 4.1:357–584; Ernesto Pontieri, *Alfonso il Magnanimo re di Napoli: (1435–1458)* (Naples: Edizioni scientifiche italiane, 1975); Alan Ryder, *The Kingdom of Naples under Alfonso the Magnanimous: The Making of a Modern State* (Oxford: Oxford University Press, 1976); idem, *Alfonso the Magnanimous, King of Aragon, Naples, and Sicily, 1396–1458* (Oxford: Oxford University Press, 1990); Musi (2013).

11. G. D'Agostino, *La capitale ambigua: Napoli dal 1458 al 1580* (Naples: Società editrice napoletana, 1979).

12. See Jerry Bentley, *Politics and Culture in Renaissance Naples* (Princeton: Princeton University Press, 1987); SN 4:471–77; Amedeo Feniello, "Les campagnes napolitaines a la fin du Moyen Âge: Mutations d'un paysage rural" (Paris: École des hautes études en sciences sociales, 2001); idem, "Gli interventi sanitari dei secoli XIV e XV," in *Napoli nel Medioevo. 4. La città del Mezzogiorno medievale* (Galatina: Congedo, 2007), 123–35.

13. Mario Santoro, "Napoli Aragonese: La cultura umanistica," SN 4:317–498; idem, "Humanism in Naples," in Albert Rabil, Jr., ed., *Renaissance*

or university of Naples. Among the major humanists whom he patronized were Bartolomeo Facio, Lorenzo Valla, Giannozzo Manetti, Panormita (Antonio Beccadelli), Giovanni Gioviano Pontano, and the noted Greek scholar George of Trebizond. Alfonso moved the royal library from Castel Capuano to the renovated Castel Nuovo and vastly increased its collection and the quality of its holdings.[14] He sponsored philosophical and literary discussions at the Academy there, and opened it up to selected students at the *Studium*. The king also turned Naples into one of the first capitals of an early modern state, establishing a permanent class of well-educated professionals and a bureaucracy drawn from the urban middle class, which he utilized to check the barons' power and to build permanent institutions of governance and diplomacy.

Despite foreign war and invasion, baronial revolt, and the devastating earthquake of 1450, Alfonso's heirs continued the beautification and enrichment of the city. Around 1400 the city's population stood at 45,000. By 1490, it had reached between 100,000 and 120,000.[15] The Aragonese seaborne empire and Naples' predominance in southern Italy brought to the city a vast network of commercial trade and manufacturing. Administrators and nobility flocked to it from all over the South and abroad. The Aragonese regularized taxation and finance, granting Naples and other cities much autonomy in local administration. Under Alfonso's son, Ferrante I (r.1458–94), manufacturing was expanded and supported throughout the kingdom, iron mines were opened in

Humanism: Foundations, Forms and Legacy, vol 1. *Humanism in Italy* (Philadelphia: University of Pennsylvania Press, 1988), 296–331; Fulvio Delle Donne, *Alfonso il Magnanimo e l'invenzione dell'umanesimo monarchico: Ideologia e strategie di legittimazione alla corte aragonese di Napoli* (Rome: ISIME, 2015).

14. Emilia Ambra, ed. *Libri a corte: Testi e immagini nella Napoli aragonese* (Naples: Paparo, 1997); Gennaro Toscano, *La Biblioteca Reale di Napoli al tempo della dinastia Aragonese* (Valencia: Generalitat Valencia, 1998).

15. Estimates vary. See Astarita (2005), 320; Antonio Calabria, *The Cost of Empire: The Finances of the Kingdom of Naples in the Time of Spanish Rule* (Cambridge: Cambridge University Press, 2002), 27. Giovanni Muto, "Urban Structures and Population," in Astarita (2013), 35–61, at 43, estimates the population at 48,000 in 1505, after the devastation of the plague of 1493.

Calabria, and the printing industry[16] was launched in Naples. The famed *Tavola Strozzi*, now at the Museo di San Martino, accurately reflects the beauty and importance of the city about 1472.[17]

Under Alfonso, first as duke of Calabria, and then as Alfonso II (r. 1494–95), Naples became the projected site of the most ambitious urban redevelopment plan of the Renaissance.[18] Architect Giuliano da Maiano replaced the Angevin walls to the east of the city and expanded them north from Castel del Carmine (Sperone) to San Giovanni a Carbonara. One stretch of these walls and several typical Aragonese towers still stand, as do their Porta Capuana and Porta Nolana. In 1487, the palace at Poggioreale was designed by Giuliano da Maiano northeast of Porta Capuana. To the west, a new expanse was added up to the area now defined by Via Toledo (Roma) and Sta. Brigida. During this period, the city became famed for its gardens and elegant villas capping the crests to the west of the city.

Despite their largesse to the city and its gains during the quattrocento, the Aragonese dynasty shared the insecurity of all late medieval and early modern dynasties throughout Europe. In 1459, Ferrante faced a serious revolt of the barons, in league with the aged René and Jean of Anjou, that he finally subdued in 1465. Throughout this period Naples remained a key player in the developing Italian balance of power. In 1480, the Turks shocked Europe with the sack of Otranto, but perhaps an even worse enemy to Naples than the Turks was the Roman papacy, which under Pope Innocent VIII was strongly allied with the house of Anjou and through it with the French Crown, stirring up a second barons' revolt in 1485/86.[19] The 1490s brought catastrophe to Naples and to Italy as a whole. With

16. See, for example, Mariano Fava and Giovanni Bresciano, *La stampa a Napoli nel XV secolo*, 3 vols. (Leipzig, R. Haupt, 1911–13; New York: Kraus Reprint, 1969); and Marco Santoro and George H. Fletcher, *La stampa a Napoli nel Quattrocento* (Naples: Istituto nazionale di studi sul Rinascimento meridionale, 1984).

17. See chapter 7, reading 132, p. 344; and Appendices, pp. 480–81.

18. See below, 36–38.

19. See chapter 1, reading 6, pp. 76–79.

Lorenzo de' Medici's death in 1492, the fragile balance of power in the peninsula collapsed in the wake of an alliance between Ludovico Sforza, duke-regent of Milan, and King Charles VIII of France.

Charles lived in the hope of reviving the Angevin claims to the Regno; and Ludovico Sforza's invitation to play his hand in Italian politics gave him the opportunity when Ferrante died in January 1494. Ferrante's son, Alfonso II, quickly allied with the papacy. But their defensive strategy failed, and Charles turned south with an army of 40,000, panicking Alfonso. In 1495 he abdicated in favor of his son Ferrante II (also called Ferdinand II or Ferrandino, r. 1495–96) and fled to a monastery in Sicily. With barons in revolt and Naples in anarchy, Charles entered the city, almost without a fight, in February 1495.[20] Giovanni Pontano, loyal minister to every Aragonese king and the leading intellectual of the Regno, greeted the French and persuaded Charles to avoid a brutal sack.

The Spanish and the Hapsburg Viceregency, 1504–c.1600

By May 1495, Charles VIII's control of the Regno was becoming untenable, given long supply lines, an untrustworthy nobility, and the heavy toll of disease. By July, Ferrante II had retaken the city, and by 1496 he had reconquered most of the Regno. But in one of the many turns of *fortuna* that would mark the history of Naples for its humanist historians, he suddenly fell ill and died in October. Ferrante's uncle Frederick (r. 1496–1501) inherited the crown. But by then the papacy had allied with the French, and in 1500 the French in turn had signed the Treaty of Granada to divide the Regno with a newly unified Spain under Ferdinand and Isabella. While Ferdinand of Aragon (Ferdinand the Catholic of Spain) had supported the Aragonese against both baronial revolt and the French, he now worked to absorb the Aragonese inheritance into the new kingdom of Spain. By 1502, the French and Spanish were fighting one another, and by 1504 Ferdinand the Catholic's lieutenant in Italy, Gonzalo Fernández de Córdoba, had won the entire Regno, thwarting Louis XII of France's invasion. The last Aragonese claimant to the throne died as a palace prisoner in Spain in 1550.

20. See chapter 1, readings 8–11, pp. 85–92.

Ferdinand the Catholic's conquest and visit in 1506 began the Spanish viceroyalty in Naples. This would last until 1734 under successive Hapsburg and Bourbon monarchies.[21] In 1517, the Hapsburg Charles I of Spain inherited the throne of Naples, and he soon added it to his domain when he was elected Emperor Charles V.[22] The most powerful monarch of his age, Charles ruled separately as king of Spain and as emperor over Germany, Austria and its eastern territories, the Low Countries, imperial Burgundy, and all the Spanish overseas empire in the Western Hemisphere and all its territories in the Mediterranean. He also inherited control over most of northern Italy from the Holy Roman Empire.

The wars of Charles V and François I (Valois) of France[23] brought further havoc to Italy and saw the sack of Rome in 1527.[24] In 1528 François's lieutenant, Odet de Foix, viscount of Lautrec, besieged Naples and cut it off with a naval blockade. Only his death, along with most of his army from the plague, and Charles V's alliance with Genoa and its fleet under Andrea Doria, saved the Hapsburg hold on the city and Regno.

Naples thus became one part of this great empire, ruled – as was Mexico or Peru – by a Spanish viceroy.[25] Under his authority sat

21. See Chenault Porter, xxvii–xxxi; Astarita (2005), 107–219.

22. See Giuseppe Galasso and Aurelio Musi, ed., *Carlo V, Napoli e il Mediterraneo: Atti del Convegno internazionale svoltosi dall'11 al 13 gennaio 2001 presso la Società napoletana di storia patria in Castelnuovo Napoli* (Naples: Società napoletana di storia patria, 2001).

23. For these events, see SN 4:1–84; Eric Cochrane, *Historians and Historiography in the Italian Renaissance.* (Chicago: University of Chicago Press, 1980), 33–54; Musi (2013).

24. See James H. Mc Gregor, *The Sack of Rome* (New York: Italica Press, 1993).

25. T. Pedìo, *Gli Spagnoli alla conquista dell'Italia* (Reggio Calabria: Editori riuniti meridionali, 1974); Antonio Calabria and John Marino, ed. and trans., *Good Government in Spanish Naples* (New York: Peter Lang, 1989); Giuseppe Galasso, *Alla periferia dell'impero: Il Regno di Napoli nel periodo spagnolo, secoli XVI–XVII* (Turin: G. Einaudi, 1994); B. Anatra and Aurelio Musi, *Nel sistema imperiale l'Italia spagnola* (Naples: Edizioni scientifiche italiane, 1994); P.L.

INTRODUCTION

a series of courts and appointed administrators. Local voices were
heard in open councils. Firmly behind these colonial officials
were the Spanish infantry, the dreaded *tercios*, so named after their
unbeatable military formations. Nevertheless, Neapolitan feelings
were respected; and Neapolitans retained the privilege of appealing
directly to the king in Spain. The surviving *seggi* kept much of their
local power and traditional membership, and each continued to send
their representative to the seat of civic government, the Tribunale di
San Lorenzo. Together these *Eletti* formed the ruling *Giunta (Junta)*,[26]
whose chief responsibility into the 1560s was overseeing the city's
Annona, or supply system.[27] Relations remained cordial as long as the
Neapolitans remained conscious of the Spanish garrisons within the
city and the vast new bastions of Castel Sant'Elmo (Belforte), its guns
aimed squarely at the city center.

The reign of viceroy Pedro de Toledo (r.1532–53)[28] marked the
conversion of Naples into a capital city of a different kind: as one
of many provincial centers in a colonial empire. Toledo revitalized
a city desolated by decades of war and neglect. He expanded the
city westward, extending the northern ramparts up the slopes of

Rovito, *Il viceregno spagnolo di Napoli: Ordinamento, istituzioni, culture di governo*
(Naples: Arte tipografica, 2003); Giovanni Muto, "A Court without a King:
Naples as a Capital City in the First Half of the 16ᵗʰ Century," in *The World
of Emperor Charles V*, Wim Blockmans and Nicolette Mout, ed. (Amsterdam:
Royal Netherlands Academy of Arts and Sciences, 2004), 129–41; Giuseppe
Galasso, *Il Regno di Napoli: Il Mezzogiorno spagnolo (1494–1622)* (Turin:
UTET, 2005); John A. Marino and Thomas J. Dandelet, ed., *Spain in Italy:
Politics, Society, and Religion 1500–1700* (Leiden: Brill, 2007); Giulio Sodano,
"Governing the City: The Capital City and the Policy of the Capital," in
Astarita (2013), 109–29.

26. Sodano (2013), 110–14; Angelantonio Spagnoletti, "The Naples Elites
between City and Kingdom," in Astarita (2013), 197–214, at 203–5.

27. Sodano (2013), 117–20; Muto (2013), 53–54; Gaetano Sabatini, "Economy
and Finance in Early Modern Naples," in Astarita (2013), 89–107, at 93–95.

28. Pedro Álvarez de Toledo y Pimentel, second marquis consort of Villafranca
del Bierzo (July 13, 1484–February 2, 1553). See Giulio Pane, "Pietro di Toledo
vicere urbanista," *Napoli Nobilissima* 14 (1975): 81–95, 161–82.

9

Monte San Martino to Castel Sant'Elmo and revamping the city's fortifications to include Pizzofalcone, the perimeters of Castel dell'Ovo, and the newly expanded Castel Nuovo. Within this enormous area of 150 hectares, the viceroy established a new urban center, focused on an innovative grid plan that housed his Spanish garrisons in buildings three stories or higher, known ever since as the Spanish Quarter. The central corridor of this new expansion, paralleling the old western walls, remains known as the Via Toledo.

To the east, Toledo transformed the old Castel Capuano into the viceregal administrative center of the city and Regno, bringing together (1540–41) into this new "Vicaria" the prison and the civil, criminal, religious, and financial tribunals. To the south, he reinforced the old Aragonese walls along the waterfront, expanded the Arsenale, and eased access to the waterfront markets around Piazza del Mercato. As we will see in chapter 4 below,[29] the viceroy accompanied this with improvements to the ancient urban core: paving the streets and destroying encroachments along them, rebuilding the water and sewage systems, installing a series of monumental fountains, and reviving the aqueduct system.[30]

Viceroy Toledo's motives were varied. The impending visit to Naples of Emperor Charles V in 1535–36 spurred his first efforts, the renewed threat of Turkish attack continued his work on defenses, and the un-renounced claims of France made defense of the city's western periphery an ongoing necessity. But Toledo also wanted to ensure that Naples functioned as the most important provincial capital of Charles V's widespread empire, and Renaissance ideals of city normalization and beautification coincided well with Naples' role in this larger political context.

Despite this attention, Pedro de Toledo saw his mission as colonial administration: he and his Spanish colleagues in the imperial bureaucracy focused almost solely on defense and the display of power, and they reconfigured the city for those purposes. They

29. Pages 218–23.

30. Sodano (2013), 120–23. See below, chapter 1, readings 13, 47–49.

saw little need to address many of the fundamental structural shortcomings of an urban fabric under extreme duress as his very policies drove masses of southern Italian nobility and countryfolk into the city.[31] Between 1500 and 1550, the already overcrowded area of Naples increased by approximately thirty percent, while its population swelled by more than forty percent.[32] By 1527, Naples' population numbered 155,000, larger than Venice or Milan and twice the size of London. By contrast, the population of Constantinople, the largest city of the Mediterranean in the early modern period, numbered 80,000 in 1478 and 400,000 around 1530.[33] Despite losses of some 60,000 in the plague of 1526–27,[34] Naples quickly recovered. By 1547, its population had reached 212,000.[35]

But Toledo did nothing to alleviate overcrowding and lack of economic opportunity within the ancient urban core. In addition, his mercantile policies favored both Florentine and Genoese commercial interests at the expense of the native Neapolitan merchant class. Such policies permanently imperiled the growth of an urban bourgeoisie that could both create excess wealth (and its resulting cultural production) within the city and Regno and

31. Spagnoletti, "Naples Elites," 197–203.

32. Cesare De Seta, *Napoli,* 5th ed. (Rome: Laterza, 1991); idem, "The Urban Structure of Naples: Utopia and Reality," in *The Renaissance from Brunelleschi to Michelangelo,"* Henry Millon and Vittorio Magnago Lampugnani, ed. (New York: Rizzoli, 1994), 349–70; C. Rusciano, *Napoli, 1484–1501: La città e le mura aragonesi* (Rome: Bonsignori, 2002); Massimo Rosi, *Napoli entro e fuori le mura: Le trasformazioni urbanistiche, demografiche e territoriali di un'antica capitale rimasta per troppo tempo vincolata dalle sue stesse mura* (Rome: Newton & Compton, 2003).

33. These figures can be disputed. See De Seta (1973, 1991), 167, 210; Cipolla (1976), 281–82; Nicholas (2003), 13–21; Astarita (2005), 320; Muto (2013).

34. David Gentilcore, "*Tempi sì calamitosi:* Epidemic Disease and Public Health," in Astarita (2013), 281–306, at 286–87.

35. Astarita (2005), 320; Muto (2013), 43.

counter the overweening policy influence of the Spanish monarchy and its dependent Neapolitan aristocracy.[36]

Viceroy Toledo remained feared and respected, acknowledged for his urban improvements but personally unpopular throughout his reign — so much so that in 1552 Charles V effectively recalled him by reassigning him to Tuscany. Charles V abdicated in 1556 and was succeeded in Spain by Philip II (1556–98) and then by Philip III (1598–1621).[37] Between 1553 and 1601 Naples was ruled by a series of twelve viceroys[38] based on the Palazzo Reale. During this "golden age," Spain retained political, material and cultural hegemony over Catholic Europe, much of Latin America and the Philippines; and it used the vast resources of these territories to wage war with the Protestant North.

Naples had also remained a haven for religious minorities,[39] dissidents and intellectuals of all types. In 1492 Jews[40] expelled from the newly unified Spain under Ferdinand and Isabella came to Naples.[41] They quickly joined the Regno's intellectual, professional and financial elites and under the Aragonese lived in four *giudecche* in the city. Financiers, such as the Abravanel, rose to prominence as royal officials, and Naples also became a center of Hebrew printing.[42]

36. On the economy of Naples and the Regno, see John A. Marino, *Pastoral Economics in the Kingdom of Naples* (Baltimore, MD: Johns Hopkins University Press, 1988); idem, "Wheat and Wool in the Dogana of Foggia: An Equilibrium Model for Early Modern European Economic History," *Mélanges de L'école Française de Rome. Moyen Âge, Temps Modernes* 100.1–2 (1988): 871–92; Calabria (2002); E. Sakellariou, *Southern Italy in the Late Middle Ages: Demographic, Institutional and Economic Change in the Kingdom of Naples, c.1440–c.1530* (Leiden: Brill, 2012).

37. For this period see Giuseppe Galasso, *Napoli capitale: Identità politica e identità cittadina. Studi e ricerche 1266–1860* (Naples: Electa, 1998), 113–43.

38. https://en.wikipedia.org/wiki/List_of_viceroys_of_Naples.

39. Peter A. Mazur, "A Mediterranean Port in the Confessional Age: Religious Minorities in Early Modern Naples," in Astarita (2013), 215–34.

40. Mazur (2013), 216–22.

41. See chapter 1, reading 7, p. 83.

42. See below, pp. 50–51.

But things changed under the Spanish. Despite Emperor Charles V's heavy reliance on their loans to finance his military campaigns, in 1541 Pedro de Toledo moved to expel the Jews, who either left for northern Italy and the Ottoman Empire or remained as *conversos*. Few Muslims had remained in the Regno since the Angevin period, and under the viceroys only an elite of refugee princes resided in the city. Pedro de Toledo also suppressed the city's humanist traditions, closing the academies and limiting the freedom of the university. In 1547, his campaign to impose the Spanish Inquisition rapidly led to a general revolt that forced Charles V to retract the gambit.[43] Protestant thought continued to be tolerated in this cosmopolitan port under the first viceroys, and a thinkers like Bernardino Ochino and Juan de Valdés were able to use their prominence to sponsor any number of noble dissidents. This relative freedom was suppressed with the arrival of the Roman Inquisition in the 1550s and the execution of Protestants in 1564.[44]

Scientific inquiry and publishing also had a mixed history in the Regno.[45] The natural science of Bernardino Telesio (1509–88) had a wide impact not only in the Regno but also among a wider European intelligentsia, including Gasendi, Descartes, and Hobbes. Giambattista Della Porta (c.1535–1615) was able to continue his scientific research and publication and his playwrighting throughout his life in Naples. Ferrante Imperio (c.1525–c.1615) used his natural history collection at Palazzo Orsini di Gravina to create a public museum and to make cutting-edge science a concern of Naples' elites. Other thinkers who combined inquiry with social and political critique were less fortunate. Giordano Bruno (1548–1600) was forced to leave the Regno after 1575. Tommaso Campanella (1568–1639), born in Stilo

43. Musi (2013), 139–40; Giovanni Romeo, "Inquisition and Church in Early Modern Naples," in Astarita (2013), 235–56. See reading 12, pp. 93–99.

44. Mazur (2013), 229–33.

45. See Nancy L. Canepa, "Literary Culture in Naples, 1500–1800," in Astarita (2013), 427–51, at 439–40; Sean Cocco, "Locating the Natural Sciences in Early Modern Naples," in Astarita (2013), 453–75 at 453–60.

in Calabria, spent over twenty-five years in a Neapolitan prison for his anti-Spanish organizing.

Despite a long tradition of seeing Spanish rule as "corruptive" to such aspects of Neapolitan life, recent historiography has begun to methodologically analyze its impact on the Regno's economy, society, culture, government, and administration.[46] The city did benefit from its membership in Spain's empire.[47] Building on its role since the late Middle Ages, when it was a net exporter of agricultural produce, by the 1550s Naples had also become a supplier to luxury markets. Florence and Venice were major markets for Neapolitan goods and raw materials; the trade within the Spanish empire remained a continuous source of wealth. Even with the gradual shift of maritime and commercial fortune to the Atlantic seaboard states, by 1605 Naples' fleet had a total tonnage of about 40,000, equal to that of Venice or Marseilles, while all of England had about 100,000 tons and Spain about 175,000.[48]

By the mid-sixteenth century, the economy of Naples had come to center on its luxury markets: "Naples had no equivalent in Christendom…. [It produced] lace, braids, frills, trimmings, silks, light fabrics (taffetas), silken knots and cockades of all colours, and fine linens. These goods travelled as far as Cologne in large quantities…. Pieces of so-called Santa Lucia silk were even resold at Florence."[49] The countryside abounded with fresh produce, and sheep for wool and food, as well as other livestock.[50] On the other side of the balance sheet, according to Giulio Cesare Capaccio (1550–1634) secretary of the city of Naples under Viceroy Juan Alonso Pimentel de Herrera

46. This historiography is briefly reviewed in Calabria (2002), 2–4.

47. See Sabatini (2013).

48. Fernand Braudel, *The Mediterranean and the Mediterranean World in the Age of Philip II*, Sian Reynolds, trans., 2 vols. (New York: Harper & Row, 1972), 1:446.

49. Braudel (1972), 1:345.

50. As reported by Nicholas Audebert in 1576. See Eric Cochrane, *Italy, 1530–1630*, Julius Kirshner, ed. (New York: Longman, 1988), 183.

(1603–10), consumption levels were equally remarkable.[51] The Regno's revenues more than doubled from about 1.3 million ducats a year in 1550 to about 2.9 million by 1600.[52] The city and its wealth played a key role in the defeat of the Turkish fleet at Lepanto in 1572.

Wealth and its display[53] and the military empire that supported it had its troubling side, however.[54] Spanish rule shifted the costs of its imperial wars in Italy from Lombardy to the Regno, forcing Naples to bear the cost of both its own and of northern Italy's economic collapse in men, arms, and commodities. The Regno's expenses[55] grew from 1.37 million ducats in 1550 (45% military, 31% public debt) to 3.3 million in 1600 (28% military, 45% public debt). Taxation became oppressive throughout the kingdom and soon began to exceed state income.[56] As Genoese bankers replaced the Florentines and took control of the Regno's finances and resources, credit (largely bond) markets became almost exclusively concentrated on financing the government's debt, and everyone with a ducat to spare invested in it, siphoning off all other available capital, starving commercial enterprises of needed investment, cutting off credit to the agricultural sector, and sinking rural society into peonage.

The Spanish never encouraged the growth of mid-sized cities in the Regno, nor a viable system of transport. Naples was thus isolated in its commercial activity, consumption and production.[57] The increasingly impoverished rural population and their feudal overlords continued to stream into the city. By 1595, the city's population would rise to somewhere between 225,000 and 300,000, twice that

---

51. See Chapter 1, reading 15, pp. 102–3.

52. Calabria (2002), 54–75.

53. See Gabriel Guarino, "Public Rituals and Festivals in Naples, 1503–1799," in Astarita (2013), 257–79.

54. Sabatini (2013), 95–102.

55. Calabria (2002), 76–103.

56. See Calabria (2002), 4–8.

57. Sabatini (2013), 93–94.

of Venice, still second in Europe only to Paris.[58] The population of the kingdom as a whole, from which the city of Naples drew its numbers and its wealth, soared between 1505 and 1595 from 1.1 million to 2.4 million.[59] Most of this new population made Naples a center of immigration unlike almost any other European capital: tightly restricted to its original tufa platform and Greek grid plan, with expansions restricted either to the Spanish Quarter or to the aristocratic villas dotting the hills of Sant'Elmo and Posillipo (as seen in the *Tavola Strozzi*), the residents of the city had little choice but to build up, and population density in this core had reached 7000 per square kilometer by 1600,[60] or roughly between that of modern Singapore and Hong Kong.[61] Naples boasted some of the very first high-rise apartments in Europe since the Roman *insulae*. These buildings still mark the core of the old city, visible, for example, all along the Via Carbonara or dotted amid the grander urban palaces of Naples's aristocracy. Complete urban renewal in Naples would have to await the Risorgimento and the often brutal Risanamento of 1887 to 1898[62] that forever removed many traces of the historic core.

SOURCES AND HISTORIOGRAPHY 1400–1600
Archives
Archival documentation for Naples before 1560 is scarce.[63] More than other Italian and European centers Naples has also suffered repeated

58. Astarita (2005), 320, cites 300,000 in the early 1600s. Calabria (2002), 27, cites 225,000 in 1596. Muto (2013), 43, cites a total of 225,769, also in 1596.

59. Astarita (2005), 319. Estimates differ. Braudel (1972), 1:408, 523 n. 355 places it closer to 3 million.

60. Galasso, *Napoli capitale*, 114.

61. Singapore: 7698/sq. km.; Hong Kong: 6553/sq. km. Manila had the world's highest density in 2007 at 41,515/sq. km. New York City had a density of 10,431/sq. km. in 2010.

62. John Santore, *Modern Naples: A Documentary History, 1799–1999* (New York: Italica Press, 2001), 187–217.

63. G. Pepe, *Il Mezzogiorno d'Italia sotto gli Spagnoli: La tradizione storio-grafica* (Florence: G.C. Sansoni, 1952); J. Mazzoleni, *Fonti aragonesi* (Naples: L'Accademia, 1957); Riccardo Filangieri di Candida, *L'Archivio di stato di*

ravages to its historical record, from occasional loses of archives during the early Middle Ages to the destruction of the royal archives during the riots against Queen Giovanna I in 1345; in the popular revolts of 1547 against the Inquisition; in 1647 under Masaniello;[64] and in 1701 during the Macchia Conspiracy against Spanish rule (in which most tax, court, and other records were destroyed); to the more recent destruction of the state archives of the High Middle Ages[65] and Renaissance in Naples on September 30, 1943 at the hands of the retreating Nazis. Bentley has estimated that 90% of the Aragonese archives have been lost.[66] Luckily, many of these were retained in duplicate in the Aragonese and then Spanish archives in Barcelona; and many copies survived in scattered locations of others throughout Italy and Spain. This renders Gaetano Filangieri's copious summaries of archival documents published in the late 1800s

---

Napoli durante la Seconda Guerra Mondiale, Stefano Palmieri, ed. (Naples: Arte Tipografia, 1996); Istituto italiano per gli studi filosofici, *Fonti per la storia di Napoli aragonese* (Salerno: Carlone, 1997); A.A. Sotelo, *Casa de Aragón de Nápoles, 1412–1503 en la historiografía italiana, siglo XV–XVIII* (Torrevieja: Áristos, 2001); Marino, "Constructing the Past," 17–19; idem, "Myths of Modernity and the Myth of the City: When the Historiography of Pre-Modern Italy Goes South," in Calaresu and Hills, 11–30; Carlos López Rodríguez and Gloria López de la Plaza, "L'Archivio della Corona d'Aragona e Napoli," *Napoli Nobilissima,* ser. 6.3 (2012): 150–55.

64. Chenault Porter, 9–16.

65. See Riccardo Filangieri di Candida, "Report on the Destruction by the Germans, September 30, 1943, of the Depository of Priceless Historical Records of the Naples State Archives," *American Archivist* (1944): 252–55; idem, et al., *Registri della Cancelleria angioina ricostruiti da Riccardo Filangieri con la collaborazione degli archivisti napoletani.* 50 vols. to date (Naples: Archivio di Stato, 1950–). An excellent guide to the archival and narrative sources before 1943 can be found in Bartolommeo Capasso, *Le fonti della storia delle province napolitane dal 568 al 1500* (Naples: Riccardo Marghier, 1902; repr. Naples: Arnaldo Forni, 1997). More recent studies include Jole Mazzoleni, ed., *Regesto della Cancelleria aragonese di Napoli* (Naples: L'Accademia, 1951–); idem, *Fonti aragonesi;* and Stefano Palmieri, "Napoli, settembre 1943," in *L'Incidenza dell'Antico: Studi in memoria di Ettore Lepore,* Claudia Montepaone, ed., 3 vols. (Naples: Luciano, 1995–96), 3:263–79.

66. Bentley, 49. George Hersey, *The Aragonese Arch at Naples, 1443–1475* (New Haven: Yale University Press, 1973), 7–8, discusses their relevance to researchers.

of critical importance; one volume is devoted to the activities of the ambitious patron Alfonso, the duke of Calabria (later Alfonso II) between 1484 and 1491, narrated by Giampietro Leostello, a priest from Volterra and member of the duke's court.[67]

Narrative Sources: Court Humanists
Narrative sources[68] have survived more robustly, often in single manuscript copies, but sometimes in multiple manuscripts and printed editions, especially from the cinquecento. Though it has recently been subject to major revision,[69] Anglophone historiography of Renaissance Naples has long followed the frame set by Eric Cochrane, who asserted that the coming of the Aragonese in the quattrocento revived Neapolitan historiography:

> Thus history writing had been dead for over a hundred years by the time Southerners once again began to take an interest in it in the second quarter of the fifteenth century, and few if any of them seem to have been at all aware of the rich historiographical heritage left them by their ancestors of the age of the Normans or the Vespers.[70]

Expanding on Cochrane's research, Jerry Bentley[71] applied these categories to the work of quattrocento historians of Naples. Bentley demonstrated the influence of Leonardo Bruni and the new

67. Gaetano Filangieri, ed., *Documenti per la storia, le arti e le industrie delle provincie napoletane,* 6 vols. (Naples: Tipografia dell'Accademia Reale delle Scienze, 1883–91).

68. Marino, "Constructing the Past," 19–28; Fulvio Delle Donne, "Il re e i suoi cronisti: Reinterpretazioni della storiografia alla corte aragonese di Napoli," *Humanistica* 11.1–2 (n.s. 5) (2016): 17–34; idem, *Politica e letteratura nel Mezzogiorno medievale: La cronachistica dei secoli XII–XV* (Salerno: Carlone, 2001); Ronald G. Musto, *Writing Southern Italy before the Renaissance: Trecento Historians of the Mezzogiorno* (New York: Routledge, 2019), 14–79.

69. See Musto, *Writing Southern Italy,* xxix–xxxi, 259–60.

70. Cochrane, 144.

71. Bentley, 1–7. For amplification and revision, see now also Guido Cappelli, Maiestas*: Politica e pensiero politico nella Napoli aragonese (1443–1503)* (Rome: Carocci editore, 2016).

Florentine historiography on such writers as Flavio Biondo and then on humanists at the Aragonese court of Naples[72] who wrote *historia*, biography, commentary, urban description and *laudatio*. These writers include Antonio Beccadelli (Panormita), Bartolomeo Facio, Lorenzo Valla, Giannozzo Manetti and Giovanni Pontano. The writings of Aragonese humanists on the subject of royal patronage, such as Bartolomeo Facio's *De Viris Illustribus* (1456).[73] Giovanni Gioviano Pontano's *De Magnificentia* (1498), translated in chapter 9, provides an erudite glimpse of royal and aristocratic patronage.[74]

The chief focus of this school included the rebirth of the Regno under the Aragonese, the revival of urban life, the arts and letters, the role of the individual and the political and ethical issues that motivate individual action in the face of constantly changing *fortuna*. These, Bentley stressed, were not mere imitations or imports of Tuscan developments but grew out of the unique context of Aragonese history and the practical experience of these authors in education, royal administration, diplomacy, and war. Whether initially attracted from elsewhere in Italy or home grown, they reflected a lay, political, and civic ethic that informed all their broadly historical work. Bentley accepted and expanded on Hans Baron's theory of civic humanism[75]

72. Bentley; Cochrane, 134–59.

73. Michael Baxandall, "Bartholomaeus Facius on Painting: A Fifteenth-Century Manuscript of the *De Viris Illustribus*," *Journal of the Warburg and Courtauld Institutes* 27 (1964): 90–107.

74. Giovanni Pontano, *I Trattati delle virtù sociali*, Francesco Tateo, ed. (Rome: Ateneo, 1965), 85–121.

75. Hans Baron, *The Crisis of the Early Italian Renaissance: Civic Humanism and Republican Liberty in an Age of Classicism and Tyranny*, 2 vols. (Princeton: Princeton University Press, 1955); idem, *In Search of Florentine Civic Humanism: Essays on the Transition from Medieval to Modern Thought*, 2 vols. (Princeton: Princeton University Press, 1988). This thesis has been criticized and modified, for example, by Jerrold E. Siegel, "'Civic Humanism' or Ciceronian Rhetoric? The Culture of Petrarch and Bruni," *Past and Present* 34 (1966): 3–48; Albert Rabil, Jr., "The Significance of 'Civic Humanism' in the Interpretation of the Italian Renaissance," in idem, *Renaissance Humanism*, 3 vols. (Philadelphia: University of Pennsylvania Press, 1988), 1:141–74. See also James Hankins, "The 'Baron Thesis' after Forty Years, and

as a key to Neapolitan historiography in the quattrocento. According to Bentley, Manetti's stylistics, Pontano's Sallustian approach to focused narrative, Panormita's political realism, and Valla's philological researches and analysis together marked Neapolitan historiography of the quattrocento as something new for the South and for humanist writing in general.

According to this schema, almost all Neapolitan historiography during the quattrocento imitated classical historians like Livy, Caesar, Suetonius, and Xenophon. It reflected a coherent political narrative; a new critical attitude toward the sources enabled by the discovery of new texts and careful philological study; a clearcut deployment of rhetorical skills to advance both utility and truthfulness; and an almost exclusive concentration on political themes that pitted the character, virtues and agency of Naples's rulers against the vicissitudes of *fortuna*.[76] What made Neapolitan historiography unique, Bentley observed, were the most startling examples of changing fortunes experienced by the Aragonese as they won and attempted to maintain their kingdom and its influence on Italy in the face of internal dissent, revolt, rival Italian machination, and foreign invasion.[77]

Building on the work of Cochrane and Bentley, but more importantly drawing on long traditions of Italian historiography, scholars at the University of Naples, Federico II have launched an intensive and decades-long study of Neapolitan historiography in the late medieval and early modern periods. Chiara De Caprio, Fulvio Delle Donne, Francesco Montuori, and Francesco Senatore are among the most prominent of this school,[78] bringing to bear deep and broad knowledge of the sources with philological and codicological research and advanced literary theory on authorship, audience, textual communities, orality and written textuality. Most

Some Recent Studies of Leonardo Bruni," *Journal of the History of Ideas* 56 (1995): 309–38; idem, ed., *Renaissance Civic Humanism: Reappraisals and Reflections* (Cambridge: Cambridge University Press, 2003).

76. Bentley, 222–41; Cappelli, 43–59, 187–224.

77. Bentley, 241–52.

78. See Bibliography.

recently Guido Cappelli has also presented a thorough study of the major Renaissance theme of *maiestas* in Neapolitan historiography in such works as Panormita's *De dictis et factis Alfonsi regis;* Giovanni Brancato's *Orationes ad Ferdinandum;* Diomede Carafa's *I doveri del principe;* Francesco Patrizi's *De regno* (the most-read political text of the cinquecento after Aristotle and Machiavelli); and Giovanni Pontano's *De principe, De obedientia,* and *De fortuna.*

Cappelli makes the convincing argument that Neapolitan humanists created an innovative model of enlightened rule, thoroughly based on classical *exempla,* keenly attuned to the political realities of the Regno, the rest of Italy and northern Europe, and fully cognizant of the need of the ruler to both exercise power and to display and exemplify the majesty of the state in his own person and behavior.[79] Neapolitan humanists turned to the secular, civic *exempla* of the Romans to guide the royal family and the state. In what Fulvio Delle Donne has termed *"umanesimo monarchico,"* secular considerations of state outweighed any lingering traditions of medieval rule.

Cappelli also joins a growing body of scholars, including Delle Donne and Francesco Senatore, who reexamine the retrospectively normative stature of Florentine "civic humanism" and question the denigration of Neapolitan forms of humanism as peripheral and second-hand, wedded too closely to monarchical developments and thus out of sync with the development of western political thought and institutions. Cappelli stresses that Naples and its new monarchy were at the forefront of European political and intellectual trends that led not to modern democratic government but rather to the *ancienne regime.* The key to Neapolitan concepts of *maiestas* is the consistent humanist program that the all-powerful state must include the ideas of justice, "mutual charity," equity, and consensus.

Narrative Sources: Civic Chroniclers
Unlike the humanist historians discussed above, the quattrocento and cinquecento also saw the continued and growing tradition of

79. As exemplified in Pontano's *The Prince,* pp. 115–38 and reading 19.

"civic chronicles" of Naples.[80] These reflected not official Aragonese policy or aspiration but the oral and visual life of the street, the documentary record of everyday life and their own perceptions of civic life and power. Without stretching such differences too far, one can say that such work reflected the existential situation of the writer immersed in the thick social context of the city.[81] These include the minor court official Loise de Rosa, Notar Giacomo, the writer known as Ferraiolo — all excerpted in the chapters below — and such chroniclers as Silvestro Guarino and Giuliano Passero. Like the author(s) of the famous trecento *Cronaca di Partenope*, they also chose to write in the Neapolitan vernacular and took their place among a circle of well informed figures who gave voice to the aspiring middle and professional classes of the city.

As opposed to the finely crafted product of humanist work, such a space maintained a constant dialogue with the reader and created text not as finished artifact but as continuous process of selection, extension, and revision. These texts also created a dialogue between the official state documents to which their authors had access via local municipal, *seggio,* and church records,[82] the printing press,

80. For analysis of these *cronache cittadine*, Francesco Senatore, "Fonti documentarie e costruzione della notizia nelle cronache cittadine dell'Italia meridionale (secoli XV–XVI)," *Bullettino ISIME* 116 (2014): 279–333; Chiara De Caprio "Spazi comunicativi, tradizioni narrative e storiografia in volgare: Il Regno negli anni delle guerre d'Italia," *Filologia Critica* 39 (2014): 39–72. For the later period, see John A. Marino, *Becoming Neapolitan: Citizen Culture in Baroque Naples* (Baltimore, MD: Johns Hopkins University Press, 2011); Chiara De Caprio, "La scrittura cronachistica nel Regno: Scriventi, tesi e stili narrativi," *Nuovi Studi Storici* 14.7 (2017): 1–42; repr. in Giampaolo Francesconi and Massimo Miglio, ed. *Le cronache volgari in Medio Evo: Atti della VI Settimana di studi medievali (Roma, 13–15 maggio 2015)* (Rome: ISIME, 2017), 227–68.

81. De Caprio, "Spazi comunicativi," 39–42 reminds us that both Machiavelli and Pontano made clear their immersion in the daily life around them that informed their ideas and work.

82. Chiara De Caprio and Francesco Senatore, "Orality, Literacy, and Historiography in Neapolitan Vernacular Urban Chronicles of the Fifteenth and Sixteenth Centuries," in *Interactions between Orality and Writing in Early Modern Italian Culture,* Luca Degl'Innocenti, Brian Richardson, and Chiara Sbordoni, ed. (London: Routledge, 2016), 129–43, at 138–42.

local gossip, report, memory, tradition, and historical and literary writing.[83]

These works differed from contemporary humanist texts in another very important regard: the incorporation of previous histories into their narratives. While Bruni might re-use the trecento chronicle of Giovanni Villani, or Flavio Biondo could incorporate any number of classical, medieval, and humanist accounts, one was never in doubt as to whose ego and authorial pen had organized the narrative and its themes. These civic chroniclers, on the other hand, did so in a way that submerged their authorial presence and questioned the very notion of single authorship in much the same way as today's online writing can often obscure individual authorship and authority.[84] For these urban historians there existed no notion of an "original text" as an abstract ideal. In addition, they molded their texts in accordance with audience expectation and contexts. While the humanists sought to enhance their own reputations — and their patronage and position — these urban historians sought rather to create a patrimony for their fellow citizens out of shared memory and experience.[85]

Apropos of this last point, throughout this book readers will also be impressed by the number of times Neapolitan writers reference their contemporaries and predecessors, whether they are humanists, civic historians, poets, or commentators on the arts. This intertextuality emerges as one of the important keys to understanding Neapolitan culture during this era: a relatively small

83. Chiara De Caprio, *Scrivere la storia a Napoli tra Medioevo e prima età moderna: Tre studi* (Rome: Salerno, 2012), 32–40; Senatore "Fonti documentarie"; De Caprio–Senatore, "Orality."

84. Eileen Gardiner notes similarities to today's digital journalism, where a story in the online *New York Times* might lead with breaking news and then supplement it with already reported background from several reporters. See Eileen Gardiner and Ronald G. Musto, *The Digital Humanities: A Primer for Students and Scholars* (New York: Cambridge University Press, 2015), 135–39. Thomas Pettitt, "Bracketing the Gutenberg Parenthesis," *Explorations in Media Ecology* 11.2 (2012): 95–114, has termed the print hiatus between manuscript and digital cultures the "Gutenberg parenthesis."

85. Senatore, "Fonti documentarie," 280.

cohort of literate and artistic minds depended upon, and constantly reinforced, the self-conscious community of arts and letters that emerged during these two centuries, forming both textual and visual communities among a wide variety of nationalities, backgrounds, and media.

HISTORIOGRAPHY OF THE ARTS
by Charlotte Nichols

Additional narrative sources include ekphrastic and other appreciations of the arts in Naples. Fra Bernardino Siciliano devotes an unusual, long poem of c.1503 to Cardinal Oliviero Carafa's sumptuous commission for the Soccorpo (1498–1506), a crypt built ex-novo beneath the high altar of the cathedral of Naples in which the newly recovered relics of San Gennaro were enshrined.[86] The priest's poem describes the process of construction with reverence, enthusiasm, and admiration. It is translated in chapter 3.

Responses to the new Spanish viceregency are embedded in the long letter of 1524 on the state of Neapolitan art sent by humanist Pietro Summonte to Marcantonio Michiel in Venice, fully translated here in chapter 9. First published in 1925, Summonte provides a very different kind of text than that of his mentor, Giovanni Pontano.[87] Rather than Pontano's ambitious humanistic formulations of *De Magnificentia*, with its references to Medicean Florence, ancient Rome, and those Neapolitan monuments that meet his mandate for *magnificentia*, Summonte here focuses on Neapolitan art produced in the two hundred years since Giotto. The result is an uneven accounting that both lists individual artists and their most notable works as well as Summonte's personal views on the arts. Despite many omissions of significant projects and a pro-Tuscan bias, in the absence of notarial documents Summonte's letter is nonetheless invaluable as a partial inventory of Renaissance works in Naples.

---

86. Franco Strazzullo, "La Cappella Carafa del Duomo di Napoli in un poemetto del primo cinquecento," *Napoli Nobilissima* 5 (1966): 62–63.

87. Fausto Nicolini, *L'arte napoletana del rinascimento e la lettera di Pietro Summonte a Marcantonio Michiel* (Naples: R. Ricciardi, 1925).

Giorgio Vasari visited Naples in the mid-1540s in the hope of gaining significant patronage from the Spanish viceroy, Don Pedro de Toledo, whose daughter, Eleonora, was married to Cosimo I de' Medici. He devotes long passages of the *Lives* to his experiences in Naples, which exude the Tusco-centricity and self-aggrandizement for which the biographies are generally known. His commentary is important, however, particularly with regard to the commissions he executed in the southern city. In contrast to Vasari, Don Pedro's patronage of urban planning and architecture projects is summarized in the ambitious narrative of Franco Strazzullo, who transcribes many relevant primary sources of information for the cinquecento.[88]

LITERATURE
by James H. Mc Gregor
Until recently, Naples has not fared well at the hands of literary historians of the Renaissance.[89] A century and a half ago Jacob Burckhardt

---

88. *Edilizia.*

89. While general introductions are not numerous, there are a lot of new works on single genres or authors that remain useful for a comprehensive picture of literature in Renaissance Naples. See Giorgio Petrocchi, "La letteratura napoletana del Rinascimento," SN 5: 281–336; M. Santagata, *La lirica aragonese: Studi sulla poesia napoletana del secondo Quattrocento* (Padua: Antenore, 1979); Alberto Asor Rosa, et al., ed., *Letteratura italiana: Storia e geografia* 7.2. *L'eta moderna.* (Florence: Einaudi, 1988); Roger Friedman, "A Bibliographical Introduction to the Study of Neapolitan Renaissance Literature," *Lettere Italiane* 44 (1992): 104–25; N. De Blasi, "Intrattenimento letterario e generi conviviali (farsa, intramesa, gliommero) nella Napoli aragonese," in *Passare il tempo: La letteratura del gioco e dell'intrattenimento dal XII al XVI secolo. Atti del convegno di Pienza, 10–14 settembre 1991,* 2 vols. (Rome: Salerno, 1993), 129-35; G. Villani, "L'Umanesimo napoletano," in *Storia della letteratura italiana,* E. Malato, ed., vol. 3.2 *Quattrocento* (Rome, Salerno, 1998), 709-62; T.R. Toscano, *Letterati, corti, accademie: La letteratura a Napoli nella prima metà del Cinquecento* (Naples: Loffredo, 2000); C. Corfiati, *Il Principe e la regina: Storie e letteratura nel Mezzogiorno Aragonese* (Florence: Olschki, 2009); Canepa, "Literary Culture;" Matteo Soranzo, *Poetry and Identity in Quattrocento Naples* (Farnham: Ashgate, 2014); Giancarlo Abbamonte, "Naples — A Poet's City: Attitudes towards Statius and Virgil in the Fifteenth Century," in Hughes–Buongiovanni, 170–88; A. Comboni

wrote an extended essay on what he called the "civilization" — by which he meant the "civic culture" — of the Renaissance in Italy. Burckhardt aimed to identify the essential change in human psychology that motivated those profound but in his view secondary changes in literature, art, and social structure that characterized the Renaissance. He found this underlying psychological dynamic in a complex of attitudes, which included a new sense of individualism, a repudiation of the ideals of feudalism, and a self-conscious and deliberate creation of rationalized forms of government. These three factors were, he argued, first represented in the despotic states of northern Italy and most perfectly exemplified in the great civic republics, Venice and Florence. With its lingering feudal structures, its agrarianism and its entrenched nobility, the early modern kingdom of Naples, comprising Sicily and southern Italy, simply did not fit Burckhardt's profile, and the notion of a Neapolitan Renaissance became something of a paradox.[90]

Was there a literary Renaissance in Naples? If so, how did it relate to the more familiar scenes and personalities of the literary Renaissance in Italy as a whole? Was it a spontaneous expression of the indigenous culture of the kingdom of Naples and of southern Italy or was it an imitative response to activities and trends that had their sources and motive forces outside the geographical and cultural limits of Neapolitan territory? Or to put the same question in other terms, was the Renaissance in Naples a local and provincial variation on themes borrowed from other regions of Italy, or was it a vital part of that national movement?

If we look at the Renaissance differently, and demand a less fundamental change in human character as the foundation for that historical period, we will see that Naples played a continual and significant role in the multiple enterprises of Renaissance literary

and T. Zanato, ed., *Atlante dei canzonieri in volgare del Quattrocento* (Florence: SISMEL-Edizioni del Galluzzo, 2017); N. De Blasi, *Saggi linguistici sulla storia di Napoli* (Naples: Società Napoletana di Storia Patria, 2017).

90. For a review of these issues see Musto, "Introduction;" idem, *Writing Southern Italy,* xix–xxi, 259–60.

culture. In a sense, Renaissance literature was a long-term work in progress, or perhaps a collection of works in progress. Different scholars and writers in different centers over a fairly long stretch of time — certainly from the time of Petrarch and Boccaccio to the mid-sixteenth century — were at work on activities that may not have had much underlying unity, but which can be identified fairly clearly.

In these terms there are three major projects that Renaissance literary writers worked on. The first is the recovery and refining of Classical Latin not just as a historical study but as a means for contemporary expression. This is a project that began in the proto-humanist circles of northern Italy sometime late in the thirteenth century and continued well beyond the end of the Renaissance.[91] The second is the development of a poetic tradition in the Italian vernacular. That tradition had roots first in Sicilian poetry in both medieval and Aragonese periods and in the poetry of southern France. But its founder and defining author was Francesco Petrarch. Petrarch's use of language, imagery, and poetic form in the collection of poems known either as the *Canzoniere* or the *Rime sparse* and in the *Trionfi* was the springboard for most of the developments in Italian lyric poetry in the Renaissance. The two works traveled together both in manuscript and in early print. The final project is less formal; it is both less literary and less self-fashioning than the other two. This is the development of the vernacular prose form called the *novella*. In the modern lexicon of literary forms the novella is a short novel but in the Italian tradition of the late Middle Ages and Renaissance, *novella* is the name for a fiction on the scale of the modern short-story. The masterpiece that defined the form and most clearly shaped its development was Boccaccio's *Decameron*.

As the selections that follow in this anthology demonstrate, Naples played a significant part in each of these three major projects. Many Neapolitan writers were involved in the development of humanist

91. See Ronald G. Witt, *The Two Latin Cultures and the Foundation of Renaissance Humanism in Medieval Italy* (Cambridge: Cambridge University Press, 2012).

Latin and all the forms of its expression. Such men as Antonio Beccadelli (Panormita), Giovanni Pontano, and Jacopo Sannazaro[92] were not simply local representatives of the movement but strong figures whose efforts spearheaded the national and international project of Latin humanism.[93] A telling example of the importance of Neapolitan humanism within Italy as a whole is offered by the volume *Poeti latini del Quattrocento*,[94] which covers the contributions of humanists throughout Italy. In a volume of some twelve hundred pages, four hundred pages are devoted to the works of Pontano and two hundred to Sannazaro; thus roughly half the volume is devoted to two Neapolitan writers.

Women also played a strong part in this literary movement. Poets like Tullia Aragona, Dorotea Acquaviva, Vittoria Colonna, Isabella di Morra and Laura Bacio Terracina all have associations with Naples and its Bay, creating what Croce called a "Mecca for women poets."[95] Vittoria Colonna (1492–1541), the famous friend of Michelangelo, was married to Ferrante Francesco d'Avalos, marquis of Pescara. She set up a court on Ischia at which Sannazaro, Pontano, Paolo Giovio, Teofilo Folengo, and Bernardo Tasso regularly attended. Maria d'Aragona (1503–68), marquisa of Vasto, also held literary court for humanists on Ischia, in Pozzuoli, and at the Palazzo d'Avalos in Chiaia; as did Roberta Carafa dei Maddaloni (c. 1509–80). Silvia Piccolomini, duchess of Amalfi and great niece of Popes Pius II and Pius III, assembled a remarkable library of the sciences and liberal arts that become a focus of literati. The patronage of royal women like Queen Isabella di Chiaromonte and of her daughter, Eleanora d'Aragona, is apparent throughout these pages.[96]

92. For Panormita, see readings 20–22, pp. 139–42. For recent work on Sannazaro, see pp. 169–83 and readings 28–30.

93. See also Canepa, "Literary Culture," 428–29.

94. Francesco Arnaldi, ed. (Milan: Ricciardi, 1964).

95. See Elisa Novi Chavarria, "The Space of Women," in Astarita (2013), 177–96, at 178; Canepa, "Literary Culture," 431–32; chapter 3, readings 33–34, 38–39, 43–44.

96. Novi Chavarria, "The Space of Women," 178–82.

The Petrarchan poetic tradition is represented by many men and three women in this volume. Perhaps the most important contribution of Neapolitan poets to the development of lyric came towards the middle of the sixteenth century, near the end of the Renaissance. These poets pushed the conventions of the Petrarchan sonnet beyond its traditional boundaries into a range of emotional expression and landscape evocation that is the forerunner of the Baroque sensibility.

In vernacular prose the towering Neapolitan figure is Masuccio Guardati, also known from the city of his birth as Masuccio Salernitano.[97] In his collection of *novelle* Masuccio shows that this supposedly northern, bourgeois and urban form of expression was completely at home in the imaginative world of the kingdom of Naples. In addition this collection includes *novelle* by Girolamo Morlini and Tommaso Costo.

In objective terms then it seems appropriate to say of Naples that it played a major role in each of the areas Renaissance literature was exploring. It played that role simultaneously with other centers, not lagging behind the pace of the Italian Renaissance, as was the case in France, where the Renaissance began in the 1530s, or England where it began only in the last decade of the sixteenth century. Naples had its own take on the multiple issues of the Renaissance, and it added its own stamp to every literary form its writers used.

Ultimately, though, the importance of Naples in the Renaissance must rest on the reader's assessment of those works that exemplify its contribution. That assessment will probably not be historically founded. A reader is more likely to judge a work on its appeal today than on its place in the scheme of literary history. It is my belief that the literature of the Neapolitan Renaissance can make a claim on our attention and can offer us much in the way of insight and pleasure, and it is my hope that what is good about the literature of the Neapolitan Renaissance has not been lost in my translations.

97. See D. Pirovano, *Modi narrativi e stili del* Novellino *di Masuccio Salernitano* (Florence: La Nuova Italia, 1991); and L. Terrusi, *El rozo idyoma de mia materna lingua: Studi sul 'Novellino' di Masuccio Salernitano* (Bari: Laterza, 2005).

THE VISUAL LEGACY OF NAPLES
by Charlotte Nichols
By 1600 Naples was considered one of the most beautiful cities in Europe, celebrated for its dramatic topography and brilliant Mediterranean setting. The lush, saturated ambiance has always encouraged sensual abandon and fervent piety, along with a frisson of danger felt particularly in the dark, narrow streets of the ancient city center where Caravaggio was disfigured in a brawl. This intoxicating atmosphere, commingling the sacred and profane, has both lured and repelled visitors, most of whom paid more attention to the views of the bay and local Roman sites rather than to the Neapolitan monuments within the walls. Indeed, those sites under consideration here have only begun to receive the level of scholarly attention long given other Italian cities to the north.

The history of the visual arts in Naples between 1400 and 1600 is distinguished by its extraordinarily aspirational patronage and cosmopolitan eclecticism. The status of the early modern city as an Angevin and Aragonese capital or Spanish viceregency; its function as a primary western Mediterranean port; and the multi-national diversity of its wealthier populations meant that the city was a conduit for artistic exchange. These factors, along with the tangible remains of the Greco-Roman past,[98] mandate that the Neapolitan artistic heritage should be considered in terms other than those used to assess developments in centers elsewhere on the peninsula with a more homogeneous population, such as communal Florence or oligarchic Venice. Despite these obvious distinctions, it was only with the shift of focus towards regionalism in the art historical scholarship of the later twentieth century that the interpretation of artistic production in Naples began to shed its long-standing historic biases — particularly those of Giorgio Vasari — favoring central and north Italian centers and to be fully considered as products of court sponsorship within the larger context of intra-peninsular and trans-Mediterranean cultural exchange.

98. See Hughes–Buongiovanni.

The fact of French and Spanish dominion in southern Italy during the period to be surveyed introduced complexities of foreign royal patronage not experienced in a comparably determining way elsewhere on the peninsula. Art functioned in a particularly distinctive manner for rulers to express authority and ingratiate themselves with the local populace. Therefore, it must be understood in terms other than those embodying an organic connection to a populace and its traditions. The ongoing prominent role of the work of non-Neapolitan artists — Catalan, Tuscan, Northern European, and Spanish among them — at the courts of the occupying French and Iberian regimes between 1400 and 1600 reflected changing political hegemonies and the adjustments of both indigenous and heterogeneous patrons to them.

A pattern of importation for major commissions had been established under the Angevins in the trecento — the Sienese Tino da Camaino's royal commemorative monuments or his design for the Certosa di San Martino, for example — and continued for centuries as a manifestation of 1. the continued political and economic connections between the kingdom and other centers including Tuscany, Rome, Dalmatia, Bruges, Valencia, and Castile; 2. the travels of artists working for specific religious orders; and 3. the presence of non-Neapolitan rulers and other patrons living in the southern capital. Distant artists tended either to send portable works from their own studios — such as Filippo Lippi, Donatello, Raphael, and Titian — or to spend relatively little time there if not required to work *in situ*.

Although this phenomenon of importation is not exclusive to Naples, it occurs with greater frequency as regimes changed; such perceived instability, together with the lack of a guild system, has been cited by historians as inhibiting the development of a distinctive Neapolitan school during the period under discussion. Conversely, it will be demonstrated that many of the foreign artists, such as Giuliano da Sangallo, did particularly innovative work on behalf of clients in Naples because of the *licenza* or freedom of experimentation facilitated by the lack of an entrenched local style and particularly proactive patrons. The reciprocal effect of Neapolitan culture on those foreign artists has only recently begun to be fully explored.

The potent combination of continuous foreign domination and cosmopolitanism has traditionally impeded scholarly assessment of the city. Prejudices against Spain on the part of Italians — and the physical distance of archives in Barcelona, Vallodolid, and Simancas[99] — meant that less attention was paid to the role of Iberia in shaping local culture. These prejudices have continued in historical researches until quite recently. The proto-baroque excesses of the later sixteenth century were contrary to neo-classical tastes as the formalization of art historical commentary evolved in the 1800s, with European scholars focused instead on the rediscovery of Pompeii and, in England, the British collectors of antiquities like Sir William Hamilton. Research was further impaired in 1943 by the Nazis' destruction of critically important archives from the Archivio di Stato in Naples and the Allied bombing of primary historical sites.[100]

Scholarly investigations undertaken in Naples for limited periods of time have traditionally been difficult for non-Neapolitan scholars. The perilous condition of buildings dating to our period due to neglect and earthquakes meant that until c.2000 they remained inaccessible to many without the laborious process of petitioning the Soprintendenza for access. Nor were they easily studied via photographs. The Tusco-centric orientation of campaigns by companies such as Alinari means that southern Italian monuments are incompletely documented by them. The copious photographic records of the various Soprintendenze in Naples are scattered among several locations and unavailable online, while requests for reproductions are often delayed. There have traditionally been no gathering points for foreign scholars analogous to those in Rome or Florence, which has been a deterrent to some.

99. For a summary of historical archives and chronicles see Marino, "Constructing the Past," in Astarita, *Companion*, 17–27; José Luis Rodríguez de Diego, "Napoli nell'Archivio di Simancas," *Napoli Nobilissima*, ser. 6.3 (2012): 155–60; López Rodríguez and López de la Plaza, "L'Archivio."

100. Riccardo Filangieri, *L'Archivio di Stato di Napoli durante la Seconda Guerra Mondiale,* Stefano Palmieri, ed. (Naples: Arte Tipografia, 1966). See above, 16–18.

Finally, the reputation of the city as dangerous or a less elite topic of study has discouraged them as well. Others, such as George Hersey, found these challenges invigorating, which resulted in his important publications about Aragonese patronage in 1969 and 1972.[101] Anthony Blunt's survey of seventeenth- and eighteenth-century Neapolitan architecture featured a valuable introductory chapter on cinquecento monuments, while the revisionist study of 2004 by Caroline Bruzelius on Angevin church architecture in Naples set the stage for the early quattrocento patronage considered here.[102]

The later twentieth century saw extraordinary efforts by Neapolitan, European, and American scholars to re-present the history of art between 1400 and 1600 in Naples within a larger Mediterranean context, fulfilling an intellectual initiative set in motion by Fernand Braudel from the 1920s on.[103] Pierluigi Leone de Castris augmented the study of Neapolitan painting in several volumes published in the 1980s and 1990s, including substantial transcriptions of documentary evidence, with a view towards the contributions of "foreign" artists, particularly those with long, influential careers in Naples.[104] Sabina

101. George Hersey, *Alfonso II and the Artistic Renewal of Naples, 1485–1495* (New Haven: Yale University Press, 1969); idem, *Aragonese Arch.*

102. In 1971 Christoph Thoenes published his comprehensive guide to Naples titled *Neapel und Umgebung* (Stuttgart: Reclam, reissued 1983). In 1974 Ludwig Heydenreich and Wolfgang Lotz illustrated Neapolitan works in their volume for the renowned Pelican History of Art series: *Architecture in Italy 1400–1600* (Penguin: Harmondsworth). Roberto Pane's lavishly illustrated and widely distributed two-volume set titled *Il rinascimento nell'Italia meridionale* also whetted scholarly appetites for Naples (Milan: Edizioni di Communità, 1975–77). Among Anglophone works, see Anthony Blunt, *Neapolitan Baroque and Rococo Architecture* (London: A. Zwemmer, 1975); Caroline Bruzelius, *The Stones of Naples: Church Building in the Angevin Kingdom, 1266–1343* (New Haven: Yale University Press, 2004); idem, and William Tronzo, *Medieval Naples: An Architectural and Urban History, 400–1400* (New York: Italica Press, 2011), which distills the 2004 study and modifies some of its findings.

103. Braudel (1972).

104. Paola Giusti and Pierluigi Leone de Castris, *Pittura del Cinquecento a Napoli, 1510–1540: Forestieri e regnicoli* (Naples: Electa, 1988); idem, *Pittura del Cinquecento*

de Cavi's seminal 2009 study of the Palazzo Reale by Domenico Fontana begun for the Spanish viceroys in 1600 presents the structure in relation to its Roman and Iberian prototypes.[105] Claire Challéat's magisterial account of Aragonese patronage with regard to non-Italian Mediterranean centers appeared in 2012.[106] Others began to situate Vasari's negative yet influential appraisal of the city as a personal reaction not only to his failure both to gain the position of Don Pedro's court artist but also even to function successfully in a multicultural city.[107] As noted above, three centuries of work in Naples by artists from other cities were traditionally deemed derivative. These began to be re-evaluated.[108] Art historical scholarship profited from the revisionist work of historians in

---

a *Napoli, 1540–1573: Fasto e devozione* (Naples: Electa, 1996); idem, *Pittura del Cinquecento a Napoli, 1573–1606: L'ultima maniera* (Naples: Electa, 1991).

105. Sabina de Cavi, *Architecture and Royal Presence: Domenico and Giulio Cesare Fontana in Spanish Naples (1592–1627)* (Newcastle-upon-Tyne: Cambridge Scholars Publishing, 2009).

106. Claire Challéat, *Dalle Fiandre a Napoli: Committenza artistica, politica, diplomazia al tempo di Alfonso il Magnanimo e Filippo il Buono* (Rome: Bretschneider, 2012). As this volume goes to press, a new partnership has been created between the O'Donnell Institute of Art History (University of Texas at Dallas) and the Museo e Real Bosco di Capodimonte to facilitate the study of Naples as a globally interconnected port city: https://www.utdallas.edu/arthistory/port-cities.

107. The second edition of Giorgio Vasari, *Lives of the Painters, Sculptors and Architects* (1568), Gaston du C. de Vere, trans. (New York: Knopf, 1912, repr. 1996), is used throughout this book. See the revisionist essays by Aislinn Loconte, "The North Looks South: Giorgio Vasari and Early Modern Visual Culture in the Kingdom of Naples," *Art History* 31 (2008): 438–59; and Thomas Willette, "Giotto's Allegorical Painting of the Kingdom of Naples," in *Gifts in Return: Essays in Honour of Charles Dempsey*, Melinda Schlitt, ed. (Toronto: Centre for Reformation and Renaissance Studies, 2012), 69–92.

108. Charlotte Nichols, "The Caracciolo di Vico Chapel in Naples and Early Cinquecento Architecture" (Ann Arbor: UMI, 1988); Bianca De Divitiis, "Giuliano da Sangallo in the Kingdom of Naples: Architecture and Cultural Exchange," *Journal of the Society of Architectural Historians* 74.2 (2015): 152–78.

several volumes of collected articles.[109] The publication in 2017 on Naples in the series titled Artistic Centers of the Italian Renaissance (Cambridge University Press) brings together the synthetic essays of European and American scholars.[110] All of these scholarly impulses are fully manifested in the indefatigable and meticulous research on fifteenth-century patronage by Bianca De Divitiis of the University of Naples and her équipe.[111]

An exhibition in 2013 at the Uffizi Gallery, titled *Norma e capriccio: Spagnoli in Italia agli esordi della "maniera moderna,"* made the connections between Spanish artists and Italy in the Renaissance visible for a larger non-scholarly audience.[112] In the 1980s this author made a long trip to Burgos in search of a small, exquisite marble sculpture of Saint Sebastian by Diego de Siloé that had been made for the altarpiece in the Caracciolo di Vico Chapel in San Giovanni a Carbonara in Naples. It was locked in a cupboard in the sacristy of a suburban church, whose nervous young curate produced it only after much persuasion. The sculpture travelled to Florence for the Uffizi's exhibition three decades later.

There are several ways to present the material culture of Naples between 1400 and 1600. One can highlight patronage by considering artistic production within a chronological framework of the foreign dynasties in power. Another approach is to use each medium as a means of organizing the overview. The latter option is followed here to showcase the way in which succeeding artists responded to shifting regimes and tastes. Related documents in this volume are cross-referenced throughout. They include a full English translation by Frederick J. Booth of Giovanni Pontano's *De Magnificentia* (1498) in chapter 9[113] and of Pietro Summonte's letter to Marcantonio Michiel

109. For example, Astarita (2013).

110. Hall–Willette.

111. See the Bibliography.

112. Tommaso Mozzati and Antonio Natali, ed., *Norma e capriccio: Spagnoli in Italia agli esordi della "maniera moderna." Exh. Galleria degli Uffizi, Florence, 5 March–26 May 2013* (Florence: Giunti, 2013).

113. Reading 164 and pp. 395–441.

in 1524 by Charlotte Nichols in chapter 10.[114] The chapters may be summarized as follows.

Urban Planning
The orthogonal grid laid down by the planners of the ancient Greek colony "Neapolis" continued to form the nucleus of the city between 1400 and 1600. The fortress-residence of Castel Nuovo, built by the Angevins and substantially rebuilt by the conquering Alfonso I, announced the city by sea. By land, friend and foe would have entered the city further uphill through such gates as the Porta Capuana on the eastern side of the city, and the Porta Reale to the west. These gateways led to the *decumani* of the venerable urban center (which was subdivided into *seggi* or administrative districts). Alfonso's promotion of a cultural agenda *all'antica* meant that he delighted in the perceived Vitruvian aspects of this historic urban plan — indeed, he planned to found an ideal city on the ruins of Bivona in southern Italy[115] — and the sovereign promoted the neighborhood as a site for the ambitious new residences of his humanist-minded Neapolitan allies.

Alfonso I initiated a number of urban improvements, but it was not until the 1480s that a systematic overhaul of the Angevin city was undertaken by the Aragonese. His grandson Alfonso, duke of Calabria, son of Ferrante I and heir to the throne (r. 1494–95), is generally credited with supervising a number of projects, which were eloquently championed by the celebrated humanist and statesman Giovanni Pontano, also the duke's former tutor, in his epic prose-poem on the mythical origins of the city, *Lepidina* (1496).[116]

The future Alfonso II focused his efforts on developing the eastern side of the city. He pushed the extant Angevin city walls further east

114. Reading 169 and pp. 447–66.

115. Bruno Figliuolo, "Sulla fondazione, fallita, della nuova città di Alfonsina in Calabria (1447)," *Archivio storico italiano* 170.634 (2012): 725–30.

116. For celebrations of Naples in relation to Vitruvius, see Vincenzo Fontana, *Fra' Giovanni Giocondo architetto 1432–1515* (Vicenza: Neri Pozza, 1988), 27–28; Geoffrey Hamburg, "Vitruvius, Fra Giocondo, and the City of Naples," *Acta Archaeologica* 36 (1965): 25; and De Seta, "Urban Structure," 352, who also notes that Duke Alfonso's utopian vision may be compared to Filarete's Sforzinda for Milan.

in the 1480s; this allowed the duke to coopt property surrounding the newly enclosed Castel Capuano, which he transformed into a sumptuous residence. He established lush private gardens outside of the castle, with a built retreat called La Duchesca for his wife, Ippolita Maria Sforza. From the castle, Alfonso could easily access his brilliant new villa named Poggioreale. Giuliano da Maiano's services were loaned by Lorenzo de' Medici for all of these commissions.

The viceroys of Naples, acting on behalf of the kings of Spain, configured the city as experienced today. The Spanish Viceroy Don Pedro de Toledo (r. 1532–53) induced both physical — and ultimately psychological — upheaval with his extensive plans for the urban development of the port city, which was emerging as an important satellite of imperial Spain in the sixteenth century. His many accomplishments with regard to urban planning over two decades include the expansion of the walls west of the street grid defining the traditional city center; uphill towards the Castel Sant'Elmo (which he vastly renovated) and in the coastal zone called the Chiaia west of Castel Nuovo; the laying of the Via Toledo running north-south from the zone west of Castel Nuovo to the new Porta Reale (adjacent to the modern Piazza Dante); the creation of the Spanish Quarter on the western side of the city to house administrative employees and soldiers; the construction of roads running northwest along the coast beyond Castel Nuovo, through the sites with many ancient ruins in Pozzuoli and on to Rome; and new roads heading south to the Sorrentine peninsula.[117]

Despite Don Pedro's enlargement of the city walls from a circumference of approximately five miles to eight, the city was dangerously overcrowded by the later sixteenth century. Its population had quadrupled during the sixteenth century alone, reaching 225,769 by 1596.[118] In addition to an influx of land-owners and others in search of employment, a major factor contributing to the crowding was the viceregal designation of land within the walls to accommodate new and expanded monastic complexes in an effort to strengthen Catholicism by making it a visually dominant

117. Franco Strazzullo, *Edilizia e urbanistica a Napoli tra XVI e XVII secolo* (Naples: Berisio, 1968), 5–24; and Pane, "Pietro di Toledo."

118. Muto (2013), 43. For population figures, see also above, p. 16 and n. 58.

force. This mandate to *"fare isola"* (or appropriate property to create a block) ultimately created a disproportionate number of churches in the city in relation to its size. To compensate for the lack of available housing, more storeys were added to pre-existing structures, thus creating the towering structures that continue to darken streets in the historic center today.

Royal and Aristocratic Residences
The proclamation of political hegemony is manifested in the residences of the Aragonese sovereigns and Spanish viceroys. While Alfonso inherited the dominant skyline of churches created by the Angevins, he rebuilt the damaged Castel Nuovo, which was one of the five royal castles.[119] It was immediately visible to those who approached the city by sea as seen in the *Tavola Strozzi* (c.1473). Alfonso proclaimed his dominion by commissioning an unusual triumphal arch (begun 1452) for the new entrance to the renovated fortress-residence. This monument faced the city center uphill; and its gateway *all'antica* announced his political, cultural, and Roman imperial ambitions in a boldly aggressive way. (He also displayed portraits of the Spanish emperors Trajan and Hadrian inside the Castel Nuovo.) The design of the Sala Grande, or the throne room (1452–57), by Guillem Sagrera commingled an Italian and Catalan aesthetic that embodied the cosmopolitan flavor often distinguishing the port cities of the Mediterranean from their inland counterparts.

The Greco-Roman site of ancient Neapolis provided the point of departure for rulers and local patrons in their visions of urban renewal. Alfonso I and his Aragonese successors promoted private building by local allies within the venerable street grid to reinforce associations with the antiquity of the city. This effort also announced a new location for the elites, who had previously settled near Castel Nuovo during the Angevin reign. Residences, such as Diomede Carafa's palace (begun 1450s) along a decumanus (Via San Biagio), incorporated visual programs that proclaimed the ancient origins of the city even as they celebrated the rulership of the reigning Aragonese sovereign. Palaces were further embellished by collections of antiquities from local sites unavailable in such quantities elsewhere on the peninsula, save Rome. These initiatives were broadcast by court humanists, including Giovanni Pontano. Building continued in the area in the early cinquecento

119. The others were the castles Belforte, Carmine, dell'Ovo, and Capuano.

with structures like the Palazzo di Capua (or Marigliano) begun by Giovanni Francesco Donadio (il Mormando).

Alfonso I's grandson, Alfonso, duke of Calabria and Alfonso II (r. 1494–95), contributed significantly to the phenomenon of *villegiatura* by building a sumptuous retreat in the 1480s, called Poggioreale, beyond the eastern walls of the city in a zone that was fertile but also potentially swampy. In so doing he echoed other patrons, such as Lorenzo de' Medici, by this time a Neapolitan ally. Lorenzo also supplied the duke with the services of Giuliano da Maiano, a Florentine artist whose star had been eclipsed by Giuliano da Sangallo. The latter was engaged in constructing Poggio a Caiano for Lorenzo, with which the Neapolitan structure and surroundings, including a nymphaeum, clearly competes. (At Lorenzo's request, Sangallo travelled to Naples to present Ferrante II with his model for a magnificent new royal palace in 1488.) Scant remains of Poggioreale survive. The villa was, however, documented by Sebastiano Serlio, and interest in it has intensified over recent decades. The estate was linked directly to the duke's residence at Castel Capuano, newly enclosed by the walls as they shifted further east. Alfonso splendidly renovated that castle as well and claimed the property now within the walls for the lush gardens greatly admired by the invading French king, Charles VIII. At this time, the coastal areas west of the city also provided settings for airies with spectacular views of the bay, thermal springs, and antiquities. The Aragonese rulers granted properties there to loyal humanists, such as Giovanni Pontano and Jacopo Sannazaro.

Nor did the Spanish viceroys shy from using palace design to communicate their ambitions in the 1500s. Don Pedro de Toledo shifted his primary residence from the fortress-palace of Castel Nuovo to one designed in 1548 by the Spaniard Fernando Maglione. As noted above, the palazzo faced westward towards a new street leading to a new gate, the Porta Romana. That gate was located near the palazzo of Luigi Carafa di Stigliano (also Palazzo Cellamare), a powerful political ally. This commission, together with the westward expansion of the city generally under Don Pedro, was reinforced by the trend to build villas beyond the Porta Romana, one of which belonged to the viceroy and another to his son, Don Garcia. High above loomed Castel Sant'Elmo (formerly the Castel Belforte), redesigned during Don Pedro's tenure by Pedro Luis Escrivá as a commanding defensive outpost. The century closed with the grand plan of c.1600 by Domenico Fontana, formerly Pope Sixtus V's architect, for a much more splendid viceregal seat. The Palazzo Reale continues to command the breezy coastal zone west of Castel Nuovo and across from the later Piazza del Plebiscito.

Ecclesiastical Projects

The Renaissance has traditionally been perceived as a period of little or no significance with regard to ecclesiastical architecture in Naples. Yet during that time, Neapolitan patronage of religious institutions was no less expressive of building trends than its medieval mendicant houses or lavish late sixteenth- and seventeenth-century churches. Almost all of the sizeable projects from 1400 to 1550 were built for reformed branches of long-established religious orders: San Giovanni a Carbonara for the Observant Augustinians begun c.1410 by King Ladislaus, Sta. Maria di Monteoliveto for the Olivetan Benedictines begun in the early 1500s, the upper and lower churches of SS. Severino e Sossio for the reformed Benedictines, and Sta. Caterina a Formello for the Observant Dominicans (1515–77).[120] One notable exception was the non-monastic Spanish national church of San Giacomo degli Spagnoli begun in 1540 under the aegis of Don Pedro de Toledo. It was designed by his Spanish building superintendent, Fernando Maglione, and administered by the Knights of Saint James, whose cult had been promoted by the Aragonese kings and Spanish viceroys. (Don Pedro's sumptuous free-standing tomb by the local sculptor Giovanni da Nola is located there.) Even the sixteenth-century churches of the new religious orders, such as the first church of the Jesuits, the Gesù Vecchio (begun in 1557), can best be understood in terms of these earlier Renaissance churches for the *riformati*. In fact, it would be difficult to find another major Italian city

---

120. Many of the new churches between 1400 and 1500 in Florence are also from the reformed or Observant branches of the orders: San Marco (Observant Dominican), Sta. Maria a San Gallo (Observant Augustinian), San Salvatore al Monte (Observant Franciscan).

in this period where their architectural patronage was so completely synonymous with trends in ecclesiastical building generally. The reformed orders developed an innovative church type in Naples and applied it consistently to a wide range of project sites. The churches were decorated by teams of artists, many of whom traveled from church to church within a given order to execute frescoes, choir stalls, and the like. Guido Mazzoni's terracotta tableau of the *Lamentation* (1490–92), incorporating portraits of the Aragonese, in Monteoliveto is particularly striking.

This distinctive church prototype may be seen at Sta. Caterina a Formello, prominently located adjacent to the Porta Capuana, and initially constructed with the participation of the Tuscan Romolo Balsimelli. The determining elements include a barrel-vaulted nave flanked on each side by identical chapels; a retro-choir; inscribed transepts; and a dome over the crossing, which was the first local, large-scale cupola since antiquity. These key elements of post-Tridentine churches were present in Naples by the 1530s and appeared in the first Jesuit church there: the Gesù Vecchio (1558) by Giovanni Tristano, the building superintendent of the Society of Jesus. All of these features recur in the plan for the Gesù in Rome, begun in 1568 by Giacomo Barozzi da Vignola. Late in the century, the architect Giuseppe Valeriano adopted a Greek cross plan for the Gesù Nuovo (begun in 1584), which incorporated part of the distinctive diamond-point façade of the Palazzo Sanseverino, probably due to the constraints of the pre-existing palace site. It is also indicative of the willingness of the Jesuits to experiment as architectural patrons, especially with a central plan that alludes to those under consideration for St. Peter's and, therefore, the papacy to which the Jesuits were so devoted. Perhaps relevant is the Neapolitan belief that Saint Peter was the founder of the Christian church in Naples.

There is one particularly significant category of ecclesiastical building patronage outside of the reformed religious orders: the commemorative chapel. The orders were often pawns in the struggle for political hegemony in Naples on the part of both the ruling dynasty and of private local patrons seeking to consolidate their position with the foreign occupier or to counter that occupation with grand, even magnificent, statements of personal or civic identity.

One example of a visual alliance by a Neapolitan patron with a foreign regime is the funerary chapel in San Giovanni a Carbonara commissioned by Sergianni Caracciolo del Sole, grand seneschal and paramour of Giovanna II of Anjou (who evidently intended to be buried in the church). Begun c. 1427, the monument takes the form of a large rotunda appended to the presbytery of the church and entered by passing under the towering tomb of the queen's brother, King Ladislaus. Sumptuously painted with frescoes by the Lombard Leonardo da Besozzo, the construct is a bold, idiosyncratic statement of power and prestige on the part of a Neapolitan aristocrat.

Antonio Todeschini Piccolomini similarly proclaimed his alliance with the Aragonese a half-century later. The Sienese nephew of Pius II had been rewarded with a marriage to Maria, daughter of Ferrante I, in return for political favors. Following her early death, c. 1470 Antonio commissioned from Antonio Rossellino a commemorative chapel for the church of Sta. Maria di Monteoliveto that copied the artist's chapel for James, the Cardinal of Portugal for San Miniato in Florence, also an Olivetan church. Scholars have generally regarded the architecture and sculpture of the Cappella Piccolomini as completely derivative. Except for the replacement of the Florentine painted altarpiece with Rossellino's large and innovative marble relief of the Adoration for the altarpiece, which heightens the overall impression of conspicuous consumption, one could agree with this comparative assessment. Far from seeming derivative, however, the chapel must have been viewed by its southern audience as a fashionable statement of power and prestige, which introduced to the Aragonese court and Neapolitan aristocracy the mode of the latest Florentine tour de force for commemorative ensembles. The commission (1470–81) would have also had the effect of rendering Angevin mortuary commissions visually obsolete. His chapel introduces a level of lavish patronage that compromises the simplicity of the original construction for the reformed Benedictines. In the same way, royal and aristocratic lay patronage at the Observant Augustinian monastery of San Giovanni a Carbonara had already altered its interior appearance.

Private citizens continued to commission highly innovative mortuary chapels, as did cardinals and bishops operating in much the same way. It is important to note the degree to which two non-monastic chapels in particular — the Pontano Chapel (begun in 1490) and Cardinal Oliviero Carafa's Soccorpo (1497–1506) by Giuliano da Sangallo — appropriate with striking originality a highly symbolic classical vocabulary that encourages civic identity in a metropolis continually occupied by foreign rulers. Giovanni Pontano, the consummate humanist and political consort of the kings of Aragon, is without precedent, parallel, or progeny in early modern commemorative ideation. Located alongside the decumanus of ancient Neapolis, his chapel takes the form of a freestanding rectangular block prominently adorned on the interior with lengthy elegies of the patron's own composition and on the exterior with moralizing apothegms written during the extraordinary political upheavals of the late fifteenth-century in Naples: the invasion of the city by Charles VIII and the subsequent battle between the French and Spanish for its control.

Cardinal Carafa's Soccorpo also announces a Neapolitan identity. Recovering the precious miracle-working relics of San Gennaro, he enshrined them in a sumptuous reinvention of a paleo-Christian crypt or basilica that features a life-sized image of himself kneeling in communion with the tomb of the bishop-saint. Cardinal Carafa thus reinforced his own claims to authority while providing the citizens of a perpetually occupied city with a locus in which their powerful early Christian religious heritage may be visually recalled. The commissions for the Pontano Chapel and the Soccorpo assert an innate "Italian-ness" in the face of continuing threats from the French.

The subjugators also felt vulnerable. Neapolitan viceroys like Pedro de Toledo were threatened in the second quarter of the sixteenth century by the preachings of persuasive heretics like Juan de Valdés and Bernardino Ochino, who appealed to a population disillusioned with the excesses and lassitudes displayed by many of the unreformed religious orders. Consequently, the viceregency promoted the foundation of the new orders — including the Jesuits and Theatines — and was hospitable to them, so long as they could be manipulated for the realization of imperial ambitions and beliefs. The orders thus became a tool of the Spanish regents in ensuring orthodoxy in Naples. This was manifested visually by the explosive expansion of monastic communities within the walls of the city. Furthermore, the Spanish viceroys in Naples openly encouraged both the construction of churches to accommodate the new orders and the renovation of the structures of the older orders. As noted, this ultimately created a disproportionate number of churches in the city — nearly 100 monasteries by 1600 — in relation to its size. Such patronage created a wealth of opportunities for local and non-Neapolitan artists who were deployed to embellish these new structures.

Painting

The cosmopolitan scope of patronage under René of Anjou (r.1438–42) and Alfonso I of Aragon (r.1442–58) defined that of the following centuries in a way that distinguished Naples from centers elsewhere on the peninsula. Alfonso imported the services of painters from Valencia; owned panels by Jan Van Eyck — supplied by his ally Philip the Good of Burgundy — in the revolutionary new oil medium; commissioned work from the north Italian court painter and illuminator Leonardo da Besozzo, whose highly decorative style had attracted Neapolitan patrons during the Angevin period; displayed Cosimo de' Medici's gift of an altarpiece by Filippo Lippi; and commissioned a polyptych from the local artist Colantonio. The latter also encountered the Sicilian prodigy Antonello da Messina in 1445 during his stay in Naples.

The presence of Tuscans in the Regno at mid-century, such as the banker Filippo Strozzi, exiled from Medicean Florence, and Antonio Todeschini Piccolomini, married to Ferrante I's daughter, reflected the ongoing interconnection of patrons, politics, ecclesiastics, and the papacy there. Lorenzo de' Medici used the talents of artists to ensure Aragonese fealty later in the century, including that of the powerful Neapolitan Cardinal Oliviero Carafa, who supplied the services of Filippino Lippi to paint his chapel of 1488 in Sta. Maria sopra Minerva in Rome. (After 1500 Carafa also commissioned Pietro Perugino, the Umbrian hard at work on behalf of Sixtus IV, to paint the *Assumption of the Virgin with San Gennaro and Cardinal Carafa* for the cathedral of Naples.)

The Spanish victory in 1503 encouraged painters from Iberia to seek work in the southern city. These included Pedro Fernandez de Murcia (Pseudo-Bramantino), who brought with him an experience of central Italian artists, as would the north Italian follower of Leonardo Cesare da Sesto. The latter had worked for Julius II alongside Raphael and Peruzzi. The presence of Raphael's altarpiece, the *Madonna del Pesce*, in San Domenico after c.1515 inspired generations of local and foreign artists in Naples, including Andrea Sabatini from nearby Salerno and Marco Cardisco from Calabria. Raphael's pupil Polidoro da Caravaggio was in Naples twice during the 1420s.

Giorgio Vasari worked in Naples in the mid-1540s, following stints in Venice and Rome. The challenges of working in a multi-cultural, chaotic city, together with his failure to gain significant commissions from Don Pedro, whose daughter Eleonora was married to Duke Cosimo I de' Medici, caused Vasari to depart within a few years. Yet the Tuscan painter did leave significant work there in the "modern manner" that he claimed to have introduced to the region. His stuccoed, frescoed vault *all'antica* for the sacristy of the prestigious foundation of Monteoliveto influenced artists like Pedro de Rubiales (Roviale), who had also worked in Farnese Rome. Don Pedro de Toledo commissioned the Spaniard to paint the chapel of Castel Capuano that had been newly transformed by the viceroy from a royal residence into an administrative center.

The explosion of monastic building in the second half of the cinquecento provided innumerable commissions from religious orders and private patrons for painters. These included Marco Pino from Siena, who remained in Naples for three decades (1551–83). He worked alongside the local artist Giovanni Battista Llama. Dirck Hendricksz from Spanish Flanders married a Neapolitan and, like Pino, had worked in Rome with practitioners of a mid-century classicism that blended the innovations of Raphael and Michelangelo. Dirck lived in Naples from the 1570s until 1609. This trio was joined by Belisario Corenzio from Greece, whose animated late-century classicism was jolted by the experience of Caravaggio. That Lombard settled in Naples in 1606 under the protection of the Colonna family after escaping from Rome, where he was wanted for murder. Caravaggio's darkly haunting work revolutionized the Neapolitan artistic landscape, and the *Flagellation of Christ* for the

De Franchis family joined Raphael's *Madonna del Pesce* (c.1515) and Titian's *Annunciation* (1557) in San Domenico, where the Aragonese royals were also buried. The brawl outside a tavern in Naples resulted in injuries that affected his ability to paint and, consequently, the style of the late paintings.

Caravaggio's gifted follower, Battistello Caracciolo, along with Corenzio and Juseppe de Ribera, formed the notorious "Cabal of Naples," whose objective in the early 1600s was to eliminate by life-threatening means any non-resident competitors for prestigious Neapolitan commissions, particularly those for the treasury of San Gennaro in the Duomo. Just as Summonte had bemoaned the lack of local talent in 1524, by 1622 cathedral officials lamented that there were no local artists capable of directing that commission.

Antiquity

The city of Naples, founded as a Greek colony, provided an extraordinary stage on which kings, poets, humanists, and patrons could indulge the early modern passion for antiquity. Not only had its Greco-Roman grid remained intact, but during the Middle Ages it was the only place on the peninsula where Greek was taught, and a constellation of Greek temples could even be visited at Paestum. Part of the Roman temple of Castor and Pollux (the Dioscuri) survived along the upper decumanus (Via Tribunali). Further away from the center, Virgil's tomb and other coastal ruins in Baia and the Campi Flegrei increasingly attracted artists, collectors, and travelers during the centuries before the discovery of Pompeii. The late quattrocento sketchbook of Giuliano da Sangallo, the *Codex Barberini* (Vatican Library), survives as a *dimostrazione* of the transformative impact of antiquities in and near the city on an artist from ruin-starved Florence.

Foreign rulers in Naples adopted an especially bombastic artistic vocabulary *all'antica* to convey dominion, as seen in Alfonso I's hubristic triumphal entrance begun in the 1450s for the renovated Castel Nuovo, a decade after defeating the Angevins. Within the castle, the king systematically displayed portraits of the Spanish emperors Trajan and Hadrian. Likewise, Neapolitan aristocrats, such as Diomede Carafa, followed suit as noted collectors of antiquities, some excavated on their own properties outside the city and displayed on the exterior and interior of their new urban palaces. Driven by the mania to possess all things ancient, cognoscenti were fully capable of inventing provenances for works such as the *Protome Carafa,* the equine head by Donatello. The humanist and poet Giovanni Pontano celebrated the Aragonese dynasty in a series of eloquent writings, including his prose-poem *Lepidina* (1496), which evoked the mythical origins of the city. Pontano was rewarded in turn with a palace and an adjacent ancient quadrifons arch, both along the same decumanus as the temple of Castor and Pollux. Here he built his commemorative chapel (begun in 1490) in the form of the ancient Roman roadside tombs embellished with inscriptions that he praises in *De Magnificentia* (1498), translated below in chapter 9.[121]

In the following century, Pietro Summonte, a disciple of Pontano whose lengthy letter of 1524 to the Venetian Marcantonio Michiel is translated in chapter 10, lauded the antiquities visible near Naples as a way of claiming superiority over other Italian centers. Spanish viceroys also laid claim to the past in attempting to link their hegemony to the Aragonese and, through them, to Rome. Don Pedro de Toledo built a villa over ancient ruins in Pozzuoli (Puteoli) and eagerly participated in antiquarian culture. The coastal road leading to Campania that he laid out during the mid-1500s facilitated access to the Campi Flegrei, which began to be visited increasingly by foreign travelers as well by the end of the century. The emerging genre of guidebook facilitated such expeditions. The most well-known of them was written by Benedetto di Falco, seven editions of which were published between 1535 and 1680.[122]

FORMS OF COMMUNICATION
by Ronald G. Musto

Orality, Manuscript, and Print
Recent research, most especially by scholars at the University of Naples, Federico II, have concentrated on the forms of communication that underlay and helped define all other structures of life, literature,

121. Pages 395–441.

122. See below, p. 477, Fig. 84.

and the arts in early modern Naples.[123] Rather than positing a series of discontinuities and successive stages between oral traditions (folk tales, urban gossip, *infamia* and rumor, official news and royal decree), manuscript culture, and the new printing press, they have carefully laid out the interconnections among all three forms. It has long been accepted among Renaissance scholars that the manuscript culture of the Middle Ages did not suddenly die with the coming of Gutenberg. Deluxe manuscripts continued to be produced for princes and wealthy bourgeois for at least a century after the invention of print; while manuscript compilations, often based on a variety of sources, continued to be created by private individuals at various social levels and with various classical and vernacular language skills. Some, like those of the Neapolitan chronicler Ferraiolo, combined oral, manuscript, and printed sources into his own custom-made manuscript; some were like Notar Giacomo, who based his work on every available source: from earlier histories and local memory, to official documentation filtered down to local administrators, to the urban networks of oral transmission that connect the palace to the street. In the other direction, Giacomo's own eyewitness and his professional role as a notary took oral testimony and transformed it into the official documentation of the court and archive.[124]

Latin and Vernacular Printers
The history of printing in Naples offers both a familiar pattern with pan-Italian developments and its own particular forms.[125] As in Rome,

123. As, for example, De Caprio–Senatore, "Orality."

124. On the role of the notariate as intermediary between official royal power and the life of the streets, De Caprio, *Scrivere*, 94–104; idem, "La scrittura cronachistica," 25–38.

125. See Fava and Bresciano, *La stampa a Napoli nel XV secolo*; Biblioteca Nazionale di Napoli, *Libri a stampa napoletani dal 1400 al 1800* (Naples: Biblioteca Nazionale, 1952); Pietro Manzi, *La tipografia napoletana nel '500* (Florence: L.S. Olschki, 1971–75); Santoro and Fletcher, *La stampa a Napoli*; Lorenzo Giustiniani, *Saggio storico-critico sulla tipografia del Regno di Napoli* (Sala Bolognese: Forni, 1985, repr. Nabu, 2012); Silvia Sbordone, *Editori e tipografi a Napoli nel '600* (Naples: Accademia Pontaniana, 1990); William Emmet Coleman and Gordon D. Piltch, *Naples, the Lost Renaissance: Neapolitan Books and Manuscripts from the Collections of the New York Public Library, Friday, November 22, 1991* (New York: City University, Graduate

Naples' printing presses were established by Germans, brought into partnership with local book dealers and scribes, often abandoned either by personal or financial changes, sometimes maintained through aristocratic and royal patronage, and focused on either the new Latin learning or the more popular forms of vernacular literatures. Several of Naples' most active printers have been well documented by Pietro Manzi and other scholars. These printers included Giovanni Paolo Suganappo, Raimondo Amato, Giovanni De Boy, Giovanni Maria Scotto, Sigismondo Mayr, Giovanni A. de Caneto, Antonio de Frizis, Giovanni Pasquet de Sallo, Giuseppe Cacchi, Giovanni Battista Cappelli and the Stamperia Stigliola.

Of these perhaps the best known is Francesco del Tuppo (1443/44–1501).[126] He was born in Naples in the *seggio* of Porto. His father was a notary and royal court official from the time of Queen Giovanna II on; and Francesco received his education there under the personal patronage of Alfonso I. Though he never completed a university education, he became a *familiaris* of King Ferrante's court. In 1471 Sisto Riessinger of Strasbourg set up the first printing press in Naples. Francesco became his associate in 1473, and in 1481 he took over his press when Riessinger left for Rome. In 1480 King Ferrante granted Francesco a privilege to sell his books throughout the Regno without toll or tax. Del Tuppo's connections to the high nobility and distinguished humanists brought him a ready audience but, like many publishers, little financial gain. He specialized in legal texts for university classroom use but also published the new Italian vernacular literature, issuing the *editio princeps* of Masuccio Salernitano's *Novellino*,[127] editions of Dante's *Commedia* (1479), Boccaccio's *Fiammetta* and *Filocolo*, a translation of the *Eroidi*, of

---

Center, 1991); Antonio Garzya, ed., *Per la storia della tipografia napoletana nei secoli XV–XVIII: Atti del convegno internazionale, Napoli, 2005, 16–17 dicembre* (Naples: Accademia Pontaniana, 2006).

126. Bentley, 58–59, 78–79; Paola Farenga, "Del Tuppo, Francesco," DBI 38 (1990), online at http://www.treccani.it/enciclopedia/francesco-del-tuppo_(Dizionario-Biografico); Samantha Kelly, ed., Cronaca di Partenope: *An Introduction to and Critical Edition of the First Vernacular History of Naples (c.1350)* (Leiden: Brill, 2011), 98–101.

127. See below, pp. 149–65, and readings 24–25.

the anonymous *Innamoramento di Rinaldo*, the most famous of all Neapolitan historical works — the *Cronaca di Partenope* (1486–90) — and in 1485 his own Neapolitan translation of Aesop's *Fables* (Fig. 77), considered the most beautiful example of quattrocento printing in Naples.[128]

Del Tuppo was also at the forefront of a new phenomenon that has recently received detailed study: the dissemination of official court news in the form of pamphlets and broadsheets. In the wake of Ferrante's suppression of the Conspiracy of the Barons, their trial, and the execution of their leaders, in 1487 Del Tuppo was commissioned and well paid to print 200 copies of the official record of the trial of Antonello Petrucci and Francesco Coppola, and from 1488 to 1490, 1000 copies for the trial of Pirro Del Balzo, Antonello Sanseverino, and Girolamo Sanseverino. De Caprio and Senatore[129] have examined how such printed material both amplified oral communication among Naples' *seggi* and made its way into new manuscript compilations, such as those of Ferraiolo and Notar Giacomo.

Hebrew Printers

The history of Jews in the Regno is a complex one, marked by official intolerance but cultural acceptance and prestige.[130] A Hebrew press[131] was established in Rome c.1469, and under Pope Sixtus IV (1471–84) others appeared in Mantua, Ferrara, Bologna, and Soncino. But by the century's end Naples became the only safe haven for Hebrew printing. The Gunzenhausers arrived in Naples from Gunzenhausen in southern Germany and set up a Hebrew press, which from 1487

128. See Alfredo Mauro, *Francesco Del Tuppo e il suo "Esopo"* (Città di Castello: Il solco, 1926).

129. "Orality."

130. Mazur, "Mediterranean Port," 216–22.

131. Joshua Bloch, "Hebrew Printing in Naples," *Bulletin of the New York Public Library* 46 (1942): 489–514; Renzo Frattarolo, *Tipografi e librai, ebrei e non, nel Napoletano, alla fine del XV secolo* (Florence: Sansoni, 1956); Emile G.L. Schrijver, "The Transmission of Jewish Knowledge through MSS and Printed Books," in *The Book: A Global History,* Michael F. Suarez, SJ and H.R. Woudhuysen, ed. (Oxford: Oxford University Press, 2013), 97–106 at 103.

to 1492 issued about twelve volumes, including the 1487 *Sefer Tehilim* (Book of Psalms, Fig. 81),[132] the *Hagiographa Variorum* with rabbinical commentaries (1487), Avicenna's medical *Canon (Ha-Kanon)*, and the first edition of Abraham Ibn Ezra's *Pentateuch* commentary (1488). After Joseph Gunzenhauser's death, his wife (or daughter) and son continued his work, assembling a team of distinguished typesetters and correctors from all over Italy.[133] Joshua Solomon Soncino, who began printing at Naples about this time, issued a prayer book of the Spanish rite for Gunzenhauser in May 1490 and a *Bible* in 1491. He remained in Naples until 1492.[134] Other Hebrew printers included Hayyim ha-Levi Ashkenazi, who in 1486 produced an edition of Immanuel Komi's *Proverbs;* Isaac ben Judah ibn Katorzi, who printed Nahmanides' *Pentateuch* in 1490; and several unnamed printers.[135]

Guidebooks and Antiquarian Works
Neapolitan writers also contributed to the phenomenon of the late Renaissance guidebook,[136] along with some French and English authors. None were written by Spaniards. Foremost among these authors and works are Benedetto di Falco's *Descrittione dei Luogi Antiqui* (published in seven editions between 1535 and 1680, Fig. 84); Pietro De Stefano, whose *Descrittione dei luoghi sacri della città di Napoli* (1560) conscientiously records objects of art and translates into Italian the inscriptions in most Neapolitan churches; and Giovanni Tarcagnota's *Del sito et lodi della città di Napoli* (1566).[137]

132. Commentary by David ben Joseph Kimhi, corrected by Jacob Baruch ben Judah Landau. Naples: Joseph ben Jacob Ashkenazi Gunzenhauser, 4 Nisan 5247 (28 March 1487).

133. See http://www.encyclopedia.com/religion/encyclopedias-almanacs-transcripts-and-maps/gunzenhauser-ashkenazi-joseph-ben-jacob

134. https://en.wikipedia.org/wiki/Soncino_family_(printers).

135. https://en.wikipedia.org/wiki/Hebrew_incunabula#Places_of_printing.

136. See Harald Hendrix, "City Branding and the Antique: Naples in Early Modern City Guides," in Hughes–Buongiovanni, 217–41.

137. Giovanni Tarcagnota, *Del sito et lodi della città di Napoli* (Naples: Giovanni Maria Scotto, 1566); Benedetto di Falco, *Descrittione dei Luoghi Antiqui di Napoli e del suo amenissimo distretto*, Ottavio Morisani, ed. (Naples: Libreria

One of the common features of these writers — frustrating for the historian — is the common lack of interest in attributing works of art. This trend has been ascribed to the antiquarian culture in which anonymous authorship is a given, although the glorification of the patron at the expense of the designing artist may also be seen as a by-product of court culture. At the end of our period Giulio Cesare Capaccio (1552–1634) was among the more prolific local antiquarians and historians, in 1606 appointed head of the antiquities of the Cumaean Campania by Viceroy Juan Alonso Pimentel de Herrera (1603–10).[138]

★

New research into such forms of communication has begun to provide us with a lively picture of the web of connections that bound together a growing capital like Naples and made it resilient to both the changing fortunes of war, disease, and natural disaster; to continued political and social upheaval; and to the rapidly increasing material base of the city. Like the forms of literary and artistic life traced above, these networks attest to the vital agency of Naples and its people in responding to challenges both internal and external and in defining their civic past, present, and future. In the concluding section of this book[139] we will present a visual essay on the forms of Neapolitan manuscript and print culture from c.1400 to c.1600.

★ ★ ★

---

scientifica editrice, 1972); Francesca Amirante, *Libri per vedere: Le guide storico-artistiche della città di Napoli* (Naples: Edizioni Scientifiche Italiane, 1995), 7–11.

138. See below, reading 16 and pp. 103–5.

139. Pages 467–78.

CHAPTER I: HISTORICAL TEXTS

FLAVIO BIONDO

Though based in Rome and Florence, Flavio Biondo (1392–1463)[1] wrote extensively on the history and chorography of the Regno and played a major part in constructing the new humanist historiography. He was born in Forlì in 1392. After a standard education in grammar, rhetoric, and poetics *(grammatica)*, the young Flavio moved to Padua. There he came under the influence of Petrarch's humanist successors before relocating to Piacenza, then to Pavia. While he studied for his law degree at the university there he met the humanist historian Pier Candido Decembrio.

Flavio had taken up his father's profession as an itinerant chancellery notary, in the Romagna, Veneto, and Lombardy.[2] By 1427 he had become secretary to the papal governor of the Romagna and entered the papal curia in Rome in 1432. Like many humanists, Biondo continued to travel widely, a practice that would become part of his research into the history and geography of all the Italian regions. But Biondo's most permanent home was Florence, and there he joined the circle of Leonardo Bruni (c.1370–1444) and began to write history in the new humanist mode. When he died in Rome in 1463 his reputation was European-wide, and his books continued to be used as basic texts for at least the next century.

1. From his Latin name, Blondus Flavius, modern scholarship often cites him as Biondo Flavio. For his life and work, see Cochrane, 34–40; Ricardo Fubini, "Biondo Flavio," DBI 10 (1968): 536–59, online at: http://www.treccani.it/enciclopedia/biondo-flavio_(Dizionario-Biografico); Biondo Flavio, *Italy Illuminated,* Jeffrey A. White, ed. and trans., 2 vols. (Cambridge, MA: Harvard University Press, 2005–16), 1:vii–xxvii; Nicoletta Pellegrino, "From the Roman Empire to Christian Imperialism: The Work of Flavio Biondo," in Sharon Dale, Alison Williams Lewin, and Duane J. Osheim, ed., *Chronicling History: Chroniclers and Historians in Medieval and Renaissance Italy* (University Park: Pennsylvania State University Press, 2007), 273–98.

2. White in *Italy Illuminated,* 1:viii–ix.

After studying Orosius, Tacitus, and Jerome, Flavio began his *Historiarum ab inclinatione romani imperii decades,* first composed between 1439 and 1453.[3] He amplified his ideas of distinct historical periods in his works on the city of Rome itself, carefully collating and critiquing the known narrative sources with the archeological remains of the city. The result was two massive works, the *Roma Instaurata* (1443–46) and the *Roma Triumphans* (1452–59). Flavio's work fused Roman imperial and Christian history with the city's new status as humanist capital. Biondo followed this up with his general history of Italy and its regions, the *Italia Illustrata* [Fig. 1], begun in 1447 and completed in 1453 and dedicated Pope Nicholas V.[4]

But the project also appears to have derived from Biondo's relationship with King Alfonso I of Naples.[5] Flavio was writing to Alfonso as early as 1443 to secure patronage and advising him on the importance of history as a guide to rule and reputation.[6] He sent the first eight books of his *Decades* to Alfonso in June 1443. He at first planned to end this work with Alfonso's triumphal entry into Naples the previous year, but his emphasis on neat periodization moved up his end date. Alfonso had urged Biondo to create a catalog of illustrious men, to "travel across and illuminate Italy" and to reconcile ancient and modern names and usage.[7] Flavio accepted the commission, wrote to Bartolomeo Facio at the Neapolitan court for advice on revisions,[8] and applied his previously successful methodologies with a chorographic comprehensiveness to all the regions of ancient Roman Italy. Flavio finally visited Naples for several months in 1451/2; and in 1453, shortly after the fall of

3. Pellegrino, 285–98.

4. *Italy Illuminated*, 4.5–9.7.

5. Pellegrino, 274 n. 7; 281.

6. Bentley, 47, 54, 222.

7. Fubini; White in *Italy Illuminated*, xi.

8. Bentley, 104.

Constantinople to the Turks, he wrote a treatise urging Alfonso to lead a crusade against them.[9]

Flavio's *Italia Illustrata* demonstrates many of the tensions between strict adherence to classical style, language and modern realities, most especially in place names and in numerous modernizations of vocabulary. His *Regno*, however, remains the ancient Roman provinces, and his discussion focuses on a careful study of ancient sources and archeological remains. Flavio's work remained selective, however, determined to some extent by the location of powerful patrons.[10] Sicily barely appears, and he makes no mention of Sardinia.

1. Biondo: Naples and Campania
Our selection is from Biondo's *Italia Illustrata*, White trans., 2:335–41.

Region 13
...But a glorious calamity that was transformed into a piece of great fortune caps all their distinctions: thanks to the loyalty they showed toward the French king René of Anjou, the Neapolitans were enduring a terrible siege at the hands of King Alfonso of Aragon when there occurred an event reminiscent of what happened in Belisarius's day: having been captured by the king entering through the channel of an aqueduct, they were brought by the king's protection and clemency to the good fortune that they currently enjoy. At last, then, King Alfonso has quite properly restored to Italy the long-abandoned custom of celebrating triumphs after a long exile.

The city of Naples has basilicas, city walls, and fortresses, and splendid private and public buildings which are a match for any in Italy. Among them is the famous convent of Sta. Chiara built by Queen Sancha of Aragon [Sancia of Majorca],[11] wife of the famous King Robert, and far outstripping all the monasteries of Italy. Near the outside of the city you can see the Carthusian monastery of San Martino, a magnificent and beautiful building. Yet all agree

9. Bentley, 164–65.

10. Pellegrino, 281.

11. See Musto (2013), 204–17, 234–38.

that one particular fortress which overlooks the sea, called the Castel Nuovo, a work worthy of the glorious memory of King Alfonso, is superior to all other works , monuments, and edifices ancient or modern now extant in Italy, no matter whether the experts in such matters consider the height and massiveness and beauty of its towers and walls or the spaciousness and ornament of its halls, rooms and individual parts....

Following the city of Naples, ancient writers describe Pompeii as being next along the coast, a town that was once very agreeable and attractive to the Romans. Cicero, for example, in arguing against the agrarian legislation of Rullus (which I have often mentioned) conveys his shock at the decemvirs putting Pompeii up for sale. Since I see that learned men who are today held in high regard at the king's court in Naples are wrong in maintaining that Pompeii and Herculaneum were where Torre del Greco is now, I shall adduce surer ancient evidence bearing on the site of Pompeii....

...(I shall show below that Herculaneum was further on and many miles away.) Certainly Turris Octavii is a town of recent foundation (its name derives from its distance from Naples) and has no traces of antiquity, beyond being the place of the elder Pliny's death, which I am sure must have occurred there. There was no other direction from which a boat could have approached the flames of Mount Vesuvius — the foolhardy inspection of which killed Pliny. In fact this entire stretch of coast, wherever rocks lie on top of earth, even on the edge of the beach, displays such clear signs of fire that only the absence of flames and smoke stops a stranger supposing that they are burning even now....

Mount Vesuvius, which is very rich in vines and agricultural land, is now called Monte Somma, because being set in full view of the city of Naples and surrounded on one side by plains and on the other mostly by the sea, it seems very large.... Virgil [suggests] what I said above regarding the Terra Laboris: the entire region that lies on both sides of the river Clanio, once called Leborine, has extremely fertile soil. Though Pliny in discussing the best land for planting vines says that all Campania, which "emits thin clouds of vapor," is very good for the best vines, I mentioned above that he wrote that in the land about Pompeii the chalk and clay are preferable to all other kinds of soil for growing vines because white sand is in turn extracted with them....

NICCOLÒ MACHIAVELLI

Machiavelli (1469–1527) is among the best known of Renaissance and all historical figures, and he has received an enormous number of studies and biographies.[12] Born into an old and distinguished Florentine family of the lower nobility, he received a standard education in grammar, rhetoric, and the Latin classics. In 1494 Florence exiled the ruling Medici and restored the republic, and Machiavelli was appointed to the chancery, and then as secretary of the governing council. In the years after 1500 he served as a diplomat to the papacy in Rome and as head of the Florentine militia, in which capacity in 1509 he defeated Pisa for the Florentines. In 1512, however, the Medici were restored to rule, and Machiavelli was deprived of his office, imprisoned, tortured under suspicion of treason, but soon released. He retired shortly after to his estate at Sant'Andrea in Percussina, and there began his full-time writing on history and political thought. Machiavelli's letter to Francesco Vettori on his visits to the local village gathering places, followed by his

12. On January 30, 2019, WorldCat served up over 5,400 books alone with Machiavelli as their prime subject. Among these see Robert Black, *Machiavelli* (London: Routledge, 2013); Corrado Vivanti, *Niccolo Machiavelli: An Intellectual Biography* (Princeton: Princeton University Press, 2013); Christopher S. Celenza, *Machiavelli: A Portrait* (Cambridge: Harvard University Press, 2015); Catherine H. Zuckert, *Machiavelli's Politics* (Chicago: The University of Chicago Press, 2017). For comprehensive bibliography see Cary J. Nederman, "Niccolò Machiavelli," in *Oxford Bibliographies in Philosophy,* at http://www.oxfordbibliographies.com/view/document/obo-9780195396577/obo-9780195396577-0268.xml; Vickie B. Sullivan and Michelle T. Clarke, "Machiavelli's Political Thought," in *Oxford Bibliographies in Political Science,* at http://www.oxfordbibliographies.com/view/document/obo-9780199756223/obo-9780199756223-0176.xml.

solitary work in his study in dialog with the ancients, is one of the most compelling self-portraits of the intellectual life that come down to us.

Machiavelli is probably best known to modern readers as the author of *The Prince* (1513);[13] but he also composed the important humanist tract, *Discourses on the First Ten Books of Titus Livy* (1517, published 1531) and his *History of Florence and of the Affairs of Italy from the Earliest Times to the Death of Lorenzo the Magnificent* (published in 1532), among the most important Renaissance works of historiography.[14] While his *Discourses* focus on how republican governments are founded and maintained, like his contemporary humanist colleagues, Machiavelli focused in the *History* — as he amply demonstrated in *The Prince* — on the empirical study of politics. He highlights the tension between individual virtue and talent and the changing vicissitudes of *fortuna*: how the ruler, or the state, rides the waves of political and military victory or disaster, of sudden illness, death, political intrigue, treachery, and other unforeseen circumstances.

Machiavelli's understanding of causality and human motivation is therefore complex, and his representation of events is always placed within a thick context of competing agencies and outlooks. The delicate Italian balance of power, and how each small action worked within a network of other actions and actors, remained central to his interpretation of history. As the largest and most powerful emerging state in that balance of power, the kingdom of Naples was therefore of key interest to Machiavelli.[15] From the perspective of the 1520s he was able to offer the Aragonese dynasty as a prime example of his humanist themes of complex causality, human virtue and changing fortune.

Our selection is taken from Machiavelli's *History of Florence and of the Affairs of Italy from the Earliest Times to the Death of Lorenzo the Magnificent*

13. See John T. Scott, *The Routledge Guidebook to Machiavelli's* The Prince (London: Routledge, 2016).

14. Cochrane, 265–70, 279–86 et passim.

15. See Carlo De Frede, *La crisi del Regno di Napoli nella riflessione politica di Machiavelli e Guicciardini* (Naples: Liguori, 2006).

(New York: W. Walter Dunne, 1901), Hugo Albert Rennert, ed. for Project Gutenberg, (EBook #2464. Last Updated: February 6, 2013.)

2. Machiavelli: On the Coming of the Aragonese

I.7 Ladislaus, king of Naples, at his death, left to his sister Giovanna [II] the kingdom and a large army, under the command of the principal leaders of Italy, among the first of whom was Sforza of Cotignuola, reputed by the soldiery of that period to be a very valiant man. The queen, to shun the disgrace of having kept about her person a certain Pandolfello, whom she had brought up, took for her husband Giacopo della Marca, a Frenchman of the royal line, on the condition that he should be content to be called prince of Taranto, and leave to her the title and government of the kingdom. But the soldiery, upon his arrival in Naples, proclaimed him king; so that between the husband and the wife wars ensued; and although they contended with varying success, the queen at length obtained the superiority, and became an enemy of the pope. Upon this, in order to reduce her to necessity, and that she might be compelled to throw herself into his lap, Sforza suddenly withdrew from her service without giving her any previous notice of his intention to do so.

She thus found herself at once unarmed, and not having any other source, sought the assistance of Alfonso, king of Aragon and Sicily, adopted him as her son, and engaged Braccio of Montone as her captain, who was of equal reputation in arms with Sforza, and inimical to the pope, on account of his having taken possession of Perugia and some other places belonging to the Church. After this, peace was made between the queen and the pontiff; but King Alfonso, expecting she would treat him as she had her husband, endeavored secretly to make himself master of the strongholds; but, possessing acute observation, she was beforehand with him, and fortified herself in the castle of Naples. Suspicions increasing between them, they had recourse to arms, and the queen, with the assistance of Sforza, who again resumed her service, drove Alfonso out

of Naples, deprived him of his succession, and adopted
Louis of Anjou in his stead....

V. 2. The affairs of Florence being in this condition,
Giovanna [II], queen of Naples, died, and by her will
appointed René of Anjou to be her successor. Alfonso, king
of Aragon, was at this time in Sicily, and having obtained the
concurrence of many barons, prepared to take possession
of the kingdom. The Neapolitans, with whom a greater
number of barons were also associated, favored René. The
pope was unwilling that either of them should obtain it;
but desired the affairs of Naples to be administered by a
governor of his own appointing.

In the meantime Alfonso entered the kingdom and was
received by the duke of Sessa; he brought with him some
princes, whom he had engaged in his service, with the
design (already possessing Capua, which the prince of
Taranto held in his name) of subduing the Neapolitans,
and sent his fleet to attack Gaeta, which had declared itself
in their favor. They therefore demanded assistance of the
duke of Milan, who persuaded the Genoese to undertake
their defense; and they, to satisfy the duke their sovereign,
and protect the merchandise they possessed, both at Naples
and Gaeta, armed a powerful fleet. Alfonso hearing of this,
augmented his own naval force, went in person to meet
the Genoese, and coming up with them near the island
of Ponza, an engagement ensued, in which the Aragonese
were defeated, and Alfonso, with many of the princes of his
suite, made prisoners and sent by the Genoese to Filippo.

This victory terrified the princes of Italy, who, being jealous
of the duke's power, thought it would give him a great
opportunity of being sovereign of the whole country. But
so contrary are the views of men, that he took a directly
opposite course. Alfonso was a man of great sagacity, and as
soon as an opportunity presented itself of communicating
with Filippo, he proved to him how completely he
contravened his own interests by favoring René and
opposing himself; for it would be the business of the former,
on becoming king of Naples, to introduce the French into

Milan; that in an emergency he might have assistance at hand, without the necessity of having to solicit a passage for his friends. But he could not possibly secure this advantage without effecting the ruin of the duke, and making his dominions a French province; and that the contrary of all this would result from himself becoming lord of Naples; for having only the French to fear, he would be compelled to love and caress, nay even to obey those who had it in their power to open a passage for his enemies.

That thus the title of king of Naples would be with himself (Alfonso), but the power and authority with Filippo; so that it was much more the duke's business than his own to consider the danger of one course and the advantage of the other; unless he rather wished to gratify his private prejudices than to give security to his dominions. In the one case he would be a free prince, in the other, placed between two powerful sovereigns, he would either be robbed of his territories or live in constant fear, and have to obey them like a slave. These arguments so greatly influenced the duke, that, changing his design, he set Alfonso at liberty, sent him honorably to Genoa and then to Naples. From thence the king went to Gaeta, which as soon as his liberation had become known, was taken possession of by some nobles of his party....

AENEAS SILVIO PICCOLOMINI (POPE PIUS II)

Aeneas (Enea) Silvio Bartolomeo Piccolomini (1405–64)[16] is among the most interesting of Renaissance figures. Born into a noble but impoverished Tuscan family near Siena, he spent his early years laboring on his family's farm. After receiving a basic Latin education, he was able to go on to the universities of Siena and Florence and began professional life as a *grammatica* teacher in Siena. In 1431 was appointed secretary to Bishop Domenico Capranica of Fermo and in 1431 accompanied him to the Council of Basel (1431–39). There Piccolomini began to make the contacts that would eventually see the young humanist entrusted with diplomatic missions on behalf of the council.

16. Craig Kallendorf, "Aeneas Sylvius Piccolomini," in *Oxford Bibliographies in Renaissance and Reformation,* at http://www.oxfordbibliographies.com/view/document/obo-9780195399301/obo-9780195399301-0065.xml.

A staunch Conciliarist (or proponent of controls of papal power, privilege and opulence, and of necessary church reforms) Piccolomini also participated in the election of Antipope Felix V. He thus came into favor with the imperial party and was named ambassador to Emperor Frederick III in Vienna. Frederick was so impressed by the young humanist that he crowned him poet laureate in 1442 and entrusted him with delicate negotiations with the Roman popes that concluded in a reconciliation between imperial and papal parties, forging a compromise in 1447 that ended the new schism. Once Piccolomini had entered holy orders, Pope Nicholas V (1447–55) appointed him bishop of Trieste and then of Siena (1450–58). Meanwhile Enea continued his diplomatic and reform efforts, all the while gaining the trust and support of high ranking churchmen. On the death of Pope Calixtus III (6 August 1458), Piccolomini suddenly (but not unexpectedly) found himself the favorite of the conclave, which elected him Pope Pius II on 3 September 1458.

As pope, the formerly free-living humanist, conciliarist, and independent intellectual and poet suddenly became the authoritarian monarch of the newly empowered papacy and Papal States. Yet Pius' reign ended in disappointment. As he prepared to lead a newly unified Christendom in a crusade against the Turks, he died in Ancona on 14 August 1464.

Piccolomini remains best known for his combination of Renaissance humanism and power politics. He was an outgoing, personable man who could easily reconcile opposing parties and viewpoints but was also an astute — and often biting — judge of character. His *Tale of Two Lovers (Historia de duobus amantibus)* of 1444 is among the most erotic of Renaissance works; while his *Memoirs,* published only in 1584, offer a wonderful series of frank insights into personalities, events, the pleasures of the table, the city, antiquities, and the countryside.

Piccolomini's memoirs remind us that Naples remained of key interest to Renaissance popes. We have excerpted this first passage on the earthquake of 1456 from *Memoirs of a Renaissance Pope: The*

Commentaries of Pius II. An Abridgment, Leona C. Gabel, ed., Florence
A. Gragg, trans. (London: George Allen & Unwin, 1960), 78.

3. *Piccolomini: Earthquake in Naples, 1456*
   During this time the kingdom of Naples was racked for
   many days by an earthquake such as our fathers cannot
   remember to have seen or heard. At Naples itself many
   splendid buildings fell, and Ariano and many other towns
   were completely destroyed. It was said that more than thirty
   thousand bodies were buried under the ruins. The people
   everywhere left the cities and moved into the country.
   There was a period of public penitence, men and women
   mortifying themselves by fasting and scourging.....

DURING THE FIRST BARONS' REVOLT, King Ferrante met the rebel
forces at the Battle of Sarno (or Nola), in the plain at the mouth of
the Sarno River, south of Mount Vesuvius. The battle was a decisive
defeat for royal forces. Piccolomini both describes the battle and
provides a detailed description of a strange new weapon: the musket.
Our selection is excerpted from *Memoirs of a Renaissance Pope,* 156–58.

4. *Piccolomini: The Battle of Sarno, 7 July 1460*
   ...While this was going on, Ferrante, king of Sicily,
   encouraged by the arrival of Simonetto and other captains
   of the Church, took the field and offered battle to the
   enemy. When they refused, he assumed the offensive and
   drove them from their position, never halting till all were
   routed and penned up in the town of Sarno. This is about
   thirty miles from Naples. Part of it lies on a high hill and
   part in the plain below. Its defense is not so much in its
   walls as in its water. From the base of the mountain crystal
   springs gush out to form the Sarno River mentioned
   above, which is so icy that it kills grass and trees and no
   fish but crabs can live in it. In this town King René's son
   Jean, the prince of Taranto, all the nobles of their party, and
   all the infantry and cavalry had taken refuge after their
   rout, since they had been unable to resist King Ferrante's
   charge. There was no doubt that in a short time hunger
   would force them to surrender or to disperse and leave
   the field to the enemy, for penned up as they were, they

could bring in no supplies, and they had already begun to consider the best route for flight.

Nothing contributed to their escape so much as the rashness of Ferrante, who was made overbold not only by his own temperament but by necessity. His soldiers excelled the enemy in bravery rather than in strength. But they were ugly and dissatisfied, demanded their pay, and made threats if the money were not forthcoming. The king had nothing to give them, and already two hundred foreign mercenaries, called musketeers *(scoppeterii)*, had deserted to the enemy because they were not paid. Ferrante feared that if any more deserted, he should have to raise the siege, and without money he could not make the soldiers do anything.

In these straits he thought it advisable to make a sudden attack on the city in the hope of storming it and satisfying his army from the spoils of the enemy. When this plan was discussed in the council, the majority agreed, but Simonetto was against it, because he thought that the enemy could not easily be dislodged from a fortified position and that they could be conquered by hunger better than by the sword. Nevertheless, he advised attacking a certain tower near the town, for if they took this, it would be impossible for the enemy to go out to forage. Simonetto's motion prevailed, but when the tower was taken at the first assault, the maddened and victorious soldiers in their wild elation could not be restrained. The rash troops disregarded the commands of their officers and entered the city gates on the heels of the fleeing enemy. There was a fierce battle within the walls where many fell. The papal forces suffered most, being massacred by the fusiliers, who, as we have said, had deserted the king.

The musket *(scoppetum)* is a weapon invented in Germany in our time. It is of iron or copper as long as a man, as thick as the fist, almost completely hollow. Powder made of charcoal from the fig or willow mixed with sulfur and niter is poured into it; then a small ball of lead the size of a filbert is inserted in the front end. The fire is applied through a small hole in the back part, and this explodes the powder with such force that it shoots out the ball like lightning with a report like a clap of thunder. This report is popularly called a *scoppium*, hence the name of the *scoppeterii*. No armor can withstand the force of this engine, and it penetrates wood also.

Therefore the royal and papal forces, though they had entered the town and had taken some prisoners, were repulsed by the *scoppeterii* with a considerable number of killed and wounded and pursued by the enemy a long distance from the town. While Simonetto was charging the enemy and trying to rally his own men, he was struck by a bullet. He was thrown from his horse and died without speaking a word. Though he would have chosen a longer life, yet this was the end he desired, for he used often to say to his friends, "May God grant me to die in the exercise of my profession and the service of the Church!" His body was found by the enemy and given honorable burial attended by Prince Jean and all the nobles.

When the news of Ferrante's defeat at Sarno was received at Siena, the French, of whom there were many in the Curia, cheered, danced about the city, lighted bonfires, abused the Catalans, jeered at the Aragonese, insulted even the pope's household, taunted the Lombards and Florentines, and struck with their fists or swords any who they thought did not sufficiently applaud their madness. They gouged out the eye of a Burgundian and killed a citizen of Siena who showed some slight disapproval of their clamor.

The pope endured all this calmly, saying to himself, *"How would they treat us in their country, should we come to them, when in our country they insult us so shamelessly? Behold, O Italian race! will you be able to endure as masters these men who are so insolent as servants? They are servants in the Roman Curia, and they put on the countenance of a ruler. What would they do if they should some day secure the papacy or come to rule Italy? Woe to thee, Italy! if thou art forced to go under their yoke! I will help thee, with all my might that thou mayst not have to endure such cruel masters, although neither Venetians nor Florentines give any aid; and their people, while they are trying to*

*subdue thee and care not to agree among themselves, are preparing
the way for foreign sovereignty over thee."*

LOISE DE ROSA

While Eric Cochrane relegated Loise de Rosa to an index entry, Jerry
Bentley opened his authoritative analysis of Neapolitan historiography
with an account of Rosa's encomium to the city.[17] Born in Pozzuoli
around October 15, 1385,[18] Loise was brought up in Naples. The
family fled to Aversa during the sack of Naples by Alfonso I. We know
little of his education, though the fact that he wrote exclusively in
the Neapolitan vernacular, without trace of Latin, indicates that he
may have received only a standard *abbaco* (business) education. He
was apparently back in Naples, serving at the royal court at the age of
twenty, when he was arrested and falsely accused of having abused a
maid of Queen Giovanna II. He died in 1475.

Loise claimed to have served in the royal bureaucracy for the
Angevin, Angevin-Durazzan, and Aragonese dynasties for a long
list of royal and noble patrons. Whatever the variety and scope
of his duties and experience,[19] like several Neapolitan historians
of the trecento and the humanists of the quattrocento, he was a
professional courtier who knew and understood the personalities,
events, official narratives, and archives of the dynasties and their
courts. He produced three major works,[20] which he himself dates
from between 1467 and 1475, though he seems to have conceived

17. Bentley, 3–7.

18. Mauro De Nichilo, "De Rosa, Loise," DBI 39 (1991): 171–74; online at:
http://www.treccani.it/enciclopedia/loise-de-rosa_(Dizionario-Biografico);
Loise De Rosa, *Ricordi: Edizione critica del Ms. Ital. 913 della Bibliothèque Nationale
de France,* Vittorio Formentin, ed. (Rome: Salerno Editrice, 1998).

19. Benedetto Croce, "Sentendo parlare un vecchio napoletano del
Quattrocento," in *Storie e leggende napoletane* (Bari: Laterza, 1948), 125, attributes much of De Rosa's record of his achievements to the "illusions of
servants." Bentley, 3, also questions his accuracy on this count.

20. All contained in Paris, Bibliothèque nationale de France, Cod. Ital. 913 (ex
10171). For editions, De Rosa, *Napoli aragonese,* superceded by De Rosa, *Ricordi.*

them some time around 1452. These included his *Memorie* or *Ricordi*, his *Elogio di Napoli* [Fig. 78], and a *Cronaca di Napoli* concluding with his tract *Lodi della donna*. The manuscript belonged to Ippolita Sforza, wife of Ferrante's heir, Duke Alfonso of Calabria, and seems to have been the product of Loise's service to the duke and duchess, duties that both Panormita and Pontano also fulfilled. His *Lodi* were written for Ippolita, while he notes that his *Ricordi* were begun as a result of a request from Don Alfonso.

Unlike that of the court humanists, Loise's work is based closely on orality and enlivened with details drawn from every level of Neapolitan society: from the conversations of the powerful in the Regno and the humanists at Castel Nuovo, to the sermons of popular preachers, deliberations of the *seggi,* and the echoing chatter in the *vicoli* of Naples. His Neapolitan vernacular was apparently untouched by the Tuscan-inflected *medio* dialect[21] used at court or by writers like Diomede Carafa, Masuccio Salernitano,[22] and others.

To see the Neapolitan Renaissance through the eyes of Loise de Rosa is to share a viewpoint on that world that is offered by no other writer. While Loise, like Pontano or Masuccio, was a successful man of the court, his writing has none of the courtier's style, diplomacy, or grace. Pontano cultivates urbanity in language and in culture. Masuccio writes in Italian rather than Latin and uses some dialect words and turns of phrase; he is unabashed in his devotion to Aragonese causes and his love for the local scene. Yet read three sentences of Loise's, and it is perfectly clear that even Masuccio's language must be a brilliantly constructed linguistic facade that bears only a minimal relation to the way most people talked, thought, or acted; and his anticlericalism, while it reflected official policy, certainly belied the intense devotion of the majority of Neapolitans.

Late in life he began to write a book without title that modern editors refer to as his *Cronache e ricordi,* or *Chronicles and Memoirs,* a mixture

21. Musto, *Writing Southern Italy,* 273–75.

22. See chapter 3, readings 24–25, pp. 149–65.

of historical and autobiographical observations on his own time and surroundings. The second chapter of this text, which is translated below, is entitled *The Praise of Naples*. The manuscript of the *Chronicles* breaks off abruptly in 1475, presumably at the point of Loise's death.

If Naples had had a chamber of commerce in 1471, Loise would have been in charge of it. He's a born booster, one hundred and fifty percent convinced that Naples is the finest, noblest, prettiest, best dressed, best fed, most wonderful and most important city in the entire world. Using a style of implied question and answer that may have its origins in the Renaissance dialogue tradition but that certainly doesn't read like any Renaissance dialogue ever penned, Loise leads his reader on to a detailed understanding of all the benefits and all the blessings of Neapolitan life. From its situation and its attributes, he moves on to a discussion of the city's provision for health and well-being. Then he turns his attention to the health of the soul and describes the great blessings available through the special indulgences granted and shared by the churches of Naples and the surrounding region. In the end he compares every other city (of course unfavorably) with Naples.

The following translation by James H. Mc Gregor is based on Loise de Rosa, "Lodi di Napoli," in Antonio Altamura, *Napoli Aragonese nei ricordi di Louise de Rosa* (Naples: Libreria scientifica editrice, 1971), 183–94.

5. *De Rosa: In Praise of Naples*

I want to tell you a good story about us Neapolitans, me, Loise de Rosa. The story is this: how the Neapolitans are by nature the best people in the world. And I'll prove it. Stay and hear my reasons.

God created the world and divided it into three parts: Asia, Africa, and Europe. If you don't know, ask, but the best of the three is Europe. The Neapolitan is born in the best part of the world because Naples is in Europe.

And furthermore: what is the best part of Europe? Do you know? If you don't know, ask. I say that the best of Europe is Italy. And I say that Naples is in the best part of Italy. Therefore, the Neapolitans are the best born.

And furthermore: What is the best of Italy? Do you know? No? Well, let me tell you, it's the kingdom of Naples, that is Sicily. Therefore Naples is the best city in the kingdom and the Neapolitan is the best born. And furthermore: what is the best of the kingdom? It's the agricultural region. The Neapolitan is from the agricultural region and so he's the best.

And furthermore: what's the best of the agricultural region, don't you know? Yes. What is it? It's Naples. Therefore the Neapolitan is the best born of all the men in the world.

Now I, Loise, have written out all these reasons about the kingdom, and now I will write about the magnificence of these Neapolitans of ours, and their virtues and of the illustrious leaders they have had in the past and have at present.

In Naples there are great numbers of knights, who live on their incomes, and there are many barons with great estates, and there are plenty of counts, marquises, and dukes, even princes and kings, all born in Naples. And I want to write about some that I know, so that you won't suspect that because I'm Neapolitan I say what I do. So now listen.

There is no need to speak of knights. The barons are plentiful and very noble men, and there are many of them from Naples. Let's talk about the counts. The count of Montoro, the count of Avellino, the count of Arena, the counts of Nicastro, Matlune, Vocchianico, and the former counts of Alife, Caiazza, and Corigliano, the present count of Brienze, and the former count of Acerra, the former marquis of Ierace, and the present duke of Melfe, the duke of Cefalonia, the prince of the Morea, the king of Arte, who used to be called the despot and know is called the king. These are all citizens born in Naples. Now, you won't find another city in the world where the citizens are counts, marquises, dukes, princes, and kings! We'll leave the cardinals and popes out of the count.

Now let's talk about the noble qualities of the city. You know that for a city to be well placed and have a good site, it needs to have four things: sea, mountains, plains, and water. Naples has them all.

And for cities to be good you need to have four additional things. Know what they are? No? I'll tell you: walls, streets, houses, and churches. And if you also have fountains, that's excellent. Naples has them all. And if the walls aren't beautiful, all the rest of them are marvelously so.

Four other things are important in a city. Know them? No? They are the four elements: water, air, fire, and earth. Naples has both surface water and spring water in perfection. It has temperate air, not hot or dry, not heavy or thin. Because of this the Neapolitans carry themselves well all over the world. Good fires because of the abundance of oak that sells at a good price. The earth is exceptional, it produces crops above and below ground that are the best in the world. That's because the kings who have ruled Naples have brought the best from each of their countries. The German rulers brought plants from Germany; the French rulers brought plants from France; the Spanish rulers have brought plants from Spain; the pope and cardinals from the Marches, from Tuscany, and the Papal States.

Do you want me to tell you about the nobility of Naples? There are some from all parts of the world. Reader, who are you? German? There are more than a hundred nobles with German wives or husbands here in Naples. No, I'm French. There are plenty from there married and unmarried. Are you Venetian? Plenty of those. No, I'm Genoese. Plenty again, and if you were Florentine, there would be plenty who are citizens here. And if you're Spanish, why the whole city is full of Spaniards. Oh, I'm from Lombardy. That's a fine people, and Our Most Illustrious Lady Duchess is from there. I'm a knight. You'll find plenty of those. I'm a count. Plenty already. I am a duke. There are dukes here. Oh, I am a prince. We have some. Oh, I am a king. We have one of those too, and he has daughters like a rabbit. Oh, I am a man-at-arms; plenty once, though now there aren't many. A child of peace; we have enough of them to fill the ships the king has made.

Oh, I am a Certosan monk. Any of those? Yes, and of the order of Saint Francis as well as that of Saint Dominic there are plenty here and also of Saint Benedict. To tell the truth, you can't name anything that isn't here in Naples.

Well fine, I'm a hunter and I really enjoy hunting; do you have falconry that is among the best in the world? Close by, close by just outside the city gates. And do you have other forms of hunting? Yes, indeed. Where? Just outside the gates. We have mallards and rabbits. Do you have wild goats? Oh yes, fine ones. In the Valle del Gaudo. And do you have hunting with dogs, I mean boar hunting? Oh yes, wonderful boar hunting in several places, but there is one in particular called Astroni, which is the royal or imperial hunt where the boar and the wild goats and deer are always plentiful because of the good forage and abundant water there. They are never hunted except by the king who holds the keys to it.

Now tell me: don't you have any recreation on the sea? Oh, we have certain grottoes, called the King's Grottos, inside there is a gentle stream that comes from the mountains; and we also have other grottoes quite close by called Chiatamone and Serapia in which there is a great fountain of fresh water. And we have the Castel dell'Ovo, which is in the sea, and we have a saying, "If you want to be happy and cool, go to Castel dell'Ovo, you'll find a place both old and new, and good Greek wine too." And I'll tell you that they spend hundreds of ducats a year in there.

Let's speak of the qualities of this excellent city of Naples. God has favored it most uniquely. Take note: within one day's journey from Naples there are sixty cities. Now just think for a minute whether there's any other city in the world that has sixty others within one day's journey....

Now tell me, do you know any other city which is endowed with so many of the things that cities ought to have for their well-being? Naples has stone and lime, we call it *pozzolana,* and it has such an abundance of wood that we load our ships with it. What beams, braces, masts, and every other kind of timbers they make! Naples has rock to make paving stones. Do you want to dig a well? Dig. You'll find lime and gravel and white stone and some black.

I want to tell you something else you won't find in any other city in the world. And I'll tell you what it is. Things are brought from every part of the world to be sold in Naples. The port comes into your mouth. And what is it you taste and smell? Whatever you can name, they bring it here. Like what? Wood for the fire and any sort of building. And what else? Oil, fish, flax, every kind of fruit and also every kind of vegetable: lettuce, broccoli, radishes, parsnips, garlic, leeks, onions, rice, almonds, semolina, capers, round breads, bread from Nola, millet bread and millet flour, and every kind of bean. Where will you find a city so endowed with all the graces of God as Naples? It even has glass, chalk, soap, sulfur, and anything else you can name.

In Naples there are many hospitals; and especially that hospice of the Virgin Mary which is call the Annunziata, a place for the infirm whether they be citizens or foreigners. A hospital with doctors, a pharmacy and women who help you. There are never as few as a hundred patients there. Now that I'm writing this, on this very day one of the masters of the Annunziata told me that they have seven hundred nursing mothers with their children, and in addition every year they marry twelve girls and provide for more indigent people both noble and non-noble than they can count.[23] Now what town or city does that?

I will tell you a marvelous thing, that on any day of the year, you can find the four seasons within one day's journey of Naples. I'm not fooling. I say: if it's winter and it's cold but you want heat, go to Pozzuoli. If it's summer and you want to be cold, go to Montevergine. No, I'd prefer spring. Go to Salerno or Amalfi, where you will find it.

Oh, I am sick with a very difficult disease, and there is no doctor who is adequate from among the best in the world. And what will I say to you? In Naples we have the medical school par excellence, and a large part of Italy comes here.

23. Compare with reading 15 below, pp. 102–3, from c. 1590.

And I'll add that there are hot water baths and warm water baths in Pozzuoli. These baths are beneficial for whatever illnesses you might have; and furthermore, when you have an incurable illness, like tuberculosis or another unknown illness, go to the bath of Subbiene Omene, which is right on the seashore at Pozzuoli; the bath of the fountain is also there and the bath of Cantariello; these three are in Pozzuoli. In Trepergole there are these others: the bath of the Arch; the bath of Rognere if you want to cure your kidneys; the bath of Vetare; the bath of the Sow; the bath of Sta. Lucia; the bath of Sta. Maria; the bath of the Cross; the Gutwrencher bath, if you want it; the Iron bath for your teeth; the bath of Tritola. There are more than enough. And by the way if you want to get your wife pregnant, take her to the bath of Sarviata and do your duty with her, because women don't get pregnant from hot water!

We've spoken enough about the consolations of the flesh, now let's talk about the soul. You won't find a city in the whole world that only one day's journey from it has three apostles who distribute holy manna: San Matteo in Salerno; Sant'Andrea in Amalfi, and San Bartolomeo in Benevento. And furthermore I'll say that Naples has the best relics in the whole world: it has the head of San Gennaro, who was the archbishop of Naples; and it has a vial of his blood, which is like a rock, and when it sees the head it turns liquid as if it had just come pouring out of the head, and it makes and has made many miracles. Now what do you think of the stupendous things in Naples?

Where will you find a city that has so many indulgences granted by God and also plenary pardons granted by the pope? And do you want me to tell you about the one given by God? The emperor had a son who had leprosy, and that son was in camp with his tents where the church of Sta. Maria stands today in Capua, where there was a small part of the ancient wall still standing with an image of the Virgin Mary painted on it. One day this son of the emperor lifted up the side of his tent and saw that painting of the Virgin Mary and he said, "O, glorious Virgin Mary, who produced a son but without sin, who was a virgin before birth and during birth and after birth; you, glorious Virgin Mary, give me grace; my sweet lady, lift this infirmity from my flesh, for I promise to shelter you from the wind and the rain. I will build you a beautiful church."

After he had said this prayer, he saw a multitude of mice go and lick the foot of that Virgin Mary and then they went and licked the foot of that son of the emperor and that very hour he was cleansed of his leprosy. Immediately the courtiers went to the emperor with the good news, and the emperor mounted his horse and the son mounted his and they met on the road and embraced each other, then they went back to thank the Virgin Mary. And at that time the foundations for the church were dug and the crowds came drawn by such an incredible miracle. And when the church was completed a letter was found on the altar, blue with letters of gold, and it said "body and soul" and that letter is not made of leather nor of cotton; nobody knows what it's made of.

The emperor sent a prince to the pope to tell him of these two miracles, the one of the mice and the one of the letter. So the pope came from Rome and he was in that church with seventeen cardinals, and he said mass and commanded the cardinals to say mass one each day; which made eighteen days in all. And the pope asked when the letter was found; and he was told that it was on the first day of August. The pope said, "The first day of August is a plenary indulgence body and soul, given by God, and I declare a plenary indulgence for the fifteenth." What other city has that?

And I also say to you: "Oh, you who wish to go to heaven, confess your sins and take the Lord's body, and go to the Trinity in Cava dei Tirreni, where there is also 'body and soul'; or go to Sta. Maria Mother of God, which is close to Nocera Superiore, which also grants 'body and soul.' Or you could go to Sta. Maria in Montevergine which is above Avellino, which is twenty miles outside of Naples on a mountain."

Now you could say to me, "I would rather not leave Naples, isn't there any place inside?" Yes sir, go to Sta. Chiara, which has plenary indulgence, "body and soul," on all the days of Christ and of the Virgin Mary, which, if I'm counting right, adds up to twenty times a year; or go to the Principio or to Sta. Croce.

And I'll say this: we have a church that is called the Ascension (which comes in those lovely days in May), and then there is "body and soul" and the whole kingdom comes. And more: at San Domenico there is a chapel of the Crucifixion, and there is a dispensation that gives you the power when you are approaching death to chose your own priest, and the dispensation gives that priest the power to absolve you "body and soul" as if it were the Jubilee. And there's another church called Sta. Maria della Grazia, which has a dispensation that if somebody has stolen a hundred ducats, say, if they give back a quarter of it, that is twenty-five ducats to the church of Sta. Maria, they are absolved for the whole hundred.

Now we've said enough about indulgences; let's talk about the very best of Naples, which I've saved for last. What's the best of Naples? You really don't know? No, what is it? It's [the *seggio* of] Capuana, because it's always been the capital of Naples, and in that part of town the best lords in the world are born — and now that we have arrived in the year 1471, they have given and continue to give kings, popes, cardinals, princes, dukes, counts, marquises, and continue to bring honor to Naples. O, noblemen of Capuana, continue to be virtuous because I have shown that you are among the best men in the entire world. So give thanks to God.

Reader, have you travelled in the world? Have you visited those famous cities like holy Rome, great Milan, beautiful Florence and gracious Naples? If you remember, there are thirteen notable things that cities ought to have: the four elements; four noteworthy features, that is mountains, plains, sea, and water; five additional features, which are walls, streets, houses, churches, and fountains. And these thirteen things aren't to be found in any city in the world if not Naples, which lacks one of them, that is walls; it has all the rest.

Let's start with the city of Rome. Have you been there? No. Well, I'll tell you of the four elements, it hasn't one that is perfect. Of the four noteworthy things it lacks three; of the five it lacks one, that is fountains. And Naples has twelve, and lacks only one of them.

Have you ever been in Venice the rich? No. Did you know that Venice is built in the sea, that it has no fresh water, neither surface water nor spring water; no mountain, no plains; it has none of the four elements. It has nothing. And of the thirteen Naples has twelve.

I haven't been in the other cities, like Milan, Florence, Paris, Genoa, Constantinople, Cairo, and all the other famous cities in the world. I'll leave them to you, reader.

Saint Isidore said that Naples is a servant of the pious, mother of hospitals, refuge of the poor, a most excellent place.

FERRAIOLO

The *Cronaca* of Ferraiolo[24] focuses on the fate of the Aragonese from 1423 through Alfonso's conquest of Naples in 1442 to February 1498 and the coming of the French. We do not know much about Ferraiolo's life.[25] He seems to have come from a family of goldsmiths active in the city through the end of the cinquecento. He notes that his father Francesco witnessed Alfonso I's triumphal entry into the city in 1442, and Ferraiolo family names appear in the registers of the Aragonese chancellery from 1479 to 1500. Whatever his education, Ferraiolo appears to have known Latin. He may have served as a minor court official under Alfonso and his successors, a lower level majordomo or seneschal, and claimed to have witnessed "with my own eyes" events around the royal family. But he was not privy to the humanist circle around the king, and his access to deliberations at court was probably second-hand via official documents made available through local administration and print.

24. Ferraiolo, *Cronaca,* Rosario Coluccia, ed. (Florence: Accademia della Crusca, 1987); Musto, *Writing Southern Italy,* 276–78.

25. Franco Pignatti, "Ferraiolo," DBI 46 (1996), online at: http://www.treccani.it/enciclopedia/ferraiolo_(Dizionario-Biografico).

His *Cronaca* survives in a single manuscript, New York, Pierpont Morgan Library, MS 801[26] [Fig. 83]. This incorporates several works: the *Fasciculus temporum*, a Latin world chronicle attributed to Werner Rolewinck,[27] a hand copy of the first print edition (1486–90) of the *Cronaca di Partenope*, Ferraiolo's father's description of Alfonso's entry into Naples,[28] an Italian translation of *The Baths of Pozzuoli* titled the *Trattato de li bagni di Pezola*,[29] and finally Ferraiolo's *Cronaca*.[30] This array of materials enabled Ferraiolo to construct a history of Naples and its environs based on information garnered from official circles but given life by his perspective of the city's streets and marketplaces, its topography, and local lore. In this regard Ferraiolo's work reflects the voice of Naples' urban classes and the orality that underlay their community of communications and memory.[31] Poetry and rhymed prose, popular sayings and metaphors from folk tale, all in the popular style of Neapolitan vernacular, make his text one of the most important monuments of vernacular prose of the late quattrocento.[32]

Its version of Rolewinck's *Fasciculus temporum* copies both the text and images in Erhard Ratdolt's printed edition (Venice 1481); while his versions of the *Cronaca di Partenope* and the *Baths of Pozzuoli* are based on the first printed Neapolitan edition of 1486–90 by Francesco

26. Many images of complete manuscript are now online at: http://ica.themorgan.org/manuscript/page/1/146991. The following comments are based on my first-hand examination of the Morgan MS and of the Morgan description at: http://corsair.themorgan.org/cgi-bin/Pwebrecon.cgi?BBID=146991&V1=1; and the detailed description, much revised, at corsair.morganlibrary.org/msdescr/BBM0801a.pdf.

27. Fols. 1r–51v.

28. Fol. 84r–v.

29. Fols. 85r–87v.

30. Fols. 88r–150r.

31. Senatore, "Fonti documentarie," 307–8; Francesco Montuori, "Come 'si costruisce' una cronaca," in *Le cronache volgari in Medio Evo: Atti della VI Settimana di studi medievali (Roma, 13–15 maggio 2015)*, Giampaolo Francesconi and Massimo Miglio, ed. (Rome: ISIME, 2017), 31–88, at 41–43.

32. De Caprio, *Scrivere la storia*, 62–68, 75–76.

del Tuppo.[33] Ferraiolo's own Neapolitan text is accompanied by 120 well-known pen-and-wash drawings of varying sizes that provide a vivid picture of events in quattrocento Naples. The manuscript also demonstrates the new access to various forms of popular and more learned texts made available to a broader public through the printing press. Ferraiolo's manuscript thus testifies to a sense of fluidity of medium, genre, language, textuality, orality, and visuality in this more popular genre of historiography.[34] The skilled (if idiosyncratic) richness of the decoration and illustrations,[35] many showing clear mastery of classical style and motifs,[36] also points to more than a naive private book of *ricordanze*. Put together, this evidence may indicate the creation of a presentation copy for a member of the court[37] or a plan for a publication,[38] a work of "recuperation"[39] designed to succeed the *Cronaca di Partenope* that would bolster civic pride, knowledge of the city's geography, topography, and traditions while confirming the place of the Aragonese in a tumultuous phase of its illustrious history.

★

33. Montuori, "Come 'si costruisce'," 37–39.

34. Francesco Montuori, "Immagini di Napoli fra trecento e quattrocento," in *Il viaggio a Napoli tra letteratura e arti*, Pasquale Sabbatino, ed. (Naples: Edizioni scientifiche italiane, 2012), 13–37, at 21–28; Senatore, "Fonti documentarie," 297–98; De Caprio–Senatore, "Orality," 142–43; De Caprio, "La scrittura cronachistica," 30–31.

35. De Caprio, *Scrivere*, 76 nn. 11–12 for bibliography.

36. For example, fols. 35r, 36r, 36v, 41r, 43r, 104r, 104v, 105r, 107r, 108r, 115v, 116r.

37. Marcello Barbato and Francesco Montuori, "Dalla stampa al manoscritto: La iv parte della *Cronaca di Partenope* trascritta dal Ferraiolo (1498)," in *Dal manoscritto al web: Canali e modalità di trasmissione dell'italiano. Tecniche, materialie e usi nella storia della lingua. Atti del XII Congresso SILFI (Helsinki, 18–20 giugno 2012)*, E. Garavelli and E. Suomela-Härmä, ed. (Florence: Cesati, 2014), 51–70, at 67.

38. Barbato–Montuori, 67, argue that such publication might have been intended for a small textual community of family or neighbors, for which the rigidity of a printed edition was inadequate.

39. Montuori, "Come 'si costruisce'," 43.

In reaction to King Ferrante's policies of stemming their feudal powers and independence the barons first revolted in 1460, but the king was able to suppress the rebellion. New tax impositions in the wake of the Turkish sack of Otranto in 1480, however, led to further baronial unrest; and with the election of Pope Innocent VIII in 1484, the Neapolitan barons found an ally against the Aragonese. Under the leadership of Girolamo and Antonello II Sanseverino, former Angevin and Guelph partisans banded together to foment another rebellion. They included the Caracciolo of Melfi, the Gesualdo of Caggiano, and the Balzo-Orsini of Altamura. But the chief organizers of the conspiracy were new nobles who has risen within the Aragonese royal administration: Antonello Petrucci, the royal secretary, and Francesco Coppola, count of Sarno.

In September 1485 the rebels seized Aquila and a few months later the principality of Salerno, capturing Federico, the duke of Calabria and heir to the throne. Ferrante met with the barons at Miglionico but had the leaders arrested. Under the guise of seeking further reconciliation, on August 13, 1486, Ferrante then arrested the remaining conspirators at a wedding in Castel Nuovo. Petrucci's sons Francesco and Giovanni Antonio, and Francesco and Antonello Coppola were executed in Naples on December 11.

Ferraiolo's record of the rebellion, trial and punishment of the barons in 1486[40] comes almost verbatim from the official documentation printed by Francesco Del Tuppo and translated here by RGM.

6. *Ferraiolo: The Conspiracy of the Barons*
   [18] In this month [of September, 1486] there was arranged the wedding of the said Marco Coppola with the daughter of the said duke of Amalfi in Castel Nuovo. The feast was arranged, and there in the Sala Grande attended the Lord King Ferrante and the Lady Queen [Juana of Aragon] and the Lady Duchess of Calabria [Ippolita Maria Sforza] and many other ladies for the said feast, and many other lords who danced and enjoyed themselves.

---

40. Ferraiolo, *Cronaca*, §18–28, pp. 13–19.

The lord king, who had been clearly informed of these many treasons, pretended he needed to talk and called the count of Sarno [Francesco Coppola] into the chamber where His Majesty was staying. But as he entered the various rooms [Coppola] found Lord Sir Inpascale, the castellan of Castel Nuovo with many men at arms, who ordered, "Keep this person right here." And they did this secretly as not to frighten off the other barons who were in the Sala Grande. They did this because His Majesty, who had been clearly informed of the many treasons of these barons, had ordered this. And His Majesty did this before anyone started to leave.

He next called in by name the Secretary, Sir Antonello de Petrucci, the said count of Policastro, and Sir Aniello Arcamone, count of Burriello, and Sir Giovanni Pau. And he did to these the same as to the count of Sarno. Also detained in the said castle were the wife and daughters of the Secretary. The houses and the possessions of all these aforesaid lords were written down; and the Court seized them as the property of traitors and rebels....

[24] On the 13th of the said month [of October], 1486, the news arrived in the city of Naples that [Federico], the most illustrious lord duke of Calabria, had entered the city of Aquila and that, in the battle that he waged to enter the city, he had slain the archdeacon of Aquila along with many other persons in the great rout he caused....

[28] On the 13th of the said month of October, 1486, the sentence was published against these said lord barons, [Francesco Coppola], the count of Sarno and the Secretary [Antonello Petrucci] and all the children of the Secretary:[41]

---

41. Petrucci's wife, Elisabetta Vassallo, had died in custody in Castel Nuovo and was buried in San Domenico. See Ferraiolo §23, p. 15.

"A platform shall be erected for the count of Sarno and the Secretary above the Citatella,[42] that stands above the gate of the said Castel Nuovo, and he is to be beheaded. In the center of Piazza del Mercato a platform is to be erected for all the sons of the Secretary. The count of Carinola is to be dragged through Naples and then is to be quartered. And the count of Policastro is to be beheaded, and his head is then to be dragged through Naples.[43]

"We also declare and decree through this, our definitive sentence, that the said Antonello, Giovanni Antonio and Francesco de Petrucci, father and sons, and Francesco Coppola are to be deprived, and thus we deprive them through this our definitive sentence, of each and every city, castle, baronage, land and realm, jurisdiction and benefice, moveable and immoveable, both feudal and allodial, and all their money, jewels, and precious possessions wherever they might be, either in the Regno or outside the Regno, of whatever nature they might be. And all the aforesaid goods, as said above, shall be applied to our court and royal fisc. And they shall be open and confiscated through this our definitive sentence, pronounced for future memory, as thus written below, completely pronounced, read and promulgated."

The said sentences were read by the Secretary of our council, Antonetto Sapone of Naples, and by Michele Richa, our scribe, who as notaries of this act have been assigned to this case. Seated for the tribunals are the below-written barons and tribunales, knights, gentlemen, merchants, and other people in great number, the said commissioners and counselors, counts and barons seated in the Sala Grande of Castel Nuovo for the tribunals.

There were present the said Antonello, Giovanni Antonio, Francesco Petrucci, father and sons, and Francesco Coppola. Of these the said Antonello Petrucci replied in this manner: "I understand the Sacred Majesty of the Lord Most Christian King, most just and virtuous, and therefore I implore God

42. Illustrated in Morgan MS 801, fol. 97v.

43. Ferraiolo described and depicted these punishments in §37, pp. 21–22. The Morgan MS, fol. 96r shows the "catafalco" clearly as a guillotine.

and the grace of Your Majesty and remit myself to the clemency and to the conscience of Your Majesty."

Giovanni Antonio Petrucci replied thus: "The Majesty of the Lord King acts justly and rightly against me because I have gravely offended Your Majesty; and therefore I remit myself to your clemency."

Francesco Petrucci replied thus: "I remit myself to the mercy and clemency of the Lord King and his wife and children."

Francesco Coppola remained silent and made no reply.

[There follow the names of the officers of the court, the attending counts and barons, the witnesses for the sentencing, and the notaries of the court. The court notary and fiscal procurator then asked to king to pass final judgement.]

The sacred majesty of the lord king, responding to the said fiscal procurator, saying, "I shall proceed to justice, as much for the republic of our Regno as for the *lese maiestas* against ourselves and against our first-born." And he fell silent....

[Subsequent illustrations in Morgan MS 801, fols. 96r–v, show Francesco Petrucci placed upon his back in a cart, surrounded by royal knights, and led to the place of execution. The same fate awaited Francesco Coppola.]

FERRAIOLO IS ALSO one of our witnesses for the expulsion of the Jews from the newly united kingdom of Spain under Ferdinand and Isabella. They followed this unification with the Alhambra Decree (also known as the Edict of Expulsion) of March 31, 1492 against the Jews. On July 30, 1492, about 40,000 Jews were expelled from the Spanish territories. Hunted out, their lands and property expropriated, huddled together in the quickest sea transport they could find (never sanitary at any time), thousands of refugees died en route. An estimated 9000 Spanish and unknown numbers from Sicily and Sardinia fled to Naples and the Regno. They arrived in Naples beginning on 18 August 1492. Soon thereafter the plague of 1493 broke out in Naples, killing an estimated 25,000 Jews (both new refugees and long-time Neapolitans) and about 30,000 Christians, out of a estimated population of about 100,000.[44]

44. Gentilcore, "*Tempi,*" 284–85.

Following a long tradition of anti-Semitic tropes, Ferraiolo places the blame for the outbreak squarely on the Jews. Ferraiolo's account may have had some historic basis, however, given the condition of refugees, their weakened conditions and susceptibility to pre-existing diseases, plague or not.[45] Our account is taken from the *Cronaca*, § 47, p. 25 and translated by RGM.

7. Ferraiolo: The Arrival of Jews Expelled from Spain
The Jews entered the city of Naples on 18 August 1492. They came from every region of Spain. They came in ships, caravels, and barks, they whom the most illustrious lord king of Spain had expelled. He[46] had decided to expel them from all his lands. Therefore they were also expelled from France[47] and from the island of Sicily, and they all arrived in Naples.

From the middle of September they began to infest Naples with the bad airs that they carried with them, which infected Naples along with the entire Regno. In the city of Naples alone there died 20,000 persons among the Christians and the Jews, without counting the rest of the Regno, where there died another 20,000 persons. And this mortality lasted from the middle of the said September until the end of the next August, for one year. It was the worst mortality that was ever recorded in Naples.[48]

FRANCESCO GUICCIARDINI
Guicciardini (1483–1540) joins his fellow Florentine and friend, Niccolò Machiavelli, among the most important historians of the Italian Renaissance.[49] Born into one of the most prominent

45. Gentilcore, "*Tempi*," 285.

46. The prime mover of the expulsion was actually Queen Isabella.

47. "Francza." Perhaps the remaining portions of Navarre, claimed by Spain; and Perpignan, restored to Spanish control in 1493.

48. Fol. 99v of the Morgan Library MS 801 contains an image of the ships arriving in Naples.

49. Cochrane, xi–xii, 171–76, 295–305 et passim; Felix Gilbert, *Machiavelli and Guicciardini: Politics and History in Sixteenth-Century Florence* (Princeton: Princeton University Press, 1985); Pierre Jodogne and Gino Benzoni,

Florentine families and allies of the Medici, Francesco received a solid humanist education in the classics. He studied law at the universities of Ferrara and Padua, and in 1505 he was appointed by the Signoria to teach law at Florence's *studium*. By 1508 he had begun his *Storie Fiorentine* and other works. Between 1512 and 1514 he served as Florentine ambassador to the court of King Ferdinand of Spain. The new Medici pope Leo X made him governor of Reggio Emilia in 1516, of Modena in 1517, and then of Parma, which he defended against the French in 1521. In 1523, he was appointed vice-regent of the Romagna by Pope Clement VII. During the French–Imperial war, Clement named Guicciardini lieutenant-general of the papal army. Although he saved Florence from imperial troops, he was unable to prevent their sack of Rome in 1527.[50] In 1531, Pope Clement named Guicciardini governor of Bologna, a post he retained until Clement's death in 1534. He then returned to Florence as an advisor to the Medici and ambassador to Emperor Charles V's court at Naples. He served the new Medici dukes into the late 1530s and then retired to Arcetri to work on his *Storia d'Italia* until his death in 1540.

Guicciardini's *History* covers the years between 1490 and 1534 and draws extensively on government archives and his own experience in politics and diplomacy. Like Machiavelli, with whom he remained in close touch as both Florentine citizen and historian, Guicciardini focused on the tangled webs of human motivation and action and devotes much attention to the affairs of Naples and the Regno as key to the dissolution to the Italian balance of power.[51] Reading his *History* can often be a complicated and difficult task as he works his way through the multipolarity of personal ambitions, political goals, and power struggles that influenced events throughout Italy. Yet these very same insights into human character and motivation, balanced against the weight of events, still makes his *History* compelling.

"Guicciardini, Francesco," DBI 61 (2004), online at: http://www.treccani.it/enciclopedia/francesco-guicciardini_(Dizionario-Biografico).

50. See Mc Gregor, *Sack*.

51. See De Frede, *La crisi del Regno*.

Our selections of Guicciardini's *History of Italy* are excerpted from his *History of Italy and History of Florence,* Cecil Grayson, trans.; John R. Hale, ed. (New York: Washington Square Press, 1964).

8. Guicciardini: On the Fall of the Aragonese

Book I. 6. ...Alfonso [II], as soon as his father was dead [25 January 1494], sent four ambassadors to the pope [Alexander VI]. The latter was showing signs of wishing to go back to his first idea of friendship with France. In a bull signed by the college of cardinals he had recently promised, at the request of the king of France, the rank of cardinal for the bishop of Saint-Malo, and at the joint expense of himself and the duke of Milan he had recruited Prospero Colonna, who used to be the king's captain, and some other military commanders....

Alfonso, to whom fear had become a good teacher, pursued with Ludovico Sforza the efforts begun by his father offering him the same concessions. Sforza, in his usual way, ingeniously fed him with various hopes but gave him to understand that he was forced to proceed with the greatest skill and care so that the war planned against others should not begin against himself. On the other hand, he never ceased pressing on the preparations in France. To do this more effectively and the better to establish all the details of what had to be arranged, and also so that there should be no delay in the execution of those plans, he sent to France — saying that he had been summoned by the king — Galeazzo da Sanseverino, the husband of his natural daughter, who was greatly favored and trusted by him.... [125–27]

7. More important than the speeches of ambassadors and the replies they received were the preparations by land and sea which were being made everywhere. Charles [VIII] has sent Pierre d'Urfé his grand equerry, to Genoa, which was ruled by the duke of Milan with the support of the Adorno faction and Giovan Luigi dal Fiesco, to prepare a powerful navy of great ships and narrow galleys. Other ships he had fitted out of Villefranche and Marseilles. It was therefore rumored at the French court the Charles intended to enter

the kingdom of Naples by sea as Jean, René of Anjou's son, had done against Ferdinand [Ferrante]....

Alfonso, on the other hand, who had never ceased preparing by land and sea, thought it was no longer possible to allow himself to be deceived by the hopes held out to him by Ludovico, and that it would be better to frighten and harry him than to attempt to reassure and sooth him. So he ordered the Milanese envoy to leave Naples and recalled his own from Milan, took possession of the duchy of Bari — which had been held by Ludovico for many years as a gift from Ferdinand — and sequestered its revenues. Nor was he content with these open demonstrations of hostility (rather than insults): but he then made every effort to lure the city of Genoa away from the duke of Milan.... [133–34]

8. These and many other issues were being discussed in many quarters, but finally the Italian war was opened by Don Federigo [Frederick] going to Genoa with a fleet beyond all doubt larger and better equipped than any seen in the Tyrrhenian Sea for many years past. He had 35 narrow galleys, 18 ships and many other smaller vessels, much artillery and 3000 soldiers for landing. Because of these preparations and because they had with them the exiles [from Genoa], they had left Naples with great hopes of victory; but they had left rather late, partly because of the difficulties which attend all great military movements, and partly because of the false hopes raised by Ludovico Sforza, and they had stopped in the ports of the Sienese to recruit as many as 4000 soldiers; all of which made it difficult to achieve what a month earlier would have been easy....

At this very time the duke of Calabria was moving toward Romagna with the land forces, intending to go on into Lombardy as first planned. But to advance freely and without leaving an enemy behind him he had to win over the state of Bologna and the cities of Imola and Forlì.... [138–40]

18. Charles [VIII] remained in Rome about a month, though he constantly sent forces to the borders of the kingdom of Naples where everything was already in such disorder that Aquila and almost the whole of the Abruzzi had raised his

standard before the king left Rome. Fabrizio Colonna had occupied the country districts around Albi and Tagliacozzo, and the rest of the kingdom was hardly less in tumult. As soon as Ferrando [Frederick] left Rome, the fruits of the people's hatred for Alfonso [II] became apparent. They also remembered the many cruelties of Ferdinand [Ferrante I] his father. Denouncing vehemently the wickedness of the government in the past and the cruelty and arrogance of Alfonso, they openly showed their welcome for the arrival of the French: so much so that the ancient remains of the Angevin faction, in comparison with the other causes, made very little difference, even though they were backed by the memory and following of the many barons who had been driven out and imprisoned at various times by Ferdinand — a thing in itself of great moment and a powerful instrument of change. So powerful, even without these stimuli, was the feeling against Alfonso throughout the kingdom.

When he heard of his son's departure for Rome, Alfonso was so afraid that — forgetting his great fame and glory, which he had won in long experience in many wars in Italy, and despairing of being able to resist this fatal storm — he decided to abandon his kingdom and give up his royal title and authority to Ferrando. He hoped perhaps that with his departure all the intense hatred would disappear and that by making king a young man of great promise who had never offended anyone and was universally popular, he would perhaps diminish his subjects' desire for the French. This decision might have been effective if taken earlier; but put off to a time when things were not only in violent commotion but had already begun to go downhill, it was powerless to prevent his ruin.... [183–84]

GUICCIARDINI WAS ALSO among the first to record the association of venereal disease in Europe with Naples. Our selection is taken from Guicciardini's *History of Italy,* Grayson, trans., 278–79.

9. Guicciardini: On Venereal Disease

Book II.13. After our account of other matters, it does not seem unworthy to report that at this period — when it was Italy's fate that all its ills should originate with the French invasion or should at least be attributed to them — the disease which the French call "the Neapolitan sickness" and what the Italians commonly called *buboes* or "French sickness," made its first appearance.

The French caught this disease in Naples, and they spread it all over Italy on their way home to France. It was either quite new or until this time unknown in our hemisphere except in the most remote parts and was for many years so horrible that it deserves to be mentioned as a grave disaster. It showed itself either in hideous boils which also became incurable sores, or with intense pains in the joints and nerves all over the body. The doctors, who knew nothing about the disease, did not employ suitable remedies but quite often wrong ones which made the symptoms much worse. Many people of every age and sex died from it, and many others were hideously deformed and became helpless and subject to almost continual agonies of pain. Indeed most of those who appear to have recovered in a short time fell again into the same misery. However, after many years the influence of the stars which had made the disease so virulent was mitigated or the appropriate cures for it became known to long experience, and it became much less malignant.

It had of its own accord also produced several types different from the first form of the disease. This was a calamity of which the men of our age might the more reasonably complain if it had fallen upon them without any fault of their own: for it is agreed by all those who have closely observed the characteristics of the disease, that it never, or hardly ever, occurs save my contagion in coitus. Yet one should rightly remove the smirch from the French name, because it was later seen that the disease was brought in from Spain to Naples and was not characteristic of that nation but brought in from those islands which, as we shall narrate at some more appropriate moment, began to be known to our hemisphere during these years through the voyages of a Genovese, Christopher Columbus. In those islands, however, this malady finds a prompt remedy through the benevolence of nature; for they cure it easily, simply by drinking the juice of a tree distinguished for its many remarkable properties.

PHILIPPE DE COMMYNES

Commynes (1447–1511)[52] was a diplomat and historian attached to both the dukes of Burgundy and the French royal house. He was born into a old French baronial family with extensive titles and holdings around Flanders. Orphaned in 1453, he entered the household of his godfather, Philip the Good (1419–1467), duke of Burgundy, and gained some reputation as a trusted knight and retainer of both Phillip and his son Charles the Bold. Believing that Commynes had saved his life at Péronne in October 1468, King Louis XI brought him into royal service as an ambassador to England and member of his inner circle. From the late 1470s he became a chief royal ambassador to the court of Lorenzo de' Medici and quickly learned the intricacies and personalities of the Italian balance of power.

Exiled in 1489 for his role in the Orleanist rebellion against King Charles VIII, Commynes began to write his *Mémoires*,[53] ending in 1501 with the death of Charles in 1498. He thus devoted a good amount of his work to Italian affairs, including those of the Regno, but from a decidedly French point of view, which excoriated the Aragonese. Our selection is taken from Desmond Seward, *Naples: A Travellers' Companion* (New York: Atheneum, 1986), 112–13.

10. De Commynes: On Alfonso II

> No man was crueler than he [Alfonso], more vicious, more corrupt, more debauched. His father [Ferrante I] was still more dangerous since no-one could ever tell what he was thinking... smiling in a friendly way, he would seize and destroy people, as he did with Jacopo Piccinino.... His near-relations and close acquaintances have informed me that he knew neither mercy nor compassion. Where money was concerned he never had had pity or forbearance for his subjects.
>
> He turned everything in the country into goods for sale and merchandise. He even had time for pig-breeding, people

52. Joël Blanchard, *Philippe de Commynes* (Paris: Fayard, 2006).

53. Philippe de Commynes, *Mémoires*, Joël Blanchard, ed., 2 vols. (Geneva: Droz, 2007).

being forced to mind his pigs for him; if they fattened, he sold them for his own profit — otherwise the people had to pay for the pigs themselves. In oil-producing districts like Apulia he and his son bought it at a fixed price which they dictated, and also corn [wheat] before it ripened; then they forced up the prices and made the people buy all their oil and corn from them — so long as their own stocks lasted, no-one else's oil was allowed to be put on the market.

If a nobleman or a baron's estate prospered, they would ask him for a loan and either take it with his agreement or else extort it by force. They confiscated everyone's stallions for their own use, so that in the end they had a herd that was far too large, stallions, mares and colts, keeping them all on their vassals' pastures, much to the latter's detriment. Both raped several women savagely. Indeed it was impossible for them to commit more evil crimes.

PIETRO SUMMONTE

In 1524 the Neapolitan humanist Pietro Summonte (1453–1526) wrote a letter with a lengthy description of Renaissance art in Naples[54] in response to a request from Marcantonio Michiel (c. 1484–1552), the noted Venetian connoisseur, historian and politician. Michiel evidently intended to use the information in a publication on Italian art. Summonte's position as former student and erudite successor to Giovanni Pontano as president of the Neapolitan Academy rendered him a suitable candidate for Michiel's task; the two had met via their mutual acquaintance, poet Jacopo Sannazaro.[55] However, the Venetian's ambitions were stymied, possibly by the sheer magnitude of the undertaking or by the news of Vasari's planned biographies. Therefore, the letter survives as an autonomous work.

Well-known only after Fausto Nicolini's publication of it in 1925, the epistle provides a rare critical overview of local accomplishments

---

54. See below, chapter 10, reading 169, pp. 447–66.

55. Ferdinando Bologna, "Qualche osservazione sulla lettera di Pietro Summonte a Marcantonio Michiel," in *Libri per vedere: le guide storico-artistiche della città di Napoli* (Naples: Edizioni Scientifiche Italiane, 1995), 185.

and as such it has secured for Summonte a certain prominence in the history of Neapolitan art.[56] His letter exudes the learned references, prejudices, pretensions, and sense of competition that one might expect of one Renaissance man of letters and politics writing to another. It is translated in full by Charlotte Nichols below in chapter 10.[57] and excerpted here. Summonte's letter blames historic circumstance for derailing a perceived trajectory: the fulfillment of Aragonese cultural patronage.

11. Summonte: On Alfonso II

[475–511] In our times the Signor King Alfonso II of beloved memory was dedicated to building and the cupidity to do great things, which, if iniquitous fortune had not robbed him so soon of his throne, without a doubt he would have adorned this city to the highest degree. He had it in mind to bring a distant river through great aqueducts into the city; and completing the grand walls of the city, in good measure already done, to extend in a straight line all the main roads within the walls of the city, to eliminate all the arcades, corners, and uneven protuberances, and thus to extend directly the transverse roads from hilltop to hilltop of the city in such a way that, both for the direction of the streets and the alleys, and also for the natural orientation of the site from the north to the south, this city would have been, beyond the beauty of its evenness, the most clean and elegant city (I say it with your indulgence) in all of Europe which in even the lightest rain would be cleaned like a plate of polished silver.

In addition to the fountains for individual houses, there would have been constructed public fountains and drinking troughs in the appropriate quarters and places, from which water would spew onto the streets,

56. Nicolini, *L'arte napoletana*. The letter is located in the Archivio di Stato, Turin, and was published earlier in part by Cornelius von Fabriczy, "Summonte's Brief an M.A. Michiel," *Repertorium für Kunstwissenschaft* 30 (1907): 143–68. Roberto Pane republished the letter in *Il rinascimento nell'Italia meridionale* (Milan: Edizioni di Comunità, 1975), 1:63–95.

57. Pages 450–66.

since those were swept in the summer, for keeping the ground without dust and clean. Besides this, he wanted also to build a sumptuous temple for the remains of the Aragonese dynasty who died here, and a great palace near Castel Nuovo in the Piazza della Coronata, in which he wanted to situate all the tribunals in different rooms, so that it would not be necessary for the merchants to go to different places, but instead here expedite whatever their business, without enduring the rain or sun or tiring themselves going here and there. Neither was His Majesty the type not to carry out the things he said after having deliberated them nor was he scared of spending. The more the plans cost, the more they pleased him.

[510–523] All of these noble and holy thoughts were interrupted and completely destroyed by the sudden barbaric invasion of Charles VIII, king of France, who caused the demise of the Aragonese family in this kingdom....

ANTONIO CASTALDO

Toward the end of 1546 Toledo wrote to his brother, the cardinal of San Sisto, who was one of the six members of the Congregation, expressing his desire to introduce the Inquisition into Naples. He also explained that he feared that doing so might lead to a successful general revolt in Naples against the Spanish. They therefore decided to procure from the pope a commission for an inquisitor against any heresy prevalent among the clergy, both regular and secular. The required commission was issued in February 1547 to the prior and the lector of the Dominican convent of Sta. Caterina. Toledo did not personally grant the *exequatur* for it but caused this to be done by the regents of the *Consiglio Collaterale*, but this precaution and the profound secrecy observed proved useless.

Our selection is taken from the *Istoria di Notar Antonio Castaldo, Libri Quattro* (Naples: Giovanni Gravien, 1769), in the summary translation in Henry Charles Lea, *The Inquisition in the Spanish Dependencies* (London: Macmillan, 1922), 70–78. Castaldo was a notary and a loyal adherent of the emperor and witnessed much of what he relates below.

12. Castaldo: The Neapolitans Revolt against the Spanish Inquisition, May 1547

Rumors spread among the people that orders had been received from the cardinals to proceed against regular and secular clerks; the old animosity against anything but the episcopal Inquisition at once flamed up and deputies were sent to the viceroy to beg him not to grant the *exequatur*. He assured them that he wondered himself at the fact; he had written to the pope that it was not Charles [V's] will or intention that the Inquisition should be introduced and that meanwhile he had not granted the *exequatur*. Little faith was placed in his statements, and the general belief was that [Pope] Paul III was eager to create strife in Naples in order to give the emperor opposition there and check his growing ascendency. It is said that he actually sent two inquisitors but, if so, they never dared to show themselves, for there is no allusion to them in the detailed accounts of the ensuing troubles.

To carry out the plot, action was commenced in a tentative way by the archiepiscopal vicar affixing at the door of his palace an edict forbidding the discussion of religion by laity and announcing that he would proceed by inquisition to examine into the beliefs held by the clergy. The very word "inquisition" was sufficient to inflame the people; cries of *serra!, serra!* were heard; and the aspect of affairs was so alarming that the vicar went into hiding, and the edict was removed.

The *seggi* of the nobles were assembled and elected deputies charged with enforcing the observance of the *capitoli,* or liberties of the city. The Seggio del Popolo was crippled, for the viceroy some months previously, in preparation for the struggle, had dismissed the Eletto and replaced him with Domenico Terracina, a creature of his own, who did not assemble his *seggio* but appointed the deputies himself. Then, on Palm Sunday [April 3], Toledo sent for Terracina and the heads of the Ottine and charged them to see that those guilty of the agitation were punished. But in place of doing this the *seggio* assembled and sent to him deputies who boldly represented the universal abhorrence felt for the Inquisition, which gave such facilities for false witness that it would ruin the city and kingdom; and they expressed the universal suspicion felt that the edict portended its introduction. The viceroy soothed them with the assurance that the emperor had no such intention; as for himself, if the emperor should attempt it, he would tire him out with supplications to desist and, if unsuccessful, would resign his post and leave the city. But, as there were people who talked about religion without understanding, it was necessary that they should be punished according to the canons by the ordinary jurisdiction. This answer satisfied the majority, but still there were some who regarded with anxiety the implied threat conveyed in the last phrase.

Then, on May 11, the patience of the people was further tested by another edict affixed on the archiepiscopal doors, which hinted more clearly at the Inquisition. At once the city rose, with cries of *armi! armi! serra! serra!* The edict was torn down; Terracina was compelled against his will to convene the Seggio del Popolo, where he and his subordinates were promptly dismissed from office and replaced with men who could be relied upon. The ejected officials could scarce show themselves in the streets, and three of them were only saved from popular vengeance by taking sanctuary. The viceroy came from his winter residence at Pozzuoli breathing vengeance. He garrisoned the Castel Nuovo with 3000 Spanish troops and ordered the popular leaders to be prosecuted.

Tommaso Aniello tore down the edict and forced Terracina to assemble the *seggio*. He was summoned to appear in court, but he came accompanied with so great a crowd, under the command of Cesare Mormile, that the judges were afraid to proceed; and when the people seized Terracina's children as hostages, Aniello was discharged. Then Mormile was cited and went accompanied by forty men, armed under their garments and carrying papers like pleaders; the presiding judge was informed of this and dismissed the case.

Finding legal measures useless, the viceroy adopted more severe methods. On May 16 the garrison made a sortie as far as the Rua Catalana, firing houses and slaying without distinction of age or sex. The bells of San Lorenzo tolled to arms; shops were closed and the people rushed to the castle, where they found the Spaniards drawn up in battle array. Blinded with rage, they flung themselves on the troops and lost some two hundred and fifty men uselessly, while the cannon from the castle bombarded the city.

Angry recrimination and threats followed; the citizens determined to arm the city, not for rebellion, as they asserted, but to preserve it for the emperor. Throughout the whole of this unhappy business, they were strenuously eager to demonstrate their loyalty and, when the news came of Charles V's victory over the German Protestants at Muhlberg, April 24, the city manifested its rejoicing by an illumination for three nights. So when, on May 22, the viceroy ordered another sortie, in which there was considerable slaughter, the citizens hoisted on San Lorenzo a banner with the imperial arms and their war-cry was *"Imperio e Spagna!"* They raised some troops and placed them under the command of Gianfrancesco and Pasquale Caracciolo and Cesare Mormile, but it was difficult to form a standing army, owing to the question of pay, as the money had to be raised by voluntary subscription.

Bad as was the situation, it was embittered when some bailiffs of the Vicariate arrested a man for debt. On the way to prison he resisted and called for aid; three young nobles stopped to enquire the cause and, during the parley, the prisoner escaped. This enraged Toledo, who had the youths arrested at night and condemned with scarce a pretext of trial. On May 24 they were brought out on the bridge in front of the Castel Nuovo, where their throats were cut by a slave and the corpses were left in blood and mud, with a placard prohibiting their removal. This gratuitous cruelty inflamed the people almost to madness; houses and shops were closed, arms were seized and crowds rushed through the streets, threatening they scarce knew what. To manifest his contempt for the populace, Toledo rode quietly through the town, where he would infallibly have been shot had not Cesare Mormile, the prior of Bari, and others of the popular leaders earnestly dissuaded reprisals.

Meetings were held in which the nobles and people formally united for the common defense, which was always regarded as a most threatening portent for the sovereign, and they resolved to send envoys to the emperor, for which office they selected the prince of Salerno, the greatest noble of the land, and Placido di Sangro, a gentleman of high quality. Toledo summoned the envoys and told them that, if their mission concerned the Inquisition, it was superfluous, for he would pledge himself within two months to have a letter from the emperor declaring that nothing more should be done about it; if it was about the *Capitoli,* he could assure them that any infraction of the city's privileges would be duly punished; if it was to complain of him, they were welcome to go. The envoys were too well pleased with their appointment to accept his offer and wait two months for its fulfillment; the people suspected the viceroy of trickery, and the envoys set out. Six days later they were followed by the marquis della Valle, sent by the viceroy to counteract their mission; the prince dallied in Rome with the cardinals, so that della Valle reached the court before him and gained the ear of the emperor.

Meanwhile crowds of exiles and adventurers, under chosen leaders, came flocking into the city, and a guerrilla warfare was organized against the Spaniards, who had advanced from house to house up to the Cancelleria Vecchia, making loopholes in the walls and shooting everyone within range. With the aid of these reinforcements the Spaniards were gradually driven back to [Sta. Maria] Incoronata. On the other hand Antonio Doria came with his galleys, bringing a large force of Spanish troops. The courts were closed.

Four things were remarkable. First, there were no homicides, assaults, or other crimes. Second, although there was no government of the city, yet food and wine were abundant and cheap, and no fraud or violence was committed on those who came with provisions. Third, although there were great numbers of exiles or bandits, with their chiefs, some of them bitterly hostile toward each other, there was no quarreling or treachery; on one occasion two mortal enemies met, each at the head of his band and a fight was expected, but one said "Camillo, this is not the time to settle our affair," to which the other replied "Certainly; let us fight the common enemy; there will be ample time afterwards for our matter." Fourth, the prison of the Vicaria was full of prisoners, some condemned to death and others held for debt, but no attempt was made to rescue them and food was sent to them as usual by women and children. Evidently the people felt that they were fighting for their liberties and would not allow their cause to be compromised by common lawlessness.

At length Toledo's preparations for a decisive stroke were completed and, on July 22, a sortie was made in force, while the guns of the fortresses and galleys bombarded the city. There was much slaughter and some four hundred houses were burnt, whose ruins blockaded the streets. Desultory fighting continued for some days and then a truce was agreed upon until the envoys should return.

On August 7 came Placido di Sangro, the bearer of a simple order, signed by Secretary Vargas, to the effect that the prince of Salerno should remain in the court, while he should return and tell the people of Naples to lay down their arms and obey the viceroy. This cruel disappointment came near producing a violent outbreak, but the prior of Bari succeeded in quieting the people and persuading them to obey the emperor. The next day, by order of the Eletti, a huge collection of arms was made, loaded on wagons and carried to the viceroy. Then the tribunals were opened and every one returned to his private business.

On August 12 the viceroy summoned the Eletti and read to them a royal *indultus*, which purported to be granted at his request, pardoning the people for their revolt, except those already condemned and seventeen other specified persons. Most of those deeply compromised had, however, already sought safety in flight. This doubtful mercy did not amount to much. A bishop came, commissioned by the emperor, to try the city for its misdeeds when, through the procurement of the viceroy, witnesses were found to swear that the cry of *Francia, Francia!* was often raised. Whether this was true or not, the letters of Dio that active negotiations had been carried on with both France and the pope, and that the sovereignty of Naples had even been offered to Cardinal [Alessandro] Farnese, the grandson of the latter.

Mendoza evidently regarded Paul III as ready to take advantage of the situation if occasion offered and, when the revolt was suppressed, he mentions that the fugitives received a warm welcome in Rome. It is not surprising therefore that the decision of the episcopal commissioner was adverse to the city, containing, among other things, a fine of a hundred thousand ducats for ringing the bells as a call to arms. The viceroy, moreover, by no means confined himself to the persons excepted from pardon, but threw into prison all the leaders whom he could seize. He had already published a considerable list of those excluded and the seventeen also grew to fifty-six, of whom twenty-six were condemned to death, although it does not appear that any were actually executed, and the prisoners were gradually liberated, twenty-four at one time, four at another and all the rest in 1553.

Among them was Placido di Sangro, whose friends could not learn the cause of his confinement and sent Luigi di Sangro to the emperor to find out. Charles said that Placido was *buon cavaliero,* but that he was a great talker and that orders had already been sent to the viceroy about him. The incident that left on the emperor the impression of Placido's loquacity is too characteristic of the former's good-nature to be omitted. Once, as he left his chamber, Placido followed him, pleading for the city; he appeared not to listen, and Placido had the audacity to pluck his mantle and ask his attention. Charles turned smilingly and said "Go on Placido, I am listening." The duke of Alva was close behind and Placido said "Signore, I can not talk, for the duke of Alva hears all I say," to which Charles replied, laughing, "Tell him not to hear it" and then obligingly drew Placido to one side and let him say all that he wanted. The conclusion of the whole business was that their arms were returned to the citizens and the emperor contented himself with the fine, but the hated viceroy kept his post until his death in 1553, and no assurance against the Inquisition was obtained.

PIETRO ANTONIO LETTIERI

Lettieri (fl. c.1560) was royal surveyor under both Pedro de Toledo, who commissioned him to restore the ancient Aqua Augusta (Serino Aqueduct), and under Perafán de Ribera, duke of Alcalà (viceroy 1559–71), who in 1560 appointed him to rationalize the water supplies of the city, continue repairs to the ancient aqueducts, drain the swamps, and remove the polluting textile mills to the east of the city. Ribera also authorized him to control the urban sprawl then beginning to cover the hillside of San Martino.[58] Our selections are excerpted from Francesco Abbate, *Storia dell'arte nell'Italia meridionale: Il Cinquecento* (Rome: Donzelli, 2001), 133–35. Readings for Lettieri ultimately derive from Lorenzo Giustiniani, *Dizionario geografico ragionato del Regno di Napoli,* 10 vols. (Naples: Vicenzo Manfredi, 1797–1895). They have been translated by RGM.

13. Lettieri: On Naples' Infrastructure
Lettieri was familiar with the Serino Aqueduct because he himself had inspected portions of it, and he had also been informed about it by Ciccio de Loffrido, a friend of Sannazaro:

> And I recall that the now deceased Messer Ciccio de Loffrido had told me several times that at the time of Sannazaro he was in Nola because of the plague then raging in Naples. When he noticed certain formations that appeared in the plain of Palma Campania he said that the Sebeto River flowed through these to Naples. I myself heard something similar from those who heard it from the mouth of [Jacopo] Sannazaro himself: the venerable Don

58. See chapter 4, reading 58, p. 224.

Constantino Sebastiano, a monk of Monteoliveto, who is still alive, and from the magnificent Lord Mario Galeotta.[59]

...I say that for two thirds of the aforesaid ancient aqueducts to be restored, it would cost 80,000 ducats at the most. And one must impose a limit on the price of the water that it carries, which the Serino Aqueduct will conduct all under the ground, except for the section near the casale of Pomigliano de Arcore where it flows over over brick arches.

LETTIERI ALSO PROPOSED the elimination of the mills on the marshland to the east of Naples,

...which are becoming more and more watered and flooded, as one sees today, instead, constructing mills using this Serino water in other more dry sections. These marshes will remain dry, and will create beautiful gardens, as it was in the mansion at the time that the Capuana was in its greatness, and that all that territory was the garden of the Castel Capuano and was called the *"mansio rosarum,"* and which at present is [still] called the mansion of roses.[60]

FOR THE CITY'S FOUNTAINS, Lettieri advises a unified system whereby,

...the waters flowing from the fountains, which abound inside the city, consolidate all the sewers and carry out to sea all the bad odors, which now cause putrefaction of the air, and also carry out all the human waste and waters of the sewers, and the rotting foundations of the houses. And it is a great hope that the city will be so purified — both inside and out — of that pollution, so as not to suffer from recurrent plagues.

LETTIERI RECORDED PLANS for the expansion of the city walls westward. This selection was translated in Anna Giannetti, "Urban Design and Public Spaces," in Hall–Willette, 46–100, at 88–92.

59. Translated from Bianca De Divitiis, "Memories from the Subsoil: Discovering Antiquities in Fifteenth-Century Naples and Campania," in Hughes-Buongiovanni, 189–216, at 204 n. 42.

60. On the gardens extending out from the Porta Capuana toward Poggioreale, see Giannetti, "Urban Design," 71–76.

The work started from the closed Porta di San Giovanni a Carbonara and the piperno tower behind the monastery, turning to the church of Sta. Maria di Costantinopoli, turning toward the monastery of San Sebastiano delle Monache, and turning again to continue upward toward Monte Sant'Erasmo, where there is the beautiful gate called Porta Reale Nuova or Toledo. There are plans to continue the walls up to the Castel Sant'Elmo. From the area of Chiaia begins a new portion of the walls with another gate called Porta Romana located just below the house and garden of the prince of Stigliano, continuing toward Castel Sant'Elmo. Another portion of the walls continues toward Castel dell'Ovo, including the area called Ecclesia and of Sta. Lucia, reaching toward Castel Nuovo.

DISCOURSE ON THE KINGDOM OF NAPLES, c.1570
This anonymous and undated report is contained in a summary State of the Royal Patrimony from 1571–72, on the last cusp of the Regno's prosperity. It is edited and translated by Antonio Calabria.[61]

14. State of the Royal Patrimony, 1571–72
The Kingdom produces… all things needed not only to sustain human life of men, but also to bring them ease and pleasure — truly a rare thing, and one which I think is not to be found in any other kingdom of which we have news. For it produces grain, barley, legumes, oil, wine, almonds… saffron… and silk not only for its own needs but also to give to other countries in great quantity, as it does in abundance, for a million in gold, with much utility for the people of the kingdom and for the king.…

Naples has …a great quantity of livestock of every sort, for its own use, and to give to others… beautiful and good horses, which are deemed more apt for war than whatsoever other horses of whatsoever other country, and most beautiful mules.

[Because of its] beautiful woods, mountains and plains, the Regno produces most excellent wines… and a great quantity of fruit of every kind in every season, and every

61. *Cost of Empire*, 9–10.

sort of game, and since it is surrounded by the seas it has great quantities of very good fish. [The kingdom also boasted] things to acquire and to preserve human health, that is, baths, geysers and hot sands, which are better and in greater number than in whatsoever other country.

[Yet, the *Discourse* goes on to warn], all the lands in the kingdom are oppressed by very heavy debts, and they have little hope of being able to redeem themselves fully or in part. In general, too, there is very great poverty, so that there can be no hope of getting even a little more out of this kingdom than at present is gotten, not even if war or plague came, which God forbid.

ROYAL *VISITAS DE ITALIA*

15. On Poverty, Prostitution, and Orphanage in Naples, c.1590
The following is excerpted from the royal Spanish *Visitas de Italia* and has been edited and translated by Antonio Calabria.[62]

...all the streets of full of [prostitutes]... and they have grown in infinite numbers. In fact, over the last few years they have come to this city from all the places in the world, because of the freedom they have to live here. They pick the best streets and the best squares, as was seen last year, when the Lord Duke of Osuna[63] kicked them out of Via Toledo, which was full of them from one end to the other....

[A gabelle tax regulates the trade], which is necessary and useful to the city of Naples... to curb and punish the women who live dishonestly, to hold in check the iniquity and licentiousness of the prostitutes and pimps, who, being evil-doers, continuously commit enormous crimes and excesses, because... the best places of thieves, blasphemers, gamblers, pimps and other criminals are almost always the houses of prostitutes....

[Yet], the secretaries and the civil and criminal officials of the High Courts of Justice [Vicaria] protect some of the whores, who are their friends and concubines, and they

62. *Cost of Empire*, 29–30.

63. Pedro Téllez-Girón, viceroy 1582–86.

frustrate the work of the said gabelle with the writs they issue..., which the judges sign simply on the secretaries' reports... and because of the connections they have with the police and the ministers of justice, it is commonplace during the holidays to see some of the secretaries going around in coaches, accompanying the whores, and so also at night, and they wrongly make them cross-dress as men....

[The large numbers of prostitutes (and the impoverished) gave rise to huge numbers of illegitimate births. Sto. Spirito in Naples alone hosted 300 girls], daughters of prostitutes, whose mothers, it is suspected, would impose on them the same life, and they stay in the said house until they are of age to get married, and then the house gives them something for their dowry, and if they don't want to get married, they become nuns....

The Hospital of Sta. Annunziata ordinarily employs 7000 [sic] wet-nurses to bring up the babies who are left at the door of the church of the Annunziata,[64] and they look after them up to the age of seven; and after that the boys are put to work, and the girls are placed in a convent... where there are usually 1200 of them, and each year about 200 of them get married, and they are given 90 ducats each in dowry....[65]

GIULIO CESARE CAPACCIO

Capaccio (1552–1634)[66] was born in Campagna d'Eboli (Salerno). After studying under the local Dominicans, he was sent to the University of Naples for a law degree, which he completed at Bologna but not before coming under the influence of the Jesuit Girolamo Casella da Nola, an expert in Syriac and Hebrew. He also

64. The famous revolving door of the Espositi, where newborns could be left anonymously, has been preserved at Sta. Annunziata.

65. By 1560 there were 32 women's religious houses in Naples with a total population of about 1700. Many religious and lay women devoted their energies to caring for such orphans, widows and abandoned wives, former prostitutes and their daughters. See Novi Chavarria, "Space of Women," 184–87.

66. See Salvatore Nigro, "Capaccio, Giulio Cesare," DBI 18 (1975) online at:http://www.treccani.it/enciclopedia/giulio-cesare-capaccio_(Dizionario-Biografico).

became friends with Cardinal Felice Peretti di Montalto, the future Pope Sixtus V, and began his close association with Neapolitan humanists and literary figures. Capaccio was the author of numerous Latin works, eclogues and other poetry, public orations, treatises on preaching, local histories, civic treatises, heraldry, emblematica,[67] biography, genealogical and antiquarian works, eventually becoming one of the founders of the Accademia degli Oziosi (1611).

Capaccio served in a variety of public offices both in Naples and in Urbino. In 1593 he was named head of the *Provveditoria* of grains and oils, a post that involved him in both fiscal administration and public works. He was appointed secretary of the city of Naples under Viceroy Juan Alonso Pimentel de Herrera (1603–10) and in 1606 tapped to examine and catalog the antiquities then being discovered around Cuma. Capaccio's antiquarian guide, *La vera antichità di Pozzuoli* is excerpted in the *Baroque Naples* volume of this series.[68] Here we present a small selection of his administrative record. This selection is translated by RGM from Galasso, *Napoli capitale,* 116.

16. Capaccio: Consumption Levels in Naples c.1600
> Naples consumes 4000 tomola[69] [120,000 kg. or 6250 bushels] of grain a day [or 2.4 million bushels a year], 30,000 botti [15.7 million litres] of wine a year in public venues alone, excluding private consumption, 1000 staia [25,480 litres] of oil, 15,000 cantaia [1.3 million kg.] of salted meats, 6000 [534,000 kg.] of cheese and 20,000 [1.8 million kg.] of fish a year. 100,000 large and small beasts are slaughtered every year, without counting young goats, chickens, and other similar animals, and more than 30,000 scudi[70] worth

67. See his *Delle imprese, trattato* (Naples: Gio. Giacomo Carlino & Antonio Pace, 1592).

68. Chenault-Porter, 26–27.

69. On weights and measures, see Calabria, *Cost of Empire,* xii.

70. The gold scudo was roughly equivalent to 1 Florentine or Roman florin or 1 Venetian ducat. See Carlo M. Cipolla, *Money in Sixteenth-Century Florence* (Berkeley: University of California Press, 1987), 65–76; Calabria, *Cost of Empire,* xiii.

of vegetables and other garden produce a month. Into the city arrive, moreover, 300 trunks of merchandise and dry goods, 6000 of sugar, 2000 of white wax and 20,000 cantaia [1.8 million kg.] of almonds a year. Neapolitans spend 400,000 ducats a year in imported clothing and 200,000 on domestic; 300,000 scudi for Venetian cloth and 200,000 for Flemish, as well as 150,000 for gold jewelry and silver work and 40,000 for pin work.

★ ★ ★

CHAPTER 2: HUMANIST THOUGHT

Neapolitan humanists wrote on a wide variety of topics, ranging from literature and poetry, to archaeology and art, to political theory and ethics. Presented elsewhere throughout this book are selections from many of these authors, including Antonio Beccadelli (Panormita), Tristano Caracciolo, Bartolomeo Facio, Jacopo Sannazaro [Fig. 2, opposite] and Pietro Summonte. Here we will concentrate on a few representative texts of philosophical, political, civic, and biographical writing by humanists at the Aragonese and Spanish courts of Naples.

GIANNOZZO MANETTI

Manetti (1396–1459)[1] was among the most illustrious of Florentine humanists and was included in chapter six of Vespasiano da Bisticci's *Lives* as among "the distinguished men who have adorned our century."[2] He was born in Florence into a family of prosperous merchant bankers. First educated in the *abbaco* to take his place in the family business, he soon entered the city's administration, serving as one of the Twelve Good Men in 1429. By 1421, however, he had already begun the study of Latin, and over the next nine years he mastered Latin, Greek, and Hebrew, first at the convent school of San Agostino and then at Sta. Maria degli Angeli, under the direction of the humanist Greek scholar Ambrogio Traversari. Among his fellow students was Tommaso Parentucelli, the future Pope Nicholas V.

Over the 1430s and 1440s Manetti continued to hold important civic offices as administrator in Florence and Tuscany and as

---

1. Cochrane, 26–27; Bentley, 122–27, 209–12; Simona Foà, "Manetti, Giannozzo," DBI 68 (2007), online at: http://www.treccani.it/enciclopedia/giannozzo-manetti_(Dizionario-Biografico). For important critical work, see Craig Kallendorf, "Giannozzo Manetti," *Oxford Bibliographies Online* (New York: Oxford University Press, 2014), online at: http://dx.doi.org/10.1093/OBO/9780195399301-0091http://dx.doi.org/10.1093/OBO/9780195399301-0091.

2. Vespasiano Da Bisticci, *Renaissance Princes, Popes, and Prelates,* W. G. Waters and Emily Waters, ed. (New York: Harper & Row, 1963), 372–95 at 372.

ambassador and orator to Milan and Genoa. By the 1440s he was already recognized as among the most important Florentine humanists as he began composing humanist tracts and philological studies of the Greek and Hebrew scriptures, on the Greek philosophers, historical work and biographies,[3] including the *Vitae Dantis et Petrarchae ac Boccacii* of c.1440.

Alfonso of Aragon invited Manetti to Naples in 1443, and again in 1445 to attend the wedding of Ferrante and Isabella di Chiaromonte (Clermont). In 1453, while he was on an embassy to the papal court, Manetti's anti-oligarchic politics and Italian diplomacy led to accusations of treason against him for conspiracy against Cosimo de' Medici. Offered a position as Pope Nicholas V's secretary, Manetti remained in Rome until the pope's death and finally moved to Naples to join Alfonso's court in 1455. There he served as a highly rewarded court councilor and as president of the Sommaria (exchequer). He remained in Naples until his death on October 27, 1459.

Despite Manetti's diplomatic orations for Florence urging Italian states to unite against Alfonso — the new Hannibal — the king and humanist enjoyed a long and close friendship. One of their long, ongoing conversations resulted in Alfonso's commissioning Manetti's treatise, *On the Dignity and Excellence of Man* in 1452. He continued to compose various works, including *De terraemotu* of 1456 following a major earthquake in Naples[4] and dedicated to King Alfonso, translations of Aristotle's *Nicomachean* and *Eudemian Ethics* and *Magna moralia*, a complete Latin translation of the Greek New Testament and of the Hebrew Psalms, and polemics.

In his dedication to the *Vita Socratis et Senecae,* excerpted below, he praised Alfonso's virtues, patronage of the arts and letters, his knowledge of the classics, distinguished (and ancient) pedigree, his military prowess, and his ability to lead Christendom in a new

3. Giannozzo Manetti, *Biographical Writings*, Stefano Ugo Baldassarri, and Rolf Bagemihl, ed. and trans. (Cambridge, MA: Harvard University Press, 2003).

4. See chapter 1, reading 3, p. 63.

crusade against the Turks. Our selection is taken from Manetti, *Biographical Writings*, 165–73.

17. *Manetti: Lives of Socrates and Seneca*

To King Alfonso of Aragon Serene and Glorious Prince
The illustrious life of the philosopher Seneca of Spain, which I wrote in Latin some time ago, I should have already sent to your majesty had I not thought its sending unworthy of your exceptional and outstanding preeminence. But recently, as you understand from the letters of our excellent [Florentine] ambassador Franco [Sacchetti], you have, to your credit, abandoned all your wars against Christian princes and peoples, and, having read through the histories and annals of Livy, you have been turning your whole mind towards the finest studies of moral philosophy. I have been informed in clear terms that it is for this reason that you have explicitly requested and required from him the aforesaid life of Seneca — who, if I may say it without offense, is agreed to be the prince of Latin philosophers. So I could not delay or refuse to dispatch it, fearing to displease Your Serenity even slightly by not sending something needed by so great and distinguished a prince and so powerful a king, especially when you had asked for it in such a kindly and liberal way. Indeed I should worship, venerate and respect you before all others because of the great abundance of your royal titles, because of the great excellence of your many realms and not least because of the admirable and almost unbelievable splendor of your numerous and great virtues; And I have a powerful and particular desire to serve, gratify and please you.

So I beseech and implore you to accept with a joyous and happy heart this little gift of ours, whatever you may think of it, as befits your singular and outstanding humanity towards men of all kinds and your outstanding goodness towards educated and learned men....

The more diligently and carefully, most serene prince, I meditate on both the noble and ancient house from which you spring and the outstanding and admirable exploits of your previous life, and note this present laudable design of your truly regal mind to study the finest kind of moral philosophy and to defeat the barbarous races, the more forcefully am I compelled to praise and admire you, to revere and respect you. For on the many occasions when I consider your exceptional marks of distinction, you generally seem to me to surpass in lineage, power, glorious deeds, virtue and learning the other princes of our time. And you seem for a long time now to have equalled your ancestors — not only those most ancient and famous kings, but also Trajan and Hadrian, Theodosius and Arcadius, Honorius and the other Theodosius who were undoubtedly Roman emperors, although born of Spanish parents.

...For even if Fortune, which generally seems to block and resist brave and high-spirited men, was strenuous in her opposition on different occasions to your valorous acquisition by means of land and naval forces of the realm of Apulia⁵ you nevertheless overcame her by long patience and an almost incredible endurance of cold, heat, starvation and sleeplessness, so that with great glory you brought the whole aforesaid kingdom of Apulia under your sway....

Thus fortified with both the freedom to speak and with the truth itself, we do not hesitate at this point in time to reiterate and affirm the things which we remember saying to you in Naples some time ago, while we were serving in the office of ambassador of the Florentine people [at the wedding of Alfonso's son, Ferrante, to Isabella di Chiaromonte]. In bestowing extraordinary and due praise on your marks of distinction as befitted that occasion, we spoke as follows: "For to say nothing of your virtues, you are descended from ancient kings and rule many great kingdoms. You have great and illustrious kings as your brothers and cousins. You have preserved many realms for yourself and thus may grace and embellish your sons with signs of royalty.

"If distinguished offspring will happen to be born from this great and wonderful marriage of your only son you will also establish those grandsons as kings in other hereditary

5. I.e., the kingdom of Naples.

realms, an outcome unexampled, I truly believe, among those famous princes of old. For in reading and paging through Hebrew, Greek and Latin books we could find no king from the creation of the world who had brothers, cousins, sons and grandsons as kings simultaneously. To these extraordinary and uncommon distinctions, seeing that they have already happened or are about to happen, thanks to this blessed and famous offspring you have newly received into your family, you have added two wonderful and almost unbelievable ones, your exceptional knowledge of many disciplines, and your fixed intention to turn against the inhuman and barbarous races — as we hope and believe you will do, given that you have made peace and concord with all Christian princes and peoples."...

This, we hope and believe, will come to pass and come to you if you leave aside other tasks and dedicate yourself entirely to the excellent study of moral philosophy and the glorious defeat of the barbarous races [the Turks]. I beg and pray that you do this with the whole strength of my body and soul, turning as much as I can with pure and devoted heart to our Lord Jesus Christ, that he may deign to grant and bestow His grace upon you for the sure preservation of Christian peoples and the conspicuous increase of the Catholic faith. And I pray earnestly that you will receive this precious grace, made ready for a soul like yours, with humility and devotion, and having received it will desire to venerate, respect and cooperate with it, so that you may attain the aforesaid prizes of morality and eternal life. Farewell in prolonged happiness; and I pray and beg that you will deign sometimes to call to mind and remember Giannozzo, your Majesty's most faithful servant.

LORENZO VALLA

The most famous of all Neapolitan humanists, and among the most influential of all Renaissance authors, was Lorenzo Valla (1407–57). As such he has been the subject of countless studies over the past century on every aspect of his work:[6] translation, philosophical, moral and philological, exegetical and religious, polemical and historical.

Valla was born in Rome in 1407 into a family of lawyers and papal curialists and grew up amid the new humanist culture. He studied under Giovanni Aurispa and Leonardo Bruni, but his outspoken and abrasive manner earned the animosity of curial humanists Antonio Loschi and Poggio Bracciolini, who prevented him from gaining a papal appointment. In 1431, through Panormita's influence, he therefore moved to Pavia to teach rhetoric at the university. But he was forced to flee for his life after publishing a treatise attacking the trecento legist Bartolus of Sassoferrato. Moving to Milan again to teach, he met Bartolomeo Facio, and in 1435 he moved to the Regno in time to accompany Alfonso of Aragon into defeat and imprisonment in Genoa following the Aragonese defeat at Ponza. During this period he probably served as a tutor to Prince Ferrante and for him began a translation of Xenophon's *Cyropaedia* as a "mirror of princes."

Once established at the Aragonese court, in the 1440s Valla began to produce a series of moral and philosophical treaties, including his *Dialectical Disputations,* in which he stressed the literary and rhetorical arts, his dialogue *On Free Will,* and his polemic *The Profession of the Religious*. In all of these he sought to promote a new lay, civic ethics while advancing philological studies. His *Elegantiae linguae latinae* of 1441 used the study of words and their historical development and contexts to correct errors about the past and to reform individual ethics and institutions in the present.[7] His *Collatio Novi Testamenti* of 1442 was a comparative study of the Latin Vulgate and the Greek New Testament that would have an enormous influence on Erasmus and all later exegetical studies.

6. Craig Kallendorf, "Lorenzo Valla," *Oxford Bibliographies Online* (New York: Oxford University Press, 2011), online at: http://oxfordbibliographiesonline. com/view/document/obo-9780195399301/obo-9780195399301-0129.xml.

7. Cochrane, 148.

Valla combined his philological, polemical, and historical interests in one of the most important Renaissance texts, his *Declamation on the Donation of Constantine* of 1440.[8] While there has been some debate over the intent of the work,[9] its Neapolitan context and thrust seems to support Bentley's contention that "it seems to me impossible to doubt the political implications of Valla's treatise."[10] These were intended to bolster Alfonso of Aragon's claims to the throne against Pope Eugenius IV's assertions of papal sovereignty and his backing of Angevin claimant René of Anjou. Bentley concedes that Valla's letters seem to indicate that Alfonso pressured the reluctant humanist to compose the work, and Valla himself acknowledged its controversial nature and the personal danger into which it placed him.[11]

This groundbreaking political application of philological method examined the text of Constantine the Great's supposed grant of the Western Roman Empire to Pope Sylvester I, which was later incorporated into Gratian's *Decretum*, the authoritative collection of canon law. Valla demonstrated thorough a careful philological comparison of historical Latin usage and internal logic that the work was actually composed around the mid-eight century, thus

8. Lorenzo Valla, *The Treatise of Lorenzo Valla on the Donation of Constantine,* Christopher B. Coleman, ed. and trans. (Toronto: University of Toronto Press, 1993); idem, *On the Donation of Constantine,* G.W. Bowerstock, ed. and trans. (Cambridge, MA: Harvard University Press, 2007).

9. Coleman in Valla, *Treatise,* 3–4; Bentley, 113–15. Bowerstock in Valla, *On the Donation,* vii–x, asserts that the work was "more reasonably seen as an extension of his literary and philosophical interests than as a political weapon" and that the work had neither impact nor appeal at the time, an interpretation laid out by Wolfram Setz, *Lorenzo Vallas Schrift gegen die konstantinische Schenkung:* De falso credita et ementita Constantini donatione: *Zur Interpretation und Wirkungsgeschichte* (Tübingen: Niemeyer, 1975). For the opposite, political interpretation see Mario Fois, *Il pensiero cristiano di Lorenzo Valla nel quadro storico-culturale del suo ambiente* (Rome: Libreria Editrice dell'Università Gregoriana, 1969).

10. Bentley, 114.

11. Valla, *On the Donation,* 2–5.1.

undermining papal pretensions to secular power. His defense of the Regno against papal claims to secular sovereignty is clear.[12]

Despite Alfonso's support, Valla's own rash personality and uncompromising search for truth brought him into conflict both with the Inquisition in Naples and with fellow Neapolitan humanists Panormita and Facio. Such controversies led Valla to ask Alfonso to be released from his service. He returned to Rome after the election of his friend Tommaso Parentucelli as Pope Nicholas V. There he devoted the last decade of his life to scholastic, liturgical, and biblical studies.

Our selection is taken from *On the Donation of Constantine*, G.W. Bowerstock, ed. and trans., 3–7.

18. Valla: Preface to On the Donation of Constantine
Many, many books have issued from my pen in almost every area of learning, and in these I have disagreed with some great authors of long established reputation. Inasmuch as there are those who feel ill treated and accuse me of recklessness and impiety, what must we imagine they are going to do now? How much will they rant against me? And if they have the chance, how eagerly and swiftly will they carry me off to punishment? I am one who writes not only against the dead, but against the living as well — not just one or two of them, but many — and not just against private persons but even against those who hold high office! What office-holders they are! The supreme pontiff, of course, who is armed not only with a temporal sword in the manner of kings and princes, but also an ecclesiastical one as well, so that you cannot find protection from him by sheltering, so to speak, under the shield of any prince, to avoid being struck down by excommunication, anathema, or execration....

I am not acting to satisfy a desire to harass anyone and to write Philippics against him — may I not be guilty of such a heinous deed —, but to eradicate error from people's minds, to remove persons from vices and crimes by admonition and reproof. I would not dare say that

12. Valla, *On the Donation*, 52–53.33.

others, instructed by me, should prune with steel the papal seat — the vineyard of Christ — which is teeming with undergrowth, and force it to bear plump grapes instead of emaciated berries. When I do this, will there not be someone who would wish to stop my mouth or his own ears, to say nothing of calling down punishment and death? If so, even if it is the pope himself, what kind of man should I say he is: a good shepherd, or a deaf snake that would not hear the voice of the charmer and would prefer to go at the charmer's limbs with a poisonous bite?

I know that for a long time people have been waiting to hear the accusation I would bring against the Roman pontiffs: a massive accusation assuredly, of either supine ignorance or monstrous avarice, which is enslavement to idols, or pride of rule, which is always accompanied by cruelty. Already for several centuries they either did not realize that Constantine's Donation was a lie and a fabrication, or else they invented it themselves. Their descendants, following the deceitful path of earlier generations, defended as true what they knew to be false — dishonoring the majesty of the pontificate, dishonoring the memory of the pontiffs of the old, dishonoring the Christian religion, and confounding everything with slaughter, collapse, and crime. They say that the city of Rome is his, that the kingdom of Sicily and Naples is his, that the whole of Italy is his....

GIOVANNI PONTANO

Pontano (1426–1503)[13] was born on May 7, 1426 in Cerrato in Umbria, where he received his *grammatica* education. His family was prominent in local politics, but his father was killed during a local uprising, and the Pontano family was left impoverished. Giovanni went on to study at Perugia, and in September 1447, he took the opportunity of Alfonso's campaign in Tuscany to introduce himself to

13. Bentley, 127–37, 176–94, 241–54, 261–65, 297–99, et passim; Pontano, *Dialogues,* Julia Haig Gaisser, ed. (Cambridge, MA: Harvard University Press, 2012), vii–xxvii; Bruno Figliuolo, "Pontano Giovanni," DBI 84 (2015), online at: http://www.treccani.it/enciclopedia/giovanni-pontano_(Dizionario-Biografico).

the Neapolitan king. Alfonso took the young man into his entourage and brought him to Naples in October 1448. There Pontano continued his studies in Greek and astrology under Gregory Tifernas, Lorenzo Buonincontri, Tolomeo Gallina, and George of Trebizond. He so favorably impressed the court with his learning and eloquence that Panormita included him in his diplomatic missions to Florence and Venice in 1451. From 1452 to 1457 he was back in Naples as tutor to Alfonso's nephew, Juan de Navarre.

Pontano's career remained assured even after Alfonso's death and Ferrante's accession. He accompanied the new king during his campaigns against both Angevin claimants and rebel barons, and by the 1460s he was serving in the offices of the royal chamberlain, protonotary, and royal councillor. After a teaching appointment in Perugia (1466–68) he returned to Naples. Ferrante granted him Neapolitan citizenship in 1471 and named him to the royal Sommaria in 1475. Pontano soon succeeded Panormita as tutor to Duke Alfonso of Calabria, and in 1471 he succeeded Panormita as president of the Neapolitan Academy, which stills bears his name.[14] From 1475 to 1482 he served as secretary to Alfonso's wife, Ippolita Sforza, and from May 1482 to Alfonso himself. In that capacity Pontano travelled with the duke to the Abruzzi and Lombardy during the War of Ferrara and acted as the chief inspiration and negotiator for the Peace of Bagnolo in 1484 that reestablished the Italian balance of power. In 1486, in the aftermath of the second barons' revolt, Pontano became royal secretary to Ferrante and chief ambassador.

Pontano's later career coincides with the collapse of the Italian balance of power, the French invasion, the end of the Aragonese dynasty, and the beginning of the Spanish hegemony. Though wealthy enough by the 1490s to own an urban palazzo and country villa and to build the Capella Pontano in the city center, he continued active and loyal service to the Aragonese. On Ferrante's death in 1494 he served as royal secretary to Alfonso II and then to King Ferrandino. He devoted all his diplomatic, oratorical, and military experience to

14. See Shulamit Furstenberg-Levi, *The Accademia Pontaniana: A Model of a Humanist Network* (Leiden: Brill, 2016).

preventing the French conquest but was on hand to present the keys of Naples to French King Charles VIII with the plea that the French spare the city from sack. He retired from active service in 1495, but he maintained his civic loyalty to Naples. His last known letter, dated May 1503,[15] urged the French King Louis XII to come to the starving city's relief as Spanish troops under *Gran Capitán* Gonsalvo de Córdoba advanced against it.

Over the past generation studies by Bentley, Ginzburg,[16] and most recently Roick[17] have produced a positive assessment of Pontano's life and work, aligning him and his intellectual circle fully with both the classical influence and civic humanism of the time and with a new pragmatic history that anticipated both Guicciardini and Machiavelli in their emphasis on human motivation, political realism, prudence, and fortitude. Guido Cappelli[18] has most recently examined the idea of *maiestas* across a variety of Neapolitan humanist works as a reflection of a new "monarchical humanism" and has offered a new appreciation of Pontano's and his colleagues' contributions to modern political thought.

Most of Pontano's works reflect this political humanism, methodically treating the public and private virtues of citizens and rulers.[19] They include *De principe* (1468),[20] *De obedientia* (1470), *De fortitudine* (1481), *De liberalitate* (1493), *De beneficentia* (1493) and, after

15. Bentley, 134.

16. Carlo Ginzburg, "Pontano, Machiavelli and Prudence: Some Further Reflections," in *From Florence to the Mediterranean and Beyond: Essays in Honour of Anthony Mohlo,* Diogo Ramada Curto and Niki Koniordos, ed., 2 vols. (Florence: Olschki, 2009), 1:117–25.

17. Matthias Roick, *Pontano's Virtues: Aristotelian Moral and Political Thought in the Renaissance* (London: Bloomsbury Academic, 2017).

18. *Maiestas.*

19. Bentley, 132–33, 220–22, 249–52; Pontano, *I libri delle virtù sociali.*

20. Translated below, reading 19, pp. 121–38.

his retirement in 1495, *De magnificentia*,[21] *De splendore*,[22] *De conviventia*, *De magnanimitate*, *De prudentia*, *De immanitate*, *De fortuna*, and *De sermone*. Between 1469 and 1501, he also composed five dialogues,[23] ranging across a variety of literary, cultural, and personal subjects, but each set against contemporary political events. He also wrote the *Baiae*, a collection of seventy-two poems on the ancient — and modern — pleasures of these baths on the Bay of Naples that recall Boccaccio's praises of the city and its environs.[24] They were published posthumously by Aldus in 1505.[25]

Much like Machiavelli, Pontano used his *De principe* (1468)[26] to argue that the ruler can overcome *fortuna* through his own virtues, most especially *prudentia*. All other civic virtues revolve around this key to successful rule.[27] To the end of his career and of the Aragonese dynasty, Pontano reflected the Neapolitan humanists' concern with combining civic virtue with service to the new monarchical state.[28] In this he reflected the general trend of humanist historiography since Bruni to acknowledge, come to terms with, and serve the emerging oligarchies of the cinquecento.

What distinguishes Pontano from the majority of his contemporaries and from the majority of those in all ages who have dedicated themselves to the revival and use of a "classical" language, is his remarkable ability to make the conventional personal. The

21. Translated below, chapter 9, reading 164, pp. 406–40.

22. See below, chapter 9, reading 165, pp. 441–43.

23. Pontano, *Dialogues*, xi–xii.

24. See Musto (2013), 224–27, 269–73.

25. See *Baiae*, Rodney G. Dennis, ed. (Cambridge, MA: Harvard University Press, 2006).

26. Guido M. Cappelli, ed. (Rome: Salerno, 2003); Cappelli, *Maiestas*, 91–98.

27. See Victoria Ann Kahn, *Giovanni Pontano's Rhetoric of Prudence* (University Park: Pennsylvania State University Press, 1983); Bentley, 206–8, 246–52.

28. Claudio Finzi, *Re, baroni, popolo: La politica di Giovanni Pontano* (Rimini: Il cerchio, 2004); Cappelli, *Maiestas*, 200–224.

extensive passage from *The Prince* below, the examples of his poetry included in chapter 3 below,[29] and Pontano's *On Magnificence* and *On Splendor* that follow in chapter 9 reflect this ability to work within borrowed conventions of style, form, and language and yet to produce intimate and deeply felt statements.

The Prince: Introduction and English Translation by James H. McGregor

THE PRINCE SHOWS BOTH the conventional and personal aspects of Pontano's work in a variety of ways. To begin with, it abounds in examples drawn from the history of the ancient world; in its very first paragraph it tells a story about Scipio Africanus, who is mentioned frequently throughout the text, as are Cyrus, Cicero, Seneca, Virgil, and Ovid as well as less famous men and women. It quite self-consciously acknowledges its indebtedness to classical sources for such information and makes explicit the connection between its extensive discussion of "majesty" and Cicero's treatment of decorum. But with equal insistence, it draws on contemporary examples, and the names of the Aragonese rulers of Naples and the poets and counsellors of the kingdom of Naples are mentioned with equal frequency and with parallel authority. For the young prince to whom the work is dedicated and for whose instruction it is intended, should, Pontano argues, shape himself to conform to both ancient and local examples; ideally he should be a Cyrus and an Alfonso, too.

While Pontano's prose displays an ease and intimacy in style and language for personal revelation and reflection that are quite enviable, it does not appear to rival the great works of the high Renaissance in Italy that share its themes and concerns. *The Prince* of Pontano certainly demands comparison with *The Prince* of Machiavelli,[30] but in reputation at least, there is no comparison. At first glance, in fact, Pontano's work seems to be exactly the kind of traditional and unself-conscious reiteration of platitudes that Machiavelli is so earnestly writing against. Pontano wants his prince to be just, merciful, and generous; to be loved rather than feared; to keep his word absolutely, and these, of course, are the very things Machiavelli counsels against.

29. Chapter 3, reading 23, pp. 143–46.

30. For recent work on Machiavelli, see above, p. 57 n. 12.

Machiavelli argues that any deficiency in substance can be overcome by the aggressive exercise of power and well engineered public-relations campaigns. But he does not appear to believe anymore than Pontano does that this is the best way for things to be.

The actual field of disagreement between the two men is pragmatic and centers on whether this is the only way things can be in the fallen and depraved world of human affairs. Pontano argues that the prince can and should work to achieve the love of those who serve him, that his security and his wider reputation are both necessarily based on this. Machiavelli argues that while such love is desirable, it is less certainly and easily attainable than fear. As recent research has stressed, rather than listen exclusively to Machiavelli and feature his works unilaterally in our teaching of the Renaissance, it might be good to open the conversation to include Pontano's well argued point of view.

In one sphere, Pontano and Machiavelli are in surprising agreement. Throughout his discussion of majesty, Pontano reveals his sense that this quality, that is innate in the prince, can be greatly enhanced through art. When he discusses those aspects of the prince's conduct and demeanor that magnify and communicate the presence of majesty, that work its magic as it were, he is quite close to Machiavelli's sense that the prince controls people by regulating the impression he allows them to receive of himself. Pontano acknowledges that his treatment of majesty derives from Cicero's treatment of decorum and so reveals that he views majesty as a kind of rhetoric, a tool of persuasion that can be deliberately manipulated. From the point of view of divine kingship, this notion is every bit as scandalous as Machiavelli's.

In speaking of the dress, voice, gesture, glance and attitude of the prince, Pontano is entering the field that is best represented for us by Castiglione's *The Courtier*. Castiglione, too, implies — if he does not acknowledge — that the style of the ideal courtier his book portrays is a kind of rhetoric of the body, that its purpose is persuasion; and that its method is primarily charm, which Castiglione calls grace. We can treat such passages in Pontano, then, as examples of the pervasiveness of rhetoric in social thinking in the Renaissance, but we can also treat them more simply as commentaries on manners. How people should dress and behave, what they should do for fun, how they should entertain and so on. If we expect to find a world of simple pleasures and straightforward values there, we will be disappointed. Pontano presents the world in general, but especially the world of the prince as full of uncertainties; a sphere of life that demands care and deliberation, unfailing self-control and an abundance of good luck. In short, while Pontano paints a rosier picture of the prince's character than Machiavelli does, he does not set him in a world that is any more forgiving.

19. Pontano: The Prince

> To Alfonso, Duke of Calabria:
> Publius Cornelius Scipio, Duke Alfonso, who for his valor was later called Africanus, when he first made himself a candidate for the office of aedile was opposed by the tribunes of the people because he had not yet reached the minimum age prescribed by the law for that office.
>
> "I am old enough," he told them, "if the Romans think I am qualified."
>
> Confident of his own abilities, even though he was underage, he did not hesitate to ask the people for this position. You had just entered adulthood and you had not asked, but your father made you viceroy of the kingdom and entrusted you with the province of Calabria, not with the intention of honoring your age but your abilities; and these are such that both the nobles and the people respect them, and all eyes are turned toward you. Scipio conducted himself so well in office that the Roman citizens had no reason to regret their choice. You must exert yourself to avoid disappointing your father and to exceed the expectations that everyone has for you that you will easily do if you do not fail yourself. And you cannot fail if you follow honest and direct advice; so that those over whom you have been placed in authority as well as all the rest of men will find in you justice, liberality, piety and mercy.
>
> Nothing is as effective in conciliating men as a reputation for justice and piety. Virgil very wisely had the character Flegias in his *Aeneid* praise justice and religion in these words: "Learn justice and respect the gods." When a ruler

is just, people spontaneously place themselves under his authority and submit to his will with a good grace, as we read of Cyrus who was regarded as a model not only of justice but of all the kingly virtues. The value for a ruler of a reputation for piety is amply demonstrated by Alexander the Great, who honored not only religion but even superstition because it enabled him to reach into the minds of his people. Not only have Cyrus, of whom we have spoken, Camillus, Scipio, and other famous men excelled in this quality, but your grandfather Alfonso exceeded all his contemporaries and many kings of the preceding centuries in this as well. We know, in fact, that he observed the rites and customs of the Christian faith so scrupulously that the most Holy Fathers could not surpass him in piety.

Those who wish to rule must first arm themselves with two essential qualities: liberality and mercy. In fact the prince who shows himself to be liberal makes friends of his enemies; collaborators of rivals; and trusted friends of the mistrustful. Indeed even strangers will come to love him, even those who live in far-off lands. As for those in whom mercy is found, all will admire them, venerate them, consider them even as a kind of God. Both of these virtues, in fact, make the prince very similar to God, Whose characteristic it is to do good to all and to pardon the guilty.

But it is also essential to avoid flattery. The prince who listens to flatterers ceases to be master of himself because he judges himself on the basis of the praise of others rather than according to his own standards. It is also imperative that you drive ambition from your court because it is the mother and nurse of many great evils. On this subject I am in agreement with my relative, Tommaso Pontano, a man well respected for his accomplishments and his wisdom, who often asserted his conviction that ambition was the plague of the city and the court. The Roman Emperor Alexander was right when he ordered the execution of a man who was overly eager to cultivate popularity as if it were the greatest good. The man was shackled above a pile of wet wood, which was then set alight, so that he died of suffocation rather than heat. The emperor considered it just that someone who made a habit of buying and selling smoke should be put to death by smoke.

The prince who never forgets he is a man will never let himself be carried away by pride; he will preserve his equilibrium, and especially when he sees things going his way, he will recall that all human affairs are governed by God, to Whom pride is especially abhorrent. Remember what you have promised and to whom. It is not enough to take account of the abilities and achievements of men, but consider their intelligence and their circumstances, too. Many other things are to be considered besides, but you ought especially to remember that nothing is more shameful than not keeping your word; and this principle is so important that even when your word is given to an enemy, in every case it is to be respected. And since faith, as the ancients said, is constancy and truthfulness in words and agreements, the prince should place nothing ahead of truth. This is exemplified by that wise custom of our ancestors according to which the Gospels are to be offered to the prince each day to kiss. For the Gospels contain the divine truth, and in offering them to the prince he is reminded daily to respect the truth and to be zealous in its defense.

Make especially sure that those who approach you find you accessible; nothing in fact is so alien from the prince, nothing earns him greater hatred than harshness and what is called contrariness. A temperate and serious courtesy, however, wins high praise. Your grandfather was particularly successful in this because he never allowed anyone to leave his presence in a state of unhappiness. And he used to repeat the maxim of Titus that no one should ever go away sad after talking with a prince.

Those who find you temperate will never dare to ask you for something improper. "Lucky Cato," Cicero used to say, "no one would dare to ask him for something unlawful." You will be judged worthy of your principate, and you will inspire hope of being a good king, if you prosecute the wicked, hate the intemperate, and drive out the untruthful. Those who try to seduce you to pleasures are to be avoided like the plague, because they can corrupt even noble minds. A man who surrenders himself to vice cannot live an ordered life. His boyhood will be shameless, his adolescence unmanly, and his old age infamous. Nero had many companions in pleasure. How did he end up? In just the same way as all the rest of those who were like him. I don't know anything that is more praiseworthy in Scipio than his courage in battle and his self-control throughout his life. With courage you will overcome your enemy two or perhaps three times in a lifetime, but with self-control you conquer yourself at every moment. And self-control is that much more admirable in that there have been and are many capable of overcoming an enemy, but those who conquer themselves are extremely rare, especially since victory itself often makes men insolent and intemperate.

The man who leads must be completely devoid of passions. Anger keeps you from seeing what is right; hatred pushes you towards iniquity; love clouds judgment; lust leads to violence; sadness urges you to revenge; and envy leads to ruin.

It is a peculiar quality of some men and one especially valuable to the prince to remain master of himself in times of adversity and not to succumb to adverse fortune. Your father Ferdinand [Ferrante I], at the very beginning of his reign, never lost heart or even changed his expression when he heard that many of the people and the nobles and indeed entire provinces had gone over to Jean of Anjou. He didn't even utter an offensive word against the traitors. When, in fact, he heard of the defection of one of the grandees — whose name I won't sully even though he had little enough care for his own reputation — he was agitated to the point of saying that he was sorry that a man of such eminence and such ancestry should demean himself and his family in that way; but he thanked God that he had not given him the slightest excuse for committing such an offense. What does this exemplify if not an unconquerable soul capable of holding its own even in great adversity? When he learned about the disaster at Sarno[31] and that with the exception

31. See chapter 1, reading 4, pp. 63–66.

of a few towns the majority of the state had abandoned the king, and Enneco Guevara and Onorato Fundano had convened the Senate to take desperate measures, Ferdinand spoke to the senators with such effect that he not only won their allegiance but convinced them that he would drive out the enemy in a short time and leave a kingdom to his sons that was more secure than the one his father had left him. In adversity you must continually bear in mind that no one reaches high position without great difficulty and danger. And who, after all, can pretend that he has a father or a mentor or a ruler so amenable and gentle that he never criticizes or corrects? It is a wise saying indeed that God chastises those whom He loves.

It's important to bear in mind that God, the ruler of human affairs, Who is always conscious of our weakness, provides in this manner for the correction of our audacity. As we see every day, good fortune leads many men to ruin, men who would have been better off had they experienced some contrary winds now and again and not always been sailing along at full tilt. On the other hand, we often see that misfortune provides an opportunity for great good. Alfonso [I], of whom I have already spoken, and of whom I will often speak again throughout this discourse, was once overcome in battle and imprisoned by the Genoese. But it was precisely because of his imprisonment that he was able to conquer the kingdom of Naples, as if he could not become victor without first being vanquished. Let me also say here that for whatever reason things brought to birth or obtained with difficulty please us more, and we hold them more dear than those we obtain by chance or retain without effort.

Opportunity is like a mirror of ourselves, and what is often said of political offices is true of opportunities as well, namely that they give the clearest evidence of what we are made of. Consequently it is very important to be temperate when you are in a position to do exactly what you want. The mind must be controlled so that it does not become proud or insolent or forgetful of its true nature. It must be trained always to consider the possibility that one will fall from liberty to servitude; from riches to poverty; from high and illustrious position to a base and obscure role in life. They tell the story of Bellerophon who was suddenly pitched into the abyss while he was riding on the winged horse Pegasus. He, as the ancient verse says, "wandered sad and miserable through strange lands." That is what happens to people whom good luck tempts to excessive pride and intemperance.

Cicero refers to a statement of Plato's that goes, "Happy the man who can in old age attain wisdom and truth." And that is a very wise saying; but in order to attain wisdom in old age, we need to lay the foundations in childhood. When the foundations are firm, as they are in a house that is well constructed, there is no danger of collapse. Even though immaturity and lack of experience keep young people from being wise, youth will build an excellent foundation for attaining wisdom if it delights as much as possible in the company of those who are considered wise. So Cicero says that as soon as he had put on the toga of a man, his own father took him to Mucius Scaevola with instructions that he was never — within the limits of possibility and decency — to leave the side of that venerable gentleman. The first duty of young people, in fact, is to learn to venerate the wise. The second is to willingly hear what they have to teach; the third is to imitate as faithfully as possible not just the words but the actions of their preceptors. With such a beginning, and always following the same road, they will arrive at last at the wisdom they seek.

Your father has chosen talented and well-respected men of every sort to mold you with their advice and precepts; and not because you are lacking in ability, but because young trees need to lean against some prop. You should listen to all of them as if they were philosophers when they speak of serious things. What better teachers could be chosen then men who have accomplished great things. Your grandfather Alfonso, to choose a familiar example, listened with incredible pleasure to the poet Antonio Panormita, when he spoke of deeds described in the old chronicles. Indeed he had the poet read to him every day from the texts of ancient writers; and even though he was often busy with very urgent matters, he never allowed anything to interfere with the time set aside for reading. It is extraordinary indeed how beneficial a habit of assiduous and diligent reading can be for the formation of character. Sallust tells us that Scipio was fond of saying that the paintings of the ancients were remarkably effective in spurring those who saw them to virtuous action. But how much more inspiring would their words and their deeds be if we could have them continually before our eyes? Your grandfather never set off on a campaign without books, and he ordered the tent where they were kept always to be set up next to his own. Since he had no other portraits through which he could contemplate Fabius, Marcellus, Scipio, Alexander, and Caesar, he looked at the books that recorded their deeds. His example in this as in so many other things should inspire you who bear his name. And while it would not be shameful for the grandfather to be surpassed in learning by the grandson, it would be base and shameful indeed for the grandson to fail to live up to the glory of his grandfather.

You must not give your assent to those who condemn reading. If they think reading is not worth learning, I can't imagine what they do consider worthwhile. In fact, by Christ, what could be more important than extensive knowledge both in the field of the natural sciences where the secrets of nature are contained and also within the realm of history that offers us the examples of great men. I presume that these detractors do not think it vain to know what is noble and what is base; what is good or evil; what is worthy of pursuit and what is to be avoided; what is beneficial to those who are ill; what is harmful to those who are healthy. Perhaps, though, they think the only thing a person needs to know is how to arrange a sumptuous banquet. Or it may be that they hold the view that letters are unmanly. If that is the case, they are completely mistaken and have, as they say, missed the point. What is more worthy of a man than to stand out from the crowd? And that learned men excel can be judged from the fact that in great enterprises and grave deliberations they always have the first rank among those whose opinions are considered. Men would not be in general agreement that children should be entrusted to grammarians for their instruction, if they were convinced that letters would be unworthy of them when they became adults. There are of course those who, in order to defend their own ignorance, in which they have perhaps the rashness to take pride, habitually defame letters and learned men, while they themselves wallow in idle uselessness. And even if there are men among the learned who are not entirely without defects, the fault is not to be attributed to learning but to the men themselves, even though it is learning that makes these faults more glaring because of its renown.

But the detractors of learning must admit that even among those who are entirely ignorant of letters, there are many who are stained and corrupted by horrible vices; and even where more egregious failings are lacking such men are inevitably guilty of rudeness and ignorance, and there is nothing less praiseworthy or more unbecoming to a man. When Rome was in a panic and incapable of deciding on a course of action for fear of Catiline and the other conspirators, the first citizens of Rome were passed over and the consulate, by common consent of the Senate and the people, was conferred on M. Tullius Cicero, even though he was a newcomer and a man born outside Rome. That confidence was not based on his ancestry or on the reputation of his hometown of Arpino, but on the outstanding literary merits of the man who brought the eloquence of the rhetorical schools into the forum and the Senate. Marino Tomacello told me that at the death of Pope Nicholas V and the succession of Calixtus [III], there was considerable fear that Giacomo Piccinino would go to war against the papacy. When certain eminent man went to the pope to warn him of this possibility, His Holiness said, "There is no reason to fear Piccinino. The church of Christ has more than three thousand learned men, and with their wisdom and counsel we can easily withstand and overcome the efforts of all the adventurers in Europe."

But there is no need for me to battle at length with these adversaries, nor does learning really need my defense, especially when it comes to you. It was necessary to touch on the issue, but there is no need to spell out its merits, and I won't say any more, especially since in singing the praises of literature it might seem that I was actually boasting of my own studies. I will give one more example, however: After Antonio Caldora had been defeated and imprisoned, your grandfather marched with his army into the ancient territory of the Peligni. When they reached a point from which the city of Sulmona could be seen, your grandfather asked if that was, as he had heard, the birthplace of Ovid. And when those present confirmed this, he saluted the city and gave thanks to the spirits of the place for having once given birth to such a great poet. And having spoken at length on Ovid's merits, and moved in the end by the grandeur of his fame, he said, "I would happily give up this region, which is neither a little nor an unimportant part of the kingdom of Naples, if in my time it were possible to have such a poet, whom I appreciate more, even though he is dead, than the lordship of all the Abruzzi."

But we cannot always be busy; sometimes even books should be put aside so that we can relax our bodies and our minds. At such times it is important that our recreations be appropriate, so that in our desire for relaxation we do not become lazy or unmanly. Our leisure should be free from worry but it should also be free from excessive softness. The wise peasant allows his fields to lie fallow while they are still fertile; but if they lie fallow too long, the same fields become overgrown with weeds and brambles. By the same token, if the mind is allowed to indulge in idleness, then people can justifiably use expressions like, "pillows of Sardanapolis," or "pigs from the herd of Epicurus," or even worse insults than you can imagine to describe us. In these pauses in our work we should look for games and recreations that restore our spirits. What Laberius says about a good companion being as important to a trip as a good vehicle also applies to recreation. And it is good to call on musicians, who delight the mind and diminish cares with their singing and playing; and actors are good to have too. Your grandfather was in the habit of shooting a bow with the young boys during the afternoon; and Augustus played ball. The various forms of hunting are very good for refreshing the mind and the body. When your father was your age, he rode regularly; and the young Cyrus, when he was staying with his grandfather, Astiage, learned how to hunt animals within the park of his estate. Once he became an adolescent, he went to hunt lions and boars in the forest. Virgil was right to praise Picus for his ability to break horses and subdue wild animals.

It is extremely important to act in such a way that you will be loved by those who are responsible for the care of your body and of your possessions. You will live more secure in this way, and once that love has taken deep root among your courtiers, it will spread more widely and propagate itself not only among your citizens and subjects, but even among strangers. When you are loved, people want you to live forever; there is no need for an army; and no one has more defenders than the man who is greatly loved. Tommaso Pontano was fond of repeating that love cannot be bought. But that other saying of his is equally wise, namely, that love goes everywhere unarmed and still sleeps securely. In order to keep the love of your staff and increase it every day, one thing is more valuable than any other, and that is that they should feel that you love them. The ancients put it better; Seneca said, "If you want to be loved, love." Those around you will feel you love them if you truly rejoice with them in their good fortune and commiserate with their sufferings. You will bind their souls to you and you will render them particularly faithful if you practice a generosity that is derived from gratitude. But this generosity must not overstep certain bounds and you must not be equally generous to everyone all the time, so that your servants don't become accustomed to receiving something every day. That way, if necessity sometimes forces you to withhold a reward or leads you to a reasonable moderation, they won't change their feelings or imagine they have received an insult from you that they must avenge. It is very important to be empathetic, a virtue in which you already excel, and that requires that you be loved not only by those who know you well, but by men in general. Cyrus, whom I particularly desire you to imitate, was for a while unable to be generous because he lacked the means to do so; at that time he won the good will of his followers through his sympathetic manner. He helped them in their work and shared their weariness. After he had conquered Assyria, he practiced every form of generosity because he reasoned that his treasure was not composed of goods but of the friends to whom he had given enormous riches. He not only rejoiced in the good fortune of his courtiers, but also in that of his subjects, and he acknowledged that it was the duty of a monarch and also a necessity for a good king to make his people happy as well.

All the same, it is less important to gain a reputation for being empathetic and generous than it is to keep yourself from those vices that are their opposites. Others must never feel that you covet those goods that are of particular importance to them. In fact, the greedy ruler soon becomes rapacious and quick to use force whether legitimately or illegitimately to gain the object of his desire. Banishments come from this and exiles, torture, and bloodshed. And that is borne out by this wise saying of Cicero's, "Kings descend to the netherworld without wounds; but tyrants rarely arrive there without suffering a violent death."

Generally speaking nothing could be more unfitting to a king and less suited to his security than to appear difficult and proud, when in fact rulers should set the standard for gentility. Inhumanity is the mother of hatred; pride of cruelty; and both are miserable guardians of a sovereign's life or kingdom. When I was a baby, Cardinal Angelotti [Fusco], who was always harsh and cruel, had his throat cut [in 1444] by a servant who had been placed in charge of his rooms. What will be the fate of tyrants if this can happen to a person who is considered sacrosanct? Tyrants in fact are always afraid, and their fears torture them night and day. They say that Massinissa, whose kingdom at one time extended through most of North Africa, did not trust his own sons but left his personal security to ferocious dogs whom he himself raised in great numbers. You can easily form a judgment about the security of his life from the single fact that he had more faith in his dogs than in his own children. Alexander of Pherus and Dionysus of Syracuse were just as insecure. When Alexander wanted to be with his wife, whom he loved desperately, he had a tattooed barbarian go ahead of him with a sword in his hand, as Cicero records, while his bodyguard went through the women's closets looking for hidden arms among their clothes. Dionysus had two wives, Aristomache and Dorida, and it is said that he never slept with either one of them without first searching their clothes. And he entered their rooms, which were surrounded by a moat, by crossing a wooden bridge. His daughters cut his hair, but when they became adults he was afraid to let them use a razor any longer so he had them burn his hair off with live coals.

It's a wise old saying, and one that is often borne out by experience, that kings always fear the abilities of others. If kings were as diligent in acknowledging talent as they are all too often in rewarding the undeserving, without doubt things would go much better for kings, and we wouldn't be witness to revolutions and see kingdoms pass from just lords to unknown masters. Since the succession of the great and rich kingdom of Naples rests on you, I exhort and implore you to follow in the footsteps of your father and grandfather, and from childhood on, accustom yourself to cultivating those men who are most renowned and most endowed with talent. Talent is the sort of thing that cannot be hidden for long. Once, a long time ago, Antonio Beccadelli [Panormita], tired out from reading, was resting in the courtyard of his villa not far from Naples on the shore at Resina. Those present were discussing virtue, and Antonio said that the light of virtue was the brightest of all things. A peasant who was passing by spoke up and said, "I don't know what virtue you're talking about; but I do know that for some time I've been trying to catch a glimpse of it without being able to."

"My good man," Antonio replied, laughing, "I'm sure you could speak quite movingly about that donkey you lost through your imprudence and haven't been able to recover, but I'm more curious to know what you think the brightest thing in the world might be?"

And the peasant answered, "the sun."

"And yet," Antonio continued, "blind men cannot see it because their eyes are darkened. Bright and splendid indeed is virtue if even blind men can see it with perfect clarity."

You must show the people that you take the greatest delight in the company of outstanding men. When they see that, they will begin to believe that you are the kind of ruler who rewards talent. And that expectation will increase day by day if it becomes known that you honor those the most who have the greatest reputation for ability. The number of talented men is small, because talent like every other good, is rare. But it works the same way as with other arts. If a prize is offered for poetry or physics, the number of people who will compete for it will be great; similarly many will attempt to develop their talents if they see hope of achieving a reward for them. Nicholas V once asked Lorenzo Valla why he showed such enthusiasm for the study of Greek when he was already old and exceptionally skilled in Latin studies. Valla replied, "So that I can have a double reward from you, Your Holiness."

★

The impressions of your subjects and others will be greatly influenced by what some people not without understanding though with little justification term "majesty."[32] Since I want to avoid arguments about diction, I hope you will forgive me if I follow the majority. Majesty then is proper to princes; it is obtained with skill and diligence and has its roots in nature. First of all, it requires that you know yourself and acknowledge that you have been assigned the role of the prince. If you understand this, you will maintain both gravity and constancy in all your words and actions. And

32. See above, p. 21.

because every one of your thoughts or actions leads either to a public or private decision, you will have to listen to many things as you deliberate and consider even more besides in order to understand the reasons behind what is said. You should not consent too quickly or always disapprove; you should convey much with your look, show yourself to be thoughtful; listen to the opinions of others as if you wanted to thoroughly examine the thoughts of those who are speaking. Don't give your opinion quickly or to more than a few; be brief and cautious in what you say. Respond sparingly and according to the quality of questions; never blame someone unless the case is very serious; give praise with gravity; restrain anger, the enemy of majesty, and never in any case let yourself be carried away beyond certain boundaries. From all this, and from other things that only nature, time, and circumstances can teach you, and about which I can give you no advice, that admiration will grow without which there can be no majesty.

I should also give you some instruction in the area of private obligations, even though I hesitate to do so for fear of speaking out of turn. Generally speaking there are many things that are appropriate in one place and utterly inappropriate somewhere else. Many customs vary according to time, place, and circumstances; and nature alone is the best guide. If we are to consider the private life or rather the reciprocal relationship between you and those who come close to you, here is the rule that you ought to obey in your dealings with others: welcome strangers kindly, listen with attention, treat them with generosity, show yourself to be accessible and kind to all. As soon as they are presented to you, try to find out what their special interests are, who their friends are, and what arts they cultivate; ask about their opinions and their political allegiances; are they sad or happy; easy to talk to or difficult. What responsibilities do they have; and what do they hope to attain; and do they come on public business or for private reasons. It is also important to learn about the habits and activities of different nations. Once you understand them, you will know better how to behave. You will invite your guests to dinner and entertain them well, speak familiarly with them on those occasions and show that you are very interested in what they have to say. Ask them as much as possible about the customs of people, the situation of cities, about everything memorable, in short, that they have seen in their travels. It is also a good idea to ask those present to discuss some issue, either a serious or a playful one, so that your guests can have an opportunity to say something interesting or amusing. When they finally get around to asking for something, you must show your generosity and magnificence, and if your dignity or their request requires it, then you must show yourself to be religious, just, chaste, and merciful too. When you say goodbye to them, speak to them kindly and courteously. Don't be satisfied with what you have given them, promise them many things yourself and offer them through the intermediacy of others.

*

This one precept is the foundation of majesty: live in such a way as to be self-consistent, maintaining faith and constancy in all your words and actions. What you find blameworthy in others, correct in yourself first; keep your mind free from guilty desires so that you can be preeminent not just in power and authority, but in piety, justice, constancy, and moderation. While you hate treachery and fraud, you must not believe everything and everyone; too many things in mortal life are uncertain and we must expect to encounter deception, error, and intrigue. The ways of truth are full of twists and turns and as the brilliant theologian Narcissus says, "Truth lives in the shadows."

*

The way you move, trivial as it may seem, is not without importance. Your walk, for example, should not be indecisive, or too determined and unrhythmic, but somewhere in the middle. No movement of your body should suggest oafishness or impulsiveness. Don't bang your hands together or wiggle your arms. Grimacing is very unbecoming; excessive laughter and snorting like someone in convulsions is exceptionally rude. It's very unsuitable to shake your head all the time. That's the sort of movement that's appropriate for a thirty-year-old horse, not a man.

Nature has made the eyes declarers of what moves through the spirit. Every hint of impudence or immaturity should therefore be eliminated from them. While every part of the body needs to be controlled, the eyes of the prince especially must follow the guidance of decency. Nothing shameful, nothing changeable, nothing cruel, envious, or vain should appear in their movements, their glances, nor in the motion of the eyebrows or the forehead.

Your clothes and a neat and suitable appearance will contribute greatly to establishing and preserving that which I call majesty. You will certainly need to change the way you dress depending on the place, your business, the season, and the weather. Old people and young people shouldn't try to look the same; peace and war demand different styles; as do good times and bad, the law court or the theater. Always dress so that you fit in; don't wear mourning clothes in a court celebrating a triumph or gorgeous multicolored silks at a funeral. And what an outrage it is that we have reached that point of impudence where there is no difference in clothing or any other ornament between a prince and a merchant. We can deplore such license, but we cannot prevent it. Styles change so radically every day that clothes that were considered the height of elegance three months ago are despised today and thrown away like so many rags. And, shameful as it is to admit, no sort of clothing is thought acceptable unless it comes from France, even if it is very often the case that Italians determine the fashion. Not every color and not every kind of cloth or silk and not all clothes and jewelry are suitable to a prince. Some clothes are only for shepherds or sailors; some colors are more suitable to young people than old, some are for servants and others for nobles. In the midst of such variety, you should chose those things that are most appropriate. And when you are in doubt, you should follow this criterion, to reject those things that seem unsuitable to the dignity of a man and the majesty of a prince.

★

I realize that this entire discussion of the cultivation and maintenance of majesty, O Duke Alfonso, which I have been carrying on, was completely overlooked by the Ancients; indeed none of those whom we still possess, as far as I know, has given precepts on this matter. What Cicero says with such precision and such good judgment about decorum applies to private persons and the political offices that private men hold for a specified period of time; it does not apply to kings, even though it may be referred to them....

There are only two things that exalt us and set us apart from the other animals: our immortal souls and our ability to speak. Speech is the index of those things we conceive or feel in our hearts and minds, and therefore it is of the utmost importance that your speech show that you have nothing within you that is shameful or stupid, cowardly or envious, proud, irresponsible, greedy, lustful, or cruel. Your speech should show that you are serious in serious situations, light-hearted and witty at play, cautious in situations of uncertainty, truthful and severe in judgment, strong in adversity and in sorrow, and easy and forthright when things are going well. Words should be suited to their subjects, and your face and body should in a decent and proper manner be in accord with your words. Make sure your words are not pedestrian, outlandish, or overly military. Pedestrian words are ignoble and ridiculous; outlandish words might be heard with a certain pleasure because of their novelty, but they will still be condemned by those who hear them; military terms are harsh and lacking in gentility. Your manner of speaking should be neither emotional nor abrupt; it should be simple, gentle and fluid. It should express what you want to say in brief but appropriate terms. Even if occasion demands that your speech be tempestuous and somewhat aggressive, and if sometimes you must wound or threaten—and none of that can happen without to some degree awakening your wrath and stirring up your emotions — nevertheless, whenever you must reproach someone or stir them to action, keep your anger under control as much as possible because wherever wrath appears there can be no majesty.

I have written this for you in brief, O Duke Alfonso, even though the material and the importance of the argument require much more extensive treatment. I am not unaware of how vast the subject is for one who wishes to teach or describe it properly. But I had no wish to set myself up as an instructor for a king. Read these things not as if they were written to teach you, but written so that you might recognize yourself and what you are to accomplish. I wrote them so that every day you might progress further towards glory....

★ ★ ★

CHAPTER 3: LITERATURE
by James H. Mc Gregor

ANTONIO BECCADELLI (PANORMITA)

Antonio Beccadelli (1394–1471),[1] known as Panormita from the Latin name of his native Palermo, served throughout the reign of Alfonso the Magnanimous and into that of the king's heir Ferrante. His family fled their native Bologna to Sicily, but in 1419 Beccadelli travelled to Florence and in 1420 returned to Bologna to study law at the university. He began his writing career at about that time, and in 1429 was named court poet to the Visconti dukes of Milan and professor of rhetoric at the University of Pavia (1430–33). He returned to Palermo in 1434 and entered the service of Alfonso the Magnanimous as librarian at the royal palace of Ziza. Alfonso soon entrusted Panormita with a variety of important administrative and diplomatic posts, including the presidency of the Sommaria (exchequer). The humanist remained close to the king throughout Alfonso's conquest of the Regno and served as royal ambassador through much of the 1450s. He soon became the dean of Naples' intellectual life, culminating in 1447 with the establishment of the Neapolitan Academy, which then passed on to the leadership of Giovanni Pontano, whose name has since been attached to it.

Panormita's best known work is his *Hermaphrodite*[2] from the 1420s, a collection of sexually explicit Latin poems that made him so notorious throughout Italy that Pope Eugenius IV threatened to excommunicate anyone found with the book. His most important

---

1. See Gianvito Resta, "Beccadelli, Antonio, detto il Panormita," DBI 7 (1970), online at: http://www.treccani.it/enciclopedia/beccadelli-antonio-detto-il-panormita_(Dizionario-Biografico);Alan Ryder "Antonio Beccadelli: A Humanist in Government," in *Cultural Aspects of the Italian Renaissance: Essays in Honour of Paul Oskar Kristeller,* Cecil H. Clough, ed. (Manchester: Manchester University Press 1976), 123–40; Cochrane, 146–48; Bentley, 84–100.

2. *The Hermaphrodite,* Holt Parker, ed. and trans. (Cambridge, MA: Harvard University Press, 2010).

historical work was his *De dictis et factis Alphonsi regis* of c.1456.[3] Panormita followed this in 1462 with two letters to King Ferrante following the *speculum principis* (mirror of princes) form, urging the king to practice both the ancient and Christian virtues of justice, moderation, chastity, gratitude, kindness, humanity, and liberality.[4] In 1469 he began his *Liber rerum gestarum Ferdinandi regis*[5] covering Ferrante's youth, his virtues, his military prowess, and his deeds. But before he could complete it, Panormita died in Naples on January 15, 1471.

The Hermaphrodite, a collection of poems about prostitutes, pimps, and their clients was an early work of Beccadelli, and it brought him immediate notoriety. It gives a sense of the men's club atmosphere that was a strong undercurrent in Latin humanism. It also serves as a foil to the sensuality of Pontano. Beccadelli describes what is today known as "the life" in frank detail. Yet the poetry is generally mechanical, more intent on titillation and the display of cleverness than a delineation of character or situation. The first poem is the form of an epitaph, a favorite genre of the humanists. The second is addressed to the book the poet is writing.

20. Panormita: The Hermaphrodite

Book 2.30
If you pause for a little and read this verse
You'll know the whore who's buried here.
I was stolen from my homeland as a child;
I left it for love; I left if for the money.
Flanders was home; I went everywhere after.
Now I'm settled down here in Siena.
My name — you've heard it — was Nichina. Houses
* were home. I was the fire they had to have.*
I was pretty and nice, perfumed and rich,
No girl in Siena had better hips;

3. *De dictis et factis Alfonsi regis,* M.Vilallonga, ed. (Barcelona: Barcono, 1990).

4. Bentley, 204–5, 224–28, 243–46.

5. *Antonii Panhormitae liber rerum gestarum Fernandi regis,* Gianvito Resta, ed. (Palermo: Centro di studi filologici e linguistici siciliani, 1968).

my skin was whiter than snow; my bed
was covered with a thick white quilt.
When a man kissed me I'd give him tongue
and keep on kissing after he'd come.
And I was great with my hands. I had a basin in my room; I
sponged myself all over and my dog licked me off.
One night a hundred guys took turns.
I was fun; I knew just what to do
but without the money, nothing seemed right.
May music sound around you, Nichina
May the earth lie light on your breast.
Let the Pleiades sing around your tomb,
the sound of Apollo's lyre ease your rest.

Book 2.36
To his book:
Go on, defy my warnings, book-of-mine, go
to Florence. There's a hot-spot in the center
of town. Here's how to find it. Go
to the Duomo or the Baptistery. Better
yet, pass straight by them, look
for the Mercato Vecchio, you're
almost at your goal, my worn out little book;
You'll know it by that special smell. Enter.
Say hello to the players and the girls
for me. The ones who take you on their laps.
Blonde Helen, sweet Mathilda will show their stuff.
You'll see Jeanette and that dog of hers; Claudia comes down
topless; Claudia
knows all the moves. Galla likes you
either way, remember, you've got it all.
Old Anna sings at the drop of a hat some
awful German song. Her breath is awful, too.
Here comes Python, the big squeeze, and
Ursula the cream of the crop. From down
the Street of Slaughtered Calves, Thais
sends word. In short there's not a whore
in town who won't be on you, all over you.
You're there to talk dirty and do whatever
you like. No blushes now. No "no." Just

> do or be done to, whatever you please.
> Remember, little book, you've got it all.

21. *Panormita: Selected Poems 8.*

To Travellers: On the Works of King Alfonso
If you come by sea, the seawall and the port,
*   by land, the eerie light of the grotto and*
*   the dried up marshlands will astonish you;*
Next my walls and the grand citadel,
*   noble houses, fountains and the wide straight streets;*
All regal works. More waits, so rest awhile.

22. *Panormita: Selected Poems 10.*

Against Lorenzo Valla
They say you write while standing on one foot;
No wonder your verses limp.

GIOVANNI PONTANO

In his Latin poetry as in his prose, Pontano speaks with a deeply personal voice.[6] The poetic forms he uses are the familiar ones common to the humanists. Odes, satires and elegies abound; epitaphs are frequent. The vocabulary too is familiar, especially the tendency to describe details of Christian worship in terms of classical deities and practices. Despite the artificiality of these formal and stylistic elements, however, the effect of the poetry is immediate and strikingly intimate. Pontano's focus on the individuals in his own life is largely responsible for this, but it goes beyond simple naming.

The Roman poets were very free with names, and their poetic code required the individualization of characters and scenes. Catullus' Lesbia is an excellent example of one such character, but every poet in the Roman world gives us persons, places, and things that are convincingly real and individual. Roman poetry presents these individuals only through highly stylized or conventionalized relationships with the poet. Despite the intensity of Catullus' feelings for his beloved and the range of emotions she inspires in him, we don't know much about her or much about what they might have done together when they weren't fighting or making love.

6. See above, pp. 115–38.

What Pontano portrays throughout his poetry, but especially in the *De Amore Conjugale* (On Married Love) is the long history of his relationship with one woman, his wife Adriana Sassone, whom he calls Ariadne in his poems. Their meeting, their marriage, their love-making, their separations, the birth of their children, and ultimately Adriana's death are all recorded in these poems. The differences between Pontano's refashioning of the conventions of classical poetry and those of even his most talented contemporaries can be seen if we compare Pontano's evocations of his love for Adriana with Beccadelli's erotic poetry from *The Hermaphrodite*. Similarly, if we compare the poems on the death of Adriana and her son Lucio with other more conventionalized epitaphs, the same contrast is apparent.

23. Pontano: Married Love

Book 1, Poem 7
To his heart:
O god you're going, going without me. Who
    will guide you? Who will show the way? Love?
Imagine he will be your guide and companion.
So Luck goes with you, returns with you, stays with you.
O god, I wish he could take me, too.
Pitiful. How many mountains, what great rivers
    deny me your love, dear Ariadne? What
    does the Arno matter to me, or the Po, or the Rhine?
Violent Mars and his weaponry mean nothing.
Death to sharp swords and bright helmets;
Peace now! Let Mars creep away in defeat.
Crowned with peace, men in love drink too much
    while love pours it on. Somebody sings a love song.
Everybody claps; they dance; they're drunk.
Somebody plays guitar; there's a flute somewhere.
In peacetime it's Ceres and Bacchus. Vintners cut
    clusters of grapes, reapers reap, apple pickers
    pick apples. Women bring food at mealtime, prize
    recipes and wine made in their own cellars.
In the afternoon breeze they attack the grain
    and fill their bins with captive wheat;
    they trample out the vintage and boil the wine

on a great fire; now they cut sweet heather
and ripe apples to be treasured up at home.
Perfect quinces are bound up with a little string.
The holy days return. Dressed to the nines
husband and wife go out to sacrifice
their first fruits, a young goat and fat lamb;
garlands are everywhere; on the way home a bagpipe
leads the villagers to a vast dinner and more wine.
Husband serves wife and wife husband. Three cheers
for the Master. The wine consecrates; the wine
that causes drowsiness awakens Love.
If only, Ariadne, if only the wind would rise
or some god whisk me to your breast. Bacchus
remember her — but keep your distance! Bring me
home to her and I will sing your praise: joy
of the afflicted, rest of the weary, sweetest of all.
If only I were planting vines, marrying them to elms;
or hoeing the soft earth with her beside me (leaving
the hard work to me) and meanwhile stealing kisses
from her lips, while I brush back the bangs on her forehead.
I envy the Arabs who take their wives to battle
behind their men on horseback handling sword and lance.
Never helpless, never alone; sharing whatever happens
in war or peace, come life come death inseparable.
That would make war beautiful. Give me a spear
and watch me ride to battle trumpets squalling.
She is beside me, I defy the enemy, I ride against
a hundred; my shield alone against a squadron.
Even if a thousand came, love would conquer all.
But no. No cold or heat should burn your face
no heavy spear should bruise your lovely hands.
Could victory matter more to me than you? Could I
expose you to the pitiless whims of burning Cancer
or the brutal winter snows? See you endure the wind
and rain? Never.
So the hell with glorious warfare
go back to where you came from, and you, Peace,
blessed Peace return; bring Love and Pleasure
with you and all the blessed works of Love.

Book 2, Poem 8
A Lullaby — To Make sleep come
Please sleep; Lucio is pleading with his eyes.
Please sleep; please sweet little sleep, please;
Lucio's singing sweetly, sleep, sweet little sleep.
Please sleep, please sweet little sleep, please.
Lucio's calling from the bedroom, sweet little sleep,
    tender little sleep, dear little sweet little sleep.
He's calling from the crib over there, little sleep.
Sleep, come to the cradle, sleep, please little sleep.
He's calling for you to put him to sleep, little sleep.
So go on little sleep, please little friend, please.
He's calling you to his pillow, sweet little sleep,
    little sleep, please, please little sleep, go on.
He wants to give you a hug, little sleep;
    slip into his arms little sleep, please little sleep.
You've done it little sleep. A father's wish:
To be restored, to be lifted. Please.

Among the Tombs. Book 2, Poem 25
On the tomb of his wife Adriana Sassone
What funeral gifts, dear wife, what can
I bring? I have no tears, no groans, no words.
For old times' sake and all your gifts of love
I bless your tomb and offer what is due.
Incense and holy water, son!
Father, recite the blessings for the honored dead.
Light the sacred candles. Even dead
    you live for me, my dear, here in my heart
(I see you living right before my eyes —
You're having fun with me, you're teasing me!)
You rule our house and all my worldly goods.
You're alive at home, Ariadne, alive in bed.
Together we walk the orchards and gardens, we pass whole days
    and nights together.
Since you are alive, old age is dear;
    your death is the life of this weary old man.

Book 2, Poem 36
On the tomb of his son Lucio Francesco
I, your father, built this tomb myself

where you could place my ashes when I died.
But fate and the twisting laws of time
have placed you here while I remain above.
Old men bury young men; fathers bury
sons. What sorrows you send me, cruel stars!
But hard as you are, the pain can't last:
the best is over; the rest is death.
I write no will for you but this.
I inherit suffering; this tomb is your legacy.

Book 2, Poem 39
On the tomb of Sancia, a Neapolitan woman
The dead woman speaks to her husband, a painter.
You couldn't bear to live without me, so
you brought me back to life in painting;
without me life meant nothing to you and
death was harder for me, too, darling.
But still, you can't beg a kiss or love,
and you can't paint our talks; a picture
brings back the body, not the body's touch;
and it's the poet's voice you hear, not mine.

Book 2, Poem 43
On an unnamed infant
Born, dead, and buried all at once;
from which realm could his name be taken?

Book 2, Poem 54
Focilla
A spark buried in a frozen bed;
no hand to set tinder to my flame.

THE RENAISSANCE IN THE VERNACULAR

Introduction

The official patronage of letters in the Neapolitan Renaissance had
two different faces. In the reign of King Alfonso, Latin literature was
officially encouraged. Under the sponsorship of Ferrante, the official
policy of the court broadened to embrace both Latin and vernacular
literature. The change of language was far more important than it
might appear, however, since with the inclusion of the vernacular
both the kinds of literature produced and the audience for literature

were transformed. The staples of humanist Latin literature, as this anthology has already displayed, included the treatise, several forms of verse such as the ode, satire, love elegy, and epitaph. The range of forms in the vernacular is quite different. Treatise writing is still important in the vernacular, but the dominant prose form is the *novella,* a work of short fiction that blends the conventions of the anecdote, the short story, and the extended example. Prose fiction was important in antiquity, but it was not particularly favored by the humanists, and so most Renaissance fiction was written in the vernacular languages. Boccaccio's *Decameron* was among the first and the most significant for shaping the limits of the genre.

Several examples of the *novella* as it was written and enjoyed in southern Italy are included here. In addition to the popular prose writing of the *novella,* there is an example of what we might call "art prose" in the *Arcadia* of Jacopo Sannazaro. Even when treatises are produced in the vernacular they can, as the example of Loise de Rosa demonstrates,[7] completely reject the norms of classical treatise writing.

The Roman elegiac poets, Horace, Catullus, Ovid, and Propertius primarily, govern the writing of Latin poetry in the Renaissance. The vernacular poetic tradition in the Neapolitan Renaissance as in the rest of Italy in the period is most closely tied to Petrarch and to the tradition of forms and themes he pioneered. Even the poetry of the sixteenth century, which is clearly moving beyond Petrarch in thematic terms, is still tied very strongly to such forms as the sonnet and sestina, which are medieval European inventions and not classical ones at all. In essence, then, as we move from the first half of the fifteenth century into the second half and beyond, the shift in language brings with it a shift in forms, styles, and models. A world dominated by the prose of Cicero and the poetry of the Roman elegists is enlarged and becomes one in which the "classics" include Italian examples. Boccaccio and Petrarch,[8] two of the three

---

7. See chapter 1, reading 5, pp. 68–76.

8. For Petrarch and Boccaccio in Naples, see Musto (2013), 224–30, 261–73, 286–87, 291–98; Musto, *Writing Southern Italy,* passim.

great founders of Italian literature, hold sway in Naples as they do elsewhere in the Italian peninsula.

The Neapolitan contribution in both the *novella* tradition and vernacular poetry is a major one. It is also the case that while Tuscany claims the so-called *Tre Corone* or Three Crowns of Italian Literature exclusively for itself, both Petrarch and Boccaccio, but especially the latter, had close and important ties to Naples. Petrarch had many Neapolitan friends and correspondents and when he decided to seek the poet's crown of laurel it was Robert of Anjou, king of Naples,[9] to whom he went for certification of his poetic abilities. Boccaccio spent most of his adolescence and young adulthood in Naples. He wrote all of his books before the *Decameron* there and many of them reflect Neapolitan themes, locales and ideas. Several of the most important *Decameron* stories are focused on Naples and its people.[10] In imitating Petrarch and Boccaccio, then, Neapolitan writers are as much reclaiming their own heritage as they are imitating Tuscan ideals.

The Novella

In the modern literary vocabulary, the *novella* is a short novel, like Charles Dickens' *Christmas Carol* or Henry James' *Turn of the Screw*. In the Middle Ages and Renaissance, *novella* is a name for a piece of fiction about the length of the modern short story. It takes its name, *novella* meaning "new" and implying "news" or "novelty," "the latest," from the fact that its subjects were usually ephemeral incidents involving people in the immediate social world of author and audience or others known by reputation. Such short fictions made their first written appearance on the Italian literary scene early in the fourteenth century. A collection of stories called *Il Novellino* offered a loose assembly of news stories, gossip, anecdotal jokes, and exemplary tales.

In the mid-trecento Boccaccio took the rough materials of the genre and added a frame story about a group of wealthy men and women who escape Florence during the Black Death of 1348 and

9. See Musto (2013), 192–256, readings 50–66.

10. See Musto (2013), reading 62, pp. 224–27; reading 73, pp. 269–73; reading 78, pp. 286–87.

take refuge in country houses where they entertain themselves with ten days of story-telling. These ten days justify the title *Decameron,* which Boccaccio applied to his framed collection of *novelle.* For the rest of the century almost no one dared to step into a field so completely dominated by a single masterpiece, but soon after the beginning of the fifteenth century writers all over Italy began to produce collections of *novelle* and to provide them with framing stories in imitation of Boccaccio.

Among these imitators were many whose story collections reflected the experiences of the newly emerging class of merchants and the equally new experiences of urban life. So pervasive is this focus and so influential is the *novella* in the Renaissance invention or discovery of the novel, which is itself often considered a bourgeois form of expression, that the *novella* is often depicted as a type of literature that aims to depict and defend the circumstances of mercantile and civic life. The culture of merchants and the culture of cities was long considered more characteristic in the Renaissance of northern than of southern Italy. According to this view — increasingly contested in recent scholarship — if we regard the *novella* as necessarily reflecting bourgeois values, then we have to see Neapolitan versions of the *novella* as somehow out of tune with this subject matter, because the Neapolitan *novella* typically was not supposed to depict the activities or values of a class that was presumably under-represented in the South.[11] If, on the other hand, we consider the *novella* to be a popular form of fictionalizing that takes its subject matter from whatever happens to be the experience and the imaginative world of its creators, then we need make no distinction between the *novella* tradition in the merchant-dominated cities of Tuscany and the north or those of the kingdom of Naples. Just as Boccaccio could move freely between the cultural centers of Florence and Naples without loss of audience or impact, so too could later writers of the South.

MASUCCIO SALERNITANO

Born Tommaso Guardati (c.1410–c.1475), Masuccio Salernitano is the most important of the Neapolitan *novellieri* or novella-writers of

11. See above, pp. 16–24; and Musto, "Introduction," in Hall-Willette, 8–11.

the Renaissance.[12] He was born in Salerno and served as secretary to Roberto Sanseverino, count of Marsico and grand admiral of the Regno, made prince of Salerno by King Ferrante I in 1463. He dedicated his work to Ippolita Maria d'Aragona (Sforza), the duchess of Calabria and wife of Alfonso, duke of Calabria. Little else is known about his life.

Masuccio is usually ranked, along with Giovanni Pontano and Jacopo Sannazaro, as one of the leading literary figures in Naples during that period. Masuccio's *Novellino,* which circulated in manuscript before its publication in 1476, is strongly influenced by the *Decameron;* it is divided into five ten-story subdivisions, and its stories are grouped around particular themes. The theme of the last day — magnaminity — is identical to Boccaccio's own. Despite these structural parallels and the fact that it is often possible to point to a particular *Decameron* story that lies in the background of his tales, Masuccio does not introduce a frame tale to give coherence to his collection. Each story is dedicated to a particular person, and the appropriateness of the story to its dedicatee is explained in a brief prologue that is more or less in the form of a letter. Then the *novella* is narrated; and in a final section, which is always headed with the name "Masuccio" the author offers his own commentary on his story. The practice is similar to that adopted by Matteo Bandello[13] in the following century. It gives scope for setting the story into some particular historical or ideal context; and it allows the author to comment on his story and to link it with others in the collection. In this way it captures something of what Boccaccio's frame also manages to suggest, namely that the stories are in commerce with life and with each other; that they are not supposed to sit quietly on the

12. See Valerie Martone and Robert L. Martone, ed. and trans., *Renaissance Comic Tales of Love, Treachery and Revenge* (New York: Italica Press, 1994), xxv–xxvii; Michael Papio, *Keen and Violent Remedies: Social Satire and the Grotesque in Masuccio Salernitano's* Novellino (New York: Peter Lang, 2000); Fabio De Propris, "Guardati, Tommaso," DBI 60 (2003), online at: http://www.treccani.it/enciclopedia/tommaso-guardati_(Dizionario-Biografico).

13. See Martone and Martone, xxiii–xxv, 77–127.

page, but that reading them is in some sense an act requiring response, commentary, discussion, and argument within a textual community.

The two stories I have translated from Masuccio are consecutive ones. They are somewhat atypical in that neither demonstrates Masuccio's frequent misogyny or his virulent and politically motivated anticlericalism. The first story is somewhat similar to Boccaccio's story of Andreuccio of Perugia[14] (*Decameron* 2.5) about an out-of-town boy who comes to Naples to buy horses. He is first overwhelmed by the town and its inhabitants, but eventually his ingenuity reasserts itself and he manages to come out ahead in the end. In Masuccio's story, the focus is on a young workman from the small town of Cava dei Tirreni not far from Naples, and the victory over obstacles is on a much smaller scale than in Boccaccio's story.

The letter of dedication describes the transformation of Cava dei Tirreni from a village of industrious weavers and masons, like the hero of the story, to a town filled with doctors, lawyers, and political figures. In that letter Masuccio wonders whether Cava has really gained anything by transforming itself in this fashion; and the story implies that the men of Cava were better off in the old days when they had trades that were in demand and when they weren't too self-important to take advantage of whatever luck brought them. While a northern writer might have presented the upward mobility and gentrification of Cava as a good thing, Masuccio regards the change from a conservative point of view.

The second story is typical of the *novella* tradition in that it focuses on a trick played by a skillful and manipulative character. It might even remind us of one of Boccaccio's stories like that of Frate Cipolla[15] about a skillful trickster who is himself the victim of a trick. Masuccio's story differs from Boccaccio's however in two very significant ways. The trickster isn't defeated intellectually but physically, and the text applauds this act. Moreover, Masuccio's heroes are nobles, and the beating the trickster receives implicitly

14. *Decameron* 2.5. See Musto (2013), 269–73, reading 73.

15. *Decameron* 6:10.

reestablishes the authority of the nobility in a way that is alien to Boccaccio.

24. Masuccio Salernitano: Novella 19

Prologue To the Virtuous and Magnificent Bernardo de Rogieri

As I tell my stories I want to commemorate my splendid friends and inscribe their names in my book for perpetual memory. Before I go on any further, therefore, I am required by the debt I owe to the memory of our perfect and singular friendship to dedicate to you this little story composed of frivolous materials. It will not only give you pleasure but also some understanding of the history of our fellow citizens from Cava dei Tirreni so that you, at present their most prudent commandant and director, can judge correctly whether her citizens were right to swerve from the path of their ancestors.

The Story

Cava dei Tirreni, a most faithful and ancient city and one that has recently attained nobility at least in part, as I've already noted, was always well supplied with exceptional builders and weavers, who were so talented in their arts or indeed "mysteries" that both in terms of goods and money they were always very well off. So much so in fact that throughout the kingdom of Naples whenever people talked about wealth they always had to mention Cava. And if the descendants of these men had followed in their father's footsteps and in the shadow of their grandfathers, they wouldn't have been reduced to that extreme of poverty in which we find them in the present day. But they scorned riches that had been acquired by demeaning labor and regarded them as base and worldly things; they chose instead to pursue the universal and unchanging excellences of virtue and nobility, and to a man they devoted themselves to careers in medicine, law, or warfare. The upshot is that now there isn't a house there in town where you won't find staffs of office, gold-plated armor or spurs, where you used to find looms or masons' tools. Which of these two patterns they ought to have followed, I leave not only to your discretion, Bernardo, but I appeal to the judgment of those from Cava who, since they have nothing better to do with their time, are in a position to offer a detailed assessment of their own situation.

Anyway, to get on with my story, let me say that in the time when the famous master builder Onofrio de Iordano had undertaken the construction of that remarkable structure, the Castel Nuovo,[16] the best part of the masters and journeymen from Cava came to Naples to work on it. And among them there were two young fellows from Priato, who were glad to have the work but who also wanted a chance to see Naples since they'd never been there. So one Sunday morning they set out as part of a large group of men from Cava. Pretty soon the two of them, who weren't used to walking far, had fallen a good way behind the rest of the group. And since they didn't know the road at all, they wasted so much time in their efforts to find the path the others had taken that it was quite late before they got even as far as Torre del Greco.

One of the two was a good deal more tired than the other, and he decided to stop right there, but the second one, who had a little more energy, thought that he might still be able to catch up with the group, and so he kept on going. But as much as he hurried, he was still on the road between Torre del Greco and Naples when night fell. By this time the poor fellow was running and really regretting the fact that he'd left his friend behind. Pretty soon he reached the Ponte Ricciardi,[17] without of course knowing where he was, and seeing the walls and the doorway, he took it for an inn. Completely worn out by this point and anxious to get in out of a light rain which had just begun to fall, he went up to the door and banged on it with a rock. When

16. He began supervising work on the castle between 1450 and 1451. See Maria Grazia Ercolino, "Giordano, Onofrio," DBI 55 (2001). Online at: http:// www.treccani.it/enciclopedia/onofrio-giordano_(Dizionario-Biografico).

17. This is the Ponte Maddalena — also known as the Ponte Guizzardo, Ricciardo, or Licciardo — at Naples' southeast corner, over the Sebeto River, on the shore adjacent to Sta. Maria del Carmine, and the site of Naples' gallows.

nobody answered, he made a virtue of necessity and settled down to wait until morning for his friend to catch up with him. He stretched out on the ground with his head against the door and finally fell into a light and fitful sleep.

Just by chance a poor tailor had set out from Amalfi on that very same day with a sackful of jackets over his shoulder which he planned to sell the following morning at the market in Naples, and he had also been overcome with fatigue at nightfall in Torre del Greco. So he stopped there with the idea that he'd get up first thing in the morning and still be able to get to Naples in time to sell his pathetic merchandise. And just a little past midnight he happened to wake up. The moon was shining so bright that this poor fellow thought it must almost be daybreak, and he got up and started walking again. When he got as far as Orti, he heard the friars there ring the bell for matins and then he realized that he still had the best part of the night ahead of him. And that's when he remembered the criminals who were executed at the Ponte Ricciardi and left to hang there and rot. And being from Amalfi, where folks are apt to be a little timid and faint-hearted anyway, and being a tailor besides, which is not a very valiant profession, he started to tremble with fear. He walked slower because he didn't dare go past the bridge, but at the same time he was afraid to turn back. He was so upset and terrified that he expected any minute that one of the hanged men would jump right out at him. Well, he finally made it to the awful place itself, there he was right at the gallows. And not a corpse stirred! He began to feel a little better. He felt like most of the danger was behind him, but just to give himself a little boost he yelled out, "Hey, hanged man, want to go to Naples?"

The guy from Cava, who hadn't been sleeping all that comfortably or soundly, had already heard the footsteps approaching and figured it was his friend. Then when he heard the invitation to go to Naples, he was sure of it, so he sang out, "Here I come!"

When the fellow from Amalfi heard that, he was certain that it was that hanged man coming to get him, and he was so scared that he just about dropped dead himself. But in a minute he kind of came to his senses, and when he saw the hanged man coming towards him, he decided it was no time to hang around, so he threw down his sack and took off towards the Maddalena yelling, "Help me, Jesus!"

When the fellow from Cava heard him calling for help and running hard, he still thought it was his friend but now he figured that he must have been jumped by somebody, so he took off after him yelling, "Don't you worry, I'm coming for you, wait for me!"

The tailor didn't find these words quite as comforting as they were intended to be, and he really took off. The guy from Cava kept coming after him, but then he tripped over the sack the tailor had dropped. He picked it up thinking it was full of more valuable stuff than it actually contained. He knew of course that his friend wasn't carrying anything, so he realized that this fellow couldn't be him and he didn't chase after him anymore. With his brand new sack over his shoulder, he walked back to where he'd already spent the bulk of the night determined to wait until daybreak for his friend or for somebody else who could direct him to Naples.

Meanwhile the tailor, shrieking and howling like one of the damned, made it to the guard-post of the bridge. The customs police stopped him and demanded to know what all the screaming was about. He told them that with his very own eyes he'd seen one of the hanged men get down from the gallows and come after him, and that the dead man had chased him all the way to the water's edge. The police found this completely believable, and no less terrified than the tailor, they ran into the guardhouse and barred the door. No one dared set foot outside until it was daybreak.

The friend from Cava, who had spent the night in Torre del Greco where he'd been joined by another man from up there, arrived just at daybreak at the Ponte Ricciardi. When he heard them talking, the fellow who'd spent the night there got up and joined them. Then he told them all about the strange things that had gone on there in the dark. The third fellow, who was familiar with the area, pretty soon pieced together what must have happened and to avoid having to give back the sack, he suggested they go back to Cava by way of Somma. That's what they did, and when they'd divided up their booty back home, they turned around again and came right back to Naples.

The tailor's story was all over the countryside within a couple of days, and everybody added his own little embellishments to it. But the central fact remained clear, and so everybody now understood that the hanged men on the Ponte Ricciardi would chase after you if you dared to cross alone at night. Consequently there wasn't a single peasant who had to go through there before daybreak who didn't make the sign of the cross over himself and his animals and recite a hundred other incantations as he made his way through that perilous locale.

Masuccio

Diverse and strange are the fears that the dead inspire in the living, and we see fresh evidence of that everyday. Now and again it happens that someone going along at night tormented by his fear sees something that isn't there and then makes up the most extraordinary and marvelous fables about it you've ever heard, as the preceding *novella* has demonstrated. Which reminds me that I wanted to write about another kind of fear, quite different from the previous one in that the victim in this one, spurred on by the burning flames of love, went voluntarily to seek out his fear, and many notable benefits came out of it, as the following will demonstrate.

25. *Masuccio Salernitano: Novella 20*

Prologue To the Illustrious Gianfrancesco Caracciolo

Knowing as I do the depth of your intellect, most virtuous Gianfrancesco, I am sure that you understand how difficult it is to grasp the full dimensions of Love's powers: how he makes the foolish wise and the wise and prudent man turn fool again; or makes the brave man timid and the fearful valiant; and how he sometimes acts as Fortune's agent to

drive rich men into abject poverty or bring poor men to
financial security. But since you have been a follower of
his since your tender years, it seems absurd for to me to
give you further information about Love's dominion and
about the multitude of wise and prudent men and women
who have been driven by his burning flames to a raw and
brutal death at their own hands. In the present story I want
instead to illustrate a hitherto unknown power of Love,
put to effect in the life of one of our noble citizens, a
man neither particularly wise nor brave who became both
intelligent and courageous once Love got hold of him.
Love was the reason he became rich, and Love won him
fame for his strength and skill at arms; so that after many
afflictions he came to enjoy great happiness.

May you also be well and happy!

The Story
It wasn't many years ago that there was a young man in
Salerno of noble and ancient family, called Iacomo Pinto,
who came from the part of town called Portanova, which
we commonly think of as the academy of wisdom in our
city; it would, however, have been more appropriate in
his case had he come from the area we call Monte, since
that's were most of our other ancient ruins are to be found.
This fellow, who was devoid of possessions and more than
a little short on common sense, did have something of a
noble soul, and he fell in love with a young and attractive
widow, the sister-in-law of our commandant; and never
having been in love before, he carried on his courtship so
carefully and discreetly that there wasn't a kid in Salerno
who didn't know all about it. And in every corner of
town, noblemen and noblewomen talked about it with
extraordinary pleasure and everybody made fun of him.
Wounded in a way he'd never known before, not caring
a bit about what people said, he pursued his love with
enormous energy and a complete lack of skill or success.

There was another nobleman from his part of town named
Loisi Pagano who found some new cause for delight almost
every day in Iacomo's imbecility. Loisi was a very intelligent,

well-mannered, likable man, and the only person in whom
Iacomo confided his burning passion. Every day Loisi had
fresh evidence that his friend's brains were scrambled in
his head; and it occurred to him that with a little luck he
could have some fun with this love affair and maybe even
do a little more. There was another man from Salerno,
a regular Svengali, who'd been pulling the wool over
people's eyes his entire life and always getting away with it.
Sometimes he pretended to be a doctor and other times a
rich merchant, even though he was just a blacksmith. And
he always introduced himself as Sir Angelo. He travelled
all over Italy, and he usually came back home filled to the
brim with cash. Loisi thought there ought to be a way to
use Iacomo's situation as a foil to go after Sir Angelo.

So one day while they were having their usual conversation
Loisi said to Iacomo, "It seems to me, my friend, that you
have little real desire to solve your problem, given that you
have a simple expedient ready to hand. You know that Sir
Angelo is the greatest magician now living on this earth, as
I can testify myself, since I've used him in several operations
and always come out a winner. And, of course, he's your
cousin on your mother's side. Why don't you go to him
and talk his magic up a little and then try to get him to use
his skills on your behalf? Because it's for sure, if he's willing
to help, you'll be entirely satisfied. But I want to warn you,
if he shows any inclination to add you to the list of those
he's suckered in the past, make sure you give him the back
of your hand with enough oomph to it so that he'll never
be able to think about conning another nobleman without
remembering you."

Iacomo was very happy to hear this and he just kept on
thanking his friend over and over. It was as if his wishes
had already come true, and he promised to do just what
his best and dearest friend had suggested. Loisi could hardly
get rid of him, and when he finally did he went out to
look for Sir Angelo and tell him what he'd set in motion.
He was counting on several days worth of entertainment
out of this situation. Sir Angelo was extremely grateful for

the catch that had dropped right into his lap and entirely without suspicion that Loisi was as interested in seeing him beaten up as he was in seeing his other friend Iacomo made a fool of. Before the two friends parted, they worked out the details of the plot between them. And not too long after that Iacomo sent for Sir Angelo, and almost in tears revealed to him his innermost and universally shared secret.

"Cousin," Iacomo began, "in times of need, friends should help each other. I have recently learned that you're a magician, and that through your wisdom you could help get me out of a bad situation. For God's sake, please, help me. I want to be able to say one day that you restored not just my lady to me but that my very life has been a gift from your hands."

Sir Angelo plopped a very obliging expression on his face and answered that as far as he was concerned, he was totally ready to serve, and moving on from point to point in the discussion he finally said, "Iacomo, I don't know how brave you are, but I want to warn you that this is going to take considerable courage on your part."

"How bad can it be?" Iacomo answered, "I mean you have to realize that Love has given me so much courage that I'm ready and willing to go all the way to hell to get what I want."

"Actually it's worse than that," Sir Angelo replied, "because what you'll have to do is speak face-to-face with a gruesome fiend called Barabas whom I have in my power to do my bidding."

"I'd speak to Old Satan himself," said Iacomo, "if that's what it takes."

"God's will be done!" replied the magician, "but how are we going to get the other things we'll need? For starters, we need a sword that's killed a man."

" I have one that belonged to my brother," Iacomo said, "he killed more than a dozen men with it."

"Well," said Sir Angelo, "we've got the one thing I thought would be the hardest; the other things will be a snap.

All the same, get some money together so that when I ask you, you'll have a fat black calf and four fat capons available. Then we wait for the new moon. And just leave everything else to me, and believe me, I'll put that mouse between your paws, whether you want to marry her or just have fun with her."

Iacomo was thrilled with the arrangements, and he said that he'd get everything taken care of before the new moon. After he'd left Iacomo, Sir Angelo went to find Loisi and tell him everything that he and Iacomo had agreed on. And before the conspirators separated, they went over everything in detail pretty much the way it turned out later to everyone's delight. And after several days had passed, in which Iacomo continually begged Sir Angelo to get on with the plan, finally one day the magician replied, "Cousin, everything's ready on my end, what about you, were you able to get your hands on everything that I asked you for?"

"Of course," Iacomo said, "I've been remarkably lucky, in fact, my sister-in-law has the nicest capons in the world, and I got hold of four of the best of them; and not only that, but I happened onto a black calf in the weirdest way, big as a bull and jet black. And it's got four horns! It's a real monster."

"Cousin," said Sir Angelo with considerable enthusiasm, "you seem an entirely different person than you were just a few days ago. Love has sharpened your wits to the point where the next thing you know you'll be teaching the Medici how to add. What other man would have been able to come up with all this stuff in such a short time?"

And then he told him to get everything together because that night he would come for him. And then he went to Loisi and they agreed on the time to meet at the spot they'd chosen. And when it was night, Sir Angelo went back to Iacomo's house.

"Ready to go?" he asked, "'cause it's time."

"Yes, indeed," Iacomo replied.

And then Sir Angelo picked up the man-killing sword and arranged the calf on his shoulders and stuck a pair of capons under each arm and they set out. They stopped among a group of abandoned houses were Loisi was already hiding with some other noblemen he'd brought along so that he'd have somebody to share the fun with. Sir Angelo turned to Iacomo and said, "Listen, cousin, we're at a point now where we can't turn back without serious risk to ourselves, so you need to hang tough. Whatever you do — I can't emphasize this enough —no matter what you see or hear, don't under any circumstances mention God or the Virgin Mary; don't cross yourself either, because if you do we'll both be sucked right into Satan's gullet. If you get scared, and people do in these situations, believe me, commend yourself to the ass that pulled the cart into Egypt. The Holy Mother and Son where in that cart, of course, but Satan doesn't need to know that."

Iacomo promised that he'd do that for sure.

"Show time," said the magician. "You'll say what you hear me say; and when we've conjured up Barabas and he says, 'throw me the tailbones,' we'll toss the chickens and we'll do the same thing with the calf when he asks for the horny-head."

Iacomo said that he'd be very happy to do that. And once Sir Angelo had repeated everything and made sure he understood, he pulled out the sword and made a big circle with it in the dirt, and drew various symbols in it; and with some embers he'd brought with him and some envelopes of stinky stuff, he produced a horrible-smelling smoke, and after he'd intoned some mumbo-jumbo that he accompanied with horrible grimaces and strange jerks of his arms and legs, he turned to Iacomo and said, "Put your left foot in the circle and tell me what you'd prefer: to see him up close in all his infernal horror or to hear him speak to you from one of those broken-down houses over there?"

The poor fellow, whom love and his own innocence had supplied with the considerable courage it had taken to reach this point, realized that the beginning of the game was already bothering him a lot so he decided that just hearing Barabas speak would be fine. Shaking all over he put his foot into the circle, and completely forgetting about that ass from Jerusalem, there wasn't a saint in heaven that he didn't call on for help. The magician could see that Iacomo really believed he'd been transported to the other world, "Call Barabas, three times," he said.

Fearing the worst, Iacomo called the first time. Loisi, who had transformed himself into a devil, set off some gunpowder with a tremendous blast that would have scared the hell out of anyone. Whether Iacomo at that point wished he'd stayed home, don't even ask. But when the magician told him to, he called Barabas the second time. The devil set off another charge even louder and more terrifying than the first one. Seeing that his pigeon was half dead with fear, the magician encouraged him, "Don't fear, cousin, we have him tied up completely with our spell; he can't hurt us at all. So go ahead and call him one more time."

Against his own better judgment, Iacomo followed orders, but he called out so quietly and fearfully that you could barely hear him. Loisi set off the third charge anyway and let out a scream that was so ghastly and blood-curdling that it just about dropped Iacomo right on the spot.

"Don't worry," said the magician, "and don't be afraid. He's our prisoner. Now you need to know what to say to make him do what you want, so just repeat out loud what I tell you to say."

He had his spell all ready, and he tried to get Iacomo to say it, but it was no use. As soon as Iacomo opened his mouth his teeth started to chatter and his legs began to shake so hard he could barely stand up. Angelo was beginning to think something might really happen to him, so he decided that things had gone far enough for the time being, and he began to recite the incantation himself. Loisi and his buddies were pretty well incapacitated with laughter. But when he noticed that the plan had changed, he wanted to make sure that he didn't come out on the losing end of the deal so he screamed out all at once, "Give me the tailbones and the horny-head."

"Throw everything to him," the magician said, "then run like hell. And don't turn around or you'll drop dead on the spot."

Iacomo, who really felt like he was in hell, was all for this plan. He threw the capons and the calf towards the deserted house and ran. He ran so fast that the champion runners in the Palio couldn't have come close to catching him. And he didn't stop till he was safe at home. A while later the magician came along, "Well, cousin," he said, "what do you think about my magic, now? And don't worry about what happened today; the next time we'll get what we came for."

"Not on your life," Iacomo said, "I wouldn't go back there to be made emperor. So please figure out some other way to work it, cousin, and I'll be in your debt forever."

"As God is my witness," said the magician, "I'll put my mind to it, and believe me one way or the other you'll get what you want."

And after reassuring him some more, he went on his way. Meanwhile Loisi had gathered up the offerings and said goodbye to his friends. He went on home to bed and when it was morning, he made arrangements for a feast to be prepared using the calf and the capons and plenty of other good things besides, and he invited Iacomo along with all the people who were in on the trick to come. Once everybody got there and started eating, it seemed like nobody could keep themselves from laughing. Then various people started yelling out "Barabas," and saying the kind of thing that made it clear to Iacomo that everybody there was making fun of him. When Loisi saw that, he figured it was time for the second part of his plan to be put into action, the part where the trickster paid for all his past crimes at the hands of his latest victim. And when dinner was over, Loisi called Iacomo over and in front of a fair number of their friends, he told him everything that Sir Angelo had done to trick him. Iacomo remembered what Loisi had told him right at the start, and so he knew that every word was true. In a black rage, Iacomo lit out in search of the so-called magician. And when he found him, without saying a single word he grabbed him by the hair and threw him to the ground and started to punch him and kick him so steadily and so hard that it's a wonder he didn't kill him. The more he kicked and hit the madder he got; finally he picked up a rock and if the crowd hadn't pried it out of his hands, which they did with enormous difficulty laughing all the time, it would have been the last trick Sir Angelo ever played.

When Iacomo came to his senses and realized what had happened, he was so ashamed that he didn't have the heart to set foot outside his house again. Finally he decided he'd have to leave town altogether. He sold a little piece of land — it was the last thing he had left — and bought himself a horse and some weapons with the proceeds and set out for foreign parts where the wars were. Aided by luck and his own strength it wasn't too long before he became a rich and famous soldier. And Love and Sir Angelo were the cause of it all. And since Iacomo has already paid off Sir Angelo for his part in the adventure, it's left to me to confirm the words I began with: wonderful, incomprehensible, and truly miraculous are the powers of the god of Love. And how fortunate are those on whom both Luck and Love turn smiling faces.

Masuccio
You hear people say all the time that when someone who isn't very smart gets tricked by somebody who is, the victim still knows enough to repay the trick and the trickster together. Without a second thought, he resorts to force. And even though the victim doesn't recover anything in the process, I'm still convinced that the con man suffers more because he's not used to being victimized. And the preceding story has shown that this is true, because Sir Angelo, recognizing that his "cousin" didn't have much common sense, put his mind to taking advantage of him. And when the victim found out about it, of course he lacked the ability to get his own back with a similar trick, so he just went after him tooth and nail. And he went at it with such determination that if help had been a little slower in coming, he would have sent Sir Angelo straight to Barabas.

GIROLAMO MORLINI

Little is known about Morlini.[18] He was probably born in Naples c.1480 and he is recorded as a jurist at the *Studium* of Naples in 1513–14 with the title *doctor in utroque iure,* lecturing on books II and IV of the *Institutes.* An historical work bearing his name, the *De bello Mediolanensi inter Franciscum I regem Gallorum et Carolum V imperatorem gesto,* narrates events between 1521 and 1525, and it is speculated that he died c.1528. He also composed in Latin at least one, one-act play, his *Comedia.* His collection of *Novelle*[19] includes some eighty-one stories, many of which have strong misogynistic themes. It was issued in Naples by the French printer Jean Pasquet de Sallo on 8 April 1520. In keeping with the political leanings of the kingdom of Naples, like Masuccio he is strongly anticlerical. In 1559, in fact, his *Novelle* were placed on the *Index of Prohibited Books* for their obscenity and anticlericalism. Nevertheless, they continued to appear in collections over the next decades and found their way into French editions during the Revolution.

While Morlini was heavily influenced by Boccaccio and Masuccio, among others, he chose to write his *Novelle* in Latin rather than the far more traditional Italian. Despite this unusual linguistic choice, his *novelle* still bear the marks of the Italian tradition. In the story that follows, Morlini tells how a clever innkeeper unloaded some mediocre wine on his credulous customers. While most writers would have focused on the innkeeper and tacitly or directly supported his ingenious trick, Morlini focuses on his Neapolitan victims. There is no sentimentality here, however, no unquestioning support for the home-town folks. Instead Morlini, himself a Neapolitan, is harshly critical of those traits of character that make his fellow citizens such easy prey to the unscrupulous innkeeper.

18. Franco Pignatti, "Morlini, Girolamo," DBI 77 (2012), online at: http:// www.treccani.it/enciclopedia/girolamo-morlini_(Dizionario-Biografico).

19. *Novelle e favole,* Giovanni Villani, ed. (Rome: Salerno Editrice, 1988).

26. Morlini: How Giovanello the Innkeeper Tricked the Neapolitans
There was an innkeeper named Giovanello whose hostelry lay outside Naples on the shore in the area of Chiaia. He'd bought fifteen casks of good wine from Caleno that he intended to sell during the summer when the price would be higher. But when summer came he wasn't able to sell a drop of it for some reason, and what was worse, the wine was beginning to turn. Nevertheless, this wise man turned his problem around and found a way to make a liability into an asset. He knew that the Neapolitans are very gullible folks who follow one behind the other like goats, and that once they start to talk the shadow of the truth never enters their heads. These traits are the origin of their confusions, their discords, and their servitude.

So when some Neapolitans happened by his inn the next morning, the innkeeper told them about an enormous dragon that had appeared not long before in the mouth of a cave on the side of Monte Posillipo and that in one bite it had eaten up a cow that was grazing nearby. Some of the local farmers banded together to kill it, he said, but they weren't able to, so they gave up and left the monster alone. Anybody with eyes could see the big opening right up there on the side of the mountain where he was still holed up. And the innkeeper pointed right at it with his hand.

These folks went running back to the city and they told everybody they knew not that they had *heard* about this dragon but that they had *seen* it with their own two eyes, and by late afternoon the news was all over town. So the next day along comes an enormous crowd of suckers, men and women of every age and rank, dying to see the dragon. And they came in such multitudes that by the end of the day the innkeeper had sold every bit of his wretched wine at an incredibly inflated price. The following day when more fools came to see the monster, the innkeeper came up to them and said, "Turn back, dear citizens, because yesterday evening the dragon flew off toward Sicily."

In great disappointment, this crowd gave up hope of seeing the monster and went back to town. But in the sarcastic and malicious spirit of the true innkeeper and to make fun of those credulous poltroons, Giovannello had painted on the wall of his inn a picture of the dragon who had helped him to sell vinegar at champagne prices.

This story demonstrates that the Neapolitans are excitable and that wherever one of them wanders through imprudence the rest follow, and even though they are all alike in this, they can't agree on anything else.

TOMMASO COSTO

Little in known of Costo's life,[20] or of his birth and death. For about forty years he served in Naples as secretary to a long list of noble families including the Carafa, Giovanni d'Avalos (from 1577 on), the son of Francesco Ferrante and Maria d'Aragona, and from 1581 to Scipione Pignatelli and his heirs, the Orsini of Gravina, and others. He was then appointed secretary to the Great Court of the Admiralty of Naples under Matteo Di Capua.

Costo was an active member of Naples literary scene, a member of the Accademia dei Sereni Ardenti, and a correspondent[21] with such fellow writers as Giovan Battista Attendolo, Giulio Cesare Capaccio, Angelo Di Costanzo, Scipione De Monti and many others. He was also a prominent editor, bringing out new editions of Tasso's *Gerusalemme liberata* (Naples 1582) and Bartolomeo Sacchi (Platina)'s *Lives of the Popes* (Venice 1592), among others.

His first literary work was *La rotta di Lepanto* (Naples 1573), republished in Naples in 1582 as *La vittoria della Lega,* and he followed this up with several well regarded historical works, including his *Giunta al Compendio dell'istoria del Regno di Napoli* (Venice 1588), his *Apologia istorica del Regno di Napoli contro la falsa opinione di coloro che biasimarono i regnicoli d'incostanza e d'infedeltà* (Naples 1613), and others.

There is little difference between the *novella* as he writes it and the work of Masuccio and Morlini a century before. Costo published his

---

20. Vera Lettere, "Costo, Tommaso," DBI 30 (1984), online at: http://www.treccani.it/enciclopedia/tommaso-costo_(Dizionario-Biografico).

21. *Lettere* (Venice: Barezzo Barezzi, 1602, repr. Naples: Costantino Vitale, 1604).

novella collection called *Il Fuggilozio,* "The Timekiller," in 1596.[22] It consists of a number of stories chosen more for their variety than for any consistent theme; the author labels his work, "a salad composed of mixed greens." The brief story included here tells how a clever priest convinced his parishioners that he could "raise up" the church in their village.

27. Costo: Il Fuggilozio, "The Timekiller"

The Church of Father Paolino is robbed; he comes up with a scheme to make the locals pay for the damage and a little more.

Certain farmers over there in the mountains around Genoa close to the border with Lombardy had built a church for themselves, and it was served by a priest named Father Paolino, who regularly said mass. And this priest had been in the parish for such a long time that he'd been able to set aside a little bit of money for himself. Now it happened one day that the church was robbed of quite a number of things, and those farmers decided that Father Paolino was well enough off that he ought to bear the cost of replacing what was stolen. The priest saw that he was in a bind and figured that the best way to pay for the stolen goods was with a trick.

He knew that the farmers in his parish weren't as poor as they were dumb, and when a few months had passed he began to talk to them about "raising up the church." "It's too low," he kept saying, "we need to raise it up." Nobody quite knew what he meant by that, but he kept after them about it until they decided to go along with his idea. They didn't have any architects or builders in their community, which meant they would have to send outside for one. But Father Paolino told them that if they could just come up with fifty *scudi,* he'd direct the project himself and see that the church was raised up in a way that would satisfy them all. They agreed to that, and pretty soon they got the money together from here and there and from one person and another.

22. Naples: Giovanni Iacopo Carlino & Antonio Pace; Venice: Barezzo Barezzi, & Compagni, 1600; with several later editions. Newly edited by Corrado Calenda, *Il fuggilozio* (Rome: Salerno, 1989).

Once he had the money in hand, Father Paolino hired men with ox-carts to collect manure from all the farms in the area. Then he had the outside walls of the church plastered all around with manure up to a height of about six feet or so. Naturally enough some of the people asked him what he thought he was doing plastering the church with manure like that, and he replied, "I'm doing it so that, come September when the rains start, what with the church being covered with manure and all, it'll start to grow just like a tree. Of course I'll add my prayers, too."

The poor boobs accepted that and didn't ask any more questions, although they were very curious to see what would happen. Well it finally got to be fall and the rains started, and every time it would rain, a little bit of the manure would wash away and the top edge of the manure layer would drop down a couple of inches. And there was so much rain that fall that within a couple of weeks the top two feet of the manure had been washed away. And when that happened, it left a dark stain all around the walls where the manure had been. When the locals saw that dark area up above the manure, they were astonished and they kept pointing to it and telling each other that the church was growing. Finally when the stain was about four feet above the manure plaster, they all went running to Father Paolino and told him that the rest of the manure should be scraped off right away because the church had been raised up just enough and they were afraid if they didn't get rid of the manure in time it might grow too much!

JACOPO SANNAZARO

While many writers of the Neapolitan Renaissance established their reputations within Italian literature in general, only Sannazaro was widely known outside Italy.[23] Because of his *Arcadia* and *Piscatorial*

---

23. See Santagata, *La lirica aragonese;* Carol Kidwell, *Sannazaro and* Arcadia (London: Duckworth, 1993); Angela Caracciolo Aricò, *L'Arcadia del Sannazaro nell'autunno dell'umanesimo* (Rome: Bulzoni, 1995); Ralph Nash, *The Major Latin Poems of Jacopo Sannazaro* (Detroit: Wayne State University Press, 1996); Carlo Vecce, *Gli zibaldoni di Jacopo Sannazaro* (Messina: Sicania,

Eclogues, which were read and imitated throughout Europe during the long period when pastoral literature was all the rage, Sannazaro became internationally known. With the waning of enthusiasm for the imaginary lives of lovesick, poetic shepherds, Sannazaro's reputation declined; and while he is still judged an historically important poet, he is seldom read, though translations of his major works are available in English and other modern languages.

Sannazaro was born in Naples c.1456, there is no precise indication of the year of his birth. As he records in the *Arcadia,* the family was an ancient and noble one originally from the Valtellina region. Dante mentions them in the *Convivio,* written in the early years of the fourteenth century. Jacopo's branch of the family followed Charles III of Durazzo to Naples and in the early part of the quattrocento rose to great prominence, but the family fortunes were in eclipse by the time of the poet's birth. His father died while Jacopo was still a child, and he was raised by his mother.

He entered the household of Alfonso, duke of Calabria in 1481, the grandson of King Alfonso to whom Pontano dedicated his *Prince.*[24] His earliest poetry was produced in this household, and two examples are included in this anthology, the brief comical "Elbows" and *A Farce.* Sannazaro, whose poetic gifts were already becoming known, became a member of the Accademia Pontaniana. His poetic career was interrupted by the expulsion of the Aragonese rulers from Naples, and he followed King Frederick into exile, returning home only after the deposed monarch's death in 1504. In the wake of Pontano's death, the members of his poetic Academy reformed themselves

---

1998); Davide Canfora and Angela Caracciolo Aricò, ed., *La Serenissima e il regno: Nel V Centenario dell'Arcadia di Jacopo Sannazaro. Atti del convegno di studi (Bari-Venezia, 4–8 ottobre 2004)* (Bari: Cacucci, 2006); *Latin Poetry,* Michael C.J. Putnam, ed. and trans. (Cambridge, MA: Harvard University Press, 2009); Pasquale Sabbatino, ed., *Jacopo Sannazaro: La cultura napoletana nell'Europa del Rinascimento. Convegno internazionale di studi (Napoli, 27–28 marzo 2006)* (Florence: L.S. Olschki, 2009); and C. Vecce, "Viaggio in 'Arcadia'," in Iacopo Sannazaro: *Arcadia,* C. Vecce, ed. (Rome, Carocci, 2013), 9-41.

24. See chapter 2, reading 19, pp. 121–38.

around Sannazaro, who, as he records in the *Arcadia,* was known by the Academic name, Sincerus or Sincero. The last decades of his life were divided between poetry and the spirited defense of Cassandra Marchese. Sannazaro antagonized almost everyone of importance in Italy in an effort to achieve justice for this woman, and the bitterness of his quarrels is attested by his epigrams. He died in 1530.

Gliommeri — "Elbows" — is the name Sannazaro gave to his earliest poems. While the name makes no literal sense, it aptly characterizes the kind of knobby and ridiculous verse the collection contains. The verse form is a popular one called *frottolato,* which has no place in the grand tradition of either classical or vernacular poetry. Each line has a strong break within it, which is emphasized by the unusual rhyme scheme. The word at the end of line one rhymes with the last word before the pause in the middle of line two, rather than with the end word of line two, as in most standard verse forms. I have not followed this rhyme scheme in my translation.

28. Sannazaro: Elbows

> *To the happy memory   of king Andy*
> *he ate peacock stew   like candy;*
> *and he liked his eggs   with jello,*
> *sandpiper sauce   and mortadella;*
> *saffron sprinkled   on rotini;*
> *mushrooms backfired   on zucchini*
> *with two or three   capons underground*
> *and pigs-feet   pickled by the pound*
> *perked up his appetite   before the main course.*
> *He was sparing with condiments   of course.*

SANNAZARO'S *Farce* is what we would call a masque. It is an allegorical court entertainment that combines the elements of a play with music and dance performances. This particular masque celebrates what we are apt to regard as a fairly shameful act, the final expulsion of the Moors from Granada by the Spanish rulers Ferdinand and Isabella in 1492. The *Farce,* however, gives no evidence of sharing our view; it celebrates the Christian victory and glories in the expulsion of Muhammad from the Spanish peninsula. It is exactly the sort of work that a court poet is called upon to produce, and while it cannot be called a masterpiece in any sense of the word, it is a competent piece of work, and it shows very clearly the official attitudes of the court as well as the routine use of court entertainment for political ends. The verse form is the *frottolato*, the same popular form used in "Elbows."

A Farce was presented March 4, 1492 in Naples in the great hall of the Castel Capuano at the celebration to honor the victory of King Ferdinand and Queen Isabella of Castile over the king of Granada on the second of February of the same year.

29. Sannazaro: A Farce

First Scene: A magnificent temple was erected in the center of the hall surrounded by twenty columns and highly ornamented. And after various noises within, MUHAMMAD in tattered clothes was pushed and pulled from the temple, and a banner was raised over the temple with a cross and the arms of Castile; then the exiled MUHAMMAD began to speak in great sadness:

MUHAMMAD: Flee, flee miserable one
don't stay to see your people subjugated
your Granada conquered; flee weary one.
Why, why delay your steps? Heaven exiles you
Fortune threatens you. Oh, unlucky one
Let it go. Accept fate. Once you had
Everything you desired and with delight
You called yourself Muhammad! Now you must
Live with your shame. O dear temple,
I love you and wonder sighing, I wonder
Who has taken you from me? Now you have abandoned
me, and I am wretched. O My Mosque
White, beautiful and pure, who will rule you now?
Now my law is ended and you are possessed
By the Christian faith; and I am alone out here.
That is what hurts me so, and can you live
Without being able to invoke my name?
Muhammad, I am he, Muhammad the ancient,
Prey to my enemy prey, prey;
Who would believe it? Once upon a time

I was their scourge and terror. *So goes the world*
Now up, now down. *Oh stars, now where*
Shall I go *where death will not be found,*
And a worse fate? *My Africa*
Will you welcome me? *Or will you fear*
Your own safety more. *As well you might*
For you must see the great Lion of Castile
Who stretches his claws *over many lands.*
Nor will he ever tire *of making war,*
Until from land to land *to my dismay*
They will have hounded me. Now what woods,
What cavern can I find *obscure and deep*
Enough to shelter me? *Wherever I flee*
I fear the same yoke *and the arrows*
Sharpened for vengeance *on my blood.*
And Grenada languishes! *Oh gods, I feel*
Her pavement tremble; *and if the Faith*
That drove me out *and now holds my throne*
Should find me, what then? Flee miserable one,
Follow your own road *don't hang back,*
Go, you're wasting time *in sobs and sorrow.*
Don't you hear the noise *grow louder and louder?*
Flee, for to capture you *she must only take one step.*

When MUHAMMAD had finished this speech, FAITH, very richly dressed and crowned with laurel, stepped from the same temple and began to speak....

When FAITH had finished her speech, she returned to the temple that was quickly raised to the ceiling of the hall. Afterwards JOY entered very ornately dressed and with three companions, all playing music on a violin *cornemusa*, flute, and rebec. JOY, who sang, played the violin and also led the other musicians. When they reached the place where the temple had been, they stopped playing, and JOY began to speak.

JOY: Whenever have the stars
Beheld such beautiful ladies and so many
Congregated before the presence
Of such a Power? In what other age

Has the world witnessed   such gentility?
Let everyone be glad and laugh   and thank God,
And feast our eyes   for here we see
A great King   seated in Majesty,
Lord of these splendid people   and a Queen
Angelic and divine,   with a glorious
Victorious Duke,   a Prince benign
And worthy of all honor,   an Admiral,
And a joyous Infante   in whom Nature
At one lucky cast   has melded together
The supreme beauty   of her Mother
And the great valor of her Father.   Oh Dukes, oh Ladies,
Why do you wear   such rich garments?
Why are you so happy?   O My Lord,
What Providence   what Grace of God invites
You to share this grand   and solemn festival?
Is there something here   or elsewhere
Which delights you?   Is that fierce and foul
Mohammed stolen off   sick and naked?
Has enemy Grenada   returned again
To her ancient Faith?   May heaven give you
Just cause always   and time and space
For pleasure and for play.   May God spare
You from all misfortune   and all treachery.
I am that Joy   who adorns Paradise
With my smile   and delights
Those shining spirits,   who with their songs
Forever glorify   their Maker,
Full of chaste love   and gentility.
I seldom show myself   here below;
And even though your eyes look on me,
You do not see or know me under this veil
As I am known in heaven.   This once
(and here she lifted the veil that had covered her face and
continued)

You will not see me   through a glass darkly
But unveiled   and beautiful and clear.
And now the earth learns   in mid-winter
To see eternal flowering,   and follows suit.

Now the peaceful ocean   is without storms;
The Heavens are tranquil   on every side;
Night becomes bright as day;   every element
Is pacified   and the planets
Grow mild and fortunate.   Oh happy age,
Oh happy men destined   for kinder years!
Now schemes and frauds   are nullified;
The vices overcome;   and now Envy
And Moorish treachery   and impious War
Are banished   from the whole earth.
Come now, come   sweet virtues
For human joy   resides in you.
Let there be none who sorrows   or complains;
Let no evil thought remain   in this hall.
Bitter sadness   come out from behind the stairs
And follow the Moors;   and you Fears,
You black and Sinful Pleasures,   you Sighs,
Let me not see you,   and be absent
All this season.   Now Dances and Songs
Come here to me,   and Games and Laughter
Rise up from your seats.   O happy band
Behold the Spring;   here are flowers,
Here sweet perfumes,   here is delight.
Laugh all of you!   Muhammad weeps alone.

When JOY had finished her speech, she scattered flowers and flowering branches, and singing as she began, she returned to where she had entered; immediately from there trumpeters all richly and uniformly dressed entered playing. Then came the FOOL followed by The Most Illustrious Prince of Capua representing the LORD KING OF CASTILE with others splendidly dressed in green brocade with silk vests and fur hats, all masked. These were followed by others dressed in the French style with gold embroidered damask capes to their feet, and gold hose, all dancing and carrying torches. Then each courtier took a Lady by the hand and danced her high and low, and then they withdrew with torches in their hands, and that concluded the celebration for that evening.

THE EXACT DATE of the composition of the *Arcadia* [Fig. 3] has not been determined. From the various manuscripts and partial or complete printings of the early part of the sixteenth century a picture emerges of a poem in progress. The earliest versions of the poem, dating back apparently to the late 1480s, would seem to have something in common with the two earlier pieces by Sannazaro included here. The language of this earlier version is very Neapolitan in flavor, and its range and cultural ambitions are quite restricted. The final printed versions of the *Arcadia* are rich with literary history and written in a literary Italian that bears the marks of Tuscan rather than Neapolitan. Despite this use of the developing national literary language, the text is closely tied to Naples as the following selection demonstrates.

Fig. 3. Sincero and the river nymph. From Jacopo Sannazaro, Arcadia. *Francesco Sansovino, ed. Venice: Franceschi, 1578.*

Most modern readers will find the *Arcadia* rough going. The language of the poem is very formal, its emotions highly stylized. The governing fiction, that of pastoral, is largely closed to the modern imagination. Most of us can't imagine that the lives of shepherds and cowherds ever were or ever could be idyllic. The pastoral genre invites us to imagine that they spent most of their time lying around composing songs while their flocks grazed untended, and that seems like an aristocrat's sentimental view of agricultural labor. But if we can accept the conventions of the genre for what they were, we can at least follow imaginatively Sannazaro's autobiographical statement of the formation of a poet equally dedicated to politics and to love.

The form of the *Arcadia* is an unusual one too in that it includes both poetry and prose. In classical poetics this combined form is known as Menippean Satire, but the best known example of the genre from the antique period is Boethius' *Consolation of Philosophy.* Given the resemblance between Sannazaro's story of falling in love and the story Dante tells of his own childhood love for Beatrice, the most obvious model for the *Arcadia* is Dante's *Vita Nuova.* Despite this important similarity, the *Arcadia* differs from the *Vita Nuova* in important ways. Perhaps the most significant of these is the dominance of prose in the *Arcadia,* where it far outweighs the verse. This emphasis on prose ties the *Arcadia* to literary trends in the Renaissance that lead forward in the direction of the novel rather than backwards to the re-evocation of medieval forms.

30. Sannazaro: Arcadia

Prose Seven

When Opico had finished his song, which the crowd had listened to with great pleasure, Carino turned to me and asked who I was and where I was from and why I was staying in *Arcadia*. And after a long sigh, as if compelled by necessity, I replied:

I cannot, gracious shepherd, without great unhappiness remember times past; which, even though I have little reason to call them happy, nonetheless, having to recount them now when I am in greater distress will be an increase of torment for me, and a sharpening of the pain of an unhealed wound, which, naturally shrinks from being touched too often. But because the release of words often brings relief of pain to the afflicted, I will answer you. Naples, as each one of you must very often have heard, lies in the must fruitful and delightful part of Italy, a famous and noble city set on the margin of the sea, and in arms and letters perhaps more blessed than any other city in the world. Built by people from Calcidia around the ancient tomb of the Siren Parthenope, it took and still retains the venerable name of the dead youth. There I was born, not from obscure origins, but, if I may be permitted, as the coat of arms of my predecessors prominently displayed in the most noble parts of the city demonstrate, descended from a most ancient and liberal ancestry, among the other young men of my age I was perhaps not the least in reputation. And the grandfather of my father — who hailed from Cisalpine Gaul, while (should we look to his origins) his ancestors came from Eastern Spain, in which two places the descendants of my family still flourish — was not only noble in his origins but for his own deeds most celebrated. He was head of a large force during the invasion of the kingdom of Naples by Charles III and for his service he was awarded possession of Sinuessa and a large part of the Falernian fields and the Massicci mountains along with the little town on the shore where the turbulent Volturno erupts into the sea, and Linterno, which, though solitary, is nonetheless famous for the memory of the sacred ashes of the divine Scipio Africanus; and in fertile Lucania he held many towns and castles under honorable title on which alone he could have lived abundantly in the style his condition required. But Fortune, much more liberal in giving than careful in conserving worldly prosperity, decreed that in the course of time, when King Charles and his legitimate successor Ladislaus had died, that the widowed realm should pass to a woman [Giovanna II]. Driven by natural irresolution and inconstancy of spirit, to her other most grievous faults she added this, that those who had been rewarded by her father and her brother with the greatest honors, she reduced through persecution and humiliation to virtual destitution. Beyond this the story of what and how many were the misfortunes and frustrations my grandfather and father suffered would be long to tell. I come to myself, therefore, who in those late years when King Alfonso of Aragon of blessed memory had passed from worldly things to a more tranquil world, under the unlucky prodigies of comets, earthquakes, and plague, after a bloody struggle I was born into poverty, or according to the wise, into modest circumstances.

As my star and the fates determined, I had scarcely reached eight years of age, when I began to feel the forces of Love; and I fell in love with the loveliness of a little girl, more beautiful and sweeter than any I had ever seen, and of noble blood; yet, I was discrete far beyond the limits of my age and kept my desire completely hidden. Playing with me in her childish way, from day to day, with her extraordinary beauty, without every being aware of it, she set my tender heart on fire. Love grew with the years and as we came to adulthood we became more inclined to love's desires. But our friendship never diminished, in fact it grew closer, which was a great cause of suffering to me. Because it seemed to me that the love, goodwill, and great affection she had for me were not directed to that end I would have preferred; and knowing myself to have that in my heart which I must not show; and not being sufficiently brave to declare myself in any way for fear I would lose in an instant what I had worked so diligently over many years to acquire; I fell into such terrible melancholy and pain, that I lost my appetite for food and sleep and became more like a shadow of death than a living man. She often asked me what was the cause of all this, but I gave her no response other than a sigh. Often, as I lay in the narrow bed in my bedchamber, I made up my mind to tell her, but all the same, when I was in her presence, I grew pale, trembled, and turned mute; so that it would have given reason for suspicion to many perhaps. But she either never understood because of her innate goodness or never wished to understood because of a cold heart, or perhaps — what is more credible —

she was so wise that she knew how to hide it better than I, though in act and word she always seemed very direct. For all these reasons I was unable to distract myself from loving her, nor could I continue in such an abject manner of life. Therefore, as a final remedy, I decided to live no longer; and I went about meditating various and strange ways of finding death. And frankly I would have ended my sad days with the noose or poison or the sharp sword, if my sorrowing heart, overcome by some cowardice, had not become afraid of what it most desired. Turning my savage thoughts into more orderly ones, I decided to abandon Naples and my father's house, imagining I would leave love and my thoughts behind with them.

But alas, it turned out quite otherwise than I had imagined. Formerly when I saw and spoke with her I loved so much, I thought myself to be unhappy because the cause of my suffering was unknown to her; now I can call myself more unhappy than any other mortal, separated from her by such great distance, and without hope of ever seeing her again perhaps or even receiving news of her, which might do me good. The worst is to recall the pleasures of my sweet homeland here in the solitude of Arcadia, where — begging your indulgence — not only does it seem impossible that men raised in the city might live with pleasure, but I can scarcely imagine that wild beasts do so. And if I suffered no other torment but anxiety of mind, which continually holds me in suspense because of the fervent desire I have to see her again, so that I am unable to form any other thought in my mind by day or night, still that would be excruciating pain.

I never see a mountain or a wilderness, that I don't imagine I will come upon her there, impossible as I know that to be. No beast or bird or branch can move that I don't turn in fear to see if she hasn't come here to learn of the miserable life I lead for her sake; likewise I can see nothing here that does not give me occasion to remember her with greater fervor and concern. And it seems to me that the hollow grottoes, the springs, the valleys, the mountains, and all the forests call her, and the trees continually whisper her name. Sometimes when I find myself among them, and look at the leafy elms circled by lush vines, it comes over me with almost unbearable intensity, how different my situation is from that of the insensate trees, who, loved by the sweet vines live continually with them in a gracious embrace, while I consume my life in sorrow and tears, separated by an infinite space of sky, earth, and sea from her I love. How many times have I wept among the solitary groves, as I saw two doves kiss each other with sweet murmurs and then in desire go searching for their beloved nest. "Fortunate ones," I have then said, "to whom it is given to sleep and wake in secure peace untouched by any hint of jealousy. Long life to your joy and to your love; while I alone remain an emblem of sadness for all living things."

It often happens that as I am watching your flocks come and go — a habit I have acquired here in your wilderness — I see among the fertile pastures a bull so thin that his bones seem hardly able to carry his withered skin. I can never see this without suffering inestimable weariness and pain, knowing that love is the source of both our miserable lives....

By why do I go on describing what must be obvious to you all? I can never hear one of you call me Sannazaro, though it was a name of honor to my predecessors, without thinking of how she used to call me Sincero, and then I sigh. Nor can I hear the sound of the pipes, or a shepherd singing, without having my eyes well up with tears; then the good times come back to me, when I heard her praise my rhymes and the verses I had written. But rather than recount each and every one of my sufferings, suffice it to say that nothing pleases me, and no celebration or game could, I will not say increase my joy, but even lessen my sorrow. And I pray to whatever god hears the words of the afflicted, that this suffering might come to an end either by a speedy death or some happier eventuality.... Then I picked up my lyre and played and sang this song:

Sincero (solo)
Like the night bird who hates the sun
I wander in lightless spaces and somber
as long as I know that day rules earth;
even when earth is covered by evening,
alone of the living I find no sleep;
I am restless and weep for my wounds.
If ever these eyes in grove or wood
beyond the reach of rays of the sun
worn down with tears should close in sleep
cruel visions, fantasies and somber
dreams depress me so at evening
I fear to lay my weary head on earth.
O Mother of us all benignant Earth,
I pray I find that graceful wood,
and lie down on one final evening,
and never stir till the blessed sun
shows his light to eyes so somber
and wakens me from eternal sleep.
Since my eyes abandoned sleep
and I left my bed to lie on earth,
my days of peace became somber;
thorns choked off the secret wood.
When mortal day comes with the sun
darkness dawns for me and evening.
My lady, by her grace one evening
appeared to me beautiful in sleep
and cheered my heart just like the sun
breaks through the clouds to light the earth;
She said to me, "Come search my wood,
pick flowers and forget what's somber."
Vanish now unspeakable and somber
thoughts, my lifelong evening;
I go to walk the fields and wood,
to lie in the grass and fall asleep
knowing now that none on earth
is luckier than I am under the sun.
Song, at evening in the east the sun
will rise and unearth the somber

kingdom before that wood rocks me to sleep.

Rhymes 6 :The Tomb of Icarus
Icarus fell here. These waves received him,
they caught his impudent feathers
when his brief surge heavenward
turned, the envy of all who come.
A flight well worth the pain and risk:
with death he bought eternal fame.
Fame purchased at such a rate
consumes the damage in the prize.
He should be happy with his fall
soaring to heaven like a dove
in a heat that height dissolves.
And now this sea sounds his name;
a wide sea, its own element,
beyond the scope of mortal tombs.

PIETRO JACOPO DE JENNARO

De Jennaro[25] was born in Naples in 1436 into a noble family associated with the *seggio* of Porto since the duecento. His father Giorgio was a prominent feudatory and was appointed the *maestro razione* in 1452. His mother, Maddalena Di Gaeta, was the daughter of Carlo, president of the Regia Camera della Sommaria and herself lady-in-waiting to Queen Giovanna II. Pietro was educated in law but began writing poetry while still in school. By the 1470s, De Jennaro was serving as an Aragonese ambassador in the Papal States and is recorded in Pesaro, Ferrara, and Venice. By 1479, he was already president of the Sommaria and served as commissioner general of the lands of Bari and Otranto. In 1482 he was named captain of the city of Cosenza, and he served as commissioner of Molise (1487–95) and of Basilicata and Cosenza (1497). He died in Naples in 1508.

25. Erasmo Pèrcopo, Pietro Jacopo De Jennaro, and Filenio Gallo, *La prima imitazione dell'Arcadia: Aggiuntevi l'Egloghe pastorali di P.J. de Jennaro e di Filenio Gallo* (Naples: L. Pierro, 1894); Sandra Niccoli, "De Gennaro, Pietro Jacopo," DBI 36 (1988), online at: http://www.treccani.it/enciclopedia/de-gennaro-pietro-iacopo_(Dizionario-Biografico).

In 1470 he probably composed his *Plutopenia*, a dialogue between Wealth and Poverty, dedicated to Federico of Aragon. He followed this with a variety of works, including his *De regimine principum* (1481) dedicated to Alfonso, duke of Calabria, the *Canzoniere* (1486), his *Pastorale* from around the same time, his *Le sei etate de la vita umana*, and his *Regimento dell'opera de li huomini illustri sopra de le medaglie* (1504). De Jennaro was also named a member of the Accademia Pontaniana

Among the best known and most popular poets in the circle of Sannazaro, De Jennaro wrote poems in the Petrarchan style. His collection of *Rime* produced in 1486 and dedicated to his beloved,[26] whom he calls "Bianca," contains a hundred and seventeen poems. All are examples of forms that Petrarch had made famous, and the bulk of them are sonnets, the favorite form of the Petrarchan tradition. In the following poem, in addition to echoes of Petrarch, there are evocations of Dante's *Divine Comedy*.

31. De Jennaro: Like the Glowworm
   Like that worm we often see
   in the season the sun most warms
   the earth, night-walking, lighting another's
   steps, himself in darkness;
   so it goes for me, for she,
   alas, will not believe my love.
   Believe what I say and know
   that love leads me along to death.
   So I am a warning beacon
   to all who sail this bitter sea,
   but ever slow to leave its pain.
   Lucky the man who remembers
   himself and his needs and sets sail
   for gentler and sweeter breezes.

26. *Rime e lettere*, Maria Corti, ed. (Bologna: Commissione per i testi di lingua, 1956).

BENEDETTO GARETH (IL CHARITEO)

Born in Barcelona in 1450, Gareth,[27] arrived in Naples some time between 1466 and 1468 as one of many from Catalonia who followed their Aragonese rulers from Spain to Naples. By 1482 he is recorded as a member of the *regio scrivano* and as *familiare* of the king's household. In 1486, when Antonello Petrucci, royal secretary of King Ferrante I, was implicated in the conspiracy of the barons, imprisoned, and finally executed,[28] Gareth succeeded him as keeper of the royal seal. Serving in this capacity until 1495, Gareth worked closely with Giovanni Pontano, who had been appointed royal secretary in Petrucci's place. Because of Gareth's excellent knowledge of the Latin classics, Pontano invited him to join the Accademia Pontaniana.

Gareth established a close working relationship with King Ferrandino (Ferdinand or Ferrante II), and when French troops of Charles VIII occupied Naples in February 1495, Gareth followed the king into exile and back in his triumphal return. The king appointed him royal secretary in place of Pontano, who some considered compromised under the French occupation. With the fall of the Aragonese (August 1501), Gareth fled Naples for Rome, where he lived for about two years among the literati of the city. Returning to Naples in September 1503, after the expulsion of the French and the ascent to the throne of Ferdinand the Catholic of Spain, Gareth was appointed governor of Nola. In these years he was part of the cultural and social circle that gathered around Constanza d'Avalos. Gareth spent his last years in precarious health and is last attested in a document of 20 April 1512. A letter by Pietro Summonte of 28 July 1515 refers to Gareth as "lo bon messer Chariteo di felice memoria."

In 1506, Gareth published the first poetry collection to which his reputation was linked: *Libro de sonetti et canzone di Chariteo intitulato*

---

27. Angela Asor Rosa, "Gareth, Benet," DBI 52 (1999), online at: http://www.treccani.it/enciclopedia/benet-gareth_(Dizionario-Biografico); Beatrice Barbiellini Amidei, *Alla Luna: Saggio sulla poesia del Cariteo* (Florence: La Nuova Italia editrice, 1999).

28. See chapter 1, reading 6, pp. 79–82.

Endymione a la Luna.[29] In November 1509 Sigismondo Mayr published *Tutte le opere volgari di Chariteo,* edited by Pietro Summonte. Gareth's poetry[30] is studied, refined, fluid, and ingenious. It has an urbanity that eluded De Jennaro and that was quickly abandoned by later poets in search of deeper emotional effects.

32. *Gareth:You, Lady, and I*
   You, Lady, and I by all we see
   are both bound for eternal pain;
   you for pride, I for excess
   zeal, for lusting for a star.
   But since my eyes oppress you,
   you will suffer more, and I
   who want no glory but your sight
   will be the only happy man in Hell.
   With you to gaze on for eternity
   I'll have a Paradise in Hell,
   a prize no smaller than the heavens.
   And if I do not lose your sun,
   the wicked spirits hold no threat.
   To suffer I must close my eyes.

VITTORIA COLONNA

Vittoria Colonna was born in Marino c.1492[31] in the Alban hills near Rome, of the illustrious family of the Colonna princes. In 1509, she married Ferrante Francesco d'Avalos, marquis of Pescara, to whom she had been betrothed since the age of three. This desirable political

---

29. Naples: Giovanni Antonio da Caneto.

30. *Le Rime di Benedetto Gareth detto il Chariteo,* Erasmo Pèrcopo, ed. (Naples: Accademia delle scienze, 1892).

31. This introduction is based on Laura Anna Stortoni, ed., *Women Poets of the Italian Renaissance: Courtly Ladies and Courtesans,* Laura Anna Stortoni and Mary Prentice Lillie, trans. (New York: Italica Press, 1997), 49–53. See also Giorgio Patrizi, "Colonna,Vittoria," DBI 27 (1982), online at: http://www.treccani.it/enciclopedia/vittoria-colonna_(Dizionario-Biografico); Abigail Brundin,T. Crivelli, and Maria Serena Sapegno, ed., *A Companion to Vittoria Colonna* (Leiden: Brill, 2016).

match solidified the Colonna's ties with Naples. Brief periods of happiness with her husband were spent at their castle on the island of Ischia in the Bay of Naples, times which she would later remember fondly in her poetry. Since Ferrante was in the service of the Emperor Charles V, then at war with François I of France, he did not remain long at her side. In 1512, the marquis was taken prisoner after the battle of Ravenna and died of wounds received in the battle of Pavia in 1525. After his death, Vittoria led a semi-monastic life in the remembrance of past happiness. The marriage was childless, and Colonna raised her husband's orphaned cousin, Alfonso del Vasto, as their heir.

Although her family urged her to remarry, she devoted herself instead to scholarship, religious reform, and pious works. Profoundly religious by nature, she became even more so in widowhood. On some moral issues, she held views similar to those of the Counter-Reformation religious reformers Ochino and Valdés, and she took an active part in the evangelical movement designed to purify and renew Catholicism. Her friendship with Ochino led the Inquisition to investigate her beliefs, saddening her final years.

As witnessed by her voluminous correspondence, she had close literary friendships with many prominent writers and scholars of her age, among whom were Bembo, Aretino, Castiglione, Molza, Ariosto, and others. She played a great role in the intellectual, social, and political life of her time, inspiring many artists. Her castle on Ischia became a meeting place for Neapolitan humanists and literati.[32] Her life as a widow was also enriched by a deep Platonic friendship (starting around 1530) with Michelangelo. For her, especially after her death, he wrote some of his most powerful verses, acknowledging her as his literary and spiritual guide.

In *The Lives of the Painters*, Vasari wrote: "Michelangelo sent a vast number of poems by his own hand, receiving answers in rhyme and in prose, to the most illustrious Marchionness of Pescara, of whose virtues he was enamored and she likewise of his; and she went many times to visit him, and Michelangelo designed for her a dead Christ

32. See above, pp. 28–29.

in the lap of Our Lady, with two little angels, all most admirable, and a Christ fixed on the cross, who, with the head uplifted, is recommending his spirit to the Father, a divine work…" The historian Condivi also wrote about their relationship in his *Life of Michelangelo*, describing at great length Vittoria's death in the convent of the Benedettine di Sant'Anna in Rome, attended by the grieving artist. She had been suffering from a debilitating illness from 1543 until her death in 1547. Ariosto, in the *Orlando Furioso* 37, hailed her as the most illustrious woman of her time.

Before her husband's death, Vittoria wrote very little, and only the *Letter* in *terza rima* written in 1512 to her husband survives from this period. This extraordinary poetic letter, of which we present only excerpts, is Colonna's most personal statement, in which she expresses the pain and anguish of the separation caused by war. *Sonnet* 1 is written to her late husband. Colonna's lyric poetry is essentially Petrarchist, and her style is complex, intellectual, and replete with many unusual conceits and rhetorical figures for which she was greatly admired. Her poetry (and especially her religious poetry) is imbued with Neoplatonism. In her times, and for several centuries afterwards, she was regarded as Italy's greatest woman poet.

Her poetry was printed for the first time in 1538,[33] without her involvement. In fact, she never personally oversaw any of the editions of her work, of which twenty came out in the sixteenth century alone. Our translations are taken from Stortoni, *Women Poets*, 67 and 55.

33. Colonna: Letter to Ferrante Francesco d'Avalos, after the Battle of Ravenna (Excerpts)
> *My highest Lord, I am writing this letter*
> *to tell you in what sadness I exist,*
> *torn among doubt and loneliness and pain….*
>   *When others asked for war, I called for peace,*
> *sufficing me that my belovèd Marquis*
> *should dwell with me content and satisfied.*
>   *Risky endeavors of war do not harm men;*
> *but we women — afflicted and forsaken —*

33. *Rime de la divina Vittoria Colonna*, Filippo Pirogallo, ed. (Parma: Antonio Viotti).

are hurt by fear and anxious care alike.
Compelled by your belligerence, you think
only of honor, and with loud war cries
you rush straight into the perils of battle.
But left behind, we, fearful and sad,
worry for you: the sister wants the brother,
the bride the bridegroom, and the mother her son.
Wretchedly lonely, I long for my husband,
for my father and son: I am at once
spouse, daughter, sister and aging mother....
Independent you live, devoid of cares
and thinking only to gain fame and acclaim —
you do not care if I yearn for your love.
My face darkened by sadness and disdain,
I lie alone in a forsaken bed,
feeling hope intertwined with bitter pain,
and tempering my sorrows with your joy....

34. Colonna: Sonnet 1
I write only to ease the inner sorrow
On which my heart feeds, wishing nothing more —
Not to add light to my belovèd sun
Who left behind on earth such honored spoils.
Reason enough have I for these laments —
Although I greatly fear to scant his glory.
Some better pen, perhaps, with wiser words
May come to raise his great name from the grave.
Pure faith, warm ardor, and consuming pain
Be my excuse to all the world, to write,
For neither time nor reason can withhold me.
Thus, bitter weeping, not delightful song,
Dark sighs, and no serene melodious voice —
Not style, but grief alone, give me the praise.

LUIGI TANSILLO

Tansillo was born in Venosa in 1510 and served under Pedro di Toledo as a naval commander against Turks and pirates, and finally as captain of justice at Gaeta. He died in Teano in 1568.[34]

34. For his works: Erasmo Pèrcopo and Tobia R. Toscano, ed., *Il canzoniere edito ed inedito secondo una copia dell'autografo ed altri manoscritti e stampe* (Naples:

Tansillo composed a variety of poetic works, including *I due pellegrini* (a dramatic eclogue, 1527), *Il vendemmiatore* (1532), le *Stanze a Bernardino Martirano* (1540) on life on the high seas; *Clorida* (1547), *Le lagrime di San Pietro* (1539–59), *La balia* (1552), *Il podere* (1560), and his best known, *Canzoniere* (published 1711), Petrarchan sonnets to a high noblewoman, Maria d'Aragona d'Avalos.

Tansillo's roots are in the Petrarchan tradition both in the choice of verse form, the sonnet, and in the underlying sympathy his poem depicts between the state of mind of the narrator and the emotional atmosphere of the world he inhabits. In this it resembles both Petrarchan convention and the fictional sympathy between poet and landscape in Sannazaro's *Arcadia*. But this relationship is pushed to an extreme, and the portrait of nature is more haunted. The poet emphasizes in fact the sense of *superbo orror* or "arrogant horror" that the wild setting evokes and it is clearly this awe-inspiring effect he seeks. Tansillo has often been compared to the Neapolitan landscape painter Salvator Rosa, and his poetry gives more than a hint of the aesthetic of the Baroque period.

35. Tansillo: Sonnet 69
> *Sheer cliffs, bitter mountains, grisly wastes*
> *and stone naked and open to the sky*
> *which clouds with great effort scarcely climb,*
> *clouds struggling to surface in obscure air.*
> *Arrogant horror, silent woods and black*
> *poisonous caves, yawning from rotten stone;*
> *wastelands lifeless and abandoned*
> *where the wandering herds are afraid to go.*
> *Like a man who has suffered torment*

Consorzio editoriale Fridericiana, 1996); *Capitoli giocosi e satirici,* Carmine Boccia, ed. (Rome: Bulzoni, 2010); *Edizione delle opere di Luigi Tansillo* (Rome: Bulzoni, 2010); *Rime,* Tobia R. Toscano, Erika Milburn, and Rossano Pestarino, ed. (Rome: Bulzoni, 2011). For studies: Gian Piero Maragoni, *La devozione e la letteratura: Sulla poesia sacra di Luigi Tansillo* (Rome: UniTor, 1991); Erika Louisa Milburn, *Luigi Tansillo and Lyric Poetry in Sixteenth-Century Naples* (Leeds: Maney, 2003).

whose heart is anguished, out of his mind,
who wanders weeping, driven by fury
So I wander among men, and if the skies
don't change, with a voice more charged
in blacker shades I will be recognized.

THE FOLLOWING SONNET, while charming, is considerably more conventional than the preceding one. It describes a *locus amoenus*, a secluded and delightful spot where shepherds might traditionally rest at midday. Here the grove is imagined as populated by classical nymphs rather than by pastoral shepherds.

36. Tansillo: Sonnet 53
The spring is cold and crisped with waves,
soft grasses green it to the edge;
the poplar, the willow and the ash
chase Phoebus, banishing his rays.
The breeze scarcely lifts the lightest
branches, it blows so gently,
while the sun at his fiery apex
receives bright homage from the fields.
Rest by the liquid emerald,
dear nymphs, and bathe your lovely feet
wearied by the sun and racing.
Sleep will repair your weariness;
green shadows and delicious cold
and fresh water will banish thirst.

JUST AS THE FIRST SONNET by Tansillo suggested a break with the Petrarchan tradition, the following one suggests a break with the allegorical or moral conventions of medieval poetry. Ignoring the command of his father, Icarus flies too high, melting the wax that holds his wings together and then plummeting to his death. For Christian poets of the Middle Ages, as for the classical poets before them, Icarus is a negative character, a figure of excess and disobedience whose fall warns humans to keep the middle way. For Tansillo, however, Icarus' transgression is so grand in itself that it more than makes up for the price he pays. Here then is another indication in Tansillo's work that a Baroque sensibility is prevailing over a more traditional one.

Sannazaro also wrote a sonnet on the Icarus theme, which I have included above.[35]

37. *Tansillo: Sonnet 26*

> *Since I opened my wings to desire —*
> *its height is reckoned by the depth*
> *of clouds — and took proud flight*
> *toward the open sky, on fire,*
> *the son of Daedalus, his wicked end*
> *cannot deflect me. It urges me.*
> *The image of my fall, my awful death:*
> *what life could hope to equal them?*
> *The voice of my heart rings in the air*
> *"Where are you taking me?" End this*
> *mad flight. He suffers who dares."*
> *But I say never fear great ruin.*
> *Being so exalted, burn to die*
> *if heaven offers death with glory.*

ISABELLA DE MORRA

Isabella de Morra (c.1520–c.1545)[36] was born into an illustrious baronial family in a remote fief of Favale, between the regions of Calabria and Basilicata near the small river Siri (today Sinni), a dismal site that in her poems De Morra often compared to an infernal

35. Pages 182–83.

36. For her poetry, see Stortoni, *Women Poets*, 114–27; *Canzoniere: A Bilingual Edition,* Irene Musillo Mitchell, ed. and trans. (West Lafayette, IN: Bordighera, 1998). For studies: Giovanni Caserta, *Isabella Morra e la società meridionale del Cinquecento* (Matera: META, 1976); Sara Adler, "The Petrarchan Lament of Isabella di Morra," in *Donna: Women in Italian Culture* (Ottawa: Dovehouse, 1989), 201–21; Juliana Schiesari, "The Gendering of Melancholia: Torquato Tasso and Isabella di Morra," in *Refiguring Women: Perspectives on Gender and the Italian Renaissance,* Marilyn Migiel and Juliana Schiesari, ed. (Ithaca, NY: Cornell University Press, 1991); Alan Bullock, "Morra, Isabella di (1520-46)," *Oxford Reference Online* (2002) at: http://www.oxfordreference.com/view/10.1093/acref/9780198183327.001.0001/acref-9780198183327-e-2117; Emilio Russo, "Morra, Isabella di," DBI 77 (2012), online at: http://www.treccani.it/enciclopedia/isabella-di-morra_(Dizionario-Biografico).

landscape. Isabella's father, Giovan Michele, had sworn allegiance to the French and therefore was banished from the kingdom of Naples in 1527. He subsequently emigrated to the court of François I, leaving his family behind. Morra was brought up without all the cultural and social advantages that benefited other noble women; rather, she was barred from any social and literary exchange.

The fief of Favale went to Giovan's firstborn son Marcantonio, and Isabella was left in the stern tutelage of her six brothers. In spite of her brothers' surveillance, with her tutor as go-between, she became involved in a secret epistolary relationship with the Spanish nobleman Don Diego Sandoval de Castro, who was married to Donna Antonia Caracciolo of Naples. As soon as the correspondence between the two lovers was discovered, the tutor, while bearing a letter to De Morra under Don Diego's wife's name, was murdered by three of the De Morra brothers. Soon after, they beat their sister to death in a fit of rage in order "to cleanse the family honor." After De Morra's death, having ambushed and killed Don Diego, the brothers were forced to flee and find refuge in France.

De Morra left thirteen poems in all, reflecting her brief, intense and tragic life. They are perhaps the most autobiographical and artifice-free in all of Italian Renaissance women's poetry, and express in an eloquent, moving way De Morra's sense of isolation, the terror of imprisonment, the hope for a freedom that never came, and the oppression of the stark, gloomy landscape around her. For the tragic events of her life as well as for the poignancy of her poetic expression, De Morra has often been compared to a Romantic poet *ante litteram*.

Paradoxically, this cultural isolation made her a more original and spontaneous poet, in that it effectively insulated her from too strict an adherence to the Petrarchan lyric mode prevailing in Italy. Her style, which she herself describes as *"amaro, aspro e dolente"* (bitter, harsh, and grieving), is a strong, concise, direct style, which at its best reminds us of Dante, whose works she knew well. She had a special gift for poetic sound effects and for evocative imagery. Her poetry has also been compared to that of Tansillo, superficially conventional but heightened in expression and emotional tone.

38. De Morra: Sonnet 3. To Her Absent Father
Translated by JHSM

> *From a mountain height where the sea*
> *is visible, I, your daughter Isabella*
> *watch for any ship with sails full spread*
> *to bring me news of you, O father dear.*
> *But my adverse and pitiless stars*
> *decree that comfort will not reach*
> *my sad heart, hope's apostate,*
> *and turn live hope to lifeless fear.*
> *At sea I see no sail fill, no oar*
> *turn the luckless, bitter water;*
> *no breeze moves on the salt desert.*
> *I pick a fight with evil luck*
> *and grow to hate the stingy height:*
> *nothing else explains my lack.*

39. De Morra: Canzone 11
Translated by Laura Anna Stortoni and Mary Prentice Lillie[37]

> *Since, cruel Fortune, you have clipped the wings*
> *Of that belov'd desire, born from my heart,*
> *So that I live deprived of every good,*
> *I shall speak out, though rough and weak my style,*
> *And tell a little of my inner pain*
> *Caused by you only, here among these thorns,*
> *Among the uncouth ways*
> *Of people lacking reason, short of wit,*
> *Where, robbed of any help,*
> *I am constrained to live a narrow life,*
> *Placed here alone, in blind oblivion.*
> *Ah, cruel one, from childhood, those few years,*
> *You have deprived me of a loving father,*
> *Who, if he has not yet traversed the river[38]*
> *Must feel the pains of death on my account,*
> *Because my suffering doubles his grief.*

37. In *Women Poets*, 123–27.

38. Acheron, river of death.

Caesar[39] forbids him yet to send me aid —
Unheard-of cruelty!
Keeping a father's heart from aid to daughter!
And so, with loosened bridle,
O cruel Fortune, you have followed me
Straight from my mother's breast and from the cradle.
This time of life, the so-called flowery age,
I have spent here, alone, dried-out, obscure,
Like a poor hermit, sightless, weak and ill,
And knowing nothing of the gift of beauty.
Pity for me indeed is dead in you
And quenched in all those others who might loosen
And carry clean away
From its harsh jail the shadow of my soul,
Which, as unsullied snow,
Is melted by the sun, so it by you
Is melted while it sadly lingers here.
I'm not allowed the proper state of woman,
Because of you, who set me in such straits
That death would be a dearer goal than life.
The sweet remembrances of my dear father
Weep all around me. Ah, my wretched fate!
To eat the bitter fruit gathered by others,
Though I have done no wrong,
My simple innocence would breed some pity
In tigers or in serpents,
But not in you, more pitiless than Procne[40]
To her own son, Medea[41] to her brother.
Of all the goods your hand gives out unjustly,
You have deprived me, leaving me a beggar.
You prove yourself always my enemy;
In this estranging, solitary hell,
You render vain every design of mine.
If I, with justice, do complain of you,
Only to ease my mind,

39. Emperor Charles V, who exiled Isabella's father.

40. She slew her own son to punish the infidelity of her husband.

41. She killed her brother in her attempt to escape from Colchis with Jason.

Those who, in ignorance, misunderstand me,
Sharply rebuke me.
Could I have only lived in some fair city,
You would be blamed, people would pity me.
The sons, who should have been a strong support
To my poor mother in her fragile age —
Because of your unjust and wicked storms,
Live in a state of helpless poverty.
And quenched in them will be the noble spirit
Left by our ancestors down to these days,
Unless from highest heaven
Pity rains down to touch the king of France,
Who, with the scales of justice,
Weighing our wrongs, could match them
with his mercy,
In true accord with my unspotted faith.
Then I might pardon you,
And let my soul desist from its complaints,
If you could do but this —
Ah, Fortune, why can you not do this much?
And let my sighs reach to that mighty king?

GALEAZZO DE TARSIA

Born in Naples in 1520, Galeazzo died in mysterious circumstances in 1553. Most of his poetry is dedicated to his wife, Camilla Carafa, as is the first example here. One of a group of three sonnets written on the death of Camilla in 1544 or 1545, the poem imagines a reunion between the two after death. These excerpts are translated by JHM from Daniele Porchiroli, ed., *Lirici del Cinquecento* (Turin: UTET, 1958), 569–616.

40. De Tarsia: Sonnet 47
Darling, you were the sunrise
of beauty and the shield on my arm,
a strong and sturdy garden wall
that never yielded to the winter.
Then you suddenly sank in the west
and I walk on alone in the dark
weeping, bitter, and sick with sorrow
remembering your shining hair and eyes.

You are lost to this earth; my pain
divides my heart in two;
my sorrow grows without end.
The time will come when I will have
another dawn, another sun
in you, and lie down in your lap.

THE SECOND POEM by Galeazzo de Tarsia is very much in the mood of Tansillo. It describes a wild natural scene, too tempestuous and troubled to reflect the norms of the Petrarchan tradition. What is even more striking is that the natural landscape, which traditionally reflects the poet's mood, here echoes his anger, an emotion that is seldom the subject of poetry.

41. De Tarsia: Sonnet 6
Storm tossed, bellowing, angry seas
tranquil an hour ago, placid even;
my life was like that; that rhythm
echoes my sorrows vast and deep.
The sleek hulled ships, the even tempered
nymphs desert them in this mood;
everything that made life good
for me vanishes in my anger.
I know there will come a time,
a season for joy to return,
when another fate could be mine.
But quiet nights and clear days
the sun at noon or setting
my tyrant blocks them always.

ANGELO DI COSTANZO

Angelo was born in Naples in 1507[42] into the Sanfremondo family in the *seggio* of Portanova near the "strada delli Costanzi." Nothing is known of his upbringing, but he seems to have received a solid humanist education. Angelo played a prominent role in Neapolitan politics. In 1536, along with Carlo Mormile, he represented the *seggio* of Portanova in the deputation appointed by the General

42. Paola Farenga, "Di Costanzo, Angelo," DBI 39 (1991), online at: http://www.treccani.it/enciclopedia/angelo-di-costanzo_(Dizionario-Biografico).

Assembly of the Regno to study the request made by Charles V for a contribution of 3,500,000 golden ducats for the new war against the Turks. As a vocal critic of Spanish policy, di Costanzo faced political marginalization and brief exiles in the 1540s. These frictions were exacerbated by Angelo's membership in the Accademie degli Incogniti and dei Sereni that, along with the degli Ardenti, were suppressed by Pedro de Toledo in 1547.

In 1553, following Toledo's reassignment, Angelo was among the embassy to Charles V urging the appointment of a new viceroy who would recognize the privileged relationship between monarchy and the Neapolitan nobility and defend the autonomy of the *seggi*. Di Costanzo's last recorded public office was in 1590 when he was again elected to the *seggio* of Portanova. He died in November 1591 in Somma.

Angelo joined the circle of poets around the aging Sannazaro and continued his literary activities despite the vicissitudes of Neapolitan politics. He produced the bulk of his sonnets and a comedy, *I Marcelli,* in the years 1546–47. Like Sannazaro, he produced works both in Latin and Italian. From 1527, when he first discussed his project with Sannazaro, to 1556 di Costanzo worked on his famous *Istoria del Regno di Napoli.* This eventually reached twenty volumes,[43] stretching from the death of Emperor Frederick II in 1250 to 1494. In the 1550s he retained membership in the Accademia del Lauro, where he joined the poets Giovanni Geronimo Acquaviva d'Aragona and Laura Bacio Terracina.[44] While he never collected his *Canzoniere* into a published volume, his poems accompanied those of Tansillo and Rota in the *Libro terzo delle rime di diversi illustri signori napoletani* published by Gabriele Giolito de' Ferrari in Venice in 1552, amplified and reprinted in 1555 and 1563.

43. Aquila: G. Cacchi, 1581. See *Historia del Regno di Napoli,* Walter Capezzali and P. Farenga, ed. (Aquila: Fondazione Cassa di risparmio della Provincia dell'Aquila, 2007); and *History of the Kingdom of Naples, 1250–1489,* Christopher David Costanzo, ed. and trans. (Charleston, SC: Create Space, 2016).

44. See below, readings 43–44, pp. 199–202.

The following poem[45] in the Petrarchan tradition was written on the death of his son.

42. Di Costanzo: Sonnet
   A dove immaculate and pure
   you soared again blessed spirit
   to God and left me alone and blind
   in this valley of black misery.
   Do you think of me ever? Do you
   miss the father who always loved you?
   Nothing on earth could replace you
   and nothing makes up for losing you.
   Sometimes in sleep, death's brother,
   my savaged soul buried in sorrow
   seals itself from sight and hearing;
   sometimes down from the Milky Way
   your shadow comes to comfort me
   wrapped in brightness like the day.

LAURA BACIO TERRACINA

Most of what we know about the life of Laura Bacio Terracina (1519–c.1577) is gleaned from her work.[46] Her family was originally from Brescia, and later moved to Rome; as a reward for helping the pope against the powerful Colonna family, it obtained the fief of Terracina. After moving to Naples some time in the quattrocento, the family gave allegiance to the Angevins. At the end of the century, the family was granted sovereignty over the territory of Vatio or Bacio, from which came the double name Bacio Terracina.

Bacio Terracina was a prolific writer, publishing nine volumes of poetry between 1548 and 1561. Early in life, she became a member of the Accademia degli Incogniti under the name of Febea. Her two-year (1545–47) membership in the Academy gave her valuable contacts with Neapolitan intellectuals, which in some cases she kept for the rest of her life. Among the poets and scholars she was in touch

45. From Achille Gallo's editions of the *Canzoniere* in *Poesie italiane e latine e prose;* and *Giunte alle rime del Costanzo* (Palermo: Gallo, 1843).

46. This introduction is based on Stortoni, *Women Poets,* 104–7.

with were the lyric poets Luigi Tansillo,[47] Anton Francesco Doni, and Lodovico Domenichi. The latter edited her volume of *Rime*,[48] which had great immediate success and gave her considerable renown as a wise and moral poet. This first book of poetry, a collection of lyrics still within the Petrarchan tradition, was so successful that it was reprinted five times in the cinquecento and twice in the seicento.

Her second book of poetry, appropriately called *Rime seconde*, was published in Florence in 1549, and was not as successful as the first. Her third, *Discorso sopra tutti i primi canti di Orlando Furioso*, was immensely popular however, capitalizing as it did on Ariosto's fame and acclaim. She later published a few more collections of poetry, all conveniently entitled *Quarte rime* (1550), *Quinte rime* (1552), and *Seste rime* (1558). For the most part these collections contain occasional and encomiastic poems — which were particularly successful due to their topicality — as well as some moralistic compositions.

Late in life, the poet married her relative Polidoro Terracina. In 1561, she published in Naples some elegiac stanzas, *Sovra tutte le donne vedove di questa nostra città di Napoli*, in which she reflects on the transitory nature of human affections and on the vanity of life, and comments on the state of widowhood in her time. She lived in Rome between 1570 and 1572, towards the end of her life, as attested by sonnets addressed to cardinals gathered there for the election of Pope Gregory XIII. Her last volume, which was not printed, contains poems imbued with mystical religious feelings.

We have selected a famous sonnet that shows Terracina's concern with the political state of Italy in her times, as well as her desire for moral and political change. We also present the best-known stanzas from Canto 37 of her *Discorso*. Both selections are taken from Stortoni, *Women Poets of the Italian Renaissance*, 108–13.

43. Bacio Terracina: Sonnet
> *I see the world astray, I see it foolish,*
> *I see that every virtue is abandoned*

47. See above, readings 35–37, pp. 189–92.

48. Venice: Giolito, 1548.

And that the Muses stand in low regard,
So that my talent is as good as buried.[49]
I see the thoughts of friends turned all to hatred
And envy; everywhere I see the good
Betrayed with ill intent by wicked people,
And heaven turned averse, to our destruction.
No one has firm respect for common good,
But all think only of their own advancement,
While every heart is filled with mundane thoughts.
And seeing this, my heart is full of hate;
So much, that from disgust, I'd rather be
Either without my eyes, or the world blinded.

44. Bacio Terracina: Commentary on the Beginning of all the Cantos of Orlando Furioso

Dedication to Veronica Gàmbara

Were there more women here on earth like you
To put a halt to those too many writers
Who, unrestrained, publish against us women
Much cruel writing, filled with bitter venom:
Then might our names reach oriental shores
Our names and fame, adorned with well-earned honors.
But since we have not ventured to oppose them,
They hold our writings in too low esteem.

Canto 37

I can't believe that those industrious writers
Have written so much blame, so little praise
Of us, that all the world is so convinced
That no one can prevail against their frauds,
For they have set our good work to one side,
And spread evil report on every hand.
Ah, had they only performed one good deed
So that we could acquire some other gift![50]

---

49. Matthew 25:25.

50. The verses in Roman type correspond to Ariosto's verses in the first octave of Canto 37 of *Orlando Furioso*.

Because, if by themselves they had been able,
These women, to produce much more good writing,
Male writers would have not been silent,
Hiding feminine talent as a wrong.
But since today we must go beg for aid
From these male writers, just for our poor living,
They have become so heated in their writing,
Since nature gives no gifts without great labor.

If only women would give up their needles,
Their thread and cloth, and would take up their studies,
I think, then, they could wound you, o male writers,
More than the Carthaginians hurt the Romans.
But since few women have done this, so little
True fame has garlanded our heads with laurel.
Not many women take the pains I speak of,
To labor night and day and never rest.

And therefore do not cease, gifted women,
To launch your ships of talent on the ocean![51]
Forget your needles, make yourselves more eager
To labor frequently with pen and paper.
Thus you can win as glorious a fame
As men of whom I bitterly complain.
And also be attentive to your reading
With highest diligence and long endurance....

Let us devote ourselves so totally
To art and to the freeing of our tongues
That we will not be silenced to the point
Of ceding victory to men's productions.
And let us free ourselves from servitude
But following holy, life-supportive reading.
If only we had devoted ourselves to studies
That make our mortal aptitudes immortal!

---

51. A reference to Dante, *Paradiso* 2 on the perils of writing.

TORQUATO TASSO
Though most often associated with the northern courts and with
Rome, Tasso was a native of the Regno.[52] He was born in Sorrento
in 1544 while his father Bernardo was campaigning in Piedmont
with his patron Ferrante, the prince of Sanseverino. He was in
fact repeatedly absent during Torquato's early childhood. In 1547
Viceroy Pedro da Toledo attempted to introduce the Inquisition in
Naples, provoking a violent uprising.[53] Representing the insurgents,
Sanseverino brought his secretary, Bernardo, to Augsburg to confer
with Emperor Charles V. In 1548, Bernardo returned to Sorrento and
in November 1551 the Tasso family moved to Naples. But in 1552,
Sanseverino and his retinue were proclaimed traitors, and all their
property was confiscated. Nonetheless, they continued to intrigue
for a military invasion of Naples against the Spanish —Tasso at Henri
II's court in Paris and Sanseverino at Suleiman the Great's in Istanbul.
These efforts failed, and Bernardo moved to Rome, barred from
his family by the decree of exile. Meanwhile Torquato had begun
his schooling at a Neapolitan convent under the Jesuit Giovanni
d'Angeluzzo until summoned to Urbino by his father who, though
impoverished and a fugitive, was well connected.

Torquato continued his education at Urbino under the best
humanist masters, with the ducal heir, Francesco Maria II della
Rovere, as one of his schoolmates. In 1559 he began composing
his chivalrous epic *Rinaldo*. In 1561 Torquato gave up law school
at Padua and began his studies in philosophy and rhetoric at the
university of Bologna. From 1565 he served as court poet to the Este
family in Ferrara, often traveling with various members of the family
on official business. During these years Tasso began to publish love
poetry, the *Discorsi dell'arte poetica,* dramas including the pastoral play
Aminta, and his epic *Gerusalemme liberata.*

52. For general introductions see *Rinaldo*, Max Wickert, ed. and trans. (New
York: Italica Press, 2017), xi–xiii, xl–xlv. See also Canepa, "Literary Culture,"
433–34.

53. See chapter 1, reading 12, pp. 93–99.

By the 1570s he was moving frequently between princely courts in Ferrara, Mantua, Urbino, and Turin, with a mysterious side trip back to Sorrento to visit his sister. In 1579 he returned to Ferrara where his increasingly erratic behavior led Duke Alfonso II to confine him for seven years in Sant'Anna Hospital. In 1587 he was released into the custody of the Gonzagas of Mantua. He spent the remainder of his life wandering through Italy, much admired but impoverished. His late travels included a stay in Naples, where he met his future biographer Giovan Battista Manso and the composer Carlo Gesualdo. Tasso died in Rome in 1595 at the monastery of Sant'Onofrio on the Gianicolo, just before Pope Clement VIII was to name him poet laureate.

Tasso never seems to have left behind his memories of Naples and its bay, and in his *Rinaldo* he used it as a magical background for one of his hero's many adventures. The following selection is taken from the episode of the palace of the queen of Naples in Canto 7. It evokes the natural beauties and antiquities of the Bay of Naples, Posillipo, Pozzuoli, Baia and its fabled frescoes and may even refer back to the golden days Tasso's father spent among his fellow humanists and literati at the court of Vittoria Colonna on Ischia.[54] It has been excerpted from *Rinaldo*, translated by Max Wickert.[55]

45. Tasso: Rinaldo, Canto 7
> *On the third day, with the sun about to gain*
> >*the mid-point twixt its east- and westward door,*
> *they saw afar the blue Tyrrhenian main*
> >*with placid wavelets strike the tranquil shore*
> *and found themselves within a blossoming plain*
> >*of such unnumbered smiling hues and more*
> > >*that its fair face, decked with such grace and art,*
> > >*might well have ravished both my soul and*
> *heart....*

> *Citron, acanthus, lily, crocus here*
> >*with swelling buds adorn the verdant lea,*
> *along with blooms that nowhere else appear*

54. See above, pp. 28–29.

55. New York: Italica Press, 2017, 199–213.

but in this place by Nature's kind decree.
Through them with rustlings that delight the ear
  a limpid stream meanders toward the sea
      over corals branching on its golden floor
      than which all Thetis holds no richer store.

No oaks or firs, beeches or pines here rise,
  but myrtles, laurels, trees of slender girth
from the hot rays of the unclouded skies
  shelter with their fresh verdant locks the earth.
Here even in hardest hearts all rudeness dies,
  and gay-plumed birds engender pleasant mirth,
      flitting from branch to branch in amorous play,
      each answering each in a soft roundelay.

This is Posillipo, where Nature excels
  herself, astonished by what she can do,
where Chloris in perpetual blossom dwells
  and fair Pomona never fades from view;
where dancing Graces weave their deathless spells
  accompanied by Love and Venus, who
      from ancient Cyprus to this place have come
      as to a worthier, more beloved home....

They climbed the regal staircase, which was all
  fashioned of living alabaster stone,
and reached a spacious, well-proportioned hall
  that overlooked the whole Tyrrhenian zone.
On all four sides fine casements, wide and tall,
  opened where first and last daylight is shown,
      and northward toward Boreas and again
      where Auster shakes his hoar head crowned with rain.

A shrine stood raised in that hall's center, made
  of shining gold with jewelry inlay,
on which a lady's picture was displayed,
  incomparably fine in every way.
Rare, godlike charms the painter there portrayed —
  kind brow, bright eyes, dark lashes soft and gay,
      a kind and chaste smile on a candid face
      seeming to welcome all with pleasant grace....

On all four walls, more images were hung
of varying persons, next each window sill,
diverse in sex and look, both old and young
diversely clad, depicted with such skill
as to Apelles might of old belong
or as Salviati[56] now commands who still
with bold pen and bright hues makes Nature keep
in her own bounds and other painters weep.

But when the knights had at full length admired,
sating their gazes with repeated view,
those works, and with delight that never tired
the hall's great treasures one by one run through,
they turned unto their escort and inquired,
for she was still standing between them, who
it was whose image the high altar crowned
and whose the panels hanging all around....

When the exquisite wines had quenched their thirst
and their importune hunger had been fed,
and their gaze fell on fine carpets interspersed —
the table cloth being off — by golden thread,
then she who of these ladies seemed the first
looked blithely at the errant knights and said:
"Dear Sirs, the time has come for you to know
the truth for which you asked a while ago.

Naples, which lies quite near here on the sea,
in olden times was ably governed by
a queen endowed with every quality
that mind or soul could be ennobled by,
but none throughout the world in courtesy
could match her, for she valued it so high
that she excelled each woman and each man
known for that virtue since the world began.

---

56. Florentine painter (1510–63). See Iris Cheney, "De Rossi, Francesco, detto il Salviati," DBI 39 (1991), online at: http://www.treccani.it/enciclopedia/de-rossi-francesco-detto-il-salviati_(Dizionario-Biografico).

She, much desiring that her courteous ways
should by unending fame be crowned,
so that in death, even as in life, her praise
for noble courtesy should still resound,
by potent sorcery — and in those days
few who could match her in that art were found —
raised up this hill-top palace for divine
Courtesy's monument and hallowed shrine.

She named the place you visit now the Inn
of Courtesy. Moreover, it was she
who had that splendid image placed within
the spot where now it stands for all to see.
She then had painted all who had ever been
renowned for courtesy, or soon would be,
and had their portraits hung to deck each wall
facing the altar that commands the hall....

GIORDANO BRUNO

Born in Nola in 1548, Giordano was educated in Naples at the Augustinian *Studium*. He entered the Dominican Order at San Domenico Maggiore in 1565. Forced to leave the Regno in 1575 because of his unorthodox teaching on topics ranging from astronomy and architecture, to philosophy and theology, to dreams and metaphysics, he wandered through Europe for many years. Returning to Venice in 1592 in the hopes of securing an academic position, he was turned over to the Roman Inquisition and finally burned at the stake on February 17, 1600 in the Campo de' Fiori where he statue now stands. Bruno is the author of many works — astronomical, other scientific, and literary.

Bruno wrote *The Candlebearer (Il Candelaio)* in Paris in 1582.[57] Full of magic, sexual ambiguities, and social satire, it is set in Naples, in the *seggio* of Nido in and around the infamous Cerriglio Tavern, also the setting of Giambattista Della Porta's *Tabernaria*. Bruno dedicated the play to an unknown Lady Morgana. The following excerpt is from Beecher, *Renaissance Comedy*, 336–38.

57. See Canepa, "Literary Culture," 439–40; Donald Beecher, ed. and trans., *Renaissance Comedy: The Italian Masters* 2 (Toronto: University of Toronto Press, 2009), 329–34.

46. Bruno: The Candlebearer (Il Candelaio)

Prologue: The Book To Those Who Drink From the Caballine Fount

All ye who suck like babes at the breast
Of the Muses and slurp their rich pottage with glee,
Turn your hearts to my plight and your ears to my plea,
And hearken, I entreat you, to my modest request.

I ask, beg and plead for a laud or encomium,
A motto, a hymn, a brief line I implore
To hide my behind or to send well before
My happy return to my pa and my mum.

Alas my desire for sartorial elegance
Is bound to be thwarted and like Bia, I know,
I'll go naked and flagrant in doing my penance.

My prick and my anus to my lady I'll show,
Like good father Adam when still in his manse
Covered only in innocence a shod he did go.

Yet these rags as I beg at my back I hear
The swift hooves of the posses of critics draw near.

To Lady Morgana B
His Ever Honored Lady

And I, to whom shall I dedicate my *Candelaio*? To whom, oh great destiny, would you have me offer my sprightly paranymph, my fine chorus leader? To whom shall I address what has, through Sirius's celestial influx, during these most sweltering hours and most searing so-called dog days, was made to rain down in my brain by the fixed stars, being showered upon me by the fair fireflies of the firmament, been instilled in my mind by the decans of the twelve signs, and blown into my inner ear by the seven wandering lights? Towards whom has it turned? I ask. Whom does it face? On whom has it set its sights?

On His Holiness? No. On His Imperial Majesty? No. On His Serenity? No. With His Highness, Most Illustrious and Reverend Lordship? No. No. No. By my faith, it will be no prince or cardinal, king, emperor or pope that shall take this candle from my hand in this most solemn offertory. It is yours by right, so it comes to you; and you will either place it in your cabinet or stick into a candleholder, oh my superlatively learned, wise, beautiful and generous Lady Morgana…

Argument and Ordering of the Play

There are three principal matters woven together in the present comedy: the love of Bonifacio, the alchemy of Bartolomeo, and the pedantry of Manfurio. However, for a distinct understanding of these subjects, a reasoned explanation of their ordering, and evidence of the artifice of this text, we will present first, of himself, the insipid lover, second the sordid miser, third the pompous pedant. Of which the insipid one lacks neither sordidness nor pomposity, the sordid one is equally insipid and pompous, and the pompous one is no less insipid and sordid than he is pompous.

★ ★ ★

CHAPTER 4: URBAN PLANNING
by Charlotte Nichols

ALFONSO I RENEWS THE CITY

Alfonso I immediately set an ambitious agenda of restoration and renewal following his victory over the Angevins in 1442, in keeping with a victor's customary pattern of projecting power through visible urban transformation. He first repaired the wartime damage to the city walls [Fig. 4] and to the Angevin royal residence of Castel Nuovo. Antonio Beccadelli (called Il Panormita),[1] the Sicilian humanist, poet, and political intermediary at the Aragonese court, summarizes in his biography the king's other accomplishments with regard to gates, aqueducts, fountains; the clearing, repaving, and widening of streets; the draining of marshes east of the city; and the initiation of new defensive wall construction. Alfonso improved roads from his fortress-residence of Castel Nuovo eastward to the new commercial center of the city previously established by the Angevins at the Piazza del Mercato and west from Castel Nuovo along the coast to Castel dell'Ovo. Alfonso also planned to found an eponymous city ("Alfonsina") on the ruins of the ancient Roman coastal town of Bivona in southwestern Calabria.[2]

The following passage is found in Panormita's biography of Alfonso I (1455), *De dictis et factis divi alphonsi* (Naples: n.p., 1585), 42, c.61, cited in Ottavio Morisani, ed., *La letteratura artistica a Napoli* (Naples: Fausto Fiorentino, 1937), 27; and here translated from the Latin by Anne Laidlaw. Beccadelli's work was also translated into Catalan.

47. Panormita: From the Biography of Alfonso I

He restored the most beautiful pier of the Neapolitan harbor, which had been breached in many places; he cleaned out and rebuilt the aqueducts; he restored the ancient fountains and built several new ones; he rerouted the public water sources — in large part diverted for a long time — into the channel of the aqueduct; he paved with black basalt the city

1. See above, pp. 19–21.

2. Figliuolo, "Sulla fondazione." For an overview of urban planning in Naples, see Anna Giannetti, "Urban Design." For aqueducts and underground water channels, see De Divitiis, "Subsoil," 195–201.

Fig. 5. I Ponti Rossi. From Raccolta di vedute del regno di Napoli e suoi contorni disegnate al vero. *Rome: D'Atri, 1850.*

streets, almost all rutted and pot-holed from old age and the frequent passage of vehicles, having banished the carts and vehicles from the city; and now, with the help of the gods, he is preparing, for the sake of the clarity and wholesomeness of the air, to dry out the swamps and drain the lakes.

DUKE ALFONSO'S WORKS

The following passage from Giovanni Gioviano Pontano's *De bello napoletano* (1499) is particularly illuminating with regard to the refurbishment, under the supervision of Alfonso, duke of Calabria, of the conduits and fountains within the Greco-Roman grid in the later quattrocento. Leon Battista Alberti, who had lived in Naples and whose writings on architecture were well known to Neapolitan humanists, devoted considerable attention to the urban role of water in Book 10 of his *De re aedificatoria* of 1452.[3] Pontano himself witnessed the repairing of aqueducts [Fig. 5] and the installation of fountains in the later quattrocento. For him, the use of water also had profound metaphorical associations with the mythical origins and rebirth of ancient Neapolis, as explored in the epic poem *Lepidina* of 1496.[4]

3. Alberti, *On the Art of Building*, 335–41. For Alberti, Vitruvius, and Neapolitan humanists, see De Seta, "Urban Structure," 352.

4. Hersey, *Alfonso II*, 18–21.

There were evidently serious issues of drainage along the down-
ward slope of the city, which Pedro da Toledo rectified in the following century.[5] This laudatory excerpt from *De bello napoletano,* an
account of King Ferrante's fight to maintain political hegemony, is
translated in Hersey, *Alfonso II,* 22, whose source is Giovanni Gravier,
ed., *Raccolta di tutti i più rinomati scrittori dell'istoria generale nel regno di
Napoli* (Naples: Gravier, 1769) 5:146–47.

48. Pontano: Duke Alfonso Improves the Water Supply
In our own time Alfonso, son of Ferrante, having extended
the walls toward the east and north, strengthened and
beautified that part of the city with thick walls of piperno.
But these things were only the beginning of what I
know he had in mind to do. Another sign of this one-
time magnificence, beside the walls, is the river that was
brought into the city by stone pipes. The ancient city was
built over these, and these pipes and open conduits were
placed under the main streets and brought to the individual
squares into which the whole city was once divided. Then
wells were erected which drew water for each quarter.
From these conduits the water went to the further parts of
the city, not only to wells in the houses of the nobles, but
also to the fountains in the quarters bordering on the sea.
The conduits and tunnels were wide and hollow, and their
course was not at all straight. This caused the water to splash
frequently, and made it healthier. The water rumbled like a
rocky river, a work of great antiquity, and an outstanding
testimony to the original glory of Naples.

Summonte's passage highlights the accomplishment of Alfonso,
duke of Calabria, who succeeded as King Alfonso II in 1494. He
served his father, Ferrante I, as the supervisor of many ambitious
royal urban projects, one of which was to continue the project of
fortification, begun by Alfonso I, to the east of the pre-existing
Angevin walls. From a coastal point near the church of Sta. Maria
del Carmine and the Porta del Mercato, the walls built from the later
1480s on continued uphill past San Pietro ad Aram, and then towards

5. Strazzullo, *Edilizia,* 50.

Fig. 6. Castel Capuano and new Aragonese walls. From Baratta Plan (1670).

the Castel Capuano: the ducal residence that would be newly enclosed by this system [Fig. 6]. The wall, made of *tufa* covered by the local *piperno* stone, continued further uphill to the church of San Giovanni a Carbonara, where it joined the extant Angevin walls running east-west. The new eastern wall was bordered by a moat, with wooden bridges facilitating entrance through the three gates on this side. The shift east meant that previously open property was bisected and built on within the expanded boundaries.

The project, with which the Tuscans Giuliano da Maiano and Francesco di Giorgio have been associated, was interrupted by the French invasion of 1495 and resumed a few years later, as documented below. The passage from Summonte's letter of 1524 is found in Nicolini, *L'arte napoletana*, 69–70, lines 475–511. Translated by CFN. Latin phrases are italicized and translated by JHM.

49. Summonte: On Duke Alfonso's City Walls
In our times the Signor King Alfonso II of beloved memory was dedicated to building and the cupidity to do great things, which, if iniquitous fortune had not robbed him so soon of his throne, without a doubt he would have adorned this city to the highest degree. *He had it in mind to bring a distant river through great aqueducts into the city;* and completing the grand walls of the city, in good measure already done.

PORTA CAPUANA

As an arresting embellishment to the rebuilt eastern walls of the city, the Porta Capuana (1485–92/94) received much attention from contemporary writers, including Summonte. They attribute the gate to Giuliano da Maiano, who seems to have been involved as well with the construction of the wall system before his death in 1490. Distinguished in Florence as a follower of Michelozzo, Giuliano arrived in Naples c.1485 at a time when Lorenzo de' Medici was deploying artists under his patronage to reinforce Aragonese fealty. The Porta Capuana stands adjacent to Castel Capuano, the residence of the dukes of Calabria, which was renovated by Duke Alfonso and newly enclosed by the wall. Sandwiched between two guard towers of the wall system, the gate takes the form of a single barrel vault flanked by fluted Corinthian columns supporting a flat entablature. The trophies praised by Summonte fill the marble relief outlining the arch on its extra-urban side. Lost is an attic relief depicting Ferrante II.[6]

The gate [Fig. 7] is on axis with the main decumanus of the city, now the Via Tribunali. The inland road to Rome lay outside of it. The duke's entourage would also have proceeded from the Castel Capuano through the Porta Capuana to Alfonso's new villa retreat at Poggioreale, discussed below.[7] Summonte tells us the following in his letter of 1524 (68, lines 330–33, translated by CFN):

6. Hersey, *Alfonso II,* 56.

7. Readings 69–71, pp. 240–46.

Fig. 7. Porta Capuana. Photo: Italica Press

50. Summonte: Giuliano da Maiano Designs Porta Capuana
Among these works… are even some of the better designs;
so it is for the gate of this city, known as the Porta Capuana,
all marble with sculpted trophies and arms.

GIORGIO VASARI, with his overt pro-Tuscan agenda, lauded Giuliano's contribution to the Neapolitan cityscape in his *Lives* several decades later. He praises the trophies of the Porta Capuana as well and cites the riches bestowed on Giuliano da Maiano by the surely grateful King Ferrante. The following passage is found in Vasari, 1:395.

51. Vasari: On Giuliano da Maiano's Porta Capuana
Giuliano also wrought the decorations of the Porta Capuana, making therein many varied and beautiful trophies; wherefore he well deserved that great love should be felt for him by that king, who, rewarding him liberally for his labors, enriched his descendants.

THE WESTERN WALLS

Notar Giacomo tells us that in September 1499, when the Regno was once again briefly under Aragonese control, King Federico began construction of new walls on the western side of the city, beyond the extant Angevin walls, which were demolished. They ran downhill from the zone of the Angevin Porta Reale (near the Piazza Gesù), enclosing the great complex of Monteoliveto (now Sant'Anna dei Lombardi) to the great consternation of the monks whose orchards were split by the construction.[8] The walls then stretched further south along what would later become the Via Toledo and terminated at Castel Nuovo. As the younger brother of Alfonso II, who had supervised the construction of the eastern walls as the duke of Calabria, Federico must have felt compelled to complete the full circuit of the city as initially projected to achieve real and symbolic closure. The king also rebuilt the defenses of Castel Nuovo that had been destroyed during the French invasion of Charles VIII in 1495.

8. Strazzullo, "La Fondazione," 108, 111 n. 22.

Notar Giacomo would have personally witnessed the wall construction. The following observation is found in his *Cronica di Napoli,* Paolo Garzilli, ed. (Naples: Stamperia Reale, 1845), 229. Translated by CFN.

52. Notar Giacomo: Naples' New Walls

...September 1499... In that month and year the walls of the city of Naples were begun, beginning at the Porta Reale and running all the way to the Castel Nuovo.

PEDRO DE TOLEDO'S URBAN RENEWAL

Don Pedro de Toledo arrived in Naples in 1532 as the viceroy of Charles V, the Spanish Hapsburg monarch. He overtly manifested his control — as had his Angevin and Aragonese predecessors — by immediately cleaning up the streetscapes. He paved streets and removed porticoes, shacks, and stalls. His biographer, Scipione Miccio, justified their purging as a means of preventing the criminal activities encouraged by such structures. Clearing them away also served political purposes by denying the local populace and their *seggi* places to gather. Don Pedro's efforts had immediately visible results also in the form of increased daylight on the constricted city streets. The viceroy received Charles V in Naples in 1535.

The following passage comes from a biography of Don Pedro written c.1600 by Scipione Miccio, "Vita di Don Pedro de Toledo," *Archivio storico italiano* 9 (1846): 18, cited by Strazzullo, *Edilizia,* 8–9. Translated by CFN.

53. Scipione Miccio: De Toledo's Street Renewal

And because in the city there were many porticoes, almost dark caverns, where at night delinquents assaulted the unsuspecting poor, he [Don Pedro] determined to knock them all to the ground... for the same reason he determined to take away the tables and counters of the artisans, which obstructed public piazzas, and concealed misdeeds at night.

Another project requiring Don Pedro's immediate attention was the improvement of the defense system of walls around the city, an initiative that King Ferdinand the Catholic had declared of paramount

Fig. 8. New Spanish bastions on the north and west. From Donato Bertelli, Napoli (1570).

importance on winning Naples in 1503.[9] The east-west Angevin walls on the northern side of the city were also to be reinforced with polyhedral bastions. Begun by 1534, Don Pedro's walls — some of which were 8.5 meters high — extended west uphill from the current Piazza Dante, where a new Porta Reale (also Porta Toledo) was placed [Fig. 8], to the present Stazione Cumana, and then traversed southwest across Monte Sant'Erasmo in sections because of the craggy slope beneath the Certosa di San Martino. A second tract enclosed the rocky zone of Pizzofalcone (Mont'Echia) along the coast (Chiatamone) and extended a short way west just inland.[10]

The gate called Porta Romana mentioned by Pietro Antonio Lettieri, surveyor for Pedro de Toledo, is particularly significant because it signaled the viceregency's westward focus. The main portal of Don Pedro's new viceregal palace, the Palazzo Vecchio (reading 76), started in 1548 by Ferdinando Maglione (Manlio) at the base of the Via Toledo, faced the street (now the Via Chiaia) begun in 1540 that lead to the Porta Romana. Through it one accessed the coastal roads recently developed

9. Strazzullo, *Edilizia*, 5.

10. Muto, "Urban Structures," 37.

to improve access to Gaeta and, ultimately, Rome.[11] This area was also the fashionable location for villa retreats, including Don Pedro's.[12]

Lettieri's description of c.1560 is found in Lorenzo Giustiniani, *Dizionario geographico – ragionato del Regno di Napoli* (Naples: V. Manfredi, 1797–1805) 6:388, and translated in Anna Giannetti, "Urban Design and Public Spaces," 88–92.

54. Tommaso di Catania: De Toledo Extends the Western Walls
The work started from the closed Porta di San Giovanni a Carbonara and the piperno tower behind the monastery, turning to the church of Sta. Maria di Costantinopoli, turning to the monastery of San Sebastiano delle Monache, and turning again to continue upward toward Monte Sant'Erasmo, where there is the beautiful gate called Porta Reale Nuova or Toledo. There are plans to continue the walls up to the Castel Sant'Elmo. From the area of Chiaia begins a new portion of the walls with another gate called Porta Romana located just below the house and garden of the prince of Stigliano, continuing toward Castel Sant' Elmo. Another portion of the walls continues toward Castel dell'Ovo, including the area called Ecclesia and Sta. Lucia, reaching toward Castel Nuovo.

Don Pedro created a nexus of intersecting roads on the western side of Naples, the most well-known of which is the Via Toledo [Fig. 9]. Developed in the 1540s, it ran north-south — in opposition to the east-west decumani of the ancient city center — and represented the general development of the western sector of the city in contrast to the eastern orientation of the late fifteenth-century expansion under Ferrante I. The wide street was outside of the earlier Aragonese wall system, but within the new walls built under Don Pedro. A new gate, the Porta Reale, was built uphill at the northern end of the street

11. The Porta Romana was strategically placed adjacent to the villa built by Giovanni Francesco Carafa di Stigliano, a powerful Neapolitan aristocrat, and expanded by his son Luigi, an ally of the viceroy. Don Pedro had developed new roads along the coast in the opposite direction towards Sorrento as well.

12. See below, reading 75, pp. 250–51.

Fig. 9. Via Toledo (67 on plan). From Antoine Lafréry, Napoli (1566).

(now Piazza Dante), and the new viceregal palace at the foot of the Via Toledo served as a terminus for the street at the southern end. Nobles were, moreover, encouraged to build near the residence along the Via Toledo as a demonstration of fealty.[13]

The street has been described as an axis delineating old and new Naples, with the grid of the venerable Angevin–Aragonese city to the east and, to the west, Don Pedro's expansion in the direction of the hill of Monte Sant'Erasmo, Pizzofalcone, and the coast. The viceroy developed a regularized street grid west of the Via Toledo in which to house the thousands of soldiers present in Naples, called the Spanish Quarter. Looming high above is Castel Sant'Elmo (formerly Belforte), a medieval fortress that was redesigned under Don Pedro's aegis.

GIOVANNI TARCAGNOTA was born north of Naples in the seaside town of Gaeta and resided for many years in Venice. A translator of Petrarch and an historian, he wrote *Del sito et lodi della città di Napoli* (Naples: Giovanni Maria Scotto, 1566) in the form of a dialogue. The following passage is found in Tarcagnota's *Del sito*, 27t, cited by Morisani, 75. Translated by CFN.

13. Hernando Sanchez, "Nation and Ceremony."

55. Giovanni Tarcagnota: Via Toledo and Other New Roads
We know that Don Pedro da Toledo, wishing to enclose the monte of Sant'Hermo [Erasmo] within the city, expanded the ancient wall, and, demolishing Porta Reale, which was at the head of the street of Nido near Sta. Chiara, transferred it to where we see it now at the head of his street that he calls Toledo. This street, which was previously outside the city, now is inside....

IN 1545 DON PEDRO put Ferdinando Magliano (Manlio), his Iberian building superintendent and urban planner, in charge of approving all construction materials (including those for sculpted or painted embellishment), the pricing of materials, fixing workers' salaries, and licensing. This decree is found in the Archivio di Stato di Napoli, *Collaterale, Curiae*, 10:251v-253, cited by Strazzullo, *Edilizia*, 13–15. Translated by CFN.

56. Don Pedro's Decree Regulating New Construction, c.1545
Because we believe that in royal structures, which are presently underway in this magnificent and most faithful city of Naples, some things have been abused and presently are being abused to the grand detriment of those royal structures, and little serving your kingly majesty, we have thought and deliberated to prevent every type of fraud and abuse to make the following ordinances:

Firstly, that no part of any work site, whether of wood, piperno, marbles, sculpture, or pictures, should be contracted without the intervention of the architect named by Your Excellence for all the buildings of the Royal Court....

Giovanni Tarcagnota wrote his *Del sito et lodi della città di Napoli* c.1566 for the stated purpose of recording the many changes to the urban fabric that had taken place under Pedro de Toledo. He relies heavily on the information provided by Pietro di Stefano in his *Descrittione dei luoghi sacri della città di Napoli* of 1560.[14] Tarcagnota, a translator of Petrarch and an historian, was born north of Naples in the seaside town of Gaeta and resided for many years in Venice.

14. Amirante, 8; Franco Strazzullo, "Un descrittore della Napoli del '500: Giovanni Tarcagnota," *Atti della Accademia pontaniana* 38 (1989): 131–40; Morisani, 73–81.

The following passage is taken from Giovanni Tarcagnota, *Del sito et lodi della città di Napoli* (Naples: Giovanni Maria Scotto, 1566); reprinted and edited by Franco Strazzullo (Naples: Banca della Provincia di Napoli, Rome, 1988), 11; and translated in Muto, "A Court without a King," 139–40.

57. *Giovanni Tarcagnota: Pedro de Toledo's Legacy*

Thirty or forty years ago these spaces were just gardens and meadows.... Everyone today knows the great change of the city. The viceroy managed to beautify it. He ordered many streets to be widened and straightened, a lot of porticos, staircases and even buildings to be demolished. People who visited it in the past could not recognize it now; however, they would surely consider it more beautiful and tidy.

VICEROY DON PERAFÁN DE RIBERA

The Spanish viceroys issued various bans during the second half of the cinquecento against private building. The areas of concern for the authorities were outside of the walls on the western side of the city, particularly on the slope beneath the Certosa di San Martino. By this period the population of Naples had surged with the increasing Spanish population; the influx of nobility lured from the feudal seats by the viceroys; and people in search of employment. The densely packed city center could not accommodate the invasion, hence the encroachment of the hillside area outside the walls. These sites also afforded fresher air and stunning views.

Don Perafan became impatient with the ongoing violations of previous bans as the following decree of 1583 makes clear.[15] Historians have interpreted this action in various ways, including a perceived threat to the agrarian economy. At the same time, restrictions forced crowding and increasingly tall structures, which in turn caused issues of sanitation. Another concern was the illegal quarrying of stone from the hillside for building material.[16] By the early seicento these types of constraints were no longer reinforced.

15. Strazzullo, *Edilizia*, 71-83.

16. Strazzullo, *Edilizia*, 80.

Franco Strazzullo, *Edilizia*, 72, published the letter from Viceroy Don Peráfan taken from *Pragmaticae, edicta, decreta, interdicta regiaque sanctiones Regni Neapolitani* (Naples; n.p., 1772), 1:311, translated here by Tania Zampini.

58. *Viceregal Decree Banning New Construction, 1583*

In recent years, and to our benefit, public announcements and bans have prohibited the erection of new buildings in the hamlets of this most pious city or on the mountain of San Martino, with the following exceptions.... At the present time, we have once again banned building construction in the aforementioned places, in the format of the previously decreed bans, [with the additional clause] that the Regia Camera be notified of any illegal building [in these areas], under penalty of fifty *once*, and any other amount previously deemed appropriate in our judgment incurred by those who have violated said bans, by the authority of which the fiscal regime will make its demands with which, in conformity with the law, transgressors must comply.

THE RELIGIOUS CONSUME CITY PROPERTY

The unflinching Spanish objective to strengthen Catholicism by making it a visually dominant force resulted in the extraordinary expansion of pre-existing monastic communities in the cinquecento. The city's population had quadrupled during the century, reaching 225,769 by 1596.[17] These inhabitants lived in a city whose walls had a circumference of about eight miles.[18] The restricted area of the city center, coupled with the aggressive development of religious orders to *"fare isola"* (to aggregate properties in order to form a single building block, Fig. 10), as advocated by the viceregency through special loopholes in real estate legislation, ultimately created a disproportionate number of churches in the city in relation to its size. In fact, the impressive monastic enclaves that many of the religious communities managed to establish in the midst of a choked urban fabric periodically incurred the hostility of an oppressed populace to the same degree that they invoked reverence.

17. Muto, "Urban Structures," 43.

18. For density figures, see Introduction, pp. 5–6.

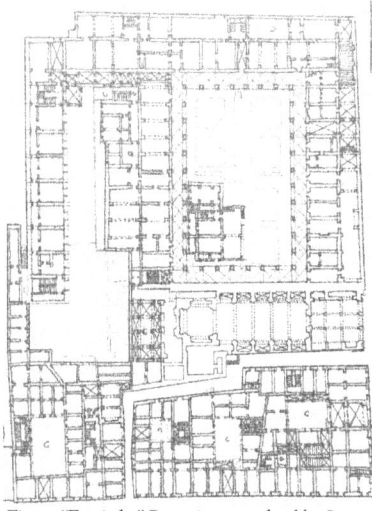

Fig. 10. "Fare isola." Properties accumulated by S. Gregorio Armeno. NACS, 327.

By the early seicento, the Spanish government recognized that the imbalance between residential and religious building practices meant that the ban against building outside the walls of the city was unsustainable. The follow- ing passage is found in *Privilegi e capitoli con altre grazie concedute alla Fedelissima Città e Regno di Napoli dalli Serenissimi re Filippo II...* (Milan: n.p., 1719), 2:82–83, cited by Strazzullo, *Edilizia,* 84, and translated by TZ.

59. *Petition to Philip II to Allow New Building Outside the Walls, c. 1600*
There have so expanded so many monasteries, churches, and other pious buildings in the city of Naples that its residential area is greatly restricted. For this reason, its citizens implore Your Highness to consider granting them license to build in hamlets and other now prohibited [construction] areas. With the tranquility now achieved under the reign of Your Highness, the population has multiplied, making it necessary for citizens to leave their birthplace and look for homes elsewhere should they not be granted such a favor. This, in turn, would consolidate the memory of Your Majesty in creating the prohibition as one to deter foreigners — who pay taxes in their own countries — from coming to cities where they live free of all charges, and not as one put in place to deprive the citizens of Naples their natural habitation.

★ ★ ★

CHAPTER 5: ROYAL & ARISTOCRATIC RESIDENCES
by Charlotte Nichols

CASTEL NUOVO

King Alfonso I's most significant act of artistic patronage was the rebuilding and embellishment of Castel Nuovo [Fig. 11, opposite], which he envisioned as the centerpiece of a modern, cosmopolitan capital city.[1] This royal project forcefully established the new ruler's hegemony and attracted attention throughout the peninsula. The imposing castle, begun by Charles I of Anjou, is prominently situated harborside, southwest of the street grid of the ancient and medieval city. Alfonso set out to rebuild the structure — severely damaged during the Aragonese–Angevin conflict — as both his primary residence and a key element of the coastal defensive system. The Majorcan Guillem Sagrera served as its *protomagister* from 1447 to 1454.[2]

The anonymous mid-quattrocento design, whose plan is trapezoidal, commingles familiar architectural elements of rounded towers and crenellation with a distinctive sloping escarpment. It was surrounded by a double moat. The king coopted the once fashionable but damaged Angevin residential area of Corregge on the city side, thus isolating Castel Nuovo in a way it had not previously been. An exotic hanging garden eventually adjoined the structure. A century later, the palaces built nearby for the Spanish viceroys supplanted Castel Nuovo's function as a royal residence, and it housed instead military personnel.

1. Other castles in the city included the Castello Belforte (later Castel Sant'Elmo) on Monte Sant'Erasmo, the Castel Capuano on the eastern side of the city near Porta Capuana, the Castel dell'Ovo on the coast below Pizzofalcone, and the Castel del Carmine at the coastal base of the eastern walls of the city. For an overview of residential design in Naples, see Gérard Labrot, "The Residence of Power," in Hall–Willette, 299–338.

2. Hersey, *Arch*, 16–18; Andreas Beyer, *Parthenope: Neapel und der Süden der Renaissance* (Munich: Deutscher Kunstverlag, 2000), 37–38; and Bianca De Divitiis, "Castel Nuovo and Castel Capuano in Naples: The Transformation of Two Medieval Castles into 'All'antica' Residences for Aragonese Royals," *Zeitschrift für Kunstgeschichte* 76 (2013): 441–47.

IN HIS *DE VARIETATE FORTUNAE* (*On the Vagaries of Fortune*) of c.1520, which chronicles the careers of the Aragonese kings, Tristano Caracciolo describes both the destruction of the castle in wartime and Alfonso's desire for a bold new structure. Caracciolo, a Neapolitan nobleman and member of Giovanni Pontano's academy of humanists, is best-known for his aristocratic perspective on Renaissance Naples.[3] The epigram attributed to Alfonso himself is quoted by Caracciolo in his *De varietate fortunae*, in Giovanni Gravier, ed., *Raccolta di tutti i più rinomati scrittori dell'istoria generale del regno di Napoli* (Naples: Gravier, 1769–72), 6:84, and translated from the Latin in Hersey, *Aragonese Arch*, 17.

60. Tristano Caracciolo: On Castel Nuovo
IF THE NAME GIVEN THIS PLACE BE OTHER THAN NEW, LET NOT
A SINGLE ONE OF ITS STONES REMAIN.

THAT ALFONSO was consciously emulating antiquity is evidenced by the following comment of Panormita, who was Alfonso's court biographer. Scholars have, in fact, noted that Vitruvius advocates the round towers and the stonework used for the exterior of Castel Nuovo.

Alfonso's attention to the binding of Panormita's copy of Vitruvius is of interest in relation to the private library housed in the castle for which he is well known. This excerpt is from Panormita's *De dictis et factis divi Alphonsi* (Naples: n.p., 1585), 36, c.44, cited by Morisani, 25, and translated from the Latin here by Anne Laidlaw.

61. Panormita: Alfonso I and Vitruvius
When he had determined to restore that famous Neapolitan fortress, he ordered the book of Vitruvius, which is titled *De architectura*, to be brought to him. The book was brought, but when Vitruvius was in front of him — it being, indeed, mine, without any decoration or binding — as soon as the king had examined it, he said that it was not fitting that this most important book, which instructed so beautifully — although we had bound it so casually — should continue to be unbound, and he ordered that it be bound by me as elegantly and as soon as possible.

3. Bentley, 276–83.

IN THE PREFACE to the second part of his *Lives*, Vasari — who was in Naples in the 1540s — includes Castel Nuovo as an example of great "disegno" by Francesco di Giorgio, along with the cathedral of Florence. He does not explain that the contributions by Francesco di Giorgio in the 1490s were limited to renovations of the outer defense system of the castle, communicating instead the impression that the Sienese architect was responsible for the entire structure. Francesco was employed by the Aragonese in conjunction with the new city walls, and c.1495 he dedicated his *Libro de architecture* and *Libro de artigliaria* to Alfonso, duke of Calabria, later Alfonso II.[4] The following passage is from Vasari 1:252.

62. Vasari: Di Giorgio as Architect of Castel Nuovo
Design grew in strength and depth; good grace was given to buildings; the excellence of that art made itself known; and the beauty and variety of capitals and cornices were recovered in such a manner, that the ground-plans of his [Brunelleschi's] churches and of his other edifices are seen to have been very well conceived... besides the great and commodious edifice that Francesco di Giorgio made in the palace and church of the duomo at Urbino, and the very strong and rich castle of Naples, and the impregnable castle of Milan, not to mention many other notable buildings of that time.

GUILLEM SAGRERA OF MAJORCA, who had designed the cathedral at Palma, made an important contribution to the interior design of Castel Nuovo, most notably in the Gran Sala or throne room (1452–57, Fig. 12). The space was directly accessed by a stairway from the main courtyard of the building, while windows on the far wall faced the harbor. A spectacular ribbed vault rising over 20 meters and punctuated by an oculus dominates the square plan. The room was evidently cherished by Alfonso, and its design serves as a reminder that the language and customs of his court were Spanish rather than Italian.[5] The walls were covered with the precious hangings prized by Alfonso, and the floor

4. De Seta, "Urban Structure," 358; and Nicholas Adams, "Castel Nuovo a Napoli," in *Francesco di Giorgio Architetto,* Franco Paolo Fiore and Manfredo Tafuri, ed. (Milan: Electa, 1993), 2:228–95.

5. In his account of the earthquake of 1456, Notar Giacomo, 97, refers to Alfonso's concern about damage to the Gran Sala.

Fig. 12. Guillem Sagrera. Gran Sala, Castel Nuovo, 1452–57. Photo: Italica Press.

paved with Hispano-Moorish tiles. Scholars speculate that the use of an oculus may have been inspired by those of Roman domical structures visible in nearby Baia.[6] The classically minded Summonte was, however, less than enthusiastic about the Sala in Castel Nuovo, as demonstrated by his *Letter* of 1524 (171, lines 469–74). Translated by CFN.

6. Arnaldo Venditti, "Presenze ed influenze catalane nell'architettura del regno d'Aragona in Napoli, 1442–1503," *Napoli Nobilissima* 13 (1974): 503–36.

63. Summonte: On Castel Nuovo's Gran Sala
    The grand room of the Castel Nuovo is indeed a great work;
    but it is Catalan, having nothing of ancient architecture.
    Your Lordship knows well that for many many years the
    only building style followed everywhere was barbarian.

ALFONSO I'S TRIUMPHAL ARCH

In a stunning tour de force of imperialist propaganda, Alfonso I commissioned two superimposed marble triumphal arches to frame the
newly relocated main entrance to Castel Nuovo [Fig. 11], inside of
which busts of the Spanish emperors Trajan and Hadrian were on display.[7] Construction began c.1452–53, and it was completed by his son
and heir, Ferrante I in 1471.[8] The gate is situated in the manner of an
ancient Roman wall system between the rounded brick towers called
Torre della Guardia and Torre di Mezzo on the castle's city facade. This
positioning has also been frequently compared to that of the classicizing
entrance to Frederick II's Castel del Monte of the 1240s in Apulia, long
part of the kingdom of Naples. The design includes four female statues
of Virtues at the top and, below, a large relief depicting Alfonso's triumphal entry into Naples on 26 February 1443 with an inscription reading
ALFONSUS REX…ITALICUS. A monumental equestrian image of the ruler
by Donatello was begun c.1453 for the upper arch, of which only the
head and neck were completed.[9] Under Ferrante I's rule, a sumptuous bronze door with scenes of the recent Aragonese triumph over the
Angevins was commissioned in 1465, along with additional sculpture
for an inner arch. The presence of such a door signals additional magnificence and the defensive nature of Castel Nuovo.

   To a quattrocento audience, the bombastic aspects of the arch echoed
the assertive dynamism of the tomb of King Ladislaus (1421) in San

7. Hersey, *Arch*, 31.

8. Hersey, *Arch*, 21–56; Beyer, *Parthenope*, 30–61. A triumphal arch was
originally planned by Alfonso for the Piazza del Duomo within the Greco-
Roman grid inhabited by the local Neapolitan aristocracy. See De Divitiis,
"Castel Nuovo," 448, for the recent bibliography.

9. See chapter 8, readings 155–156, pp. 382–84.

Fig. 13. Pisanello. Triumphal Arch, 1448–50. Museum Boijmans Van Beuningen, Rotterdam. Photo: De Agostini Picture Library / Bridgeman Images.

Giovanni a Carbonara.[10] A drawing by Pisanello [Fig. 13], which may be a preparatory study for the built arch, recalls this soaring Angevin project.[11] The more classicizing style of Alfonso's commission, together with its location facing the city, meant that the arch served as an audacious statement of dominion by the victorious Aragonese, who were continually beset with Angevin challenges to their legitimacy.[12]

The principle artists documented as involved with the arch's construction include Pere Joan of Tarragona, the Aragonese superintendent of works, and the sculptor Pietro da Milano, who arrived in Naples via Ragusa. He probably knew the Arch of the Sergii in Pula (Croatia), with which the lower arch at Castel Nuovo is frequently compared.

BARTOLOMEO FACIO DEDICATED his *De viris illustribus* (*On Famous Men*) of 1456 to Alfonso I, in whose court the humanist figured

10. The tomb's patron, Giovanna II, had named Alfonso as her heir in 1421 and then disinherited him.

11. See readings 79–81, pp. 257–60.

12. Other ambitious and status-conscious Italian rulers were aware of Alfonso's project to rebuild Castel Nuovo, such as Francesco I Sforza, engaged c.1455 in the expansion of his Castello di Porta Giovia in Milan (Hersey, *Arch*, 67).

prominently as a royal biographer and tutor. The following passage celebrating the arch is found in *De viris illustribus* (1454–55, Florence: n.p., 1745), 78, transcribed in Hersey, *Aragonese Arch*, 67, and translated here from the Latin by Anne Laidlaw.

64. Bartolomeo Facio: Alfonso's Triumphal Arch
> Alphonso built a castle with a triumphal arch, in magnificence, construction, (and) detail second to none in the whole world.

IN HIS *Lives,* Vasari notes the contributions of Giuliano da Maiano, his Tuscan compatriot, to the ongoing decoration of Castel Nuovo later in the quattrocento during the reign of Ferrante II (r. 1458–94), while erroneously implying that the Florentine Giuliano was the arch's designer as well.[13] Unremarked by contemporary observers is the unusually large size of the central relief showing Alfonso I's triumphal procession into Naples that spans the entire width of the arch [Frontispiece, Figs. 1 and 12].[14] As such, its measurements eclipse those of the ancient reliefs it recalls and introduces to the Renaissance a bold new narrative format in stone for exterior decoration. Later Neapolitan altarpieces would match its precocity. The following excerpt is found in Vasari's life of Giuliano da Maiano (1:395).

65. Vasari: Giuliano da Maiano and Alfonso's Triumphal Arch
> Working in sculpture, likewise, for the said King Alfonso, then duke of Calabria, he [Giuliano da Maiano] wrought

13. Summonte (67, ll. 313–19) attributes the arch to Francesco Laurana, also from Dalmatia, who executed a series of portrait busts for the Aragonese royals.

14. See Hersey, *Arch*, 63, for a contemporary document regarding the actual triumphal procession led by Alfonso on 26 February 1443, during which Julius Caesar recognizes Alfonso as his imperial reincarnation. He notes that the car itself was preserved as a relic in the church of San Lorenzo Maggiore until 1580. For earlier triumphal processions by conquering monarchs, see Beyer, *Parthenope*, 32–34. For the relationship of the relief's background to the tomb of Parthenope, founder of the city, see ibid., 46–51. For the political aspects of Alfonso's patronage, see Pietro Corrao, "Progettare lo Stato, Costruire la Politica: Alfonso il Magnanimo e i regni italiani," in *Il Principe Architetto,* Arturo Calzona, et al., ed. (Florence: L.S. Olschki, 2002), 23–39.

scenes in low-relief over a door (both within and without) in the great hall of the Castle [Nuovo] of Naples; and he made a marble gate for the castle after the Corinthian order, with an infinite number of figures, giving to that work the form of a triumphal arch, on which stories from the life of that king and some of his victories are carved in marble.

THE RELIEF shows the victorious king seated on a horse-drawn cart covered by a baldachin, while the entourage accompanies him on foot. Porcellio de' Pandoni, a Neapolitan member of the Aragonese court, participated in the actual procession. He names Isaia di Pisa as author of the arch; the sculptor is elsewhere mentioned in documents connected with the relief itself. By overtly linking him to both Pope Eugenius IV and Alfonso I, Porcellio underscores the artist's desirability and even the ongoing support of the papacy for the king.

Porcellio's poem entitled "Ad Immortalitatem Isaiae Pisani marmorum celatoris" ("To the Immortality of Isaia of Pisa sculptor of marbles") begins with evoking Phidias, Polykleitos, and Praxiteles. This section is translated from the Latin in Hersey, *Arch*, 46 (with his brackets), who cites Angelo Battaglini, "Memoria sopra uno sconosciuto egregio scultore del secolo XV," *Dissertazioni dell'Accademia romana di archeologia* 1 (1821), 117.

66. *Porcellio de' Pandoni: Isaia di Pisa, Sculptor of Alfonso's Triumphal Arch*
 The marvelous monument of Eugenius' tomb will be witness [to Isaia's talent]

> *And the royal arch of Alfonso;*
> *That man of triumphal virtue and strong arms,*
> *At Naples chose [Isaia] from a large group [of competitors].*

THE ARISTOCRACY BUILD *ALL'ANTICA:*
THE PALACE OF DIOMEDE CARAFA

Diomede Carafa began the ambitious rebuilding of his family residence [Fig. 14] on a decumanus (now the Via San Biagio) of the ancient city in the 1450s, the design of which befitted his status as a culturally sophisticated member of the city's — and peninsula's — cultural elite. Carafa was a Neapolitan aristocrat and an early ally of Alfonso I and later

Fig. 14. Palazzo Diomede Carafa, 1450s. Detail of main portal. Photo: Italica Press.

became Ferrante I's most trusted advisor; the king named him count of Maddaloni in 1465.[15] He was friends with Cosimo de' Medici, whose own palace in Florence was underway by 1446.[16]

The palace's siting signaled an alliance with the new Aragonese order, whose Roman imperial aspirations were complemented by the building projects by loyalists within the Greco-Roman street grid. Alfonso I would have resided in Castel Capuano while Castel Nuovo was being reconstructed, and the new building on the decumanus represented a shift away from the fashionable location of trecento Angevin residences near the Castel Nuovo in the Corregge quarter.

15. Franca Petrucci, "Carafa, Diomede," DBI 19 (1976), online at: http://www.treccani.it/enciclopedia/diomede-carafa_(Dizionario-Biografico).

16. Filippo Strozzi, long resident in Naples, commissioned a *scrittoio* for Carafa on behalf of Piero de' Medici. See Eve Borsook, "A Florentine *scrittoio* for Diomede Carafa," in *Art the Ape of Nature: Studies in Honor of H. W. Janson,* Moshe Barasch and Lucy Freeman Sandler, ed. (New York: Abrams, 1981), 91–96. See Soranzo, *Poetry and Identity,* 64–66, for the impact of Florentine literary culture on that of Naples in the 1470s.

Fig. 15. Palazzo Penna. Detail of main portal. Photo: Italica Press.

The Carafa facades are constructed of identical rectangular stone tufa blocks, suggesting the *opus isodomum* described by the Roman author Vitruvius — to whom Alfonso was devoted — in his *De architectura*.[17] The Palazzo Penna (c.1406, Fig. 15) nearby serves as an important prototype for the design. This sense of an impenetrable plane complements the linearity of the decumanus, also praised by Vitruvius, and would have contrasted meaningfully with early trecento Angevin

17. Beyer, *Parthenope*, 84–135; Bianca De Divittis, *Architettura e committenza nella Napoli del Quattrocento* (Venice: Marsilio, 2007) 43–135; idem, "Building in Local *All'Antica* Style: The Palace of Diomede Carafa in Naples," *Art History* 3 (2008): 505–22; and idem, "Subsoil," 192–93.

palaces in the neighborhood, many of which had porticoes. The portal of the Palazzo Carafa, with its flat lintel and classicizing embellishments recalls Alberti, who visited Naples. Niches intended for sculpture punctuated the façade, and busts of the patron and his wife appear at the corner of the building.

Antiquities from Carafa's vast collection, some of which had been excavated on his properties outside the city, were also on display in the palace's courtyard.[18] They included the *Protome Carafa*, a bronze equine head now attributed to Donatello, that was a gift from Lorenzo de' Medici. An ancient column with a bronze equestrian monument of Ferrante I stood at the center. It survives, albeit in an altered position. The courtyard also featured a hanging garden, enjoyed by such prestigious guests as Sigismondo d' Este. Diomede Carafa's nephew, Cardinal Oliviero Carafa, emerged as a major patron and collector later in the century.

A portion of the dedicatory inscription on the lower edge of the lintel of the exterior portal is translated here by Tania Zampini. Far from a bold classicizing inscription, it is illegible from the street. Heraldic emblems are, however, prominently displayed in the carved wooden door, and Ferrante's coat of arms were on view in the courtyard.

67. Dedicatory Inscription on Palazzo Diomede Carafa
IN HONOR OF THE KING AND HIS MOST NOBLE BIRTHPLACE.

18. Readings 155–157, pp. 382–86. See Bianca De Divitiis, "New Evidence for Diomede Carafa's Collection of Antiquities. II," *Journal of the Warburg and Courtauld Institutes* 73 (2010): 335–45. For Giuliano da Sangallo's drawings of works in Carafa collection, see idem, "New Evidence for Diomede Carafa's Collection of Antiquities. I," *Journal of the Warburg and Courtauld Institutes* 70 (2007): 106–10. The courtyard of the Palazzo Carafa features an exterior staircase and flat Catalan arches, seen also at Castel Nuovo.

THE PALACE OF ROBERTO DI SANSEVERINO

Another privileged patron and royal favorite, Roberto di Sanseverino, initiated a similarly ambitious palace construction on a site given to him by Ferrante I, for whom he had fought in the battle of Ischia and who would also name him prince of Salerno. Located at the western end of the lower decumanus, the residence was closer to the Aragonese residence at Castel Nuovo than the Palazzo Carafa.

Designed by Novèllo da San Lucano by 1470, the palace [Fig. 16] was situated near the church of Sta. Chiara and the Angevin Porta Reale in an area less densely packed than that of Carafa's neighborhood; this in turn allowed for a spacious courtyard and gardens beyond. It was distinguished by the use of diamond-shaped stones of piperno, anticipating the façade of the more well-known Palazzo Bevilacqua in Bologna by some twenty years.[19] At the end of the 1500s, the palace was converted into the church of the Gesù Nuovo, and its columned

Fig. 16. Palazzo Sanseverino, Novello da San Lucano, 1470. Now the Gesù Nuovo. Detail of façade. Photo: Italica Press.

19. Maria Ann Conelli makes connections between the stonework of the palace and the new scarps of Castel Nuovo (which have their roots in Iberian prototypes). See her "The Gesù Nuovo in Naples: Politics, Property and Religious" (Ann Arbor: UMI, 1992), 36–40. For the patronage of the Sanseverino family, see Watson, 155–58.

courtyard and vast gardens were destroyed. The distinctive façade was, however, incorporated into that of the new church.

The original palace was lauded by many including Giovanni Pontano, who declared it a *magnificam domum* (magnificent house) in chapter 7 of his treatise *De magnificentia*.[20] Pontano had previously dedicated *De principe* (1468)[21] and *De obedientia* (1470) to Roberto di Sanseverino, who died decades before *De magnificentia* appeared. Pontano evidently felt comfortable in his criticism of the patron's building practices in relation to those of Orso Orsini, count of Nola, a prominent counselor and negotiator for the Aragonese whom he praised elsewhere for his personal conduct.[22] The following passage is found in chapter 7. It is titled "Honor must be followed in making expenditures" (Tateo, ed., 178) and translated here by Frederick Booth.

68. Pontano: Palazzo Sanseverino
> When he was building a magnificent home in Naples, Roberto, the prince of Salerno, was said to have abused his people greedily and lawlessly to pay for the quarrying and transporting of stone from Lucania. On the other hand, Orso of Nola observed justice so that not even one rock was used in the buildings he erected in Nola unless it was bought for a fair price. Despite that, Roberto acquired the reputation of a generous prince, while Orso was considered rather stingy.

POGGIOREALE
Alfonso, duke of Calabria and the future Alfonso II (r. 1494–95), is best known for his *villa suburbana* at Poggioreale [Figs. 17–19], which, save for a few traces, no longer exists (1487–92; destroyed 1789). The project was part of the duke's larger plan of residential embellishment and construction on the eastern side of the city where he also transformed the Castel Capuano, long the residence of the dukes of Calabria and far removed from Castel Nuovo, into a splendid palace

20. Chapter 9, reading 164, pp. 406–40.

21. Chapter 2, reading 19, pp. 119–38.

22. Georgia Clarke, "The Palazzo Orsini in Nola: A Renaissance Relationship with Antiquity," *Apollo* 144 (1996): 44–50.

admired throughout the peninsula. He also built a small retreat called La Duchesca for his wife, Ippolita Maria Sforza, in the adjacent gardens.[23] An allé flanked by plantings led from the Porta Capuana at the eastern end of the central decumanus to the villa at Poggioreale, built *ex-novo* a few miles away; this zone was populated by recreational residences or *delizie*. The structure was damaged by the French invasion of 1528, then used as a retreat by the Spanish viceroys through the 1600s, and subsequently fell into decay.

Poggioreale is of great interest with regard to villa design and *villegiatura* generally in the late quattrocento, although studies have consistently been stymied by the lack of physical evidence.[24] The plan [Fig. 19], recorded by Baldassare Peruzzi and Sebastiano Serlio, shows a rectangular structure with corner towers and a sunken courtyard. Based on the evidence of Joampiero Leostello and others, Giuliano da Maiano of Florence has traditionally been named as the principle

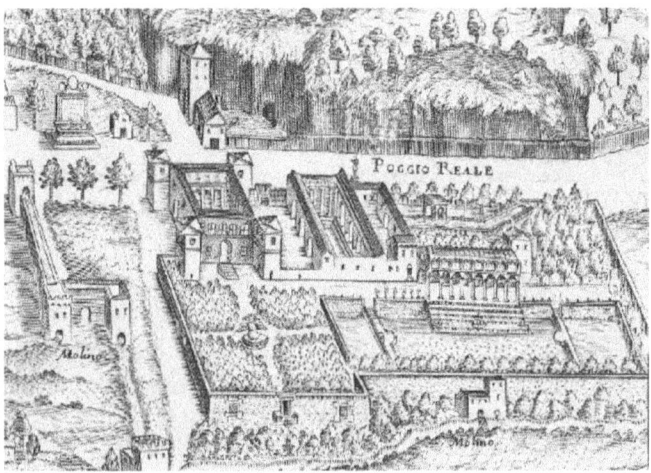

Fig. 17. Villa at Poggioreale. Alessandro Baratta, Naples (1670). Detail.

23. See De Divitiis, "Castel Nuovo," 462–71.

24. See the extensive study, with digital reconstructions, by Paola Modesti, *Le delizie ritrovate: Poggioreale e la villa del rinascimento nella Napoli aragonese* (Florence: Olschki, 2014). She includes an inventory of descriptions of the villa, 197–213.

architect *("disegnatore").*[25] A follower of Michelozzo and architect of the Florentine Opera del Duomo, Giuliano had earlier enjoyed the patronage of Lorenzo de' Medici, who, however, replaced him in 1485 with Giuliano da Sangallo as architect of Sta. Maria delle Carceri in Prato and, later, as architect of his villa at Poggio a Caiano outside of Florence. The shift in Lorenzo's preference for Sangallo in turn freed Da Maiano for other projects; he arrived in Naples by the mid-1480s, where he collaborated on the new eastern defensive walls, designed the Porta Capuana (from which one accessed the road to Poggioreale), refurbished Castel Capuano, and designed La Duchesca.

Lorenzo's tradition of lending the services of artists in his employ to his allies worked to Giuliano's great advantage in that he was given the responsibility and freedom to execute far more ambitious projects for the court of Naples than in ostensibly republican Florence. Like Lorenzo at Poggio a Caiano, Alfonso appears to have been very involved with Poggioreale in the princely tradition of participation in construction projects, surely with the input of his humanist advisors, such as Giovanni Pontano.[26] Giuliano da Sangallo, Francesco di Giorgio Martini, Fra' Giocondo da Verona, and Luca Fancelli have also been named in association with it following, or even preceding, Giuliano's death in 1490.[27]

The project is given considerable attention by Giampietro Leostello, a priest from Volterra who eventually joined Duke Alfonso's court and recorded his daily activities from 1484 to 1491. Known as the *Effemeridi,* the chronicle is written in the Italian vernacular with some Latin phrasing. The manuscript was taken by Charles VIII

25. Leostello, in Filangieri, *Documenti,* 1:132.

26. F.W. Kent, *Lorenzo de' Medici and the Art of Magnificence* (Baltimore, MD: Johns Hopkins University Press, 2004), 102.

27. See the anguished letter from Duke Alfonso to Lorenzo de' Medici about Da Maiano's replacement, transcribed in Doris Carl, "Giuliano da Maiano und Lorenzo de' Medici," *Mitteilungen des Kunsthistorischen Institut von Florenz* 37 (1993): 255. Giuliano da Maiano was rewarded for his service to the Aragonese with a tomb in the newly built church of his design, SS. Severino e Sossio.

Fig. 18. Villa at Poggioreale. Viviano Codazzi (c.1641). Musée des Beaux-Arts et d'Archéologie de Besançon. Wikimedia.

to France — whose experience of the gardens of Poggioreale are reflected in his chateau at Amboise — and now is housed at the Bibliothèque Nationale de France, Paris.[28] The details he provides range from the duke's personal habits to issues of diplomacy and patronage. In his many passages about Poggioreale, Leostello emphasizes the economic benefits of new construction, echoing the rationale for sumptuous expenditure put forth by a number of Renaissance theorists, including Alberti and Pontano. Leostello's passage celebrates the duke's far-flung munificent patronage.

It is found in his *Effemeridi delle cose fatte per il Duca di Calabria (1484–91)*, in Filangieri, *Documenti*, 1:323; and translated in Hersey, *Alfonso II*, 23.

69. Giampietro Leostello: Duke Alfonso and Poggioreale

> He greatly delighted in building, which he did in numerous lovely spots, so that he made many poor men rich, and many builders who had four or five daughters to marry off, though they had formerly been poor, were now very easily able to find husbands for these daughters... because

28. Filangieri, *Documenti*, 1:52–79; Morisani, 25–43.

of the money coming from these builders' hands from the constant construction of palaces and fine houses, such as Poggioreale, two miles from Naples, or La Duchesca, as well as many gardens and farms. Oh, where did he not build? In Calabria, in Apulia, in Gaeta, in Casa di Principe. On both sides [of Naples] he dedicated himself to this work.

THE IMPORTANCE OF POGGIOREALE within the larger context of Renaissance villa construction is underscored by its appearance in Book III (1540) of Sebastiano Serlio's *Tutte l'Opere d'Architettura et Prospettiva* [Fig. 19]. The lengthy passage and drawings are based on information conveyed by Serlio's mentor in Rome, Baldassare Peruzzi, and by the Venetian Marcantonio Michiel, who visited the site c.1510 and to whom Summonte addressed his famous letter.[29] Serlio's description and drawings are of great importance to scholars, who continue attempts to reconstruct the ambitious design of the destroyed villa.[30] His plan shows a tower at each of the four corners of the building, giving it a fortified aspect in the manner of late medieval villas. However, the plan also shows a sunken central courtyard *all'antica* surrounded by a colonnaded portico; this courtyard had an elaborate hydraulic system for the instant flooding of guests, as Serlio notes with great delight. Alluded to by Serlio are subsidiary pavillions, *a vivaio* (fishpond), extensive gardens, and the first known Renaissance nymphaeum. The freshwater supply at the villa also served the citizens of Naples.[31]

Due to the wide circulation of Serlio's treatise, the plan for Poggioreale became a point of departure for structures elsewhere in Europe, including Robert Smythson's Wollaton Hall (Nottingham,

29. See chapter 10 below.

30. See Modesti for a complete overview of scholarly research.

31. Bruce Edelstein, "'Acqua viva e corrente': Private Display and Public Distribution of Fresh Water at the Neapolitan Villa of Poggioreale as a Hydraulic Model for Sixteenth-Century Medici Gardens," in *Italian Renaissance Cities: Artistic Exchange and Cultural Translation,* Stephen Campbell and Stephen Milner, ed. (Cambridge: Cambridge University Press, 2004), 187–220.

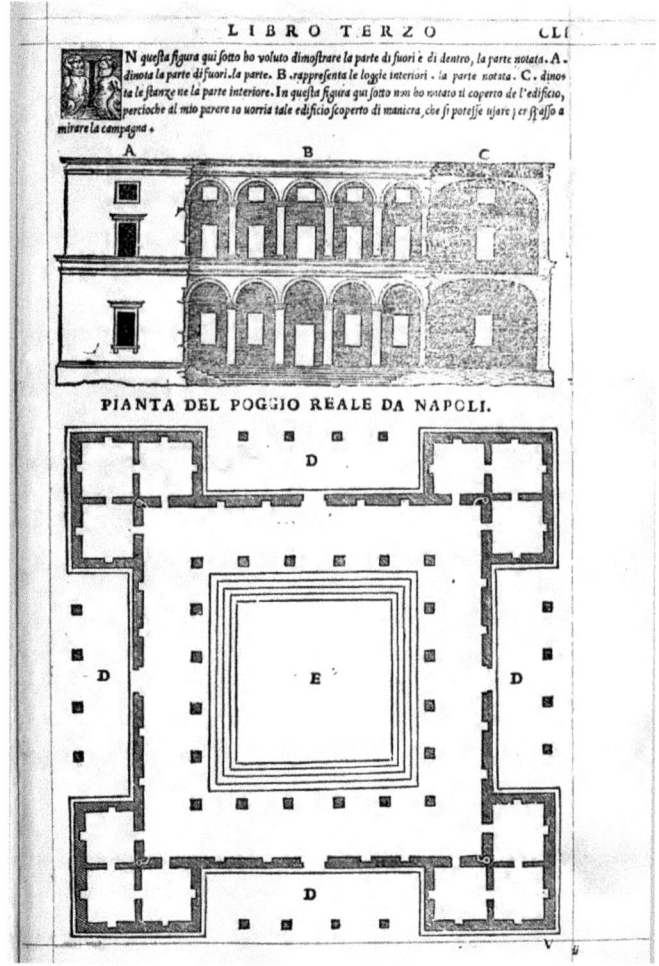

Fig. 19. Villa at Poggioreale, plan. Sebastiano Serlio, Delle antichità (1540), 3:157.

1580–88).[32] This excerpt is from Sebastiano Serlio, *Delle antichità: Il terzo libro di Sebastiano Serlio Bolognese* (Venice: n.p., 1540), fol. 121 r–

32. Deborah Howard, "Sebastiano Serlio: Influence," online at: www.oxford-artonline.com.

122v, in Serlio, *On Architecture,* Vaughan Hart and Peter Hicks, trans. (New Haven: Yale University Press, 1996), 1:240–41.

70. *Sebastiano Serlio: Poggioreale*
Of all the cities in Italy, Naples is called "noble" not only for its exceedingly noble manners, its great barons, castellans, counts, its innumerable gentlemen, and grand nobility, but also for being more blessed with gardens and places of pleasure than anywhere else in Italy. Among the many pleasant and charming spots which are outside the city there is a palace which is called Poggioreale, which King Alfonso had built for his pleasure in the time when Italy used to be happy and more united — she is now, however, unhappy because of her discords. This palace has a most beautiful shape for a modern building and is very well partitioned, such that a nobleman and his entourage could be lodged in each of the corners since there are six good rooms — not including those underground and some secret chambers. ... Of those most beautiful formal gardens with their different enclosures, the kitchen gardens, the most abundant fruits of every sort, the freshwater fish pools and rivers, the places for game fowl both large and small, the stables richly stocked with every breed of horse and of many other beautiful things, I shall say nothing because Master Marcantonio Michiel, noble patrician in this city and very well versed in architecture — who has seen much and from whom I got this and other things — discussed them at great length in a letter in Latin addressed to one of his friends.

SERLIO'S ALLUSION TO NAPLES as an earthly paradise is also reflected in the early observation of Charles VIII, almost certainly to the gardens at Poggioreale, during his invasion of Naples in 1495. Memories of Alfonso's villa evidently shaped the French king's own garden at the chateau of Amboise, to be tended by an Italian gardener named Pasella da Mercigliano. Charles' quotation is partially translated in Kent, *Lorenzo de' Medici*, 117, citing Terry Comito, "Renaissance Gardens and the Discovery of Paradise," *Journal of the History of Ideas* 32 (1971): 483–506, at 483.

71. Charles VIII: Poggioreale
You would not believe the beautiful gardens that are in this city, because, on my honor, it is so full of beautiful and singular things that it lacks only Adam and Eve to make of it an earthly paradise.

LA DUCHESCA

In addition to transforming the Castel Capuano into a palatial residence, Alfonso commissioned a series of gardens for it, to be linked with the gardens of a new retreat called La Duchesca in honor of Ippolita Maria Sforza, the duke's wife. This commission of 1488 is recorded by Leostello; the duchess died that year. Designed by Giuliano da Maiano, the two-story casino was built on land appropriated by Alfonso from the Angevin convent of Sta. Maria Maddalena. The notoriously aggressive Alfonso petitioned the nuns to use the building as a residence for his courtiers, offering to install them in the nearby community of Sta. Caterina a Formello, whose Celestines in turn were paid 1500 ducats to move to San Pietro a Maiella. Once installed in the former convent of the Maddalena, the courtiers fell fatally ill, prompting both the immediate departure of remaining courtiers and speculation about divine retribution for having displaced the nuns.[33] This development, together with Alfonso's abdication in 1495, evidently prevented further work on La Duchesca, and the sisters eventually returned to their original habitat at Sta. Maria Maddalena. The grounds of La Duchesca would be used by Don Pedro de Toledo for housing high-ranking administrators in his law courts after transforming the nearby Castel Capuano, formerly a royal residence, into the seat of the judicial courts. No trace of La Duchesca survives.

Leostello's neutral commentary (1:297, 304–5) about the displacement reflects his personal proximity to the future Alfonso II. His entry is dated 17 January 1490. Translated by CFN.

---

33. Gennaro Aspreno Galante, *Guida sacra della città di Napoli*, Nicola Spinosa, ed. (Naples: Società Editrice Napoletana, 1985), 168.

72. Leostello:Alfonso Displaces the Nuns of Sta. Maria Maddalena
He [Alfonso] got up at a good hour and rode to Sta.
Caterina Formello. There he arranged certain things
in preparation for the nuns of the Maddalena... the
Magdalena recently renamed [the] church Santa Maria of
the Martyrs adjacent to his [Alfonso's] castle. Its nuns were
transferred to Sta. Caterina a Formello; and the monks
who were in that church were sent to San Petro Maiella
and were well provided for there.

A PALACE FOR KING FERRANTE

The Florentine artist Giuliano da Sangallo was engaged by Lorenzo
de' Medici in 1488 to design an elaborate palace just inland from
Castel Nuovo seemingly at the request of Ferrante I, who evidently
no longer wished to reside in the venerable castle-fortress.[34] The project survives as yet another manifestation of Lorenzo's use of artistic
patronage to further his own political interests in the southern capital.
But it also reflects Giuliano's experience of Neapolitan culture, architecture, and ancient ruins. By the time of the commission, Giuliano
had emerged as a distinguished architect whose ability to embellish
the neo-Brunelleschian architectural idiom with an antiquarian vocabulary earned him the premier position among Lorenzo's court
architects.

Sangallo's unexecuted plan [Fig. 20] is extraordinarily ambitious
and rivals ancient structures in its complexity and decorative ornamentation; the design implies a detailed study of treatises by Vitruvius
and Alberti as well as of Roman ruins. He proposes a tripartite colonnaded atrium, a sunken colonnaded courtyard, a large hall whose
walls are punctuated by niches framed by columns, and an octagonal
tempietto all'antica (seemingly inspired by the temple of the Cumaean
Sibyl near Naples) with a similar wall articulation. The plan shares
certain features with Sangallo's other Neapolitan projects and his later
Palazzo Medici on the Via Laura in Florence, and it anticipates aspects

34. Bianca de Divitiis, "Giuliano da Sangallo." Identifying the function of the
building has been obscured by Summonte's description (70, ll. 497–513) of
it as a tribunal, which De Divitiis rejects. Vasari also comments on Sangallo's
design (1:698–99).

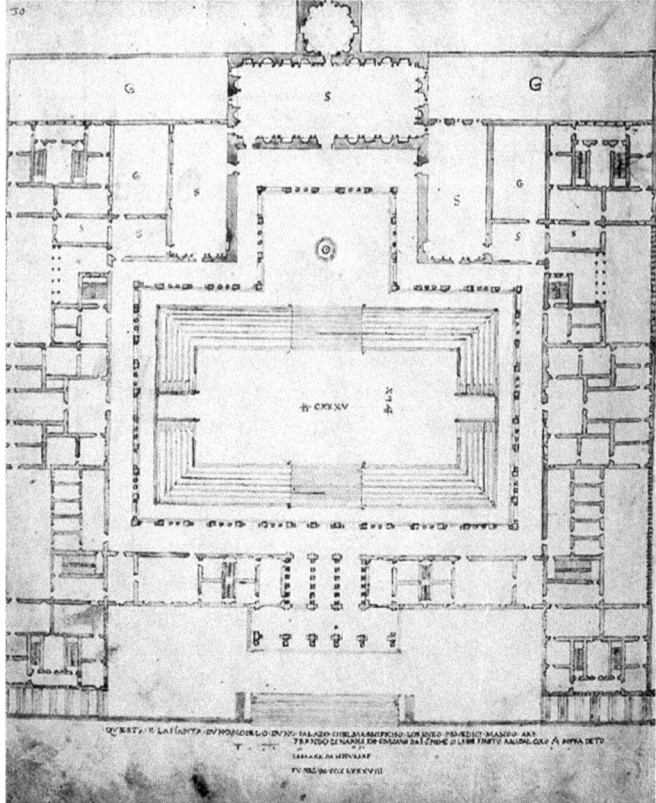

Fig. 20. Giuliano da Sangallo. Palazzo Ferrante (Tribunale), plan, 1488. Codex Barberini Latina 4424, 39v.

of Bramante's vision for the Cortile del Belvedere at the Vatican. The fact that Giuliano was designing a structure for a Neapolitan king gave him license to experiment with grandiose forms in a way that would have been inappropriate for ostensibly republican Florentine patrons, such as Lorenzo himself.

The first-person notation on a drawing for the unrealized project in Giuliano's sketchbook, the Codex Barberini, follows here and indicates Giuliano's role in both executing and delivering the model to the Aragonese. Given Lorenzo's own interest in architecture one may, however, assume a collaborative role between Giuliano, Lorenzo, and the royal patron in developing the model. The following section is taken from the Biblioteca Apostolica Vaticana, Codex Barberini Latina 4424, fol. 39v, and reproduced in Cristiano Huelsen, ed., *Il Libro di Giuliano da Sangallo* (Leipzig: Harrassowitz, 1910). Translated by CFN.

73. Giuliano da Sangallo: Plan for King Ferrante's Palace
This is a plan of a model of a palace that the Magnificent Lorenzo de' Medici sent to King Fer[nan]do of Naples and I, Giuliano da Sangallo, as soon as I had finished it, went with the model described above. 5 10 15 20 measured in braccie. This was in 1488.

SANNAZARO'S VILLA IN POSILLIPO
The utopian villa settings, or *delizie*, developed by Duke Alfonso and others resonated in the descriptions of a number of humanists in the Aragonese court, such as Giovanni Pontano and Jacopo Sannazaro,[35] who had direct experience of them. Sannazaro's royal patron, King Frederick of Aragon (r.1496–1501), awarded him a country estate (or *massaria*), called the Villa Mergellina, in 1499 on the coast west of the city in the area known as Posillipo. Pontano had similarly been given property in this area, where Alfonso, duke of Calabria, also had a *delizia*.

Sannazaro's epigram below records the gift, while playfully commenting on its location and its associated menial labor. Nonetheless, the views of the Bay, the Sorrentine Peninsula, Capri, and Ischia would have been spectacular. Moreover, it was near the tomb of Virgil and the celebrated Campi Flegrei with its many antiquities.[36] The Villa Mergellina was eventually destroyed c.1530 during the conflict with the French. A church built by Sannazaro survives there and houses his tomb. His epigram is translated in Ralph Nash, *Arcadia and Piscatorial Eclogues* (Detroit, MI: Wayne State University Press, 1966), 9.

35. For Sannazaro, see Soranzo, 71–88; and above, chapter 3, pp. 169–83 and readings 28–30.

36. See De Divitiis, "Memories" 211–12; Hendrix, "City Branding."

74. *Sannazaro: Epigram for his Villa Mergellina*
You have given me the desire of being a writer, Frederick,
While you draw every talent to your praises.
Lo, a suburban seat, and new estates you give:
You made a poet, now you are making a peasant.

DON PEDRO'S VILLA AT POZZUOLI

Following the devastating earthquake of 1538 in the volcanic area of Pozzuoli on the coast, Don Pedro de Toledo rebuilt the town, along with a villa for himself. The residence was situated on the ruins of the ancient Greco-Roman colony of Puteoli and evidently had a sizeable library filled with books on antiquarian topics, a large garden, and painted decoration by Vasari.[37] Thermal springs celebrated in humanist literature were nearby. By this time, the coastal zone west of Naples had eventually replaced inherently marshy locations outside the eastern walls as an ultra-fashionable location for the retreats of wealthy Neapolitans and the Spanish viceregency. The phenomenon reflects Don Pedro's general interest in developing the western sections of the city. Franco Strazzullo, *Edilizia*, 18, cites Raimondo Annecchino, *Storia di Pozzuoli e della zone flegrea* (Pozzuoli: n.p., 1960), 192, who quotes the sixteenth-century writer Filonico Alicarnasseo (Costantino Castriota). Translated by CFN.

75. *Filonico Alicarnasseo: Don Pedro de Toledo's Villa in Pozzuoli*
Once he had bought many useful and delightful things in Pozzuoli and had his imperial chambers built there, he would leave Naples for that place with only two staffers, staying there awhile with those whose company he personally enjoyed most. For that reason he earned the resentment of many officials, ministers, barons, and knights, leaving in Pozzuoli many beautiful residences and palaces almost uninhabited.

37. Pane, "Pietro di Toledo," 85.

PALAZZO VECCHIO

Don Pedro's expansion of the city westward was overtly signaled by the establishment of a new viceregal palace of c.1550 designed by Ferdinando Maglione (Manlio) at the southern end of the Via Toledo, today the Piazza Trieste e Trento. The structure is adjacent to Castel Nuovo, which it replaced as the principle viceroy's residence, and represented an expanded center of power by land and sea. Antoine Lafréry [Fig. 21] provides precious evidence of the design in his map of 1566, which shows a square plan with a large courtyard and two corner towers (*casa-torre*) framing the main facade.[38] High walls project from either side of the structure and enclose the large park behind. As such, the fortified design is very different from those of the nobility, such as the Palazzo Orsini di Gravina (1513–49, Fig. 22), executed by Gabriele D'Angelo and Francesco de Palma and descended from Bramante's Palazzo Caprini. After 1600 the palace was known as Palazzo Vecchio because Domenico Fontana's new palace was underway.

The portal of Toledo's Palazzo Reale displayed the coat of arms of Charles V and looked west towards the coastal Chiaia region and Pozzuoli, which he developed. This orientation was particularly significant in a larger geographic sense as well, because it faced the

Fig. 21. Lafréry, Naples (1566). Detail showing Via Toledo and Palazzo Vecchio (48 on plan).

38. As noted by De Cavi, *Architecture and Royal Presence*, 159.

Fig. 22. Palazzo Orsini di Gravina. Photo: Italica Press.

street begun in 1540 (now the Via Chiaia) that lead to the new gate called the Porta Romana. Through it one accessed seaside roads recently developed to improve access to Gaeta and, ultimately, Rome. From it Don Pedro could also gaze up at Castel Sant'Elmo, impressively redesigned by his Valencian architect Pedro Luis Escrivá. On a nearby slope was the recently built Spanish Quarter housing military personnel. Within the context of the city plan, the palace may be seen as a western center of authority balanced on the eastern side by the Castel Capuano, the former Aragonese-Angevin residence also newly renovated by Don Pedro (1537 f.) as a judicial administrative center.

Giulio Cesare Capaccio, *Il Forestiero* (Naples: G.D. Roncagliolo, 1634), 852, cited in De Cavi, 164, and Labrot, 318, provides a rare source of evidence for the Palazzo Vecchio, [Fig. 23] which was eventually subsumed by Fontana's building. His commentary notes the

Fig. 23. Anonymous, 18th c. Via Toledo and Palazzo Vecchio (Vicereale) abutting the new Palazzo Reale. Fondazione F. Zeri. Wikimedia.

defensive aspects of the design in relation to the civic unrest incurred by events such as the proposed Spanish Inquisition.

76. *Giulio Cesare Capaccio: Don Pedro de Toledo's Palazzo Vecchio*
    Don Pedro de Toledo made another house that more resembled a fort since it was built in tumultuous times.

AVILLA WITH A VIEW
The following imagined dialogue is set on the loggia of the Villa Pignatelli. It is excerpted from Giovanni Tarcagnota's *Del sito et lodi della città di Napoli*[39] as transcribed by Strazzullo, *Edilizia*, 21, and translated by TZ.

77. *Tarcagnota: The View from Villa Pignatelli*
    Have you ever in your life seen a more beautiful view than this? Should it also be used in one of these Flemish paintings, who would not call it the most exquisite thing in the world?... Our spirit is lifted simply when we look at a verdant tree; our soul is revived each time we turn our eyes to the calm and placid waves of the sea. And the more our

39. See chapter 4 above, p. 223 and reading 55.

Fig. 24. Palazzo Reale. Domenico Fontana, begun 1600. Photo: Italica Press.

sight and spirit and soul are reborn, the more happily they rejoice, admiring, all at the same time, so many and such grand buildings, of which we are now reading, so many pleasant hills, and so many and such beautiful flowered plants, alongside such an equally peaceful sea. This, to my view, is a most charming and enjoyable sight.

DOMENICO FONTANA'S PALAZZO REALE

Domenico Fontana arrived in Naples in 1592, with the title of "Ingegnere del Regno," a title that evoked much jealousy from his local professional peers. He had gained considerable fame for recently repositioning the Egyptian obelisk in front of St. Peter's in Rome under the aegis of Sixtus V. In 1600 Viceroy Fernando Ruiz, count of Lemos, announced that Fontana would develop plans to expand substantially the viceregal palace not far from Castel Nuovo that Don Pedro had built a half-century earlier at the southern end of the Via Toledo,[40] thus reinforcing both Spanish hegemony in Naples and its role as an outpost of the Hapsburg monarchy.

Fontana's design for the three-story structure [Fig. 24] echoes his monotonous formula for the papal palace in Rome on the Quirinal

40. See above, reading 76 and pp. 251–53.

Hill (1580s).[41] The lowest level has multiple arcuated openings, framed by single pilasters, and the upper two stories feature rows of windows with triangular and segmental pediments that are also framed by single pilasters.[42] Sections of Don Pedro's palace were eventually absorbed into this structure or demolished, and the new palazzo was expanded under the Bourbons in the eighteenth century.

Belisario Corenzio decorated the viceroy's apartment with scenes of the *Deeds of Alfonso the Magnanimous* and the *Deeds of Ferrante of Aragon* (1607–14) to reinforce the longstanding Iberian presence in the city.[43] The palace facade would become a backdrop for elaborate court pageantry. Giovan Carlo Scaramelli, the Venetian ambassador to Naples, documents the initiation of the palace project as recorded in the *Corrispondenze diplomatiche veneziane* (Rome: Istituto Poligrafico e Zecca dello Stato: Libreria dello Stato, 1991–), 3:288, translated in Sabina De Cavi, *Architecture and Royal Presence*, 159.

78. Giovan Carlo Scaramelli: Costs of Fontana's Palazzo Reale

His Excellency has obtained permission from his Majesty to spend 200,000 ducats on a royal palace adjacent to that which he now inhabits […]. For these extraordinary but ongoing expenses, fiefs and other royal incomes have been alienated, and they are also selling bonds on the open market, with a guaranteed income of 13 percent and more.

★ ★ ★

41. De Cavi, *Architecture and Royal Presence,* 160, suggests that papal politics may have in fact been involved in this commission during a jubilee year.

42. See De Cavi's comparisons to Spanish prototypes, 190–212.

43. De Cavi, 96–98.

CHAPTER 6: CHURCHES AND RELICS
by Charlotte Nichols

SAN GIOVANNI A CARBONARA

The rebuilding of the Augustinian monastery of San Giovanni a Carbonara was the first building project of the quattrocento in Naples and the last of the major Angevin churches. Moreover, it was one of the few Renaissance structures to be commissioned *ex-novo*, as the need to accommodate the new religious orders had been satisfied by the building surge of the previous century. The document below indicates that San Giovanni was commissioned c.1400 by King Ladislaus of Anjou-Durazzo. The architect and its precise dates of construction are unknown. The king was evidently attracted to the resident Piedmontese monk Fra Cristiano Franco, an advocate of the Observant Augustinian rule eventually introduced at San Giovanni. Thus, just as the Angevin sovereigns had been engaged with the controversial Franciscan Spirituals, so, too, did Ladislaus embrace a mendicant reformer.

The design of the church, with its aisle-less plan and squared presbytery-choir, continues the trend towards simplicity seen in trecento Angevin churches in Naples. The lack of chapels may suggest that the king intended for San Giovanni a Carbonara to have exclusively royal patronage. Private chapels were later appended to the structure in an ad hoc manner.[1]

The Renaissance source below is cited in an eighteenth-century compilation of summaries of earlier documents, probably destroyed in 1943, for San Giovanni a Carbonara: Naples, Archivio Storico di Napoli, Monasteri Soppressi 6079, *Platea del Regal Monastero di S. Gio. a Carbonara* (1730–62), 1:2r. Translated by CFN.

79. Platea del Regal Monastero di S. Gio. a Carbonara: King Ladislaus and the Last Angevin Church

    Around 1400 Ladislaus, king of Naples, full of esteem and devotion for these religious [Augustinian monks] and for

---

1. Charlotte Nichols, "Ecclesiastical Architecture and the Religious Orders," in Hall–Willette, 101–70, at 101–9. The church was damaged during World War II.

Fig. 26. Andrea da Firenze. Tomb of King Ladislaus, c.1428. Detail of Ladislaus on horseback. Photo: Italica Press.

Fra Cristiano Franco of renowned virtue and saintliness, not wanting the anxieties about the original building to continue any longer, built near that small church and inadequate convent a much larger new temple with the same name of San Giovanni Battista, which is that still standing today.

KING LADISLAUS died in 1414, following his occupation of Rome and aggressive military campaigns further north. His sister and heir, Giovanna II, undertook the patronage of a royal tomb c.1428, which takes the form of an enormous wall monument behind the high altar of San Giovanni a Carbonara [Fig. 25]. The following inscription from a now dismembered tomb in Ancona identifies the sculptor of the Neapolitan monument as the Florentine Andrea da Firenze (1388–1455), also called Andrea di Onofrio, Andrea di Nofri and Andrea Ciccione. However, scholars have questioned its authorship.[2]

Reaching from floor to ceiling, the tomb's massive gothicizing framework includes seated images of Ladislaus and Giovanna II and is surmounted by an equestrian image of the ruler with the inscription: DIVUS LADISLAUS [Fig. 26]. The latter is a strikingly secular reference to the military prowess of a man who threatened Florentine independence early in the quattrocento and whose motto was *"Aut*

2. Nicholas Bock, "Antiken und Florenzrezeption in Neapel, 1400–1450," in *Opere e giorni: Studi su Mille anni di arte europea,* Klaus Bergdolt and Giorgio Bonsanti, ed. (Venice: Marsilio, 2001), 243–47. For trecento Angevin tombs, see also Tanja Michalsky, "Tombs and the Ornamentation of Chapels," in Hall–Willette, 233–98, at 233–47.

Caesar aut nullus." As such the imagery and size of this project would have been inappropriate in the carvers' native republic of Florence. Nor was the tomb admired a century later, as seen in Summonte's condemnation of gothicizing works in his letter of 1524 below.[3]

The design of the monument makes direct reference to Angevin prototypes, both in terms of design and placement, such as that of King Robert the Wise in Sta. Chiara, commissioned from Pacio da Firenze in the mid-trecento by his grand-daughter and successor, Giovanna I. The tombs patronized by the Giovannas each represent an ostentatious display of power and *magnificentia* within the austere architectural settings of mendicant churches.

The inscription on the tomb of Simone Vigilante, bishop of Senigallia, originally in San Francesco alle Scale, Ancona, is partially cited by Riccardo Filangieri di Candida, *La Chiesa e il monastero di San Giovanni a Carbonara* (Naples: L. Lubrano, 1924), 39.

80. Inscription on the Tomb of Simone Vigilante
>   THE WORK OF ANDREA OF FLORENCE WHO ALSO EXECUTED
>   THE TOMB OF KING LADISLAUS.

THE POET AND HUMANIST Jacopo Sannazaro composed an epigram about the sepulchral equestrian image of Ladislaus in San Giovanni a Carbonara, two lines of which are excerpted here. Humanists like Sannazaro and other members of Giovanni Pontano's erudite academy met frequently at the church c.1500, when he may have composed the verses found in Jacopo Sannazaro, *Poemata ex antiquis editionibus accuratissime descripta* (Padua: Cominus, 1719), 120, translated in Hersey, *Aragonese Arch*, 170.

81. Sannazaro: An Epigram for the Tomb of King Ladislaus
>   *Admire the floating stone in snowy columns,*
>   *Visitor, and the horseman who sits upon its crest.*

THE AUDACITY OF LADISLAUS' TOMB in San Giovanni a Carbonara is matched by the design of the Caracciolo del Sole Chapel of the same date [Fig. 27] and to which it is both adjacent and competitive.

3. Chapter 10, reading 169, ll. 320–28, pp. 458–59.

In 1427 the powerful Neapolitan aristocrat Sergianni Caracciolo — Giovanna II's seneschal and lover, whom she later had killed — commissioned a large funerary chapel appended to the choir on the main axis of the church and entered through the lower level of the king's tomb. The architect and exact dates of construction are unknown. Dedicated to the Nativity of the Virgin, the chapel is circular in plan and domed, precociously suggesting a funerary pantheon. It may also be seen as evoking late medieval lady chapels. The inherent classicism of the design renders it very different than its bombastic and gothicizing royal frontispiece. The design of the chapel could have been motivated by an acoustical agenda as well, since the space appears to have doubled as a retro-choir for the hermetic monks who were famous for their music.[4]

The dual function of the space as a funerary chapel and retro-choir is reflected in the chapel's two superimposed fresco cycles signed by Leonardo da Besozzo and Perrinetto da Benevento, the styles and subjects of which also signal the coexistence of private magnificence and a monastic observance at San Giovanni. This excerpt is recorded in the *Platea*, 1:24r.[5] Translated by CFN.

82. The Audacious Chapel of Sergianni Caracciolo
The chapel under the name of the Nativity of the Holiest Virgin Mary, found in our church behind the tomb of King Ladislaus, was built by Sergianni Caracciolo, duke of Venosa, count of Avellino, and grand seneschal of the kingdom of Sicily, in the year 1427 as seen in the document of a book of 1427, with the many expenses for this chapel....

ANOTHER EXTRAVAGANT DISPLAY of munificence at the Augustinian church of San Giovanni a Carbonara is the circular, domed commemorative chapel commissioned by Galeazzo Caracciolo di Vico

4. Nichols, "Ecclesiastical Architecture," 123–24; Franca Trinchieri Camiz, "Augustinian Musical Education and Redemption in the Fifteenth-Century Caracciolo del Sole Chapel, Naples," *Imago Musicae* 5 (1998): 41–64; Bock, (2008), 19–23; Michalsky, "Tombs," 253–56. See also below, reading 119, pp. 321–22.

5. Transcribed in Nichols, "Caracciolo di Vico," 196–99.

Fig. 27. San Giovanni a Carbonara. Cappella Caracciolo del Sole, Tomb of Sergianni Caracciolo, 15th c. Photo: Armando Mancini. Wikimedia.

Fig. 28. Giuliano da Sangallo. Caracciolo di Vico Chapel, S. Giovanni a Carbonara, c.1514–17. Photo: IlSistemone. Wikimedia.

c.1514 [Fig. 28]. His choice of San Giovanni as a site was motivated by the location of the pantheon for his Angevin kinsman Sergianni Caracciolo and his evident affinity for the order itself; he had attended the fashionable humanist gatherings at San Giovanni c.1500 led by Egidio (Giles) of Viterbo, the erudite and pious Augustinian reformer who was in residence there.[6] Like Sergianni, Galeazzo's allegiance to a foreign ruler — although Aragonese rather than Angevin — was legendary. He successfully led the troops for Ferrante I of Aragon against the Turks in 1480 and travelled as a diplomatic envoy on behalf of the new Neapolitan viceregency to Segovia in 1505 to meet with Ferdinand of Aragon and Castile, recently ordained by Pope Julius II as a Catholic king and newly victorious over the French as king of Naples. In 1506 King Ferdinand would come to Naples for a sojourn of several months.

6. Nichols, "Caracciolo di Vico," 140–41. On Giles of Viterbo, see Francis X. Martin, *The Writings of Giles of Viterbo* (Louvain: Institutum Historicum Augustinianum, 1979); Germana Ernst and Simona Foà, "Egidio da Viterbo," DBI 42 (1993), online at: http://www.treccani.it/enciclopedia/egidio-da-viterbo_(Dizionario-Biografico).

Dedicated to Mary Queen of Heaven, the Caracciolo di Vico Chapel is located to the immediate left of the high altar, its marble entrance abutting the side of the tomb of the Angevin King Ladislaus and the entrance to Sergianni's chapel-choir, which is also circular in plan and vaulted. The placement of a centrally planned structure in proximity to the high altar of a church recalls such well-known prototypes as the mausolea-chapels adjacent to Old S. Peter's in Rome, but it should also be understood in relation to the particular space constraints of the site.

The lower story, in place by 1517, is subdivided into four interlocking triumphal arches of white marble with contrasting *rosso antico*; it possesses an ambitious marble Doric order of paired half-columns on high pedestals that supports a heavy classicizing entablature copied from the Theater of Marcellus in Rome. The chapel (9.3 meters in diameter) is surmounted by a coffered hemispherical dome (15.5 meters in height, Fig. 29). This author attributed the Bramantesque design to Giuliano da Sangallo. The similarities to the plan and elevation of Bramante's Tempietto, the new martyrium of Peter in Rome commissioned by Ferdinand

Fig. 29. S. Giovanni a Carbonara, Caracciolo di Vico Chapel, dome. Photo: Miguel Hermoso Cuesta. Wikimedia.

and Isabella, imply direct knowledge of it on the part of Caracciolo who knew the king personally.[7]

Also of particular interest is Raphael's domed chapel for Agostino Chigi in the Augustinian church of Sta. Maria del Popolo in Rome, which was begun in the same year as the Caracciolo di Vico Chapel; it is perhaps significant that Chigi had an office in Naples.[8] The two allude to Hadrian's Pantheon, which by the early cinquecento was emerging as a model for Marian churches and commemorative chapels.

Caracciolo's munificent patronage would have been viewed by his Neapolitan and Iberian contemporaries as a lavish display of *magnificentia* reviving and competing with that of Oliviero Carafa's Soccorpo following the drought of patronage during the crippling French and Spanish struggles for the Regno in the late fifteenth and early sixteenth centuries.[9] The Cappella Caracciolo di Vico may be seen as means of proclaiming — despite his Spanish alliances — the Neapolitan origins, wealth, and position of Galeazzo Caracciolo as the indigenous aristocrat renegotiated his position in relation to the newly established viceregency and resulting influx of Iberian nobility. Later in the century Diego de Siloé used the Neapolitan chapel as a model for prominent commissions in Spain.[10]

7. Nichols, "Ecclesiastical Architecture," 113–20.

8. The chapel can be compared to the contemporary Marian funerary chapel by Raphael for Agostino Chigi at the Augustinian church of Sta. Maria del Popolo, Rome, in its function as a dynastic mortuary chapel after the Pantheon, dedication to Mary, use of precious materials and monumental decorative forms all'antica, and in its integration of sculpture and architecture. See Nichols, "Ecclesiastical Architecture," 114–16.

9. Nichols, "Ecclesiastical Architecture," 120; and, reading 100, pp. 290–97.

10. Nichols, "Caracciolo di Vico," 105–14. Diego de Siloé, who worked on the altarpiece for the Caracciolo Chapel, planned the cathedral of Granada for Charles V in the new capital city as a symbol of the re-Christianization of Moorish Spain. Siloé then replicated the typology of the cathedral for that of Guadix, seat of the oldest bishopric in Spain and an important ecclesiastical center. His chapel dedicated to San Torquato (1549), appended to the left of the high altar, copies the Caracciolo Chapel's location and plan precisely.

THE ANGLED INTRADOS of the chapel's entrance is boldly engraved near eye-level in large letters with a dedicatory inscription facing in the direction of the altar, the royal tomb of Ladislaus, and the entrance to Sergianni Caracciolo's mortuary enclosure. By the mid-cinquecento it was credited to the humanist-poet Jacopo Sannazaro, a personal friend of Galeazzo.[11] Humanists gathered informally in the church during Giles of Viterbo's sojourn there.

The date of dedication is the Epiphany, which is also the subject of the chapel's carved altarpiece. The inscription is translated here from the Latin by Anne Laidlaw and Derek Moore.

83. The Caracciolo di Vico Chapel

TO YOU QUEEN OF HEAVEN, I GALEAZZO CARACCIOLO, ON WHOM YOU HAVE CONFERRED YOUR MANY BLESSINGS, AND INDEED FROM WHOM YOU HAVE KEPT MANY ILLS, GRATEFULLY AND WITH JOY DEDICATE THIS PURE MARBLE CHAPEL WITH AN ALTAR, STATUES, AND EVERY REFINEMENT, AND HEREBY PAY MY TITHE.

IN THE YEAR OF OUR SALVATION BORN OF YOU, VIII [VI] JANUARY 1516.

THE SCULPTED ALTARPIECE (c. 1516–19) for the Caracciolo di Vico chapel by the Spaniards Bartolomé Ordóñez and Diego de Siloé [Fig. 30] copies the distinctive format of the quattrocento retable of white marble and *rosso antico* in the chapel of Maria d'Aragona at Sta. Maria di Monteoliveto. Here King Ferrante I, whom Galeazzo served, appears in the carved relief in the guise of a Magi.[12] Thus, the altarpiece coopted a Florentine prototype of 45 years earlier for the chapel of an Aragonese princess and, with the overt inclusion of Ferrante I of Aragon's portrait, reminded the viewer of Galeazzo Caracciolo's primary role in service to him while protecting the Regno from the Turks. In so doing he signaled the longevity of his support of the Spanish. The commissioning of Ordóñez and Siloé, who themselves were the recipients of royal Iberian commissions, strengthens this announcement in direct contrast to the Angevin support proclaimed

11. See Nichols, "Caracciolo di Vico," 36; and below, reading 101, pp. 297–98.

12. Nichols, "Ecclesiastical Architecture," 117; idem, "Diego Siloé," in *The Encyclopedia of Sculpture*, Antonia Bostrum, ed. (Chicago: Fitzroy-Dearborn/ Routledge, 2004), 3:1567–69; Michalsky, "Tombs," 280–82.

Fig. 30. Bartolomé Ordóñez and Diego de Siloé. Altarpiece of Adoration of the Magi. Caracciolo di Vico Chapel, S. Giovanni a Carbonara. Photo: Miguel Hermoso Cuesta. Wikimedia.

in the previous century by his ancestor Sergianni Caracciolo in the choir-chapel a few feet away in San Giovanni a Carbonara.[13]

13.   Charles V commissioned Marco Cardisco for an altarpiece after 1518 for the royal chapel at Castel Nuovo. It showed the emperor, Alfonso II, and Ferdinand II in the guise of the Three Magi. It is now at the Museo Civico in Naples.

In his letter of 1524 (lines 360–65), Summonte comments on the chapel, noting its Doric order but not the dome, and praises the altarpiece. Translated by CFN.

84. Summonte: Spanish Sculptors in Naples

In the church of San Giovanni a Carbonara, in the Doric chapel begun for Signor Galeazzo Caracciolo and now directed by his son Signor Colantonio, is a marble altarpiece with the three Magi, Our Lord, Our Lady, and other figures made by two Spaniards, Diego [de Siloé] e Bartolameo Ordogno [Ordóñez]: a very good thing.

VASARI OBTAINED A COMMISSION at San Giovanni a Carbonara during his Neapolitan sojourn of 1544–45 and isolates the Caracciolo Chapel in his *Lives* (1:866–67). He identifies the sculptor of the statuette of St. John (now missing) that flanked the relief as Girolamo Santacroce of Naples, although he mistakenly attributes the architecture to him as well; Santacroce would have been about fourteen years of age at the time that the chapel was begun.[14] His Italian chauvinism is displayed in his remarks about "a Spaniard," or Bartolomé Ordóñez, who carved the relief of the high altar.

85. Vasari Mis-Attributes the Caracciolo di Vico Chapel

Girolamo Santa Croce of Naples, although he was snatched from us by death in the very prime of life, at a time when greater things were looked for from him, yet showed in the works of sculpture that he made at Naples during his few years, what he would have done if he had lived longer; for the works that he executed in sculpture at Naples were wrought and finished with all the lovingness that could be desired in a young man who wishes to surpass by a great measure those who for many years before his day have held the sovereignty in some noble profession. In San Giovanni a Carbonara at Naples he built the chapel of the marchese di Vico, which is a round temple, partitioned by columns and niches, with some tombs carved with much diligence. And because the altar-piece of this chapel, made of marble in half-relief and representing the Magi bringing their offerings to

14. Nichols, "Caracciolo di Vico," 169.

Christ, is by the hand of a Spaniard, Girolamo executed in emulation of this work a St. John in a niche, so beautifully wrought in full-relief, that it showed that he was not inferior to the Spaniard either in courage or in judgment....

THE AUTHORS OF THE EARLIEST GUIDEBOOKS to Naples, including Giovanni Tarcagnota, do not attempt an attribution of the design. Thus, the pattern of anonymity with regard to the designing architects for major and remarkable Neapolitan commissions continues into the sixteenth century and is characteristic of the approach of cinquecento authors of Campanian guidebooks in general, unlike authors elsewhere in Italy.[15] The following passage is found in Tarcagnota, *Del sito e delle lodi della città di Napoli*, 79–80. Translated by CFN.

86. Tarcagnota: The Caracciolo di Vico Chapel
Neither the date nor architect of the Caracciolo di Vico Chapel in San Giovanni Carbonara is known, but with its incredible beauty and magnificence it leaves the spirit of whomever sees it well satisfied and content.

SANT'ANGELO A NILO

A prominent commission of the late 1420s is the tomb of Cardinal Rinaldo Brancacci in Sant'Angelo a Nilo by the Florentines Donatello and Michelozzo c.1427. The private chapel, originally part of a charitable institution, is adjacent to the family palace and prominently situated on the *decumanus inferioris*, now via San Biagio de' Librai, of the ancient city.[16] Brancacci negotiated King Ladislaus' acceptance of Pope John XXIII (Baldassarre Cossa, a Neapolitan native) during the papal schism of the early quattrocento. His sepulcher, also by Donatello and Michelozzo, is in the Baptistry in Florence.

The Brancacci Tomb [Fig. 31] follows the models set a century earlier by the Sienese Tino di Camaino for royal Neapolitan monuments in which classicizing caryatids support a reclining effigy beneath a gothicizing tabernacle. Therefore, Donatello

15. Amirante, 9.

16. Dieter Girgensohn, "Brancaccio, Rinaldo," DBI 13 (1971), online at: http://www.treccani.it/enciclopedia/rinaldo-brancaccio_(Dizionario-Biografico).

Fig. 31. Donatello. Tomb of Cardinal Rinaldo Brancacci, Sant'Angelo a Nilo, 1427. Photo: Italica Press.

and Michelozzo establish a visual continuum with the Angevin monuments at a time when Naples was still under French rule. However, the Tuscans include the classicizing triumphal arch substructure seen in their other Florentine works, and Donatello's relief of the *Assumption of the Virgin* provided the southern capital with an example of his innovative painterly use of *rilievo schiacciato*.

The document translated here makes clear that Brancacci's commission was essentially a mail-order operation; executed at the sculptors' studio in Pisa, near the marble quarries of Carrara, the tomb was then shipped to Naples and assembled *in situ*. These circumstances are markedly different than Leonardo da Besozzo's long tenure in the city as mandated by the nature of his commission in fresco. The following passage from Michelozzo's cadastre (*catasto*) of 1427 is translated in H.W. Janson, *The Sculpture of Donatello* (Princeton: Princeton University Press, 1963), 88.

87. *Donatello's Tomb for Cardinal Brancacci in Sant'Angelo a Nilo*
Donatello and Michelozzo have done about one quarter of the work on the tomb of Cardinal Rainaldo da Brancacci of Naples, which they are doing in Pisa; they expect to receive a total of 850 florins for this commission and have already been given 300 florins, with the understanding that they will bear all expenses, including the transportation of the monument to Naples.

THE FOLLOWING RECORD indicates that Cosimo de' Medici facilitated the commission from Donatello and Michelozzo for the Neapolitan tomb shortly after Brancacci became cardinal. Brancacci was living in Florence during the papacy's residency there. The date of completion, 1428, is also given. The Medici family continued to lend the services of Florentine artists for major royal and aristocratic projects in Naples throughout the quattrocento in exchange for political favors, therefore establishing artistic hegemony. The document is in Florence, Archivio di Stato di Firenze, MAP 153, fol. 26, as cited by James Beck, "Donatello and the Brancacci Tomb in Naples," in *Florilegium Columbianum: Essays in Honor of Paul Oskar Kristeller*, Karl-Ludwig Selig and Robert Somerville, ed. (New York: Italica Press, 1987), 125–45, at 131.[17]

17. The degree to which the cardinal himself was involved in the choice of Donatello is unclear; see Ronald W. Lightbown, *Donatello and Michelozzo*, 2 vols. (London: Harvey Miller, 1980), 2:296.

88. Cosimo de'Medici Arranges the Commission for Brancacci's Tomb
On 23 March 1428 he [Messer Rinaldo Cardinale
de'Brancacci] paid 850 florins *di camera* for his tomb, as
commissioned by Cosimo de' Medici and Company
from Donato di Niccholò and Michelozo di Bartolomeo,
carvers, who have undertaken said tomb.

STA. MARIA DI MONTEOLIVETO

As a reward for the support of Pius II[18] in his fight for the throne of
Naples, Ferrante I awarded in 1459 Antonio Todeschini Piccolomini
of Siena, the pope's nephew, the title of "Maestro Giustiziere," the
duchy of Amalfi, and his daughter Maria in marriage. Piccolomini
took the surname of d'Aragona at that time. Maria died in 1469
at the age of 18, leaving three children. Piccolomini turned to
the Olivetan monastery of Sta. Maria Vergine di Monteoliveto
(Sant'Anna dei Lombardi) in Naples [Fig. 32], whose order had
been co-founded by his ancestor Ambrogio Piccolomini near Siena.
The Olivetan prior of San Miniato al Monte in Florence assisted
Piccolomini c.1470 in commissioning Antonio Rossellino, at work

Fig. 32. Monteoliveto (S. Anna dei Lombardi). Entrance showing exterior of Piccolomini Chapel at left. Photo: Italica Press.

18. Aeneas Silvius Piccolomini. See chapter 1, readings 3–4, pp. 61–66.

Fig. 33. Antonio Rossellino. Altarpiece with Nativity. Piccolomini Chapel, Monteoliveto, c.1470. Photo: Italica Press.

on that church's chapel of the Cardinal of Portugal, as designer of the funerary chapel of Maria d'Aragona [Figs. 33–34]. He replicated the chapel of the Cardinal of Portugal in San Miniato so closely that the Neapolitan work has traditionally been considered derivative.

The chapel's neo-Brunelleschian design is important within the larger context of Neapolitan architecture, however. It features a square plan, a triumphal arch system in piperno, and pendentives

Fig. 34. Antonio Rossellino. Tomb of Maria d'Aragona. Piccolomini Chapel, Monteoliveto, c.1470. Photo: Italica Press.

supporting a domical vault. This modularity meant that the chapel could be more easily imitated than idiosyncratic constructions such as the chapel of Sergianni Caracciolo, and it became a popular prototype for later Neapolitan patrons, including Marino Curiale.[19] Moreover, the construction of the chapel marks the introduction of a lavish level of patronage that runs counter to the simplicity of the

19. See reading 89 below, p. 275.

original construction for the reformed Benedictines in the way that the lay patronage at the Observant Augustinian monastery of San Giovanni a Carbonara altered its spare interior.[20]

Vasari errs in noting only that the tomb is "similar to the other in every respect save in the figure of the dead." Unremarked by him is the importance of Rossellino's substitution of a large sculpted altarpiece of the Nativity in place of a traditional painted image. In terms of its size, it forms an interesting ecclesiastical counterpart to the huge triumphal relief for the entrance to Castel Nuovo. While Donatello incorporated sculpted reliefs into his tombs, such as the *Assumption* for the Brancacci Tomb discussed above, their large-scale use for altars was unprecedented in Renaissance art. Rossellino's *Nativity* [Fig. 33] functions as an important harbinger of the Baroque taste for sculpted retables.

There may have been an additional motivation beyond Piccolomini's own oblique connection to the cardinal via his papal uncle for the decision to appropriate Rossellino's ensemble for his wife's funerary chapel at Monteoliveto in Naples. The Cardinal of Portugal's coat of arms include the vertical stripes of the house of Aragon to which his mother belonged. Included in the border of heraldic insignia inside the chapel are the arms of Ferrante I, then king of Naples. In the Neapolitan chapel of Maria d'Aragona, the Aragonese arms were entwined with those of her husband Antonio Todeschini Piccolomini. The Cardinal of Portugal was a distant cousin of King Ferrante I of Naples, whose daughter Antonio had married, and Ferrante also had blood relations to the successive queens of Portugal. Thus, the overt physical connections between the two chapels may even be viewed as a stroke of diplomatic genius on the part of Antonio Piccolomini, a relative newcomer to Naples and the house of Aragon.

Far from seeming derivative, however, the chapel must have been viewed by its southern audience as a fashionable statement of power and prestige, which introduced to the Aragonese court and Neapolitan aristocracy the mode of the latest Florentine tour de force for commemorative ensembles. The commission (1470–81) would

20. Nichols, "Ecclesiastical Architecture," 123–24; and Michalsky, "Tombs," 256–61.

have also had the effect of rendering Angevin mortuary commissions visually obsolete. His chapel introduces a level of lavish patronage that compromises the simplicity of the original construction for the reformed Benedictines in the way that the royal and aristocratic lay patronage at the Observant Augustinian monastery of San Giovanni a Carbonara altered its interior appearance.

Moreover, the chapel's architecture is important within the context of Neapolitan architecture. Located to the left of the entrance facade, its design was easily replicated; and this, together with its seeming modernity and royal associations, meant that the Piccolomini Chapel would become an influential prototype for other Neapolitan patrons. In fact, the elevation of the Cappella Piccolomini was immediately copied, albeit clumsily, by local architects for the pendant chapel (c.1489) of the powerful Marino Curiale (Correale) of Sorrento, count of Terranova and majordomo for Queen Giovanna II and the Aragonese.

The following passage is found in Vasari's life of Antonio and Bernardo Rossellino, 1:469.

89. Vasari: The Piccolomini Chapel at Sta. Maria di Monteoliveto
   This tomb of the cardinal was erected in 1459; and its form, with the architecture of the chapel, gave so much satisfaction to the duke of Malfi, nephew of Pope Pius II, that he had another made in Naples by the hand of the same master for his wife, similar to the other in every respect save in the figure of the dead. For this, moreover, Antonio made a panel containing the Nativity of Christ and the Manger, with a choir of angels over the hut, dancing and singing with open mouths, in such a manner, that he truly seems to have given them all possible movement and expression short of breath itself, and that with so much grace and so high a finish, that iron tools and man's intelligence could effect nothing more in marble. Wherefore his works have been much esteemed by Michelagnolo and by all the rest of the supremely excellent craftsmen.

THE DOCUMENTS TRANSLATED BELOW confirm the attribution to Antonio Rossellino and cite the Spannocchi Bank of Siena, which had a branch in Naples, as the financial agents for the transaction. They are from Florence, Archivio di Stato, Corporazioni religiose soppresse dal governo francese, 168, San Miniato al Monte, vol. 155, contratti, livelli e oblighi, 1453–1513, fol. 41 transcribed in Italian in Doris Carl, "New Documents for Antonio Rossellino's Altar in Sant'Anna dei Lombardi, Naples," *The Burlington Magazine* 138 (1996): 320, docs. 1, 4. Translated by CFN.

90. Surviving Documents for the Piccolomini Chapel
    1. I record that up to the month of February 1470 Father Giuliano of Florence had from the monastery of Sta. Maria of Monteoliveto outside Naples our monastery 130 florins larghi as a letter of credit by the Spagnochi [Spannocchi] of Naples directed to Rabatti and Chanbi whose money we have in deposit here in the monastery, and which money is said to be for the altarpiece of the chapel of the duchess of [A]malfi, which is in said monastery....

    4. On 19 May 1474 twenty florins were given to master Antonio sculptor, as is written in his hand and for us from the bank of Francesco Chochi, which money we gave him to buy the marbles for the altarpiece he is making for said brothers of Naples....

THE PRESENCE OF A ROYAL ARAGONESE CHAPEL in Monteoliveto transformed the church into a highly desirable venue for other wealthy Neapolitans and Spaniards. Marino Curiale commissioned a chapel in the late 1480s as a pendant to the Cappella Piccolomini, whose architecture it copies.[21] Benedetto da Maiano had been entrusted to finish the Piccolomini Chapel after Antonio Rossellino's death, and, significantly, he also carved a large relief of the *Annunciation* for Curiale's chapel. The following passage from Vasari is found in his life of Benedetto da Maiano, 1:544.

91. Vasari: The Terranova Chapel Copies the Piccolomini Chapel
    Having afterwards gone to Naples by reason of the death of his uncle Giuliano, whose heir he was, Benedetto, besides certain works that he executed for that king,

21. Erminia Pepe, "Le tre cappelle rinascimentali in Santa Maria di Monteoliveto a Napoli," *Napoli Nobilissima* 37 (1998): 97–116.

made a marble panel for the count of Terranuova in the monastery of the monks of Monteoliveto, containing an Annunciation with certain saints, and surrounded by very beautiful boys, who are supporting some festoons; and in the predella of the said work he made many low-reliefs in a good manner.

VASARI RECORDS the continuing importation of artists for commissions in Monteoliveto, including Fra Giovanni da Verona's intarsia for the chapel of Paolo Tolosa (1507–8). The patron was a wealthy Catalan merchant who controlled the supply of grain to Naples and made significant loans to the house of Aragon.[22] Securing a chapel in a church favored by Alfonso, duke of Calabria, reflected Tolosa's standing at court.

The intarsia panels feature elaborate perspectival urban views. Fra Giovanni had recently supplied choir stalls for the Tuscan abbey of Monteoliveto Maggiore. The panels in the Cappella Tolosa were later moved to the sacristy painted by Vasari in the same church. The Olivetan network may have facilitated the acquisition of an altarpiece by Pinturicchio, employed by the Piccolomini in Siena, for the same chapel. See Vasari, 1:575. The following passage is embedded in Vasari's life of Raphael (1:722).

92. Vasari: The Chapel of Paolo Tolosa
And it is certain that in that craft [perspective-views in inlaid woodwork] there was never any man more able than Giovanni either in design or in workmanship: of which we still have proof... in the sacristy of Monteoliveto at Naples, and also in the choir of the chapel of Paolo da Tolosa in the same place, executed by that master.

GUIDO MAZZONI OF MODENA, who had familial connections with the d'Este family, made a major contribution to Monteoliveto in the form of a terracotta group depicting the Lamentation (1490–92, Fig. 35). The multi-figured, life-size ensemble evokes the north Italian tradition of a polychromed tableau vivant, which Mazzoni infused with an

22. Pasquale Maione, "Paolo Tolosa e la sua cappella nella chiesa di Monteoliveto," *Samnium* 15 (1942): 43–46.

Fig. 35. Guido Manzoni. Lamentation. Monteoliveto (S. Anna de' Lombardi). Photo: Il Sistemone. Wikimedia.

elevated sense of drama. His highly emotive style evidently appealed to the Aragonese patron, Alfonso, duke of Calabria. As noted by Vasari, the religious figures comprise a gallery of royal Aragonese portraiture, whose realism was admired by Charles V on his visit to Naples in 1535–36.[23] Such groups anticipate the extraordinary Neapolitan *presepe* tradition.[24] Mazzoni followed Charles VIII to France in 1496 after the king's withdrawal from Naples. There, Mazzoni became a royal court artist and designed Charles' tomb at Saint-Denis. The following passage is found in Vasari's life of Giuliano da Maiano, 1:396–97.

93. Vasari: Guido Mazzoni's Lamentation
> …in his youth he [Benedetto da Maiano] was the rival of a sculptor named Modanino da Modena, who worked in terracotta, and who wrought for the said Alfonso a Pietà with an infinite number of figures in the round, made of

23. De Cavi, 108. Timothy Verdon, "Mazzoni, Guido," www.oxfordartonline. com,; Grazia Vaccari, "Guido Mazzoni: Lamentation," *Encyclopedia of Sculpture* (New York and London: Fitzroy Dearborn, 2004), 2:1027–28; Hersey, *Alfonso II*, 118–24; Massimo Ferretti, "A Court Artist: Neapolitan Lamentations. Guido Mazzoni in Naples," *FMR Magazine* 88 (1997): 48–58.

24. See Jessica Hughes, "'No Retreat, Even When Broken': Classical Ruins in the *Presepe Napoletano*," in Hughes–Buongiovanni, 284–308.

terracotta and colored, which were executed with very great vivacity, and were placed by the king in the church of Monteoliveto, a very highly honored monastery in the city of Naples. In this work the said king is portrayed on his knees, and he appears truly more than alive; wherefore Modanino was remunerated by him with very great rewards.

SAN DOMENICO
In the course of reporting a serious fire in 1506 at the Angevin foundation of San Domenico, Notar Giacomo (295–96) mentions that the bodies of Alfonso I, Ferrante I and Ferrante II may have been burned.[25] The church was favored by Alfonso in keeping with the Iberian affinity for the Dominican Order.[26] After 1494 San Domenico served as a burial place for Aragonese royalty in power between 1442 and 1501; their bodies were kept in a wooden choir near the crossing of the church and later moved to the sacristy.[27] De Cavi speculates that Domenico Fontana may have been involved with the re-systemization of this "*capilla real*" in the late 1500s at the request of Philip II.[28] Angevin rulers had been buried nearby at Sta. Chiara. Translated by CFN.

94. Notar Giacomo: San Domenico as the Burial Place of Aragonese Royalty
On the 29th of December 1506 from Tuesday overnight to Wednesday at 6:30 in the morning they found San Domenico in Naples burned.... some say "yes" and others "no" that the bodies of the most serene kings Alfonso I, Ferrante I and Ferrante II, which were elevated near the high altar, were burned.

25. The king's will stated that his body was to be returned to Spain; Biagio Ferrante, "Il Cinquecentesco Restauro dei Feretri Aragonesi in S. Domenico Maggiore," *Napoli Nobilissima* 23 (1984): 73.

26. Alfonso I created a "slargo" behind the church, with a staircase from which he could address the citizens. By so doing, he re-directed attention away from the nearby Angevin foundation of Sta. Chiara; see Yoni Ascher, "The Church and the Piazza: Reflections on the South Side of the Church of San Domenico in Naples," *Architectural History* 45 (2002): 92–112.

27. De Cavi, 119.

28. Ibid., 121–32.

THE PONTANO CHAPEL

The Pontano Chapel at Sta. Maria Maggiore is an extraordinary and unusual public statement of private ambition. Commissioned c.1490 by Giovanni Pontano, consummate humanist and political envoy of the house of Aragon, the monument [Fig. 36] is situated diagonally across from his palace (now demolished) along a decumanus (Via Tribunali) of the ancient city, near the remains of an ancient quadrifons arch surmounted by a medieval tower given to Pontano by Ferrante I, and adjacent to the church of Sta. Maria Maggiore.[29]

The architect of the chapel is unknown. The present author notes the similarity of its revetment to the lower story – originally five bays

Fig. 36. Pontano Chapel, c.1490. General view showing decumanus, medieval bell tower built over Roman ruins. Photo: Italica Press.

29. See Nichols "Caracciolo di Vico," 135–37; and Bianca De Divitiis, "*Pontanus Fecit:* Inscriptions and Artistic Authorship in the Pontano Chapel," *California Italian Studies* 3.1 (2012): 1–36.

wide – of the Palazzo Ruccellai, Florence, by Alberti c.1450 [Fig. 37], the home of Bernardo Ruccellai, with whom Pontano was well acquainted. The blocky shape, streetside placement, and spare adornment in the form of Pontano's own inscriptions recall that of ancient Roman tombs, which the humanist himself celebrates in his treatise *De magnificentia* (1498)[30] as important contributions to a city's beauty and testimony to the exemplary actions of virtuous men. Thus, the Neapolitan humanist ensures the survival of the ancient tomb type by adopting an aggressively antique style for his own funerary chapel. However, its prominent position within the city walls defies ancient tradition and ostensibly constitutes an aspirational example of hubristic self-fashioning also acted out by other humanists elsewhere in Italy. Pontano, a native of Umbria, was married to a Neapolitan aristocrat, Adriana Sassone.

Fig. 37. Leon Battista Alberti. Palazzo Ruccellai, Florence. Photo: Miguel Hermoso Cuesta. Wikimedia.

Pontano's *De Magnificentia* is found in Pontano, *I Trattati delle virtù sociali*, Tateo ed., 192, 203, and translated here from the Latin by Frederick J. Booth.

95. Pontano: The Pontano Chapel

Among private works we include tombs, which are either of one person or single families. Nevertheless, in a wonderful way they contribute to the ornamentation of cities. Our ancestors wished these to be sacred; they have a certain wonderful power of exciting people to glory and virtue, especially when they are built for well-deserving

30. See chapter 9, reading 164, pp. 406–40.

men. So great, however, was the iniquity of the times and
the neglect and wickedness of men themselves, that a later
age let them collapse into their ruins. So, here and there
throughout Italy the stones lie toppled and overturned as
though by troops and siege weapons....

For truly, what are these images and the magnificent kind
of burial, other than a public and eternal testament to the
virtues and deeds of the man who passed from life and of the
gratitude of those who erected statues or built tombs with the
greatest eagerness in regard to the virtue of the living and to
the honor of the kind that must be regarded in life and death?

PONTANO RECREATES the ancient Roman roadside tomb championed
in his *De Magnificentia* in an effort to resurrect the city's ancient
architectural legacy in a way that would resonate with Italian viewers
generally and fellow humanists particularly; the chapel also functions
as a contemporary billboard. On the exterior of the structure
Pontano's own moralizing inscriptions constitute embellishment in
lieu of sculptural ornament.[31] These phrases are of contemporary
relevance in that they prescribe an intellectualized behavior for a
populace torn first by Aragonese political turmoil and then by the
battles between Spain and France for their city (c. 1490–1505).

The overtly political allusions expressed in the epigrams are unusual
for a commemorative monument and reflect Pontano's difficulties in
negotiating his own political position during the invasion of Charles
VIII of France in 1495 and the disintegration of the Aragonese regime.
The inscriptions on the exterior of the Pontano Chapel were the
source of great interest to humanists and were often copied.[32]

Pontano's enshrining these texts within the context of his own
funerary monument raises larger issues about the role of the word in
his literary *oeuvre*. In the dialogue *Aegidius*, Pontano announces that

31. See Nichols, "Giovanni Pontano's Funerary Chapel in Naples:
Renaissance Commemoration and the Word." Forthcoming.

32. Marino Sanuto, *Diarii di Marino Sanuto* (Venice: F. Visentini, 1890),
27:274, cited by Cornel von Fabriczy, "Summontes Brief an M.A. Michiel,"
Repertorium für Kunstwissenschaft 30 (1907): 145n.

the "Word" is fundamental to his account of Creation, that the word is both human and godly; godly in the sense that Christ is the word; human in the sense that Christ as an incarnation of the word revealed himself in the history of humanity. Pontano goes on to say that the Word possesses power over life and death, implying that it can save men who are bound by history.[33]

The following three inscriptions from the exterior of the Pontano Chapel are translated in Carol Kidwell, *Pontano: Poet and Prime Minister* (London: Duckworth, 1991), 217.

96. The Pontano Chapel: Exterior Inscriptions

THE STATE GROWS THROUGH DARING AND ACTION, NOT THROUGH THOSE COUNSELS THAT THE TIMID CALL CAUTIOUS.

SUPERIOR MEN IGNORE THE ABUSE OF THE WICKED FROM WHOM EVEN PRAISE IS FOUL.

DO NOT OFFER ONLY YOURSELF AS AN EXCEPTIONAL MAN, BUT TRAIN ANOTHER LIKE YOURSELF FOR YOUR COUNTRY.

THE INSCRIPTIONS decorating the chapel's interior [Fig. 38] are more private in nature and offer a glimpse into Pontano's sorrow at the loss of his wife, Adriana (d. 1490), and son, Lucio Francesco (d. 1498). As such, the word is given a physical structure and text acquires the permanence of stone. The following inscription on the interior of the Pontano Chapel is translated by Julia H. Gaiser.

97. The Pontano Chapel: Interior Inscription

I, THE FATHER, WAS BUILDING THIS TEMPLE TO GOD WHERE YOU, MY SON, MIGHT BURY MY ASHES.

THE FOLLOWING PROSE-POEMS, also translated by Julia H. Gaiser, appear in book form in Pontano's *De Tumulis* of 1502.[34] Elsewhere in *De Tumulis* Pontano describes both the physical structure of tombs

33. Rainer Weiss, "The Humanist Rediscovery of Rhetoric as Philosophy: Giovanni Giovano Pontano's Aegidius," *Philosophy and Rhetoric* 13 (1980): 33.

34. See also the translation by James H. Mc Gregor, chapter 3, reading 23, pp. 145–46. In the later twentieth century the Pontano Chapel functioned as a storehouse for folding chairs and was mostly inaccessible to visitors.

Fig. 38. Pontano Chapel, Interior. Photo: Italica Press.

and the role that words play in making tombs live: *"vigeant tumuli."* Implicit are the issues regarding the primacy of the word itself and the relative efficacy of stone and paper in conferring fame and immortality.

98. The Pontano Chapel: Inscriptions from De Tumulis

ALAS, THE UNLUCKY POWER OF FATE AND VARIABLE LAW OF TIME, FOR I AS THE FATHER, SON, AM BUILDING YOUR TOMB.

AS A PARENT, I PLACE FUNERAL OFFERINGS FOR MY BOY AND AS AN OLD MAN A BURIAL PLACE FOR MY SON.

ALAS, WHAT THE CRUEL STARS PREPARE, BUT WHATEVER THEY PREPARE, LET IT BE BRIEF, FOR THE BEST TIME OF MY LIFE HAS BEEN SPENT. THE REST OF MY LIFE WILL BE A FUNERAL.

AS A FATHER, HEIR OF GRIEFS, I PLACE THIS FOR YOU INSTEAD OF MAKING YOU HEIR OF PATRIMONY, AND YOU TAKE THIS TOMB AS YOUR PATRIMONY.

AN INSCRIPTION, NOW LOST, near the high altar of the Pontano Chapel (c. 1490) indicated that the arm-bone of Livy had been interred there. Alfonso I had been given the relic on behalf of the republic of Venice in 1451,[35] and it had subsequently passed to Pontano, the Aragonese prime minister, in the later quattrocento. The presence of such a relic in a humanist's chapel dedicated to the Virgin and to St. John the Evangelist is a consummate example of the coexistence of the pagan and Christian within the Renaissance cultural milieu. It also showcases the limb with which one writes.

The inscription is transcribed in Riccardo Filangieri, "Il Tempietto di Gioviano Pontano in Napoli," in *In onore di Giovanni Gioviano Pontano del V centenario della sua nascita* (Naples: Accademia Pontaniana, 1926), 16, after Laurentius Schrader, ed., *Monumentorum Italiae* (Helmstedt: Jakob Lucius, 1592), c. 231. Translated by Derek Moore.

99. Pontano: Inscription about the Arm-Bone of Livy

THE ARM OF T. LIVIUS, WHICH ANTONIO PANORMITA OBTAINED FROM THE PADUANS, GIOVANNI PONTANO ARRANGED AFTER MANY YEARS TO BE SET IN THIS PLACE.

THE SOCCORPO

A Franciscan monk called Fra Bernardino Siciliano penned a fascinating poetic account, rare in Renaissance literature, of the most important Neapolitan commission of the late fifteenth century: the *Soccorpo (Succorpo)* or crypt for the relics of San Gennaro [Fig. 39] commissioned by Cardinal Oliviero Carafa for the cathedral. The description of 1503–5, translated below, forms part of a larger work dedicated to the life of Gennaro, famous as a fourth-century martyr and bishop of Benevento, who would eventually become the patron saint of Naples. Gennaro's relics included his blood, which first liquefied in 1389; from that point on annual liquefaction was interpreted as an auger of good fortune for the city, while failure to liquefy portended imminent civic disaster (reading 112 below).

Fra Bernardino's poetic efforts were surely motivated by the return to Naples in 1497 of the additional relics recently discovered at the abbey of Montevergine, whose commendatory abbot was the powerful, aristocratic cardinal. Carafa himself negotiated their return

35. B.L. Ullman, "The Post-Mortem Adventures of Livy," *Studies in the Italian Renaissance* 51 (1973): 54–58.

Fig. 39. Duomo, Soccorpo. Photo: Nicole Riesenberger.

through mediation with Pope Alexander VI and the Aragonese monarchy; the actual transfer of the relics was effected by his brother and successor as archbishop of Naples, Alessandro Carafa. Immediately thereafter, work began on Carafa's *Soccorpo* (1497–1506), to be built *ex-novo* beneath the high altar of the cathedral of Naples. The crypt ultimately served as a mortuary chapel for other members of the Carafa family, many of them Neapolitan archbishops.

Fra Bernardino's manuscript is dedicated to Oliviero Carafa. Its 53 folios reflect the monk's education; he evidently had a degree in canon law and signed the introductory letter to the work with "Bernardinus Siculus, professor Minorum Decretum doctor." Written in hendecasyllables and laced with Sicilianisms, he uses the octave format of classic Italian literature. The manuscript is divided into five sections: 1. life of San Gennaro; 2. *On his blood* and the translation of his relics; 3. elegy to Cardinal Oliviero Carafa; 4. description of the Carafa Chapel and the *Soccorpo* of Saint Gennaro; and 5. conclusion with an oration to San Gennaro. Of particular significance for the history of Neapolitan art is the fourth section translated here, which comprises thirty verses and describes the crypt commissioned by Oliviero Carafa for the cathedral of Naples to showcase the relics of the saint.

In the absence of a formal contract for the *Soccorpo*, Fra Bernardino's poem survives as a valuable eyewitness account of the most important artistic commission of the late quattrocento. After first lauding the construction as the "empress of all chapels," he provides a detailed description of it. Marveling at its lavishly carved white marble revetment, he carefully notes that the crypt takes the form of a miniature basilica measuring, in Neapolitan palms, the equivalent of 10.20 meters long, 8.75 meters wide, and 3.86 meters high. Two rows of Ionic columns support a flat ceiling whose elaborately carved coffers contain reliefs of the Madonna and several early Neapolitan saints.

Fra Bernardino goes on to describe the niches with altars that line the walls. An apse contains an episcopal throne. The pavement consists of inlaid polychrome marbles of Cosmatesque pattern. This design reinvents local paleo-Christian sources such as the subterranean basilica in the catacombs of San Gennaro outside the city walls [Fig. 40], the crypt of Sta. Candida at San Pietro ad Aram that housed the relics of the first seven Neapolitan saints, and the early Christian *ipogea* of Probus Anicius at Old St. Peter's and of St. Lorenzo at San Lorenzo fuori le mura, Rome, of which Carafa was titular cardinal and patron.

While the verses resonate with Fra Bernardino's reverence for the new crypt, they also include several key pieces of information about it. Verses 6–16 indicate that a freestanding sepulcher-altar containing a Christ-like effigy of the saint surrounded by an iron grille was to stand in the crypt. This work was never executed, and Fra Bernardino's description is the lone piece of evidence for its intended appearance. Verse 21 indicates that the kneeling effigy of Cardinal Carafa was to be placed between the two entrance stairs to the chapel facing the sepulcher, a position analogous to that occupied by the work

Fig. 40. Ipogeum of the Catacomb of San Gennaro. Print by C.F. Bellerman, Hamburg, 1839.

today. Thus, the image of Carafa was evidently intended to be seen as communing with the sepulcher of San Gennaro, forming a tableau of intercession on the viewer's behalf.

Towards the end of the section, verse 26 identifies the supervising artist as Tommaso Malvito di Como, an attribution later echoed by Summonte in his letter of 1524. In the absence of other documentation, Fra Bernardino's citation of Tommaso Malvito has been taken as evidence that he conceptualized the crypt as well as supervised its construction. However, Malvito, head of a thriving workshop of Lombard sculptors, was primarily a designer of tombs rather than an architect.

A formal analysis of the *Soccorpo*'s aggressively *all'antica* design and sophisticated engineering, highly precocious by any standards of the day, suggests instead affinities with the work of Giuliano da Sangallo.[36]

36. For the attribution of the Soccorpo to Giuliano da Sangallo, see Nichols, "Caracciolo di Vico," 96–97; Daniela del Pesco, "Oliviero Carafa e il Succorpo di San Gennaro nel Duomo di Napoli," in *Donato Bramante: Ricerche, proposte, riletture,* Francesco Paolo di Teodoro, ed. (Urbino: Accademia Raffaello, 2001), 143–205. See also Michalsky, "Tombs," 272–75. Michelozzo's mid-quattrocento tabernacles for miraculous images at SS. Annunziata, Florence, and Sta. Maria dell'Impruneta provide the modular prototype deployed at the Soccorpo.

Given Carafa's close relationship to Lorenzo de' Medici, who lent the services of Filippino Lippi as the artist for the cardinal's chapel in Sta. Maria sopra Minerva (Rome), such a connection with Giuliano, chief architect to Lorenzo, is plausible. The *Soccorpo* is a brilliant example of both the princely *magnificentia* — Fra Bernardino gives the cost as 10,000 ducats in verse 27 and Summonte also comments on it — lauded by Pontano,[37] and of the daring precocity of Neapolitan design, already seen in the Pontano Chapel, in the late quattrocento.

With regard to the relics of San Gennaro brought to Naples in 1497 by Archbishop Alessandro Carafa, Fra Bernardino notes in section 3 of his manuscript that "the pest did not proceed, after the saint came into Naples; because of his many virtues and merits, the plague ceased." It is precisely at this moment that St. Januarius (Gennaro) joins Saints Roch and Sebastian as a plague saint. Fra Bernardino's perception of the healing powers of Gennaro's relics thus gives yet another dimension to the function of the *Soccorpo*. In a time of plague and great political uncertainty following the French invasion of 1494, the crypt becomes a locus of civic identity in which the image of Carafa may be seen as a powerful Neapolitan prince of the church who petitions San Gennaro to protect the citizens of his city from catastrophe. Using visually evocative forms, Carafa enhances his own episcopal authority in Spanish and French dominated Naples by promoting an alliance with a popular local saint-bishop, from whom he is intended to be seen as directly descended. In so doing he creates an important touchstone for Neapolitans.

Cardinal Carafa's *Soccorpo* also announces a Neapolitan identity. By recovering the precious miracle-working relics of San Gennaro and enshrining them in a sumptuous reinvention of a paleo-Christian crypt or basilica that features a life-sized image of himself kneeling in communion with the tomb of the bishop-saint, Cardinal Carafa reinforces his own claims to authority while providing the citizens of a perpetually occupied city with a locus in which their powerful early Christian religious heritage may be visually recalled.[38]

37. See chapter 9 and reading 164.

38. Nichols, "Plague," 28-33.

Fra Bernardino's poem is found in the Biblioteca Nazionale di Napoli, Fondo Brancacciano, V.A.12, ff. 40r–51r, and is transcribed, with important commentary, by Strazzullo, "La Cappella Carafa."[39] It is translated here by David Beneteau, Derek Moore, and CFN.

100. Fra Bernardino Siciliano: Poem about the Commission and Construction of Oliviero Carafa's Soccorpo in the Cathedral

I

A succorpo [the Cardinal] built
in his cathedral
both so gorgeous and so singular
that I believe the world has made nothing like it:
furthermore, it cannot be stated how fine it is,
being even more beautiful than people say:
it is the empress of all chapels
no matter how rich or beautiful others may be.

II

Of fine and select marble
the whole structure is made:
I have seen it clearly.
There are finely formed
pilasters, eighteen smooth and straight:
there are also ten reinforced columns,
handsomely placed
on bases with capitals.

III

Forty-eight palms long
is the socta corpo,
and fifteen palms high
with a gleaming ceiling,
and it is thirty-six palms wide.
In it are carved many saints
very elegant and adorned,
they are tall, handsome and well defined.

39. See also Franco Strazzullo, *Quinto centenario della traslazione delle ossa di San Gennaro da Montevergine a Napoli 1497–1997* (Naples: Edizioni Scientifiche Italiane, 1996), 42–93.

IV

The image of the empress
of paradise, modest virgin,
mother of our redeemer,
it pleases me to place here first.
I bless the hand that
made it, represented with such feeling:
she holds omnipotent Christ to her breast,
In her arms her devoted son.

V

The first pope, zealous prince,
apostle of Christ, Saint Peter,
who holds in that triumphant court
the keys of heaven's gates, a true shepherd,
and there is also Paul, elegant doctor,
who departed this world together,
and bequeathed their boundless gifts,
in this succorpo are sculpted.

VI

There are also the seven patron saints
of Naples, supreme and regal city:
the four evangelists of course,
as well as the four doctors of the Church:
who seem to be living people,
their limbs so well formed and natural.
only the breath of life
they lack, and speech, but nothing else.

VII

To adorn each saint
The master mason decorated them
with four seraphs at the corners,
Finishing each in this manner.
Such adornment suits them so well
that those who see it are full of admiration:
the master is revered for this work,
the stone is fine, it seems like alabaster.

VIII

Also sculpted there is that Philistine
decapitated by David's hand,

who stood against the Hebrew people
So strong he was, known as Goliath.
And also that Holofernes, so guilty,
by Judith's hand beheaded:
each figure in relief, well sculpted
by that very expert Master.

IX
Four triumphal chariots
are also sculpted there and much adorned by
the very magisterial sun and moon,
Mercury with Jove adorned,
another depiction worth not a little.
I haven't written of everything, you know:
for brevity's sake I won't include them,
I am sure you will agree.

X
Thirteen altars there are in this space,
behind each is a niche
half round, and laboriously adorned,
of whitest marble and very articulated.
Such work had not been seen in these parts,
nor do we expect to see another similar:
everyone delights in beholding
such a completely unique work.

XI
In the middle of this succorpo will be built
A sepulcher worthy and excellent:
in this the master has prepared
with all his five senses,
both to please that very agreeable saint
and to comfort those who view it,
and to please that cardinal
and to comfort all mortals.

XII
The master wants to sculpt four animals
of equal shape and similar appearance,
on these he intends to support
that great sepulcher of the perfect man.

They are called harpies by everyone:
I understand them to have the head of an eagle,
the arms, chest and stomach of a woman,
with a single lion's foot.

XIII

And then in resemblance to Christ,
who lies dead in the sepulcher,
an angel of light was seen
overhead, and another on foot in the garden
to gladden that sorrowful heart
of the Magdalen, so very wan:
that adroit master wishes to represent
this event in the sepulcher he must make.

XIV

Two angels he intends to sculpt
around the body of San Gennaro,
one at his head, I understood it recounted
by the master, who has no equal,
and one at his feet in accordance with his ability,
a work which is so rare:
he will surely not be stingy in showing
all his talent and unique skill.

XV

And above the sepulcher of such value,
eight palms long and four wide,
they will place a high altar:
the master has recounted to me.
The altar table is beauteous and of great whiteness,
they have measured it at ten palms in length,
there will be five colonettes per side,
or actually little piers.

XVI

All around there will be a worthy grate
of wrought iron with its strong bars,
which has been arranged in an outstanding setting
with its locked and strong gates,
and masterfully arranged
by great masters with their clever ways:

with good fortune the work proceeds,
and happy will be all who see it.

XVII

The floor and pavement they wish to make
completely in inlay of great value:
the stone is fine, lovely and singular
with various and different colors:
the masters do not cease to labor
on this most beauteous work.
It will be inlay such as this
to bring pleasure in the succorpo.

XVIII

Two great stairs of great value
are a worthy embellishment in the succorpo,
of twenty steps, of beautiful workmanship,
and measuring ten palms per side,
each in a piece of white color.
Everyone descends happily to the pleasing crypt;
with heart truly consoled
the devout descend and ascend.

XIX

In between these stairs are placed two gates
of equal form and similar appearance;
they will be of metal, fine and strong,
sculpted completely in proper fashion;
again the seven patrons of good fortune
will be shaped effectively:
the chosen master named above
is prepared to make these worthy gates.

XX

At the head of each stair will go
two great columns very well ornamented,
above which a beam they will make,
of finest marble adorned.
Its length they've measured
At fifty and one palm, you know.
Such beautiful columns have been measured
Fifteen palms with their capitals.

XXI

Outside the grate and between the two stairs
stands a prie-dieu polished and smooth;
here will be that worthy cardinal
on bended knees with bare head
before the saint, of immortal life:
his hands are joined with such feeling,
his pleasing gaze towards the shepherd
whom he takes for his worthy defender.

XXII

Three very excellent windows there are certainly
in the succorpo, you know:
all are on the eastern side,
polished, large, beautiful and measured:
all make that place so bright,
the aforesaid works illuminated,
and they are sealed by a double grate,
each very lovely and each glazed.

XXIII

At the foot of that stair a recessed cupboard
the exceptional master will put in place,
so that there can effectively
be conserved the sacred objects,
and all in one place clear and neat,
each one with such craftsmanship made.
Another recessed cupboard appears beside this one,
all have seen it at the foot of the other stair.

XXIV

At the head of each stair with honor,
according to the reason I have heard said,
there will be two worthy niches for ashes
of those who does not want to be buried;
which is conceded by the highest shepherd
who can absolve if he so wishes
at one's death, with such power,
from the punishment and guilt of all sins.

XXV

It certainly does not appear unreasonable
to narrate the many qualities

of this succorpo and of the great patron
of this most noble city;
and that which I say is not mere hearsay;
but things seen, clear, and proven.
The truth has been told to me with certainty
by he who in this art appears crowned.

XXVI
Thomas is his pleasing name
by many people certainly recognized,
and Malvito is his surname,
who has sculpted well many figures,
and his city is called Como.
In the art of sculpture trained,
he was raised in that wholesome city
in the grand duchy of Milan.

XXVII
My low intellect tried to figure out
what the expense will be,
for that which one actually sees
and for what will come in the future;
and about this he gave
the right and truthful response.
He has told me the absolute truth
that it will reach ten thousand ducats.

XXVIII
At all times, moments, days and hours,
except the major saints' days,
in the existing work they labor
those who are expert and learned laborers.
That worthy cardinal takes great care
to send that work forward:
he has put all his effort
In that succorpo until it is finished.

XXIX
The devoted worthy work will be finished,
which is worth a lot,
it is certainly necessary that the worthy and excellent
cardinal establish dowries.

*I'm not going to specify the amount
because I don't know which rumor to believe,
but I think that it will be excellent.*

XXX
*I've already heard about the endowment
from a man worthy of honor:
and he told me how he came to know it,
but he did not hear it from that great lord
who will provide it,
according to his status of great wealth:
however, my heart has advised me
that he will leave it in his will.*

SANNAZARO'S CHAPEL AND TOMB

Jacopo Sannazaro commissioned a chapel c.1524. It was to be built near Virgil's tomb on the grounds of his villa at the coastal site of Mergellina, deeded to him by the king in 1499. The chapel — for which he commissioned a *presepe* from the Neapolitan sculptor Giovanni da Nola — was dedicated to Sta. Maria del Parto or St. Mary of Childbirth, and as such it forms the physical counterpart of Sannazaro's poem titled *De partu virginis* (1521). Dedicated to Leo X, the poem celebrates the Annunciation and the prophecy of a new golden age in keeping with Pope Leo's own cultural agenda.[40]

The excerpt that follows from *De partu virginis* (1:19–30) includes a vow to build the church and is translated by Nash, *Major Latin Poems*, 33, ll. 18–30.

101. Sannazaro Vows to Build a Chapel
But chiefly you, O Gracious Mother, the certain hope of men, the certain hope of the gods, whom a thousand armed bands attend, and the whole militia of high heaven with all their chariots, their standards, their clarions and trumpets, joining their multitudes to the singing circle about you — if to your

40. Sannazaro was one of the poets included in Raphael's Parnassus in the Stanza della Segnatura for Julius II. *De partu virginis* was inspired by a sermon preached by the celebrated humanist-theologian Giles of Viterbo at San Giovanni a Carbonara, a venue popular with Pontano's Academy c.1500.

Fig. 41. Giovanni Angelo Montorsoli. Tomb of Jacopo Sannazaro, S. Maria del Parto. Photo: Mentnafunangann. Wikimedia.

shining temple I bring the garlands that are due; if for you I establish abiding altars in the carven rock, whence lovely Mergellina rising high from her steep summit looks down on the foaming waves, and comes in view for the approaching sailor while yet he is far away; if rightly I sing your praises, if I bear witness to your rituals and offerings and your day, and your assemblies everywhere renowned, when yearly we observe the celebration of the blessed birth; Goddess, instruct your poet ignorant of the way and unaccustomed to the work, and aid him now benignly in his fearsome enterprise.

SANNAZARO ALSO BUILT a larger church called San Nazaro above Sta. Maria del Parto to house his tomb, effectively creating a double-church. Sannazaro had bequeathed the church to the order of the Servants of Mary, who, following the poet's death in 1530, turned to the Florentine Giovanni Angelo Montorsoli, himself a Servite, to execute the tomb (1536/37–1543, Fig. 41). Thus, as with the Piccolomini Chapel in Monteoliveto, the inter-relationship of the houses of a particular order facilitated the selection of the artist for the commemorative monument. Montorsoli, who had visited Naples and perhaps left because of the threat of the "Turkish army," worked together with Bartolomeo Ammanati in Pisa and Carrara on the commission for the tomb exported from there to Naples, thus repeating Donatello and Michelozzo's exportation of the Brancacci Tomb from the same locale a century earlier. Seated Michelangelesque figures of Apollo and Minerva frame a relief with Arcadian mythological figures, and a portrait bust of Sannazaro rests on a sarcophagus above them.[41]

Vasari's recounting of the project was motivated by the involvement of the Florentine sculptor Giovanni Agnolo Montorsoli (patronized by Duke Cosimo I de' Medici), by his admiration for Sannazaro, and by his own first-hand familiarity with the project which he would have seen newly completed in Naples. His unusually detailed account describes the sculptor as involved with several projects for both Cosimo I and other patrons simultaneously. It provides important testimony of the degree to which sculptors worked in a variety of locations on a single commission and of the way in which works of art themselves were moved around. Vasari sees this as one means of gaining exposure — where admiration for one project results in another — as with the Genoese response to sculptures for the Neapolitan tomb. Sannazaro's poetry was known throughout Europe, and his tomb later became a popular stop on the Grand Tour.

This passage is from Vasari's life of Fra Giovanni Agnolo Montorsoli, 2:539–42.

41. Marc Deramaix and Birgit Laschke, "'Maroni musa proximus ut tumulo': L'église et le tombeau de Jacques Sannazar," *Revue de l'Art* 95 (1992): 35–36; Michalsky, "Tombs," 284–87.

102. Sannazaro Builds a Second Church for His Tomb

...the Frate... went on to Naples in the hope that he might have to make the tomb of Jacopo Sannazaro, a gentleman of Naples, and a truly distinguished and most rare poet. Sannazaro had built at Mergellina, a very pleasant place with a most beautiful view at the end of the Chiaia, on the shore a magnificent and most commodious habitation, which he enjoyed during his lifetime; and coming to his death, he left that place, which has the form of a convent, with a beautiful little church, to the Order of the Servite Friars, enjoining on Signor Cesare Mormerio and the Lord Count d'Aliffe, the executors of his will, that they should erect his tomb in that church, built by himself, which was to be administered by the above-named friars. When the making of it came to be discussed, Fra Giovanni Agnolo was proposed by the friars to the above-named executors; and to him, after he had gone to Naples, as has been related, that tomb was allotted, for his models had been judged to be no little better than the many others that had been made by various sculptors, the price being a thousand crowns. Of which having received a good portion, he sent to quarry the marbles Francesco del Tadda of Fiesole, an excellent carver whom he had commissioned to execute all the squared work and carving that had to be done in that undertaking, in order to finish it more quickly.

...the Turkish army having entered Puglia and the people of Naples being in no little alarm on that account... [the Frate] gave the executors to understand that he would do the work either in Carrara or in Florence, and that at the appointed time it would be finished and erected in its place....

To Carrara the Frate went very willingly, hoping with that opportunity to carry forward the above-mentioned tomb of Sannazaro, and in particular a scene with figures in half-relief... he went off to Genoa... yet without altogether neglecting the tomb of Sannazaro... After this the Genoese, seeing the tombs and figures made for the tomb of Sannazaro, and much liking them, desired that the Frate should execute a St. John the Evangelist for their cathedral church....

Finally Fra Giovanni Agnolo departed from Genoa and
went to Naples, where he set up in the place already
mentioned the tomb of Sannazaro, which is composed in
this fashion. At the lower corners are two pedestals, on each
of which are carved the arms of Sannazaro, and between
them is a slab of one *braccio* and a half on which is carved
the epitaph that Jacopo wrote for himself, supported by two
little boys. Next, on each of the said pedestals is a seated
statue of marble in the round, four *braccia* in height, these
being Minerva and Apollo; and between them, set off by
two ornamental consoles that are at the sides, is a scene two
braccia and a half square in which are carved in low-relief
Fauns, Satyrs, Nymphs, and other figures that are playing
and singing, after the manner which that most excellent
man has described in the pastoral verses of his most learned
Arcadia. Above this scene is placed a sarcophagus of a very
beautiful shape in the round, all carved and very ornate, in
which are the remains of that poet; and upon it, on a base in
the centre, is his head taken from life, with these words at the
foot — ACTIUS SINCERUS — accompanied by two boys with
wings in the manner of Loves, who have some books about
them. And in two niches that are at the sides, in the other
two walls of the chapel, there are on two bases two upright
figures of marble in the round, each of three *braccia* or little
more; these being St. James the Apostle and St. Nazaro.
When this work had been built up in the manner that has
been described, the above-mentioned lords, the executors,
were completely satisfied with it, and all Naples likewise.

MONTORSOLI AFFIXES HIS NAME only to the plinth of the monument.
Continuing the fashionable imitation of Apelles' signature, the use
of the imperfect tense *"faciebat"* echoes Michelangelo's inscription
of authorship on his Roman *Pietà*. His assistant, Ammanati, is not
mentioned.

*103. Giovanni Agnolo Montorsoli Uses "Faciebat" in the Inscription for the
Tomb of Sannazaro*

> BROTHER GIOVANNI ANGELO FLORENTINE OF THE SERVITE
> ORDER MADE THIS.

P<small>IETRO DE</small> S<small>TEFANO</small>'<small>S</small> exhaustive post-Tridentine catalogue of Neapolitan churches includes a detailed, deliberately prosaic — "so as not to appear affected and intended for all" —description of Sannazaro's chapel and a translation of its Latin inscriptions into Italian. He is, however, characteristically unspecific with regard to the chapel's authorship, alluding to Montorsoli's fame but failing to identify him by name. He does, however, cite Genoa, from which Vasari claims he brought the sculptures, instead of Pisa as the site of manufacture.

De Stefano's lack of attribution characterizes Neapolitan guidebooks of the cinquecento. Little is known about him, and the valuable guide written in 1560 was not republished, perhaps because of the appearance of Cesare d'Engenio's *Napoli Sacra* in 1623.[42] De Stefano's comment is found in his *Descrittione dei luoghi sacri della città di Napoli* (Naples: Amato, 1560), 23–24. Translated by CFN.

104. Pietro de Stefano: Sannazaro's Tomb
...a tomb of marble that was made in Genoa by a brother of the aforementioned order, a very famous sculptor.

T<small>HE LITERARY RELATIONSHIP</small> of Sannazaro's bucolic poetry to that of Virgil, and the physical proximity of San Nazaro to the tomb of the Roman poet at Posillipo, itself the subject of fervent cult, provides the focus for the inscription.[43] Although Vasari attributes it to Sannazaro, the inscription was composed by Sannazaro's friend Pietro Bembo, the Venetian-born humanist, patron, and future cardinal.[44] "Sincerus" refers to Jacopo's academic name of Actius Sincerus. Bembo's inscription for the tomb of Jacopo Sannazaro is translated in Kidwell, *Sannazaro and Arcadia*, 169.

105. Pietro Bembo: Virgil and the Inscription for Sannazaro's Tomb
P<small>LACE FLOWERS BY THE SACRED ASHES, HERE IS THAT</small> S<small>INCERUS</small> C<small>LOSEST TO</small> V<small>IRGIL IN HIS POETRY AS IN HIS TOMB.</small> H<small>E LIVED</small> 72 <small>YEARS.</small> H<small>E DIED IN</small> 1530.

42. Amirante, 19.

43. J.B. Trapp, "The Grave of Vergil," *Journal of the Warburg and Courtauld Institutes* 62 (1984): 1–31. See also Abbamonte, "Naples: A Poet's City."

44. Deramaix and Laschke, 40 n.106.

SAN GIACOMO DEGLI SPAGNOLI

Don Pedro de Toledo's establishment of a church-hospital complex c.1540 dedicated to the apostle James, patron saint of Spain, near the Castel Nuovo and towards the western end of the city that he was developing, created a prominent focal point for the cult in a city whose population was increasingly Iberian; the church was also a counterpoint to the powerful cult of San Gennaro that centered around his relics in the cathedral on the eastern side of the city.[45] Its architect was Ferrante Manlio (Maglione), the Spanish royal architect who later designed a new residential palace for the viceroy nearby (reading 76). Administered by the Knights of Saint James, the lay administration of the church seems to have been analogous to that of the Angevin church of Sant'Eligio. The plan incorporated a three-aisled basilica with a dome over the crossing.

In the second edition of his *Vite*, Vasari discusses the tomb of Don Pedro de Toledo [Fig. 42], the centerpiece of San Giacomo, and the patron whom Vasari hoped to serve as court painter. Vasari would have known Giovanni da Nola's monument of 1540–46 from his sojourn in Naples and through Cosimo I de' Medici and Eleonora de Toledo, Pedro's daughter. However, he provides considerably less detail than that given to Sannazaro's tomb, undoubtedly due to the authorship of a local Neapolitan artist called Giovanni da Nola (da Mirigliano). Nola had executed c.1522 the tomb of Don Ramón de Cardona, an earlier Spanish viceroy, which was sent to San Nicolas in Bellpuig, Catalonia.

The grand and unusual marble monument for Don Pedro takes the form of a free-standing square slab with a raised platform on which rest kneeling figures of the viceroy and his wife, María Osorio de Pimentel, at a *prie-dieu*; the platform is decorated on three sides with reliefs depicting Don Pedro's major victories and Charles V's entry into Naples.[46] Standing figures of virtues anchor each of the four corners. The work thus develops a royal tomb

45. Sanchez, 168–69.

46. Claudia Roth Pierpont, "Giovanni da Nola and the Monument of Don Pedro da Toledo: A Study in Sixteenth-Century Neapolitan Sculpture," (UMI, 1988); Michalsky, "Tombs," 287–88.

type of Spanish and French origin. Although Vasari critiques the Neapolitan sculptor's lack of design, the tomb in fact displays a strikingly bold mixture of piety and overt political propaganda in the development of a commemorative type that became increasingly popular.

Don Pedro was visiting Eleonora in Florence in 1552 when he died and was buried at the Duomo there. Thus, as Vasari points out (1:867–68), Nola's tomb was never sent to Spain as seemingly intended. The monument's eventual placement, at the direction of Don Garcia de Toledo, the viceroy's son, behind the high altar in the newly established Spanish national church calls attention to Don Pedro's role as the church's founder.

Vasari was much more favorably disposed towards the younger (and short-lived) Neapolitan sculptor Girolamo Santacroce whose talents he discusses in comparison. [47] The Tuscan would have known the work of both sculptors first-hand.

Fig. 42. Giovanni da Nola. Tomb of Don Pedro de Toledo, S. Jacopo degli Spagnoli. Photo: Italica Press.

47. Vasari, 1:866–67.

106. Vasari: Pedro de Toledo Builds the Church of San Giacomo
Old as he was, Giovanni da Nola, who was a well practised
sculptor, as may be seen from many works made by him at
Naples with good skill of hand, but not with much design,
still remained alive. Him Don Pedro di Toledo, marquis of
Villafranca, and at that time viceroy of Naples, commissioned
to execute a tomb of marble for himself and his wife; and
therein Giovanni made a great number of scenes of the
victories obtained by that lord over the Turks, with many
statues for the same work, which stands quite by itself, and
was executed with much diligence. This tomb was to have
been taken to Spain; but, since that nobleman did not do this
while he was alive, it remained in Naples. Giovanni died at
the age of seventy, and was buried in Naples, in the year 1558.

IN THE INTRODUCTORY SECTION on architecture for the edition
of 1550 for the *Lives,* Vasari highlights the desirability of Carrara
marble by noting that it was exported outside of Italy. He uses Nola's
monument of Don Pedro as an example, believing in the later 1440s
that it was destined for Spain. Vasari may have chosen this work to
showcase as it allowed him to celebrate the largesse of his own patron,
Duke Cosimo I de' Medici. In this section, he describes Nola's work
as excellent. As noted, Cosimo was the husband of Don Pedro's
daughter, Eleonora de Toledo; she in turn functioned as a conduit for
cultural exchange with Spanish Naples.

The passage is from Giorgio Vasari, *Le vite de' più eccellenti pittori scultori
e architettori nelle redazioni del 1550 e 1568*, Rosanna Bettarini and Paola
Barrocchi, ed. (Florence: Sansoni, 1966), 1:44–45. It is translated by CFN.

107. Vasari: The Carrara Marble of Don Pedro's Tomb
Today the moderns quarry this type [Carrara marble] for
their statues and not only for use in Italy, but it is shipped
to France, England, Spain, and Portugal; as we see today for
the tomb made in Naples by Giovanni da Nola, excellent
sculptor to Don Pedro da Toledo viceroy of that kingdom,
that all the marbles were given and brought to Naples by the
most illustrious and excellent Signore Cosimo de' Medici,
duke of Florence, a work they are bringing to Spain.

Fig. 43. S. Gregorio Armeno. Nave with nun's corretto. Photo: ho visto nina volare. Wikimedia.

SAN GREGORIO ARMENO

The prestigious Benedictine church of San Gregorio Armeno, which housed an extensive collection of relics, was renovated during the post-Tridentine surge of monastic building in the late sixteenth century. Embedded within the ancient street grid of the city, its new tripartite atrium (1574–80) supported an innovative nuns' choir [Fig. 43] that was level with the cloister they inhabited.[48]

Fulvia Caracciolo, a member of one of the prestigious aristocratic families sheltered at San Gregorio, wrote a history of the monastery in which she describes the elevated choir space as one of privilege. Here the nuns spent several hours a day out of view of the laity and close to the ceiling painted by Dirck Hendricksz of Flanders (reading 149).

Fulvia Caracciolo's brother, Francesco Caracciolo, eventually was proclaimed a saint — and later a patron saint — of Naples itself. Her history of the church is found in the Archivio di Stato di Napoli, ASN, Monasteri soppressi, San Gregorio Armeno, 3435, Caracciola, "Borro ó sia Esemplare, fol. 126r, translated in Helen Hills, *Invisible Cities: The Architecture of Devotion in Seventeenth-Century Neapolitan Convents* (Oxford: Oxford University Press, 2004), 148.

48. Del Pesco, "Oliviero Carafa," 326; Hills, 151–55.

108. Fulvia Caracciolo: San Gregorio Armeno, Nuns, and Sacred Spaces
They received the veil from the abbess. One day after
Vespers, the nuns' hair was cut short, and after a few months,
or years, depending on their age, they took the second rank
which were certain [privileged positions] in the choir.

GESÙ NUOVO

The second half of the cinquecento saw an extraordinary surge of
ecclesiastical construction in Naples, which visually communicated the
authority of Catholicism. Of particular note are the building projects
undertaken in Naples by the Order of the Society of Jesus, whose
energetic mission of preaching and education had generally appealed to
the Spanish need to establish orthodoxy.[49] The Jesuits appropriated land
at the western end of the lower decumanus, near the Angevin church of
Sta. Chiara, for their first church, *case professe,* and *collegio.* Eventually, the
order acquired the Palazzo Sanseverino, which had been constructed
c.1470 by Novèllo da San Lucano for Roberto Sanseverino, prince of
Salerno. Its distinctive diamond-point façade was incorporated into that
of the new second church, called Gesù Nuovo [Fig. 44], begun in 1584
by the Jesuit architect Giuseppe Valeriano.[50]

Giovanni Battista del Tufo's lengthy poetic homage to Naples of
1588 celebrates a number of Neapolitan monuments, including the
Palazzo Sanseverino, in the form of unsophisticated non-rhyming
free verse. An aristocrat and promoter of the viceregency, Tufo gives
no indication of the controversy surrounding the Jesuits' acquisition
of the structure.

The poem in his *Ritratto o modello delle grandezze, delizie o meraviglie
della nobilissima città di Napoli,* 1588, is partially transcribed in Morisani,
Letteratura artistica, 69. Translated by CFN.

*109. Giovanni Battista del Tufo: Poem about the Gesù Nuovo and the
Palazzo Sanseverino*
> Also is that of Salerno
> Today under different governance

49. Nichols, "Ecclesiastical Architecture," 151–56.

50. Conelli, 46–52.

Fig. 44. Gesù Nuovo, exterior. Photo: Italica Press.

The prince constructed near S. Chiara
Shows proud and rare,
Whose façade in front
Is all marble and diamond points;
And its height is
Equal to its width
That one or the other, whether near or far
Is difficult for the eye to determine.

This palace so proud
The Jesuits now have for their residence.

A LETTER OF 1584 to Cardinal Ferdinand de' Medici from Pietro Riccardi, his Tuscan agent in Naples, in fact documents the resentment of the Neapolitans about the Jesuit acquisition of the Palazzo Sanseverino and reflects the strong undercurrent of tension between the Spanish viceroy and his Neapolitan subjects. The degree to which Pedro Giron was identified with the Jesuit cause in the letter underscores both the alliance of the viceregency with the Jesuits (and other reformed orders), through whom the Spanish hoped to obliterate all forms of heresy, including Protestantism, as well as the degree to which the aristocratic palace symbolized Neapolitan pride.

Riccardi's letter also notes the prominent location of the palace on the western side of the ancient Greco-Roman grid near the new Via Toledo. The sloping piazza in front of the church gave the facade a particular prominence.[51] The creation of a Jesuit enclave fulfilled the Tridentine mandate to *"fare isola"* (aggregating property to make an isolated block) within the city walls, itself another very controversial issue.

The letter from Riccardi to Cardinal Ferdinand de' Medici is dated 23 March 1584 and included by Alfred de Reumont, *The Carafas of Maddaloni: Naples under Spanish Dominion* (London: Henry G. Bohn, 1854), 258, as cited in Conelli, "Gesù Nuovo," 46–47.

110. Pietro Riccardi: Neapolitans Resent the Jesuit Acquisition of Palazzo Sanseverino
> The Neapolitans are angry in their language against His Excellency [Pedro Giron, duke of Osuna] on account of the preference shown to the Jesuits at the sale of the palace of the prince of Salerno. The commonality of Naples tried hard at the same time to get possession of it, because they wished that the [palace] might keep its original form, since it contributed particularly to the ornament of the town, and was so advantageously situated. But the fathers, who strive after undivided power, have overcome all difficulties, and obtained their object, and already is the building begun.

51. Conelli, 52–54.

RENAISSANCE NAPLES: A DOCUMENTARY HISTORY

SAN MARTINO

The Carthusian monastery of San Martino, on Monte di Sant'Eramo high above the city of Naples, was also a major construction site in the late sixteenth century. Unlike the project for the Gesù, however, the scheme involved the renovation and expansion of a trecento Angevin foundation whose original architects included the Sienese Tino di Camaino. Traditionally the object of munificent patronage and known within the order as an intellectual center, the prior Severo Turbolo used his own fortune to transform the complex into a sumptuous display of wealth and architectural sophistication.[52] He turned to the Florentine sculptor-architect Giovanni Antonio Dosio to realize this ambition; Dosio had previously been employed by the Carthusians to renovate the cloister of Sta. Maria degli Angeli in Rome. Dosio contributed a design for the cloister of San Martino as well, whose gleaming neo-Brunelleschian forms would be embellished by Cosimo Fanzago in the following century [Fig. 45]. The following document recorded by the notary Aniello Rosanova in 1591 is summarized by Gaetano Filangieri, *Indice degli artefici delle arti maggiori e minori* (Naples: Tipografia dell'Accademia Reale delle Scienze, 1891), 5:173.

111. Aniello Rosanova: Expanding the Carthusian Monastery at San Martino
On 7 June 1591, the Neapolitan master Raymo Bregantino, Felice de Felice and Fabrizio de Guido da Carrara marble-workers... promise to consign to said monastery San Martino all the marbles that will be necessary for the church of said monastery, which will be worked to the complete satisfaction of the Most Reverend Father Prior of said monastery and of Gio. Antonio Dosio architect of said monastery....

52. V. Spinazzola, "La Certosa di S. Martino. I. Notizie Storiche della Certosa di S. Martino, 1325–1900," *Napoli Nobilissima* 11 (1902): 101; Daniela del Pesco, "Alla ricerca di Giovanni Antonio Dosio: Gli anni napoletani," *Bolletino dell'Arte* 71 (1992): 15–66; John Nicholas Napoli, "From Social Virtue to Revetted Interior: Giovanni Antonio Dosio and Marble Inlay in Rome, Florence, and Naples," *Art History* 31 (2008): 523–46; Nichols, "Ecclesiastical Architecture," 145–51.

Fig. 45. S. Martino, Cloister. Photo: Italica Press.

RELICS

Among the many relics that fill Neapolitan churches (as they did most great and small churches throughout Europe), the most famous Neapolitan relics are those of San Gennaro (Januarius), an early Christian bishop who eventually became patron saint of the city in the seventeenth-century. During the Renaissance, Gennaro's miraculously liquefying blood was housed at the cathedral that bears his name. Notar Giacomo, 97, refers to the astonishing survival of the carafes containing the blood in his account of the catastrophic earthquake of 1456. Translated by CFN.

112. Notar Giacomo: Carafes with San Gennaro's Miraculous Blood Survive the Earthquake of 1456

In the year 1456, on Saturday the 4th of December, at the eleventh hour [about 5:30 AM] into Sunday there was a great earthquake in the city of Naples that lasted for more than a day causing the Neapolitans to camp out at San Giovanni a Carbonara and at Piazza del Mercato in tents and pavilions: it was this way throughout the Regno… I believe that Naples was the hardest hit, and the most buildings fell in Naples, such as San Giovanni Maggiore, San Pietro Martire, the tower of the Duomo where the blood of the glorious San Gennaro was [preserved]. And miraculously two beams were found on the glass ampullae [*carrafelle*], under which they didn't suffer any damage.

FOLLOWING A WELL-ESTABLISHED European tradition, a court document of 2 April 1466 indicates that a heart-shaped container was planned to hold the heart of Alfonso I as a *"glorioso ricardacio."* Alfonso had died in 1458 and the copper and silver object was commissioned by his son, Ferrante I, from "Andria Galasso." Although never executed, it was intended to be placed in the triumphal arch of Castel Nuovo.[53]

The document issued on behalf of King Ferrante is reprinted in Hersey, *Aragonese Arch*, 71, doc. 26, and excerpted here from the Italo-Catalan by Derek Moore.

113. A Heart-Shaped Reliquary for Alfonso I's Heart

30 June 1466. On said day, by the order of His Lordship the king, 8 ducats 4 tarens were given to Master Andrea Galasso, silversmith… in partial payment… for a heart-shaped container, to hold and preserve the heart of his glorious Lordship the king Don Alfonso, of immortal memory, whch is to be placed in the triumphal arch of Castel Nuovo.…

53. Hersey, *Arch*, 55.

ONE OF THE FASCINATING ASPECTS of Duke Alfonso's ecclesiastical patronage in relation to his development of the eastern part of Naples was his transferal to Sta. Maria Maddalena in 1489 of the relics of 240 "corpi dei BB. Martiri Idruntini," the martyrs of Otranto.[54] Alfonso had led the papal troops overland in the critical campaign of 1480–81 against the Turks, who had penetrated the Italian peninsula at Otranto on the Ionian coast.[55] Here the Turks had slaughtered hundreds of citizens at the beginning of the siege. Proclaimed martyrs, their remains were eventually transported to Naples by the Aragonese. It is believed that Alfonso intended to construct a memorial for the relics, although this never occurred.[56] They were moved in 1500 from Sta. Maria Maddalena to a chapel in Sta. Caterina a Formello, where they remain today. This public display of the duke's piety was compromised by his maneuvering with regard to the same two churches.

Joanpiero Leostello provides this account in his *Effemeridi*, 1:304–5. Translated by CFN.

114. Leostello: Duke Alfonso Brings the Relics of the Martyrs of Otranto to Sta. Maria Maddalena
    12 February 1490.

> And on this day the charitable priest of Otranto came and he brought ten cases of bones of the dead who were cut to pieces by the Turks, which the aforementioned illustrious lord wanted to place in the Magdalena

54. Michele Furnari, "L' insula di Santa Caterina a Formello: Fondazione, crescita e sviluppo attraverso i contributi della cartografia storica (1500–1880)," in *Santa Caterina a Formello: Vicende di un'insula napoletana,* Martino Canonico, ed. (Naples: Electa, 1996), 39 n. 5.

55. For the role of the Aragonese troops in the crucial battle of Otranto, see Kenneth Setton, *The Papacy and the Levant (1204–1571)* (Philadelphia: American Philosophical Society, 1976–84), 2:343–5, 364–75.

56. Fra Renaldi stated that the relics were "destinata per cappella reale," excerpted by Gerardo Cilento, "La fabrica della Chiesa," in *Santa Caterina a Formello*, 117–25 at 118. Sta. Maria Maddalena was renamed Sta. Maria dei Martiri when the relics were moved there in 1489.

recently renamed the church Sta. Maria of the Martyrs adjacent to his castle, whose nuns were transferred to Sta. Caterina de Formello; and the monks who were in that church were sent to San Pietro Maiella and were well provided for there....

THE MADONNA DELLA BRUNA was one of the most powerful miracle-working images in Naples. Located in the crypt of Sta. Maria del Carmine on the eastern side of the city near the coast, the panel's nickname calls attention to the pigment used for the flesh-tones of the Virgin and Child that had darkened with age. Notar Giacomo (234) records that the panel was taken to Rome by the Confraternity of Sta. Caterina in celebration of the Jubilee during the Easter season of 1500.[57] Translated by CFN.

Fig. 46. S. Maria del Carmine, High Altar with Madonna della Bruna. Marble frame by Bartolomé Ordóñez and Diego Siloé. Early 16th c. Photo: Maurizio Rea. Wikimedia.

115. Notar Giacomo: The Miracle-Working Properties of the Madonna della Bruna

On Tuesday 7 April 1500 the confraternity of Sta. Caterina departed from the city of Naples taking with them the venerable altarpiece of Our Lady embracing the Child called Sta. Maria della Bruna, and they brought it to Rome where when in procession it worked more miracles for several men from a variety of places and on Saturday the 25th on the day of St. Mark this confraternity returned with said altarpiece where in Naples it worked many miracles on the deaf, blind and lame from almost everywhere in the kingdom....

57. Filangieri, *Documenti*, 3:283–4, 348–63.

GIULIANO PASSERO'S ACCOUNT differs from that of Notar Giacomo by stating that Pope Alexander VI ordered the Madonna della Bruna be returned from Rome to Naples due to insufficient indulgences. A sumptuous carved marble tabernacle [Fig. 46], attributed to Bartolomé Ordóñez and Diego de Siloé, was later commissioned for the high altar of Sta. Maria del Carmine in the early sixteenth century to house the Sta. Maria della Bruna.

Passero's journals chronicle Neapolitan history from 1100 to 1530: Giuliano Passero, *Giornali*, Vincenzo Altobelli, ed. (Naples: Orsini, 1785), 121, cited by Filangieri, *Documenti*, 3:284. Translated by CFN.

116. Giuliano Passero: Pope Alexander VI sends the Madonna della Bruna back to Naples
> When the image arrived in Rome, Pope Alexander VI was skeptical of these miracles — no indulgence had been established for this image, neither at St. Peter's nor at other sites in Rome. So he told those who had brought it that they must leave immediately and return to Naples....

NOTAR GIACOMO comments (213) on the miraculous liquefaction of San Gennaro's blood when it was united with other recently discovered body parts of Gennaro. Additional relics of the saint were discovered c.1480 at the abbey of Montevergine, of which Cardinal Oliviero Carafa was commendatory abbot. Negotiations between Carafa, Ferrante I, and the papacy for their removal to the cathedral of Naples began in 1490 and were not concluded until c.1497. However, the nuns at Montevergine vehemently protested the transferal, which Notar Giacomo states took place in the middle of the night during an outbreak of the plague. The subsequent reuniting of Gennaro's relics resulted in the liquefaction of the blood. Translated by CFN.

117. Notar Giacomo: The Liquefaction of Gennaro's Blood when Unified with Other Newly Recovered Relics
> On the 13th of January 1497... on a Sunday at two in the morning the Neapolitan archbishop, Alessandro Carafa, entered the city of Naples, bringing with him the body of the glorious San Gennaro, the prize from the sanctuary of Sta. Maria Montevergine.... because of the plague there was

not a large crowd… when this body was put with the head
and blood of the saint, the blood liquefied.

AN ACCOUNT OF 1557 describes a tabernacle set up in honor of San
Gennaro in the old treasury of the cathedral. The miraculous blood
and other relics of the saint were transferred from the *Soccorpo* of the
cathedral (completed 1511, see reading 100 above) to the old treasury
in the first half of the cinquecento, perhaps following 13 January
1527 when a vow was made during an outbreak of the plague to
construct a new tabernacle and chapel in honor of Gennaro. The
more accessible location in the old treasury was a temporary one, in
anticipation of a new structure to house the relics.[58] Construction on
the sumptuous new treasury — present home of the relics — would
not begin until the seventeenth century. The silver image of San
Gennaro probably refers to the reliquary bust of 1304 commissioned
by Charles II of Anjou from Etienne Godefroyd, Guillaume de
Verdelay, and Milet d'Auxerre.

A text of 1557 included by F. Girolamo Maria di Sant'Anna, *Istoria
della vita, virtù e miracoli di S. Gennaro…* (Naples: S. Abbate, 1733), 315,
is cited by Franco Strazzullo, *La real cappella del Tesoro di S. Gennaro:
Documenti inediti* (Naples: Società editrice napoletana, 1978), 175.
Translated by CFN.

*118. F. Girolamo Maria di Sant'Anna: San Gennaro's Relics Are Moved
from the Soccorpo to the Old Treasury of the Cathedral*
Above the high altar of the three altars that are in that
chapel [Old Treasury], is a niche or window carved into
the wall and divided in two parts adorned with taffeta with
gold stars; in the first part there is a beautiful tabernacle
of gilded silver made with two orders of columns above
a silver vessel and between the order of four columns,
before which there is a silver image of San Gennaro bishop
and martyr; and between the other four columns of the

58. See Charlotte Nichols, "Plague and Politics in Early Modern Naples: The
Relics of San Gennaro," In *Sickness and in Health: Disease as Metaphor in Art and
Popular Wisdom*, Laurinda Dixon, ed. (Newark: University of Delaware Press,
2004), 23-44.

second order there is a round silver tabernacle [the case] with transparent glass pieces on each side, in the midst of which are two ampoules with the blood of the blessed San Gennaro, one larger and almost full and another smaller one, almost empty, and on each side of this tabernacle there is a silver angel.

★ ★ ★

CHAPTER 7: PAINTING
by Charlotte Nichols

THE LAST ANGEVINS

Sergianni Caracciolo del Sole was the grand seneschal of the Regno during the reign of Queen Giovanna II, and her paramour. (The queen later ordered his execution.) For the large, domed funerary chapel dedicated to the birth of the Virgin, he commissioned Leonardo da Besozzo[1] to paint a monumental Marian fresco cycle [Fig. 47, opposite page]. The mausoleum, which doubled as a monk's choir, was appended to the presbytery of the Augustinian church of San Giovanni a Carbonara, a church rebuilt by Giovanna's brother King Ladislaus and located near the royal residence of Castel Capuano. The towering and ornate tomb of Ladislaus, placed behind the high altar of the church, in fact frames the entrance to the Caracciolo Chapel, thereby reinforcing Sergianni's powerful position in the Angevin regime.[2] With telling symbolism, the Coronation of the Virgin is located on the other side of the royal tomb wall.

Around 1427 Leonardo da Besozzo brought to Naples the Gothic International style practiced by his father, Michelino, at the court of the Visconti in Milan and Pavia, where the younger artist also produced illuminated manuscripts. The Lombard's Marian scenes reflect Sergianni's urbanity and wealth by means of contemporary

1. For the dates of the commission, see Gennaro Toscano, "Leonardo da Besozzo à Naples: Un peintre du gothique tardif à l'époque des derniers rois de la dynastie angevine," in *Pierre, lumière, couleur: Études d'histoire de l'art du Moyen Age en l'honneur d'Anne Prache*, Fabienne Joubert and Dany Sandron, ed. (Paris: Presses de l'Université de Paris-Sorbonne, 1999), 417–21; idem, "Aggiunte a Leonardo da Besozzo," *Arte medievale* n.s. 3 (2005): 2:125–37; Challéat, *Dalle Fiandre a Napoli*, 109–10; Giovanna Cassese, "Leonardo (de' Molinari) da Besozzo," www.oxfordartonline.com; Serena Romano, "Patrons and Paintings from the Angevins to the Spanish Hapsburgs," in Hall–Willette, 171–232, at 189–92.

2. Two fresco paintings of Saint John the Baptist and Saint Augustine, attributed to Leonardo da Besozzo, are also seen between the caryatids at the lower level of the tomb of King Ladislaus.

Fig. 48. Leonardo da Besozzo. Nativity of the Virgin (above) with scene of Augustinian Hermits by Perrinetto da Benevento (below). Caracciolo del Sole Chapel, S. Giovanni a Carbonara. Photos: Italica Press.

fashionable accoutrements; the patron himself appears in an elaborate contemporary headdress throughout and is shown observing the Nativity scene from the bottom stair[3] [Fig. 48].

3. The double role of the centrally planned space as a private mortuary chapel and monks' choir is underscored by the two diverging themes of Leonardo's frescoes and Perrinetto da Benevento's comparatively rustic scenes from the *Thebaid* beneath them, which would have served as poignant reminders to monks, close to eye-level, of the hermitic ideals of work, prayer, and solitude. Jean-Claude Richard de Saint-Non's eighteenth-century

The artist's signature in Latin reportedly appears at the bottom of the *Nativity of the Virgin* in the Caracciolo del Sole Chapel. It has been translated here.

119. Leonardo da Besozzo Decorates the Chapel of Sergianni Caracciolo del Sole

LEONARDO DA BESOZZO OF MILAN PAINTED THIS CHAPEL AND THIS TOMB.

LEONARDO'S FLORID STYLE, rich in decorative effects, also appealed to King René of Anjou, the last Angevin king of Naples, where he ruled for a few tumultuous years (r. 1438–42) before being ousted by Alfonso I. Immediately on inheriting the kingdom in 1438, he commissioned from Leonardo a lavishly illustrated book of hours, *The Codex Santa Marta* (Naples, Archivio di Stato di Napoli), which celebrated his Angevin ancestors in Naples. Leonardo stayed on in Naples following Alfonso's ascension, executing a few works for him in the 1450s, which are now lost.

In the 1430s, as a prisoner of Philip the Good, duke of Burgundy, René of Anjou was exposed to a luxurious court life and to the art of Flanders, a taste that other royals shared.[4] Moreover, the Angevin king was himself evidently quite knowledgeable about the processes of Flemish painting, as Pietro Summonte indicates in his informative letter to Marcantonio Michiel in Venice in 1524. René may have learnt about them from Barthélemy van Eyck, who is thought to have been in Naples briefly before the invasion of 1442 and was later with the former king in France.[5]

René's short reign and the tendency of court historians beginning in the mid-quattrocento to privilege the cultural accomplishments of their conquering Aragonese patrons mean that his influence has

engraving in fact shows the *Thebaid* covered with fabric, perhaps to emphasize the grander aspects of the decoration for certain occasions. See Nichols, "Ecclesiastical Architecture," 109–13.

4. Joan Isobel Friedman, "René I, 4th Duke of Anjou," online at: http://www.oxfordartonline.com.

5. Challéat, 119 and 133.

traditionally been diminished. However, the king should be viewed as having promoted in Naples the cosmopolitan court life and taste for luxury objects for which Alfonso was celebrated. René established an influential Burgundian-style court in Provence following his defeat by the Aragonese in 1442; in what may be interpreted as a form of cultural retribution, he eventually lured a number of artists from Naples including Francesco Laurana.[6]

A section of Summonte's letter to Michiel follows here from the transcription in Nicolini, *L'arte napoletana*, 159, (lines 63–64). Translated by CFN.

120. Summonte: René of Anjou as a Painter and Collector of Flemish Art
    King Raniero [René], himself an accomplished painter dedicated to his art, although in the Flemish style, ruled for a short time here and was then expelled by King Alfonso I.

ALFONSO I AND HISPANO-NETHERLANDISH STYLE
Tangible evidence of Alfonso I's importation of Spanish artists to Naples and his taste for the Hispano-Netherlandish style[7] survives in the form of various documents and letters concerning the Valencian painter Jacomart Baco (also called Jaime Baco), who arrived there by order of the king c.1443.[8] Among Jacomart's missing Neapolitan works is the large and evidently heavy altarpiece in which the Virgin appears to Alfonso, thus signaling to the newly conquered populace their ruler's piety and alliance with the divine. The painting on panel — no doubt with richly gilded, stiff, and angular figures in the Hispano-Netherlandish manner — was the centerpiece of the votive church of Sta. Maria della Pace, erected in Campo Vecchio near

6. François Robin, *La Cour d'Anjou-Provence: La vie artistique sous le règne de René* (Paris: Picard, 1985), 81.

7. For Alfonso I and painting, see Romano, "Painting and Patrons," 190–94.

8. For Catalan documents about Jacomart's transfer to Naples and other works, see Elias Tormo y Monzó, *Jacomart y el arte hispano-flamenco cuatrocentista* (Madrid: Blass y cia, 1913), 96–119; and Claudie Bessort, "Jacomart [Baco, Jaime]," www.oxfordartonline.com. Alfonso also brought the Valencian painter Lluis Dalmau to Naples (Challéat, 106).

which the Aragonese had encamped on the eastern side of the city. Castel Capuano, Alfonso's first residence in Naples, was also located here. Installations of high altarpieces, such as that of Duccio's *Maestà* in the cathedral of Siena in 1311, were occasions of great celebration throughout the peninsula and are often well-documented. Sta. Maria della Pace was severely damaged during the earthquake of 1456.

Camillo Minieri Riccio, "Alcuni fatti di Alfonso I d'Aragona dal 15 aprile 1437 al 31 maggio 1458," *Archivio storico per le provincie napoletane* 6 (1881): 243–44, paraphrases a document of 1444 on moving Jacomart's altarpiece, citing the Archivio Storico delle Provincie Napoletane, *Cedole di Tesoreria* (Cedole 8, anno 1444, f. 38v). Minieri Riccio's summary, translated here by CFN, is included by Challéat, 107.

121. Cedole di Tesoreria: Jacomart Baco of Valencia Comes to Naples and Paints an Altarpiece for Alfonso I
    The painter Master Jacomart Baco, having finished the painting of the miracle of Sta. Maria della Pace which had been commissioned from him by the king, had that painting transported from his house to Castel Capuano in Naples. King Alfonso then had this painting taken from Castel Capuano to Campo Vecchio — this move took ten porters.

ALFONSO I DECREED Jacomart's altarpiece in Sta. Maria della Pace as the destination of an annual procession celebrating his conquest of Naples. The passage below demonstrates the way in which the king, who was personally devoted to St. George, integrated the local religious in a lavish ritual that ultimately underscored his own hegemony. The Aragonese court in Naples was generally known for its sumptuous pageantry as later recorded by humanists in the royal entourage, such as Giovanni Pontano.

Camillo Minieri-Riccio, "Alcuni Fatti," 417-18, reconstructs a description of the procession based on the *Cedole di Tesoreria, Archivio storico delle provincie napoletane* (cedole 23, anno 1453, f. 345. t. 346; cedole 30 anno 1456, f. 227). His summary is cited by Challéat, 107, and translated here by CFN.

122. Cedole di Tesoreria: Alfonso I's Annual Procession to Sta. Maria della Pace
This procession began with eight men in Turkish dress who carried the standard of St. George with the vermilion cross, then followed by 210 archers who were brothers of the confraternity of St. George. With lit candles in hand they accompanied King Alfonso together with the archbishop and all the ecclesiastic orders in this general procession, who, leaving the cathedral of the city went as far as the church of Sta. Maria della Pace in Campo Vecchio, where on arrival, the king gave a chalice of silver, which was gilded inside and out, to this confraternity, to be given to whichever archer would make the best shot in a game of crossbows. Then the king, having previously prepared bread, wine, fruit, and other things in abundance, allowed the archers and all of the people accompanying them to refresh themselves.

ALFONSO'S GROWING LIBRARY — probably inspired by the example of Philip the Good and the need to compete with other collector-rulers[9] — was augmented by a commission of c. 1455–58 for an illuminated manuscript on the princely sport of falconry titled *De scientia venandi per aves* (*On the Science of Hunting with Birds*, Fig. 49). The essay was originally written in Arabic by the ninth-century author Moamin and translated into Latin by Theodorus of Antioch c. 1250 at the request of Frederick II Hohenstaufen, who ruled the Regno at that time.[10] Alfonso's coat of arms appears at the bottom of the first page, part of which is translated here. The king shared the predilection for falcons, which he is documented as having received as a gift from Philip the Good, duke of Burgundy.[11]

9. For the library established by Alfonso I, see the revisionist article by Rowan Watson, "Fit for a King? The Alfonso of Aragon Hours and Baronial Patronage in Late Fifteenth-Century Naples," in *Under the Influence: The Concept of Influence and the Study of Illuminated Manuscripts*, John Lowden and Alixe Bovey, ed. (Turnhout: Brepols, 2007), 154.

10. See Musto, *Medieval Naples,* 124–43.

11. Challéat, 26. For falconry, see also Pontano's *De Magnificentia,* chapter 20 (Tateo, 216); and Luke Syson and Dillian Gordon, *Pisanello: Painter to the Renaissance Court* (London: National Gallery and Yale University Press, 2001), 82–83.

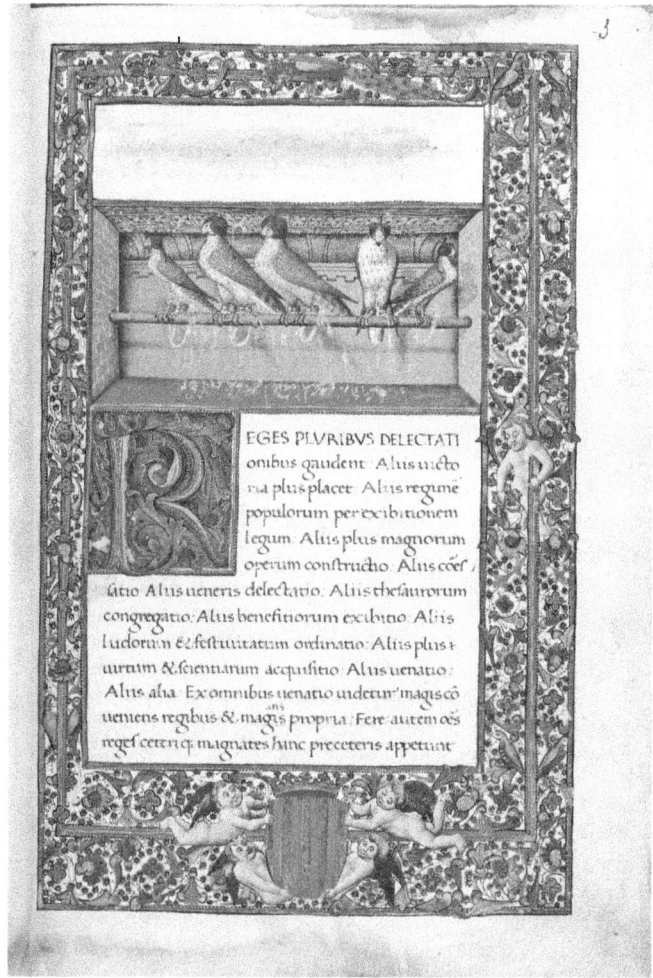

Fig. 49. On the Science of Hunting with Birds (De scientia venandi per aves).
Bienecke Rare Book and Manuscript Library,Yale University. Mss. 446, fol. 1v. Photo: Beinecke Library.

Folio 1r of the Beinecke Library's manuscript [Fig. 49] demonstrates both a decorative sensibility and naturalism that would have provoked the admiration and amusement of elite viewers with whom the king competed and shared his little treasure measuring 10 x 6 inches. Of particular note are the black and gold tiles at the top of the page, the shadows cast by the birds themselves, and the inclusion of their droppings.[12] The popular treatise, known throughout Europe, was later translated into the Neapolitan dialect for Ferrante I, son of King Alfonso.

An excerpt describing falconry as the kingliest of activities from *De scientia venandi per aves* (New Haven, Beinecke Library, Mss. 446, fol. 1v) is translated here from the Latin by Anne Laidlaw with Lilian Randall.

123. Alfonso I Commissions a Manuscript on Falconry
For entertainment, kings take delight in all kinds of things. For some, victory pleases most. For others, control of subjects through the promulgation of laws. Some, the construction of great works. Some, riotous Bacchanalian drinking. Some, the delights of love. Some, the amassing of treasures.... Hunting, above all, seems more suitable and appropriate for kings. For, to be sure, almost all kings and others of high estate seek out hunting in preference to the list above.... All sensations are a source of delight; all body parts perform their tasks more perfectly; the ruinous choice of the possession of love and other faults are abated; sadness, the depressing preoccupation with worry, excessive Love, on the contrary, after hunting all hopelessness is abandoned and driven away.... And if the exercise be light

12. Moamin, *De scientia venandi per aves* (New Haven, CT: Beinecke Rare Book & Manuscript Library, MS 446), http://brbl-dl.library.yale.edu/vu-find/Record/3592283; Ranee Katzenstein, "A Neapolitan Book of Hours in the J Paul Getty Museum," *The J Paul Getty Museum Journal* 18 (1990): 79, notes that the painting *Five Falcons in an Aviary* echoes the style of the Master of the Offices because of its similarity to the Hours of Alfonso dated 1455–68 (Naples, Biblioteca Nazionale, Ms. I B 55) and a Book of Hours for a Catalan merchant in Naples of c.1460 (Los Angeles, J. Paul Getty Museum, Ms Ludwig IX 12; 83.ML.108), online at: http://www.getty.edu/art/collection/objects/1396/unknown-maker-book-of-hours-italian-about-1460). For Alfonso's Book of Hours, see Antonella Putaturo Donati Murano, "Libri miniati per Alfonso e Ferrante," in *Libri a corte: Testi e immagini nella Napoli aragonese,* Emilia Ambra, ed. (Naples: Paparo, 1997), 13–39, 105–7, plates 1–4.

and moderate, it strengthens the normal body temperature, drives out excesses, restores the limbs calmly and agreeably, and spurs the appetite for food.... Also birds caught alive are a more splendid and wonderful means of hunting. Using them, a man has sheer joy and delight. Having studied this, Moamin the falconer composed this book about hunting in Arabic, and divided it into four thematic sections, which Theodorus, at Caesar's order, has translated into Latin.

ALFONSO I'S TASTE for Italian and Netherlandish art was recorded by Bartolomeo Facio in his *De Viris Illustribus* (*On Famous Men*) of 1456, a classicizing work dedicated to the king in whose court the humanist figured prominently as a royal biographer and tutor, following stints in Verona, Florence, Genoa, and Lucca.[13] The Latin treatise celebrates ninety-two men whose accomplishments are divided by categories, two of which are devoted to painters and sculptors. The artists include Gentile da Fabriano, Jan van Eyck, Pisanello, Rogier Van der Weyden, Lorenzo and Vittore Ghiberti, and Donatello, many of whom were associated with the most prestigious of Italian and other court circles, including those of the Medici, d'Este, and Philip the Good of Burgundy.

The prologue *De Pictoribus/On Painters* is presumably indicative of the kind of discourse taking place among the *literati* of Alfonso's court to whom Facio would have first presented *De Viris Illustribus*. He comments on the debate made famous by Horace about the merits of painting versus poetry (*ut pictura poesis*) that would become increasingly popular in Italian centers in the following century.[14] His criteria for excellence specify that naturalistic representation must be enhanced by communicating "interior feelings and emotions," sentiments echoed in the writings of his contemporary Leon Battista

13. For Facio's career at the Neapolitan court of Alfonso I, see above, pp. 18–21, 233; Bentley, 100–108; Morisani, *La letteratura artistica*, 9–24; P. Viti, "Bartolomeo Facio," DBI 44:113–21, online at: http://www.treccani.it/enciclopedia/bartolomeo-facio_(Dizionario-Biografico); Jill Kraye, "Bartolomeo Facio," www.oxfordartonline.com.

14. See Baxandall, "Bartholomaeus Facius," 92–96.

Alberti. Particular praise is given here and throughout the treatise to the use of realism and perspective, which Jan Van Eyck and Rogier Van der Weyden achieved through their innovative use of the new medium of oil painting. For this Facio subsequently praises them.

This excerpt is from the prologue to Bartolomeo Facio, *De Viris Illustribus*, Bibliotheca Apostolica Vaticana, Vat. Lat. 13650, fol. 38r–39r, translated from the Latin in Michael Baxandall, "Bartholomaeus Facius," 98.

124. *Facio: Alfonso I's Collection of Paintings*

Now, let us come to the painters, though it might perhaps have been more appropriate to put the painters after the poets. For there is, as you know, a certain great *affinity* between painters and poets: *a painting is indeed nothing else but a wordless poem*. For truly almost equal attention is given by both to the invention and arrangement of their work. No painter is accounted excellent who has not distinguished himself in representing the properties of his subjects as they exist in reality… it requires the representation not only of the face or countenance and the lineaments of the whole body, but also, and far more, of its interior feelings and emotions, so that the picture may seem to be alive and sentient and somehow move and have action… painting should not only be embellished by a variety of colors but, far more, that it should be, so to speak, enlivened by a certain vigor. And, let it be said, what is true of painting is also true of carved and cast sculpture and of architecture, all of which crafts have their origin in painting; for no craftsman can be excellent in these branches of art if the science of painting is unknown to him. However, let us pass on without further discussion to write of those few painters and sculptors who have distinguished themselves in our time; and out of the infinite number of their works, we shall mention only those of which we have acquired some distinct knowledge.

In his *De Viris Illustribus* Facio lauds Jan van Eyck as "the leading painter of our time" and compares him with Pliny, praise that would reflect well on his own Aragonese patron as a collector of the northern works, of which relatively few existed in Italy. Jan van Eyck was the celebrated court artist of Philip the Good of Burgundy, the great taste-maker of Europe, with whom Alfonso was intertwined politically. Alfonso would have acquired a taste for the art of Flanders in his native Valencia, which actively traded with Bruges. The astonishing realism of works in the new oil medium *("ars nova")* captured the luminosity of precious objects, fabrics, and skin and had immense appeal to royals, aristocrats, and merchants alike. Jan's works were considered the most desirable and valuable paintings one could possess, and thus conferred considerable prestige on their owners as well.[15] Indeed, the humanist Giovanni Pontano refers to Alfonso's esteem for Jan van Eyck in relation to the mandatory magnificence of gifts in his *De Magnificentia* (1498).[16] The works cited by Facio as belonging to Alfonso I are lost, but echoes of them are thought to survive in the work of Colantonio and miniaturists at the court of Naples.[17]

Especially important are Facio's comments on Jan van Eyck, about whom information is less readily available in other contemporary

15. Gabriella Befani Canfield, "The Reception of Flemish Art in Renaissance Florence and Naples," in *Petrus Christus in Renaissance Bruges, An Interdisciplinary Approach*, Maryann W. Ainsworth, ed. (New York: The Metropolitan Museum of Art, 1995), 37; Paula Nuttall, "Jan Van Eyck's Paintings in Italy," in *Investigating Jan van Eyck*, Susan Foister, ed. (Turnhout: Brepols, 2000), 169–82; Paula Nuttall, *From Flanders to Florence: the Impact of Netherlandish Painting 1400–1500* (New Haven and London: Yale University Press, 2004); Bernard Aikema, "Netherlandish Painting and Early Renaissance Italy: Artistic Rapports in Historiographical Perspective," in *Cultural Exchange in Early Modern Europe*, 4: *Forging European Identities*, Herman Roodenburg, ed. (Cambridge University Press, 2007), 102–5. See also Paula Nutthall, "The Medici and Netherlandish Painting," in *The Early Medici and Their Artists*, Frances Ames-Lewis, ed. (London: Birbeck College, University of London, 1995), 137–38. For a Saint Jerome by Jan owned by Cosimo de' Medici, see Challéat, 21–42.

16. See chapter 9 and reading 164.

17. Challéat, 45–71, 88–92.

fifteenth-century Italian sources. Van Eyck was the court painter of Philip the Good and the most celebrated artist of his time. Facio tells us that Alfonso in fact owned a triptych, now lost, of 1430 that was displayed in his private apartments and included panels of the Annunciation, St. Jerome in his study, St. John the Baptist, and, on the reverse, donor portraits of Battista di Giorgio Lomellini and his wife. [18] Jan's stunning manipulations of the new medium of oil painting resulted in extraordinarily life-like portraiture, as Facio notes. The patron, a Genoese merchant whose family had long been connected with Bruges, traveled from Genoa (near Facio's home town of La Spezia) to Naples on a diplomatic mission in 1444, at which time Alfonso may have acquired the painting, perhaps in connection with the Peace of Lodi in which both Naples and Genoa participated.

Facio also describes Jan van Eyck's *Mappamondo* of c.1436–44 for Philip the Good, which was evidently transferred to Alfonso, in whose court cartography was actively studied. [19] The work, now lost, may have been a gift from the Burgundian duke c.1456 during the period in which the two were planning a crusade to the Holy Land to be launched from the Mediterranean kingdom. Thus, ownership of such a precious work was emblematic of art and gift-giving as a tangible demonstration of the continuing alliance between, and interdependence of, the two courts. Philip had also made King Alfonso a member of his elite chivalric Order of the Golden Fleece in 1446.

Facio records Alfonso's interest in collecting works by Jan van Eyck in the following passage from *De Viris Illustribus*, fol. 41v–42v, translated from the Latin in Baxandall, "Bartholomaeus Facius," 102.

125. Facio: Alfonso I, Philip the Good, and Jan Van Eyck
    Jan of Gaul has been judged the leading painter of our time. He was not unlettered, particularly in geometry and such arts as contribute to the enrichment of painting, and he is thought for this reason to have discovered many things about the properties of colors recorded by the ancients and

18. Challéat, 25, 51–71. Vasari notes the degree to which Alfonso and others in the Regno celebrated Jan van Eyck (*Lives*, 1:426.)

19. Challéat, 36–42.

learned by him from reading Pliny and other authors. His is a remarkable picture in the private apartments of King Alfonso, in which there is a Virgin Mary notable for its grace and modesty, with an angel Gabriel, of exceptional beauty and with hair surpassing reality, announcing that the Son of God will be born of her; and a John the Baptist that declares the wonderful sanctity and austerity of his life, and Jerome like a living being in a library done with rare art: for if you move away from it a little it seems that it recedes inwards and that it has complete books laid open in it, while if you go near it is evident that there is only a summary of these.

On the outer side of the same picture is painted Battista Lomellini, whose picture it was — you would judge he lacked only a voice — and the woman whom he loved, of outstanding beauty; and she too is portrayed exactly as she was. Between them, as through a chink in the wall, falls a ray of sun that you would take to be real sun-light. His is a circular representation of the world, which he painted for Philip, prince of the Belgians, and it is thought that no work has been done more perfectly in our time; you may distinguish in it not only places and the lie of continents but also, by measurement, the distances between places....

KING ALFONSO owned works by another northerner, Rogier van der Weyden, who had been employed by Philip the Good and in Italy by Leonello d'Este.[20] According to Facio, these constituted a series of *"linteis picturae"* with scenes from the *Passion of Christ*, now lost, which adorned a grand room in the king's newly rebuilt Castel Nuovo. Although Baxandall translates this phrase as "tapestries," others argue that the term refers to "painted linen cloth."[21] Alfonso had, however, collected Flemish tapestries while resident in Valencia,

20. Lorne Campbell and C. Périer, "Rogier van der Weyden," www.oxford-artonline.com. Rogier himself was in Italy by 1450.

21. Baxandall, 104; Paula Nuttall, "'Panni dipinti di Fiandra': Netherlandish Painted Cloths in Fifteenth-Century Florence," in *The Fabric of Images: European Paintings on Textile Supports in the Fourteenth and Fifteenth Centuries,* Caroline Villers, ed. (London: Archetype Publications, 2000), 109–10. Challéat, 22–23, argues in favor of interpreting the term as tapestries.

Fig. 50. Colantonio. Deposition for San Domenico, Maggiore. After Rogier van der Weyden's tapestries for Castel Nuovo. Photo: Sailko. Wikimedia.

and this expensive, exalted medium would have showcased the king's wealth and sophistication to a far greater degree than painted cloth. Ownership of these extremely costly, impressively large, and

CHAPTER 7 ✵ PAINTING

conveniently portable woven commodities were both requisite status symbols throughout the courts of Europe and a source of competition among patrons who guarded them zealously against damage.[22]

Rogier's lost work influenced the compositions of Italian artists working in Naples, such as Colantonio's *Deposition* at San Domenico Maggiore [Fig. 50] and those of the artists in Alfonso's scriptorium.[23]

Facio *(De Viris Illustribis)* describes the hangings in Alfonso's collection in Baxandall, "Bartholomaeus Facius," 104–6, who relies on Brescia, Biblioteca Queriniana, Ms A.II.2, for a missing folio in Vat. Lat. 13650.

126. Facio: Alfonso I Acquires Wall Hangings by Rogier van der Weyden
Rogier of Gaul, a pupil and fellow-countryman of Jan, has produced many matchless monuments of his art.... His also are the famous tapestry pictures in the possession of King Alfonso. Again, the Mother of God, dismayed of hearing of the capture of her son yet, even with flowing tears, maintaining her dignity, a most perfect work; likewise the abuse and pain that Christ our Lord patiently suffered from the Jews, and in this you may easily distinguish a variety of feelings and passions in keeping with the variety of the action.

SUMMONTE (162–63, lines 184–99) also describes Rogier's work for Alfonso and supplies additional information, such as the cost and the fact that they had been removed to Ferrara by Isabella del Balzo, wife of King Frederick, following the Aragonese loss of Naples in the late fifteenth century and the king's death in France. Marcantonio Michiel would have been familiar with the Flemish works surviving in Venetian collections.[24] This selection is translated by CFN. Original Latin phrases are italicized and translated by JHM.

22. Marina Belozerskaya, *Luxury Arts of the Renaissance* (Los Angeles: J. Paul Getty Museum, 2005), 98–100.

23. Challéat, 71–80.

24. Jennifer Fletcher, "Marcantonio Michiel, 'che ha veduto assai,'" *The Burlington Magazine* 123 (1981): 606; Aikema, 105.

127. Summonte: The Fate of Rogier van der Weyden's Works
And even though we hesitate a little to speak of things from
Flanders, I shall not fail to mention the three tapestries [*panni
di tela*] made in that country by the famous master Rogier,
son-in-law of the other grand master Jan, who at first illuminated books *or, as we say today,* drew miniatures.[25] But Rogier
worked only in large figures. These three pieces showed the
Passion of Christ Our Lord, with large figures, as I said, in
which, among other notable things, was this: the figure of
Jesus Christ, in every position and gesture he made, was identical, without varying a single hair. A feat so skillful that it
incited great admiration in whomever saw it. Such was their
public fame that signor King Alfonso I bought these three
pieces for 5000 ducats in Flanders. Now they must be in the
possession of the poor Queen Isabella in Ferrara, wife of the
signor King Federico of beloved memory.

SUMMONTE INTRODUCES his section on Netherlandish art by lavish-
ing praise on the work of a local artist, Niccolò Colantonio (c.1420–
60), who spent most of his career in Naples during the reigns of
René of Anjou and Alfonso I. It is assumed that in his earlier works
Colantonio absorbed and transmitted some aspects of the style of
Jacomart Baco, whom he encountered at court.[26]

Summonte describes him as skilled in the Flemish manner and
claims that Colantonio taught King René the art of mixing colors.
While he received commissions from Alfonso, the painter did not
achieve the stature of court artist, perhaps because of his Italian origins.[27] Colantonio's works reflect his immediate experience with the
now lost paintings of Jan Van Eyck in Alfonso's collection and therefore are of particular interest for historians. Summonte proudly states

25. Nicolini, *L'arte napoletana*, 234. Nicolini, 233, interprets Summonte's term
"panni di tela" (painted cloths) as *"arazzi."* Rogier's works were stored in the
guardaroba of the Torre dell'Oro at Castel Nuovo until 1501, when they were
taken by the deposed king Federico d'Aragona to France; upon his death in
1504 Isabella del Balzo (originally from Naples) took them to Ferrara.

26. Challéat, 107.

27. Challéat, 113–16.

that Colantonio taught the brilliant young Antonello da Messina (1430–79) to paint in oil.

Summonte applauds Colantonio's copy of a Flemish *Saint George and Dragon* but does not name its artist. It is probably the painting of the same title by Jan that Alfonso purchased c.1444.[28] The faithfulness of Colantonio's copy to the original, with its luminosity and exceptional realism, earns high marks from Summonte, attesting to the degree to which copying was deemed a praiseworthy skill in the Renaissance. Equally revealing is Summonte's phrase "the Flemish style, which was the only one marketable." The prestige of the northern mode of painting associated with courts like that of Philip the Good of Burgundy both inspired and compelled patrons to commission similar works.

Two of Colantonio's royal commissions may have carried with them a subtext relevant to the religious-political concerns of the time. In the 1440s Alfonso commissioned from Colantonio a polyptych titled *Saint Francis Giving the Rule* for the prestigious church of San Lorenzo, in the *sala capitolare* of which the king's authority over the kingdom had been confirmed in 1443.[29] The arms of the house of Aragon appear in the pavement design of the central panel. (*Saint Jerome in his Study Removing a Thorn from the Lion's Paw* [Fig. 51] is the subject of another panel; the fifth-century saint wears Franciscan robes.)

Alfonso, along with other rulers, such as Leonello d'Este, actively promoted the canonization of the Observant Franciscan Bernardino

28. Facio does not mention Jan van Eyck's painting of St. George, which may have been purchased on behalf of Alfonso in Bruges 1444 by a Valencian merchant there: Challéat, 24–25, 46–51. The figure of St. George appeared in the tympanum of the Arch of Alfonso at Castel Nuovo.

29. Sections of the altarpiece are housed at the Museo di Capodimonte, Naples. See a reconstruction of the polyptych in Ferdinando Bologna, "La 'Cona' degli ordini francescani di Colantonio nella chiesa di San Lorenzo a Napoli," in *Il polittico di Colantonio a San Lorenzo,* idem., ed. (Naples: Electa Napoli, 2001), 34. See idem, "Colantonio," DBI 26 (1982): http://www.treccani.it/enciclopedia/colantonio_(Dizionario-Biografico); and Giovanna Cassese, "Colantonio," www.oxfordartonline.com.

Fig. 51. Colantonio. Saint Jerome in his Study Removing a Thorn from the Lion's Paw, from the polyptych of Saint Francis Giving the Rule, for San Lorenzo, 1440s. Museo di Capodimonte. Wikimedia.

da Siena who died in 1444 in Aquila. Alfonso's daughter-in-law, Isabella Chiaromonte, later commissioned the altarpiece ex-voto of St. Vincent Ferrer in honor of a Spanish saint — born in Valencia and canonized in 1455 by the Spanish pope, Calixtus III — of whom she was a devout follower. The saint was a legendary peacemaker, and the commission may have coincided with the First Conspiracy of the Barons against Ferrante I in the same year.[30]

Summonte's passage (160–62, lines 99–182) is an important source of information about Colantonio. Translated by CFN. Latin phrases are italicized and translated by JHM.

128. Summonte: Colantonio's Skill in the Flemish Manner
From this time on we did not have in these parts a celebrated [single master], foreigner or native, until our Neapolitan

30. Challéat, 114.

master Colantonio, a person much inclined towards the
art of painting and who, if he hadn't died young, would
have been capable of great things. Due to circumstances, he
himself never attained perfection in the drawing of ancient
works, as did his disciple Antonello da Messina, a man, as I
understand it, known to you. The profession of Colantonio
was, in the manner of the time, Flemish in inspiration. He
was dedicated to that style and considered going there. But
King Raniero [René] kept him here, and he [Colantonio]
taught him [René] the technique of mixing colors. There
are four works by Colantonio in Naples....

The second work by Colantonio is in San Pietro Martire.
The figure is of St. Vincent Confessor in a boat that endures a storm with fierce waves and turbulent clouds; it
strikes fear in all who see it. Really a thing of great imagination. The third is in San Lorenzo. The figure of St. Jerome
is seated in his study, where there are many books of varying shapes and sizes..., with certain cartouches affixed to
the wall with wax, some sections of which appear to be
floating. This work is quite celebrated by our painters, not
for its conformity to present standards but more for its imitation of ancient models. He had the great dexterity to imitate whatever he wanted; this imitation being done in the
Flemish style, which was the only one marketable.

During his time a [rather well done] true-to-life portrait
of the head of Charles of Burgundy arrived. Colantonio
made a copy of this work that was owned by a merchant; and, having made the copy so precise that it was
impossible to tell one from another, he substituted it for
the original, which the merchant kept until Colantonio
revealed his clever trick. Similarly he made a copy of a
Flemish picture of St. George, a panel of approximately
two and a half palmi by four: a praiseworthy work in
which one sees the knight *all completely bent over and leaning hard on his lance,* whose tip had penetrated the mouth
of the dragon and formed a bulge on the other side. It
was something to see the good knight leaning so far forward and pushing so forcefully against the dragon that
the right leg pulling on the saddle seemed almost outside

RENAISSANCE NAPLES: A DOCUMENTARY HISTORY

the stirrup. Against the left leg the image of the dragon is beautifully reflected in the armor, as in a mirror. In the saddle-bow appeared a certain rustiness which, on the shiny surface of the metal, was very obvious.

In sum, the good Colantonio copied the entire painting in such a way that one couldn't tell his from the original if not for a tree that in the former was brambles and in the latter, according to the patron's wishes, is a careful study of the chestnut. This very same picture is now in Naples in the wardrobe of the illustrious signora duchess of Milan. The portrait of the duke of Burgundy, which some time ago our Jacopo Sannazaro saw in Naples, is not here.

ANTONELLO DA MESSINA, an exceptionally precocious artist celebrated for his mastery of oil painting and well known for his "dramatic close ups" of the Virgin Annunciate, arrived from his native Messina in Naples c. 1445. There he would have seen the works of Jan van Eyck and encountered Colantonio. Summonte describes the Sicilian artist only as the pupil of Colantonio. Vasari, however, prefers to emphasize the influence of Jan, the celebrated court artist of Philip the Good; he describes in particular the effect that Jan's Lomellini triptych had on the Sicilian. A detailed comparison of the glazing techniques of the three artists indeed suggests that Antonello's method is much closer to that of Jan.[31] Giorgio Vasari discusses Antonello's Neapolitan sojourn in his *Lives* (1:426–27).

129. Vasari: On Antonello da Messina

But certain Florentines, who traded between Flanders and Naples, sent to King Alfonso I of Naples a panel with many figures painted in oil by Jan, which became very dear to that king both for the beauty of the figures and for the novel invention shown in the coloring; and all the painters in that kingdom flocked together to see it, and it was consummately

31. Joanne Wright, "Antonello da Messina: The Origins of His Style and Technique," *Art History* 3 (1980): 41–60; idem, "Antonello da Messina," www.oxfordartonline.com. See also Aikema, 131; Giacchino Barbera, "The Life and Work of Antonello da Messina," in *Antonello da Messina: Sicily's Renaissance Master*, Gioacchino Barbera, ed. (New Haven: Yale University Press, 2005), 51. Vasari's claim that Antonello went to Flanders has been discredited.

extolled by all.... Antonello da Messina... then, going once
on some business of his own from Sicily to Naples, heard that
the said King Alfonso had received from Flanders the aforesaid panel by the hand of Jan of Bruges, painted in oil in such
a manner that it could be washed, would endure any shock,
and was in every way perfect. Thereupon, having contrived
to obtain a view of it, he was so strongly impressed by the
liveliness of the colors and by the beauty and harmony of that
painting, that he put on one side all other business and every
thought and went off to Flanders.

ALFONSO OWNED FLORENTINE PAINTINGS as well, a reflection of the
long-established political connections between the republic and the
kingdom of Naples. In 1455 he ratified the Peace of Lodi, which
outlined an ongoing mutual protection of the peninsula with Milan,
Venice, and the papacy. Cosimo de' Medici commissioned an altarpiece for the king from Filippo Lippi, a Carmelite monk favored by
the Medici, perhaps to quell rumors that Cosimo was double-dealing
with the French at a time when the Aragonese faced an Angevin
pretender to their throne.[32]

In an exchange of letters dated 1457 and 1458 Giovanni di Cosimo
de' Medici (Cosimo's son and general manager of the Medici bank), Fra
Filippo Lippi, and the Medici agent in Naples, Bartolommeo Serragli,
discuss the work: a *Madonna and Child with Saints* (now lost), with panels
of *Saint Anthony Abbot* and *The Archangel Michael* (Cleveland Museum
of Art, Fig. 52). St. Anthony Abbot and St. Michael were Alfonso's patron saints and also appear on the triumphal arch at Castel Nuovo.[33]
The text of the first letter (20 July 1457) indicates that Lippi had received considerable direction from Giovanni, presumably regarding the
ornamentation of the piece, since the painter makes sure to mention
that particular aspect of the work. Although the Florentine is generally

32. Caroline Elam, "Art and Diplomacy in Renaissance Florence," *Royal Society
of Arts Journal* 136 (1988): 816, who also partially translates this letter. Vasari, *Lives*,
1:437, refers to the painting and locates it in the "Chapel of the Castle."

33. Jeffrey Ruda, *Fra Filippo Lippi: Life and Work with a Complete Catalogue*
(London: Phaidon, 1993), 444; https://commons.wikimedia.org/wiki/
File:Lippi,_sant%27antonio_abate,_san_michele_arcangelo_2.jpg.

Fig. 52. Filippo Lippi. St. Anthony Abbot and the Archangel Michael, 1458. Cleveland Museum of Art. Wikimedia.

influenced by Masaccio, the style of the surviving wings for the altar-piece does in fact include considerable gilding and luminous painted highlights, elements that would have appealed to Alfonso's decorative sensibilities.[34] The correspondence includes important documentation of the importance of frames in the mid-quattrocento by including Lippi's sketch for an extremely ornate and costly gothicizing frame with pinnacles, to be executed independently of the panel. As such, it would

34. For a stylistic analysis, see Ruda, 197–99.

have complemented the architecture of Castel Nuovo's royal chapel, for which the altarpiece was probably destined.[35]

Medicean gift-giving for political purposes related to Naples recurs later in the century. In 1488 Lorenzo de' Medici would similarly consign the services of Filippo's son, Filippino Lippi, to decorate the Roman chapel of the powerful Neapolitan cardinal Oliviero Carafa at Sta. Maria sopra Minerva in exchange for Carafa's support of the nomination of his son Giovanni as cardinal.[36]

Filippo Lippi's letter to Giovanni di Cosimo de' Medici, now at the Archivio di Stato di Firenze, Cat. D4, doc. 21, II.1, is translated in Jeffrey Ruda, *Fra Filippo Lippi* (London: Phaidon, 1993), 36–38.

130. Filippo Lippi: Cosimo de' Medici's Commission of an Altarpiece for Alfonso I

20 July 1457. I did what you ordered me about the panel and held myself to the line on everything. The Saint Michael is so perfect that for the armor of his it's [sic] silver and gold and likewise his wings.... Now Giovanni, I am here absolutely to be your slave and I will produce. I have had fourteen florins from you and I wrote to you there would be an outlay of thirty and it should be that because of the beauty of ornament... and so you'll be well informed I send you the drawing of how the carpentry is done, and height and width, and for love of you I don't want to get from you more than a hundred florins [for] labor, ask anybody else. I beg you to answer because I'm dying here and would like to leave, and if I've been presumptuous in writing to you forgive me, and I will always do whatever more and whatever less will please your reverence. Valete.

TEN MONTHS LATER Giovanni de' Medici commented on Alfonso's positive reception of the sumptuous piece, as described by

35. The royal chapel, once the setting for frescoes by Giotto, appears to have been razed following damage from the earthquake in 1456. See De Divitiis, "Castel Nuovo and Castel Capuano," 460.

36. Vasari, 1:443: "...he [Lorenzo de' Medici] sent his [Filippo's] son Filippino to Rome to paint a chapel for the cardinal of Naples."

Bartolommeo Serragli. The "error" to which Giovanni refers may be the impregnation of an Augustinian nun by Fra Filippo.[37] The letter from Giovanni di Cosimo de' Medici to Bartolommeo Serragli is also at the Archivio di Stato, Cat. D4, 21.III.1, and translated in Ruda, 40.

131. Giovanni di Cosimo de' Medici: Letter Praising the Altarpiece by Fra Filippo Lippi

27 May 1458. In the last days I've had several of your letters, from which I understand that you have presented the panel to His Majesty the king, and that he was highly pleased with it, and so we've had a good laugh about Fra Filippo's error....

THE TAVOLA STROZZI

Since its discovery in the Palazzo Strozzi, Florence, in 1904, the *Tavola Strozzi* (Naples, Museo Nazionale di San Martino) has provoked intense scholarly discourse on a variety of topics, including its patronage, authorship, subject, function, and pictorial representation.[38] The large painted panel shows a panoramic view of Naples as seen from the harbor, with the Castel dell'Ovo at far left and San Pietro ad Aram at far right. Scholars agree that the scene depicts King Ferrante I's victory near Ischia over Jean of Anjou, pretender to the throne, in July of 1465. The document below has been interpreted by some to suggest that the panel was sent from Florence to Naples in 1473 as a gift from Filippo Strozzi to King Ferrante I, although this view has been challenged following its technical examination in 2006.

The panel seems to have been made for Ferrante by a Tuscan artist, possibly Benedetto da Maiano, and intended for the *spalliera* (back) of a *lettuccio* (a day-bed or couch) or for a *cassone*. (Previous attributions

37. Ruda, 40.

38. Giulio Pane, *La Tavola Strozzi tra Napoli e Firenze: Un'immagine della città nel quattrocento* (Naples: Grimaldi & C. Editori, 2009); Mario del Treppo, "Le avventure storiografiche della Tavola Strozzi," in *Fra storia e storiografia: Scritti in onore di Pasquale Villani*, Paolo Marcy and Angela Massafra, ed. (Bologna: Mulino, 1994), 483–515; Stefano Palmieri, "La 'Tavola di Casa Strozzi': Variazioni sul tema," *Napoli Nobilissima* 8 ser. 5 (2007): 171–82; Roberto Taito, http://www.tavolastrozzi.it/#progetti.

include Francesco Pagano or the Florentine cartographer Francesco Rosselli.) The urban subject matter of the painting reflects the ongoing interest in cartography generally and city views in particular during the later quattrocento and may be compared to *vedute* in the background of paintings by the Florentine painter Domenico Ghirlandaio and others.[39] The *Tavola* is reproduced below, with a key, in the Appendix, pp. 480–81.

In the mid-fifteenth century, Filippo Strozzi, scion of the family banking empire, was perhaps the most influential Florentine resident of Naples, where he lived nearly twenty-five years. In 1466 the Medici lifted the ban keeping him in exile there in exchange for Strozzi's activities on behalf of the Medici in the southern capital. As the date (1472–73) of the document attests, after his return to Florence, Strozzi maintained his ties with prominent Neapolitans and the Aragonese; he named his son Alfonso in honor of the duke of Calabria. The gift of an expensive Florentine panel (as well as figs and sausages!) for King Ferrante undoubtedly signals his desire to secure further his connection to the royal family on behalf of the Strozzi, and it represents a continuation of the trend of Florentine gift-giving to Aragonese royalty for political gain. The fact that the *Tavola Strozzi* includes warships with the Strozzi arms clearly demonstrates the degree to which Filippo Strozzi wished to be seen as integral to the Aragonese effort to maintain supremacy in the kingdom of Naples.

Moreover, Filippo Strozzi functioned as a purveyor of Florentine taste to a Neapolitan audience. He had ordered a *lettuccio*, a quintessentially Florentine product, from Giuliano da Maiano for the powerful Neapolitan aristocrat and politician Diomede Carafa in 1466; Lorenzo de' Medici had commissioned a *lettuccio* for his own palace in 1470.[40] Strozzi alludes to Florentine achievements even in the ledger entry: hence *"di prospettiva."* In addition, Strozzi bestows

39. Pane, 156–57.

40. Del Treppo, 496–97; Dario Covi, "A Documented *Lettuccio* for the Duke of Calabria by Giuliano da Maiano," in *Essays Presented to Myron P. Gilmore,* Sergio Bertelli, ed. (Florence: La Nuova Italia Editrice, 1978), 121–30.

other *lettuccie,* Flemish panels and tapestries, ancient marbles, and local Tuscan produce on his Neapolitan friends.[41]

The following document (Florence, Archivio di Stato di Firenze, *carte Strozziane,* Serie V, cc. 95–96), is transcribed from the original Italian in Del Treppo, "Le avventure storiografiche," 510–11. Translated by CFN.

132. Filippo Strozzi: Naples and the Tavola Strozzi
92. Herewith I [Filippo Strozzi] will note many thanks given to friends in Naples from 24 November 1472 to 2 June 1473....

To His Majesty King Ferrante

1 *lettuccio* of walnut of 6 *braccia* with *cassone* and *spalliera* and very beautiful cornices in which one finds inside a perspective of Naples the castle and its surroundings, which cost 110 *fiorini larghi*....

FERRANTE I'S PATRONAGE
The commissioning of manuscripts by culturally aspirational heads of state in the quattrocento continued under the aegis of Alfonso I's son, Ferrante I, and his grandson Alfonso II, who housed a library at his residence in the refurbished Castel Capuano on the eastern side of the city.[42] An edition of Plutarch's *Heroum clarissimorumque virorum divinae sentenciae* was translated from Greek into Italian c.1481 by Giovanni Albino, the erudite Aragonese librarian and secretary, who dedicated it to Ferrante I and Alfonso, duke of Calabria (the future King Alfonso II), as exemplary "heroes."[43] For folio 1r of the volume Cristoforo Maiorana of Naples painted fashionable and elaborately classicizing architectural frames animated by putti and grotesques.

Following is a section of the dedication to Plutarch's *Heroum clarissimorumque* translated by Albino, Biblioteca Nazionale di Napoli, Ms. XII.E.34, cat. n. 23 and Leg. VII, fol. 3r. It is partially transcribed in Ambra, 123.

41. Del Treppo, 498–515.

42. Murano, 13–39; Ambra, catalogue entry 23, 123. Watson, 154.

43. Ambra, 123.

133. Giovanni Albino: Dedication of his Translation of Plutarch to King Ferrante I
To refresh the weary of mind… so that Your Majesty and
the greatness of mind of your most illustrious son, Alfonso,
duke of Calabria, take your place among the heroes and be
a shining example for posterity.

THE FRENCH INVASION

In February of 1495 the recently crowned Alfonso II abdicated the
throne to his son Ferrandino (Ferrante II) before the invasion of
Charles VIII of France. Francesco Guicciardini records in his *History
of Italy* the demise of the Aragonese in Naples[44] and the export of
artistic treasures from the city by the deposed sovereign. Alfonso
fled to an Olivetan monastery in Mazara, Sicily, taking with him
many portable works of art, presumably manuscripts and small sculptures, paintings, and other precious objects. One of these may have
been the bust of a boy, perhaps Ferrandino, by Francesco Laurana
(Museo Nazionale, Palermo). Guicciardini's selection is translated
by Desmond Seward, ed., *Naples: A Travellers' Companion* (New York:
Atheneum, 1986), 73–74.

134. Guicciardini: King Alfonso II Flees to Sicily with Works of Art
…Alfonso left Naples, accompanied by four light galleys
which were laden with treasure. While he was leaving, he
shook all over, as though the French were already upon
him, trembling with fear at the slightest noise like a man
who was frightened that heaven and earth were plotting
against him. He fled to Mazara, a Sicilian town with which
he had recently been presented by King Ferrante of Spain.

THE FRENCH PLUNDERING of goods from Naples following their invasion of the city in 1495 is also documented in fascinating detail by
a Monsieur Sorcier in 1495 who indicates their final destination as
Charles VIII's castle at Amboise. Thus, the letter survives as important
confirmation of the increasingly insatiable French appetite for Italian
objects. Sorcier indicates that tradesmen of unspecified professions were
brought to France by Charles VIII as well. Many works later arrived in
France when the deposed Aragonese king, Frederick, fled there in 1501.

44. See chapter 1, reading 8, pp. 85–87.

Such transfers of works have rendered many of them untraceable.

Sorcier's comments are transcribed by Ludovic Lalanne, "Transport d'oeuvres d'art de Naples au Château d'Amboise en 1495," *Archives de l'art français* 3 (1852–53): 305, translated here from the French by David Beneteau.

135. Monsieur Sorcier: Charles VIII Plunders Naples and Returns to France
In front of me.... Notary and secretary of our lord the king, Nicolas Fagot, dyer and tapestry-maker of the king, acknowledges having received from monsieur Jehan Lalemant, advisor and general receiver of the king, in Normandy, the sum of 398 *livres* and five sols *tournois*, for a total payment of exactly 1593 *livres tournois*, given to him by the afore-mentioned gentleman for what remained owed to him for the handling, carriage, and transportation from Naples to the city of Lyons of several tapestries, books, paintings, marble and porphyry stones, and other furnishings that the aforementioned gentleman instructed him to transport; all these items weigh about 87 thousand pounds, and he is also instructed to transport the items from the city of Lyons to the castle of Amboise for the decoration and furnishing of that castle; he is also responsible for the feeding of 22 working men for 34 days at a rate of 40 *sols* per day; these men were brought from Naples to work their trade, at his pleasure; from the above-mentioned sum Monsieur Fagot has kept, and considers himself satisfied with, 398 *libres* and 5 sols *tournois*, and the receiver of this sum accepts it with my signature, upon his request, this 24th day of December, in the year 1495.

Signed, Sorcier.

THE LOMBARD SCHOOL IN NAPLES

The Lombard Cesare da Sesto is credited with bringing to southern Italy a style shaped first by his mentor Leonardo da Vinci and then by Raphael and Peruzzi, with whom he worked in Rome on projects for Pope Julius II. Cesare may have gone to Naples after the powerful Cardinal Oliviero Carafa commissioned a devotional image from him c.1510–11. The *Adoration* for Sant'Arcangelo (Baiano) mentioned below by Summonte — who could have known the artist personally — is now lost. Other surviving works may be compared to the carved marble *Adoration* (c.1516–c.1519) of the same theme by the Spaniard Bartolomé Ordóñez for the altar of the prestigious Caracciolo di Vico Chapel in San Giovanni a Carbonara. A comparison of the two works in different media is useful in relation to the number of quattrocento altarpieces in relief for Neapolitan churches and the emerging *paragone* in the sixteenth century. Cesare's later *Adoration*, the "*Pala Kress*" (San Francisco, Fine Arts Museums, Legion of Honor, Kress Collection, Fig. 53) is indebted to Raphael's *Madonna of the Fish*[45] for the Neapolitan church of San Domenico.[46] Summonte briefly describes Cesare's lost altarpiece in his letter of 1524 (164, lines 234–39). Translated by CFN.

136. Summonte: Cesare da Sesto Brings Central and Northern Italian Classicism to Naples
> One may see in the church of Sant'Arcangelo delle Monache a large altarpiece of good workmanship, done by a master Cesare of Milan.

PEDRO FERNÁNDEZ DE MURCIA, also known as Pseudo-Bramantino, arrived in Naples c.1503–7 following a stint in Milan, where he would have absorbed the style of Leonardo. Thus, the Spaniard forms part of the first group of non-Neapolitan artists bringing with them to the south an experience of late quattrocento and early cinquecento northern and central Italian art. His arrival coincided with — or was occasioned by — the tenure of the first viceroy of Naples, Gonzalo Fernández de Cordóba, *El Gran Capitán,* who had recently led the Spanish to victory over the French for control of the southern kingdom. Pedro's descent south may have been facilitated in Rome through the powerful Neapolitan Cardinal Oliviero Carafa; the ceiling of the chapel of his brother Ettore Carafa in San Domenico Maggiore is engagingly

45. See pp. 350–59 and Fig. 54 below.

46. Annalisa Perissa Torini, "Un Artista Lombarda nell'Italia del Sud," in *Leonardo & Cesare da Sesto nel Rinascimento Meridionale,* Nicola Barbatelli, ed. (Poggio a Caiano: CB Edizioni, 2013), 45–61. Exh. Chiostro di Santa Maria del Rifugio, Abbadia della Santissima Trinità July 6–September 30, 2013, Cava de'Tirreni; Andrea Beyer, "Cesare da Sesto," www.oxfordartonline.com.

Fig. 53. Cesare da Sesto. Madonna and Child with St. John the Baptist and St. George. San Francisco, Fine Arts Museums. Photo: Gift of the Samuel H. Kress Foundation.

decorated in the illusionistic Lombard manner of Bramantino.

By 1510 Pedro received the commission for a lavish two-tiered altarpiece of the Madonna and Child with Saints John the Baptist and Peter in the prestigious church of San Gregorio Armeno, the lower side panels of which may be his *Seated Papal Saint* at the Fogg Art Museum and *San Biagio* in the Museu d'Art de Catalunya,

Barcelona.[47] Scholars differ in their identification of the panel in Cambridge as Pope Gregory or Pope Damasus, whose entire head the nuns of San Gregorio believed to possess among their huge cache of relics. Pedro returned to Rome in 1514 during the heyday of Medicean papal patronage under Leo X, where he was further immersed in the pictorial language of Raphael and Michelangelo.

One document for the altarpiece in San Gregorio Armeno mentions Pedro's involvement and praises both the gilding and blue pigment used for the altarpiece. It is transcribed in Filangieri, *Documenti*, 3:152 from the notarial documents (Archivio di Stato di Napoli) of Cesare Malfitano, 1511–12, carta 217. The original notarial archive from this period was deliberately destroyed by the retreating Germans outside of Naples in 1943. Translated by CFN.

137. Cesare Malfitano: Pedro Fernández (Pseudo-Bramantino) in Naples
On this day (7 Jun. 1512) in the monastery of the Sancti Ligorii [San Gregorio Armeno] of Naples in our presence are… the most reverend Abbess Tarsilla of said monastery… [who] presented fifty ducats… [for] an altarpiece recently painted by the master Petro Ispano… whose gold will be perfect and the blue of the best that one can find in Naples except for ultramarine blue… said altarpiece will incite lasting praise.…

RAPHAEL AND HIS INFLUENCE

Summonte describes Raphael's altarpiece known as the *Madonna del Pesce* (*Madonna of the Fish,* Fig. 54), for a private chapel in San Domenico Maggiore, which arrived in Naples c.1515. The church was associated with St. Thomas Aquinas and the site of tombs for local aristocratic families, such as the Caracciolo and Carafa. Members

47. Marco Tanzi, *Pedro Fernández da Murcia lo Pseudo Bramantino* (Milan, Leonardo Arte: 1997), 9–13, 116–18; Paola Giusti and Pierluigi Leone de Castris, *Pittura del Cinquecento a Napoli, 1510–1540: Forastieri e regnicoli* (Naples: Electa, 1988), 13–35, 265–68; Barbara Agosti, "Artisti spagnoli e fonti italiane," in *Norma e capriccio: Spagnoli in Italia agli esordi della "maniera moderna,"* Tommaso Mozzati and Antonio Natali, ed. (Florence: Giunti, 2013), 159–61; Mario Marubbi in ibid., 300. For an overview of sixteenth-century painting in Naples, see Romano, "Painting and Patrons," 202–24.

of the Aragonese royal dynasty were also buried in San Domenico, adding greatly to its prestige as a location for a mortuary chapel.

Raphael's *sacra conversazione* includes the Virgin holding the infant Christ, St. Jerome, and the Angel with Tobias who dangles his familiar attribute of the fish. Summonte includes the name of Giambattista del Doce, who had a chapel in the church; historians suggest that the donor may instead be Girolamo del Doce, given the presence of Saint Jerome in the scene.[48] The rounded, ample form of Mary recalls Raphael's signature Madonna type. The altarpiece had an immediate impact on other artists in the city both foreign (Cesare da Sesto) and local (Andrea Sabatini da Salerno). Thus, Raphael's export to Naples was important to the diffusion of early cinquecento Roman painting in southern Italy, and the Umbrian's legendary *grazia* continued to permeate the work of Neapolitan commissions for most of the remaining century. The *Madonna del Pesce* was eventually taken to Madrid in 1644 by the Spanish Viceroy Ramiro de Guzman, duke of Medina de las Torres, and hangs today in the Prado.

Summonte briefly mentions Raphael's altarpiece in San Domenico in his letter of almost a decade after its installation (164, lines 245–50). Translated by CFN.

138. Summonte: Raphael's Altarpiece for San Domenico Maggiore
> In the same church, in the chapel of signor Ioan Battista del Duce, is the Angel with Tobias, done by the hand of Raphael of Urbino. Of these craftsmen I need not say more, as they and others are already more noted in this same city than in their own hometowns.

ANDREA SABATINI from Salerno was influenced by Raphael, as may be seen in his limpid *Deposition* of the later 1510s formerly in Sta. Teresa degli Studi, Naples (now at the Museo di Capodimonte).[49]

48. Jürg Meyer zur Capellen, *Raphael: A Critical Catalogue of his Paintings* 2. *The Roman Religious Paintings, ca. 1508–1520* (Landshut: Arcos, 2005), 117. Vasari mentions the painting in his *Lives* (1:728), which he would have seen in situ 1544–45.

49. Giovanni Previtali, ed., *Andrea da Salerno nel rinascimento meridionale* (Florence: Centro Di, 1986), 214; Riccardo Naldi, "Andrea Sabatini [da

Fig. 54. Raphael. Madonna del Pesce (Madonna of the Fish), for S. Domenico Maggiore, c.1515. Museo Nacional de Prado. Photo: Wikimedia.

As a local artist, his work was evidently a source of pride for the Neapolitan Summonte, who mentions him in his letter (164, lines 251–52). Translated by CFN.

Salerno]," www.oxfordartonline.com; Giusti and Leone de Castris, *Pittura del Cinquecento a Napoli, 1510–1540*, 87–186, 271–78.

139. Summonte: Raphael Influences Andrea Sabatini da Salerno
There are today others of ours who are promising: Andrea
da Salerno....

RAPHAEL AND HIS PUPIL GIULIO ROMANO are associated with a portrait of Doña Isabel de Requesens i Enríquez [Fig. 55], the wife of
the Spanish viceroy resident in Naples, a painting that was previously
identified as a portrait of Giovanna d'Aragona.[50] The circumstances
surrounding its conception in 1518 reflect the political complexities
of the time. The powerful cardinal Bernardo Dovizi of Bibbiena facilitated the painting from central Italian artists on behalf of a Florentine
pope (Leo X) for a French king (François I) of the Catalan wife
of Charles V's viceroy (Don Ramón de Cardona) at Naples, whose
kingdom the French had recently lost to Spain yet still coveted.

Doña Isabel's sumptuous garment and headdress of red velvet may
in fact be seen as responding to the various constituencies named
above through a composite of references to the Spanish and French
traditions of courtly dress, to central Italian and Venetian painted prototypes, and to the taste of François I himself (who had evidently
coveted Don Ramón's mistress in Ferrara). Scholars disagree about
the extent to which Raphael participated in the design and execution of the portrait, which has also been discussed with regard to its
erotic underpinnings.[51] Giulio Romano evidently visited Naples to
do preliminary drawings; there he would have absorbed the powerful
visual legacy of a kingdom in which the championing of conspicuous
consumption through extravagant dress had long played an important role. The painted setting may be discussed in relation to both
the Villa Farnesina, where Raphael and Giulio worked on behalf of
Agostino Chigi (who had an office in Naples), and to the sumptuous
royal villa at Poggioreale. The painting was sent to Fontainebleau soon

50. Michael P. Fritz, *Giulio Romano et Raphaël: La vice-reine de Naples ou la
renaissance d'une beauté mythique*, Claire Nydegger, trans. (Paris: Louvre, 1997).

51. Jürg Meyer zur Capellen, *Raphael: A Critical Catalogue of His Paintings, 3.
The Roman Portraits, ca. 1508–1520* (Landshut: Arcos, 2008), 27–29, 150–54.

Fig. 55. Raphael and Giulio Romano. Portrait of Dona Isabel de Requesens i Enríquez, c.1518. Louvre. Photo: mbzt. Wikimedia.

after its completion. Summonte refers to a portrait of Doña Isabel de Requesens in Naples by the Venetian Paolo de Agostini. [52]

Vasari describes the commission and the location of the painting in his section of the *Lives* on Giulio Romano (2:118–9).

52. Summonte, 164, ll. 217–33.

Fig. 56. Antonio Solario. Scene from the Life of Saint Benedict. SS. Severino e Sossio, Grand Cloister, c.1515. Photo: Wikimedia.

140. Vasari: Raphael and Giulio Romano Portray the Spanish Viceroy's Wife

...sent to King Francis of France... the portrait of the vice-queen of Naples, wherein Raffaello did nothing but the likeness of the head from life, and the rest was finished by Giulio. These works, which were very dear to that king, are still in the king's chapel at Fontainebleau in France.

A LARGE FRESCO CYCLE with *Scenes from the Life of Saint Benedict* survives in the cloister of the Benedictine monastery of SS. Severino e

Sossio in Naples. [Fig. 56] They are generally attributed to the Venetian Antonio Solario, nicknamed "Lo Zingaro" for his peripatetic travels. The cycle echoes the scale of those at other Benedictine cloisters, such as the one by Il Sodoma and Luca Signorelli c.1495–1506 at the abbey of Monteoliveto Maggiore near Siena. Many of Solario's episodes show Benedictines in the act of building, an initiative in which the order was actively engaged at the time. Although the painted inscription below with his initials — inferring G. Antonio De Solario — suggests that the date of completion is 1515, Summonte does not mention the series by the Venetian in his letter of 1524 to Michiel, leading scholars to conclude that the frescoes were executed at a later time.[53] The painted inscription is located on the base of the painted pilaster next to the fourteenth fresco of *Scenes from the Life of Saint Benedict* in the cloister.

141. A Venetian Paints the Cloister of SS. Severino e Sossio
   G.AN.DS.XVR

POLIDORO DA CARAVAGGIO, a Lombard and another of Raphael's gifted disciples, arrived in Naples from Rome in 1523–24 and returned again following the Sack of Rome in 1527. Summonte tells us that there he was commissioned to paint a series of monochromatic facades in the manner of ancient reliefs, a style for which Polidoro was well known in Rome. Ludovico Montalto commissioned the frescoes for the courtyard of his palace in the prestigious *seggio* of Nido.[54]

Montalto was a controversial and high-ranking operative in the entourage of the Spanish viceroys, a member of the Accademia Pontaniana, and a friend of the poet Jacopo Sannazaro. Polidoro painted altarpieces for two Neapolitan churches as well, including Sta. Maria delle Grazie alla Pescheria, of which some sections survive including the *tondi* of

---

53. Maria Cristina Chiusa, "Antonio Solario [lo Zingaro]," http://www.oxfordartonline.com.

54. See Pierluigi Leone de Castris, "Polidoro" www.oxfordartonline; idem, *Polidoro da Caravaggio* (Naples: Electa Napoli, 2000), 173–77, 287–322; Marco Nicola Miletti, "Montalto, Ludovico," DBI 75 (2011), online at http://www. treccani.it/enciclopedia/ludovico-montalto_(Dizionario-Biografico).

an *Annunciation* (Capodimonte, Fig. 57) re-discovered in the 1980s. Summonte describes the newly completed frescoes for Montalto in his letter of 1524 (164–5, ll. 253–8). Translated by CFN.

142. Summonte: Polidoro da Caravaggio Works in Naples
   [Maestro] Polidoro da Caravaggio, famous for works in monochrome, although quite young, just painted the four walls of the courtyard and a loggia in the house of Signor Ludovico di Montalto, where there are some lovely things, for the most part derived from the example of the Column of Trajan.

VASARI'S PREJUDICES in favor of central Italian art and bitter memories about his own experience in Naples are reflected in his account of Polidoro da Caravaggio's time there (1523–24, 1527–28). He uses Polidoro both to champion the *"moda moderna"* and to denigrate Naples as an artistic center, stating that it was dependent on the importation of artists from elsewhere to establish standards of artistic modernity.[55] Vasari describes the Neapolitan lack of interest in Raphael's gifted disciple, whose style was so naturalistic as to give "the appearance of life," and cites the local aristocrats as being more interested in horses than artists. This comment echoes the earlier complaint of Summonte and is found in Vasari's life of Polidoro along with the following passage (1:896).

143. Vasari: On Polidoro's Treatment in Naples
   Polidoro turned his steps to Naples; but on his arrival, the noblemen of that city taking but little interest in fine works of painting, he was like to die of hunger. Working, therefore, at the commission of certain painters, he executed a Saint Peter in the principal chapel of Sta. Maria della Grazia.... It came to pass that Polidoro, living in Naples and seeing his talents held in little esteem, determined to take his leave of men who thought more of a horse that could jump than of a master whose hands could give to painted figures the appearance of life. Going on board ship, therefore, he made his way to Messina, where, finding more consideration and more honor, he set himself to work; and thus, working continually, he acquired good skill and mastery in the use of color.

55. Loconte, 450–52; Willette, "Giotto's Allegorical Painting," 77–78.

Fig. 57. Polidoro da Caravaggio, Annunciation. Sta. Maria delle Grazie alla Pescheria. Photo: Sailko. Wikimedia.

VASARI ACKNOWLEDGES that the considerable topographic charms of Naples could in fact be nurturing for some artists, such as Marco Calavrese (Cardisco, d. 1542), a native of Calabria. Vasari waxes particularly poetic on the beauty of the Bay but also claims that it prevented Marco from reaching Rome, a paradigmatic center of the artistic universe.[56] He attempts to explain Marco's success there as a result of his musical nature (susceptible to the Sirens' call), which also thwarted him from working in Rome, and his personal appeal to potential patrons, for which Raphael was also well known. Vasari praises the Calabrese's altarpiece of c. 1540 for Sant'Agostino alla Zecca (now at the Museo di Capodimonte) as an example of the *"maniera moderna"* because of its debt to the central Italian styles of Raphael and Polidoro — whose work was accessible to him in Naples — and to that of Raphael's local follower, Andrea Sabatini da Salerno.[57] Marco died before Vasari arrived in Naples in 1544. Vasari gives Marco Calavrese his own chapter in the *Lives* (1:930–31).

56. Loconte, 443; Willette, "Giotto's Allegorical Painting," 82–83.

57. Barbara Agosti, "Introduzione," in Marco Cardisco, *Giorgio Vasari: Pittura, umanesimo, religioso, immagini di culto*, Riccardo Naldi, ed. (Naples: Arte'm, 2009), 7–9; Giusti and Leone de Castris, *Pittura del Cinquecento a Napoli, 1510–1540*, 226–53, 281–83.

144. Vasari: On Marco Cardisco from Calabria

When the world possesses some great light in any science, every least part is illuminated by its rays, some with greater brightness and some with less; and the miracles that result are also greater or less according to differences of air and place. Constantly, in truth, do we see a particular country producing a particular kind of intellect fitted for a particular kind of work, for which others are not fitted, nor can they ever attain, whatever labors they may endure, to the goal of supreme excellence. And if we marvel when we see growing in some province a fruit that has not been wont to grow there, much more can we rejoice in a man of fine intellect when we find him in a country where men of the same bent are not usually born. Thus it was with the painter Marco Calavrese, who, leaving his own country, chose for his habitation the sweet and pleasant city of Naples. He had been minded, indeed, on setting out, to make his way to Rome, and there to achieve the end that rewards the student of painting; but the song of the Siren was so sweet to him, and all the more because he delighted to play on the lute, and the soft waters of Sebeto so melted his heart, that he remained a prisoner in body of that land until he rendered up his spirit to heaven and his mortal flesh to earth.

Marco executed innumerable works in oils and in fresco, and he proved himself more able than any other man who was practicing the same art in that country in his day. Of this we have proof in the work that he executed at Aversa, ten miles distant from Naples; and, above all, in a panel-picture in oils on the high-altar of Sant'Agostino, with a large ornamental frame, and various pictures painted with scenes and figures, in which he represented St. Augustine disputing with the heretics, with stories of Christ and saints in various attitudes both above and at the sides.

In this work, which shows a manner full of harmony and drawing towards the good manner of our modern works, may also be seen great beauty and facility of coloring; and it was one of the many labors that he executed in that city and for various places in the kingdom.

Marco always lived a gay life, enjoying every minute to the full, for the reason that, having no rivalry to contend with in painting from other craftsmen, he was always adored by the Neapolitan nobles, and contrived to have himself rewarded for his works by ample payments.

VASARI WORKS IN NAPLES

Vasari comments extensively in the *Lives* (1550, 1568) on his own work in Naples following his residency there of 1544–45. The Tuscan assumes a lofty, proselytizing role as the purveyor of the *"maniera moderna"* to the unsophisticated, obtuse patrons of southern Italy. Following extended stays in Venice and Rome, Vasari went further south evidently hoping to secure the vice-regal patronage of Don Pedro de Toledo, the Spanish viceroy, whose daughter, Eleonora, had married Duke Cosimo I de' Medici in 1539. Vasari recounts towards the end of the passage below that he eventually received from Don Pedro a commission to decorate a chapel in the garden at his villa in Pozzuoli and then to decorate two other *loggie* at the same retreat. This project ended badly because of a skirmish between his two patrons — the Spanish viceroy and the monks of Sta. Maria di Monteoliveto — also involving the painter's own workmen; the conflict terminated any progress on the frescoes at Pozzuoli and resulted in Vasari's decision to leave Naples altogether. While Vasari's bitter account of what he perceived as dysfunctional conditions for successful employment in the multicultural city suggests a personal vendetta, it also provides a fascinating glimpse into the general animosity of Neapolitans towards Spanish occupation in the mid-sixteenth century.[58]

Prior to this debacle, Vasari had received his first Neapolitan commission c.1544 from the Olivetans (Order of White Benedictines) to embellish the refectory vault and walls for the prestigious church-monastery of Monteoliveto (now Sant'Anna dei Lombardi). Following a pattern of in-house support of artists by the religious orders, Vasari had been engaged previously by the Olivetans elsewhere in Italy and was drafted by Don Giammatteo d'Aversa in Naples at the

---

58. Loconte, 440–45; Willette, "Giotto's Allegorical Painting," 72–80. For Vasari in Naples, see also Leone de Castris, *Pittura del Cinquecento,* 95–123.

urging of other patron-abbots.[59] The wealthy Neapolitan foundation had been founded in the early fifteenth century and was dear to the Aragonese. It was, in fact, a site well-suited to Vasari's self-promotion. Not only did the order itself have Tuscan origins, but Monteoliveto was also the repository for the artistic efforts of a number of central Italian artists, including Antonio Rossellino and Giuliano da Maiano, who had similarly imported the "modern" to the southern kingdom. Here Vasari even presents himself as a sixteenth-century counterpart to the Florentine painter Giotto, whom he portrays as having similarly enlightened, even rescued, the Neapolitan court of Robert of Anjou more than two centuries earlier.[60]

Vasari adorned the refectory's pointed arch system of vaulting [Fig. 58] in the spirit of the decorative tradition *all'antica* inspired by the rediscovery of the Domus Aurea and established in Rome by Raphael and his followers decades earlier, with the objective of both "dazzling" and instructing the locals in the "modern manner." The account of the commission for Monteoliveto is in fact useful for its detail about cutting into the gothicizing original vault made of tufa. Grotesque ornament in white and painted stucco frames geometric compartments frescoed with astrological signs and religious allegories. Vasari also contributed six oil paintings with the Parables of Christ for the long wall and two triptychs for the end walls of the space. Other work at Monteoliveto includes his *Presentation at the Temple* for the high altar of the church that he claims to have executed "with a new invention." *Christ Appearing to the Apostles* for the Olivetan abbot general recalls the heroic figures of Raphael's tapestries for the Sistine Chapel.[61]

59. Pierluigi Leone de Castris, "Napoli 1544: Vasari e Monteoliveto," *Bollettino d'Arte* 66 (1981): 117–34; Liana Cheney, "Vasari and Naples: The Monteolivetan Order," in *Parthenope's Splendor: Art of the Golden Age in Naples*, Jeanne Chenault Porter and Susan Scott Munshower, ed. (University Park, PA: Pennsylvania State University, 1993), 56.

60. Loconte, 445; Willette, "Giotto's Allegorical Painting," 73–74; Leone de Castris, *Giotto a Napoli*.

61. Leone De Castris, *Pittura del Cinquecento*, 14.

Fig. 58. Giorgio Vasari. Monteoliveto (S. Anna Dei Lombardi), Sacristy, 1544–45. Photo: Italica Press.

Vasari's lengthy commentary provides important information about his commissions in Naples (*Lives,* 2:1037–39).

145. Vasari: On His Commission for the Sacristy of Sta. Maria di Monteoliveto
In that same year of 1544, I was invited to Naples by Don Giammateo of Aversa, general of the monks of Monteoliveto, to the end that I might paint the refectory of a monastery built for them by King Alfonso I; but when I arrived, I was for not accepting the work, seeing that the refectory and the whole monastery were built in an ancient manner of architecture, with the vaults in pointed arches, low and poor in lights, and I doubted that I was like to win little honour thereby. However, being pressed by Don

Miniato Pitti and Don Ippolito da Milano, my very dear friends, who were then visitors to that order, finally I accepted the undertaking. Whereupon, recognizing that I would not be able to do anything good save only with a great abundance of ornaments, dazzling the eyes of all who might see the work with a variety and multitude of figures, I resolved to have all the vaulting of the refectory wrought in stucco, in order to remove by means of rich compartments in the modem manner all the old-fashioned and clumsy appearance of those arches. In this I was much assisted by the vaults and walls, which are made, as is usual in that city, of blocks of tufa, which cut like wood, or even better, like bricks not completely baked; and thus, cutting them, I was able to sink squares, ovals, and octagons, and also to thicken them with additions of the same tufa by means of nails.

Having then reduced those vaults to good proportions with that stucco-work, which was the first to be wrought in Naples in the modern manner, and in particular the façades and end-walls of that refectory, I painted there six panels in oils, seven *braccia* high, three to each end-wall. In three that are over the entrance of the refectory is the manna raining down upon the Hebrew people, in the presence of Moses and Aaron, and the people gathering it up; wherein I strove to represent a variety of attitudes and vestments in the men, women, and children, and the emotion wherewith they are gathering up and storing the manna, rendering thanks to God. On the end-wall that is at the head is Christ at table in the house of Simon, and Mary Magdalene with tears washing His feet and drying them with her hair, showing herself all penitent for her sins; which story is divided into three pictures, in the centre the supper, on the right hand a buttery with a credence full of vases in various fantastic forms, and on the left hand a steward who is bringing up the viands.

The vaulting, then, was divided into three parts; in one the subject is Faith, in the second Religion, and in the third Eternity, and each of these forms a center with eight Virtues about it, demonstrating to the monks that in that refectory they eat what is requisite for the perfection of their lives. To enrich the spaces of the vaulting, I made them full of grotesques, which serve as ornaments in forty-eight spaces for the forty-eight celestial signs; and on six walls down the length of that refectory, under the windows, which were made larger and richly ornamented, I painted six of the parables of Jesus Christ which are in keeping with that place; and to all those pictures and ornaments there correspond the carvings of the seats, which are wrought very richly.

And then I executed for the high-altar of the church an altar-picture eight *braccia* high, containing the Madonna presenting the Infant Jesus Christ to Simeon in the Temple, with a new invention. It is a notable thing that since Giotto there had not been up to that time, in a city so great and noble, any masters who had done anything of importance in painting, although there had been brought there from without some things by the hands of Perugino and Raffaello. On which account I exerted myself to labor in such a manner, in so far as my little knowledge could reach, that the intellects of that country might be roused to execute great and honourable works; and, whether that or some other circumstance may have been the reason, between that time and the present day many very beautiful works have been done there, both in stucco and in painting.

Besides the pictures described above, I executed in fresco on the vaulting of the strangers' apartment in the same monastery, with figures large as life, Jesus Christ with the Cross on His shoulder, and many of His saints who have one likewise on their shoulders in imitation of Him, to demonstrate that for one who wishes truly to follow Him it is necessary to bear with good patience the adversities that the world inflicts.

For the general of that order I executed a great picture of Christ appearing to the Apostles as they struggled with the perils of the sea, and taking St. Peter by the arm, who, having hastened towards Him through the water, was fearing to drown; and in another picture, for Abbot Capeccio I painted the Resurrection. These works carried to completion,

I painted a chapel in fresco for the Lord Don Pedro de Toledo, viceroy of Naples, in his garden at Pozzuoli, besides executing some very delicate ornaments in stucco; and arrangements had been made to execute two great *loggie* for the same lord, but the undertaking was not carried into effect, for the following reason. There had been some difference between the viceroy and the above-named monks, and the constable went with his men to the monastery to seize the abbot and some monks who had had some words with the Black Friars in a procession, over a matter of precedence. But the monks made some resistance, assisted by about fifteen young men who were assisting me in stucco-work and painting, and wounded some of the bailiffs; on which account it became necessary to get them out of the way, and they went off in various directions.

VASARI GOES ON to describe with much grumbling his commission of 1545 from the erudite future cardinal Antonio Seripando for the mortuary chapel of his brother Antonio in the Augustinian church of San Giovanni a Carbonara, where Seripando was then *vicario* and where the elite tomb of King Ladislaus and chapels of the Caracciolo family were located.[62] Vasari may have met the cardinal in Rome. The chapel, commissioned by Girolamo together with his brother Giacomo, was completed in 1539 and housed a tomb that showcased epigraphs of the humanist but not his effigy.[63] (Seripando's vast library housed on the second floor above the chapel was widely celebrated.) Vasari's contribution, executed following the departure of his assistants described above, brought figural representation to the space with a large altarpiece showing the Crucifixion [Fig. 59] and set in the artist's trademark stucco frame. Seripando was a papal legate to the Council of Trent, and the corporeal immediacy of the *Crucifixion* echoes the Counter-Reformation mandate for powerful devotional images.

62. See above, readings 82–83, pp. 260–67.

63. Riccardo Naldi, "Il Crocefisso per Girolamo Seripando e il suo contesto," in *Giorgio Vasari: Pittura, umanesimo, religioso, immagini di culto*, Marco Cadisco, ed. (Naples: Arte'm, 2009), 107–35.

Fig. 59. Giorgio Vasari. Crucifixion. S. Giovanni a Carbonara, 1545. Photo: Armando Mancini. Wikimedia.

On returning to Rome after his untimely departure from Naples, Vasari also painted multiple scenes of the Old Testament and the life of St. John the Baptist for the sacristy of San Giovanni. The following excerpt from the *Lives* describes the Tuscan's last Neapolitan commission (2:1039).

146. Vasari: On Painting the Seripando Chapel in San Giovanni a Carbonara

And so I, left almost alone, was unable not only to execute the *loggie* at Pozzuoli, but also to paint twenty-four pictures of stories from the Old Testament and from the life of St. John the Baptist, which, not caring to remain any longer in Naples, I took to Rome to finish, whence I sent them, and they were placed about the stalls and over the presses of walnut-wood made from my architectural designs in the sacristy of San Giovanni Carbonara, a convent of Eremite and Observantine Friars of St. Augustine, for whom I had painted a short time before, for a chapel without their church, a panel-picture of Christ Crucified, with a rich and varied ornament of stucco, at the request of Seripando, their general, who afterwards became a cardinal. In like manner, halfway up the staircase of the same convent, I painted in fresco a St. John the Evangelist who stands gazing at Our Lady clothed with the sun and crowned with twelve stars, with her feet upon the moon.

SPANISH NAPLES, A CENTER OF PAINTING

The viceroy Don Pedro de Toledo granted the Spanish artist, Pedro de Rubiales (Roviale), the prestigious commission of 1547–48 to paint the Cappella della Sommaria in Castel Capuano [Fig. 60] with large scenes from the Passion of Christ below and Christological themes above.[64] He was one of several artists assembled by Don Pedro to embellish his many private and civic projects, which included the refurbishing of the castle — formerly the residence of Angevin and Aragonese royalty — to house the viceregal civil and penal tribunals. The document below describes the embellishment in 1548 of a Spanish galley in Naples, for which Pedro painted a banner and also names him as author of the paintings for the chapel. It is adjacent to a large chamber, the Sommària, now known as the Corte d'Appello.

Like his compatriot Pedro Fernández de Murcia earlier in the cinquecento, the Spanish painter brought with him a recent experience of mid-century Rome, working, according to Vasari, with Francesco Salviati (who had painted the chapel for Eleonora de Toledo, Don Pedro's daughter, in the Palazzo Vecchio, Florence) and other Tuscans at the Palazzo della Cancelleria in Rome.[65] Pedro's decoration for the chapel at Castel Capuano in fact reflects Vasari's recently completed and lavish ensemble of stucco, fresco, and oil for the refectory at Monteoliveto. Primarily represented are events from the Passion of Christ. The altarpiece in oil shows the Pietà with adventurous chiaroscuro atmospherics below the right arm of Christ and a discreet depiction of Pedro's project for the Castel Sant'Elmo under construction. This and other scenes include familiar Michelangelesque physical torsions and the energy of mid-century central Italian painting. Pedro later prepared models for the anatomical illustrations in Juan de Valverde's *Historia de la composición del cuerpo humano* (Rome, 1556).

64. Roberto Middione, "Pedro de Rubiales at the Sommària: Justice and the Viceroy," *Franco Maria Ricci* (FMR) 8 (2005): 27–52; Nicole Dacos, "De Pedro de Rubiales a 'Roviale spagnuolo,'" *Boletín del Seminario de Estudios de Arte y Arqueología* 75 (2009): 107–14; Gennaro Toscano, "Roviale, Francesco," www.oxfordartonline.com.

65. Vasari, 2:326, 582, 1042; Pierluigi Leone de Castris, *Pittura del Cinquecento a Napoli, 1573–1606: L'ultima maniera* (Naples: Electa, 1991), 136.

Fig. 60. Pedro de Rubiales. Pietà. Castel Capuano, Cappella della Sommaria, 1547/8. Photo: Fiore Silvestro Barbato. Il Sistemone. Wikimedia.

The document below is one of the few cinquecento references to Pedro's commission for the Neapolitan chapel in Castel Capuano. It is found in the Archivio di Stato di Napoli, *Cedole della Tesoreria*, vol. 298, n.p., transcribed in Ulisse Prota-Giurleo, *Scritti inediti e rari* (Naples: Arte Tipografica, 1988), 84, and cited in Dacos, "De Pedro de Rubiales," 111. Translated by CFN.

147. Roviale Spagnuolo Paints a Chapel for Don Pedro de Toledo
The second [banner], of green damask, was entrusted to the Spanish painter Pedro Roviales of Albuquerque, who painted the image of the Pietà of Our Lord, the four Evangelists, the Mysteries of the Passion, and other ornamentation.

MARCO PINO, a Sienese native, had worked with Pedro de Rubiales on prominent Roman commissions and later commanded the attention of patrons in Naples between 1551 and 1583 during the resurgence of commissions for paintings in the Counter-Reformation period. He contributed numerous altarpieces and frescoes for the private chapels of Neapolitan and Spanish patrons in the increasingly populous city. One large altarpiece is the *San Michele Archangelo* of 1573 [Fig. 61] for the prestigious church of Sant'Angelo a Nilo, founded by Cardinal Rinaldo Brancacci and the location of the cardinal's tomb by Donatello and Michelozzo (c. 1425).

Giovanni Paolo Lamozzo from Milan, a painter and pioneer in theoretic writing about art, names Marco as a pupil of Michelangelo in the section of his late sixteenth-century treatise about the *figura serpentinata*, or the positional S-curve in the shape of a flame, championed by the legendary Florentine. His *San Michele* demonstrates the expressive figural torsion *("furia")* advocated by Michelangelo along with his experience of working with Perino del Vaga — a pupil of Raphael and practitioner of *"grazia"* or grace — in Rome on prestigious papal commissions during the pontificate of Paul III Farnese.[66] The exuberance seen in his astonishing number of Neapolitan commissions foreshadows the animated fervor of Baroque works and influenced Belisario Corenzio, another foreigner who had a long career in Naples.

66. Fiorella Sricchia Santoro and Andrea Zezza ed., *Marco Pino: Un protagonista della "maniera moderna" a Napoli. Restauri nel centro storico* (Naples: Electa, 2003), 87–89. Giovan Bernardo Lama, a local artist, assisted Pino. See also Leone de Castris, *Pittura del Cinquecento, 1573–1606*, 185–232, 335–37.

Fig. 61. Marco Pino. S. Michele Arcangelo. S. Angelo a Nilo, 1573. Wikimedia.

Lomazzo's oft-cited passage on the *figura serpentinata* is from his *Trattato dell'Arte della Pittura* (Milan, 1584), 22–24, translated in John Shearman, *Mannerism* (Harmondsworth: Penguin, 1967), 81.

148. Giovanni Paolo Lamozzo: Marco Pino of Siena Works in Naples
Michelangelo once gave this advice to his pupil Marco da
Siena, that one should always make the figure pyramidal,
serpentine, and multiplied by one, two, or three. And in this
precept, it seems to me, is contained the secret of painting,
for a figure has its highest grace and eloquence when it is
seen in movement — what the painters call the *Furia della
figura*. And to represent it thus there is no better form than
that of a flame, because it is the most mobile of all forms and
is conical. If a figure has this form it will be very beautiful....
The painter should combine this form with the *Serpentinata*,
like the twisting of a live snake in motion, which is also the
form of a waving flame.... The figure should resemble the
letter "S".... And this applies not only to the whole figure,
but also to its parts.

DIRCK HENDRICKSZ CENTEN (Teodoro d'Errico) was one of many
Northern artists to seek their fortunes in Naples during the later
sixteenth century following his tutelage under Taddeo and Federico
Zuccaro in Rome. A native of Amsterdam, then under Spanish imperial rule, Dirck arrived in Naples in the 1570s and eventually married
a Neapolitan, as had his compatriot Cornelius Smet. He profited there
from the ecclesiastical building boom of the Counter-Reformation,
which provided numerous opportunities over four decades to adorn
the new or newly renovated ecclesiastical settings. The commissions
to paint the wooden soffits for the naves of the prestigious churches
of San Gregorio Armeno and, later, Sta. Maria Donnaromita reflect
the esteem in which he was held. The document below names him as
an elected consul for the Neapolitan Corporation of Painters (1593–
94).[67] He returned to Amsterdam in 1609 following the death of his
second wife and painter-son, who had assisted him in his workshop.

The passage below is from Filangieri 6:84–85, quoting Archivio
Notarile di Napoli, notary Cristoforo Cerlone, ann. 1579–80. Translated
by CFN.

67. Leone de Castris, *Pittura del Cinquecento a Napoli, 1573–1606*, 31–64,
330–32; Carmela Vargas, "Hendricksz. (Centen), Dirck [Teodoro d'Errico],
www.oxfordartonline.

Fig. 62. Belisario Corenzio. Cappella di Sant'Ugo. Certosa di San Martino. Photo: Sailko. Wikimedia.

149. Cristoforo Cerlone: Dirck Hendricksz of Flanders Succeeds in Naples
14 June 1595. Among the other elections of consuls held in the church of Santo Luca on the 6th day of November 1594 were held the elections of the consuls of painters and gilders... on the said day were named the magnificents Giovanni Andrea Magliuolo, Teodoro Gerrico... for the art of painting....

BELISARIO CORENZIO lived in Naples for most of his life. Originally from Greece, Belisario absorbed the lessons of several other non-Neapolitan artists working there after arriving in 1570: Marco Pino, Dirck Henricksz, and Cornelius Smet. [68] Thus, his work reflects the disparate stylistic trends of the late sixteenth and early seventeenth centuries: ranging from a reinvented classicism to Caravaggesque realism. The transformation of the Angevin foundation of the Certosa di San Martino, on a spectacular site overlooking the city, into a model of Carthusian *richesse* provided great opportunities for fresco painters in the 1590s, two of whom were the Giuseppe Cesare (the Cavaliere d'Arpino) and Belisario Corenzio.

68. Anonymous. "Corenzio, Belisario," www.oxfordartonline.

The former arrived from Rome by 1591 bringing to the venerated church a recent experience of commissions for the Farnese family, which in turn influenced the Greek-born artist. The vaulted areas of the church sanctuary consist of frescoed images within geometrically shaped compartments framed by stucco borders in relief [Fig. 62]. The document below of 1592 confirms Belisario's participation in the decoration for the chapel of San Nicola, and he also worked in the chapel of Sant'Ugo. In both, the classicizing muscularity of Raphael's late work is fused with the narrative clarity mandated for sacred works during the Counter-Reformation.[69]

The church of the Certosa would later be embellished with the exuberant *pietra dura* revetment by Cosimo Fanzago and the darkly dramatic oil paintings by the Spaniard Juseppe de Ribera (1638–43), both of which continue to claim the viewer's attention at the expense of the comparatively pale frescoes. Ribera, along with Corenzio and Battistello Caracciolo, formed the notorious "Cabal of Naples," whose objective in the early 1600s was to eliminate by life-threatening means any nonresident competitors for prestigious Neapolitan commissions, particularly those for the treasury of San Gennaro in the cathedral.

Gaetano Filangieri di Satriano (5:141) also summarizes the document in which Belisario enters into an agreement with Don Giustino de Urso Giustini de Urso, procurator of the Certosa. It is from the Archivio Storico di Napoli, notary A. Rosanova, prot. 20, cc. 411–412, cited in Leone de Castris, *Pittura del Cinquecento*, 324.

150. Belisario Corenzio at the Certosa di San Martino
He painted in the church of San Martino in Naples the chapel to the left upon entering for the sum of 220 ducats.

MICHELANGELO MERISI DA CARAVAGGIO arrived in Naples in 1606 under the protection of the powerful Colonna family following his hasty retreat from Rome on a murder charge. He immediately attracted many potential patrons, including the Spanish viceroy and members of his circle. After completing his well-known altarpiece of the *Seven Acts of Mercy* in 1606 for the Pio Monte della Misericordia,

69. Leone de Castris, *Pittura del Cinquecento a Napoli, 1573–1606*, 179–92, 324–26.

Fig. 63. Caravaggio. Flagellation. S. Domenico Maggiore, 1607. Museo di Capodimonte. Wikimedia.

a patron for whom Belisario Corenzio had recently worked, he evidently undertook a *Flagellation of Christ* [Fig. 63] for the de Franchis family, which was closely allied with the viceregency. The altarpiece was to be placed in the new family chapel in San Domenico,[70]

70. Vincenzo Pacelli, "New Documents Concerning Caravaggio in Naples," *The Burlington Magazine* 119 (1977): 820–26; Andrew Graham-Dixon,

Fig. 64. Titian. Annunciation. S. Domenico Maggiore, 1557. Museo di Capodimonte. Photo: Sailko. Wikimedia.

Caravaggio: A Life Sacred and Profane (New York: Norton, 2011), 339–49; and John T. Spike, *Caravaggio* (New York: Abbeville Press, 2001), 192–96.

which was the church of Thomas Aquinas, Tommaso Campanella, and Giordano Bruno and the original repository of Aragonese royal remains. The site of mortuary chapels of the most prestigious local families, San Domenico had its reputation further enhanced by the imported altarpieces of Raphael's *Madonna del Pesce* (c. 1515, Fig. 54) and Titian's *Annunciation* (1557, Fig. 64).[71]

Caravaggio's visceral realism and dynamic reinterpretation of the familiar theme of Christ's scourging — seen in Sebastiano del Piombo's Michelangelesque fresco in San Pietro in Montorio, Rome — provided a stylistic jolt and compelling alternative to the classicizing idiom dominant for most of the preceding century.[72] His sense of the momentary in a shadowy and violent pictorial world exuded a familiar reality to Neapolitan viewers and inspired a number of followers there, such as Battistello Caracciolo.

On returning from Malta to Naples in 1609, Caravaggio was attacked and disfigured outside of the tawdry Taverna del Cerriglio; his injuries affected his ability to paint. Thus, the city on whom his style had such a decisive impact was also the site of a decisive alteration to that style. He died at Porto Ercole the next year en route to Rome, following his pardon for the murder that had driven him to Naples.

The following document is found in the Archivio di Stato Banco di Napoli, Banco dello Spirito Santo, *Giornale copia polizze*, matr. 44, D.100, 11 May 1607, and copied in Vincenzo Pacelli, "New Documents," 820.

151. Giornale Copia Polizze: Payments to Caravaggio
From Tomase di Franco, 100 ducats for Michelangelo Caravaggio, who will be paid 250 ducats upon completion of the project for which we are still waiting....

★ ★ ★

71. Harold Wethey, *The Paintings of Titian: The Religious Paintings*, 3 vols. (London: Phaidon, 1969), 1:72–74.

72. Caravaggio's altarpiece of Saint Andrew of 1606–7, evidently painted for the Neapolitan viceroy Don Juan Alfonso de Pimental, is in the Cleveland Museum of Art. Pacelli, 826–29, at: https://www.clevelandart.org/art/1976.2.

CHAPTER 8: THE TASTE FOR ANTIQUITIES
by Charlotte Nichols

ALFONSO I's LETTER OF THANKS sent in 1446 to the powerful cardinal Lodovico Trevisan signals the king's increasing obsession with Greco-Roman antiquities. He describes with great enthusiasm the receipt of a reclining female figure, on which he confers the name "Parthenope": the Greek Siren whose body had come ashore at Paleopolis (now Pizzofalcone).[1] The king goes on to ask the cardinal's opinion of the new setting he designed for the sculpture, and he concludes the missive with a distich composed by the Sicilian humanist Antonio Beccadelli (Il Panormita), later the author of a series of commentaries on Alfonso's life titled *De dictis et factis Alphonsi*.[2] The verse blatantly links the mythical Greek founder of Naples to Alfonso, a savior through whom she and the city are born anew.

Lodovico Trevisan had been educated in Padua by the humanist Vittorino da Feltre, an experience that prepared him well for elite cultural activities during his pursuit of ecclesiastical high office. As archbishop of Florence, Trevisan had entré to sophisticated antiquarians and himself became a noted collector. He was appointed by his fellow Venetian, Eugenius IV, to the cardinalate as treasurer in 1440. Alfonso I's claim to the kingdom of Naples was ratified by the pope, and Trevisan's gift served as tangible evidence of support. The cardinal's portrait was later painted by Andrea Mantegna, the Gonzaga court artist.

The letter, originally written in Catalan, is translated into Italian in Benedetto Croce, "Una lettera inedita di Alfonso d'Aragona," *Napoli Nobilissima* 1 (1892): 128. Translated by CFN. The Latin couplet is translated in Hersey, *Arch*, 25.

152. Alfonso I: Letter on a Sculpture of Parthenope
> My lord, I received your letter and all the gifts that not only satisfied and delighted the corporeal senses but also those

1. De Divitiis, "Castel Nuovo and Castel Capuano," 455–58.

2. On Panormita, see above, chapter 3, pp. 139–42 and readings 20–22; Bentley, 84–100, 224–27.

spiritual; for which I see that I cannot give you adequate thanks, if in trying I risk exhausting the virtue of your patience. I tell you, O my lord, that when the first statue and the pictures arrived I was out hunting and didn't return until sunset, having not eaten; yet I deliberated whether to first satisfy the soul or the body; and I saw them without delay, and I assure you that they are of such perfection, especially the sculpture, that each day I contemplate it with no less delight than the first time. And, because, to a true friend all things must be told, I share with you my thought and my invention on the manner of installing it to know your opinion. I want it to represent the statue of the city of Naples, which, battered repeatedly by war, now having obtained peace, is at rest. I include here the verses that I have had composed; I write you of other matters through my secretary, offering myself always to your honor and pleasure.

Written by my hand in Castel Nuovo on 22 March 1446.

— King Alfonso — to Cardinal d'Aquilea.

I am that Parthenope, vexed with war for many years,
Now at last, reborn through Alfonso, I rest in peace.

153. Pisanello Designs Bronze Medals Celebrating Alfonso I
Alfonso I's patronage of Antonio Pisano, known as Pisanello, was facilitated by the politically expedient marriage of the king's natural daughter, Maria d'Aragona, to his ally Leonello d'Este of Ferrara in 1444. For that occasion the marquis commissioned a commemorative medal from Pisanello [Fig. 66], an innovation for which the artist is often credited. Inspired by Roman coins and medals, these portable, precious, and personalized objects quickly became a mandatory collectable for sophisticated rulers. Pisanello supplied Alfonso with three medals upon his arrival in Naples as court artist c.1448.

The medals for the king of 1449 follows Pisanello's established formula: a profile bust of the patron surrounded by motifs and inscriptions, with allegorical emblems on the reverse. The obverse portrait of Alfonso seen in the version at the Staaliche Museen, Berlin, is accompanied by a helmet embellished with an open book on one side and a crown and the date on the other. The

Fig. 66. Pisanello, Medal of Alfonso I obverse (L), and reverse (R). National Archeological Museum of Spain. Photo: Luis Garcia (Zaqarbal). Wikimedia.

words DIVUS ALFONSUS REX, TRIUMPHATOR, PACIFICUS appear at the top and bottom of the obverse respectively. DIVUS is an obvious allusion to deified Roman emperors; it also appears beneath the equestrian monument atop the tomb of King Ladislaus, Alfonso's Angevin predecessor. The idea of Alfonso as a triumphant bringer of peace echoes sentiments in the king's letter to Cardinal Trevisan cited above.

The reverse of the medal displays the words LIBERALITAS AUGUSTA (imperial generosity) with birds of prey devouring a deer; below is Pisanello's name. The bird in the center is usually identified as an eagle, complementing the imperialist implications of AUGUSTA. The other birds surely include the falcons to which Alfonso was so devoted as hunting companions (reading 123 above). Pisanello was well known for his drawings from nature of birds and hunters.

The medal was undertaken at the time that Alfonso began to contemplate the entrance gate for the newly refurbished Castel Nuovo, with which Pisanello has been associated.[3] The artist was celebrated by Alfonso's court humanist, Bartolomeo Facio, in his *De Viris Illustribus* of 1456.

The helmet on the obverse of the version of the Berlin medal now in Madrid (National Archeological Museum) is inscribed with the Latin phrase VIR SAPIENS DOMINATUR ASTRIS. It signals Alfonso's

3. See p. 232 and Fig. 13.

reputed love of learning as befitted the wise king-warrior.[4] Alfonso was famous for his library and evidently read to his soldiers from Livy, whose arm bone he possessed.[5] The Latin is translated here by Derek Moore.

THE DIVINE ALFONSO TRIUMPHANT KING AND PEACEMAKER

WISE MAN RULED BY THE STARS.

THE ARAGONESE were evidently eager to secure the services of Donatello, who had partnered with Michelozzo to execute Cardinal Rinaldo Brancacci's tomb in Sant'Angelo a Nilo some years earlier. In a letter of 1452 to Doge Francesco Foscari, Alfonso I describes his wish to employ the Florentine. At that time Donatello was working on the *Gattamelata*: a monumental, bronze equestrian sculpture in Padua of the condottiere Erasmo da Narni who served the Republic of Venice, and the doge. As the following entries demonstrate, Alfonso I aspired to a similar commission. The tradition of equestrian sculpture figured into the recent history of royal imagery in Naples; one crowned the tomb (c.1428) of the Angevin king Ladislaus in San Giovanni a Carbonara. A painted portrait of Alfonso on horseback was commissioned for Castel Capuano, where he resided during the rebuilding of Castel Nuovo.[6]

The letter is found in Juan Ainaud de Lasarte, "Alfonso the Magnanimous and the Plastic Arts of His Time," in *Spain in the Fifteenth Century 1369–1516*, Roger Highfield, ed. (London: Macmillan, 1972), 203, who in turn cites Jordi Rubió, "Alfons 'el Magnánim' rei de Nápols, i Daniel Florentino, Leonardo da Bisuccio, i Donatello," in *Micellània Puig I Cadafalch* I (1947–51): 25–35.

4. See Joanna Woods Marsden, "Art and Political Identity in Fifteenth-Century Naples: Pisanello, Cristoforo di Geremia, and King Alfonso's Imperial Fantasies," in *Art and Politics in Late Medieval and Early Renaissance Italy: 1250-1500*, Charles M. Rosenberg, ed. (Notre Dame, IN: University of Notre Dame Press, 1990), 11–37; Beyer, *Parthenope*, 59–61; Hersey, *Arch*, 27–29; Syson and Gordon, *Pisanello*, 123–25.

5. See chapter 6, reading 99, p. 285.

6. Hersey, *Arch*, 24.

154. Alfonso I: Letter to Francesco Foscari to Employ Donatello
26 May 1452

Most Illustrious Duke, our beloved friend, we have heard of the skill and cunning of the mind of Master Donatello in making bronze and marble statues, it has been our great desire to have him with us and in our service for a while....

IN HIS FIRST EDITION of the *Vite* (1550) Vasari, himself resident in Naples a few years earlier, described as antique an equine head (*protome*) in Diomede Carafa's legendary collection [Fig. 67]. He later attributed it to Donatello in the second edition (1568), without, however, tying it to a specific commission. The conflicting nature of his passages portends the subsequent scholarly debate about the provenance of the piece.[7] Documents recently discovered by Francesco Caglioti in the Archivio di Stato, Florence, involving Bartolommeo Serragli, Alfonso I's Tuscan art agent, offer convincing evidence of Donatello's authorship. They refer to Alfonso's wish for a large bronze horse in 1453 and note payments to Donatello in 1456 drawn from the Neapolitan royal treasury for a large "*fusione*" (smelting) of bronze.[8] Donatello would have had access to the ancient bronze horse head in the Medici collection, now in the Museo Archeologico Nazionale, Florence.

The fifteenth-century bronze head thus appears to have been part of an unfinished commission for an equestrian monument in the upper arch of Alfonso's marble entrance to the Castel Nuovo, as seen in Pisanello's drawing of c.1448–1450.[9] The statue's projected height of five meters is compatible with the physical space of the arch.[10]

7. Hersey, *Arch*, 53–55; Beyer (2000), 131–33. Summonte attributes the head to Donatello in his letter of 1524 (ll. 302–12).

8. Francesco Caglioti, "'La Testa Carafa' e il mito della poeta Virgilio, mago e protettore di Napoli," lecture filmed for RAI series titled "L'altra lingua degli italiani," 23 October 2012, filmed at Palazzo Reale, Naples. Online at http://www.raiscuola.rai.it/articoli-programma-puntate/laltra-lingua-degli-italiani-%e2%80%9cla-testa-carafa%e2%80%9d-e-il-mito-del-poeta-virgilio-mago-e-protettore-di-napoli/19917/default.aspx.

9. See above, Fig. 13, p. 232.

10. Caglioti (2012).

Vasari's commentary is found in his life of Donatello, translated in Gaston du C. de Vere, 1:370.

155. Vasari: Diomede Carafa's Bronze Horse by Donatello
> In the house of the count of Matalone, in the same city, there is a head of a horse by the hand of Donato, so beautiful that many take it for antique.

THE MONUMENT PLANNED for the Arch of Alfonso remained incomplete following the king's death in 1458, and the bronze head described above evidently languished in the studio of Donatello, who died in 1466. King Ferrante completed the arch in 1471, the year in which Lorenzo de' Medici sent – seemingly at the request of Ferrante – the equine bust to Diomede Carafa, Alfonso's most trusted advisor and long-time friend of the Medici family.[11] This act by the new head of family represents the continuing Medici investment in gift-giving to their southern ally – famous as breeders of horses – for political purposes.

The bronze head was displayed in the courtyard of the Palazzo Carafa, one of the most well-known sculpture gardens in Naples [Fig. 67]. Fevered myth-making *all'antica* thereafter conferred a Roman provenance on the piece, which confounded later scholarship and resulted in its donation in 1809 to the Museo Archeologico Nazionale in Naples, where it remains today. A terracotta copy immediately replaced the original in the courtyard.

The letter is found in Gaetano Filangieri, "La testa di cavallo in bronzo gia' di casa Maddaloni," *Archivio Storico per le provincie napoletane* 7 (1882): 416, and transcribed in Hersey, *Aragonese Arch*, 72, doc. 32.

11. See Cagliotti (2012).

Fig. 67. Donatello's Protome Carafa in the cortile of Palazzo Diomede-Carafa. Pompeo Sarnelli, Guida de' Forestieri... di Napoli. Naples: A. Bulifon, 1688.

156. Diomede Carafa: Letter Thanking Lorenzo de' Medici for the Gift of the Horse 12 July 1471
Magnificent Lord... I received the horse's head that Your Lordship was gracious enough to send me, a gesture for which I remain so very pleased as it was something that I desired, and I thank you several times for this. I am letting you know that I have placed it well in my house so that one sees it from every side, promising you that it will remind not only me of you, but my children, who will continue to have you before them, and they will be obliged to appreciate the love that it shows.... If I may serve Your Lordship, I am ready....

VASARI DESCRIBES the way in which Giuliano da Sangallo barters with King Ferrante for antiquities — a portrait bust of Hadrian, a sleeping Cupid, and a female nude — for Lorenzo de' Medici as a form of homage for Giuliano's services regarding his Palazzo de' Tribunali.[12] Vasari demonstrates the premium that the culturally minded Florentine placed on Roman art. Sangallo's sketchbooks, such as the Barberini Codex,[13] continue to be an invaluable source of information for the ruins near Naples.

12. For sleeping Cupids in the Medici collections, see Kathleen Weil-Garris Brandt, "Sogni di un Cupido dormiente smarrito," in *La giovinezza di Michelangelo*, Kathleen Weil-Garris Brandt, ed. (Florence and Milan: ArtificioSkira, 1999), 315–23. Alfonso I had displayed reliefs of the Spanish emperors Trajan and Hadrian at the Castel Nuovo; see Hersey, *Arch*, 31; De Divitiis, "Castel Nuovo," 454.

13. BAV, MS Barberini 4424.

The following section from Vasari's life of Giuliano and Antonio da Sangallo is translated in *Lives*, 1:699.

157. Vasari: Giuliano da Sangallo Chooses Antiquities in Naples for Lorenzo de' Medici

After Giuliano had been some time in Naples, he sought leave from the duke to return to Florence; whereupon he was presented by the king with horses and garments, and, among other things, with a silver cup containing some hundreds of ducats. These things Giuliano would not accept, saying that he served a patron who had no need of silver or gold, but that if he did indeed wish to give him some present or some token of approbation, to show that he had been in that city, he might bestow upon him some of his antiquities, which he would choose himself. These the king granted to him most liberally, both for love of the Magnificent Lorenzo and on account of Giuliano's own worth; and they were a head of Emperor Hadrian, which is now above the door of the garden at the house of the Medici, a nude woman, more than life-size, and a Cupid sleeping, all in marble and in the round. Giuliano sent them as presents to the Magnificent Lorenzo, who expressed vast delight at the gift, and never tired of praising the action of this most liberal of craftsmen, who had refused gold and silver for the sake of art, a thing which few would have done. That Cupid is now in the *guardaroba* of Duke Cosimo.

SUMMONTE COMMENTS ADMIRINGLY in his *Letter* of 1524 on the famed Temple of Castor and Pollux [Figs. 68–69], sections of whose pronaos are still visible from the decumanus of the ancient city, today the Via Tribunali. This location was adjacent to the Forum, the "umbilical center" referred to by the humanist. The inscription announces that the marble temple was dedicated by the freedmen Tarsus and Pelagon during the reign of the emperor Tiberius (14-37 CE), who had numerous properties on the Bay and Capri. Its Greek lettering overtly links the structure to the Hellenic origins of the site, and the pediment may have included a figure of Parthenope, the mythical founder of the city.[14] He deplores the ninth-century renovation of the

14. See Rabun Taylor, "The Temple of the Dioscuri and the Mythic Origins of Neapolis," in Hughes–Buongiovanni, 39–63, at 46.

Fig. 68. S. Paolo Maggiore (Temple of the Dioscuri). Column from pronaos. Photo: Italica Press.

temple as a church dedicated to San Paolo. The medieval church was replaced in the late sixteenth century by Fabrizio Grimaldi's structure for the Theatine Order,[15] in which the side walls of the peristyle were integrated into the walls of the nave. The new church masking the remains of the Temple of the Dioscuri (Castor and Pollux) was then rededicated to SS. Pietro and Paolo (San Paolo Maggiore).

The following passage from Summonte's letter is found in Nicolini, 173, ll. 543–56. Translated by CFN. Text in italics translated from the Latin by JHM.

158. Summonte: The Ancient Temple of Castor and Pollux in Naples

Briefly on the monuments of ancient architecture that remain among us, accept this. In the middle of this city, almost in its umbilical center, where the church of San Paolo is today, the pronaos and cornice of the ancient Temple of Castor and Pollux is all still intact, with certain grand and fluted columns, with the beautiful pediment and with the Greek inscription, which I will not send you because I think you have read it. That temple is inland from the coast. According to Your Lordship, you admired it when you were here, and on the inside it is all ruined. The epistyle columns and other parts of it were then converted into tombs, church doors, and other modern works, and certainly wrongfully, taking those precious and at one time well placed marbles and using them barbarically in French and German works.

ANDREA PALLADIO also admired the temple for its Corinthian order and includes drawings of it in the section on ancient temples in his *I Quattro Libri* (1570). He seems to have known the temple first-hand, perhaps sketching it on a visit to Naples c. 1547. Palladio comments on the architectural iconography that had emerged for temples

15. See Fulvio Lenzo, "*Ex dirutis marmoribus*: The Theatines and the Columns of the Temple of the Dioscuri in Naples," in Hughes–Buongiovanni, 242–65. The Theatines were co-founded by Gian Pietro Carafa (later Paul IV), whose ancestors included the great antiquarians Diomede and Oliviero Carafa. He chose the well-known site of the Temple of the Dioscuri for a new Theatine church. For its authorship, see Lenzo, 241.

Fig. 69. S. Paolo Maggiore (Temple of the Dioscuri). Anonymious sketch, c.1675. Paris, Bibliothèque nationale de France, Cabinet des Estampes VB 132 (L, 1), Fo. P64623.

dedicated to the Dioscuri in the early first century CE; here two foliate spirals within the Corinthian capital intertwine as symbol of twins' devotion.[16] The passage thus also constitutes a fascinating insight on the topic of deviation from the classical template by Renaissance architects. It is found in Andrea Palladio, *I Quattro Libri di Architettura* (Venice: Franceschi, 1570), 4:24, and translated in Andrea Palladio, *The Four Books on Architecture*, Robert Tavernor and Richard Schofield, trans. (Cambridge: MIT Press, 1997), 95.

16. Douglas Lewis, *The Drawings of Andrea Palladio* (Washington: International Exhibitions Foundation, 1981), 177. See Lenzo, 251.

159. Andrea da Palladio: The Temple of Castor and Pollux in Naples
In Naples, in one of the most beautiful parts of the city
between the Piazza del Castello and the Vicaria, can be seen
the portico of a temple built and consecrated to Castor and
Pollux by Tiberius Julius Tarsus and Pelagon, a freedman of
Augustus, as is evident from this Greek inscription.... That is,

TIBERIVS IVLIVS TARSVS IOVIS FILIIS, ET VRBI, TEMPLVM, ET QUAE
IN TEMPLO / PELAGON AVGVSTI LIBERTVS ET PROCURATOR
PERFICIENS EX PROPRIIS CONSECRAVIT.

This means that Tiberius Julius Tarsus began to build this
temple and the things inside for the sons of Jupiter (that
is, Castor and Pollux) and for the city, and that Pelagon,
a freedman and commissioner of Augustus, finished
and consecrated it with his own money. This portico is
Corinthian. The intercolumniations are more than one
and a half diameters but less than two. The bases are Attic;
the capitals are carved with olive leaves and exquisitely
executed; the designs of the caulicoli below the rosette are
extremely beautiful, and they entwine with each other and
appear to grow from the leaves in the upper part that cover
the other caulicoli which support the horns [*corno*] of the
capital; from this, as from many other examples scattered
throughout this book, one can see that the architect is not
forbidden to abandon common practice once in a while,
provided that such variation is elegant and natural. In the
tympanum is a sacrifice carved in high relief by a first-class
sculptor. Some say that there were two temples there, one
round and the other rectangular [*quadrangulare*]; one can
see no trace at all of the round one and in my opinion
the rectangular one is modern. Accordingly, omitting
the body [*corpo*] of the temple, I have included only the
elevation of the façade of the portico in the first woodcut
and its members [*membro*] in the second....

IN THE MANNER OF MANY HUMANISTS, Sannazaro was an art
collector and expert on antiquities as well as a poet. So indicates
the commentary of Giampietro Leostello, a priest from Volterra,
who recorded the daily activities of the future King Alfonso II from
1484 to 1491. Here he describes Sannazaro's erudite presentation to

the French ambassador of the antiquities housed at the Carthusian monastery of San Martino located high above the city.

The passage from Leostello is found in his *Effemeridi*, cited in Filangieri, *Documenti*, 1:283.

160. Leostello: Sannazaro Shows Antiquities to the French Ambassador
5 December 1489

> At a good hour he [Alfonso, duke of Calabria] got up and... rode to San Martino where he met the ambassador of the most holy king of France... and had Magnifico Jacobo Sannazaro poet show him all the antiquities on which he was an expert.

PIETRO SUMMONTE CONCLUDES his famous *Letter* of 1524 with an evocative description of the many Greco-Roman ruins surrounding the Bay of Naples [Figs. 70–71], which had become the site of antiquarian excavations with increasing frequency by the early cinquecento.[17] As such, this section of the epistle functions as an embryonic version of later Neapolitan publications that celebrated in greater detail many of these same monuments. One thinks of the writings of Giovanni Villano (1526), Benedetto di Falco (1549), Ferrante Loffredo (1570), and Scipione Mazzella (1591).[18] Like Summonte, these authors penned their enthusiastic descriptions during continued Spanish occupation; for them antiquity was both a visible link to their own non-Hispanic heritage and a means of promoting the city for growing crowds of tourists.

Summonte's cataloguing of the antiquities of the region near Naples is consistent with efforts elsewhere in Italy — such as Raphael's earlier letter to Pope Leo X — in which the ruins confer an authority on the historic legacy of the city: "many ancient ruined buildings that ruled the world." Echoing *De Magnificentia* by his mentor, Giovanni Pontano, Summonte competitively claims a larger

17. See De Divitiis, "Memories from the Subsoil"; and Hendrix, "City Branding."

18. See Ammirante, *Libri per vedere*, 359; and Marino, "Constructing the Past," 24–25.

Fig. 70. Circle of Jan Brueghel the Elder. View of the Temples of Venus and of Diana in Baia from the south, c.1594. Metropolitan Museum of Art. Purchase, Mrs. Carl Seldon Gift, 1965. Accession Number: 65.209.

population of ruins "than even in Rome." In his time, the baths and natural springs at Baia and Pozzuoli continued to nourish libidinous appetites, and thus the ruins [Figs. 70–71] functioned as a backdrop to a variety of physical activities, archaeological and otherwise. Summonte's passage is found in Nicolini, 174–75, ll. 598–615.

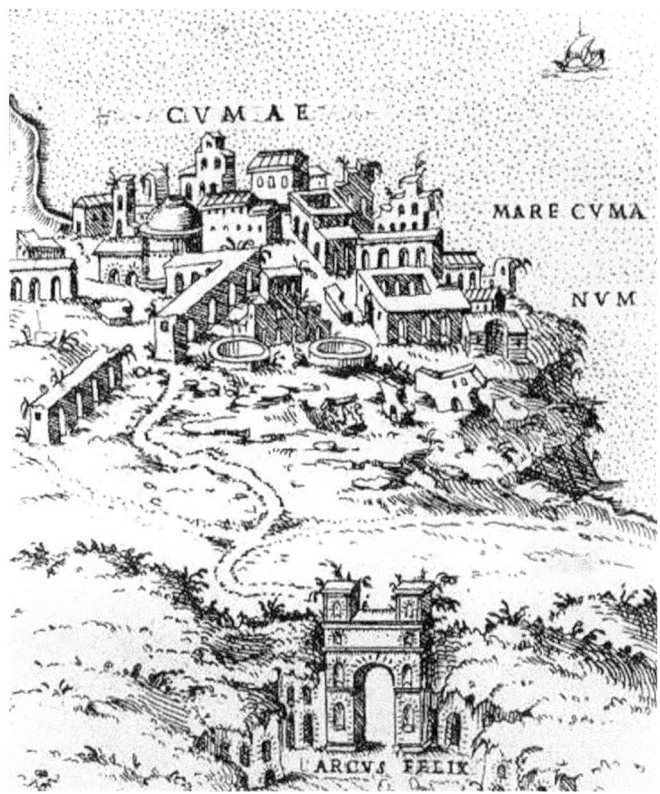

Fig. 71. Mario Cartaro, Cuma, *1584. Source: Archeoflegrei.*

161. *Summonte: On the Greco-Roman Legacy of the Bay of Naples*
But who needs to dwell on these details? Notwithstanding that
we have at Baia, Cuma, Pozzuoli many ancient ruined buildings
that ruled the world. Where one sees, beyond the baths, villas,
and tombs, the beautiful amphitheaters, circuses, pools, and the
huge reservoirs of sweet waters, made for the use of the armed
Romans fighting Africa, to where a part of the great aqueduct
system feeding the reservoirs, in such a way that all Monte
Miseno is empty inside and is reinforced by pillars, something
really stupendous to imagine. I neglect many pools next to the
sea, not only in Baia and Pozzuoli, but also in Posillipo, near

the Castel dell'Ovo and Castel Nuovo, including the port of Naples. Therefore there are all ancient buildings, from the peak of Monte Miseno through all of Baia as far as Pozzuoli and the forum of the Vulcans, today called La Solfatura [the Sulphur Springs], that now appear to be mountains and woods, more even than in Rome, *namely* baths, amphitheaters, circuses, and other similar things.

JACOPO SANNAZARO penned the poetic sequel to Summonte's factual observations in an elegy titled "On the Ruins of Cumae, a Most Ancient City." Renowned poet and head of the literary Academy at Naples, Sannazaro owned a villa spectacularly sited at Pozzuoli overlooking the Bay of Naples.[19] The villa was originally deeded to him by Frederick of Aragon in the late 1490s and was situated at the threshold to the area around Cuma, the first of the Greek settlements near the Bay. The area's topographic splendor, suggestive ruins, and deep antiquity were celebrated by Sannazaro, who laments Cuma's demise in this work of c. 1535. The description is a useful reminder of the way in which the Renaissance visitor experienced ancient sites as crumbling and wildly overgrown.

This selection of Sannazaro's Latin elegy is from Nash, *Major Latin Poems*, 174–75.

162. Sannazaro: On the Ruins of Cumae
Here once the walls of Cumae held their sway,
the primal glory of the Tyrrhene bay;
from alien shores the traveler hasted here
to seek the tripods of the Delian seer,
and wandering sailors, making port at night,
read the clear signs of that Daedalian flight,
where now the towering forest holds concealed
within its shades the beasts of wood and field.
Where once the Sybil's leaves the fates unrolled,
the shepherd now shuts in his evening fold;
the council halls of reverend fathers grave
are now the dragon's nest and serpent's cave.
The courtyards once with noble statues graced

19. See chapter 5, reading 74, p. 250.

— headlong they lie, by their own weight defaced;
thresholds once hung with monuments divine
— the grass o'ergrows the deity and his shrine.
Adornments, arts, of chamber and of hall,
ashes and graves — one ruin drives down all.
And where was once a home (now home no more)
the roving hunter spears the bristling boar....

THE COASTAL ROAD laid down by Don Pedro de Toledo west of Naples facilitated access to the ruins in Posillipo, above which he had built his villa with its vast library of antiquarian manuscripts. The viceroy also had put in a road leading to Sorrento. Such highways allowed travelers of varying nationalities to delight in the spectacular scenery of the bay and many ancient sites. [20] One of them was Jerome Turler, from Saxony, who wrote *De Peregrinatione, et Agro Neapolitano* in 1574. The two volumes represent both the enthusiasm of non-Italians and the developing genre of guidebook; they were so successful that they were published in English the following year. Turler enthusiastically describes the beauty of the bay and Neapolitan monuments. One passage is particularly striking for his description of the vineyards in the region of Pompeii, whose ancient city was as yet undiscovered.

Turler's passage is found in the anonymously translated volume *The Traveller* (1575) (Gainesville, FL: Scholars' Facsimiles & Reprints, 1951), 188–89.

163. Jerome Turler: A Saxon Discovers Naples and Drinks Pompeiian Wine
  There is also another place not far from Naples of no less
  delight than any of the above recited, at the fourth stone
  from the city, at the foot of the hill of Vesuvius... there
  grows great wine... which some call Vinum Pompeianum
  or Pompeian wine; which is very good and perfect, and
  much commended by the writings of sundry men.

★ ★ ★

20. Beate Stocke, "Foreign Impressions of Neapolitan Art in the Sixteenth Century," *Renaissance and Reformation* 24.4 (1988): 275, who notes that Turler had studied law in Padua and eventually became mayor of Leisnig.

CHAPTER 9: GIOVANNI PONTANO

by Charlotte Nichols with Frederick J. Booth

PONTANO'S *DE MAGNIFICENTIA*

by Charlotte Nichols

Giovanni Pontano (1422–1503, Fig. 72, opposite) was the most prolific and erudite humanist-statesman to serve the Aragonese.[1] His *De Magnificentia (On Magnificence)* is one of a series of essays published in 1498 about the social virtues: *On Liberality, On Beneficence, On Magnificence, On Splendor, On Conviviality.* It takes the form of an address to the poet Gabriele Altilio, bishop of Policastro — rather than to a royal patron — with whom Pontano attempted to negotiate a peace treaty between Innocent VIII and Ferrante I in Rome c. 1486. Together the two spent much time inspecting the ruins there. Pontano evidently began the project on magnificence that year, although it was not published until 1498. The group of essays constitutes a remarkably complete, if relatively understudied, prescription of conduct for the aspiring gentleman-patron that eloquently encompasses the most sophisticated thinking on the subject in the late quattrocento.

The Aristotelian notion of magnificence as a public virtue had been promoted by Thomas Aquinas and, since the trecento, by Italian writers such as the Milanese Galvano Fiamma and Leonbattista Alberti.[2] Literally translated as magnificence, *magnificentia* also

---

1. See above, Introduction, pp. 18–21; chapter 2, pp. 115–38, and reading 19.

2. See Cole, *Virtue and Magnificence*; Louis Green, "Galvano Fiamma, Azzone Visconti and the Revival of the Classical Theory of Magnificence," *Journal of the Warburg and Courtauld Institutes* 53 (1990): 98–113; A.D. Fraser Jenkins, "Cosimo de Medici's Patronage of Architecture and the Theory of Magnificence," *Journal of the Warburg and Courtauld Institutes* 33 (1970): 162–70; G. Guerzoni, "*Liberalitas, Magnificentia, Splendore:* The Classical Origins of Italian Renaissance Lifestyles," in *Economic Engagements with Art*, N. De Marchi and C.D.W. Goodwin, ed. (Durham, NC: Duke University Press, 1999), 222–78; Christine Smith, *Architecture in the Culture of Early Humanism* (New York: Oxford University Press, 1992), 40–53; James Lindow, *The Renaissance Palace in Florence: Magnificence and Splendor in Fifteenth-Century Italy* (Aldershot, UK and Burlington, VT: Ashgate, 2007), 9–19.

connotes generosity, grandeur, and *arête* or nobility of spirit; this attitude is presented as a desirable form of civic duty because it brings honor both to the individual practitioner of magnificence and to the community in which the patron lived. Pontano predictably augments the authority of quattrocento patronage by relating it to that of the ancients. For example, he likens Cosimo de' Medici's founding of libraries in Florence to Ptolemy's new library at Alexandria, emphasizing as well the similarity of the two patrons in "directing private wealth to the public good" even as he flatters the Regno's Florentine allies.[3] Thus, the glorification of *magnificentia* was intertwined with the economic success that defined, indeed created, early modern Europe.[4]

Pontano's dual role as humanist and peripatetic Aragonese prime minister meant that he was well acquainted with the leading ancient and contemporary writers, patrons, and monuments. His text therefore provides invaluable insight into the machinations of artistic patronage both in Naples and throughout the peninsula, and he demonstrates by specific example. Alfonso I is routinely praised for his magnificence: "Nothing in that age seems more magnificent than the solemn services or public games put on by him."[5] Despite acclaim for his Aragonese employers, they too emerge as occasional targets: "Alfonso decided to surround Naples with new and ample walls. He desired to do this secretly, so that he could impose a new tax on the people, and this detracted from his benevolence and glory."[6] Nor does he refrain from criticism of the local aristocracy: "Roberto [Sanseverino], the prince of Salerno, was criticized quite a bit because in the palaces in Naples he allowed many things which

---

3. Chapter 11; Tateo, 188.

4. Patricia Rubin, "Magnificence and the Medici," in *The Early Medici and Their Artists,* Francis Ames-Lewis, ed. (London: Birbeck College, University of London, 1995), 43.

5. Chapter 13; Tateo, 198.

6. Chapter 7; Tateo, 176.

should have been marble to be made from third-rate stone."[7] In addition to discussing architecture as the most ostensible form of magnificence, Pontano also provides recommendations regarding the rituals of magnificence; public games, donations, gifts, hospitality, funerals, and marriage are all addressed in his treatise. His remarks on gifts are particularly revealing for their reflections of contemporary taste: for example, "What did this same Alfonso hold in more favor than a painting by the artist Giovanni [Jan Van Eyck]?"[8] Alfonso's high standards of etiquette are also revealed: he "also presented them with gifts most magnificently, in accordance to each one's dignity."[9] Elsewhere, Pontano also provides codes of virtuous behavior, as seen in his comments on the gifts given by the Roman historian Tacitus to the Ostiense: "It was a great gift worthy of him and the people of Ostia, and the goal was not the hope of return, and the reason why the gift given was most honorable."[10] Pontano again champions private motives on behalf of the public good.

The treatise is also fascinating for the way in which it sheds light on Pontano's activities as a patron. Particularly interesting is the relationship of De Magnificentia to the humanist's own commemorative monument: the Pontano Chapel, a blocky free-standing structure begun c.1490 and located in the heart of Naples.[11] Pontano lauds the Roman tradition of roadside tombs, saying that "in a wonderful way they contribute to the ornamentation of cities," and "have a certain wonderful power of exciting people to glory and virtue, especially when they are built for well-deserving men."[12] By commissioning just such a structure, Pontano implies that persons of less than princely stature, such as himself, may also achieve magnificence.

7. Chapter 9; Tateo, 180.

8. Chapter 19; Tateo, 212.

9. Chapter 18; Tateo, 210.

10. Chapter 19; Tateo, 216.

11. See above, chapter 6, pp. 280–85 and readings 95–99.

12. Chapter 11, Tateo, 192.

De Magnificentia is fully translated below by Frederick J. Booth from the Latin text as transcribed in Giovanni Pontano, *I Trattati delle virtù sociali*, Francesco Tateo, ed. (Rome: Bulzoni, 1999), 163–219.

TRANSLATOR'S NOTE

by Frederick J. Booth

Johannes Jovianus Pontanus, to use his Latin name, was a prolific and extremely talented writer of Latin prose and poetry. The extraordinary scope of his work includes astronomy, bucolic, elegiac, lyric, poetry, dialogues, philology, poetics, and prosody. His work was widely read by and became a model for Neo-Latinists of the quattrocento and cinquecento in Europe and later in America.[13]

As its title might suggest, Giovanni Pontano's *De Magnificentia* is written in the style of Cicero's philosophical works *(De Legibus, De Amicitia, De Senectute, De Officibus,* etc.). Pontano's work is essentially an attempt to define what magnificence is, and then to limit and refine the definition through concrete examples of the character, actions, and accomplishments of magnificent men. The style of *De Magnificentia* is rather eccentric and does not lend itself easily to a modern English rendition. Pontano's prose style, like Cicero's, ranges from the grandiloquent to the succinct and varies with his subject matter. When he deals with abstractions, Pontano's Latin can be unwieldy and hard to follow. He is much more accessible when he enhances his abstractions with concrete details.

Giovanni Pontano was an accomplished classicist, and in *De Magnificentia* he draws on the works of Cicero, Suetonius, Virgil, Martial, and Livy for literary and historical allusions, as well as quotations. Often his "own" Latin is simply a reworking of his source's language.

13. Josef Ijsewijn, *Companion to Neo-Latin Studies.* Part 1: *History and Diffusion of Neo-Latin Literature,* 2nd. ed. (Leuven: Leuven University Press, 1990); Josef Ijsewijn with Dirk Sacré, *Companion to Neo-Latin Studies.* Part 2: *Literary, Linguistic, Philological and Editorial Questions,* 2nd. ed. (Leuven: Leuven University Press, 1998), passim.

Perhaps it is easiest to appraise the prose style of *De Magnificentia* by comparing a passage or two with their sources. In his discussion of funerals, Pontano refers to a passage from Cicero's *De Legibus*. The imitation is readily apparent. The words and ideas are almost identical, but have been altered grammatically to fit into the syntax of the treatise.

In the passages below, Pontano's Latin is in italics, followed by my English translation and Cicero's original Latin, again followed by an English translation.

Sometimes Pontano acknowledges his source, as in chapter 15, where he rephrases Cicero, *De Legibus* 2.63.

> *Quod ipsum ad eundem etiam Cecropem refertur, humato corpore, ac post obductam terram postque satas illic fruges, epulae sequerentur, quas inirent, ut Cicero refert; propinqui coronat.*[14]

This is the very custom that Cercrops instituted: After the corpse is buried, and after the grave is covered, and after the earth is sown, feasts follow that the relatives approach wearing garlands, as Cicero mentioned.

> *Nam et Athenis iam ab illo primo rege Cecrope, ut aiunt, permansit hoc ius terra humandi, quam quom proximi inierant obductaque terra erat frugibus obserebatur, ut sinus et gremium quasi matris mortuo tribueretur, solum autem frugibus expiatum, ut vivis redderetur. Sequebantur epulae quas inibant propinqui coronati.*

For in Athens, as they say, this custom of burial in the earth has remained since their first king, Cercrops. After the relatives had arrived, and the earth had been covered and sown with grain, so that the lap and breast as of a mother might be given to the dead, and the soil purified with grain, and returned to the living. Feasts followed which the relatives entered crowned with garlands.

Pontano is closely paraphrasing Cicero's Latin, which he recasts as indirect statement. In the earlier work, Cicero had employed a nominative subject and finite verbs *obductaque terra erat frugibus obserebatur* (and the earth had been covered and it was sown with

14. Tateo, 200.

grain). Pontano changes the nominatives to accusative subjects of indirect discourse and the finite verbs into infinitives: *ac post obductam terram postquas satas illic fruges* (and after the earth had been covered and grain sown there).

Pontano's final words, *epulae sequerentur, quas inirent, ut Cicero refert, propinqui coronati,* reverse the word order of Cicero's *sequebantur epulae* and change Cicero's imperfect indicatives *sequebantur* and *inibant* to the imperfect subjunctives *sequerentur* and *inirent,* in accordance with the grammatical demands of indirect discourse.

In the following passage found at the end of chapter 14, however, Pontano never mentions his source, Suetonius:

> *Iulius Caesar edidit spectacula varii generis, munus etiam gladiatorium ac ludos per singulas etiam urbis regiones, omnium linguarum istrionibus adhibitis, Circenses venationes, dierum quinque naumachiam quoque, effosso lacu, in quem deductis triremibus ac quadremibus, pugnatum est, tanto hominum ad spectandum confluxu, ut, quod tecta eos non caperent, sub taberaculis agerent.*[15]

Julius Caesar produced spectacles of various kinds, shows of gladiators and plays for each district of the city, presenting actors using all languages, hunts in the Circus, and even a naval battle that lasted five days with an artificial lake dug out into which were brought triremes and quadriremes. So many people attended that the lodgings could not hold them and they were put up under tents.

Suetonius had in fact written in *The Deified Julius,* 39:

> *edidit spectacula varii generis: munus gladiatorum, ludos etiam regionatim urbe tota et quidem per omnium linguarum histriones, item circenses athletes naumachium…. Ad quae omnia spectacula tantum undique confluxit hominium, ut plerique advenae aut inter vicos aut inter vias tabernaculis positis manerent….*

He produced spectacles of various kinds, shows of gladiators and plays region by region through the entire city, performed by actors of all languages, as well as races

15. Tateo, 198.

in the circus, athletic contests and a naval battle.... So many people flowed in to see these spectacles, that many strangers stayed in tents pitched among the streets and roads.

Pontano has rewritten the passage from Suetonius, keeping much of its vocabulary and subtly changing grammatical constructions. For instance, where Suetonius used the verb *confluxit*, Pontano uses the noun, *confelexu*, for the identical effect. Pontano writes: *per singulas etiam urbis regions* (through each single region of the city); Suetonius had written *regionatim urbe tota* (in the entire city, region by region). Many other passages are equally close to their sources and reveal Pontano as a great assimilator and imitator of his classical precedents.

The vocabulary of *De Magnificentia* is that of classical Latin, but by Pontano's time many words incorporated both ancient and contemporary meanings. *Templum*, for instance, may refer to a temple or to a church. Since Pontano takes his examples of magnificence from both ancient and more recent or contemporary events, double meanings are common.

Sometimes Pontano relies on etymology to reach a definition. *Magnificentia*, he reminds us, is derived from *magna*, great things, and *facere*, to make or do.[16] Simply enough, magnificence is the making of great things, as the Latin clearly states. Likewise, he derives the word for moderation, *mediocritas*, from the Latin *medius*, middle.

When Pontano discusses an abstraction, his Latin often becomes convoluted, unwieldy, and confusing. For example, Pontano begins his comparison of magnificence and moderation in chapter 4 with

> *Ea quoniam medioctitas quaedam est, ut dixi, ac satis constat magnificum ipsum, ut pro decore ac dignitate agat, magnum se et quidem in magnis sumptibus praebere debere, placet hac in parte et hoc potissimum loco quaerere, quonam pacto, si magnum eum esse et in magnis versari sumptibus oportet, mediocritatem secuturus*

16. Chapter 1, Tateo, 164.

ac retenturus sit, cum acuti quidam, magis quam docti homines, nimis etiam superciliose contendant, mediocritatem ac sumptuum magnitudinem nullo modo posse simul consistere.[17]

Moderation is a certain quality, as I said, and it is clear enough that the magnificent man, in order to act in the service of honor and dignity, ought to prove himself great by great expenditures. It is appropriate, if it is fitting that a great man be conversant with great expenditures, to investigate as eagerly as possible by what arrangement the great man should pursue and continue to observe moderation, even when certain sharp-minded and more than learned men contend excessively and too sternly that moderation and great extravagance cannot coexist.

The Latin sentence is seventy-three words long (in a language that does not have articles), and of Ciceronian length and complexity. There are fifteen verbs, many of which are rather vague and flexible in meaning (*consto, ago*). Since Pontano's sentences tend to be long and even run-ons, I have broken down many of them to more manageable English units. In the excerpt above, for instance, I have divided the passage into two sentences, but I also have tried to retain a feel for the complexity of the Latin. I have also changed many of Pontano's passive verbs into the active voice, which is more natural in English.

Pontano employs a similarly abstract style in his discussion of moderation when he attempts to establish logically the presence of a middle in anything that possesses magnitude. Likewise, his discussions of *dignitas* or of the moral benefits of triumphs or gift-giving begin in abstract terms that Pontano clarifies with relevant examples.

Pontano was an accomplished Latinist capable of close imitations of many classical styles. Odd as it may seem in this context, Pontano's hendecasyllabic verses, inspired by Catullus' lyrics, exhibit a terse, streamlined style.

17. Tateo, 172–74.

When he is supporting complicated point with particulars, Pontano's Latin can be direct, lucid, and even amusing. Observe how Pontano remarks on the stupidity of one emperor in chapter 3:

> *Varius Augustus, qui Heliogabalus agnominatus est, naves honustus mergi in portum iussit, magni animi esse dicens. Quo quid vanius dici possit, vix intelligo.*[18]

The emperor Varius, who is also called Heliogabalus, ordered heavily-laden ships to be sunk in the sea, saying that this was the sign of a great mind. I can hardly understand what could be called more useless than this.

The language is clear and to the point. A few words create a clear picture of Heliogabalus' stunt and leave no doubt as to Pontano's opinion of it. Sometimes Pontano supports his assertions with lists the length of short catalogues. In chapter 1, he lists the works appropriate to the magnificent man:

> *Quamobrem magnifici quidem opera videntur nobiles aedes, egreria templa, theatra, porticus, via stratae, moles in mare iactae et siqua sunt alia generis eiusdem.*[19]

The magnificent man's accomplishments consist of palatial buildings, splendid temples, theaters, porticoes, paved roads, jetties built in the sea, and other things of this kind.

In short, Pontano's Latin can range from circumlocution to the clear evocation of detail.

Pontano's style is detached, and he reveals little of himself in this treatise, but occasionally we do get a glimpse of the author. The treatise is addressed to Pontano's friend, Bishop Gabriele Altilio (1440–1501) to encourage him in the pursuit of magnificence. Even the address to a friend suggests the Ciceronian convention of writing philosophy in the form of dialogues or conversations. Pontano seldom speaks of himself, but we do learn that he had traveled and seen the sights of Italy with Altilio. He specifically mentions that they had gone together to Rome on a diplomatic mission to the pope.

18. Tateo, 170–72.

19. Tateo, 166.

We also catch a glimpse of the eyewitness account of the traveling archaeologist, as Pontano recalls ruins near Naples where lead pipes inscribed with the name of the emperor Claudius could still be seen.

Since Pontano clearly admires magnificence, when he gives examples of behavior that falls short, he cannot disguise a certain contempt. For instance, in chapter 9, we see Roberto Sanseverino of Salerno allowing builders to skimp on materials:

> *in aedibus Neopolitanis multa e lapide ignobili, quae marmor requirerent, fieri passus sit.*[20]

in the palaces in Naples he allowed many things which should have been marble to be made from third-rate stone.

We can feel Pontano's outrage at Nero's depravity in chapter 3:

> *Dii immortales, quantam pecuniae summam, quanta cum turpitudine Nero Domitius Augustus effudit, cum impurissimum illud spectaculum commentus lacum effodit, triremesque deduxit, quas nudae mulieres, nocturno tempore, ad incensos cereos remis agerent! Quid spectaculo hoc impurius aut sumptibus tantis perditius dicas?*[21]

Immortal gods, how much excessive money the Emperor Nero poured forth with so much indecency, when having devised the most lewd spectacle he befouled the lake, leading naked women rowing in triremes through the night time, to the light of burning tapers! What could you say is more lewd than this spectacle or more depraved than so great an outlay of money?

The sophisticated Pontano even exhibits a naive sense of humor. In discussing gifts in chapter 19[22] he describes a "donkey" that King Ferrante II received as a gift from an Eastern monarch. The gift attracted tourists from far-off places. *"Quid asino vilius"* "What is cheaper than a donkey?" he asks, seeming perplexed. Pontano continues: "One thing

20. Tateo, 180.

21. Tateo, 170.

22. Tateo, 214.

made it remarkable, that it had colored hair, and displayed a striped body with different colored parallel stripes."

A zebra!

In chapter 10, Pontano brings our attention to Licinus, a freedman of Augustus, and a barber by profession, who was wealthy enough to erect a lavish tomb for himself. Pontano quotes the following elegiac couplet:

> *Marmoreo Licinus tumulo iacet, at Cato parvo,*
> *Pompeius nullo; credimus esse deos?* [23]

> Licinus lies in a marble tomb, but Cato lies in a small one, Pompey in none; do we believe there are gods?

A footnote in Tateo's text attributes the quotation to Martial's Epigram VIII.3, v. 6, but this is incorrect. While Martial does mention the barber and his tomb:

> *altaque cum Licini marmora pulvis erunt,*

> and when Licinus' lofty marble blocks will be dust,

the couplet quoted by Pontano is not by Martial, but is but widely attributed to Publius Terentius Varro Atacinus (82 BCE–c.35 BCE). [24]

Ultimately, the charm in the work is in these details from ancient history or more contemporary events that Pontano enlists as supports for his abstractions. We see Alexander the Great unwisely rewarding a precious crown to Promachus as the prize in a wine-drinking contest. We read about the early attempts to drain swamps, level mountains, or to dig tunnels through them. We admire the building projects of Periclean Athens as well as the far more elaborate projects of Augustus and his successors in Italy and elsewhere. We observe wealthy Romans surpassing their predecessors in the extravagance

23. Tateo, 182.

24. A.S. Hollis, ed., *Fragments of Roman Poetry c.60 BC–AD 20* (Oxford: Oxford University Press 2007), 213 n. a; Franz Buecheler and Alexander Riese, ed., *Anthologia Latina sive poesis Latinae supplementum* (Leipzig: Teubner 1894), 319.

of their spectacles or games; Caesar and Pompey vying in their triumphs; or, Alphonso staging a wedding outside of Naples with shows, music, hunts, feasts, and wine-fountains set up near the beach. These precise descriptions, which Pontano employs to support his arguments, are what remain in our minds. This translation is based on Tateo (2nd ed., 1999).

164. Giovanni Pontano: On Magnificence

Prologue[25]

There are those who say that magnificence is the enjoyment of the use of money, Gabriel Altilius, and in my opinion and based on my understanding of the subject, they speak and think correctly; since, first of all, the practitioners of magnificence order the construction of public monuments and harbors, the jetties built in the sea, and the sacred temples of the immortal gods and other buildings which seem to provide usefulness as well as security for people.

You have traveled with me over a good part of Italy, you have seen harbors made by our ancestors on the most wave-beaten shores, you have crossed rivers spanned by the strongest and longest bridges, you have gone through the greatest swamps after they were drained by our ancestors, you have admired baths covered by the most ample and expensive vaulted ceilings, you were not able to marvel enough at the steepest cliffs made passable and the mountains that were tunneled through with great labor and even greater skill, and at the greatest expense, to provide a passageway. What affords more advantages or safety for human life than these accomplishments? Therefore, correctly and truthfully they have said that magnificence is the enjoyment of the use of money, since it provides for the common advantage and safety of citizens as well as foreigners, along with the most noble pleasure possible.

When I set out for Rome with you as my companion, to see Pope Innocent VIII and try to arrange peace with

25. The incipit reads: "The book about magnificence by Johannes Giovanni Pontano, addressed to Gabriel Atilius, Bishop of Policastro, begins." Tateo, 164–66.

King Ferrante, (good gods!) you scrutinized so many aqueducts, and an abundance of sights with the closest attention, and I would say that you thought the size of the buildings competed with the vastness of the empire.

Afterwards, when you had said much about the antiquity of the temples, you delivered a sermon about religion, which you thought to be inborn in people, the greatest aid for the race of mortals. However, to that power that is inborn in people you said that instruction added much. But the greatest addition was made by the majesty of the shrines and the holiness of the priests, when our ancestors entrusted many magnificent works to the care of the priests as a gift from the people. Then, as your sermon continued, you professed that you did not know whether the venerable and holy magnificence of sacred buildings provided more for the convenience of the city dwellers, or for piety and the worship of the gods.

I have set about to discuss this subject in this book, especially at your urging, you, illustrious, brilliant in the priestly office, who have urged me many times openly, and even through my friends, to write on this subject.

1. The similarities and differences between magnificence and generosity[26]
The very word "magnificence" is able to explain to us what it is and even how it differs from generosity. Since the word is used as the result of doing *(faciendis)* great things *(magnis)*, it is appropriate that it include great expense, for great things cannot be done on a small expenditure. Therefore, magnificence shares with generosity a common condition: neither one exists without the spending of money. And even though bravery also excels and accomplishes great deeds itself, nevertheless it is concerned with other matters; for the brave man accomplishes great deeds by going to meet dangers, while the magnificent man avoids danger by accomplishing great things at great expense.

For this reason the magnificent man's accomplishments consist of palatial buildings, splendid temples, theaters,

26. Tateo, 164–67.

porticoes, paved roads, jetties built in the sea, and other things of this kind, none of which pertains to generosity, for generosity only provides money, and only gives in order to benefit others by giving. The magnificent man, however, spends more than the generous man gives, and appears more extravagant than a donor. Although the expenditure must be made by a man of the type who is magnificent, the same man might also be generous, although not necessarily would a generous man himself be magnificent, inasmuch as magnificence surpasses generosity in magnitude.

Further, the liberal man desires to be useful and beneficial to others, but the magnificent do more things for the pleasures of others, as when they spend money on games and shows in the theaters, and present public hunts in the arena, which was the custom of the greatest Roman leaders. Although the magnificent and the generous man are both pleasing to the people, the generous man pleases them through one advantage by which he benefits often and much the person to whom he gives, while the magnificent man pleases them through the pleasure he offers. Porticoes and paved roads for public and private use and lavish gifts are advantageous to those receiving them, and games and hunts and other kinds of spectacles seek to provide for the minds of the citizens pleasure and relaxation from business and work. For these reasons, the generous man practices generosity with regard for others, not for himself, while the magnificent man is lavish even toward himself, as when he builds extravagant and costly houses or roomy villas and private porticoes.

From these facts it is clear how generosity and magnificence differ and how they are alike. Here ends the discussion that you requested.

2. The definition of magnificence, and what its purpose is[27]

There is, I think, a certain moderation in expenses, and even in doing great things with discrimination, although not in all cases nor in the same way. For a lot of money is spent in preparing a fleet, and, surely, fortifying cities

27. Tateo, 166–69.

for war incurs the greatest expenditure, which makes the citizens safer from the enemy. But victory seems to be the purpose of preparing fleets, as the security and the safety of the citizens is seen to be the purpose of fortifying cities.

Since the purpose of magnificence, as of other virtues, is that the magnificent man accomplishes great things gratuitously, he is content in this alone, that his work be beautiful in itself, that it be worthy, that it be noble, and that it bring about great results, and in accomplishing these things he behaves in a becoming fashion. The place of magnificence can be seen in building and equipping a fleet, as Marc Antony showed, who ruled Egypt with Cleopatra, and it may also be seen in building walls, as the walls of Babylon teach, with the greatest admiration of people.

3. What are the limits of magnificence?[28]
There are, however, two types of men who depart from this moderation: those who are called mediocre, since they do not carry themselves with enough dignity and honor, and those whom even the most excessive expenditures cannot satisfy. Even the name of these is to a certain degree considered not appropriate enough: They are called the "wind blown "(*i.e.,* fickle) by certain people, for they are delighted to pour money to an amazing degree into things that are not magnificent. Mediocrity itself is born from the petty mind that is in these people or from a meager patrimony. In these cases, an evil will is at fault, bred by necessity, born from want.

Therefore, a poor man cannot be magnificent, because riches are the very tools of magnificence. But "fickleness," that vice not yet clearly defined that consists in pouring out expenditures of this kind, is born completely from the mind. Even if the resources are inexhaustible, which seems most difficult to believe in such dissipation, how can he who willingly rejects moderation and measure, and who in fact has no discrimination, be considered at all praiseworthy?

28. Tateo, 168–72.

As in all other things, judgment must be observed in spending, and discrimination must be applied to works and spectacles. For even if great expenditure is becoming to a magnificent man, seeing that great things cannot be done without it, nothing that lacks its own moderation and measure can be called truly great in those things that pertain to praise. The fault in this is, first of all, that a principle of measure and moderation was not observed, and secondly, that money poured into these works is not fitting, nor was it spent for an honorable reason. Therefore, it happens that no discrimination whatsoever was applied to this expenditure.

Immortal gods, how much excessive money the Emperor Nero poured forth with so much indecency, when having devised the most lewd spectacle he befouled the lake, leading naked women rowing in triremes through the night time, to the light of burning tapers! What could you say is more lewd than this spectacle or more depraved than so great an outlay of money?

They say that the Athenian Demades spent an incredible amount of money on the vilest pursuits. One example of his squandering suffices to teach us not only how immoderately he used his money, but also how unjustly. In Athens, the law prohibited foreigners from dancing at the games in the theater, and there was a fine of many thousand drachmas for anyone who sponsored such games. At his own games Demades brought one hundred foreigners to dance in the theater, and, as a result, paid a fine of one hundred thousand drachmas. What could be more shameless than this wastefulness?

Nor does Alexander of Macedon seem altogether praiseworthy to me, since he gave a crown worth a talent to Promachus, a most drunken man, the winner of a wine–drinking contest. Would anyone rightly seem worthy of that valuable an award for such a foul victory? However, there may perhaps be some excuse for doing these things in a funeral procession.

Emperor Varius, who is also called Heliogabalus, ordered heavily-laden ships to be sunk in the sea, saying that this was the sign of a great mind. I can hardly understand what could be called more useless than this. Gaius (Caligula), who succeeded Emperor Tiberius, in one year used up not only the tremendous wealth amassed by Tiberius, but also an additional two billion seven thousand sesterces.[29] Why be surprised? He employed the gem-studded decks and multicolored sails of the Liburnian galleys, on which he even set up hot baths, porticoes, and great dining rooms all around, with grape vines and small fruit trees on board, whose shade protected him from the sun. In gluttonous feasting among dances and songs, he sailed the coast of Campania. The same man thought nothing of the cost of building palaces or villas. Cliffs of hard rock were cut down; in one place mountains were leveled to the ground; in another, by heaping up earth, the field was raised to the height of mountain ridges; jetties were built in the deep and stormy sea, and he did all these things so swiftly, that it was a capital offense to cause delay. At last he was most intent on completing these projects, which he knew from the judgment of others could not be done.

From these examples it should be most manifest that men of this kind waste money and squander it through shame; they do not use it magnificently, and all that they do pertains to the most foul pleasure and ostentation. Although they want to appear magnanimous, they display their riches no less shamelessly than idly. Many things show that these people have no discrimination. They are most unrestrained in those ventures that are dishonorable or are in no way expedient either publicly or privately, or which are neither truly praiseworthy nor honorable. And even if these qualities are by chance present, however, when they want to show off their money and resources, and are eager to attract a multitude to admire them, they seek another end than that which ought to be the end of magnificence, and they spend too much beyond moderation and decorum.

29. A bronze coin in wide circulation in the late Republic and Empire. The equivalent of 4 denarii, 1000 equalled 1 solidus.

These same kind of men, for whom it is appropriate to be lavish, often draw back their hands. Why? Because on small works, where it is least fitting, they spend much more than is right; on the important works they spend either too much or too little. Because they act so immoderately, they retain none of their money. After these words, let us return to the subject of magnificence.

4. Magnificent moderation consists of great expenditures[30]
Moderation is a certain quality, as I said, and it is clear enough that the magnificent man, in order to act in the service of honor and dignity, ought to prove himself great by great expenditures. It is appropriate, if it is fitting that a great man be conversant with great expenditures, to investigate as eagerly as possible by what arrangement the great man should pursue and continue to observe moderation, even when certain sharp-minded and more than learned men contend excessively and too sternly that moderation and great extravagance cannot coexist.

Clearly, moderation is considered to be from the middle, as its name indicates. We say that anyone who acts so that he never deviates from the middle either on this side or that is practicing moderation. Because if the middle has a deviation from this side and from that, it must be contained in breadth.

However, since breadth itself is some kind of quantity, it is an indication that the middle itself is something of the same kind. Moreover, great and small refer to the same kind of thing; since the middle and the great are considered to be in the same class, moderation, which is measured from the middle, ought be judged to be a quantity. From this it clearly follows that, since it is possible to find the mean in great spending, it is necessary that one follow moderation. For there is nothing great that does not have a middle, nor is there any magnitude without a middle.

In addition, if too much or too little are called measures (for all quantities are measurable), even the great, when it comes to the concept of measurement, will have its own

30. Tateo, 172–75.

dimension. In every dimension it is possible to find a greater and lesser, and therefore a mean, which lies between the two, since it partakes of neither part. It is necessary to reach this even in great spending.

Therefore, even in great spending, with which the magnificent man is involved, moderation, which is the guideline of other virtues and even of magnificence, must be observed.

5. The expenses with which magnificence is involved[31]
Since great expense is incurred in many things, it remains to be seen on what things the magnificent man spends his money. We wish to know not only how freely he spends, but with what pleasure and desire. For if beautiful and magnificent things bring delight, what then is more beautiful or delightful than doing great things? And if these things delight, it seems necessary that they be done with the greatest eagerness.

But money is spent, as was said, on many things, as in procuring country property, which is the quality of a rich man and a good head of the household, or as in buying for a price, which is the quality of a rich merchant, in which the most and greatest expenses are involved. Nevertheless this is not the mark of the magnificent man; since it is rather because of his works and gifts, that he is called magnificent. Although he is involved in magnificent works, and rather freely, nevertheless he shows the greatness of his mind by conferring great gifts, no less often than freely.

This will, therefore, be the milieu of the magnificent man, in which he will exercise the greatness of his mind and will make those great outlays, and it will be a pleasure for him to do and to have done this.

6. The works themselves ought to correspond to great expenditure[32]
This greatness of mind, which we say is the essence of the magnificent man, is apparent not only in making great expenditures but even in those works which are done;

31. Tateo, 174–77.

32. Tateo, 176–77.

and it is fitting that they bear witness to this greatness. In the first place, care must be observed that the works justify the cost and that they be of great expense and be judged great and worthy of the expense. It would be pointless and worthy of great reproach to undertake a thing so that the scope of the expense not only be unseen in the resulting works, but also be truly missed by everyone.

That intention ought to be the natural disposition and concern of the magnificent man, so that when he thinks well of the worth of a project he ignores its price and he considers only how he might proceed to undertake the most beautiful works, since it is the mark of the mediocre man to be sparing with money. Let the calculation of counting up and saving be far from his mind, for in no other way will his works be realized with honor and dignity.

Even this must be desired and preferred, that the works create a feeling of wonder for those viewing and contemplating them; and Virgil[33] wishes to show this when he says:

> ...and the great menacing
> walls and the cranes as high as the sky.

7. Honor must be followed in making expenditures[34]
Great expenditures should be made for the sake of honor, because, as with other virtues, honor should be a premise of magnificence. Otherwise, the works are not able to attain just approval, as when Alfonso decided to surround Naples with new and ample walls. He desired to do this secretly, so that he could impose a new tax on the people, and this detracted from his benevolence and glory. But his works should not be praised, as if they were undertaken honorably, when they were accomplished through theft of money and harm to the citizens.

When he was building a magnificent home in Naples, Roberto [Sanseverino], the prince of Salerno, was said to have abused his people greedily and lawlessly to pay for the

33. *Aeneid* IV.88.

34. Tateo, 176–79.

quarrying and transporting of stone from Lucania. On the other hand, Orso [Orsini] of Nola observed justice so that not even one rock was used in the buildings he erected in Nola unless it was bought for a fair price. Despite that, Roberto acquired the reputation of a generous prince, while Orso was considered rather stingy.

I hear from people in Ferrara that Borso d'Este built certain spectacular houses and villas that he gave to some of his friends. Who would not praise this? Nevertheless, the motivation for the gifts of the buildings did not lack baseness, and it is well known that he made people favorably disposed to him through the flower of his youth.

8. In making expenditures, public utility and adornment must be retained[35]

It is not only fitting to see that great expenses are undertaken for the sake of honor, and that they lack injustice, but also that they be spent on those works whose purpose seems useful and necessary, so that the reasons for undertaking them may be justified. To pour much money into things for which there is little need and which are of no use is the mark of a man of too little consideration and intelligence. For many things have been done by princes and kings of states, not so much for the sake of usefulness and convenience as for ornamentation, by those who desire magnificence or care more about outward appearance. And if those works have been undertaken for the public good, although they look toward magnificence, they ought to carry their magnitude and beauty before themselves, which is a sign of decorum and ornamentation.

Certain people ascribe the greatest praise to the Roman princes for their sewers, because only their usefulness was sought and no ornamentation was required. Nevertheless, the very amplitude and their tremendous extent and their strong-vaulted ceilings are able to recommend their builder concerning magnificence. Even though the sewers themselves lack ornamentation, they are of no small benefit to the cities.

35. Tateo, 178–79.

9. *What dignity is made of* [36]
Therefore, since magnificence consists of making great expenditures, it is especially necessary that the size of the expenditure be lavish and done with dignity, without which it is neither admirable nor properly commended. Dignity itself ought to be obtained through these things especially: ornamentation, amplitude, the excellence of the material, and the permanence of the work. For without skill nothing either great or small is able to be praised justly.

That which lacks ornament is insignificant because it is made of cheap material and insures no permanence, and it assuredly is not able to be great nor does it deserve to be. And in ornamentation, because it enhances the work more than anything else, it is praiseworthy to exceed the mean since we see that nature itself exceedingly desires ornament and beauty in a wonderful way. In contrast, when size far exceeds the norm, it cannot be appreciated, since it detracts from the dignity of the work. This is the fault of the patron of the work, no less than the architect, for it is necessary that moderation and measure be in each single thing.

The material has a great role to play. When it is seen to be cheaper and not properly examined, it detracts from the patron where it is least fitting and even leads to the suspicion of avarice.

And what is worse than this is that it is proper that the magnificent man not notice or care at what price a thing comes, or in what way money might be saved, but that he create a work as beautiful as possible. Roberto, the prince of Salerno, was criticized quite a bit because in the palaces in Naples he allowed many things that should have been marble to be made from third-rate stone. And many times I have heard his son Antonello accusing him, saying that he should have corrected this.

The permanence of the work must be looked after as much as possible, and it is able to teach this: That each very noble man is intent upon the name and reputation of permanence, and that the desire for this is inherent in

36. Tateo, 178–81.

man. For this reason buildings, especially public ones, to the extent that they are more lasting, bring greater praise to the builder. Permanence either consists of these materials or may be obtained through them; and to discuss all these things more subtly is the property of other disciplines.

It is fitting that the magnificent man be eager for and knowledgeable about these things, since it is shameful not to know the means by which you arrive at that which you greatly desire. To know what is appropriate for his art is the quality of an artist. How much more he who follows virtue and who is intent on doing great things ought to know about these very things! No one who is ignorant is able to act rightly; if he succeeds in something either accidentally or haphazardly, there is no reason for praise.

Therefore, the magnificent man ought to be desirous of these pursuits and above all to know what is worthy. And it is right for the magnificent man to conduct himself with dignity not in small matters but in those things that are and appear great.

10. First of all, a system of dignity must be observed[37]
Dignity itself, which we are now considering, must not be thought of from one point of view and must be realized through many factors. The rationale of the builder must be considered and his resources examined so that he does not become laughable or forget himself and his ancestors or find that his resources are unequal to the task that he has begun. Regal works befit kings, and it is a quality of him to whom enough money is available to make great expenditures. To do otherwise would be to stray from right reason.

The Sicilian Belfiore, not an uneducated man, did not have enough presence of mind. When already an old man he began his home at Catania, and although he had amassed a fair amount of money, he used it all up on the foundation. The money was used up wastefully when he abandoned the task that he had begun. A certain friend of his chastised him because he, a private man with hardly great means,

37. Tateo, 182–85.

should not have attempted such a great foundation, which would exhaust the means of a king. "But," Belfiore replied, "I did this so that when I had departed from life posterity would think that I was a great man from these foundations." Clearly this was an empty and stupid idea. It must be seen, therefore, that expenditure should be in proportion to resources and that the work itself should befit its patron.

Lucinus, although a barber, was made most wealthy, and his tomb reflected his means. That age, however, judged nothing more unworthy than that a man of the lowest social condition lie buried like a king. Because of his indignation about the matter the poet[38] wrote:

> *Licinus lies buried in a marble tomb, but Cato is in a small one*
> *Pompey in none: Do we believe in the gods?*

In these matters the first consideration is that dignity, which certain people call decency, be retained. A sense of proportion must be observed, as well, so that the works themselves be worthy. But it seems to me that two questions must be asked. First, are the works that are being undertaken worth doing and undertaking? Second, if the works seem worthy, do they have that dignity that we say is obtained from the size, the excellence of the material, the ornamentation, permanence, and art and is derived from the works themselves?

The very location where something is built and the time of building must be considered, for time and place bring dignity if proportion is observed; otherwise, if it is neglected, the works give rise to indignity and the deserved rebuke of knowledgeable people. Just as the Athenians placed the Parthenon of Pallas Athena on the Acropolis at Athens, so also did the Roman king place the Temple of Jupiter on the Capitoline Hill at Rome, taking into consideration the tremendous dignity of the places themselves.

When Hannibal was harassing the Roman state, what could have been more dishonorable than to undertake the

38. Attributed to Publius Terentius Varro Atacinus. See *Aeneid* IV.88.

building of a theater in the city or making roads through Italy? For these things are not suitable for disastrous times but for happy ones, and the suspension of public works was imposed in times of grief, and the theater was not adorned.

Not only should a sense of proportion be observed in undertaking works, and the outlay should be of great expense, but it should also be done with great pleasure. The patron thus provides for beauty and ornamentation as if unconcerned about spending money.

They say that Cosimo [de' Medici] of Florence often used to summon his hired workers and architects and exhort them in a pleasant and friendly manner to devote themselves to their work not only properly but even without delay: Why would they dally if they wished to save him money? And especially in these things, it seems to me that dignity must be sought and considered, the dignity, which I have said, some call decency. Just as these very things produce dignity, unwavering dignity gives birth to admiration.

Great expenditures and great works, artfully made from the same exceptional and imported material, gracefully decorated, overlooking the heights, and built solidly with an eye toward the future, not only are themselves thought to be admirable but also make their patrons themselves admirable, whom every kind of person honors with praise and even wonder. Why? Because the buildings themselves, since they were the work of that kind of man, attract people from the most distant lands to see and admire them and beckon poets and writers to praise them.

11. The works of a magnificent man?[39]
Now we must examine in more detail what kind of works are appropriate for magnificent men, some of which are public, others private. The public ones are porticoes, temples, jetties built in the sea, paved roads, theaters, bridges, and other things of this sort. The private works are magnificent buildings, extravagant villas, towers, and tombs.

39. Tateo, 184–93.

So, it follows that those who are magnificent are especially versed in those works that are going to last for a longer time. Buildings are more famous to the extent that they are more durable, and to the extent that their usefulness is longer lasting, so much more do they recommend the works and their patrons.

Caesar did not consider it enough to drain the Pontine Swamps, by which he provided for the welfare of the local populace in a wonderful way, but he laid a road through the middle of the swamps supported by the many bridges he had built so that the trip into the city might be shorter and more convenient. And even today the ruins of the bridges can be seen in many places with a singular magnificence, and even these remains are a source of wonder for the people viewing and contemplating them. Emperor Claudius employed thirty thousand men for eleven years in continuous work when he tried to drain the Fucine Lake, which oftentimes flooded the neighboring fields. Even now the ruins remain and will remain as a benefit to many generations.

What is more to be admired among the monuments of Rome than the many aqueducts, the height of which, in certain places, is said to have been a hundred and nine feet? History tells us that Emperor Constantine saw to it that the sand of Puteole [Pozzuoli] was transported by ships from the shore of Baia and mixed with lime so that the framework would be more sound and the Byzantine walls would be longer lasting; surely he did not spare expense. Apulia, the region of the Samnites, and Campania bear witness to the most magnificent expenditure of Nerva and Trajan in laying roads and building bridges with a column erected every single mile to note the distance. And I remember when the lead pipes, of astounding thickness on which the name of the emperor Claudius was inscribed, were discovered between the ruins at Baia and Puteole.[40]

There are ruins of brick substructure near the Sarno in the areas of Campania, Nola, and Accerania and a subterranean

40. That is, the Serino Aqueduct or Acqua Augusta. See chapter 1, reading 13, pp. 99–100; and De Divitiis, "Memories from the Subsoil," 195–205.

tunnel through the mountains. There is also a most sizeable aqueduct, forty miles long, extended first to Naples, then Puteole, Baia, Cumae and the buildings scattered along the coast. What can I say about the baths built at Rome by the noblemen or on the coasts of Baiae or Cumae, or the harbors made at Ostia and Pirgi, or the Julian jetty at the Lucrine Lake? As Virgil[41] says,

So many towns fortified by hand on steep cliffs.

Hannibal, terrified by the size of the walls, changed his plan to besiege Naples. The walls of Babylon are counted among the wonders of the world.

The Neapolitan tunnel is attributed to Marcus Cocceius, the grandfather of the emperor Nerva, who was in charge of the water supply at Rome, but it may have been some other Cocceius. It received the greatest praise for the skill of the architecture. The neighboring people call it a truly wonderful work, and it is convenient for those making the journey. Another tunnel also exists, which is called Sejanus', where Monte Pausilipo extends into the sea and the journey around the mountain is impeded by fallen rocks. In the fields near Cumae and near Lake Avernus there are two very impressive tunnels of similar construction, which time has mostly destroyed, that exhibit wonderful workmanship, huge expenditure, and a great concern for the public good.

I find from reliable sources that King Charlemagne of the Gauls had joined the banks of the Rhine at Magunza [Mainz] with a bridge, where the width of the river is one half mile. They say that many porticoes were made by the private citizens and by the nobles for the magnificence of their cities and the citizens, and even for the use of foreigners. Not only in the city of Rome but in various places in Italy amphitheaters still exist, although for the most part they have fallen into ruin. You could say that no kings of our age are capable of building like this. The ruins on the shores of Baia and Puteole are able to deter even the richest kings from building.

41. *Georgics* II.156.

In our time, Cosimo of Florence imitated this ancient magnificence in establishing churches and villas and in building libraries. Not only did he resume these practices, but it seems to me he first restored the custom of directing private wealth to the public good and to the ornamentation of the fatherland; and not a few people, although endowed with less property, are eager to emulate him. Ptolmey was most extravagant in collecting books and building the library at Alexandria; and Lucullus, among other praises of splendor and magnificence, was commended for his well-stocked and ornate library, which was open to all; he even built porticoes for the public to walk through.

Augustus was not content merely to have built that most noble Temple of Apollo on the Palatine, and the forum with the Temple of Mars the Avenger and the Temple of Thundering Jupiter on the Capitoline, and the Portico with its Latin and Greek library, he even managed to build many things with his own money but under someone else's name, such as the portico and basilica under the names of Lucius and Gaius. Likewise, he used the names of Livia and Octavia when he built the Theater of Marcellus. And to control the Tiber's floods, he not only dredged the channel, but he also widened the banks, and so made the passage easier. He also built Via Flaminia direct to Rimini.

In addition to these accomplishments, he restored the sacred buildings that had fallen from age or been consumed by fires, and after they were restored he decorated them with the most opulent gifts. Suetonius writes that Augustus endowed the treasury of Capitoline Jove with sixteen thousand pounds of gold, as well as jewels and pearls and fifty million sesterces, all in one donation. And even then he urged the noblemen to increase the magnificence of the state; one of those nobles was Marcus Agrippa, who built the Pantheon at Rome, which stands intact to this day. These are examples of the public works in which magnificence must be employed.

It remains now for me to say something about private works. Even if magnificence shines most brightly in public works, nevertheless, the magnificent man ought to have palaces in the city and villas in the country, constructed lavishly and in accord with his social standing, since they serve to ornament the city and give prestige to the owner. For any nobleman who spends his wealth on these kinds of projects, a paltry and mean house is a disgrace, for it appears to be an indication of a stingy and avaricious mind.

Augustus was more frugal in his personal life. He lived in a modest palace and was bored with lavish and elaborate surroundings. Suetonius says that Augustus tore down the overly extravagant palace built by his granddaughter Julia. On the other hand, Julius Caesar ordered a villa in Nemi that he had built at great cost to be demolished because it did not entirely suit his taste.

Cicero relates that Gaius Octavius had much prestige and regard among the citizens because he had built a magnificent home. Far-flung villas added much to Cosimo's prestige, as did his palace, which he found old and neglected, but then restored to grandeur. To me, he seems to have done this in order that posterity might learn how to build. Even if Emperor Nero was excessive in these projects, his great desire for magnificence must not be disapproved of; rather, we wish he had retained some moderation.

Gaius Maecenas, while he received praise in many other things, should also receive praise for that most lofty tower that later generations call the Tower of Maecenas. At Perugia and in Siena, and in certain other towns in Italy even today, the highest towers seem to attest that it was the boast of the citizens of status to raise up their square towers, and they seem to me to have competed among themselves especially in regard to height.

Among private works we include tombs, which are either of one person or single families. Nevertheless, in a wonderful way they contribute to the ornamentation of cities. Our ancestors wished these to be sacred; they have a certain wonderful power of exciting people to glory and virtue, especially when they are built for well-deserving men. So great, however, was the iniquity of the times and the neglect and wickedness of people themselves, that a later age let the tombs collapse into their ruins. So, here and there throughout Italy the stones lie toppled and overturned as though by troops and siege weapons.

Indeed, in building these monuments a sense of proportion should be observed, by which the reputation of the person for whom it is built and of the one who built it might be judged correctly. For the fame of the Tomb of Mausolus or of the Pyramids will not die unless writing itself dies.

There was a most commendable custom of constructing either monuments to victory or arches, which today they call triumphal, so that some testimony of the deeds of our ancestors might remain. In these our ancestors employed so much magnificence as the arches themselves attest. What is more wonderful than marble columns, only two of which remain in Rome? To me, on account of their height, the elegance and variety of their sculpture, and especially because of their scarceness, they seem to ornament not only the city but the world itself.

12. Concerning some magnificent men[42]
Although we have been a little longwinded in explaining these subjects, nevertheless it has been pleasing since we have been discussing magnificent works. Now we discuss certain magnificent men, so that we do not seem to cheat them of their deserved fame.

Pompey surpassed all of his contemporaries in this kind of virtue, because he built the most noble porticoes and the most magnificent theater. Caesar Augustus excelled in founding and restoring temples and in ornamenting the city with every kind of magnificence, and he rightly bragged that he had received a city of brick and left a city of marble. Emperor Claudius was famous for the aqueduct leading water into the city, which was called Claudian after him, and also for many other works. Emperor Nero was even more excessive in this kind of thing. Domitian seems to have wished to compete with the earlier emperors in magnificence.

42. Tateo, 192–97.

Trajan did not allow himself to be surpassed by others in this or any other kind of praise, except by his son Hadrian, who surpassed by far his father and all who ever were. The entire world glorified and praised him because of his works, and he wanted to have his name inscribed in only one temple built by his father Trajan. Hadrian restored as many old temples as he built new ones. Emperor Severus followed his example in restoring the public buildings that had collapsed by the fault of time.

Among the Greeks the Athenian Nicias seems to have received the greatest praise, but there was no small desire for praise in Pericles, because when he was summoned into court by the people because of the great expense of the buildings he said: "Let these costs be taken up by me myself and not by the Athenian people, and I will inscribe my name on these works."

Artemisia can deservedly be called the most magnificent of all women, unless Semiramis, the Assyrian queen, should wish to challenge this praise of her. The pyramids bear witness to the magnificence of the Assyrian and Egyptian kings.

Of the later emperors, Probus has been praised in a wonderful way because he built bridges, temples, and royal porticoes and he dredged the mouths of many rivers and drained swamps. He excelled even in the burial of Aradionus, whom he conquered in a single battle, and he bore witness to the magnitude of his mind when he built a tomb that was three hundred feet wide. Not a few monuments of Diocletian are standing in Rome and Dalmatia. Theodosius, too, must be placed rightly among the magnificent princes, even if, when Constantinople was recently captured, the savagery of the Turks destroyed many of his monuments.

Frederick [III] of Sicily built many fortresses, temples, and even more palaces in Apulia, Calabria, and also Sicily. Paul II, the Roman pope, ordained the greatest splendor and elegance in many things. An early death deprived him of leaving testimony to his building projects. Nicholas V was great and generous in building a library that his successor

Calixtus [III] destroyed in a few days. Recognizing Calixtus' degenerate mind, Cardinal Dominicus Capranicus said, when he learned that Calixtus had been made pope by the College [of Cardinals]: "How foolishly the fools have elected a fool." Pope Sixtus [IV], who succeeded Paul, made a bridge that was named after him,[43] and he made roads in a great part of the city. He made new churches and repaired the old ones, and he spared no expense in decorating the city.

13. What things must be considered by the magnificent man[44]

While he is displaying and constructing his works, the magnificent man should take care that he does not lack anything himself, whether in making manifest his own greatness, or in observing dignity, or in securing admiration of others. He ought to measure out precisely and to spend that which is owed to the gods and to men.

Besides, our ancestors showed that there were different ways suitable for erecting statues in temples or in porticoes. Some of the statues were equestrian, others dressed in togas, some in another style of dress, and a choice must be made among the men who, with their deeds, might be the subjects of the statues. It also must be considered what was the opinion or feeling of all the citizens or many of them, and what they approved of or what they expected, so that we do not appear to have cared too little about fame or about people's opinion of us, even if it is thoughtless and imprudent.

Therefore, he ought to make great and proper expenditures in those things that pertain to rituals, morals, and public institutions. Not only should this be not neglected by the magnificent man but ought to be attended to most diligently. For what is more noble than to treat the immortal gods with magnificence?

In this kind of activity the ancient Romans and the Greeks excelled in a wonderful way, as the countless gifts they sent to Apollo at Delphi and numerous games, dedicated religiously

43. Ponte Sisto over the Tiber in Rome.

44. Tateo, 196–99.

and put on so magnificently, demonstrate. And what did the seven officials (the *epulones*), to whom was entrusted the task of preparing the public feasts and spectacles, show if not the greatest desire for displaying magnificence on such an occasion? What did those officials show, who were responsible for the entire populace's food supply?

In his own day, King Alfonso [I] surpassed all the kings of that age in procuring and providing things for the pomp of religious services or the vestments of the priests. He had many statues of holy men and women and statues of the twelve apostles molded in silver. Nothing in that age seems more magnificent than the solemn services or public games put on by him.

14: Concerning the public games[45]
Since we have mentioned the games, we must not pass over this area in silence. Some are produced for the sake of piety, such as those the Roman consuls dedicated as the Secular Games, like those that are celebrated today in the solemn services at the feast of St. John the Baptist in Florence, and at Rome and Naples and in many towns in Italy in honor of the Holy Eucharist. Others are presented for the pleasure of the people, such as the equestrian shows and those that are performed on the stage, which have as their goal the pleasure of the spectators, which is why they are called spectacles. Among this type are hunts, which were put on in the circus, and sea battles.

These were the kinds of shows the Roman people were once eager to see, and the magnitude of the cost is easily understood from these examples that I offer. Pompey, in the most celebrated spectacles, even put on hunts. Elephants were even led into the arena (clearly a horrifying sight) as well as lions, a great number of which were killed. Hadrian brought a thousand wild animals into the stadium at Athens, and another thousand for his birthday when he offered gladiatorial shows for six days. I have found that the elder Gordian was so generous, that at the same time, on the same days, in all the cities of Etruria, Campania, and

45. Tateo, 198–99.

Umbria, he gave stage presentations and games in which young men performed for four days. What could be called or considered more magnificent? Julius Caesar produced spectacles of various kinds, shows of gladiators and plays for each district of the city, presenting actors using all languages, hunts in the Circus, and even a naval battle that lasted five days with an artificial lake dug out, into which were brought triremes and quadriremes. So many people attended that the lodgings could not hold them, and they were put up under tents.

15: Concerning donations, public gifts, and even funerals[46]

Since those who wish to be magnificent should neglect or overlook none of the things by which magnificence is achieved and that they think are pleasing to people and that the citizens think are a delight to witness, it would not be out of place to say something about triumphs, weddings, funerals, public gifts, or monetary donations. From the examples presented we understand more clearly what is appropriate for them. Donations were given to the people, and gifts were given to soldiers by the nobles, so that they might bear witness to the nobles' own magnificence, or so that the people might be favorably disposed toward them.

Emperor Aurelian, whose saying was that nothing is more pleasant than the satisfied Roman people, three times gave donations to the Roman people; and to gifts of oil and bread he even added pork, and white long-sleeved tunics, and other tunics made from African and Egyptian linen, and also handkerchiefs, which the people might use in cheering for him. Alexander Severus gave three gifts to the soldiers and the same number of donations to the people, in which he even distributed meat, which it had hardly been the custom to provide before. Caesar more than once provided public feasts and grain to the plebes, and also gifts for the soldiers. King Alexander, after he had invited nine thousand Macedonians to dinner, gave each one a golden cup.

46. Tateo, 200–205.

Let us now approach the subject of funerals. Among the outstanding institutions of old, they are above all worthy of commendation, because they honored with greater magnificence the lives of these people who had been most noble, whose funerals were magnificently furnished from sometimes private and sometimes public funds. Games were sometimes put on, which were called funerary. Hadrian, in those spectacles that he produced in honor of his father Trajan, ordered balsam (an aromatic unguent) and saffron to be sprayed through the steps of the theater, and in honor of his mother-in-law also gave fragrances to the people. The senate, knights, people, and the soldiers omitted nothing that could be offered at the funeral of Lucius Sulla. No less affection and even more pageantry was shown at the funerals of Julius and Octavian.

But what seems to me the best possible custom is that eloquent men were invited who praised the good deeds of the dead in their speeches. These testimonials are clearly worthy of their subjects' virtue, a not small incitement for other men to act in a well-deserving way. Moreover, each honor of a funeral pertains to the living, for of what import is a person feeling nothing about the human condition, whether he enjoys the tranquility from the gods themselves or, on the contrary, is tortured among those below?

The praise of our ancestors is a hereditary good since the children and grandchildren are accustomed to be respected because of the merits of their ancestors. This was instituted by Cercrops the Athenian, when it was ordained to offer the praise of the dead man in the presence of his relatives. Furthermore, the gratitude of posterity in attending the funerals of their ancestors does not go unrecognized. Why? Because the later generations of the families of the dead man and even other citizens are stimulated to gain merit in the eyes of their descendants and it seems unjust to act ungratefully toward the dead, who both privately and publicly endured many hardships in a hard and severe life and by far have bestowed the most and greatest benefits.

They call funerals and those things termed offerings to the dead "the just desserts of the dead." The appellation itself is worthy, but the practice itself is more worthy and most appropriate to a civilly ordered state. What is more useful or honorable for the citizens themselves, in any city in which there is a place for virtue, than that they honor those who are most deserving, those who gave birth to, raised, and educated them, and to invite not only their descendants but even the entire citizenry and the population of the world to the funerals? This motivated construction of statues and sepulchers to well deserving citizens both dead and living; and in well governed states in all ages I see that the greatest care has been taken both privately and publicly of their statues and tombs.

But let us return to the subject of funerals. Hannibal, although a savage barbarian, by the rules of war did not want the Romans killed by his soldiers to lack the honor of a burial and funeral, even in the middle of the heat of war. Emperor Probus, who as I said, killed Aradionus in single combat, honored the dead man with a magnificent tomb. By these examples, to which the deed itself lends support, they should be stimulated fervently to prepare funerals lavishly and to build tombs and erect statues.

Did not poets too, in their commendation of virtue and of illustrious men, bear witness in their poems that games were put on at the funerals of the heroes, and that feasts were held? So from those heroic times, I think, is derived what today is observed in many cities in Italy, that on the same days as the funeral, after feasts are prepared, the relatives arrive at the house of the dead man for a meal so that funeral itself is deprived of no kind of honor. This is the very custom that Cercrops instituted. After the corpse is buried, and after the grave is covered, and after the earth is sown, feasts follow that the relatives approach wearing garlands, as Cicero mentioned. In another place, rich feasts are prepared and arranged by the relatives, at which the family in mourning is fed and sits in grief: a clearly civilized form of consolation.

Ferrante [I], king of Naples, provided funerals of extraordinary ostentation not only for his wife Isabella [di Chiaromonte], but also for his daughter Eleanora [d'Aragona]; daughter-in-law Ippolita [Maria Sforza]; and even for Francesco [I, Sforza] and Bianca [Maria Visconti], the nobles of Milan; and for Ippolita's parents; and Juan, the king of Aragon; his uncle Mathias, the king of Hungary; and his brother, Federico, the general, all of whom departed from life in diverse places. He sponsored funerals with a certain rare magnificence and splendor. It is difficult to explain how his son, Alfonso [II], was so generous that he spent seventeen thousand golden sovereigns[47] on his father's funeral.

In this praiseworthy custom the Christians surpass everyone else, because they annually celebrate most devoutly the funeral days of holy men and women. They even conduct funeral services to their memory and erect churches and altars, and added to these are the celebration of feast days; some give their name to some tasks. In all expressions of honor and gratitude to them we must not appear forgetful of their birth and social rank. Even if the honors to the deceased seem excessive, we must admit that we cannot express thanks for their good deeds in any other manner. For truly, what are these images and the magnificent kind of burial, other than a public and eternal testament to the virtues and deeds of the man who passed from life and of the gratitude of those who erected statues or built tombs with the greatest eagerness in regard to the virtue of the living and to the honor of the kind that must be regarded in life and death?

George of Trebizond,[48] who nourished the greatest love of antiquity with us in his presence when we were young, used

47. The historic Italian *lira*, up until the 20th century, was roughly the equivalent of the British pound sterling, or sovereign. The basis of the Neapolitan curency c.1500 was the ducat, a gold coin fixed at 10 *carlini* and equivalent to 10 Italian *lire* in 1914. See Calabria (2002), xiii–xv.

48. Noted humanist, philosopher, and logician, 1395–1486. See John Monfasani, *George of Trebizond: A Biography and a Study of his Rhetoric and Logic* (Leiden: Brill, 1976); idem, ed., *Collectanea Trapezuntiana: Texts, Documents, and Bibliographies of George of Trebizond* (Binghamton, NY: RSA, 1984).

to say that he had read from a good author, that the citizens of Tomi had collected money from the public and had built a magnificent tomb (they use the Greek word) before the gate of the city in a most celebrated place for the poet Ovid, who had passed his last day among them, on account of the nobility of his genius; although Ovid was a foreigner and had been banished by the Roman emperor.

It is an established fact that even King Theodoric, although he was a barbarian and an overthrower of the Roman Empire, founding the headquarters of his kingdom at Ravenna, nevertheless took care in restoring the tomb of Augustus at Rome. Why? Because it was a very ancient custom, in honor of a friend or any benefactor of the country, to build a tomb for him, not because his ashes and bones were buried there, but only as a great tribute to his memory, and to magnify his illustrious name. For this reason it happens that often many tombs of the same man are found in different places.

Truly, on this subject, many things of old, whether private or public, offer themselves as examples to you, for which reason let us pass on to other subjects that must be discussed.

16: Concerning marriage[49]
We do not want to pass over untouched the area that pertains to marriage. If in anything people have followed reason, so that they differ most from the beasts, it seems to me especially that they pursue marriage for the purpose of offspring, in which they show most clearly how much desire for propriety nature has implanted in them, and how much of a desire for temperance and prudence. Above all in this way we are able to take care that women do not have intercourse promiscuously, and we judge that we are able to know best by this method to whom each child belongs. Therefore marriage was instituted to satisfy the natural desire for offspring, and to solidify the state more firmly, since families and relatives and the whole state are bound together by links of this kind.

49. Tateo, 204–7.

As a result, marriages were rightly considered to be of great honor by princes and private men both ancient and of our times. In celebrating this rite, one maintains a duty to attain a certain splendor and magnificence. In his later years, Ferrante [I], king of Naples, demonstrated this in the wedding of his daughter-in-law Ippolita Maria and his son Alfonso [II], and he invited all the princes and all the republics of Italy to it; and the spokesmen sent by them were received with exceptional courtesy. The feasts were celebrated for several days; orchestras and grandstands were arranged at great cost, these were covered here in purple and silk, there with embroidered cloth; horse races took place with luxurious trappings of men and horses; most sumptuous feasts were also provided.

And while it would seem that this wedding lacked nothing, even more noteworthy was the wedding that the father Alfonso prepared for his granddaughter Eleanor, [of Portugal] given in marriage to Frederick III, the emperor of Germany, in which the emperor himself was present with almost all of the German nobility, and many princes of Portugal, who had accompanied Eleanor from Portugal. At this wedding a show of hunting was put on, four miles from Naples, in a place reserved by the kings for hunting. Tents were pitched in the fields near the Agnonian meadows, fountains of various varieties of wine were set up along the shore, meals were prepared at which more than thirty thousand people reclined. Those who came to watch returned home loaded with enough food for many days. I would not know whether the Sun had ever seen anything more magnificent.

But let us leave for now the kings. What man from the class of the plebes does not celebrate marriage with a certain luxury? So much more it suits one who has the means not only to carry himself in such a way that he not seem miserly but that he comport himself as magnificently as he can. It is of the utmost importance that he be mindful of his circumstances. Demades the Athenian was accused, although he was very rich, because he brought the splendor of kings to his son's wedding, more than was fitting for a respectable citizen.

Chapter 17: Concerning triumphs[50]
Now is the time to take up the reason for triumphs: that the public honor must be conferred on the virtue of the private citizen, and others must be inspired by this example to virtue and glory. A triumph that was owed to Trajan was produced for him after his death. Therefore, in the pomp of a triumph, where the splendor of the victor appears more illustrious, the reins of the triumphant one are relaxed, so that the display is as magnificent as possible. Rightly, there is public rejoicing for the safety of the army when the enemy is captured and killed and victory is born from virtue. In fact, more and freer festivity was allowed, and in these shows the people's happiness was indulged.

When greatness of spirit was held on to even amid war and the most serious dangers, to not retain it in pomp of this kind and to allow it to be conquered by greed, what is it other than to disgrace the victory and debase that loftiness of spirit by saving money? Pompey was magnificent in his triumphs, and Caesar employed no less magnificence. Since I do not seem to want to follow a chronological list of triumphs, it is pleasing to refer to the triumph of Aurelian after he had conquered Odaenathus and Zenobia, who had occupied Egypt for themselves, and Tetricus, who did the same in Gaul. He rode up the Capitoline Hill with three chariots, embellished with silver and gold and many gems, royal luxury indeed. One of them belonged to Odaenathus. A second Zenobia had built for herself, in which she intended to enter Rome, which she had promised to herself through her insolence. A third had been sent to him as a gift from the Persian king. And a fourth was even added to these, which had belonged to the king of the Goths, a chariot with four deer yoked to it. It is said in the prayer in memory of this that he sacrificed the deer to Capitoline Jove.

50. Tateo, 208–11.

Twenty elephants led the procession, two hundred tamed wild beasts of diverse types, four tigers, giraffes, and from his own ranks eight hundred matched pairs of gladiators, conquered people with plaques identifying their nations: Goths, Alans, Rhodians, Samartians, Franks, Suevi, Vandals, Germans, Palmyrans, Egyptians. Among these were ten women who had been captured fighting in manly clothing alongside the Goths. Since a great number of these women had been killed in battle, their plaque indicated that they traced their origin to the Amazons. Tetricus himself was led dressed in a chlamys dyed scarlet, a greenish yellow tunic, and Gallic pants, with his son, whom he had named the emperor of the Gauls. Zenobia herself, adorned with many gems, was led in, bound by golden chains. Golden crowns of their states were carried before them.

Besides these captives there were Blemii [an ancient Ethiopian tribe], Exomitae [Abyssinians], Arabs, Eudaemones [Arabians], Indians, Bactrians, Iberians, Saracens, and Persians; and all proceeded with their own gifts. The Roman senate and people embellished that procession very greatly, having divided up the cost among the social orders. There were detachments of the priestly colleges, so many knights in armor with an entire army, that nine hours after the procession began to walk, it had hardly reached the Capitoline. After the triumph itself there followed staged shows, games in the Circus Maximus, hunts, gladiatorial games, and naval battles. Along with bread and wheat, garlands were given to the people.

18: Concerning receiving guests[51]

Even in receiving guests, since hospitality is justly to be praised and ought to bring great enhancement to the state, not only must we be sure to be generous toward our guests, but even more so that we be magnificent. Since this custom is much commended among private citizens, how much more should it shine forth in princes and kings? Among them it is not enough that hospitality be generous, unless it be splendid and magnificent.

51. Tateo, 210–12.

But we shall discuss splendor later. Now let us speak about magnificence, so that in exercising this dignity, about which much has been said already, can be retained. We must keep in mind the person being welcomed, and the host. One's ancestry, age, and the times must all be considered scrupulously.

King Alfonso was great in this point because he not only received liberally and splendidly those who had brought themselves to him but also presented them with gifts most magnificently, in accordance to each one's dignity, omitting no kind of honor in welcoming them. And since we have arrived at the subject of gifts and the grace of them, and just as in these there exists a certain seasoning of all magnificence, we will speak about this next.

19: Concerning gifts[52]

First of all, gifts themselves should be worthy of the one giving them and the one receiving them; for what motive is there for gratitude, if they are fitting to neither of the two? So they even ought to be grand, for what magnificence are they able to have when they are paltry?

However, sometimes even small gifts provide the greatest pleasure for the receiver, as his expression and attention reveal. For the cost of the gift itself does not usually move boys and girls as much as the beauty and ornamentation and what today is called elegance, even as cups from the finest glass, which we now call crystal, delight a girl more than a silver cup, and a toy horse delights a boy more than a Tarentine.

Sometimes the rarity itself sets the value. It is said that Alfonso jumped with too much joy when Cyriacus of Ancona[53] presented him with amber, in which was preserved a fly with spread wings. The gift was clearly very small, but to the prince, who valued it not so much for its cost as for its

52. Tateo 212–17.

53. Ciriaco de' Pizzicolli, 1391–c. 1454, humanist and archaeologist, known for his travels. See his *Life and Early Travels,* Charles Mitchell, ed. (Cambridge, MA: Harvard University Press, 2015).

rarity, its uniqueness made it most precious. Sometimes too, artistry renders gifts attractive. What did this same Alfonso hold in more favor than a painting by the artist Giovanni [Jan van Eyck]? There are those who prefer the smallest vase made of what is called porcelain to vases made of silver or gold, which are even more costly. Sometimes the excellence of a gift is judged not so much from its cost as from its beauty, uniqueness, rarity, and artistry.

In the same way, that magnitude which befits the magnificent man, must at times be judged not so much by cost as by those criteria by which, as we said, it is customary to estimate the value of gifts. In honor of Phailus, an energetic and powerful athlete, Alexander of Macedon is said to have sent many awards to the people of Croton, gifts that clearly the victory itself made great and pleasing more than their price. On the contrary, it is not the size but the price itself that commends certain gifts, such as gems and pearls. Therefore the magnitude of a gift sometimes must be measured by cost and sometimes by rarity, but its worth must be gauged rather by him who receives it.

It is fitting that the magnificent man be a careful appraiser of these values. Recently, the king of Syria sent to King Ferrante, among other gifts, a spotted camel[54] and an ass, which is known to have been taken from the easternmost regions. What is cheaper than an ass? Many people came from the most far away places to see it. One thing made it remarkable, that it had colored hair, and displayed a striped body with different colored parallel stripes.[55] Among these gifts there were many precious objects; nevertheless, the two animals, being exotic, had not been seen before, and rendered the gifts more excellent.

Sometimes variety and sometimes quantity account for the greatness of a gift, as when Heiron of Syracuse saw to it that a great amount of barley and wheat and an equal

54. I.e., a giraffe.
55. A zebra.

amount of clothing were brought to Rome. Sometimes the good will of the giver makes the gift itself more valuable, as when the Roman people were in so great a calamity, with so many of the people leaving, that the government and the people of Naples sent forty golden bowls as a gift to them. Who of the people to whom the gifts were sent would doubt that the donor possessed a liberal and magnificent spirit, or doubt the necessity of acting magnificently?

King Tigranes sent six thousand talents as a gift to Pompey the Great. It seems then that the Greek nobles vied with the kings of Egypt and Syria in the magnitude of the gifts that they sent to Apollo. They wanted to do this not to seem magnificent, but rather so that their actions would be pleasing to the god. Agesilaus was of this type, who, after his affairs had been conducted well by him and according to his ideas, saw to it that more than a hundred talents were sent to the god every two years as a tithe.

Alfonso employed magnificence not only toward others but even toward his soldiers, whom he adorned with golden cuirasses and bosses and silk clothing for each man's honor, and sometimes even with pants interwoven with silver and gold. As a result, nothing more splendid was seen in any army at that time. They say that when Muzio Sforza was about to engage in close combat with Alfonso, and while his soldiers were looking for a sign by which to distinguish an enemy from a friend, he replied that whomever they saw magnificently adorned and splendidly embossed, they should consider him to be the enemy.

Certain gifts are not so great in themselves, so much as the authority and great majesty of those who send them render great, as when the senate and the people of Rome presented any well deserving king with an ivory chair and senatorial robes. The gift demonstrated the senate's and people's judgment of the king. Gifts of this kind are that much more illustrious and rare, because they are not given to those seeking them, but are freely given to those who well deserve them.

All in all, the purpose of a gift should not be to generate a return, and if it consists of a dishonorable pleasure, and if anyone pursues this kind of goal, by no means will I deem him magnificent, but given to pleasure, and even a merchant of those things that men share with beasts. Nor does he seem much better if he pursues a utilitarian goal by giving great gifts, so that a little while later, he might receive even greater ones. This trait is especially shameful among kings, whose minds should be free of suspicion and avarice, although in our time hardly any other kind of men engage more assiduously in trade. When they wish to show their magnificence, they pursue actors, buffoons, and flute players with the most lavish gifts. By contrast, when they offer gifts to well-deserving people, they do it not so much because they want to, but that they might avoid the suspicion of stinginess or pursuit of ulterior motive.

In both of these cases the worst vice is seen, for virtue does not allow for anything false or artificial, nor is virtue able to do anything properly without discernment. Aulus Vitellius is said to have had no moderation or discernment. Not only did he give away his own property, but he was even generous with that of others. He seems to me be more precisely called a profligate or tyrant than a magnificent man.

But Hadrian, who they say surpassed all kings in the magnificence of his gifts, did no such thing. For just as he was most magnificent in bestowing gifts, so he abstained scrupulously from the property of others, and he practiced discernment most prudently. Emperor Tacitus gave a hundred columns of Numidian stone as a gift to the people of Ostia. Each one was twenty three feet, when the gift was measured around. It was a great gift worthy of him and the people of Ostia, and the goal was not the hope of return, and the reason why the gift given was most honorable. For the emperor wanted the people of Ostia to use his gifts by engaging in the public work that they had started.

20: On keeping animals at home[56]

One of the trappings of magnificence is to raise wild animals at home, such as bears, leopards, and lions. Alfonso was very dedicated to breeding falcons. His son Ferrante is thought to surpass his father and all other kings about whom there is any report, not only in falconry but also in raising horses and dogs, which he acquired from the most far-off lands at great expense.

We do not consider those people praiseworthy who raise birds and tame flocks to put on spectacles in order to influence many people with their gifts, or those who, for the sake of building elegantly and magnificently, take away from the deserving or desert those who should have been embraced. Nor should magnificence lack justice, but when justice is observed, magnificence should be considered honorable and valuable. On account of excellent works in the eyes of citizens and foreigners, the report of a man's virtue usually leads to admiration of him. Who would not admire magnificent things?

Magnificent men have been trained to undertake what has to be done. They do not spare money, but they act in such a way that they seem oblivious of expense, provided that the work itself turns out to be magnificent and outstanding of its kind. Thus, if anyone should wish to compete with them, he would be undertaking severe difficulties. A man would not easily be surpassed if, in order to attain that dignity about which we have spoken, he seemed forgetful of the cost. He might for these reasons appear greater in the context of his great works and become most magnificent.

There are in addition two other types of these virtues, one of which is concerned with household decorations and furnishings, the other with banquets, which we will discuss next.

56. Tateo, 216–19.

PONTANO'S *DE SPLENDORE*
by Charlotte Nichols

De Splendore follows *De Magnificentia* sequentially in Pontano's treatise on the social virtues. It is dedicated to Chariteo, the Catalan Benedetto Gareth,[57] who succeeded Pontano as prime minister under Ferrante II. In this treatise, Pontano investigates the role of luxury goods with which an interior is furnished and provides as well a list of those items particularly in vogue. By distinguishing between magnificence and splendor, the humanist makes a new and important distinction between public and private forms of display, as the following passages demonstrate.[58]

They are found in Giovanni Pontano, "*De Splendore*" in *I Trattati delle virtù sociali*, Tateo, ed., 1:224, 4:232. The treatises were originally published in 1498. Translated by DM.

165. The Difference between Splendor and Magnificence
…It is not unjustified to closely link splendor to magnificence, since it also involves large expenditures and has certain commonalities, namely, money. But magnificence derives its name from the concept of grandeur and pertains to buildings, spectacles, and gifts, while splendor pertains to that which is resplendent particularly in the ornamentation of the home, in the care of the body, in the furnishings, and in the arrangement of various objects: thus the relative virtues deal with the "splendid" things…. Furthermore, magnificence reveals itself more in public works and in those destined for a longer life, while splendor is more concerned with private matters and does not neglect something impermanent or minor….

We call ornamental objects those that we acquire not so much for use as for embellishment and splendor, such as statues, paintings, tapestries, couches, ivory chairs, fabric encrusted with gems, boxes and jewel-cases painted

57. See chapter 3, reading 32, p. 186.

58. Evelyn Welch, "Public Magnificence and Private Display: Giovanni Pontano's *De splendore* (1498) and the Domestic Arts," *Journal of Design History* 15 (2002): 214–15.

with Arabic designs, little crystal vases, and other such things with which one adorns the house according to circumstances and prepares dressers and tables. The sight of them is pleasing and brings prestige to the master of the house, because many visit the house and admire it. But ornamental objects, which one recommends to be as magnificent and varied as possible, must be displayed properly: there is one type of object suitable for the *salone*, another for the ladies' quarters. Moreover, some are destined for daily use, others reserved for feast days. And above all it seems to be that splendor should be accompanied by cleanliness and neatness. It is known that Julius Caesar was very attentive to this and acquired adornments, statues, and pictures of ancient provenance with great care and much expense. In this way the house of the splendid man will appear always merry through elegance and ornament; and not only the home but all the people who live there will revel in the exquisite splendor of the master of the house, which will accentuate the beauty and elegance of the women and the dignity and refinement of the men....

IN A SECTION OF *De Splendore* titled "Collections of gems and pearls," Pontano notes the intense competitiveness of Alfonso with the legendary collector, Jean, Duc de Berry (d. 1416); this complements Pontano's general observation that Italian rulers imported French fashions. Known best as a patron of illuminated manuscripts, the duke's taste for the precious included rare gems, many of which he gave to the church housing his commemorative monument, the Sainte-Chapelle in Bourges. Pontano's account of Alfonso's determination to equal or best the duke reflects the continuation of standards of *richesse* set by northern rulers and previously introduced to Naples by the Angevins, but he also subtly communicates the caliber of the collection of his Neapolitan patrons. Pontano in fact gives Alfonso and the duke equal billing as role models for Pope Paul II (Pietro Barbo of Venice).

The following passage from *De Splendore* is found in Tateo, chapter 7, p. 238. Translated by DM.

166. Alfonso I Competes with the Duc de Berry

Before King Alfonso, the Duc de Berry outshone all other princes of his time in his search for and acquisition of gems of every type and pearls. His was famous everywhere for his splendor.... After his death, Alfonso did not rest until he succeeded in achieving such pre-eminence, buying all the rarest gems and precious stones. Furthermore, even when he knew that a gem was not for sale, with great sums of money he would obtain permission to see it. Pope Paul II, pontifex maximus, seeming to envy these two princes, sought to emulate them....

IN CHAPTER 5 OF *De Splendore*[59] Pontano comments on the sources of such consumer goods and the negative impact that Alfonso's acquisitiveness had on the local market. One senses, in fact, some personal frustration on Pontano's part with the dealers' preferential treatment of royals. Translated by DM.

167. Alfonso I Affects Market Prices for Luxury Goods

With a variety of ornaments King Alfonso marvelously adorned both the royal palace where he lived, the church where he celebrated sacred functions, and the residences of his many ambassadors. Nonetheless, as if spreading so much largesse were not enough, he practically plundered tapestries from France and gems from Syria by offering enormous prices. In fact, he corrupted artisans and merchants because they sold excellent objects to him only.

ALFONSO I'S PATRONAGE demonstrates an aspirational desire to equal that of other European royals, for which Giovanni Pontano heralded him as the archetype of the magnificent man. However, the king evidently was impatient with overt signs of vanity in others with regard to self-presentation. In his fifteenth-century *Vite de' uomini illustri,* the noted Florentine bookseller Vespasiano da Bisticci states that, unlike the humanists at the Aragonese court, he wanted to humanize Alfonso. He then recounts an amusing incident whereby a foppish ambassador from Siena suffered public humiliation at the

59. Tateo, 235.

king's instigation. It should also be noted that Siena was a political foe of Florence during the author's lifetime, while Cosimo de' Medici, Vespasiano's client, and Alfonso I had been allies.

Vespasiano provides a bit of fashion history by recounting the following tale. The taste for black clothing — also worn by Philip the Good of Burgundy — would eventually pervade royal European courts in the following century, while the reference to brocade alludes to a luxury commodity available only to the very wealthy.

The passage is found in Vespasiano da Bisticci, *The Vespasiano Memoirs: Lives of Illustrious Men of the XVth Century,* William George and Emily Waters, trans. (Toronto: University of Toronto Press, rprt. 1997), 73. The biography of Alfonso, originally written in the vernacular, is based on the version in Florence (Biblioteca Marucelliana, MS A 76) and was published along with the other lives by Cardinal Angelo Mai in 1839 (ibid., 8).

168. Vespasiano da Bisticci: Alfonso I's Harassment of the Sienese Ambassador for Dressing Extravagantly

Sometimes the king would divert himself with some merry joke or sport. There was once in Naples a Sienese ambassador who, after the way of this people, was very haughty, and as the king mostly wore black clothes with a buckle to his cap and a chain of gold round his neck — being seldom seen clad in silk or brocade — this ambassador, when he had audience with the king, would always wear garments of the richest gold brocade. The king often jested with those about him concerning this wearing of brocade, and one day he said, laughing, to one of his gentlemen, "Certes, I should like to alter the color of that brocade." So he fixed that audience should be given in a very poor apartment and commanded that everybody should hustle the Sienese ambassador in his brocaded coat. On the morrow the poor man in his finery was pushed and hustled by the king himself, as well as by all the ambassadors, so that none of those who knew the story could keep from laughing when the court was over at seeing how this brocaded coat, which was crimson, trimmed with fur and with golden fringe, was marred and spoilt. When the king saw him go out of the room in this plight, he could not keep from laughing, and for several days he did nothing but laugh over this story of the Sienese ambassador, who never knew that the king had played this trick on him.

★ ★ ★

IOANNIS IOVIANI PONTANI.

BELLI, QVOD FERDINANDVS SENIOR
NEAPOLITANVS REX CVM IO-
ANNE ANDEGANIENSIVM
DVCE GESSIT, LI-
BRI SEX.

CHAPTER 10: SUMMONTE'S LETTER
by Charlotte Nichols

INTRODUCTION

In 1524 the Neapolitan humanist, editor and publisher Pietro Summonte (1463–1526) composed a lengthy description of Renaissance art in Naples in response to a request from Marcantonio Michiel (c.1484–1552), the noted Venetian connoisseur, historian, and politician.[1] Summonte describes the period in which he wrote the letter as *"his tenebris."* The dark times to which he refers is the early viceregency of Naples, beginning in 1503, when the city morphed from an Aragonese capital into the major eastern outpost of a new, ambitious Spanish imperial enterprise. The Aragonese cultural milieu in which Summonte had come of age during the later quattrocento, with its solicitous nurturing of artistic and literary endeavors, had been replaced, it seemed, by a disengaged bureaucracy. The mournful tone of Summonte's letter reflects his frustration about the perceived lack of courtly patronage in a way that was echoed later by humanist Piero Valeriano following the Sack of Rome in 1527.[2] Summonte's sense of loss was surely exacerbated by the prolonged ill-health he describes at the beginning of his missive. He died in 1526, two years after sending the letter to Michiel, and is buried in Sant'Eligio Maggiore, Naples.

Summonte organizes his description of the art of Naples from c.1300 to 1524 into the categories of painting, sculpture, architecture, urban design, and ancient monuments; and he presents a chronological account of local developments within each discipline. This format may have been dictated by Michiel, for whom the tradition of the biographical narrative would have been unfamiliar.[3] Summonte's

1. Marino, "Constructing the Past," 11, identifies the concept of "failed" history in relation to Naples.

2. Julia Haig Gaisser, trans. and ed., *Piero Valeriano on the Ill Fortune of Learned Men: A Renaissance Humanist and His World* (Ann Arbor: University of Michigan Press, 1999), 25, 40–49.

3. Fletcher, "Marcantonio Michiel," 603.

discussion of sculpture is further subdivided by material hierarchies: marble, terracotta, wood, intarsia, and leatherwork. However, the letter should be understood as the personal assessment of a royal insider and humanist rather than an objective inventory of works.[4] There are, in fact, many omissions and errors of fact. Summonte does incorporate observations on the relationship of art to politics of which he, as a former member of the Aragonese court and holder of many political offices, was acutely aware. The writer's deep distress over the circumstances — namely, the French and Spanish invasions — that thwarted Alfonso II's ambitions as patron in the late quattrocento is somewhat tempered by his satisfaction with the work of local talents, such as Giovanni da Nola, Girolamo Santacroce, and Giovanni Donadio (il Mormando) in the early decades of the sixteenth century.

Summonte is both competitive with and sensitive to the taste and special interests of his correspondent: Venice has great painters, but Naples has Roman ruins and many Florentine works. Thus, while he self-consciously acknowledges the greatness of Mantegna and Giovanni Bellini ("Although I know of what I must write of similar material as a Neapolitan to a Venetian, it seems as though I am pouring water into the sea…"), Summonte lists with pride the many surviving ancient ruins (including the temples at Paestum), which he states are on a par with Rome, and which, of course, were lacking in Venice. Also in direct response to the Venetian connoisseur, he writes with a critic's eye of the Flemish paintings in Naples and of Italian artists, like Colantonio, working in the Flemish style in the mid-1450s, even as he implies that the taste for that style had passed. The Renaissance reverence for the ability to imitate life or to copy Flemish prototypes permeates his narrative in this section.

4. For Summonte's literary embellishments, see Adele Hentsch-Massaro, "Alcune riflessioni sulle ekphraseis nell'epistola di Pietro Sumonte a Marcantonio Michiel (Napoli, 20 marzo 1524)," in *Il più dolce lavorare che sia: Mélanges en l'honneur de Mauro Natale*, Frédéric Elsig, Noémie Etienne, and Grégoire Extermann, ed. (Milan: Silvana Editoriale, 2009), 351–57.

Summonte, following the example of his mentor Pontano and in anticipation of Vasari, pays particular homage to the art of Florence as the font of every positive development in recent artistic history.[5] He exalts in particular Giotto, Donatello, and Alberti at the expense of "barbarous" works in the German, French, or Catalan manner. Sculpture, he tells us, recovered the greatness of Greek and Roman antiquity with the Florentines, yet he does not mention the tomb by Donatello (with Michelozzo) commissioned by Cardinal Rinaldo Brancacci for his private Neapolitan chapel, Sant'Angelo a Nilo.[6] In terms of contemporary Florentine architecture, he pedantically parrots Alberti, who had visited Naples, in faulting Brunelleschi's use of arches on columns instead of piers but fails to recognize the remarkable infiltration of the Brunelleschian idiom in late quattrocento Neapolitan architecture, seen in the church of Sta. Maria di Monteoliveto.

Summonte complains, moreover, that "until now… we have not had a building worth mentioning," ignoring smaller scale but truly remarkable works, such as the free-standing funerary monument of his mentor, humanist Giovanni Pontano, and the impressive Renaissance palaces of patrons like Diomede Carafa, whose collection of antiquities is, however, cited. In fact, these omissions are symptomatic of Summonte's greater interest in painting and sculpture rather than the buildings that they embellish, although he does list the names of several architects working in Naples.

Summonte wrote the letter in Italian sprinkled with Latin phrases that allude to proverbs or known quotations. The latter have been translated by James H. Mc Gregor and are in italics. Some awkwardness in Summonte's use of the vernacular is kept. The subdivisions in the text are maintained, but the line indications are approximate due to the translation. Excerpts from Summonte's letter included elsewhere in this volume and are indicated by appropriate reading numbers after the section. Translated by CFN.[7]

5. Summonte edited Pontano's works.

6. See chapter 6, readings 87–88, pp. 268–71.

7. Summonte's letter is reprinted in Fausto Nicolini, *L'arte napoletana del rinascimento e la lettera di Pietro Summonte a Marcantonio Michiel* (Naples: R. Ricciardi,

169. Summonte: Letter to Marcantonio Michiel, 1524
20 March 1524

[1–14] My magnificent Signor Marco Antonio,

Your Lordship has every reason to be displeased with me,
since I have not responded to your many letters. What is
more, I believe that you must think me obstinate, rude, and
impracticable, saying to yourself — what I endure for art!
Pietro seemed genial and polite: now I see he is totally the
opposite. *Faith is never secure!* You just can't trust anyone in
this world! *Which is to say it is true, as Cicero states, that "many
measures of salt are to be eaten together before becoming friends."*
However, Signor Marco Antonio, I wish now to avail
myself of the customary saying of the charlatan lawyers:
"Hear both sides if you want to judge correctly."

[15–26] *This entire winter, if you haven't heard, has been very
unfortunate for me; I've suffered a very serious pleurisy, the effects of
which are such that now after four months I seek no other remedy
than bed rest.* From the 22nd of November I have been ill;
I have been completely bedridden for two months and a
half, always suffering and in grave danger; then, the sickness
having eased, I have been and continue to be unable to
do much of anything. *All my hope, in truth, rests in you.
Receive, therefore, as is fair, my excuse with an open mind. So that
afterwards you may not only excuse me, but pity my misfortune.*

[26–32] Now I am responding to your three letters: the one
from 17 August, the next from 2 November and the third
from 1 December, all three copious and written with care.
As for the fourth, which your Lordship says to have sent me
by "pigeon" with the book of our Messer Ambrosio, it still
has not reached me, nor has the book.

[34–44] And, leaving all else aside, I will get straight to
your request for information regarding painting, sculpture,
architecture, and monuments of esteemed antiquity.

1925), 157–75; and in Roberto Pane, *Il rinascimento nell'Italia meridionale* (Milan:
Edizioni di Comunità, 1975), 1:63–95. CFN is grateful to David Beneteau, to
Derek Moore, and to Tania Zampini for her editing of sections of this translation.

Although I know what I must write of such material as a Neapolitan to a Venetian, it seems as though I am pouring water into the sea *(these and all other laudable disciplines flourish there);* really I am compelled by love and reverence, which rightly I convey to your Lordship, writing to you about what little I can find *in these dark times.* I am certain that I will not meet your expectations, but I hope that at least your Lordship will appreciate my good intentions.

[45–71] Getting to the point, I say that painting, which according to general opinion suffered for centuries, was reawakened by the Florentines, as was sculpture and all the fine arts including the study of letters; this is confirmed by Pontano towards the beginning of his book *De bello napoletano.* Being as he was altogether lacking in the theory and art of painting, Cimabue the painter — if we are to believe Dante — painted in a disordered manner, as befits that crude era. With his successor, Giotto, painting took a great leap forward. As your Lordship knows, so they appeared to Dante, *if I remember correctly:*

In painting Cimabue was thought to hold the field.
And now Giotto has the cry.[8]

Now then, I say that in our region this art has been little celebrated. I am convinced that this is due to our kings, who are concerned with tending only to war, tournaments, supplies for their horses, hunting — and loving and prizing only things associated with them. King René, himself an accomplished painter dedicated to his art, although in the Flemish style, ruled for a short time here and was then expelled by King Alfonso I.[9] Other past kings, who were Italophiles and gathered here distinguished painters, sculptors, architects, and artisans, were, to our disgrace, too quickly exiled and snuffed out, to the extent that they were prevented from leaving any great monuments to themselves.

8. Dante Alighieri, *The Divine Comedy: Purgatorio,* John D. Sinclair, trans. (New York: Oxford, 1961), 2:147.

9. Summonte refers here to René of Anjou, the last Angevin king of Naples (r. 1438–42). See Introduction, pp. 3–6, 44; chapter 7, p. 322, reading 120.

[71–79] In this city there are, however, some paintings in Giotto's own hand, as seen in the church of the nuns of Sta. Chiara: this church is all painted by his hand. In the monastery are other different paintings, or small panels, with images of saints, which were done for Queen Sancia, wife of King Robert, who, after her husband's death, dedicated her life to God and took up residence in the aforementioned monastery where these same paintings then remained.[10]

[80–87] Giotto skillfully painted all the walls of the chapel of Castel Nuovo with scenes of the Old and New Testament. Then in the time of King Ferrando the Elder, an advisor and poor judge of such things, evaluating them to be of little worth, covered them up to give the walls a new look; this caused great displeasure then and now to those with some judgment.

[88–94] In the church of Sta. Maria [In]coronata, near Castel Nuovo, are some paintings by disciples of Giotto, in which one sees the clothes and accessories from the time of Boccaccio and Petrarch.[11] In the church of San Luigi, which stands next to the archbishopric on the forum side, are also some other things by Giotto's disciples, including one known as Farina.

[95–98] The chapel said to be that of Messer Artuso, next to San Giovanni Maggiore,[12] is all painted by descendants of Giotto's disciples in the time of King Ladislaus.

[99–111] From this time on we did not have in these parts a celebrated [single master], foreigner or native, until our Neapolitan master Colantonio, a person much inclined towards the art of painting and who, if he hadn't died young, would have been capable of great things. Due to circumstances he himself never attained perfection in the drawing of ancient works, as did his disciple Antonello

10. For Giotto in Naples, see Willette, "Giotto's Allegorical Painting;" Loconte, "The North Looks South;" and Leone de Castris, *Giotto a Napoli.*

11. See Vitolo, *La chiesa della Regina.*

12. Summonte refers to the Cappella Pappacoda.

da Messina: a man, as I understand it, known to you. The profession of Colantonio was, in the manner of the time, Flemish in inspiration. He was dedicated to that style and considered going there. But King René kept him here, and he taught him the technique of tempera painting.

[112–129] There are four works by him in Naples. One in the church of San Severino, of Our Lady with Child in her arms, flanked by St. John on one side and St. Catherine on the other. In the upper part are a Crucifixion and an Annunciation of the Angel to Our Lady. In the darkness surrounding the Crucifixion, there is a shadow so astonishing, it frightens those who look upon it. And in the lower part of the altarpiece, which is the best, there are the twelve Apostles whose faces are so lively and so different one from the other that they inspire admiration. Furthermore, there is another singular device: Our Lord and St. James Minor are so similar as to be indistinguishable to all who see them. However, the subtlety of this experienced painter manifests itself in the following way: that is, by giving Our Lord a certain superior majesty and to St. James, who somehow appears inferior, an air befitting his station: something so difficult that it is almost impossible to express in painting.

[130–134] The second work by Colantonio is in San Pietro Martire. The figure is of St. Vincent Confessor in a boat that endures a storm with fierce waves and turbulent clouds; it strikes fear in all who see it. Really a thing of great imagination.[13]

[135–142] The third is in San Lorenzo. The figure of St. Jerome seated in his study, where there are many books of varying shapes and sizes,… with certain cartouches affixed to the wall with wax, some sections of which appear to be floating. This work is quite celebrated by our painters, not for its conformity to present standards but more for its imitation of ancient models.[14]

13. This panel is at the Museo di Capodimonte, Naples.

14. The *Saint Jerome* is part of a polyptych for San Lorenzo and is now located in Naples at the Museo di Capodimonte; see Challéat, 55–56.

[143–149] The fourth is in Sta. Maria la Nova, in the chapel under the preaching pulpit. Here is Our Lord, painted on a tablet, leaving a building: a work from Flanders, for which Colantonio then supplied two angels by his hand, on two sides, with great similarity of appearance, workmanship, skin tone, and in the color of the cloth with which the angels are dressed, so that one is compelled to think that they are by the same hand.

[150–183] He had the great dexterity to imitate whatever he wanted; this imitation being done in the Flemish style, which was the only one marketable.[15] During his time a [rather well done] true-to-life portrait of the head of Charles of Burgundy arrived. Colantonio made a copy of this work that was owned by a merchant; and, having made the copy so precise that it was impossible to tell one from another, he substituted it for the original, which the merchant kept until Colantonio revealed his clever trick. Similarly he made a copy of a Flemish picture of St. George, a panel of approximately two and a half *palmi* by four: a praiseworthy work in which one sees the knight *all completely bent over and leaning hard on his lance,* whose tip had penetrated the mouth of the dragon and formed a bulge on the other side. It was something to see the good knight leaning so far forward and pushing so forcefully against the dragon that the right leg pulling on the saddle seemed almost outside the stirrup. Against the left leg the image of the dragon is beautifully reflected in the armor, as in a mirror. In the saddle-bow appeared a certain rustiness which, on the shiny surface of the metal, was very obvious. In sum, the good Colantonio copied the entire painting in such a way that one couldn't tell his from the original if not for a tree that in the former was brambles and in the latter, according to the patron's wishes, is a careful study of the chestnut. This very same picture is now in Naples in the wardrobe of the illustrious duchess of Milan. The portrait of the duke of Burgundy, which some time ago our Jacopo Sannazaro saw in Naples, is not here.

15. Colantonio's *Saint George* copies a lost work by Jan Van Eyck. Challéat, 45–51, at 46, discusses St. George's importance for Alfonso. See above readings 125, 128.

[184–199] *And even though we hesitate a little* to speak of things from Flanders, I shall not fail to mention the three tapestries [reading 126] made in that country by the famous master Rogier, son-in-law of the other grand master Joannes [Jan], who at first illuminated books *or, as we say today,* drew miniatures. But Rogier worked only in large figures. These three pieces showed the Passion of Christ Our Lord, with large figures, as I said, in which, among other notable things, was this: the figure of Jesus Christ, in every position and gesture he made, was identical, without varying a single hair. A feat so skillful that it incited great admiration in whoever saw it. Such was their public fame that Signor King Alfonso I bought these three pieces for 5000 ducats in Flanders. Now they must be in the possession of the poor Queen Isabella in Ferrara, wife of the Signor King Federico of beloved memory.

[200–208] Signor Sannazaro has today in his possession a small little picture with the figure of *Christ in Majesty:* a good work by someone called Petrus Christ[us], a well-known painter in Flanders older than Johannes [Jan] and Rogier.

This is what I can offer in our account of things from Flanders. Your Lordship finds himself in a place where he might more fully inform and involve himself to the heart's content and to complete satisfaction about things foreign and Italian.

[209–216] Now returning to our painters, I state that we have had no notable painter here since Colantonio. For about forty years we had here a master Costanzo, a Lombard who lived in this city: better at drawing than anything else, he painted a room in Poggioreale, the building made by Signor King Alfonso II of beloved memory.[16]

[217–226] Next we have had in recent years a young Venetian of yours, [called] Paolo de Augustini, who well

16. See Andrea S. Norris, "Costanzo," DBI 30 (1984), online at: http://www.treccani.it/enciclopedia/costanzo_res-73f1e857-87eb-11dc-8e9d-0016357eee51_(Dizionario-Biografico).

demonstrated his training in the distinguished Venetian school but who died in his youthful prime.[17] From his hand comes the image of Sannazaro portrayed from life from the waist up. He likewise portrayed the illustrious Lady Isabella di Requesens, a beautiful woman, wife of the *former* Don Raimondo di Cardona, our viceroy. And he did other works here, well esteemed. He was a disciple of Giovanni Bellini.

[227–233] After Paolo, another youth came here called Ioan Battista Fiorentino, who also did, on a wooden panel, Sannazaro from life, the aforementioned illustrious Donna Isabella di Requesens, the illustrious Signora Donna Joanna d'Aragona, a shapely woman, wife of the illustrious Signor Ascanio Colonna, and the illustrious signora duchess of Amalfi, still a woman of great beauty. And there are other things of his still here.

[234–239] One may see in the church of Sant'Arcangelo delle Monache a large altarpiece of good workmanship, done by a Master Cesare of Milan [reading 126].

In Sta. Maria delle Grazie another altarpiece of the *Visitation*, done by a Master Pietro, who was a hermit. He was Sardinian.

[240–252] In San Domenico an altarpiece, in which Our Lord is taken from the cross and placed on a winding-sheet, by the hand of Mantegna to whom, as you know better than the rest of us, painting owes quite a lot, since it was through him and later your Giovanni Bellini that antiquity began to renew itself. In the same church, in the chapel of Signor Joan Battista del Duce, is *The Angel with Tobias*, done by the hand of Raphael of Urbino. Of these craftsmen I need not say more, as they and others are already more noted in this same city than in their own hometowns [reading 138].

There are today others of ours who are promising: Andrea da Salerno and Stefano di Caiazza, among others [reading 139].

17. Angela Catello, "De Agostini, Paolo," DBI 33 (1987), online at: http://www.treccani.it/enciclopedia/paolo-de-agostini_(Dizionario-Biografico).

[253–258] [Maestro] Polidoro da Caravaggio, famous for works in monochrome, although quite young, painted today the four walls of the courtyard and a loggia in the house of Signor Ludovico di Montalto, where there are some lovely things, for the most part derived from the example of the Column of Trajan [reading 142].

[259–274] In the art of illumination *or, as we more often say,* miniatures, we have had a singular craftsman in our times: Joan Tedeschino; a man, besides the excellence of this art, of an even more exemplary life. He was the son of a German, born in Lombardy, and he lived a long time in Naples until the end of his life. In the beginning this man followed the work of the Flemish School; then he imitated exclusively the works of a Gasparo Romano, who worked in the manner of the ancients, in such a way that the Tedeschino reached a sublimity [unequaled by others]. *Which, indeed, was not difficult for the man* because, besides great talent, he was a person of great patience with painting. He would take a round piece of paper with a circumference the size of one of your Venetian coins, and there he would be for a month or more drawing, resolved and vigilant. There are many works by him in this city.

[275–295] Of Gasparo Romano *this we know:* that he illuminated [that is, drew in miniature] the beautiful Pliny of the very reverend and illustrious signor Cardinal Don Juan d'Aragona, son of the Signor King Ferrando I; in said Pliny, at the beginning of each book, is a work of such charm and of such excellence that one could not wish for more. And, among the other works, there is *Nature*, painted with her parts and attributes, prescribed by a learned man of that time, Messer Lucio Fosforo, which is one of the beautiful and rare things that one sees in our times. This is a thin woman, of wondrous beauty, in the manner of the ancients, who holds a globe in front of her chest and spews milk from her breasts. This Pliny, which in the judgment of all who see it is something divine, together with other very precious books in the rich library of our kings, was a pawn in the uprisings in this kingdom against the Florentine merchants: since then no one

knows what happened to it. A similar unhappy ending befell
the poor craftsman Gasparo who, with his wealth of talent,
unwilling to rest on his laurels, gave himself to architecture
and, working in the house of the cardinal of San Giorgio,
now recently deceased, fell from the structure and died.

[296–301] *All sculpture, obliterated after the collapse of the Greek
and Roman states, lay in shadow until it was revived, as I said
above, by men of Florence. Who, as our Pontano says in* The
History of the Neapolitan State, *through great study of the best
exemplars and by their own nature understood it.*

[302–312] There was in Florence at the time of our
forefathers Donatello, a crude and simple man in every way,
except in sculpture, of which, in the judgment of many, we
have not seen better. He made many original things and, as
he was skilled in his craft, he executed with ease and speed
many works, which today may be seen in various places.
In this city, in the house of the signor count of Matalone
[Diomede Carafa], by the hand of Donatello, is a beautiful
bronze head and neck of a colossal horse. In the same
house there are many marble antiquities of various kinds
[reading 155].

[313–319] In the entrance of our Castel Nuovo there is a
triumphal arch, made about eighty years ago (by the hand
of the master Francisco Schiavone) in the time of King
Alfonso I of glorious memory: not bad works for those
times. He also made a marble image of the same king,
which, in the judgment of those who have seen it, always
has been reputed as extremely lifelike [readings 64–66].

[320–341] I could also at this point name many marble portals
of churches, many tombs made for past kings: however, they
are of bad design, even if they are rich in marble. In sum, they
stink of the modern[18] and of the bad times in which these
works were made; which, as your Lordship knows better
than we, for a certain time in this land, as in other parts, they
made only flat things, German, French, and barbarian things:

18. Summonte is referring to the gothicizing decoration of Angevin
churches.

whose mistake was also in architecture. Among these works, I will offer again the marble door of signor prince of Salerno and that of the church of Sant'Agostino, which even display some of the better designs; so does the gate of this city, known as the Porta Capuana, all marble with sculpted trophies and arms. (There was in this city thirty-five years ago a young Florentine called Adriano, who made a statue of Pontano in bronze, and also a medal of him, which you can see here today.) In the house of Signor Berlengiero Carafa and Messer Antonio Rota are two doors in an agglomerate, like that formerly brought from the island of Chios: something very pleasing to the eye.

[341–345] In our cathedral, under the high altar, is a grand chapel, called "Soccorpo," all in marble and set on columns of great cost. The craftsman was of our time: the Lombard Master Tommaso [Malvito] from Como, accompanied by many of his followers [reading 100].

[346–356] In the church of Monteoliveto, in the chapel of the signor duke of Amalfi, there is an large altarpiece of precious marble, on which is carved the *Nativity of Our Lord* with some beautifully carved shepherds, made in Florence by Antonio Borri called Rossellino. In the same church, in the chapel of the signor count of Terranova, is the *Annunciation*, also of good marble, with other figures, made by the hand of Benedetto da Maiano, Florentine, brother of Giuliano da Maiano, the architect who designed the building of Poggioreale, sent by Lorenzo de' Medici to do this work for Signor King Alfonso II [reading 89].

[357–366] In the church of San Domenico is the chapel of the signor count of Sanseverino, made by Andrea da Fiesole and the Lombard Matteo.

In the church of San Giovanni a Carbonara, in the Doric chapel begun for Signor Galeazzo Caracciolo and now directed by his son Signor Colantonio, is a marble altarpiece with the three Magi, Our Lord, Our Lady, and other figures made by two Spaniards, Diego [de Siloé] and Bartolameo Ordogno [Ordóñez]: a very good thing [readings 83–84].

[367–377] Now also emerging in this city is a young man, Ioan di Nola, who first was a master in wood inlay, for which he was very well respected. Now he has given himself entirely to the work of marble. These days he is working on a great marble tomb for the illustrious Signor Don Raimondo di Cardona, who will take it to Catalonia.

Another rising star, younger, about twenty-two years old, is Jeronimo Santacroce, who was first a goldsmith: then he switched to marble with such an excellent talent that he will without a doubt be great at his craft as long as he lives. He has made a portrait medal of Sannazaro and a marble Apollo: objects well thought of here by everyone.

[378–389] Of that which I now write to your Lordship I am certainly embarrassed to say: *when you are in this city, within its walls here and there, which enclose all these good arts, you will better understand and describe them than I can.* Nonetheless, to obey your orders, I will make sure not to subject my honor to prejudice.

A work in terracotta is in Monteoliveto, the *Lamentation of Our Lord from the Cross*, with the figures of King Ferrando I and King Alfonso II of beloved memory, well done from life, by the hand of Paganino di Modena, *brought here earlier* with the patronage of Signor King Alfonso II [reading 93].

[390–408] In the church of Sant'Eligio, is a great work in relief, in the chapel of the Lanii, by the hand of Master Domenico Neapolitano, an extremely inventive person.

We have here a wooden relief of the *Nativity of Our Lord,* made for the church recently built for Signor Jacobo Sannazaro *at the foot of* Monte Posillipo, a place called Mergellina; this *Nativity* is of the same classical manner as Sannazaro's depiction in his divine work "De partu virginis." And here there are also many other figures, all by the hand of the previously noted master Joan di Nola. Also by him in the sacristy of Monteoliveto is a *Crucifixion* all in wood, so well done that it did not need either gypsum or any other color. This youth first, as a woodcarver, was a disciple of a Master Pietro da Bergamo, who called himself "Venetian;" by the hand of that Master Pietro is the portal of this city's Annunziata, a praiseworthy work in half-relief.

[409–426] In Monteoliveto is a work of intarsia in the sacristy, all worked in inlay and perspective, by the hand of a renowned craftsman, Fra Joan [Giovanni] da Verona, a monk in the same order of San Benedetto of the White Robes. In this work Fra Joan was aided by a Master Geminiano, a Tuscan from Colle or a Florentine, and by Master Imperiale of Naples; the two of which, although they worked and helped in this intarsia work, themselves by trade were masters of relief. In this church of Monteoliveto is a chapel of the same work, also by the hand of Fra Joan. The choir of this church, worked in inlay with some things in perspective, is by the hand of Master Joan Francesco and by Master Prospero, brother and disciple of this Joan Francesco da Rezzo. By their hand also is the beautiful choir in the church of San Martino of the Carthusians, of the same type [reading 92].

[428–442] In our times there has been in this city an excellent Neapolitan, also unique in his art, I mean in the art of working in leather, commonly called the "art of *stuccio*," that is the making as much for sheaths for weapons as for other storage containers and similarly for book covers. By this fellow, among other admirable things, was an inkstand, which I saw, along with fifty little boxes in which to conserve jewels and similar exquisite things, in addition to the cubby-holes to store the adornments of the inkstand. Likewise a triumphal arch with one hundred little boxes. In the building of those two works was such an imitation of ancient things and so many accurate intaglio images, typical of this kind of work, that it amazed whomever saw such new things. So said Master Masone di Mais, brother of a learned man, Messer Juniano [Maio], teacher of Signor Jacopo Sannazaro in the study of the humanities.

[443–468] Architecture, for many years neglected, started, as I said at the beginning, to recover about one hundred years ago in Florence. That city must not be denied its due, since there not only painting, sculpture, architecture with the other honorable mechanical arts began to be revived, but also the study of letters. I won't take long to refer to the name of many noble craftsmen who have come from that prominent city, because Your Lordship will have already read the beginning of the commentary by Messer Cristoforo Landino on the work of Dante.[19] However, then the architects of Florence *(pardon me, best of cities)*, by wanting to be too faithful to their own genius and not completely conforming to antique things and to the noble concepts of the extremely ingenious Messer Leon Baptista degli Alberti, their citizen, they entered in many serious errors (errors, I say, of true pertinacity); and thus they have corrupted ancient things with modern errors, such as placing arches on columns, which is great heresy in architecture, since always in antiquity one found them placed over piers: this makes great sense, because, resting on a column, the four angles of the square of the arch appear suspended in mid-air. I say the same of other errors, which are incurred by too much faith in genius and the presumption to experiment.

[469–474] Until now in this city, as Your Lordship could have seen when you were here, we have not had building worth mentioning. The grand room of the Castel Nuovo is indeed a great work; but it is Catalan, *having nothing of ancient architecture.* Your Lordship knows well that for many many years the only building style followed everywhere was barbarian.

[475–511] In our times the Signor King Alfonso II of beloved memory was dedicated to building and the cupidity to do great things, which, if iniquitous Fortune had not robbed him so soon of his throne, without a doubt he would have adorned this city to the highest degree. *He had it in mind to bring a distant river through great aqueducts into*

19. Florence: Niccolò della Magna, 1481. See Cristoforo Landino, *Comento sopra la Comedia I–IV,* Paolo Procaccioli, ed. (Rome: Salerno, 2001); Simona Foà, "Landino, Cristoforo," DBI 63 (2004), online at: http://www.treccani.it/enciclopedia/cristoforo-landino_(Dizionario-Biografico).

the city; and completing the grand walls of the city, in good measure already done, to extend in a straight line all the main roads within the walls of the city, to eliminate all the arcades, corners, and uneven protuberances, and thus to extend directly the transverse roads from hilltop to hilltop of the city in such a way that, both for the direction of the streets and the alleys, and also for the natural orientation of the site from the north to the south, this city would have been, beyond the beauty of its evenness, the most clean and elegant city *(I say it with your indulgence)* in all of Europe that in even the lightest rain would be cleaned like a plate of polished silver.

In addition to the fountains for individual houses, there would have been constructed public fountains and drinking troughs in the appropriate quarters and places, from which water would spew onto the streets, since those were swept in the summer, for keeping the ground without dust and clean. Besides this, he wanted also to build a sumptuous temple for the remains of the Aragonese dynasty who died here, and a great palace near Castel Nuovo in the Piazza della Coronata, in which he wanted to situate all the tribunals in different rooms, so that it would not be necessary for the merchants to go to different places, but instead here expedite whatever their business, without enduring the rain or sun or tiring themselves going here and there. Neither was His Majesty the type not to carry out the things he said after having deliberated them; nor was he scared of spending. The more the plans cost, the more they pleased him [reading 73].

[510–523] All of these noble and holy thoughts were interrupted and completely destroyed by the sudden barbaric invasion of Charles VIII, king of France, who caused the demise of the Aragonese family in this kingdom.

This unfortunate man, before his coronation, while he was duke of Calabria, began to carry out his great building projects and, in order to build Poggioreale, brought to these parts some of the most esteemed architects: Giuliano da Maiano Fiorentino, Francesco [di Giorgio] da Siena, Master Antonio

Fiorentino, even though they made mostly equipment for wars and fortresses; and moreover the good and singular Fra Jucundo [Giovanni Giocondo] da Verona was here [reading 69].

[524–535] Wars, then, and the invasion of the barbarians, as I said, have had a direct impact on our achievements. We have now Joan Mormando, who in the judgment of everyone lacks only princes and grand signori to make use of his optimal disposition and ability. From the first he was a maker of organs, then he converted to architecture and to the total imitation of ancient things. It can be said for sure, despite the fact that he only built a few houses because of little available land, that since he gave himself completely to the study and consideration of classical antiquities he deserves to be praised highly.

[536–543] And because Your Lordship asks me again *which I would add as a (to use your word) corollary,* the vestiges of ancient buildings in this our region, *and in every part, to the extent that I can, I will follow your example,* even though I have already written you about this, rightly one could say my *"bad luck."* Be that as it may, at least in the eyes of Your Lordship I will be considered obedient.

[544–556] *Briefly on the monuments of ancient architecture that remain among us, accept this.* In the middle of this city, almost in its umbilical center, where the church of San Paolo is today, the pronaos and cornice of the ancient Temple of Castor and Pollux is all still intact, with certain grand and fluted columns, with the beautiful pediment and with the Greek inscription, which I will not send you because I think you have read it. That temple is inland from the coast, according to Your Lordship you admired it when you were here, and on the inside it is all ruined. The epistyle columns and other parts of it were then converted into tombs, church doors and other modern works, and certainly wrongfully, taking those precious and at one time well-placed marbles and using them barbarically in French and German works [readings 158–159].

[557–569] In the houses of Signor Annibale di Capua, in the houses of Messer Soardino de' Suardi, one discerns two theaters where there are still many tall remains of an immense fabric. Here the marble image of Vespasian and Titus, larger than life-size, has been excavated; and when you are inside you can see the accurate likeness and great vaults *even though* many modern things were built around it. Of this city I will say nothing else. I pray Your Lordship read the end of Pontano's *Historia rerum Neapolitanarum, where he speaks at length about this matter,* as much on things within Naples as outside it.

[570–585] Beyond the great grotto made by hand (a Roman work), towards the sea, where the beautiful little island of Nisida is, one sees clearly the remains of a circus, where there are shrubs and woods today, in addition to the other circus that is in Pozzuoli in the Ciceronian villa. *There is an amphitheater near Pozzuoli.* The castle that today is at Acerra and the castle of Suèssola are both ancient theaters. One sees in ancient Capua the grand amphitheater with other buildings, mostly intact, today called the Capuan Burlasci; all of which I think Your Lordship has already seen. I will not mention that which Your Lordship may have already seen: the theaters and aqueducts still intact, *of the river Lyrim,* today called Garigliano, where the ancient Minturne holdings were, the remains of which are now part of the Traiecto territory.

[585–597] In the building thought to be the palace in which Augustus died, near Nola, according to Your Lordship, one can learn from our Messer Antonio, are many great ruins of blocks of volcanic rock, of which most were transferred to the palace recently constructed in Nola for Signor Orsi Ursino [Orso Orsini], count of Nola, and to the building for Signor Carlo Carafa, count of Aeròla, in Naples. I have intended to go to the island of Capri to see the *surviving* remains of the buildings of Tiberius. In Paestum or Poseidonia, a ruined city, the ancient walls are intact, for the most part with towers, and inside are three Doric temples, of great blocks of quarried stone and travertine. One sees not far from Paestum the ancient city of Velia, where there are still many ruins.

[598–615] But who needs to dwell on these details? Notwithstanding that we have at Baia, Cuma, Pozzuoli many ancient ruined buildings that ruled the world, where else can one see, beyond the baths, villas, and tombs, beautiful amphitheaters, circuses, pools, and the huge reservoirs of sweet waters, made for the use of the armed Romans fighting Africa? Where else can one find a part of the great aqueduct system feeding the reservoirs in such a way that all Monte Miseno is empty inside, reinforced by pillars — something really stupendous to imagine? That is to say nothing of the many pools next to the sea, not only in Baia and Pozzuoli, but also in Posillipo, near the Castel dell'Ovo and Castel Nuovo, including the port of Naples. In sum, from the peak of Monte Miseno through all of Baia as far as Pozzuoli and the forum of the Vulcans, today called La Sulfatura [the Sulphur Springs], there are ancient buildings that now appear to be mountains and woods, so numerous, not even Rome can boast so many baths, amphitheaters, circuses, and other similar things [reading 161].

[616–624] I beg Your Lordship, when it occurs to you to honor me by writing, not to use anymore that large, uneven paper, which you use occasionally; because having kept letters from friends, in the manner that I keep them, your paper doesn't measure the same as the others in length and width, so that I am unable to preserve it alongside the letters from my friends, among whom Your Lordship's, in your saintly good taste, I wish to place.

[625] And because I greatly wish to pay the contumacy of my late response, I beg you again to confirm in two lines by letter that you and Messer Ambrosio have received this letter.

Farewell.

Naples. XX March MDXXIIII. SUMMONTIUS TUUS

★ ★ ★

CHAPTER 11: BOOK PRODUCTION
by Ronald G. Musto

Fig. 74. Late Angevin–Durazzan manuscripts. Dante, Purgatorio *XXXII, with commentary by Francesco da Buti, c.1425. Naples, BN MS XIII.C.1, fol. 133r.* The manuscript shows the influence of Umbrian and Tuscan artists on Neapolitan production.

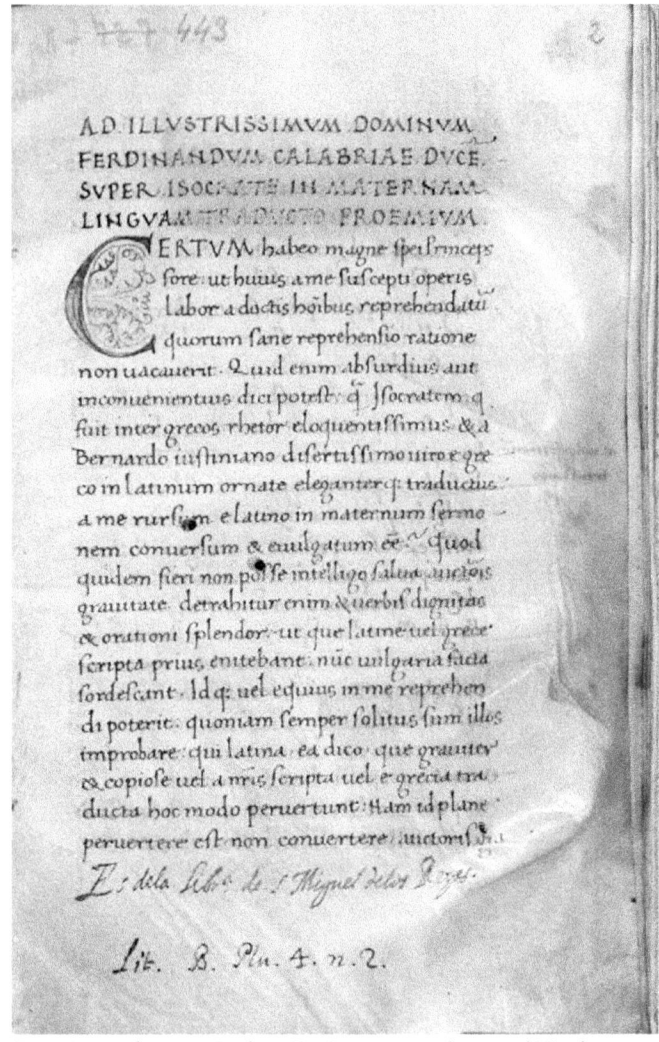

Fig. 75. Aragonese humanism. Bartolomeo Facio, Isocratis sermo de regno ad Nicoclem regem, *before 1457. València, Biblioteca Històrica, MS 0443, fol. 2r.* Dedicated to Ferdinand (Ferrante), duke of Calabria. Written in a humanist book hand, the manuscript offers testimony to both the new formal qualities of, and the place of patronage for, humanist scholarship.

Fig. 76. Aragonese humanism. Pliny, Natural History, *1465. Naples, BN, MS. V.A.3,*
fol. 1r. The manuscript was commissioned by Gherardo, protonotary of the
Aragonese kingdom of Sicily, and produced in Palermo by Giovan Marco
Cinico. Both its content and its formal qualities provide evidence of the strong
influence of the new humanist culture on the Aragonese court.

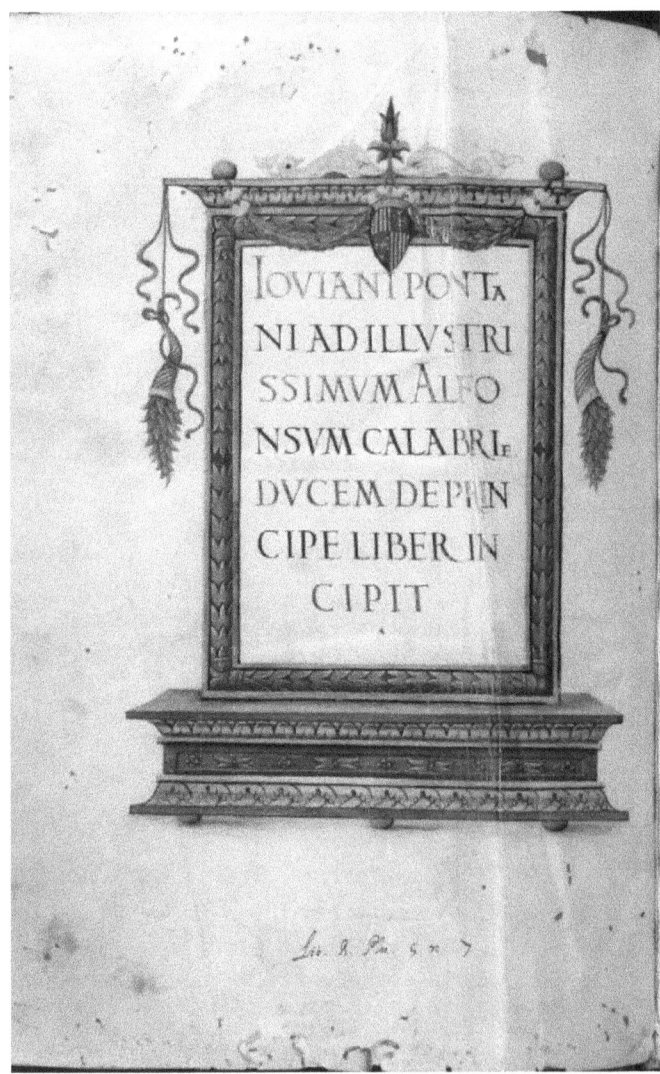

IOVIANI PONTA
NI AD ILLVSTRI
SSIMVM ALFO
NSVM CALABRIE
DVCEM DE PRIN
CIPE LIBER IN
CIPIT

Fig. 77. Aragonese humanism. Giovanni Pontano, De Principe, 1480–94. Valencia, Biblioteca Histórica, MS 0052, fol. 1v. Dedicated to Alfonso, duke of Calabria. Pontano's work equals that of Machiavelli for its political realism. For the De Principe, see pp. 115–38 and reading 19,

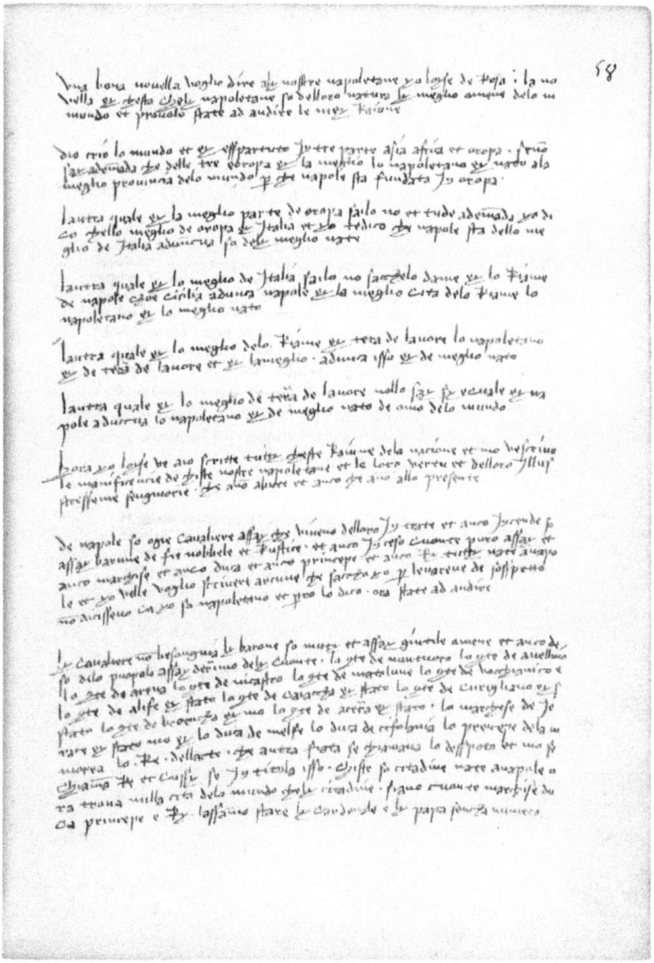

Fig. 78. Neapolitan Civic Historians. Loise de Rosa, Elogio di Napoli. *c.1470. Paris, BnF, MS italien 913, fol. 58r. Source: Gallica.* A strong vernacular, civic tradition coexisted with the more formal humanist scholarship and book production at court. See above, Introduction, pp. 18–21. For the *Elogio,* see reading 5.

Fig. 79. Aragonese liturgical commissions. The Breviarum Romanum *of Ferrante of Aragon, c.1480. Naples, BN MS I.B.57. fol. 11r.* The manuscript was commissioned for the young Prince Ferdinand (Ferrante), son of Alfonso I. He kneels in prayer at the bas-de-page in a space strongly reminiscent of the Soccorpo. (See reading 100 and Fig. 39.) The juxtaposition of the traditional devotional book with classically inspired decorative programs and architectural features is typical of Aragonese tastes.

APOLOGVS.

Vardando uno polito & groſſo boye la rana deſideroſa de eſſere coſſi groſſa como lo boye comenzo ad infiareſe in modo che ſtaua per perire Lo figliolo della rana incomenzo cuſſi ad dire alla matre. Matre mia

Fig. 80. Vernacular Printing in Naples. Aesop moralisatus. *Naples: Francesco del Tuppo, at Germani fedelissimi, 1485.* Del Tuppo was an author, editor, translator and publisher, whose print edition of the *Cronaca di Partenope* (1486–90) would have a major impact on both Neapolitan and Italian-wide historiography. His *Aesop,* which he himself translated into Neapolitan, is considered the most beautiful of Neapolitan incunabula. See above, Intoduction, pp. 49–50.

Fig. 81. Hebrew Printing. Psalms, with the Commentary of David Kimhi. *Naples: Joseph ben Jacob of Gunzenhausen, 1487. Photo: Library of Congress.* By 1500 Naples had became the only safe haven for Hebrew printers in Italy. The Gunzenhausers arrived in Naples from Gunzenhausen in southern Germany and set up a Hebrew press, which from 1487 to 1492 issued about twelve volumes. The Soncinos also began printing in Naples in the 1490s. See Introduction, pp. 50–51.

Fig. 82. *Greek Studies.* Liturgica ad usuam ecclesiarum Italo–Graecarum, *c.1500. Naples, BN, MS II.A.35, fol. 3r.* The manuscript was commissioned by Andrea Matteo III Acquaviva, duke of Atri, and composed by several scribes. It testifies to the widespread humanist interests of Naples' aristocracy and to the continued importance of Greek culture in the Regno.

Fig. 83. Vernacular history. Ferraiolo, Cronaca. c.1498. New York, Morgan Library, MS 801, fol. 112r. Into his manuscript Ferraiolo incorporated oral testimony, eye-witness and first-hand report, poetry, official court documents and large sections of such printed histories as the *Cronaca di Partenope* to create a localized civic history for his fellow Neapolitans. See above, Intoduction, pp. 48–50 and readings 6, 7.

Fig. 84. The taste for antiquities. Benedetto di Falco, Descrittione dei luoghi antichi di Napoli e del suo amenissino distreto. *Naples: Mattio Cancer, 1568.* Originally published in 1548, Falco's work saw many editions into the 17th century as the number of foreign visitors increased. It set the standard for early modern guides to the city, combining local traditions from Virgil to Sannazaro, a survey of ancient monuments, and new urbanistic studies. See Introduction, pp. 51–52.

Fig. 85. Science in Naples. Bernardino Telesio, De rerum natura iuxta propria principia. *Naples: Giuseppe Cacchi, 1570. Photo: Library of Congress.* Telesio was among Naples' new scientific class. His work had a wide impact not only in the Regno, but also among a wider European intelligentia. See Introduction, pp. 13–14.

APPENDICES

ONLINE RESOURCES

INTERACTIVE MAP: http://www.italicapress.com/index287.html

ONLINE BIBLIOGRAPHY: http://www.italicapress.com/index346.html

IMAGE GALLERIES
The URL for each site is derived from taking the URL (e.g., http://www.flickr.
com/photos/80499896@N05/albums/) and adding the specific site number. (e.g.,
2157696413689622). The numbers of images in each gallery is the total uploaded as of
November 15, 2018.

Site Gallery	#	Images
Aragonese Walls	72157696413689622	5
Cappella Pontano (Pontano Chapel)	72157669624845747	51
Castel Capuano	72157630808244632	16
Castel Nuovo	72157630165392752	43
Castel Sant'Elmo (Belforte)	72157630808796440	7
Certosa di San Martino	72157630152166968	10
Gesù Nuovo	72157696408633282	9
Duomo	72157630152316564	30
Palazzo Cuomo	72157693779023910	2
Palazzo Diomede Carafa	72157671710258708	31
Palazzo Gravina (Orsini di)	72157693779206940	25
Palazzo Marigliano	72157699629377975	5
Palazzo Reale	72157697999459221	4
Porta Capuana	72157697947862081	11
Porta Nolana	72157699184423964	9
S. Angelo a Nilo	72157638636071455	6
S. Domenico Maggiore	72157630148664544	37
S. Giovanni a Carbonara	72157630164220128	26
S. Gregorio Armeno	72157699236342844	2
S. Paolo Maggiore	72157630150918068	14
Sta. Caterina a Formello	72157696416781442	22
Sta. Maria Donnaregina	72157630164795244	25
Sta. Maria la Nova	72157699593050475	17
Sta. Maria di Monteoliveto	72157693779325380	10

Total images as of 2/01/2019   417

Castelluccio di Pizzofalcone Castel Nuovo (6) Castel Sant'Elmo (3

Castel dell'Ovo Sta. Croce Torre dell'Oro Certosa di S. Martino (7)

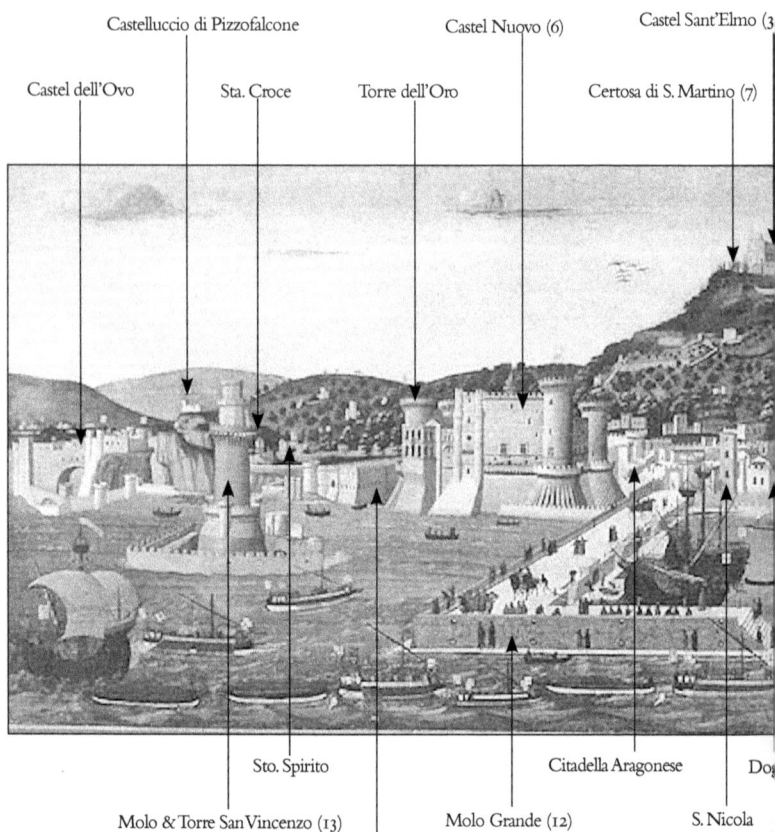

Sto. Spirito Citadella Aragonese Dog

Molo & Torre San Vincenzo (13) Molo Grande (12) S. Nicola

Palace of the Angevin Princes

THE TAVOLA STROZZI

The Tavola Strozzi is a panoramic panel painting of the bay, city and environs of Naples. It was discovered by Corrado Ricci in 1901 in the Palazzo Strozzi in Florence. The scholarly consensus now identifies it as the celebration of the Aragonese defeat of Jean of Anjou on 7 July 1465 at the naval battle of Ischia. The painting is tempera on wood, 82 x 245 cm., now in the Museo di San Martino. It was most likely a cassone panel, or perhaps the headboard of a bed, designed by Benedetto da Maiano. It has been convincingly dated now to between 1465 and 1478, most likely to 1472/73. The crispness of its detail provides a remarkably accurate visual source for the early modern city.

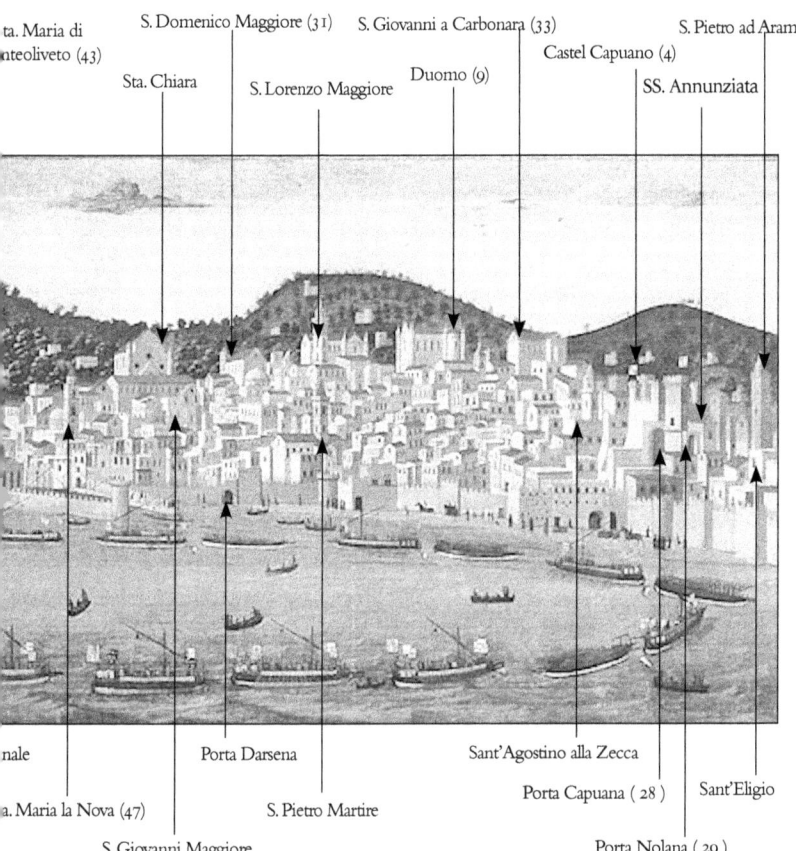

ta. Maria di
nteoliveto (43)

S. Domenico Maggiore (31)

Sta. Chiara

S. Lorenzo Maggiore

S. Giovanni a Carbonara (33)

Duomo (9)

Castel Capuano (4)

S. Pietro ad Aram

SS. Annunziata

nale

a. Maria la Nova (47)

Porta Darsena

S. Pietro Martire

S. Giovanni Maggiore

Sant'Agostino alla Zecca

Porta Capuana (28)

Porta Nolana (29)

Sant'Eligio

The perspective point of the Tavola is either from a ship off the Molo Grande or from the tower on the Molo itself, as argued in a recent analysis by Roberto Taito (http://www.tavolastrozzi.it/studio.htm). Scholarly consensus had settled on Francesco Rosselli or Francesco Pagano as its painter, but this has been cast into doubt by Pane (2009), 94–119, 141–67, who cites the lack of documentary evidence and attributes it to an unknown Tuscan painter, perhaps in Florence or Siena (141), who executed it from perspective drawings carried out in Naples. The image has been discussed and analyzed at length. See, for example, Di Mauro (1992); De Seta (1997), 11–53; and most recently in Pane (2009). Labels are to identifiable sites and several are also keyed to the map below, pp. 482–83.

MAP OF
RENAISSANCE
NAPLES

Source: Italica Press, "Renaissance
Naples," Google Maps.

See Alphabetical Key with thumb-
nails below, pp. 484–86; and links to
online Italica Press Image Galleries,
above, p. 479.

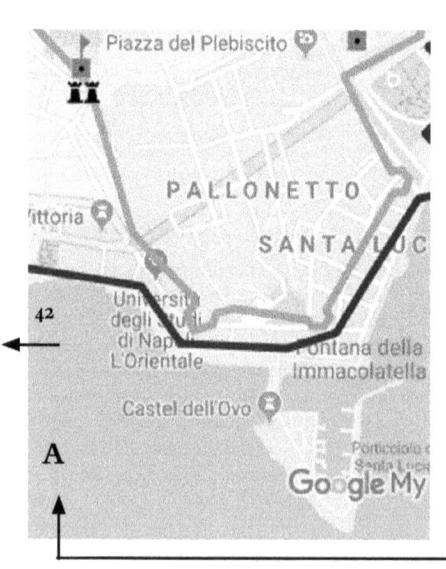

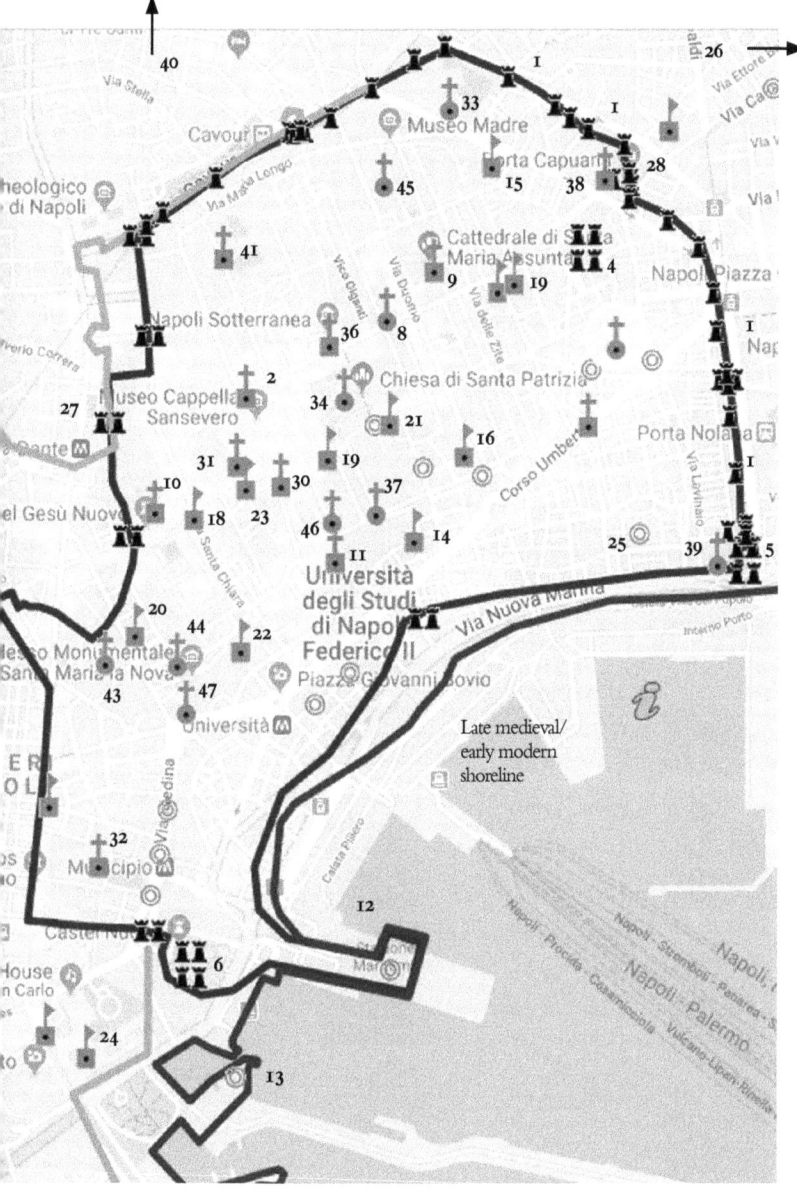

ALPHABETICAL KEY TO MAP

 1. Aragonese Walls

 9. Duomo: Soccorpo

 2. Cappella Pontano (Pontano Chapel)

 10. Gesù Nuovo (Palazzo Sanseverino)

 3. Castel Sant'Elmo, (Belforte, Sant'Erasmo)

 11. Gesù Vecchio

 4. Castel Capuano

 12. Molo Grande

 5. Castel del Carmine (Sperone)

 13. Molo & Torre San Vincenzo

 6. Castel Nuovo

 14. Palazzo Bonifacio

 7. Certosa di S. Martino

 15. Palazzo Caracciolo d'Oppido

 8. Chiesa dei Girolomini

 16. Palazzo Cuomo

 17. Palazzo Diomede Carafa

 25. Piazza del Mercato

 18. Palazzo Filomarino

 26. Poggioreale

 19. Palazzo Gianni Caracciolo

 27. Port'Alba

 20. Palazzo Gravina (Orsini di)

 28. Porta Capuana

 21. Palazzo Marigliano (di Capua)

 29. Porta Nolana

 22. Palazzo Penna

 30. S. Angelo a Nilo

 23. Palazzo Petrucci

 31. S. Domenico Maggiore

 24. Palazzo Reale

 32. S. Giacomo degli Spagnoli

485

33. S. Giovanni a
Carbonara

41. Sta. Maria delle
Grazie a Caponapoli

34. S. Gregorio
Armeno

42. Sta. Maria del
Parto

35. Spanish Quarter

43. Sta. Maria di
Monteoliveto (Sant'
Anna dei Lombardi)

36. S. Paolo
Maggiore (Temple
of Dioscuri)

44. Sta. Maria
Donnalbina

37. SS. Severino e
Sossio

45. Sta. Maria
Donnaregina

38. Sta. Caterina a
Formello

46. Sta. Maria
Donnaromita

39. Sta. Maria del
Carmine

47. Sta. Maria la
Nova

40. Sta. Maria della
Sanità

48. Villa Carafa
(Palazzo Cellamare)

BIBLIOGRAPHY

ARCHIVES & MANUSCRIPTS

Brescia. Biblioteca Queriniana. Ms. A.II.2.

Capaccio, Giulio Cesare. *Provveditoria Records.*

Corrispondenze diplomatiche veneziane. Rome: Istituto Poligrafico e Zecca dello Stato: Libreria dello Stato, 1991–.

Discourse on the Kingdom of Naples, c.1570. State of the Royal Patrimony, 1571–72.

Filangieri, Gaetano, ed. *Documenti per la storia, le arti e le industrie delle provincie napoletane.* 6 vols. Naples: Tipografia dell'Accademia Reale delle Scienze, 1883–91.

Filangieri di Candida, Riccardo, et al. *Registri della Cancelleria angioina ricostruiti da Riccardo Filangieri con la collaborazione degli archivisti napoletani.* Naples: Archivio di Stato, 1950–.

Florence. Archivio di Stato. *Carte Strozziane,* Serie V.

—. Archivio di Stato. Cat. D4, doc. 21, II.1.

—. Biblioteca Marucelliana. Ms. A 76.

Lettieri, Pietro Antonio. *Reports.* In Francesco Abbate, *Storia dell'arte nell'Italia meridionale: Il Cinquecento.* Rome: Donzelli, 2001, 133–35; excerpted from Lorenzo Giustiniani, *Dizionario geografico ragionato del Regno di Napoli.* 10 vols. Naples: Vicenzo Manfredi, 1797–1895.

Los Angeles. J. Paul Getty Museum. Ms Ludwig IX 12; 83.ML.108. Online at: http://www.getty.edu/art/collection/objects/1396/unknown-maker-book-of-hours-italian-about-1460.

Mazzoleni, Jole, ed. *Fonti aragonesi.* Naples: L'Accademia, 1957.

—. *Regesto della Cancelleria aragonese di Napoli.* Naples: L'Accademia, 1951–.

Naples. Archivio di Stato. Banco di Napoli, Banco dello Spirito Santo. *Giornale copia polizze,* matr. 44, D.100.

—. *Cedole di Tesoreria.*

—. *Collaterale, Curiae.*

—. Monasteri Soppressi. San Gregorio Armeno, 3435, Caracciola.

—. Monasteri Soppressi 6079, Platea del Regal Monastero di S. Gio. a Carbonara (1730–62).

Naples. Biblioteca Nazionale. Fondo Brancacciano, Ms. V.A.12.

—. Biblioteca Nazionale. Ms. I B 55. Hours of Alfonso I.

—. Biblioteca Nazionale. Ms. XII.E.34. Plutarch, *Heroum clarissimorumque.* —. *Privilegi e capitoli con altre grazie concedute alla Fedelissima Città e Regno di Napoli dalli Serenissimi re Filippo II…* Milan: n.p., 1719.

—. *Visitas de Italia.*

New Haven. Yale University. Beinecke Library. Ms. 446. Moamin, *De scientia venandi per aves.* Online at: http://brbl-dl.library.yale.edu/vufind/Record/3592283.

New York. Pierpont Morgan Library. MS 801. Selections online at: http://ica.themorgan.org/manuscript/page/1/146991.

Paris. Bibliothèque nationale de France. Cod. Ital. 913 (ex 10171).

Rome. Biblioteca Apostolica Vaticana. Codex Barberini Latina 4424.

—. Bibliotheca Apostolica Vaticana. Vat. Lat. 13650. Bartolomeo Facio, *De Viris Illustribus.*

Vario, Domenico Alfeno. *Pragmaticae, edicta, decreta, interdicta regiaque sanctiones Regni Neapolitani.* Naples: Cervonio, 1772.

PRIMARY

Alberti, Leon Battista. *On the Art of Building in Ten Books.* Joseph Rykwert, Neil Leach, and Robert Tavernor, trans. Cambridge, MA: MIT Press,1988.

Alighieri, Dante. *The Divine Comedy: Purgatorio.* John D. Sinclair, trans. New York: Oxford, 1961.

Altamura, Antonio, ed. *Napoli Aragonese nei ricordi di Loiuse de Rosa.* Naples: Libreria scientifica editrice, 1971.

Arnaldi, Francesco, ed. *Poeti latini del Quattrocento.* Milan: Ricciardi, 1964.

Bacio Terracina, Laura. *Poems.* In Stortoni, *Women Poets,* 108–13.

Beccadelli, Antonio (Panormita). *De dictis et factis divi Alphonsi.* Naples: n.p., 1585.

—. *De dictis et factis Alfonsi regis.* M. Vilallonga, ed. Barcelona: Barcono, 1990.

—. *Liber rerum gestarum Fernandi regis.* Gianvito Resta, ed. Palermo: Centro di studi filologici e linguistici siciliani, 1968.

—. *The Hermaphrodite.* Holt Parker, ed. and trans. Cambridge, MA: Harvard University Press, 2010.

Beecher, Donald, ed. and trans. *Renaissance Comedy: The Italian Masters* 2. Toronto: University of Toronto Press, 2009.

Biondo, Flavio. *Italy Illuminated.* Jeffrey A. White, ed. and trans. 2 vols. Cambridge, MA: Harvard University Press, 2005–16.

Bisticci, Vespasiano. da *Renaissance Princes, Popes, and Prelates.* W. G. Waters and Emily Waters, ed. New York: Harper & Row, 1963; repr. as *The Vespasiano Memoirs: Lives of Illustrious Men of the XVth Century.* Toronto: University of Toronto Press for RSA, 1997.

Bruno, Giordano. *The Candlebearer (Il Candelaio).* Gino Moliterno, ed. Ottawa: Dovehouse Editions, 2000.

Buecheler, Franz, and Alexander Riese, ed. *Anthologia Latina sive poesis Latinae supplementum*. Leipzig: Teubner 1894.

Capaccio, Giulio Cesare. *Il Forestiero*. Naples: G. D. Roncagliolo, 1634.

Caracciolo, Tristano. *De varietate fortunae*. In Giovanni Gravier, ed., *Raccolta di tutti i più rinomati scrittori dell'istoria generale del regno di Napoli*. Naples: Gravier, 1769–72.

Castaldo, Antonio. *Istoria di Notar Antonio Castaldo, Libri Quattro*. Naples: Giovanni Gravien, 1769, in the summary translation in Henry Charles Lea, *The Inquisition in the Spanish Dependencies*. London: Macmillan, 1922, 70–78.

Commynes, Philippe de. *Mémoires*. Joël Blanchard, ed. 2 vols. Geneva: Droz, 2007.

Costo, Tommaso. *Il Fuggilozio*. Naples: Giovanni Iacopo Carlino & Antonio Pace, 1596.

——. *l Fuggilozio*. Venice: Barezzo Barezzi, 1600

——. *l Fuggilozio*. Corrado Calenda, ed. Rome: Salerno, 1989.

——. *Lettere*. Venice: Barezzo Barezzi, 1602; repr. Naples: Costantino Vitale, 1604.

De Jennaro, Pietro Jacopo and Filenio Gallo. *La prima imitazione dell'Arcadia: Aggiuntevi l'Egloghe pastorali di P.J. de Jennaro e di Filenio Gallo*. Erasmo Pèrcopo, ed. Naples: L. Pierro, 1894.

Del Tufo, Giovanni Battista. *Ritratto o modello delle grandezze, delizie o meraviglie della nobilissima città di Napoli*. Olga Silvana Casale and Mariateresa Colotti, ed. Rome: Salerno, 2007.

De Morra, Isabella. *Canzoniere: A Bilingual Edition*. Irene Musillo Mitchell, ed. and trans. West Lafayette, IN: Bordighera, 1998.

——. In Stortoni, *Women Poets*, 114–27.

De' Pandoni, Porcellio. "Ad Immortalitatem Isaiae Pisani marmorum celatoris." In Angelo Battaglini, "Memoria sopra uno sconosciuto egregio scultore del secolo XV." *Dissertazioni dell'Accademia romana di archeologia* 1 (1821): 117.

De' Pizzicolli, Ciriaco. *Life and Early Travels*. Charles Mitchell, ed. Cambridge, MA: Harvard University Press, 2015.

De Rosa, Loise. *Ricordi: Edizione critica del Ms. Ital. 913 della Bibliothèque Nationale de France*. Vittorio Formentin, ed. Rome: Salerno Editrice, 1998.

De Stefano, Pietro. *Descrittione dei luoghi sacri della città di Napoli*. Naples: Amato, 1560.

De Tarsia, Galeazzo. *Sonnets*. In Daniele Porchiroli, ed. *Lirici del Cinquecento*. Turin: UTET, 1958, 569–616.

Di Costanzo. Angelo. *Canzoniere* in *Poesie italiane e latine e prose; and Giunte alle rime del Costanzo*. Palermo: Gallo, 1843.

—. *Historia del Regno di Napoli*. Walter Capezzali and P. Farenga, ed. L'Aquila: Fondazione Cassa di risparmio della Provincia dell'Aquila, 2007.

—. *History of the Kingdom of Naples, 1250–1489*. Christopher David Costanzo, ed. and trans. Charleston, SC: Create Space, 2016.

Facio, Bartolomeo. *De viris illustribus*. Florence: C. Tanzini, 1745.

Falco, Benedetto di. *Descrittione dei luoghi antiqui di Napoli e del suo amenissimo distretto*. Ottavio Morisani, ed. Naples: Libreria scientifica editrice, 1972.

Ferraiolo. *Cronaca*. Rosario Coluccia, ed. Florence: Accademia della Crusca, 1987.

Galante, Gennaro Aspreno. *Guida sacra della città di Napoli*. Nicola Spinosa, ed. Naples: Società editrice napoletana, 1985.

Gareth, Benedetto (il Chariteo). *Le Rime di Benedetto Gareth detto il Chariteo*. Erasmo Pèrcopo, ed. Naples: Accademia delle scienze, 1892.

—. *Rime e lettere*. Maria Corti, ed. Bologna: Commissione per i testi di lingua, 1956.

Giustiniani, Lorenzo. *Dizionario geographico-ragionato del Regno di Napoli*. Naples: V. Manfredi, 1797–1805.

Gravier, Giovanni, ed. *Raccolta di tutti i più rinomati scrittori dell'istoria generate nel regno di Napoli*. Naples: Gravier, 1749.

Guicciardini, Francesco. *History of Italy and History of Florence*. Cecil Grayson, trans.; John R. Hale, ed. New York: Washington Square Press, 1964.

Guicciardini, Luigi. *The Sack of Rome*. James H. Mc Gregor, ed. and trans. New York: Italica Press, 1993.

Hollis, A.S., ed. *Fragments of Roman Poetry c.60 BC–AD 20*. Oxford: Oxford University Press 2007.

Kelly, Samantha, ed. Cronaca di Partenope: *An Introduction to and Critical Edition of the First Vernacular History of Naples (c.1350)*. Leiden: Brill, 2011.

Lamozzo, Giovanni Paolo. *Trattato dell'Arte della Pittura*. Milan, 1584. In John Shearman, *Mannerism*. Harmondsworth: Penguin, 1967, 81.

Landino, Cristoforo. *Comento sopra la Comedia I–IV.* Paolo Procaccioli, ed. Rome: Salerno, 2001.

Leostello, Joampiero. *Effemeridi delle cose fatte per il Duca di Calabria (1484–1491)*. Gaetano Angerio Guglielmo Filangieri, ed. Naples: Società napoletana di storia patria, 1883.

Machiavelli, Niccolò. *History of Florence and of the Affairs of Italy from the Earliest Times to the Death of Lorenzo the Magnificent*. New York: W. Walter Dunne, 1901. Hugo Albert Rennert, ed. for Project Gutenberg. EBook #2464. Last Updated: February 6, 2013.

Manetti, Giannozzo. *Biographical Writings*. Stefano Ugo Baldassarri and Rolf Bagemihl, ed. and trans. Cambridge, MA: Harvard University Press, 2003.

Martone, Valerie, and Robert L. Martone, ed. and trans. *Renaissance Comic Tales of Love, Treachery and Revenge*. New York: Italica Press, 1994.

Morisani, Ottavio, ed. *La letteratura artistica a Napoli*. Naples: Fausto Fiorentino Editore, 1937.

Morlini, Girolamo. *Novelle e favole*. Giovanni Villani, ed. Rome: Salerno Editrice, 1988.

Notar Giacomo. *Cronica di Napoli*. Paolo Garzilli, ed. Naples: Stamperia Reale, 1845.

——. Chiara De Caprio, ed. Rome: ISIME. Forthcoming 2019.

Passero, Giuliano. *Giornali*. Vincenzo Altobelli, ed. Naples: Orsini, 1785.

Piccolomini, Aeneas Silvio. *Memoirs of a Renaissance Pope: The Commentaries of Pius II. An Abridgment*. Leona C. Gabel, ed.; Florence A. Gragg, trans. London: George Allen & Unwin, 1960.

Pontano, Giovanni. *Baiae*. Rodney G. Dennis, ed. Cambridge, MA: Harvard University Press, 2006.

——. *De principe*. Guido M. Cappelli, ed. Rome: Salerno, 2003.

——. *Dialogues*. Julia Haig Gaisser, ed. Cambridge, MA: Harvard University Press, 2012–.

——. *I Trattati delle virtù sociali*. Francesco Tateo, ed. 2nd ed. Rome: Bulzoni, 1999.

Prota-Giurleo, Ulisse. *Scritti inediti e rari*. Naples: Arte Tipografica, 1988.

Sangallo, Giuliano da. *Il Libro di Giuliano da Sangallo*. Cristiano Huelsen, ed., Leipzig: Harrassowitz, 1910.

Sannazaro, Jacopo. *Arcadia and Piscatorial Eclogues*. Ralph Nash, ed. and trans. Detroit: Wayne State University Press, 1966.

——. *Gli zibaldoni di Jacopo Sannazaro*. Carlo Vecce, ed. Messina: Sicania, 1998.

——. *Latin Poetry*. Michael C.J. Putnam, ed. and trans. Cambridge, MA: Harvard University Press, 2009.

——. *Poemata ex antiquis editionibus accuratissime descripta*. Padua: Cominus, 1719.

——. *The Major Latin Poems of Jacopo Sannazaro*. Ralph Nash, ed. Detroit: Wayne State University Press, 1996.

Sanuto, Marino. *Diarii di Marino Sanuto*. Venice: F. Visentini, 1890.

Schrader, Laurentius, ed. *Monumentorum Italiae*. Helmstedt: Jakob Lucius, 1592.

Sefer Tehilim (Book of Psalms). Commentary by David ben Joseph Kimhi, corrected by Jacob Baruch ben Judah Landau. Naples: Joseph ben Jacob Ashkenazi Gunzenhauser, 4 Nisan 5247 (28 March 1487).

Serlio, Sebastiano. *Delle antichità: Il terzo libro di Sebastiano Serlio Bolognese*. Venice: Sessa, 1540.

——. *On Architecture*. Vaughan Hart and Peter Hicks, trans. New Haven: Yale University Press, 1996.

Seward, Desmond, ed. *Naples: A Travellers' Companion*. New York: Atheneum, 1986.

Stortoni, Laura Anna, ed. *Women Poets of the Italian Renaissance: Courtly Ladies and Courtesans*. Laura Anna Stortoni and Mary Prentice Lillie, trans. New York: Italica Press, 1997.

Strazzullo, Franco, ed. *La real cappella del Tesoro di S. Gennaro: Documenti inediti*. Naples: Società editrice napoletana, 1978.

Summonte, Pietro. Letter to Marcantonio Michiel. In Cornelius von Fabriczy, trans. "Summonte's Brief an M.A. Michiel." *Repertorium für Kunstwissenschaft* 30 (1907): 143–68.

——. In Fausto Nicolini. *L'arte napoletana del rinascimento e la lettera di Pietro Summonte a Marcantonio Michiel*. Naples: R. Ricciardi, 1925, 157–75.

——. In Roberto Pane. *Il rinascimento nell'Italia meridionale*. Milan: Edizioni di Comunità, 1975, 1:63–95.

Tansillo, Luigi. *Capitoli giocosi e satirici*. Carmine Boccia, ed. Rome: Bulzoni, 2010.

——. *Edizione delle opere di Luigi Tansillo*. Rome: Bulzoni, 2010.

——. *Il canzoniere edito ed inedito secondo una copia dell'autografo ed altri manoscritti e stampe*. Erasmo Pèrcopo and Tobia R. Toscano, ed. Naples: Consorzio editoriale Fridericiana, 1996.

——. *Rime*. Tobia R. Toscano, Erika Milburn, and Rossano Pestarino, ed. Rome: Bulzoni, 2011.

Tarcagnota, Giovanni. *Del sito et lodi della città di Napoli*. Naples: Giovanni Maria Scotto, 1566; repr. Franco Strazzullo, ed. Naples: Banca della Provincia di Napoli, Rome, 1988.

Tasso, Torquato. *Rinaldo*. Max Wickert, ed. and trans. New York: Italica Press, 2017.

Turler, Jerome. *The Traveller*. Gainesville, FL: Scholars' Facsimiles & Reprints, 1951.

Valeriano, Piero. *Piero Valeriano on the Ill Fortune of Learned Men: A Renaissance Humanist and His World*. Julia Haig Gaisser, trans. and ed. Ann Arbor: University of Michigan Press, 1999.

Valla, Lorenzo. *On the Donation of Constantine*. G.W. Bowerstock, ed. and trans. Cambridge, MA: Harvard University Press, 2007.

——. *The Treatise of Lorenzo Valla on the Donation of Constantine*, Christopher B. Coleman, ed. and trans. Toronto: University of Toronto Press, 1993.

Vasari, Giorgio. *Le vite de' più eccellenti pittori scultori e architettori nelle redazioni del 1550 e 1568*. Rosanna Bettarini and Paola Barrocchi, ed. Florence: Sansoni, 1966.

—. *Lives of the Painters, Sculptors and Architects*. Gaston du C. de Vere, trans. New York: Knopf, 1912; 2nd ed., repr. 1996.

SECONDARY

Abbamonte, Giancarlo. "Naples — A Poet's City: Attitudes towards Statius and Virgil in the Fifteenth Century." In Hughes–Buongiovanni, 170–88.

Adams, Nicholas. "Castel Nuovo a Napoli." In *Francesco di Giorgio Architetto.* Franco Paolo Fiore and Manfredo Tafuri, ed. Milan: Electa, 1993, 2:228–95.

Adler, Sara. "The Petrarchan Lament of Isabella di Morra." In *Donna: Women in Italian Culture*. Ottawa: Dovehouse, 1989, 201–21.

Agosti, Barbara. "Artisti spagnoli e fonti italiane." In *Norma e capriccio: Spagnoli in Italia agli esordi della "maniera moderna."* Tommaso Mozzati and Antonio Natali, ed. Florence: Giunti, 2013, 159–61.

—. "Introduzione." In Marco Cardisco, *Giorgio Vasari: Pittura, umanesimo, religioso, immagini di culto*. Riccardo Naldi, ed. Naples: Arte'm, 2009, 7–9.

Aikema, Bernard. "Netherlandish Painting and Early Renaissance Italy: Artistic Rapports in Historiographical Perspective." In *Cultural Exchange in Early Modern Europe 4. Forging European Identities.* Herman Roodenburg, ed. Cambridge University Press, 2007, 100–137.

Ainaud de Lasarte, Juan. "Alfonso the Magnanimous and the Plastic Arts of His Time." In *Spain in the Fifteenth Century 1369–1516*. Roger Highfield, ed. London: Macmillan, 1972, 193–225.

Ambra, Emilia, ed. *Libri a corte: Testi e immagini nella Napoli aragonese*. Naples: Paparo, 1997.

Amidei, Beatrice Barbiellini. *Alla Luna: Saggio sulla poesia del Cariteo*. Florence: La Nuova Italia editrice, 1999.

Amirante, Francesca. *Libri per vedere: Le guide storico-artistiche della città di Napoli*. Naples: Edizioni scientifiche italiane, 1995.

Anatra, B., and Aurelio Musi. *Nel sistema imperiale l'Italia spagnola*. Naples: Edizioni scientifiche italiane, 1994.

Annecchino, Raimondo. *Storia di Pozzuoli e della zone flegrea*. Pozzuoli: Commune di Pozzuoli, 1960; 2nd. ed. Pozzuoli: A. Gallina, 1996.

Anonymous. "Corenzio, Belisario." At: www.oxfordartonline.

Ascher, Yoni. "The Church and the Piazza: Reflections on the South Side of the Church of San Domenico in Naples." *Architectural History* 45 (2002): 92–112.

Asor Rosa, Alberto et al., ed. *Letteratura italiana: Storia e geografia 7.2. L'eta moderna.* Florence: Einaudi, 1988.

Asor Rosa, Angela. "Gareth, Benet." DBI 52 (1999). Online at: http://www.treccani.it/enciclopedia/benet-gareth_(Dizionario-Biografico).

Astarita, Tommaso. *Between Salt Water and Holy Water: A History of Southern Italy.* New York: Norton, 2005.

——. ed. *A Companion to Early Modern Naples.* Leiden: Brill, 2013.

Barbato, Marcello, and Francesco Montuori. "Dalla stampa al manoscritto: La iv parte della *Cronaca di Partenope* trascritta dal Ferraiolo (1498)." In *Dal manoscritto al web: Canali e modalità di trasmissione dell'italiano. Tecniche, materialie e usi nella storia della lingua. Atti del XII Congresso SILFI (Helsinki, 18–20 giugno 2012).* E. Garavelli and E. Suomela-Härmä, ed. Florence: Cesati, 2014, 51–70.

Barbera, Gioacchino. "The Life and Work of Antonello da Messina." In *Antonello da Messina: Sicily's Renaissance Master.* Gioacchino Barbera, ed. New Haven: Yale University Press, 2005, 17–30.

Baron, Hans. *The Crisis of the Early Italian Renaissance: Civic Humanism and Republican Liberty in an Age of Classicism and Tyranny.* 2 vols. Princeton: Princeton University Press, 1955.

——. *In Search of Florentine Civic Humanism: Essays on the Transition from Medieval to Modern Thought.* 2 vols. Princeton: Princeton University Press, 1988.

Baxandall, Michael. "Bartholomaeus Facius on Painting, A Fifteenth-Century Manuscript of the *De Viris Illustribus.*" *Journal of the Warburg and Courtauld Institutes* 27 (1964): 90–107.

Beck, James. "Donatello and the Brancacci Tomb in Naples." In *Florilegium Columbianum: Essays in Honor of Paul Oskar Kristeller.* Karl-Ludwig Selig and Robert Somerville, ed. New York: Italica Press, 1987, 125–45.

Belozerskaya, Marina. *Luxury Arts of the Renaissance.* Los Angeles: J. Paul Getty Museum, 2005.

Bentley, Jerry. *Politics and Culture in Renaissance Naples.* Princeton: Princeton University Press, 1987.

Bessort, Claudie. "Jacomart [Baco, Jaime]." At: www.oxfordartonline.com.

Beyer, Andreas. "Cesare da Sesto." At: www.oxfordartonline.com.

——. *Parthenope: Neapel und der Süden der Renaissance.* Munich: Deutscher Kunstverlag, 2000, 37–38.

Biblioteca Nazionale di Napoli. *Libri a stampa napoletani dal 1400 al 1800.* Naples: Biblioteca Nazionale, 1952.

Black, Robert. *Machiavelli.* London: Routledge, 2013.

Blanchard, Joël. *Philippe de Commynes.* Paris, Fayard, 2006.

Bloch, Joshua. "Hebrew Printing in Naples." *Bulletin of the New York Public Library* 46 (1942): 489–514.

Blunt, Anthony. *Neapolitan Baroque and Rococo Architecture.* London: A. Zwemmer, 1975.

Bock, Nicholas. "Antiken und Florenzrezeption in Neapel, 1400–1450." In *Opere e giorni: Studi su Mille anni di arte europea*. Klaus Bergdolt and Giorgio Bonsanti, ed. Venice: Marsilio, 2001, 243–47.

Bologna, Ferdinando. "Colantonio." DBI 26 (1982). Online at: http://www.treccani.it/enciclopedia/colantonio_(Dizionario-Biografico).

—. "La 'Cona' degli ordini francescani di Colantonio nella chiesa di San Lorenzo a Napoli." In *Il polittico di Colantonio a San Lorenzo,* ed. idem. Naples: Electa, 2001, 9–33.

—. "Qualche osservazione sulla lettera di Pietro Summonte a Marcantonio Michiel." In Ammirante, *Libri per vedere,* 181–93.

Borsook, Eve. "A Florentine *scrittoio* for Diomede Carafa." In *Art the Ape of Nature: Studies in Honor of H. W. Janson*. Moshe Barasch and Lucy Freeman Sandler, ed. New York: Abrams, 1981, 91–96.

Braudel, Fernand. *The Mediterranean and the Mediterranean World in the Age of Philip II*. Sian Reynolds, trans. 2 vols. New York: Harper & Row, 1972.

Brundin, Abigail, T. Crivelli, and Maria Serena Sapegno, ed. *A Companion to Vittoria Colonna*. Leiden: Brill, 2016.

Bruzelius, Caroline. *The Stones of Naples: Church Building in the Angevin Kingdom, 1266–1343*. New Haven: Yale University Press, 2004.

—. and William Tronzo, *Medieval Naples: An Architectural and Urban History, 400–1400*. New York: Italica Press, 2011.

Bullock, Alan. "Morra, Isabella di (1520-46)." *Oxford Reference Online* (2002). At: www.oxfordreference.com/view/10.1093/acref/9780198183327.001.0001/acref-9780198183327-e-2117.

Caglioti, Francesco. "'La Testa Carafa' e il mito della poeta Virgilio, mago e protettore di Napoli." Lecture filmed for RAI series, "L'altra lingua degli italiani." 23 October 2012, filmed at Palazzo Reale, Naples. Online at: http://www.raiscuola.rai.it/articoli-programma-puntate/laltra-lingua-degli-italiani-%e2%80%9cla-testa-carafa%e2%80%9d-e-il-mito-del-poeta-virgilio-mago-e-protettore-di-napoli/19917/default.aspx.

Calabria, Antonio. *The Cost of Empire: The Finances of the Kingdom of Naples in the Time of Spanish Rule*. Cambridge: Cambridge University Press, 2002.

—. and John Marino, ed. and trans. *Good Government in Spanish Naples*. New York: Peter Lang, 1989.

Camiz, Franca Trinchieri. "Augustinian Musical Education and Redemption in the Fifteenth-Century Caracciolo del Sole Chapel, Naples." *Imago Musicae* 5 (1998): 41–64.

Canepa, Nancy L. "Literary Culture in Naples, 1500–1800." In Astarita (2013), 427–51.

Canfield, Gabriella Befani. "The Reception of Flemish Art in Renaissance Florence and Naples." In *Petrus Christus in Renaissance Bruges: An Interdisciplinary Approach*. Maryann W. Ainsworth, ed. New York: Metropolitan Museum of Art, 1995, 35–42.

Canfora, Davide, and Angela Caracciolo Aricò, ed. *La Serenissima e il Regno: Nel V Centenario dell'Arcadia di Jacopo Sannazaro. Atti del convegno di studi (Bari-Venezia, 4–8 ottobre 2004)*. Bari: Cacucci, 2006.

Capasso, Bartolommeo. *Le fonti della storia delle provincie napolitane dal 568 al 1500*. Naples: Riccardo Marghier, 1902; repr. Naples: Arnaldo Forni, 1997.

Cappelli, Guido. Maiestas*: Politica e pensiero politico nella Napoli aragonese (1443–1503)*. Rome: Carocci editore, 2016.

Caracciolo Aricò, Angela. *L'Arcadia del Sannazaro nell'autunno dell'umanesimo*. Rome: Bulzoni, 1995.

Carl, Doris. "Giuliano da Maiano und Lorenzo de' Medici." *Mitteilungen des Kunsthistorischen Institut von Florenz* 37 (1993): 235–56.

—. "New Documents for Antonio Rossellino's Altar in Sant'Anna dei Lombardi, Naples." *The Burlington Magazine* 138 (1996): 318–30.

Caserta, Giovanni. *Isabella Morra e la società meridionale del Cinquecento*. Matera: META, 1976.

Cassese, Giovanna. "Colantonio." www.oxfordartonline.com.

—. "Leonardo (de' Molinari) da Besozzo." www.oxfordartonline.com.

Catello, Angela. "De Agostini, Paolo." DBI 33 (1987). Online at: http://www.treccani.it/enciclopedia/paolo-de-agostini_(Dizionario-Biografico).

Cava de' Tirreni. Exh. Chiostro di Santa Maria del Rifugio, Abbadia della Santissima Trinità July 6–September 30, 2013.

Celenza, Christopher S. *Machiavelli: A Portrait*. Cambridge, MA: Harvard University Press, 2015.

Challéat, Claire. *Dalle Fiandre a Napoli: Committenza artistica, politica, diplomazia al tempo di Alfonso il Magnanimo e Filippo il Buono*. Rome: Bretschneider, 2012.

Cheney, Iris. "De Rossi, Francesco, detto il Salviati." DBI 39 (1991). Online at: http://www.treccani.it/enciclopedia/de-rossi-francesco-detto-il-salviati_(Dizionario-Biografico).

Cheney, Liana, "Vasari and Naples: The Monteolivetan Order." In *Parthenope's Splendor: Art of the Golden Age in Naples*. Jeanne Chenault Porter and Susan Scott Munshower, ed. University Park: Pennsylvania State University, 1993, 48–124.

Chiusa, Maria Cristina. "Antonio Solario [lo Zingaro]." At: www.oxfordartonline.com.

Cilento, Gerardo. "La fabrica della Chiesa." In *Santa Caterina a Formello: Vicende di un'insula napoletana*. Martino Canonico, ed. Naples: Electa, 1996, 117–25.

Cipolla, Carlo M. *Money in Sixteenth-Century Florence*. Berkeley: University of California Press, 1987.

Clarke, Georgia. "The Palazzo Orsini in Nola: A Renaissance Relationship with Antiquity." *Apollo* 144 (1996): 44–50.

Cocco, Sean. "Locating the Natural Sciences in Early Modern Naples." In Astarita (2013), 453–75.

Cochrane, Eric. *Historians and Historiography in the Italian Renaissance*. Chicago: University of Chicago Press, 1980.

——. *Italy, 1530–1630*. Julius Kirshner, ed. New York: Longman, 1988.

Cole, Alison. *Art of the Italian Renaissance Courts: Virtue and Magnificence*. London: G. Weidenfeld and Nicolson. 1997.

Coleman, William Emmet and Gordon D. Pilch, ed. *Naples, the Lost Renaissance: Neapolitan Books and Manuscripts from the Collections of the New York Public Library, Friday, November 22, 1991*. New York: City University, Graduate Center, 1991.

Comboni A., and T. Zanato, ed. *Atlante dei canzonieri in volgare del Quattrocento*. Florence: SISMEL-Edizioni del Galluzzo, 2017.

Comito, Terry. "Renaissance Gardens and the Discovery of Paradise." *Journal of the History of Ideas* 32 (1971): 483–506.

Conelli, Maria Ann. "The Gesù Nuovo in Naples: Politics, Property and Religious." Ann Arbor: UMI, 1992.

Corfiati, C. *Il Principe e la regina: Storie e letteratura nel Mezzogiorno Aragonese*. Florence: Olschki, 2009.

Corrao, Pietro. "Progettare lo Stato, Costruire la Politica: Alfonso il Magnanimo e i regni italiani." In *Il Principe Architetto*. Arturo Calzona, et al., ed. Florence: Olschki, 2002, 23–39.

Covi, Dario. "A Documented *Lettuccio* for the Duke of Calabria by Giuliano da Maiano." In *Essays Presented to Myron P. Gilmore*. Sergio Bertelli, ed. Florence: La Nuova Italia editrice, 1978, 121–30.

Croce, Benedetto. "Sentendo parlare un vecchio napoletano del Quattrocento." In *Storie e leggende napoletane*. Bari: Laterza, 1948.

——. "Una lettera inedita di Alfonso d'Aragona." NN 1 (1892): 127–28.

Dacos, Nicole. "De Pedro de Rubiales a 'Roviale spagnuolo.'" *Boletín del Seminario de Estudios de Arte y Arqueología* 75 (2009): 107–14.

D'Agostino, G. *La capitale ambigua: Napoli dal 1458 al 1580*. Naples: Società editrice napoletana, 1979.

—. "Il mezzogiorno aragonese (Napoli dal 1458 al 1503)." SN 4.1:357–584.

De Blasi, Nicola. "Intrattenimento letterario e generi conviviali (farsa, intramesa, gliommero) nella Napoli aragonese." In *Passare il tempo: La letteratura del gioco e dell'intrattenimento dal XII al XVI secolo. Atti del convegno di Pienza, 10–14 settembre 1991.* 2 vols. Rome: Salerno, 1993, 129–35.

—. *Saggi linguistici sulla storia di Napoli.* Naples: Società napoletana di storia patria, 2017.

De Caprio, Chiara. "La scrittura cronachistica nel Regno: Scriventi, tesi e stili narrativi." *Nuovi Studi Storici* 14.7 (2017): 1–42; repr. in Giampaolo Francesconi and Massimo Miglio, ed. *Le cronache volgari in Medio Evo: Atti della VI Settimana di studi medievali (Roma, 13–15 maggio 2015).* Rome: ISIME, 2017, 227–68.

—. *Scrivere la storia a Napoli tra Medioevo e prima età moderna: Tre studi.* Rome: Salerno, 2012.

—. "Spazi comunicativi, tradizioni narrative e storiografia in volgare: Il Regno negli anni delle guerre d'Italia." *Filologia Critica* 39 (2014): 39–72.

—. and Francesco Senatore. "Orality, Literacy, and Historiography in Neapolitan Vernacular Urban Chronicles of the Fifteenth and Sixteenth Centuries." In *Interactions between Orality and Writing in Early Modern Italian Culture.* Luca Degl'Innocenti, Brian Richardson, and Chiara Sbordoni, ed. London: Routledge, 2016, 129–43.

De Cavi, Sabina. *Architecture and Royal Presence: Domenico and Giulio Cesare Fontana in Spanish Naples (1592–1627).* Newcastle-upon-Tyne: Cambridge Scholars Publishing, 2009.

De Divitiis, Bianca. *Architettura e committenza nella Napoli del Quattrocento.* Venice: Marsilio, 2007, 43–135.

—. "Building in Local *All'Antica* Style: The Palace of Diomede Carafa in Naples." *Art History* 3 (2008): 505–22.

—. "Castel Nuovo and Castel Capuano in Naples: The Transformation of Two Medieval Castles into 'All'antica' Residences for Aragonese Royals." *Zeitschrift für Kunstgeschichte* 76 (2013): 441–47.

—. "Giuliano da Sangallo in the Kingdom of Naples: Architecture and Cultural Exchange." *Journal of the Society of Architectural Historians* 74.2 (2015): 152–78.

—. "Memories from the Subsoil: Discovering Antiquities in Fifteenth-Century Naples and Campania." In Hughes-Buongiovanni, 189–216.

—. "New Evidence for Diomede Carafa's Collection of Antiquities I." *Journal of the Warburg and Courtauld Institutes* 70 (2007): 106–10.

——. "New Evidence for Diomede Carafa's Collection of Antiquities II." *Journal of the Warburg and Courtauld Institutes* 73 (2010): 335–45.

——. "*Pontanus Fecit:* Inscriptions and Artistic Authorship in the Pontano Chapel." *California Italian Studies* 3.1 (2012): 1–36.

De Frede, Carlo. *La crisi del Regno di Napoli nella riflessione politica di Machiavelli e Guicciardini.* Naples: Liguori, 2006.

Delle Donne, Fulvio. *Alfonso il Magnanimo e l'invenzione dell'umanesimo monarchico: Ideologia e strategie di legittimazione alla corte aragonese di Napoli.* Rome: ISIME, 2015.

——. "Il re e i suoi cronisti: Reinterpretazioni della storiografia alla corte aragonese di Napoli." *Humanistica* 11.1–2 (n.s. 5) (2016): 17–34.

——. *Politica e letteratura nel Mezzogiorno medievale: La cronachistica dei secoli XII–XV.* Salerno: Carlone, 2001.

Del Pesco, Daniela. "Alla ricerca di Giovanni Antonio Dosio: Gli anni napoletani." *Bolletino dell'Arte* 71 (1992): 15–66.

——. "Oliviero Carafa e il Succorpo di San Gennaro nel Duomo di Napoli." In *Donato Bramante: Ricerche, proposte, riletture.* Francesco Paolo di Teodoro, ed. Urbino: Accademia Raffaello, 2001, 143–205.

Del Treppo, Mario. "Le avventure storiografiche della Tavola Strozzi." In *Fra storia e storiografia: Scritti in onore di Pasquale Villani.* Paolo Marcy and Angela Massafra, ed. Bologna: Mulino, 1994, 483–515.

De Nichilo, Mauro. "De Rosa, Loise." DBI 39 (1991): 171–74. Online at: http://www.treccani.it/enciclopedia/loise-de-rosa_(Dizionario-Biografico).

De Propris, Fabio. "Guardati, Tommaso." DBI 60 (2003). Online at: http://www.treccani.it/enciclopedia/tommaso-guardati_(Dizionario-Biografico).

Deramaix, Marc, and Birgit Laschke. "'Maroni musa proximus ut tumulo:' L'église et le tombeau de Jacques Sannazar." *Revue de l'Art* 95 (1992): 25–40.

De Reumont, Alfred. *The Carafas of Maddaloni: Naples under Spanish Dominion.* London: Henry G. Bohn, 1854.

De Seta, Cesare. *Napoli.* 5th ed. Rome: Laterza, 1991.

——. *Napoli fra Rinascimento e Illuminismo.* 2nd ed. Naples: Electa, 1997.

——. "The Urban Structure of Naples: Utopia and Reality." In *The Renaissance from Brunelleschi to Michelangelo.* Henry Millon and Vittorio Magnago Lampugnani, ed. New York: Rizzoli, 1994, 349–70.

Edelstein, Bruce. "'Acqua viva e corrente': Private Display and Public Distribution of Fresh Water at the Neapolitan Villa of Poggioreale as a Hydraulic Model for Sixteenth-Century Medici Gardens." In *Italian Renaissance Cities: Artistic Exchange and Cultural Translation.* Stephen

Campbell and Stephen Milner, ed. Cambridge: Cambridge University Press, 2004, 187–220.

Elam, Caroline. "Art and Diplomacy in Renaissance Florence." *Royal Society of Arts Journal* 136 (1988): 813–26.

Ercolino, Maria Grazia. "Giordano, Onofrio." DBI 55 (2001). Online at: http://www.treccani.it/enciclopedia/onofrio-giordano_(Dizionario-Biografico).

Ernst, Germana, and Simona Foà. "Egidio da Viterbo." DBI 42 (1993). Online at: http://www.treccani.it/enciclopedia/egidio-da-viterbo_(Dizionario-Biografico).

Fabriczy, Cornel von. "Der Triumphbogen Alfonsos I am Castelnuovo zu Neapel. "*Jahrbuch der königlichen preussischen Kunstsammlungen* 20 (1899): 3–30, 125–58.

Farenga, Paola. "Del Tuppo, Francesco." DBI 38 (1990). Online at http://www.treccani.it/enciclopedia/francesco-del-tuppo_(Dizionario-Biografico).

—. "Di Costanzo, Angelo." DBI 39 (1991). Online at: http://www.treccani.it/enciclopedia/angelo-di-costanzo_(Dizionario-Biografico).

Fava, Mariano, and Giovanni Bresciano. *La stampa a Napoli nel XV secolo*. 3 vols. Leipzig, R. Haupt, 1911–13; repr. New York: Kraus Reprint, 1969.

Feniello, Amedeo. "Les campagnes napolitaines a la fin du Moyen Âge: Mutations d'un paysage rural." Thèse doctorat. Paris: École des hautes études en sciences sociales, 2001.

—. "Gli interventi sanitari dei secoli XIV e XV." In *Napoli nel Medioevo 4. La città del Mezzogiorno medievale*. Galatina: Congedo, 2007, 123–35.

Ferrante, Biagio. "Il Cinquecentesco Restauro dei Feretri Aragonesi in S. Domenico Maggiore." NN 23 (1984): 69–75.

Ferraro, Italo. *Napoli: Atlante della città storica*. 9 vols. Naples: CLEAN, 2002–.

Ferretti, Massimo. "A Court Artist: Neapolitan Lamentations. Guido Mazzoni in Naples." *FMR Magazine* 88 (1997): 48–58.

Figliuolo, Bruno. "Pontano Giovanni." DBI 84 (2015). Online at: http://www.treccani.it/enciclopedia/giovanni-pontano_(Dizionario-Biografico).

—. "Sulla fondazione, fallita, della nuova città di Alfonsina in Calabria (1447)." *Archivio storico italiano* 170.634 (2012): 725–30.

Filangieri, Gaetano. *Indice degli artefici delle arti maggiori e minori*. Naples: Tipografia dell'Accademia Reale delle Scienze, 1891.

—. "La testa di cavallo in bronzo gia' di casa Maddaloni." *Archivio storico per le provincie napoletane* 7 (1882): 407–20.

Filangieri di Candida, Riccardo. "Il Tempietto di Gioviano Pontano in Napoli." In *In onore di Giovanni Gioviano Pontano del V centenario della sua nascita*. Naples: Accademia Pontaniana, 1926, 103–39.

——. *La Chiesa e il monastero di San Giovanni a Carbonara*. Naples: L. Lubrano, 1924.

——. *L'Archivio di stato di Napoli durante la Seconda Guerra Mondiale*. Stefano Palmieri, ed. Naples: Arte Tipografia, 1996; repr. Istituto italiano per gli studi filosofici, Fonti per la storia di Napoli aragonese. Salerno: Carlone, 1997.

——. "Report on the Destruction by the Germans, September 30, 1943, of the Depository of Priceless Historical Records of the Naples State Archives." *American Archivist* (1944): 252–55.

Finzi, Claudio. *Re, baroni, popolo: La politica di Giovanni Pontano*. Rimini: Il Cerchio, 2004.

Fletcher, Jennifer. "Marcantonio Michiel, 'che ha veduto assai.'" *The Burlington Magazine* 123 (1981): 602–8.

Foà, Simona. "Landino, Cristoforo." DBI 63 (2004). Online at: http://www.treccani.it/enciclopedia/cristoforo-landino_(Dizionario-Biografico).

——. "Manetti, Giannozzo." DBI 68 (2007). Online at: http://www.treccani.it/enciclopedia/giannozzo-manetti_(Dizionario-Biografico).

Fois, Mario. *Il pensiero cristiano di Lorenzo Valla nel quadro storico-culturale del suo ambiente*. Rome: Libreria Editrice dell'Università Gregoriana, 1969.

Fontana, Vincenzo. *Fra' Giovanni Giocondo architetto 1432–1515*. Vicenza: Neri Pozza, 1988.

Frattarolo, Renzo. *Tipografi e librai, ebrei e non, nel Napoletano, alla fine del XV secolo*. Florence: Sansoni, 1956.

Friedman, Joan Isobel. "René I, 4th Duke of Anjou." At: www.oxfordartonline.com.

Friedman, Roger. "A Bibliographical Introduction to the Study of Neapolitan Renaissance Literature." *Lettere Italiane* 44 (1992): 104–25.

Fritz, Michael P. *Giulio Romano et Raphaël: La vice-reine de Naples ou la renaissance d'une beauté mythique*. Claire Nydegger, trans. Paris: Louvre, 1997.

Fubini, Ricardo. "Biondo Flavio." DBI 10 (1968): 536–59. Online at: http://www.treccani.it/enciclopedia/biondo-flavio_(Dizionario-Biografico).

Furnari, Michele. "L'insula di Santa Caterina a Formello: Fondazione, crescita e sviluppo attraverso i contributi della cartografia storica (1500–1880)." In *Santa Caterina a Formello*, 13–41.

Furstenberg-Levi, Shulamit. *The Accademia Pontaniana: A Model of a Humanist Network*. Leiden: Brill, 2016.

Galasso, Giuseppe. *Alla periferia dell'impero: Il Regno di Napoli nel periodo spagnolo, secoli XVI–XVII*. Turin: G. Einaudi, 1994.

——. *Il Regno di Napoli: Il Mezzogiorno spagnolo (1494–1622)*. Turin: UTET, 2005.

—. *Napoli capitale: Identità politica e identità cittadina. Studi e ricerche 1266–1860.* Naples: Electa, 1998.

—. and Aurelio Musi, ed. *Carlo V, Napoli e il Mediterraneo: Atti del Convegno internazionale svoltosi dall'11 al 13 gennaio 2001 presso la Società napoletana di storia patria in Castelnuovo Napoli.* Naples: Società napoletana di storia patria, 2001.

Gardiner, Eileen, and Ronald G. Musto. *The Digital Humanities: A Primer for Students and Scholars.* New York: Cambridge University Press, 2015.

Garzya, Antonio, ed. *Per la storia della tipografia napoletana nei secoli XV–XVIII: Atti del convegno internazionale, Napoli, 2005, 16–17 dicembre.* Naples: Accademia Pontaniana, 2006.

Gentilcore, David. "*Tempi sì calamitosi:* Epidemic Disease and Public Health." In Astarita (2013), 281–306.

Giannetti, Anna. "Urban Design and Public Spaces." In Hall–Willette, 46–100.

Gilbert, Felix. *Machiavelli and Guicciardini: Politics and History in Sixteenth-Century Florence.* Princeton: Princeton University Press, 1985.

Ginzburg, Carlo. "Pontano, Machiavelli and Prudence: Some Further Reflections." In *From Florence to the Mediterranean and Beyond: Essays in Honour of Anthony Mohlo.* Diogo Ramada Curto and Niki Koniordos, ed. 2 vols. Florence: Olschki, 2009, 1:117–25.

Girgensohn, Dieter. "Brancaccio, Rinaldo." DBI 13 (1971). Online at: http://www.treccani.it/enciclopedia/rinaldo-brancaccio_(Dizionario-Biografico).

Giusti, Paola, and Pierluigi Leone de Castris, *Pittura del Cinquecento a Napoli, 1510–1540: Forestieri e regnicoli.* Naples: Electa, 1988.

—. *Pittura del Cinquecento a Napoli, 1540–1573: Fasto e devozione.* Naples: Electa, 1996.

—. , *Pittura del Cinquecento a Napoli, 1573–1606: L'ultima maniera.* Naples: Electa, 1991.

Giustiniani, Lorenzo. *Saggio storico-critico sulla tipografia del Regno di Napoli.* Sala Bolognese: Forni, 1985, repr. Nabu, 2012.

Graham-Dixon, Andrew. *Caravaggio: A Life Sacred and Profane.* New York: Norton, 2011.

Green, Louis. "Galvano Fiamma, Azzone Visconti and the Revival of the Classical Theory of Magnificence." *Journal of the Warburg and Courtauld Institutes* 53 (1990): 98–113.

Guarino, Gabriel. "Public Rituals and Festivals in Naples, 1503–1799." In Astarita (2013), 257–79.

Guerzoni, G. "'*Liberalitas, Magnificentia, Splendore:* The Classical Origins of Italian Renaissance Lifestyles." In *Economic Engagements with Art.* N. De Marchi and C.D.W. Goodwin, ed. Durham, NC: Duke University Press, 1999, 222–78.

Hall, Marcia B., and Thomas Willette, ed. *Artistic Centers of the Italian Renaissance: Naples.* New York: Cambridge University Press, 2017.

Hamburg, Per Gustav. "Vitruvius, Fra Giocondo, and the City of Naples." *Acta Archaeologica* 36 (1965): 106–25.

Hankins, James. "The 'Baron Thesis' after Forty Years, and Some Recent Studies of Leonardo Bruni." *Journal of the History of Ideas* 56 (1995): 309–38.

—. ed., *Renaissance Civic Humanism: Reappraisals and Reflections.* Cambridge: Cambridge University Press, 2003.

Hendrix, Harald. "City Branding and the Antique: Naples in Early Modern City Guides." In Hughes–Buongiovanni, 217–41.

Hentsch-Massaro, Adele. "Alcune riflessioni sulle ekphraseis nell'epistola di Pietro Sumonte a Marcantonio Michiel (Napoli, 20 marzo 1524)." In *Il più dolce lavorare che sia: Mélanges en l'honneur de Mauro Natale.* Frédéric Elsig, Noémie Etienne, and Grégoire Extermann, ed. Milan: Silvana Editoriale, 2009, 351–57.

Hernando Sanchez, Carlos José. "Nation and Ceremony: Political Uses of Urban Space in Viceregal Naples." In Astarita (2013), 158–61.

Hersey, George. *Alfonso II and the Artistic Renewal of Naples, 1485–1495.* New Haven: Yale University Press, 1969.

—. *The Aragonese Arch at Naples, 1443–1475.* New Haven: Yale University Press, 1973.

Hills, Helen. *Invisible Cities: The Architecture of Devotion in Seventeenth-Century Neapolitan Convents.* Oxford: Oxford University Press, 2004.

Heydenreich, Ludwig, and Wolfgang Lotz. *Architecture in Italy 1400–1600.* Penguin: Harmondsworth, 1974.

Howard, Deborah. "Sebastiano Serlio: Influence." At: www.oxfordartonline.com.

Hughes, Jessica. "'No Retreat, Even When Broken': Classical Ruins in the *Presepe Napoletano.*" In Hughes–Buongiovanni, 284–308.

—., and Claudio Buongiovanni, ed. *Remembering Parthenope: The Reception of Classical Naples from Antiquity to the Present.* Oxford: Oxford University Press, 2015.

Ijsewijn, Josef. *Companion to Neo-Latin Studies.* Part 1: *History and Diffusion of Neo-Latin Literature.* 2nd. ed. Leuven: Leuven University Press, 1990.

—. with Dirk Sacré. *Companion to Neo-Latin Studies.* Part 2: *Literary, Linguistic, Philological and Editorial Questions.* 2nd. ed. Leuven: Leuven University Press, 1998.

Janson, H.W. *The Sculpture of Donatello*. Princeton: Princeton University Press, 1963.

Jenkins, A.D. Fraser. "Cosimo de Medici's Patronage of Architecture and the Theory of Magnificence." *Journal of the Warburg and Courtauld Institutes* 33 (1970): 162–70.

Jodogne, Pierre, and Gino Benzoni. "Guicciardini, Francesco." DBI 61 (2004). Online at: http://www.treccani.it/enciclopedia/francesco-guicciardini_ (Dizionario-Biografico).

Kahn, Victoria Ann. *Giovanni Pontano's Rhetoric of Prudence*. University Park: Pennsylvania State University Press, 1983.

Kallendorf, Craig. "Aeneas Sylvius Piccolomini." *Oxford Bibliographies in Renaissance and Reformation*. At http://www.oxfordbibliographies.com/view/document/obo-9780195399301/obo-9780195399301-0065.xml.

—. "Giannozzo Manetti." *Oxford Bibliographies Online*. New York: Oxford University Press, 2014). At:http://dx.doi.org/10.1093/OBO/9780195399301-0091http://dx.doi.org/10.1093/OBO/9780195399301-0091.

—. "Lorenzo Valla." *Oxford Bibliographies Online*. New York: Oxford University Press, 2011). At: http://oxfordbibliographiesonline.com/view/document/obo-9780195399301/obo-9780195399301-0129.xml.

Katzenstein, Ranee. "A Neapolitan Book of Hours in the J. Paul Getty Museum." *The J. Paul Getty Museum Journal* 18 (1990): 69–98.

Kidwell, Carol. *Pontano: Poet and Prime Minister*. London: Duckworth, 1991.

—. *Sannazaro and* Arcadia. London: Duckworth, 1993.

Kent, F.W. *Lorenzo de' Medici and the Art of Magnificence*. Baltimore: Johns Hopkins University Press, 2004.

Kraye, Jill. "Bartolomeo Facio." At: www.oxfordartonline.com.

Labrot, Gérard. "The Residence of Power." In Hall–Willette, 299–338.

Lalanne, Ludovic. "Transport d'oeuvres d'art de Naples au Château d'Amboise en 1495." *Archives de l'art francais* 3 (1852–53): 305–6.

Lenzo, Fulvio. "*Ex dirutis marmoribus*: The Theatines and the Columns of the Temple of the Dioscuri in Naples." In Hughes–Buongiovanni, 242–65.

Leone de Castris, Pierluigi. "Napoli 1544: Vasari e Monteoliveto." *Bollettino d'Arte* 66 (1981): 117–34.

—. *Pittura del Cinquecento a Napoli, 1573–1606: L'ultima maniera*. Naples: Electa, 1991.

—. "Polidoro." At: www.oxfordartonline.

—. *Polidoro da Caravaggio*. Naples: Electa, 2000.

Lettere, Vera. "Costo, Tommaso." DBI 30 (1984). Online at: http://www.treccani.it/enciclopedia/tommaso-costo_(Dizionario-Biografico).

Lewis, Douglas. *The Drawings of Andrea Palladio.* Washington: International Exhibitions Foundation, 1981.

Lightbown, Ronald W. *Donatello and Michelozzo.* 2 vols. London: Harvey Miller, 1980.

Lindow, James. *The Renaissance Palace in Florence: Magnificence and Splendor in Fifteenth-Century Italy.* Aldershot, UK: Ashgate, 2007.

Loconte, Aislinn. "The North Looks South: Giorgio Vasari and Early Modern Visual Culture in the Kingdom of Naples." *Art History* 31 (2008): 438–59.

López Rodríguez, Carlos, and Gloria López de la Plaza. "L'Archivio della Corona d'Aragona e Napoli." *NN* ser. 6.3 (2012): 150–55.

Maione, Pasquale. "Paolo Tolosa e la sua chiesa nella chiesa di Monteoliveto." *Samnium* 15 (1942): 43–46.

Manzi, Pietro. *La tipografia napoletana nel '500.* Florence: Olschki, 1971–75.

Maragoni, Gian Piero. *La devozione e la letteratura: Sulla poesia sacra di Luigi Tansillo.* Rome: UniTor, 1991.

Marino, John A. *Becoming Neapolitan: Citizen Culture in Baroque Naples.* Baltimore, MD: Johns Hopkins University Press, 2011.

—. "Constructing the Past of Early Modern Naples: Sources and Historiography." In Astarita (2013), 11–34.

—. "Myths of Modernity and the Myth of the City: When the Historiography of Pre-modern Italy Goes South." In *New Approaches to Naples c. 1500–1800: The Power of Place.* Melissa Calaresu and Helen Hills, ed. Farnham: Ashgate, 2013, 11–30.

—. *Pastoral Economics in the Kingdom of Naples.* Baltimore, MD: Johns Hopkins University Press, 1988.

—. "Wheat and Wool in the Dogana of Foggia: An Equilibrium Model for Early Modern European Economic History." *Mélanges de l'école française de Rome. Moyen Âge, Temps Modernes* 100 (1988): 871–92.

—. and Thomas J. Dandelet, ed. *Spain in Italy: Politics, Society, and Religion 1500–1700.* Leiden: Brill, 2007.

Martin, Francis X. *The Writings of Giles of Viterbo.* Louvain: Institutum Historicum Augustinianum, 1979.

Marubbi, Mario. "Pedro Machuca e Pedro Fernández tra Roma, Napoli e la Lombardia." In *Norma e capriccio: Spagnoli in Italia agli esordi della "maniera moderna."* Tommaso Mozzati and Antonio Natali, ed. Florence: Giunti, 2013, 300–305.

Mauro, Alfredo. *Francesco Del Tuppo e il suo "Esopo."* Città di Castello: Il solco, 1926.

Mazur, Peter A. "A Mediterranean Port in the Confessional Age: Religious Minorities in Early Modern Naples." In Astarita (2013), 215–34.

Meyer zur Capellen, Jürg. *Raphael: A Critical Catalogue of His Paintings.* Landshut: Arcos, 2005–8.

—. 2. *The Roman Religious Paintings, ca. 1508–1520.*

—. 3. *The Roman Portraits, ca. 1508–1520.*

Michalsky, Tanja. "Tombs and the Ornamentation of Chapels." In Hall–Willette, 233–98.

Middione, Roberto. "Pedro de Rubiales at the Sommària: Justice and the Viceroy." *Franco Maria Ricci* (FMR) 8 (2005): 27–52.

Milburn, Erika Louisa. *Luigi Tansillo and Lyric Poetry in Sixteenth-Century Naples.* Leeds: Maney, 2003.

Miletti, Marco Nicola. "Montalto, Ludovico." DBI 75 (2011). Online at http://www.treccani.it/enciclopedia/ludovico-montalto_(Dizionario-Biografico).

Minieri Riccio, Camillo. "Alcuni fatti di Alfonso I d'Aragona dal 15 aprile 1437 al 31 maggio 1458." *Archivio storico per le provincie napoletane* 6 (1881): 243–44.

Modesti, Paola. *Le delizie ritrovate: Poggioreale e la villa del rinascimento nella Napoli aragonese.* Florence: Olschki, 2014.

Monfasani, John. *George of Trebizond: A Biography and a Study of his Rhetoric and Logic.* Leiden: Brill, 1976.

—. ed. *Collectanea Trapezuntiana: Texts, Documents, and Bibliographies of George of Trebizond.* Binghamton, NY: RSA, 1984.

Montuori, Francesco. "Come 'si costruisce' una cronaca." In *Le cronache volgari in Medio Evo,* 31–88.

—. "Immagini di Napoli fra trecento e quattrocento." In *Il viaggio a Napoli tra letteratura e arti.* Pasquale Sabbatino, ed. Naples: Edizioni scientifiche italiane, 2012, 13–37.

Mozzati, Tommaso, and Antonio Natali, ed. *Norma e capriccio: Spagnoli in Italia agli esordi della "maniera moderna."* Exh. *Galleria degli Uffizi, Florence, 5 March–26 May* 2013. Florence: Giunti, 2013.

Murano, Antonella Putaturo Donati. "Libri miniati per Alfonso e Ferrante." In *Libri a corte: Testi e immagini nella Napoli aragonese.* Emilia Ambra, ed. Naples: Paparo, 1997, 13–39, 105–7, plates 1–4.

Musi, Aurelio. "Political History: The 'Neapolitan Nation'." In Astarita (2013), 131–51.

Musto, Ronald G. "Introduction: Naples in Myth and History." In Hall – Willette, 1–33.

—. *Medieval Naples: A Documentary History, 400–1400.* New York: Italica Press, 2013.

—. *Writing Southern Italy before the Renaissance: Trecento Historians of the Mezzogiorno.* New York: Routledge, 2019.

Muto, Giovanni. "A Court without a King: Naples as a Capital City in the First Half of the 16ᵗʰ Century." In *The World of Emperor Charles V.* Wim Blockmans and Nicolette Mout, ed. Amsterdam: Royal Netherlands Academy of Arts and Sciences, 2004, 129–41.

—. "Urban Structures and Population." In Astarita (2013), 35–61.

Naldi, Riccardo. "Andrea Sabatini [da Salerno]. At: www.oxfordartonline.com.

—. "Il Crocefisso per Girolamo Seripando e il suo contesto." In *Giorgio Vasari: Pittura, umanesimo, religioso, immagini di culto.* Marco Cadisco, ed. Naples: Arte'm, 2009, 107–35.

Napoli, John Nicholas. "From Social Virtue to Revetted Interior: Giovanni Antonio Dosio and Marble Inlay in Rome, Florence, and Naples." *Art History* 31 (2008): 523–46.

Nederman, Cary J. "Niccolò Machiavelli." In *Oxford Bibliographies in Philosophy.* At: www.oxfordbibliographies.com/view/document/obo-9780195396577/obo-9780195396577-0268.xml (accessed 14 Aug 2017).

Niccoli, Sandra. "De Gennaro, Pietro Jacopo." DBI 36 (1988). Online at: http://www.treccani.it/enciclopedia/de-gennaro-pietro-iacopo_(Dizionario-Biografico).

Nichols, Charlotte. "The Caracciolo di Vico Chapel in Naples and Early Cinquecento Architecture." Ann Arbor: UMI, 1988.

—. "Diego Siloe." *The Encyclopedia of Sculpture.* Antonia Bostrum, ed. Chicago: Fitzroy-Dearborn/Routledge, 2004, 3:1567–69.

—. "Ecclesiastical Architecture and the Religious Orders." In Hall–Willette, 101–70.

—. "Giovanni Pontano's Funerary Chapel in Naples: Renaissance Commemoration and the Word." Forthcoming.

—. "Plague and Politics in Early Modern Naples: The Relics of San Gennaro." In *Sickness and in Health: Disease as Metaphor in Art and Popular Wisdom.* Laurinda Dixon, ed. Newark: University of Delaware Press, 2004, 23–44.

Nigro, Salvatore. "Capaccio, Giulio Cesare." DBI 18 (1975). Online at: http://www.treccani.it/enciclopedia/giulio-cesare-capaccio_(Dizionario-Biografico).

Norris, Andrea S. "Costanzo." DBI 30 (1984). Online at: http://www.treccani.it/enciclopedia/costanzo_res-73f1e857-87eb-11dc-8e9d-0016357eee51_(Dizionario-Biografico).

Novi Chavarria, Elisa. "The Space of Women." In Astarita (2013), 177–96.

Nuttall, Paula. *From Flanders to Florence: the Impact of Netherlandish Painting 1400–1500*. New Haven: Yale University Press, 2004.

—. "Jan Van Eyck's Paintings in Italy." In *Investigating Jan van Eyck*. Susan Foister, ed. Turnhout: Brepols, 2000, 169–82.

—. "'Panni dipinti di Fiandra': Netherlandish Painted Cloths in Fifteenth-Century Florence." In *The Fabric of Images: European Paintings on Textile Supports in the Fourteenth and Fifteenth Centuries.* Caroline Villers, ed. London: Archetype Publications, 2000, 109–17.

—. "The Medici and Netherlandish Painting." In *The Early Medici and Their Artists*. Frances Ames-Lewis, ed. London: Birbeck College, University of London, 1995, 135–52.

Pacelli, Vincenzo. "New Documents Concerning Caravaggio in Naples." *The Burlington Magazine* 119 (1977): 820–26.

Palmieri, Stefano. "La 'Tavola di Casa Strozzi': Variazioni dul tema." NN 8 ser. 5 (2007): 171–82.

—. "Napoli, settembre 1943." In *L'Incidenza dell'Antico: Studi in memoria di Ettore Lepore*. Claudia Montepaone, ed. 3 vols. Naples: Luciano, 1995–96, 3:263–79.

Pane, Giulio. *La Tavola Strozzi tra Napoli e Firenze: Un'immagine della città nel quattrocento*. Naples: Grimaldi & C. Editori, 2009.

—. "Pietro di Toledo vicere urbanista." NN 14 (1975): 81–95, 161–82.

Pane, Roberto. *Il rinascimento nell'Italia meridionale*. Milan: Edizioni di Communità, 1975–77.

Papio, Michael. *Keen and Violent Remedies: Social Satire and the Grotesque in Masuccio Salernitano's Novellino*. New York: Peter Lang, 2000.

Patrizi, Giorgio. "Colonna, Vittoria." DBI 27 (1982). Online at: http://www.treccani.it/enciclopedia/vittoria-colonna_(Dizionario-Biografico).

Pedìo, T. *Gli Spagnoli alla conquista dell'Italia*. Reggio Calabria: Editori riuniti meridionali, 1974.

Pellegrino, Nicoletta. "From the Roman Empire to Christian Imperialism: The Work of Flavio Biondo." In Sharon Dale, Alison Williams Lewin, and Duane J. Osheim, ed. *Chronicling History: Chroniclers and Historians in Medieval and Renaissance Italy*. University Park: Pennsylvania State University Press, 2007, 273–98.

Pepe, Erminia. "Le tre cappelle rinascimentali in Santa Maria di Monteoliveto a Napoli." NN 37 (1998): 97–116.

Pepe, G. *Il Mezzogiorno d'Italia sotto gli Spagnoli: La tradizione storiografica*. Florence: G.C. Sansoni, 1952.

Petrocchi, Giorgio. "La letteratura napoletana del Rinascimento." SN 5:281–336.

Petrucci, Franca. "Carafa, Diomede." DBI 19 (1976). Online at: http://www.treccani.it/enciclopedia/diomede-carafa_(Dizionario-Biografico).

Pettitt, Thomas. "Bracketing the Gutenberg Parenthesis." *Explorations in Media Ecology* 11.2 (2012): 95–114.

Peyronnet, Georges. "I Durazzo e Renato d'Angiò, 1281–1442." SN 3:335–436.

Pierpont, Claudia Roth. "Giovanni da Nola and the Monument of Don Pedro da Toledo: A Study in Sixteenth-Century Neapolitan Sculpture." Ph.D. Diss., Institute of Fine Arts, New York University, 1988.

Pignatti, Franco. "Ferraiolo." DBI 46 (1996). Online at: http://www.treccani.it/enciclopedia/ferraiolo_(Dizionario-Biografico).

—. "Morlini, Girolamo." DBI 77 (2012). Online at: http://www.treccani.it/enciclopedia/girolamo-morlini_(Dizionario-Biografico).

Pirovano, D. *Modi narrativi e stili del* Novellino *di Masuccio Salernitano*. Florence: La Nuova Italia, 1991.

Pontieri, Ernesto. *Alfonso il Magnanimo re di Napoli (1435–1458)*. Naples: Edizioni scientifiche italiane, 1975.

Porter, Jeanne Chenault. *Baroque Naples: A Documentary History, 1600–1800*. New York: Italica Press, 2000.

Previtali, Giovanni, ed. *Andrea da Salerno nel rinascimento meridionale*. Florence: Centro Di, 1986.

Rabil, Albert, Jr., "The Significance of 'Civic Humanism' in the Interpretation of the Italian Renaissance." In idem, ed. *Renaissance Humanism*. 3 vols. Philadelphia: University of Pennsylvania Press, 1988, 1:141–74.

Resta, Gianvito. "Beccadelli, Antonio, detto il Panormita." DBI 7 (1970). Online at: http://www.treccani.it/enciclopedia/beccadelli-antonio-detto-il-panormita_(Dizionario-Biografico).

Robin, François. *La Cour d'Anjou-Provence: La vie artistique sous le règne de René*. Paris: Picard, 1985.

Rodríguez de Diego, José Luis. "Napoli nell'Archivio di Simancas." NN ser. 6:3 (2012): 155–60.

Roick, Matthias. *Pontano's Virtues: Aristotelian Moral and Political Thought in the Renaissance*. London: Bloomsbury Academic, 2017.

Romano, Serena. "Patrons and Paintings from the Angevins to the Spanish Hapsburgs." In Hall–Willette, 171–232.

Romeo, Giovanni. "Inquisition and Church in Early Modern Naples." In Astarita (2013), 235–56.

Rosi, Massimo. *Napoli entro e fuori le mura: Le trasformazioni urbanistiche, demografiche e territoriali di un'antica capitale rimasta per troppo tempo vincolata dalle sue stesse mura*. Rome: Newton & Compton, 2003.

Rovito, P.L. *Il viceregno spagnolo di Napoli: Ordinamento, istituzioni, culture di governo*. Naples: Arte tipografica, 2003.

Rubin, Patricia. "Magnificence and the Medici." In *The Early Medici and Their Artists*. Francis Ames-Lewis, ed. London: Birbeck College, University of London, 1995), 37–49.

Rubió, Jordi. "Alfons 'el Magnánim' rei de Nápols, i Daniel Florentino, Leonardo da Bisuccio, i Donatello." *Micellània Puig I Cadafalch* 1 (1947–51): 25–35.

Ruda, Jeffrey. *Fra Filippo Lippi: Life and Work with a Complete Catalogue*. London: Phaidon, 1993.

Rusciano, C. *Napoli, 1484–1501: La città e le mura aragonesi*. Rome: Bonsignori, 2002.

Russo, Emilio. "Morra, Isabella di." DBI 77 (2012). Online at: http://www.treccani.it/enciclopedia/isabella-di-morra_(Dizionario-Biografico).

Ryder, Alan. *Alfonso the Magnanimous, King of Aragon, Naples, and Sicily, 1396–1458*. Oxford: Oxford University Press, 1990.

—. "Antonio Beccadelli: A Humanist in Government." In *Cultural Aspects of the Italian Renaissance: Essays in Honour of Paul Oskar Kristeller*. Cecil H. Clough, ed. Manchester: Manchester University Press 1976, 123–40.

—. *The Kingdom of Naples under Alfonso the Magnanimous: The Making of a Modern State*. Oxford: Oxford University Press, 1976.

Sabatini, Gaetano. "Economy and Finance in Early Modern Naples." In Astarita (2013), 89–107.

Sabbatino, Pasquale, ed. *Jacopo Sannazaro: La cultura napoletana nell'Europa del Rinascimento. Convegno internazionale di studi (Napoli, 27-28 marzo 2006)*. Florence: Olschki, 2009.

Sakellariou, E. *Southern Italy in the Late Middle Ages: Demographic, Institutional and Economic Change in the Kingdom of Naples, c.1440–c.1530*. Leiden: Brill, 2012.

Santagata, Marco. *La lirica aragonese: Studi sulla poesia napoletana del secondo Quattrocento*. Padua: Antenore, 1979.

Santore, John. *Modern Naples: A Documentary History, 1799–1999*. New York: Italica Press, 2001.

Santoro, Fiorella Sricchia, and Andrea Zezza ed. *Marco Pino: Un protagonista della "maniera moderna" a Napoli. Restauri nel centro storico*. Naples: Electa, 2003.

Santoro, Marco, and George H. Fletcher, *La stampa a Napoli nel Quattrocento*. Naples: Istituto nazionale di studi sul Rinascimento meridionale, 1984.

Santoro, Mario. "Napoli Aragonese: La cultura umanistica." SN 4:317–498.

—. "Humanism in Naples." In Albert Rabil, Jr. ed. *Renaissance Humanism: Foundations, Forms and Legacy* 1. *Humanism in Italy.* Philadelphia: University of Pennsylvania Press, 1988, 296–331.

Sbordone, Silvia. *Editori e tipografi a Napoli nel '600.* Naples: Accademia Pontaniana, 1990.

Schiesari, Juliana. "The Gendering of Melancholia: Torquato Tasso and Isabella di Morra." In *Refiguring Women: Perspectives on Gender and the Italian Renaissance.* Marilyn Migiel and Juliana Schiesari, ed. Ithaca, NY: Cornell University Press, 1991, 233–62.

Scott, John T. *The Routledge Guidebook to Machiavelli's* The Prince. London: Routledge, 2016.

Senatore, Francesco. "Fonti documentarie e costruzione della notizia nelle cronache cittadine dell'Italia meridionale (secoli XV–XVI)." *Bullettino ISIME* 116 (2014): 279–333.

—. "The Kingdom of Naples." In *The Italian Renaissance State.* Andrea Gamberoni and Isabella Lazzarini, ed. New York: Cambridge University Press, 2012, 30–49.

Setton, Kenneth. *The Papacy and the Levant (1204–1571).* Philadelphia: American Philosophical Society, 1976–84.

Setz, Wolfram. *Lorenzo Vallas Schrift gegen die konstantinische Schenkung:* De falso credita et ementita Constantini donatione. *Zur Interpretation und Wirkungsgeschichte.* Tübingen: Niemeyer, 1975.

Shearman, John. *Mannerism.* Harmondsworth: Penguin, 1967.

Siegel, Jerrold E. "'Civic Humanism' or Ciceronian Rhetoric? The Culture of Petrarch and Bruni." *Past and Present* 34 (1966): 3–48.

Smith, Christine. *Architecture in the Culture of Early Humanism.* New York: Oxford University Press, 1992.

Sodano, Giulio. "Governing the City: The Capital City and the Policy of the Capital." In Astarita (2013), 109–29.

Soranzo, Matteo. *Poetry and Identity in Quattrocento Naples.* Farnham: Ashgate, 2014.

Sotelo, A. A. *Casa de Aragón de Nápoles, 1412–1503 en la historiografía italiana, siglo XV–XVIII.* Torrevieja: Áristos, 2001.

Spagnoletti, Angelantonio. "The Naples Elites between City and Kingdom." In Astarita (2013), 197–214.

Spike, John T. *Caravaggio.* New York: Abbeville Press, 2001.

Spinazzola, V. "La Certosa di S. Martino 1. Notizie Storiche della Certosa di S. Martino, 1325–1900." NN 11 (1902): 97–103.

Stocke, Beate. "Foreign Impressions of Neapolitan Art in the Sixteenth Century." *Renaissance and Reformation* 24.4 (1988).

Strazzullo, Franco. *Edilizia e urbanistica a Napoli tra XVI e XVII secolo.* Naples: Berisio, 1968.

—. "La Cappella Carafa del Duomo di Napoli in un poemetto del primo cinquecento." NN 5 (1966): 62–63.

—. "La Fondazione di Monteoliveto di Napoli." NN 3 (1963): 103–11.

—. *Quinto centenario della traslazione delle ossa di San Gennaro da Montevergine a Napoli 1497–1997.* Naples: Edizioni scientifiche italiane, 1996.

—. "Un descrittore della Napoli del '500: Giovanni Tarcagnota." *Atti della Accademia Pontaniana* 38 (1989): 131–40.

Sullivan, Vickie B., and Michelle T. Clarke. "Machiavelli's Political Thought." In *Oxford Bibliographies in Political Science.* At: www.oxfordbibliographies. com/view/document/obo-9780199756223/obo-9780199756223-0176. xml (accessed 14 Aug 2017).

Syson, Luke, and Dillian Gordon. *Pisanello: Painter to the Renaissance Court.* London: National Gallery Company & Yale University Press, 2001.

Taito, Roberto. Tavola Strozzi Project. At: http://www.tavolastrozzi. it/#progetti.

Tanzi, Marco. *Pedro Fernández da Murcia lo Pseudo Bramantino.* Milan, Leonardo Arte: 1997.

Taylor, Rabun. "The Temple of the Dioscuri and the Mythic Origins of Neapolis." In Hughes–Buongiovanni, 39–63.

Terrusi, L. *El rozo idyoma de mia materna lingua: Studi sul 'Novellino' di Masuccio Salernitano.* Bari: Laterza, 2005.

Thoenes, Christoph. *Neapel und Umgebung.* Stuttgart: Reclam, 1983.

Torini, Annalisa Perissa. "Un Artista Lombarda nell'Italia del Sud." In *Leonardo & Cesare da Sesto nel Rinascimento Meridionale.* Nicola Barbatelli, ed. Poggio a Caiano: CB Edizioni, 2013, 45–61.

Tormo y Monzó, Elias. *Jacomart y el arte hispano-flamenco cuatrocentista.* Madrid: Blass, 1913.

Toscano, Gennaro. "Aggiunte a Leonardo da Besozzo." *Arte medievale* n.s. 3 (2005): 2:125–37.

—. *La Biblioteca Reale di Napoli al tempo della dinastia Aragonese.* Valencia: Generalitat Valencia, 1998.

—. "Leonardo da Besozzo à Naples: Un peintre du gothique tardif à l'époque des derniers rois de la dynastie angevine." In *Pierre, lumière, couleur: Études d'histoire de l'art du Moyen Age en l'honneur d'Anne Prache.* F. Joubert and D. Sandron, ed. Paris: Presses de l'Université de Paris-Sorbonne, 1999, 417–21.

—. "Roviale, Francesco." At: www.oxfordartonline.

Toscano, T.R. *Letterati, corti, accademie: La letteratura a Napoli nella prima metà del Cinquecento*. Naples: Loffredo, 2000.

Tramontana, Salvatore. *Il Mezzogiorno medievale: Normanni, svevi, angioini, aragonesi nei secoli XI–XV*. Rome: Carocci, 2018.

Trapp, J.B. "The Grave of Vergil." *Journal of the Warburg and Courtauld Institutes* 62 (1984): 1–31.

Ullman, Berthold L. "The Post-Mortem Adventures of Livy." *Studies in the Italian Renaissance* 51 (1973): 54–58.

Vargas, Carmela. "Hendricksz. (Centen), Dirck [Teodoro d'Errico]." At: www.oxfordartonline.

Vecce, C. "Viaggio in 'Arcadia'." In *Iacopo Sannazaro, Arcadia*. C. Vecce, ed. Rome, Carocci, 2013, 9-41.

Venditti, Arnaldo. "Presenze ed influenze catalane nell'architettura del regno d'Aragona in Napoli, 1442–1503." NN 13 (1974): 503–36.

Verdon, Timothy. "Mazzoni, Guido." At: www.oxfordartonline.com. (Accessed Aug 24, 2016).

Vaccari, Grazia. "Guido Mazzoni: Lamentation." *Encyclopedia of Sculpture*. New York: Fitzroy Dearborn, 2004, 2:1027–28.

Valerio, Vladimiro. *Piante e vedute di Napoli dal 1486 al 1599: L'origine dell'iconografia urbana europea*. Naples: Electa, 1998.

Villani, Giovanni. "L'Umanesimo napoletano." In *Storia della letteratura italiana*. E. Malato, ed. 3.2 *Quattrocento*. Rome, Salerno, 1998, 709-62.

Viti, P. "Bartolomeo Facio." DBI 44:113–21. Online at: http://www.treccani.it/enciclopedia/bartolomeo-facio_(Dizionario-Biografico).

Vivanti, Corrado. *Niccolo Machiavelli: An Intellectual Biography*. Princeton: Princeton University Press, 2013.

Watson, Rowan. "Fit for a King? The Alfonso of Aragon Hours and Baronial Patronage in Late Fifteenth-Century Naples." In *Under the Influence: The Concept of Influence and the Study of Illuminated Manuscripts*. John Lowden and Alixe Bovey, ed. Turnhout: Brepols, 2007, 151–60, 225-28.

Weil-Garris Brandt, Kathleen. "Sogni di un Cupido dormiente smarrito." In *La giovinezza di Michelangelo*. Kathleen Weil-Garris Brandt, ed. Florence: ArtificioSkira, 1999, 315–23.

Weiss, Rainer. "The Humanist Rediscovery of Rhetoric as Philosophy: Giovanni Giovano Pontano's Aegidius." *Philosophy and Rhetoric* 13.1 (1980): 25–42.

Welch, Evelyn. "Public Magnificence and Private Display: Giovanni Pontano's *De splendore* (1498) and the Domestic Arts." *Journal of Design History* 15 (2002): 211–28.

Wethey, Harold. *The Paintings of Titian: The Religious Paintings*. London: Phaidon, 1969.

Wickham, Chris. *Early Medieval Italy: Central Power and Local Society 400–1000*. Ann Arbor: University of Michigan Press, 1989.

—. *The Inheritance of Rome: A History of Europe from 400 to 1000*. London: Penguin, 2010.

Willette, Thomas. "Giotto's Allegorical Painting of the Kingdom of Naples." In *Gifts in Return: Essays in Honour of Charles Dempsey*. Melinda Schlitt, ed. Toronto: Centre for Reformation and Renaissance Studies, 2012, 69–92.

—. "Giorgio Vasari's Critique of Art and Patronage in Naples." In Hall–Willette, 34–45.

Witt, Ronald G. *The Two Latin Cultures and the Foundation of Renaissance Humanism in Medieval Italy*. Cambridge: Cambridge University Press, 2012.

Woods Marsden, Joanna. "Art and Political Identity in Fifteenth-Century Naples: Pisanello, Cristoforo di Geremia, and King Alfonso's Imperial Fantasies." In *Art and Politics in Late Medieval and Early Renaissance Italy, 1250–1500*. Charles M. Rosenberg, ed. Notre Dame, IN: University of Notre Dame Press, 1990, 11–37.

Wright, Joanne. "Antonello da Messina." At: www.oxfordartonline.com.

—. "Antonello da Messina: The Origins of his Style and Technique." *Art History* 3 (1980): 41–60.

Zuckert, Catherine H. *Machiavelli's Politics*. Chicago: University of Chicago Press, 2017.

★ ★ ★

INDEX

A

F

Fabius 127
Fabriano, Gentile da 327
Facio, Bartolomeo 5, 19, 54, 107,
112, 379; Alfonso I 233, 327–33;
*Isocratis sermo de regno ad Nicoclem
regem* 468; Valla 114
Fagot, Nicolas 346
Falco, Benedetto di 48, 52, 389,
477
Fancelli, Luca 241
Fanzago, Cosimo 310, 372
fare isola 38, 224–25, 309
Farina, master 452
Farnese, Alessandro, cardinal 98
Favale 192, 193
Federico, duke of Calabria. *See*
Frederick, king.
Felice, Felice de 310
Felix V, antipope 62
Feltre, Vittorino da 377
Ferdinand and Isabella of Spain 7,
12, 82, 171, 172, 262, 263–64;
Ferdinand of Spain, king 84,
185, Naples' walls 218; Isabella
of Spain, queen 83
Fernández de Cordóba, Gonzalo
347
Fernandez de Murcia, Pedro
(Pseudo-Bramantino) 46,
347–49, 366
Ferraiolo 23, 49, 51, 76–83; *Cronaca*
476
Ferrante (Ferdinand, Ferrandino)
I, king: antiquities 383–84; arch
of Alfonso I 382; battle of Ischia
342; battle of Sarno 63–65;
Beccadelli 140; Carafa 235,
237; Castel Nuovo 231, 452;
Commynes 89–90; conspiracies
of barons 50, 79–83, 124–25,
185, 336; death 7; del Tuppo 49;
falconry 440; Guicciardini 87;

heraldic arms 274; infrastructure
5, 36; Isabella di Chiaromonte
108, 110; Latin literature
146–47; library 326, 468;
palaces 247; patronage 344–45;
Pontano 116, 213, 280, 431, 433;
portraits 265, 460; relics 312–15;
Sanseverino 150, 238; *Tavola
Strozzi* 342–43; tomb 279;
Turks 262; urban expansion
220; Valla 112. *See also* Isabella di
Chiaromonte.
Ferrante (Ferdinand, Ferrandino)
II, king: building projects 39;
Castel Nuovo 233; da Maiano
217; French invasion 345–46;
Gareth 185; Magus 266;
Pontano 116–17, 404, 407, 437;
portraits 215; tomb 279
Ferrante, Francesco 167
Ferrer, Andreu 313
Ferrer, Vincent, St. 336, 337
Fiamma, Galvano 395
Filangieri, Gaetano 17, 372
Fiorentino, Antonio 463; Ioan
Battista 456
Florence: Archivio di Stato 381;
Baptistry 268; church construc-
tion 40n; duomo 229; human-
ism 53; Medici 24, 396; Museo
Archeologico Nazionale 381;
Opera del Duomo 241; Palazzo
Medici 247; Palazzo Ruccellai
281; Palazzo Strozzi 342, 480;
Poggio a Caiano 39; popula-
tion 30; republic 26; S. Agostino
107; S. Marco 40n; S. Miniato al
Monte 42, 271–72; S. Salvatore
al Monte 40n; SS. Annunziata
288; Sta. Maria a San Gallo 40n;
Sta. Maria degli Angeli 107; Sta.
Maria dell'Impruneta 288; trade
14; Twelve Good Men 107;

*Production of This Book Was Completed on
15 February 2019 at Italica Press,
Clifton, Bristol, United Kingdom.
It Was Set in Adobe Bembo,
Adobe Bembo Expert &
Montotype Botanical
Ornaments*

Lightning Source UK Ltd.
Milton Keynes UK
UKHW010637170319
339288UK00001B/34/P